GNOME/GTK+
Programming Bible

GNOME/GTK+
Programming Bible

Arthur Griffith

IDG Books Worldwide, Inc.
An International Data Group Company

Foster City, CA ✦ Chicago, IL ✦ Indianapolis, IN ✦ New York, NY

GNOME/GTK+ Programming Bible

Published by
IDG Books Worldwide, Inc.
An International Data Group Company
919 E. Hillsdale Blvd., Suite 400
Foster City, CA 94404
www.idgbooks.com (IDG Books Worldwide Web site)

The image of the Linux penguin, Tux, was created by Larry Ewing (lewing@isc.tamu.edu) using the Gimp (http://www.gimp.org) and was subsequently modified for use by IDG Books Worldwide on this book's cover by Tuomas Kuosmanen (tigert@gimp.org). Tuomas also used the Gimp for his work with Tux.

Library of Congress Card Number: 00-101008

ISBN: 0-7645-4640-6

Printed in the United States of America

10 9 8 7 6 5 4 3 2 1

1B/RV/QT/QQ/FC

Distributed in the United States by IDG Books Worldwide, Inc.

Distributed by CDG Books Canada Inc. for Canada; by Transworld Publishers Limited in the United Kingdom; by IDG Norge Books for Norway; by IDG Sweden Books for Sweden; by IDG Books Australia Publishing Corporation Pty. Ltd. for Australia and New Zealand; by TransQuest Publishers Pte Ltd. for Singapore, Malaysia, Thailand, Indonesia, and Hong Kong; by Gotop Information Inc. for Taiwan; by ICG Muse, Inc. for Japan; by Intersoft for South Africa; by Eyrolles for France; by International Thomson Publishing for Germany, Austria and Switzerland; by Distribuidora Cuspide for Argentina; by LR International for Brazil; by Galileo Libros for Chile; by Ediciones ZETA S.C.R. Ltda. for Peru; by WS Computer Publishing Corporation, Inc., for the Philippines; by Contemporanea de Ediciones for Venezuela; by Express Computer Distributors for the Caribbean and West Indies; by Micronesia Media Distributor, Inc. for Micronesia; by Chips Computadoras S.A. de C.V. for Mexico; by Editorial Norma de Panama S.A. for Panama; by American Bookshops for Finland.

For general information on IDG Books Worldwide's books in the U.S., please call our Consumer Customer Service department at 800-762-2974. For reseller information, including discounts and premium sales, please call our Reseller Customer Service department at 800-434-3422.

For information on where to purchase IDG Books Worldwide's books outside the U.S., please contact our International Sales department at 317-572-3337 or fax 317-572-4002.

For consumer information on foreign language translations, please contact our Customer Service department at 800-434-3422, fax 317-572-4002, or e-mail rights@idgbooks.com.

For information on licensing foreign or domestic rights, please phone +1-650-653-7098.

For sales inquiries and special prices for bulk quantities, please contact our Sales department at 800-434-3422 or write to the address above.

For information on using IDG Books Worldwide's books in the classroom or for ordering examination copies, please contact our Educational Sales department at 800-434-2086 or fax 317-572-4005.

For press review copies, author interviews, or other publicity information, please contact our Public Relations department at 650-653-7000 or fax 650-653-7500.

For authorization to photocopy items for corporate, personal, or educational use, please contact Copyright Clearance Center, 222 Rosewood Drive, Danvers, MA 01923, or fax 978-750-4470.

is a registered trademark or trademark under exclusive license to IDG Books Worldwide, Inc. from International Data Group, Inc. in the United States and/or other countries.

ABOUT IDG BOOKS WORLDWIDE

Welcome to the world of IDG Books Worldwide.

IDG Books Worldwide, Inc., is a subsidiary of International Data Group, the world's largest publisher of computer-related information and the leading global provider of information services on information technology. IDG was founded more than 30 years ago by Patrick J. McGovern and now employs more than 9,000 people worldwide. IDG publishes more than 290 computer publications in over 75 countries. More than 90 million people read one or more IDG publications each month.

Launched in 1990, IDG Books Worldwide is today the #1 publisher of best-selling computer books in the United States. We are proud to have received eight awards from the Computer Press Association in recognition of editorial excellence and three from Computer Currents' First Annual Readers' Choice Awards. Our best-selling *...For Dummies®* series has more than 50 million copies in print with translations in 31 languages. IDG Books Worldwide, through a joint venture with IDG's Hi-Tech Beijing, became the first U.S. publisher to publish a computer book in the People's Republic of China. In record time, IDG Books Worldwide has become the first choice for millions of readers around the world who want to learn how to better manage their businesses.

Our mission is simple: Every one of our books is designed to bring extra value and skill-building instructions to the reader. Our books are written by experts who understand and care about our readers. The knowledge base of our editorial staff comes from years of experience in publishing, education, and journalism — experience we use to produce books to carry us into the new millennium. In short, we care about books, so we attract the best people. We devote special attention to details such as audience, interior design, use of icons, and illustrations. And because we use an efficient process of authoring, editing, and desktop publishing our books electronically, we can spend more time ensuring superior content and less time on the technicalities of making books.

You can count on our commitment to deliver high-quality books at competitive prices on topics you want to read about. At IDG Books Worldwide, we continue in the IDG tradition of delivering quality for more than 30 years. You'll find no better book on a subject than one from IDG Books Worldwide.

John J. Kilcullen

John Kilcullen
Chairman and CEO
IDG Books Worldwide, Inc.

WINNER

*Eighth Annual
Computer Press
Awards ≥1992*

WINNER

*Ninth Annual
Computer Press
Awards ≥1993*

WINNER

*Tenth Annual
Computer Press
Awards ≥1994*

WINNER

*Eleventh Annual
Computer Press
Awards ≥1995*

IDG is the world's leading IT media, research and exposition company. Founded in 1964, IDG had 1997 revenues of $2.05 billion and has more than 9,000 employees worldwide. IDG offers the widest range of media options that reach IT buyers in 75 countries representing 95% of worldwide IT spending. IDG's diverse product and services portfolio spans six key areas including print publishing, online publishing, expositions and conferences, market research, education and training, and global marketing services. More than 90 million people read one or more of IDG's 290 magazines and newspapers, including IDG's leading global brands — Computerworld, PC World, Network World, Macworld and the Channel World family of publications. IDG Books Worldwide is one of the fastest-growing computer book publishers in the world, with more than 700 titles in 36 languages. The "...For Dummies®" series alone has more than 50 million copies in print. IDG offers online users the largest network of technology-specific Web sites around the world through IDG.net (http://www.idg.net), which comprises more than 225 targeted Web sites in 55 countries worldwide. International Data Corporation (IDC) is the world's largest provider of information technology data, analysis and consulting, with research centers in over 41 countries and more than 400 research analysts worldwide. IDG World Expo is a leading producer of more than 168 globally branded conferences and expositions in 35 countries including E3 (Electronic Entertainment Expo), Macworld Expo, ComNet, Windows World Expo, ICE (Internet Commerce Expo), Agenda, DEMO, and Spotlight. IDG's training subsidiary, ExecuTrain, is the world's largest computer training company, with more than 230 locations worldwide and 785 training courses. IDG Marketing Services helps industry-leading IT companies build international brand recognition by developing global integrated marketing programs via IDG's print, online and exposition products worldwide. Further information about the company can be found at www.idg.com.   1/26/00

Credits

Acquisitions Editor
Laura Lewin

Development Editors
Kathi Duggan
Andy Marinkovich

Technical Editor
Jason Luster

Copy Editors
Victoria Lee
Mildred Sanchez

Project Coordinators
Linda Marousek
Marcos Vergara

Quality Control Specialists
Laura Taflinger
Chris Weisbart

Graphics and Production Specialists
Robert Bihlmayer
Jude Levinson
Michael Lewis

Book Designer
Drew R. Moore

Illustrator
Mary Jo Richards
Karl Brandt

Proofreading and Indexing
York Production Services

Cover Illustration Design
Peter Kowaleszyn, Murder By Design,
San Francisco

About the Author

Arthur Griffith has been programming computers for 25 years. He has several years experience in graphics programming, including X11 and motif. His broad experience includes oil and gas monitoring, satellite communications, insurance company databases, real-time controls, and hardware diagnostic systems. He specializes in writing computer language interpreters and compilers, and has implemented several special-purpose languages. Among the books he has written are *Java Master Reference* and *COBOL For Dummies*. He is also the co-author of *Peter Norton's Complete Guide to Linux*. Arthur lives in Homer, Alaska, and is now a full-time writer. You can contact him at arthur@belugalake.com.

For Mary

Preface

In This Book

If you want to write a GNOME application, you've come to the right book.

This book is composed of one example program after another, and each example is accompanied by an explanation. Each example is also a complete running program designed to demonstrate just one thing.

My personal preference, when exploring or learning something new about software, is to have a simple example that shows me just what I want and nothing else. Software is complicated enough that it becomes impossible to explain all the nuances without showing an example, and an example can be very confusing unless the key parts of it are explained.

The documentation of a program can be included as comments in the code, or it can be separate text supplied along with the code. The examples in this book have no embedded comments because each one is accompanied by text that explains it. Leaving out comments produces a cleaner format that makes it easier for a reader to see the structure of the program. Most of the code is printed in the book with line numbers so the explanations can refer to specific lines.

What You Will Need

If you know how to program in C, have access to a Linux computer, and are able to download files from the Internet, this book will supply you with the know-how you need to write GNOME applications.

There is a version of the development software on the CD, which is described in Appendix A. Alternatively, see Appendix B to get the latest version of everything. Appendix B contains a list of all the software you will need, and where it can be found on the Internet.

Subject to Change

GNOME is large, powerful, and moving fast. Fortunately, it is also very friendly.

GNOME is an ongoing project. New things are being added constantly. Because of its open source status, this growth will probably continue for the life of GNOME and GTK+.

From time to time new methods for getting things done will be added, and it is possible that some of the techniques described in this book will become outdated. But everything in the book should continue to work. Being deprecated is not the same as being obsolete—the old function calls will still work, it's just that a new (and hopefully better) way of doing it will have been added. In some cases, there may be output during the compile stating that some function or other has been deprecated—this is so you can take the opportunity to upgrade your program to a new way of doing things.

How to Use This Book

The book is divided into three parts. The first part is one continuous tutorial covering the basics of GNOME/GTK+ programming. The second part is also comprised of tutorials, but the chapters can be taken in order on an as-needed basis. The third part was not intended to be read sequentially—it is more of a reference section, as are Appendixes C through G.

Appendix A or B: Installing the Software

If you have a late model Linux on a CD, you will have most of the software and may have it all. If not, you have two options. You can install it from the CD supplied with this book, or you can retrieve it from the Internet. Appendix A discusses the CD and Appendix B discusses the Internet.

Chapter 24: From Win32 to Gnome

If you are a Win32 programmer, start by reading Chapter 24. This chapter is a point-by-point comparison of two programs—one written for Win32 and the other written for GNOME. There are some basic differences, but the underlying concepts behind writing a GNOME application are very much like those behind writing a Win32 application.

Part I: Getting Started

This part of the book starts from the very beginning and puts the pieces together until you are able to create applications that display buttons, labels, and other widgets with whatever size, shape, and position you would like them to be. The first chapter explains some of the background information—mostly having to do with the libraries available and the structure of GNOME and GTK+ code.

Chapter 2 is where the programming starts. This chapter describes the options available for displaying its main window and allowing the user to configure it and to shut it down. Chapter 3 expands on this by adding popup windows and dialog boxes. Chapters 4 and 5 both cover the subject of managing windows as a group, and controlling their actions, sizes, and so on. Chapter 6 takes a peek under the hood and explores name and ID information, how the main message loop works, and how it can be used to process in the background and for timing. This is a GUI interface, after all, so Chapter 7 shows you how to add graphics to the windows. Chapter 8 is devoted to examples that show you how to create menus and toolbars, and how to include special things on them such as toggle buttons and icons.

Part II: Step by Step

This part could be studied from front to back, or you can skip around from one place to another. There are a few references from one chapter to another, but, for the most part, each chapter is independent of the others.

Chapter 9 is devoted to a special canvas window that can be used to hold other widgets, line drawings, filled polygons, text, and so on. If the canvas window is more than you really need, Chapter 10 explores a simple window that exposes its drawing area to a set of primitive drawing functions. Chapter 11 explains how GNOME handles color, and how you can control it inside your program. Chapter 12 digs into the details of listening and responding to the mouse and keyboard. There are literally thousands of fonts available, and you can use them all in your program with the information offered in Chapter 13. Every window is constructed from a basic software unit known as a *widget*. Chapter 14 digs down into a widget and shows you how you can perform some of the basic widget tricks of setting special styles, sending messages to a widget, and controlling the life cycle of the widget.

Chapter 15 shows how to write an applet (a program that appears on the panel bar across the bottom of the GNOME desktop window). Chapter 16 has examples of dragging and dropping between a pair of applications. The GTK+ multiple-document interface is described in Chapter 17. Chapter 18 contains an example of what it takes to write a widget, and Chapter 19 deals with internationalization and configuration.

Part III: References and Mechanics

The chapters in this part of the book are mostly intended for reference. Chapter 20 contains examples of setting things up for automatic compilation. A GNOME/GTK+ application consists mostly of gluing widgets together. Chapter 21 is an alphabetic list of the GTK+ widgets. Chapter 21 is an alphabetic list of the GNOME widgets. Chapter 23 covers a few of the basic Linux operations, like starting a new process and getting the system time. Chapter 24 is a sort of a Rosetta stone comparison of Win32 and GNOME.

The Cross Reference Appendixes

There is a lot of software here, and a normal human needs some way to get a handle on it. The appendixes contain reference information that can be very helpful in finding things.

Appendix	Lists	Contains
C	Inheritance	When dealing with an object, it is possible to access the data and functions of all of its base classes. This appendix lists all the base classes for each object.
D	Arg	You can set configuration values inside a widget by passing the value and the name of the argument. This appendix contains a list of the available arguments.
E	Enums	Throughout GNOME and GTK+, enumerated types are used as values. This appendix contains a table organized by types and lists all of the available constant names.
F	Signals	Your program receives information from a widget by connecting to the widget's signals. This appendix lists the signals available in each widget.
G	Returns	Each GNOME and GTK+ object and data type is listed with the names of the functions that return it.

Example Code

Most things described in this book include actual code samples. As much as possible, these examples are complete running programs. In the past, I have found that a simple example—an example that demonstrates just one thing—was most useful to me when I needed to figure out (or be reminded) how to do something. Each example is intended to demonstrate one, or possibly two, specific things.

The examples are not really meant to demonstrate some kind of "correct" coding practice, or even the "correct" way to do a particular job. There is no correct way because, in GNOME and GTK+, there is usually more than one way to get any particular job done. And the overall style and design of a program is up to the programmer.

All of the example code, along with the make files for it, can be found here:

```
http://www.belugalake.com/book/gnomebible
```

Acknowledgments

I want to thank all of the GNOME software developers. This group has created an excellent graphical user interface. They have a right to be proud of what they have done. And I owe a debt of gratitude to the many members of the GNOME developer's group who took the time to answer my questions and help keep me on the right track.

John Osborn came up with the original concept for this book. He defined the original scope of the book, and then helped keep me in line when I tended to wander. And I need to thank Elyn Wollensky for keeping me in touch with the realities of writing.

I want to thank Laura Lewin for putting things together in such a way that the book became a reality. Kathi Duggan has the ability to keep everything in motion. Kathi kept track of every chapter and graphic as it moved from one stage of production to another, and from one person to another. I feel more secure in putting my name on the book because Jason Luster checked everything and pointed out my technical errors and omissions. Victoria Lee showed me how to convert my strange phrasing into sentences that someone could actually read and understand. Amy Barkat is very particular about the quality of graphics and kept me busy cleaning things up.

And, as always, that special lady who makes everything happen: Margot Maley at Waterside.

Contents at a Glance

Contents

• •

Getting Started

What Is This Thing Called GNOME?

This chapter introduces you to the basic concepts behind
writing a GNOME application program. I believe you will
find that writing a GNOME application is surprisingly easy to
do — and that process begins in Chapter 2 — but there are
some things you need to know first. Once you have an idea of
the structure of things, and of the naming convention, then the
existing code is much easier to read and you quickly should
become proficient at programming a GNOME application. If
you have written GUI programs before, you probably are
familiar with most of the concepts in the chapter, but you
may want to look through it anyway.

It's a Jumble Out There

GNOME has the advantage of being based on other software —
some of it has been around for a short while and some of it has
been around for a number of years. The software libraries are
gathered from several different sources. There are many
hundreds of man-years involved in software development to
bring us where we are today. Figure 1-1 shows the relationship
among the various software elements that make GNOME work.
But there is more to it than shows up in the diagram — many
applications include other libraries (such as image manipulation,
database, security, or special communications software) making
the diagram for a specific application even larger.

Figure 1-1: The levels of software for a GNOME application in Linux

While the figure shows each level isolated from levels other than those immediately above and below it, this is not quite true. All of the functions in the levels below are available. For example, a GTK+ function can make a direct call to an X function, and a GNOME application can make a direct call to a C library function.

The Software Levels

The following is a brief description of the contents of each of the levels shown in Figure 1-1.

C

There are actually two groups of C function calls. There are functions in the C standard library, such as printf() and memcpy(), and there are Linux system calls, such as open() and mkdir(). Because C was born and raised in a UNIX environment, it's not always easy to determine into which category a function falls.

glib

This is a library of C functions, macros, and structures that are used by GDK, GTK+, GNOME, and also used in an application. It contains functions for memory allocation, string formatting, date and time, I/O, and timers. It also has utility functions for linked lists, arrays, hash tables, trees, quarks, and caches. One of the crucial functions handled by glib is the main loop, which enables GNOME to handle multiple resources simultaneously and, at the same time, execute functions in the applications program.

X

This is the graphics library that contains the low-level functions used to control the display. All the fundamental windowing functions are included — these are functions that display the windows and respond to the mouse. This library has become very stable over the years and the version numbers rarely change. Currently, it is version 11 release 6 (also known as X11R6).

GDK

The *GIMP Drawing Kit*. GDK is primarily a library of functions that simplify the programmer's access to the functions of X. The X library is very low-level — it consists of a large number function that each do a specific and relatively simple task. GDK creates data structures to hold window configuration information and provide functions that can use this data to perform consistent tasks simply. For example, a color is stored in a `GdkColor` struct. There are functions that can use this struct to allocate the color in the color map automatically. If there is no room in the color map, it finds the existing color that is the closest fit.

GTK+

The *GIMP Toolkit*. The GTK+ library organizes the functions available from GDK into objects. Mostly these objects are displayable things such as buttons, labels, text-entry windows, and so on. An object of this sort is known as a *widget*. A widget can be very simple, or it can contain a number of other widgets and be quite complicated. These objects simplify things by providing color, size, position, mouse, keyboard, fonts, and other necessary items in single packages with standard interfaces.

GNOME

In a way, the GNOME library is a specialized extension of the GTK+ library. The GNOME desktop environment was developed to control the entire desktop and a GNOME application often uses some of the GNOME objects and functions to interface with some of the desktop widgets. GNOME leaves the basic widgets to GTK+ and adds some very specialized, and more complicated, widgets of its own. For example, the `GnomeAbout` widget includes, in one widget, the complete popup About box with lists of names, descriptive text, icon, and standard colors. You also can construct menus from relatively simple tables passed to a single function call.

Application

A GNOME application program is a program that calls `gnome_init()` to initialize the windowing capabilities, constructs one or more windows to be displayed, and then goes into a loop waiting for the keyboard or mouse.

Naming Conventions

There is a naming convention that helps in keeping things straight. In almost every case, you can look at the name of something (function, object, or whatever) and tell immediately which library it belongs to. Table 1-1 lists the prefixes and the types of things they usually represent. You may find an exception here and there, but they are rare because most open-source programmers are aware of the importance of clarity. At the very least, this naming convention gives you the freedom to select your own names simply by avoiding the known prefixes. One approach is to invent your own prefix and use it for everything in your application.

Table 1-1	
The Prefix Naming Convention	
Prefix	*Indicates*
G	Unless it is one of other G prefixes in this table, this is a data structure defined in glib.
g	A glib data type.
g_	A glib function.
Gdk	An object or data structure in the GDK library.
gdk_	A GDK function.
GDK_	A constant or macro defined in GDK. Most constants are defined as enum members.
Gnome	An object or data structure in the GNOME library.
GNOME_	A constant or macro defined in GNOME. Most constants are defined as enum members.
gnome_	A GNOME function.
Gtk	An object or data structure in the GTK+ library.
gtk_	A GTK+ function.
GTK_	A constant or macro defined in the GTK+ library. Most constants are defined as enum members.

Let Me Count the Ways

With any software development system, there is more than one way to write code to get a particular job done. This is even truer of an open software system like GNOME because there are so many programmers involved in developing the underlying functions. All GNOME hackers have their own notions about how things should be done, and the notions of every hacker vary (to some degree or other) from the notions of all others when writing GNOME code. This is not necessarily a bad thing—in fact it leads to a lot of variety and flexibility in the system.

But it does mean there is no single "standard" way to write GNOME code. For example, there are at least five different function calls that can be used to display a simple message box with an OK button. And, on top of that, there are a number of functions that can change the appearance of a message box once it is constructed.

The moral of this story is that if you get something to work, but it doesn't work exactly the way you would like, look around a little bit and you probably will find something that will make it do what you want. If not, consider it an invitation to become a hacker and modify or add a function, and offer the modifications back into the open source pool.

C Object Run

Object-oriented programming is simply a method of organizing the data and the code. Nothing more, nothing less. It is a type of organization that works very well. There are object-oriented languages (C++ and Java, for example) that automate most of the things that need to be done for a program to be composed of objects. C is not even remotely object-oriented. The GTK+ and GNOME libraries are all written in C, and the API consists only of C function calls. However, the code is written in an object-oriented fashion.

Part of the object-oriented structure is imposed by the pattern of function calls, and some of it by agreed-upon convention.

There are advantages and disadvantages to this form of organizing the code. Because the language is C, the code is much simpler and easier to read than if it were written in, say, C++. Also, the source code is more portable simply because a mature C compiler exists on just about every computer made. However, because the object orientation is not a part of the language itself, it has to be simulated. There are certainly places where the object structure is broken (inadvertently or otherwise). And it is easy for an application to break the structure.

There are several characteristics of objects, but the three important ones related to GNOME and GTK+ are *encapsulation*, *inheritance*, and *methods*.

Encapsulation

A characteristic of an object is that it encapsulates its data. That is, the data can be accessed only through function calls designed for that purpose. In object-oriented speak, these functions are called *methods*.

Because the objects are defined as C structs, there is nothing to prohibit you from reading and writing the values directly. But it is not a safe practice because you may miss taking some necessary action that goes along with changing the value. For example, say there is a field called width inside the struct of an object, and you want to increase it to make the window wider. To do this, call the function that sets the width instead of just poking the value in the field because there are probably other actions that the object must take to cause the new width value to actually change the window. Calling a function to set the value automatically takes care of these other items. Even if you take a peek at the source and observe that the function is doing nothing except setting a value, you still need to follow this rule because the next version could change that function to do something and your application could cease to work.

There are a few exceptions, but not many. This mostly happens with very simple objects. Some objects don't have functions defined for some of the fields, making it necessary to read and write the values directly. Most of the exceptions you come across will be in GDK because it wasn't designed to be object-oriented in the first place.

Inheritance

Whenever the code for a new object is written, it is based on an existing object. The code describing the object — the plan or blueprint of the object — is called a *class*. The class that the new class inherits from is called a *base class*. For example, the push button class named GtkButton uses another class named GtkBin as its base class. In turn, GtkBin inherits from another class, and that class from another, and so on until GtkObject is used as the base class. GtkObject is the only class that does not inherit from another class. All classes ultimately inherit from GtkObject. The following is the entire inheritance sequence of the GtkButton:

```
GtkButton->GtkBin->GtkContainer->GtkWidget->GtkObject
```

Note   Widgets, and widget operations, are very important to GNOME and GTK+. Every class that has GtkWidget somewhere in its heritage is a widget.

This inheritance is created by relationships inside the structs. Each struct includes the entire struct of its base class. And the base class struct is included as the first item in the struct. For example, the beginnings of the structs defining GtkButton look like this:

```
struct GtkButton {
    GtkBin bin;
    . . .

struct GtkBin {
    GtkContainer;
    . . .

struct GtkContainer {
    GtkWidget widget;
    . . .

struct GtkWidget {
    GtkObject object;
    . . .
```

As you can see from this organization, every class includes all of the data from all of its base classes. And, because the data of the base class is always at the very top of the struct, it is possible to cast a class to any of its base classes. This makes it possible to call the methods of any class in the inheritance, as explained in the next section.

Note
We are all guilty of allowing some laziness to creep in by not using the terms *class* and *object* consistently. Strictly speaking, a *class* is the definition code that is used to construct an object, while an *object* is a particular instance of the class. The process of creating an object is *instantiation*. That is, there is only one definition of the GtkButton class, but your program can have dozens of GtkButton objects. You will see and hear the term GtkButton used when referring to either the class or the object.

Methods

A *method* is used to create a new object from a class. For example, a GtkButton can be created by this function call:

```
GtkWidget *button;
button = gtk_button_new_with_label("Label");
```

All functions that create objects have the word new in their name. The function gtk_button_new_with_label() creates a button that displays the text "Label". Although the item created is a GtkButton object, its address is stored in a GtkWidget pointer. This is possible because of an object-oriented capability known as *polymorphism*. Polymorphism simply means that any object can be treated exactly as if it were one of its base classes. Using a GtkWidget pointer has some programming advantages because there are so many GUI interface functions that operate on GtkWidget objects.

When calling a method to operate on an existing object, the address of the specific object is passed as the first argument. For example, once the button is properly assigned to a position in a container, it can be displayed with the following function call:

```
gtk_widget_show(button);
```

The pointer data type of button is GtkWidget, so the function accepts it the same as it does any other widget. The methods of all the classes in the inheritance can be called by using the special casting macros. For example, to change the appearance of the decoration surrounding a button from the default appearance of beveled edges to a simple undecorated button, use the following:

```
gtk_button_set_relief(GTK_BUTTON(button),GTK_RELIEF_NONE);
```

Also, it is possible to store keyed data in an object with the following function call:

```
gtk_object_set_data(GTK_OBJECT(button),"key",data);
```

There are also the casting macros `GTK_BIN()` and `GTK_CONTAINER()`. In fact, there is a casting macro defined for *every* widget in GTK+ and GNOME. These macros do a bit more than simple casting. When your application is running, there is a test that makes sure the cast is valid. This verification can save a lot of the time you could waste chasing mysterious bugs.

The Things That Widgets Do

A widget can work in concert with other widgets, and with other parts of your program, but a widget essentially is a standalone object that requires function calls be made to retrieve or set data inside it. Most widgets have a window that appears on the display, but some special-purpose widgets never show a window.

The most common special-purpose widget is a *container*. A container widget is one that assumes the responsibility of controlling the size and position of one or more other widgets. For example, if you have a dialog box with OK and Cancel buttons that displays a line of text, there is some sort of container widget positioning and sizing the two buttons and the text window.

There are many kinds of container widgets. Some organize their child widgets in rows, columns, tables, while others arrange them one on top of the other and supply tabs so the user can switch from one to another. And because a container is a widget, and it also can contain widgets, a container can be used as the child widget in another container widget. You can, for example, have a container that organizes its child widgets into a column, and each member of the column can be another container that arranges its members into a row, a table, and so on.

Signals and Callbacks

Communication with the outside world (mouse and keyboard) is the responsibility of each widget. Your program doesn't have to continuously check to see, for example, whether a button has been pressed. Instead, you instruct the widget to call a function in your program whenever the button is pressed.

When a hardware action takes place—usually a keyboard keystroke, a movement of the mouse, or the pressing of a mouse button—an *event* is sent to your program. The event is translated into a *signal*. While an event has a one-for-one relationship with hardware, a signal does not. For example, a mouse button press is a single event and is translated into a signal, but a pair of mouse button presses close together also issues another signal for the double-click. In this example, two events generate three signals.

Events also come from the X window manager whenever there is some sort of change on the display. An event is issued whenever a window first appears, becomes hidden, changes size, becomes visible, is closed, or is moved. These all translate into signals and are made available to your applications.

There are also signals that originate inside widgets. Whenever it is moved, a scrollbar issues a signal with the information on its new position. A list issues a signal indicating which of its members the mouse selected. A toggle button indicates its state whenever it is turned on or off. A toolbar sends a signal to indicate that its orientation has changed from horizontal to vertical.

All of these signals are available to your program. All you have to do is tell the widget which signal you wish to receive, and what function is to be called to receive it. Because the widget calls you, the function is known as a *callback function*.

Enter glib of GIMP

There is a graphics utility program named *GIMP (GNU Image Manipulation Program)* that is distributed with most, if not all, Linux systems. The developers of GIMP created glib so they could simplify and standardize their software development. This library contains data type definitions, macros, data structures, and a large collection of utility function calls. The items from glib are used to create the GDK, GTK+, and GNOME libraries. This makes it very convenient for you to use them to create your application—in fact, there are some GTK+ and GNOME function calls that require a glib data type as an argument.

The Fundamental Data Types

There are a number of data types defined in `glib`. This is a matter of standardization and portability. The size of an `int` may be 16 bits on one machine and 32 bits on another. Also, a `char` may be unsigned on one system and signed on another. For example, if your code uses `gint32` instead of `int`, and `gchar` instead of `char`, your source code has a much better chance of being portable across platforms.

Note
You will find inconsistencies in the code. There are places, for example, where an `int` is used interchangeably with a `gint`. Since programmers all have their own style, and there are a lot of programmers involved in developing open-source software, things are bound to vary a bit. This is a small price to pay for the amazing amount and quality of software produced by the open-source process.

All of the primitive type definitions begin with the prefix letter g. An unsigned integer always begins with the prefix gu. This program lists all the primitive types and sizes:

```
/** gshow.c **/
#include <gnome.h>

int main(int argc,char *argv[])
{
    g_print("gchar:          %d\n",sizeof(gchar));
    g_print("guchar:         %d\n",sizeof(guchar));
    g_print("gint8:          %d\n",sizeof(gint8));
    g_print("guint8:         %d\n",sizeof(guint8));
    g_print("gshort:         %d\n",sizeof(gshort));
    g_print("gushort:        %d\n",sizeof(gushort));
    g_print("gint16:         %d\n",sizeof(gint16));
    g_print("guint16:        %d\n",sizeof(guint16));
    g_print("gint:           %d\n",sizeof(gint));
    g_print("guint:          %d\n",sizeof(guint));
    g_print("gint32:         %d\n",sizeof(gint32));
    g_print("guint32:        %d\n",sizeof(guint32));
    g_print("glong:          %d\n",sizeof(glong));
    g_print("gulong:         %d\n",sizeof(gulong));
    g_print("gint64:         %d\n",sizeof(gint64));
    g_print("guint64:        %d\n",sizeof(guint64));
    g_print("gfloat:         %d\n",sizeof(gfloat));
    g_print("gdouble:        %d\n",sizeof(gdouble));
    g_print("gpointer:       %d\n",sizeof(gpointer));
    g_print("gconstpointer:  %d\n",sizeof(gconstpointer));
    g_print("gboolean:       %d\n",sizeof(gboolean));
    exit(0);
}
```

The following is a makefile that can be used to compile this program. The gnome-config utility is used to set the environment necessary to compile and link GNOME programs. This process is described in detail in Chapter 2.

```
CC=gcc
LDLIBS=`gnome-config --libs gnomeui`
CFLAGS=-Wall -g `gnome-config --cflags gnomeui`

gshow: gshow.o
```

The definitions with names that end with the numbers 8, 16, 32, and 64 are the same length regardless of which platform is used. The other definitions may be different lengths (as defined by the C language). The 64-bit integers gint64 and guint64 are the ones declared in C as `long long`. When the program is run on an x586 based version of Linux, the output looks like this:

```
gchar:          1
guchar:         1
gint8:          1
guint8:         1
gshort:         2
gushort:        2
gint16:         2
guint16:        2
gint:           4
guint:          4
gint32:         4
guint32:        4
glong:          4
gulong:         4
gint64:         8
guint64:        8
gfloat:         4
gdouble:        8
gpointer:       4
gconstpointer:  4
gboolean:       4
```

Table 1-2 lists the definition names of the maximum and minimum values contained in some of the data types. There are also some macros defined, as shown in Table 1-3.

Table 1-2 Names of Extreme Values		
	Minimum	*Maximum*
gshort	G_MINSHORT	G_MAXSHORT
gint	G_MININT	G_MAXINT
glong	G_MINLONG	G_MAXLONG
gfloat	G_MINFLOAT	G_MAXFLOAT
gdouble	G_MINDOUBLE	G_MACDOUBLE

Table 1-3 **Some Useful Macros**	
XXXX	***XXXX***
ABS(a)	The positive value of a is returned.
MAX(a,b)	The numeric value a and b are of the same data type, and the macro returns the larger of the two.
MIN(a,b)	The numeric values a and b are of the same data type, and the macro returns the smaller of the two.
NULL	This is the address value assigned to a pointer to signify that it points to nothing.
TRUE and FALSE	There are many functions that require a gboolean type for an argument. One of these names can be used to pass a constant representing either a true or false condition. Also, if you write a function that returns a gboolean type, it can return one of these names.

Utility Functions of glib

This section introduces some of the functions that you will encounter throughout the code — and probably use throughout your application. There are many more functions than the ones I list here, but these are the ones you will encounter in GDK, GTK+, and GNOME source code. Also, you will find a few of them in the example code in this book and, because they can be so handy, you may want to use them yourself.

The functions listed here fall roughly into three categories: memory management, string manipulation, and textual output. There is some overlap among them — for example, a string duplication function may need to allocate memory.

g_free(gpointer mem)
The previously allocated block of memory at mem is returned to the system.

g_print(gchar *format,...)
This function is analogous to the standard C function printf(). It sends the format string to the standard output after inserting into it the other values passed as arguments.

g_printerr(gchar *format,...)
This function sends the format string to standard error after inserting into it the other values passed as arguments.

gchar *g_strconcat(gchar *,...)

Memory is allocated that is sufficient to hold all the strings passed in as arguments, the strings are concatenated into it, and its address is returned.

gchar *g_strdup(gchar *str)

This function allocates the memory necessary to hold the string, copies the string into the new memory, and returns its address.

gchar *g_strdup_printf(gchar *format,...)

Memory is allocated to hold a new string. The string is created according to the format (along with the optional data items) and a pointer to its address is returned.

gchar *g_strerror(gint errnumber)

When a C system call or standard C library call encounters an error condition, it stores the error code in the global value errno. This function converts the error number to a descriptive string.

gchar *g_strndup(gchar *str,gint num)

Memory is allocated that is large enough to hold a string of num characters, str is copied into it, and its address is returned.

gint g_str_equal(gchar *s1,gchar *s2)

This function returns TRUE if s1 is identical to s2.

gint g_strcasecmp(gchar *str1,gchar *str2)

This function performs a caseless compare (that is, *A* is equal to *a*) and returns TRUE if the strings are found to be identical.

gpointer g_malloc(gulong size)

This function allocates a new block of memory of size bytes and returns its address.

gpointer g_malloc0(gulong size)

This function allocates a new block of memory of size bytes, initializes it to zero, and returns its address.

gpointer g_memdup(gpointer mem,guint size)

The pointer mem is the address of size bytes. A new block of memory of the same size is allocated, the contents of mem is copied into it, and its address is returned.

gpointer g_realloc(gpointer mem,gulong size)

This function changes the size of a previously allocated block of memory. If the function finds it necessary to make a memory allocation to get `size` memory bytes, the data from `mem` is copied to the new location, `mem` is deleted, and the new address is returned.

gpointer memmove(gpointer dest,gpointer src, guint size)

The contents of `src` are copied into `dest`. Because `size` bytes are copied, both `dest` and `src` are assumed to be large enough. The return value is the `dest` pointer.

void g_strdown(gchar *str)

All uppercase letters in `str` are converted to lowercase.

void g_strup(gchar *str)

All lowercase letters in `str` are converted to uppercase.

Perusing the Source

GNOME is on the move. In fact, all of Linux is on the move. The development of the software outruns the development of the documentation, so from time to time, you will find it necessary to look through some of the source code to see what is going on. Although the clarity of the code varies from simple and obvious to totally obscure, there is a way to find the section of code you want to look at immediately. If you load all the source into directories underneath a single subdirectory, you can run this script and create a complete index of everything in the source code:

```
find . -name "*.c" -print >/tmp/clist
find . -name "*.h" -print >/tmp/hlist
cat /tmp/clist /tmp/hlist >/tmp/taglist
rm -f /tmp/clist
rm -f /tmp/hlist
ctags -L /tmp/taglist
rm -f /tmp/taglist
```

The result is that a file named `tags` is constructed in the local directory. This file is a database of the names and locations of every publicly accessible function, defined constant, struct, enum, and so on that is found in the C source files of all the subdirectories. The format of the tags file is the same for the vi editor; so, f or example, to locate a function named `gnome_app_new()`, type this on the command line:

```
vi -t gnome_app_new
```

The same script can be modified to generate a tag file for the emacs editor by adding the -e option to ctags, or by using etags like this:

```
etags -L /tmp/taglist
```

Summary

The GNOME development software does not stand alone. It is built on top of GTK+, GDK, glib, and X. Much of this software has matured over the years, and some of it is brand new. Other software libraries are used in GNOME applications for things such as communications and database access. When you write your GNOME application, you take advantage of literally hundreds of man-years of software development. Here are some of the basics covered in this chapter:

✦ While everything is written in C, the GTK+ and GNOME libraries are organized into a collection of objects in such a way that your program can predict and control their actions.

✦ Creating and using objects in C requires organization and discipline on the part of the programmer — but the rewards are worth it.

✦ The fundamental, displayable item is called a widget. There are dozens of widgets and, because of the object structure, they can all be dealt with in a standard manner.

✦ A GNOME application is event driven. That is, it spends most of its time displaying widgets and waiting for the user to do something with the mouse or keyboard. When the user does take action, a signal causes a callback function to execute passing the information to the application.

✦ There are times when there is nothing else you can do but go into the source code of the libraries you are using. Having the source code available is an enormous advantage when you need detailed information.

In the next chapter, you'll learn how to write some simple GNOME programs.

✦   ✦   ✦

Displaying a Window

O ften the mechanics of getting started can be confusing, especially when you are working with a new system or new software. This chapter demonstrates the construction of some very simple programs.

Getting Set Up

This chapter contains all the basic information you will need for writing a program that displays a window.

But, before you can do any programming, there is certain software that you need to install and configure. To be able to write a GNOME program, you must be running in the GNOME environment, have access to the C compiler, and have the GNOME and GTK+ libraries installed. Appendix A contains the complete list of everything you will need and how to install each item.

If you want a copy of all the source code in the book, you can find it at:

```
http://www.belugalake.com/book/gnomebible
```

The Hello World Program

The first thing to do is make sure things are set up so you can compile and link programs. In an empty directory, create a file named helloworld.c that contains the traditional hello world program:

```
/** helloworld.c **/
#include <stdio.h>
int main(int argc,char *argv[]) {
    printf("hello, world\n");
    exit(0);
}
```

You can compile it from the command line this way:

```
gcc helloworld.c -o helloworld
```

The gcc program recognizes the .c extension as being a C program. It compiles the program and links it with the standard libraries and, because of the -o option, writes the resulting executable to the file named helloworld. If there were no -o, the executable would have been named a.out. Type **./helloworld** and the program runs showing this output:

```
hello, world
```

Note You can use either cc or gcc. The file /usr/bin/cc is a symbolic link to /usr/bin/gcc. There is a similar program named /usr/bin/g++ that contains some additional features for C++.

The program gcc is sort of a "Jack of all trades" in the world of compiling and linking. In the command line that compiles the program, gcc assumes the program with the .c suffix is a C source code program. As shown in Table 2-1, there are other suffixes recognized by gcc.

Table 2-1
Suffixes Recognized by gcc

Suffix	File Contents
.a	A library file containing one or more object files (also called an *archive file*)
.c	Source code of a C program
.C	Source code of a C++ program
.cc	Source code of a C++ program
.cxx	Source code of a C++ program
.h	A preprocessor file
.i	Source code of a C program that already has been preprocessed
.ii	Source code of a C++ program that already has been preprocessed
.m	Source code of an Objective-C program
.o	An object file produced from compiling or assembling source code
.s	Source code of an assembly language program
.S	Source code of an assembly language program that needs to be preprocessed

Compiling and linking using gcc from the command line is simple enough, until the program being compiled gets more complicated. For a large program with multiple modules, you need to specify all the source modules and libraries on the command line. It is much simpler to use a *make file*. Create a file named makefile (or Makefile, **if you prefer) that contains this:**

```
helloworld: helloworld.c
```

To the left of the colon is the name of the executable file. To the right of the colon is the file the executable depends on. Enter the command:

```
make
```

One of two things happens. Either the program is compiled and stored on disk, or it does nothing at all. If there is a helloworld program already in the directory, and it is older than helloworld.c, it will not be compiled because there is no need — in other words, there has been no change to the source code.

The reason this compiles without specifically using the gcc command is that there are rules built into make that define how to create one file type from another. This is not just limited to C and C++. Make has rules for a number of languages. If you are terminally curious and want to get a list of them (it's quite a long list), you can enter this command:

```
make -p -f /dev/null >makelist
```

The -p option causes make to list all of its internal settings. The reason the -f option is used to specify /dev/null as the make file is that make normally reads the make file from the current directory, and the information from makefile would intermingle with the predefined information.

There are so many options and characteristics to make that it would take a large part of this book to explain them all. The make files used in this book are not that complicated, but they do require compiling and linking multiple program modules, as well as use specific libraries to resolve external references. As an example, here is another hello world program with two source files. The first one is named helloworld2.c:

```
/** helloworld2.c **/
#include <stdio.h>
void hellomath(double);
int main(int argc,char *argv[]) {
    printf("hello, world\n");
    hellomath(2.45);
    exit(0);
}
```

This is the mainline of a new hello world program. It is just like the previous program, except that it contains a call to the function named `hellomath()`. That function is defined in the file `hellomath.c`:

```
/** hellomath.c **/
#include <math.h>
#include <stdio.h>
void hellomath(double value) {
    printf("sine: %g\n",sin(value));
}
```

The mainline calls the function to have the value of the sine of 2.45 displayed. A make file that compiles and links the program looks like this:

```
LDLIBS=-lm

helloworld2: helloworld2.o hellomath.o

helloworld2.o: helloworld2.c

hellomath.o: hellomath.c

clean:
    rm -f helloworld2
    rm -f *.o
```

The first line of the make file specifies that the math library is to be included as part of the linking process. The variable `LDLIBS` is known to the rules - the ones that already exist in make - as information that is to be passed to the linker. We are using the `sin()` function, so we need the math library to be linked with the program. The `-l` option to name a library is a sort of shorthand for the real file name. The linker automatically precedes the name with `/usr/lib/lib` and then tags `.a` on the end. Thus, the option `-lm` names the math library, which is `/usr/lib/libm.a`.

The `helloworld2` executable is produced by linking the object files `helloworld2.o` with `hellomath.o` and any specified libraries. However, before the linker can take over, the dependencies on the next two lines are checked to determine whether the source code needs to be compiled into an object. If an object file is missing, or if the source is newer than the existing object file, it will be compiled.

There is a special command at the bottom of the make file that has no dependencies (which means it will always execute), and it can be used to delete the output files - thus forcing a complete compile and link on the next make command. It can be invoked like this:

```
make clean
```

The list of commands for clean can be anything - just as you would enter it from the command line. It is common to have special labels in make files for things such as make install (to copy files to other locations) or make force (which does a clean followed by a recompile).

Note   The make utility originated in the early days of UNIX and has some quirks left over from those early days. The one that is most likely to trip you up is that the tab character is part of the syntax. The two rm statements in the previous example must be indented by tabs, not simply spaces. It you get some kind of strange error message out of make, then check your tabs. Missing tabs can cause make to misinterpret a statement and issue an error message for what it thought it had found.

Here is another make file that does exactly the same thing as the previous one, but is a bit more explicit:

```
CC=gcc
LDLIBS=-lm
CFLAGS=-Wall -g

helloworld2: helloworld2.o hellomath.o
    $(CC) $(LDLIBS) helloworld2.o hellomath.o -o helloworld2

helloworld2.o: helloworld2.c
    $(CC) $(CFLAGS) -c helloworld2.c

hellomath.o: hellomath.c
    $(CC) $(CFLAGS) -c hellomath.c

clean:
    rm -f helloworld2
    rm -f *.o
```

Here the LDLIBS is set just as it was in the previous example, but the arguments to the linker are specified instead of being allowed to default. The commands used to compile the two source modules also are specified, and they use the variable named CFLAGS to pass arguments to gcc. The -Wall option tells the compiler to issue a warning for anything it finds — even some that work but are considered bad coding practices. This option is used in all the examples in this book to make sure the code is as clean as possible. The -g option causes debugging information to be compiled in with the code and you can use a symbolic debugger on the program. If you use this, you will want to remove the debugging information before you put the program into production since it causes the object files to be very large. You can remove the debug information from an object file with strip, or you can remove -g from CFLAGS and compile everything again.

There is a lot more to make than described here, but this is enough to get started compiling and linking programs. Some of the other things, such as linking with third-party libraries and establishing dependencies on header files, will pop up here and there. The make files in this book are as simple as is reasonably possible.

A Window from GTK+

GNOME software is actually built on top of GTK+, so we need to be able to compile and link with GTK+ before we can compile and link with GNOME. A GTK+ program is capable of managing windows, the mouse, and the keyboard. In fact, several of the graphical programs in this book don't have to call on GNOME to do any of the work because GTK+ is such a complete GUI package.

This program displays a simple window:

```
/** gtkwin.c **/
#include <gtk/gtk.h>

int main(int argc,char *argv[])
{
    GtkWidget *topLevelWindow;

    gtk_init(&argc,&argv);
    topLevelWindow = gtk_window_new(GTK_WINDOW_TOPLEVEL);
    gtk_widget_show(topLevelWindow);
    gtk_main();
    exit(0);
}
```

All of the GTK+ *include files* are in the directory /usr/include/gtk. The directory /usr/include is the standard include file directory so, to specify the location of gtk.h, it is only necessary to tell the compiler its directory name relative to /usr/include. And although there are dozens of include files for GTK+, it is only necessary to name this one because it includes all the others.

All GTK+ programs start with a call to gtk_init(). This function locates and opens the display, and initializes things like colors and signal handlers. The command line arguments passed into the program are passed on to gtk_init(), which reads and strips off any arguments intended for it and leaves the others in place. This technique enables the command line arguments to be addressed in either GTK+ or your application. Any arguments GTK+ doesn't understand, it leaves on the argv array for your application to address. It makes every effort to understand the arguments. However, if GTK+ can't use them, it passes them on down to GDK, which in turn passes them on to the X Window System. If an argument is used at any level, it is removed from argv.

The function get_window_new() is called to create *top level* window. The main window of any program is a top-level window. While a program can have more than one top-level window, it is more common to create one top-level window and create the other windows as dialogs attached to the top-level window. This example only has one window, so it is at the top level.

The function gtk_widget_show() displays the top-level window with all of its glorious defaults. The default size is 200 x 200 pixels, it has a gray background, and it uses the name of the program as the title of the window. The decoration around the outside of the window varies depending on the display manager, but Figure 2-1 shows what it looks like being run with GNOME.

Figure 2-1: The default window

Besides not doing anything other than displaying a blank window, this application completely ignores the mouse and keyboard, and doesn't stop running even when its window is closed. To stop it, you need to enter Ctrl+C from the terminal window you used to start it. If it is running in the background, you need to issue a kill command.

The call to gtk_main() is the blocking call that waits for instructions to come in through an event queue while the window is being displayed. In this example, because there are no responses specified for the keyboard and mouse, the arrival of input is ignored completely. In a normal program, gtk_main()is supplied with a list of functions to call on the arrival of specific events.

There are many ways of constructing a make file that will compile this program. I chose this particular format for its simplicity; it's easy to modify and expand for other tasks:

```
CC=gcc
LDLIBS=`gtk-config --libs`
CFLAGS=-Wall -g `gtk-config --cflags`

gtkwin: gtkwin.o
    $(CC) $(LDLIBS) gtkwin.o -o gtkwin

gtkwin.o: gtkwin.c
    $(CC) $(CFLAGS) -c gtkwin.c

clean:
    rm -f gtkwin
    rm -f *.o
```

Note There are better ways to create a make file. As a software project grows and contains more and more files, the make file becomes more and more cumbersome. It is best to automate certain aspects of make-file creation. I explain automatic make-file generation in Chapter 20.

In this make file, two variable names (`CFLAGS` and `LDFLAGS`) are defined to hold some information needed for the compiling and linking process. The `CFLAGS` contains a list of `gcc` arguments that are required for compilation, and `LDFLAGS` contains a list of `gcc` arguments that are required for linking. Usually, this is a very confusing task, but GTK+ has made it very simple by supplying a program (a script, actually) that generates the arguments automatically. This reduces the possibility of error and, as a bonus, automatically updates our make files to fit with any new releases of GTK+. You can see the generated arguments by entering these commands:

```
gtk-config --cflags
gtk-config --libs
```

Notice how `gtk-config` is used in the make file. A pair of backward tic marks - not the single quote mark – surrounds the command. This instructs `make` to execute the command and read the output from it as the string to store in the variable. The generated settings are all that is needed for the `LDFLAGS` variable. However, from the way `CFLAGS` is defined in the make file, you can see that it is possible to add other arguments on the line. The option `-Wall` turns on the highest level of warning messages and `g` causes debugging information to be included.

A Window That Closes

Most programs have a built-in "Close" option on a menu or toolbar. Also, the user can use the mouse to select the cross at the upper-right corner of a window to instruct the window to close. Selecting Close from the menu that pops down from the upper-left corner of the window is the same as selecting the cross at the upper right. Either way, an event is sent to the program informing it that the window is to be closed. To work properly, the program should intercept the event and make some decisions about what to do. The program can even refuse to allow the window to close. Mainly, the event mechanism provides the program an opportunity to flush buffers, close files, drop communication links, and whatever else nice programs do when they clean up behind themselves.

This program displays the default window and sets up a pair of functions to bring the program to a clean halt:

```
/** closewin.c **/
#include <gtk/gtk.h>
```

```
gint downCount = 0;

gint eventDelete(GtkWidget *widget,GdkEvent *event,
        gpointer data);
gint eventDestroy(GtkWidget *widget,GdkEvent *event,
        gpointer data);

int main(int argc,char *argv[])
{
    GtkWidget *topLevelWindow;

    gtk_init(&argc,&argv);
    topLevelWindow = gtk_window_new(GTK_WINDOW_TOPLEVEL);
    gtk_signal_connect(GTK_OBJECT(topLevelWindow),
            "delete_event",
            GTK_SIGNAL_FUNC(eventDelete),
            NULL);
    gtk_signal_connect(GTK_OBJECT(topLevelWindow),
            "destroy",
            GTK_SIGNAL_FUNC(eventDestroy),
            NULL);
    gtk_widget_show(topLevelWindow);
    gtk_main();
    g_print("Done!\n");
    exit(0);
}
gint eventDelete(GtkWidget *widget,GdkEvent *event,
        gpointer data) {
    g_print("Attempt number %d\n",++downCount);
    if(downCount > 2)
        return(FALSE);
    return(TRUE);
}
gint eventDestroy(GtkWidget *widget,GdkEvent *event,
        gpointer data) {
    g_print("Shutting down\n");
    gtk_main_quit();
    return(0);
}
```

This program displays the same default window as the programs in the previous example, but this one has code that allows for a controlled and tidy shutdown. The program begins with calls to gtk_init() and gtk_window_new() as in the previous example. This is followed by two calls to the function gtk_signal_connect().

The function gtk_signal_connect() relates an event to a specific function. There are four arguments passed to it. Every event is associated with a specific window, so the first argument is the window from which the event is expected. The second argument is the name of the event. The third argument is the name of the function to be called every time the event occurs. The macro GTK_SIGNAL_FUNC() simply casts the function to the type GtkSignalFunc(). The last argument is an optional pointer that you can use to pass data to your event-handler function.

When this program runs, the function gtk_widget_show() displays a window and gtk_main() goes to sleep waiting for some input from the window. The only window input that can have any meaning is either a "delete_event" or a "destroy" event because those are the only event handlers that are registered with the system. When you use the mouse to try to close the window, a "delete_event" is received by gtk_main() and the event is used as an argument in the call to eventDelete(). The value of downCount is incremented and, if it is less than 2, the eventDelete() function returns FALSE to prevent any further action. The window does not close and the program continues to run. On the other hand, if downCount is 3 or more, eventDelete() returns TRUE. This TRUE return causes the window to be classed immediately as closing and a "destroy" event is issued that causes a call to the function eventDestroy(). There is a call to gtk_main_quit() that causes the blocking call to gtk_main() to release and return. The program makes a clean exit. Running the program produces the following output:

```
Attempt number 1
Attempt number 2
Attempt number 3
Shutting down
Done!
```

As you can see from the order in which things occur, there are three places that your program can take control and clean up things before shutting down. It may not be a good idea to rely on the "delete_event" function for clean up because it is possible to have a "destroy" event arrive from some other source. It is probably best to rely on the "delete_event" only if you want to have the option of refusing to close the window. Otherwise, just put in a simple dummy that always returns TRUE. If you have work to do at shutdown, do it either in the "destroy" callback function, or in the mainline following the call to gtk_main().

The call to gtk_main_quit() is necessary. Without it, the call to gtk_main() continues to wait for an event on a nonexistent window. This is what happened in the previous example, and is the reason you had to kill the program after you closed the window.

Callbacks and Events

All GNOME and GTK programs are based on events being received and acted upon. As we just saw in the previous example, the mainline of the program sits and waits on an input queue for the arrival of an event and, when an event arrives, a function is called. A function called because of the arrival of an event is called a *callback function* because it is the GTK system that calls these functions in your program.

The events are handled in order, one at a time. Whenever `gtk_main()` reads an event from the queue, it checks to see if there are any callback functions that are assigned to it (there can be more than one) and, if so, these functions are called. When the last of these functions has returned, `gtk_main()` reads the queue looking for the next event.

There are events issued from locations other than a window. Your program can place events in the queue. For example, it is possible to set a period of time for an event to be hidden in the queue and this mechanism can set timers that will cause functions to be called. The queue also can be used for interprocess communications because other programs, by knowing the ID of your window, can place events in your queue.

A Window with a Button

The graphical elements are all widgets. There are menu widgets, label widgets, scroll bar widgets, and in this example, button widgets. This example displays a simple window with a push button and, when the mouse selects the button, reports that the button has been pushed:

```
/** buttonwin.c **/
#include <gtk/gtk.h>

gint eventDelete(GtkWidget *widget,
        GdkEvent *event,gpointer data);
gint eventDestroy(GtkWidget *widget,
        GdkEvent *event,gpointer data);
void eventButton(GtkWidget *widget,
        GdkEvent *event,gpointer data);

int main(int argc,char *argv[])
{
    GtkWidget *topLevelWindow;
    GtkWidget *pushMeButton;

    gtk_init(&argc,&argv);
    topLevelWindow = gtk_window_new(GTK_WINDOW_TOPLEVEL);
    gtk_signal_connect(GTK_OBJECT(topLevelWindow),
            "delete_event",
            GTK_SIGNAL_FUNC(eventDelete),
            NULL);
    gtk_signal_connect(GTK_OBJECT(topLevelWindow),
            "destroy",
            GTK_SIGNAL_FUNC(eventDestroy),
            NULL);
    pushMeButton = gtk_button_new_with_label("Push me!");
    gtk_signal_connect(GTK_OBJECT(pushMeButton),
            "clicked",
```

```
                   GTK_SIGNAL_FUNC(eventButton),
                   NULL);
          gtk_container_add(GTK_CONTAINER(topLevelWindow),
                   pushMeButton);
          gtk_container_set_border_width(
                   GTK_CONTAINER(topLevelWindow),30);
          gtk_widget_show(topLevelWindow);
          gtk_widget_show(pushMeButton);
          gtk_main();
          exit(0);
   }
   void eventButton(GtkWidget *widget,
          GdkEvent *event,gpointer data) {
       g_print("The button was pushed!\n");
   }
   gint eventDelete(GtkWidget *widget,
          GdkEvent *event,gpointer data) {
       return(FALSE);
   }
   gint eventDestroy(GtkWidget *widget,
          GdkEvent *event,gpointer data) {
       gtk_main_quit();
       return(0);
   }
```

This example builds on the previous one by adding a push button and a function that will be called whenever the button is pushed. This is done using the same callback procedure that we used to close the windows and the programs. The button (which is a widget) is created by calling gtk_button_new_with_label() and specifying the text for the button label. The button works just fine even without a callback function assigned to it, but your program will never know when the button is pushed. The call to gtk_signal_connect() specifies that the function eventButton() is to be called whenever the button is clicked. The program displays the window shown in Figure 2-2.

Figure 2-2: A simple push button

The click does not occur until you release the mouse button. When the mouse pointer is placed over the button, and the left mouse button is pressed, the button changes color to show that it is reacting to being selected. For the button to be clicked, the left mouse button must be pressed and released while the mouse pointer is inside the button. After pressing the left button, if you drag the mouse pointer outside of the button's rectangle before releasing, there is no click and no callback.

Once the button is created, and its callback designed, it is necessary to attach it to the window. This is done by a call to the function gtk_container_add(). Placing widgets in a window can be complicated and time consuming, and I cover this in Chapters 4 and 5. To keep things simple for now, place the button in the center of the window by calling gtk_container_set_border_width() to specify the size of the border that is to run around the edges of the top-level window. This border stays fixed no matter what the size of the window, and the only thing in the window is a button, so when the program is run and its top-level window is resized, the button stretches to fit as the margins around it stay the same.

A Window from GNOME

The code required to produce a GNOME window is very similar to the code to produce a GTK window. GNOME is a set of additions built on top of GTK and, for the most part, the functionality of GTK is left intact. GNOME takes full advantage of this situation - as you can see in this example program that displays a GNOME window:

```
/** gnomewin.c **/
#include <gnome.h>

int main(int argc,char *argv[])
{
    GtkWidget *topLevelWindow;

    gnome_init("gnomewin","1.0",argc,argv);
    topLevelWindow = gnome_app_new("gnomewin","Gnome Window");
    gtk_widget_show(topLevelWindow);
    gtk_main();
    exit(0);
}
```

This program is very similar to the program presented earlier named gtkwin. There are only two differences. This program calls gnome_init() instead of gtk_init() to initialize the system and the function gnome_init() calls gtk_init() to initialize the graphics. But it also does some other initialization that is specific to GNOME. The second difference is that this program calls the function gnome_app_new() to create the window, whereas the previous program called gtk_window_new().

There are four arguments to gnome_init(). The first argument is the ID string of the application and the second is its version number. The last two arguments are the ones found on the incoming command line. Notice argc is passed by value (instead of by address as was done earlier), which means that no arguments can be removed from the argv array because any change the function makes to argc will be lost.

The function gnome_app_new() creates a top-level application window by calling gtk_window_new(). The window is returned as a GtkWidget, just as in the previous programs. The first argument is the name of the application program.

This name is used internally by GNOME to identify the program. The second argument is the name title to be displayed at the top of the window as shown in Figure 2-3.

Figure 2-3: A simple GNOME window

Just like with the GTK make files in the earlier examples, there is a script that helps create the make file. The make file to compile gnomewin looks like this:

```
CC=gcc
LDLIBS=`gnome-config --libs gnomeui`
CFLAGS=-Wall -g `gnome-config --cflags gnomeui`

gnomewin: gnomewin.o
    $(CC) $(LDLIBS) gnomewin.o -o gnomewin

gnomewin.o: gnomewin.c
    $(CC) $(CFLAGS) -c gnomewin.c

clean:
    rm -f gnomewin
    rm -f *.o
```

The script named gnome-config is used to declare the options that are passed to gcc to compile and link programs. Using the back tic (grave accent mark) to surround the statement causes the script to execute and the output from the execution is assigned to the variable name. This is the same thing that was done earlier with gtk-config, except gnome-config has a few more options.

Note   There is more than one advantage to using gnome-config. It greatly simplifies writing make files because you don't have to remember to include the name of every library and make sure every compiler option is set correctly. Even better is that when you upgrade to a newer version of GNOME, your make files don't have to be changed. The new version of gnome-config automatically makes the adjustments for you.

In this make file, the variable CFLAGS is set to hold the options necessary for compiling, and LDLIBS is set for linking. You can see what these values are by using gnome-config from the command line. The actual values are certain to change from one software release to the next; but to give you an idea of what's involved, enter this command:

```
gnome-config --cflags gnomeui
```

The output it produces looks like this:

```
-I/usr/include -DNEED_GNOMESUPPORT_H -I/usr/lib/gnome-libs/
include -I/usr/X11R6/include -I/usr/lib/glib/include
```

As you can see, the compile option line mostly is made up of a list of directories containing include files. There is one variable definition. The only things you need to add are the include directories, if any, for your own application and any compiler settings you would like to make (such as the -Wall and -g options in this example). To get the list of libraries required, enter this:

```
gnome-config --libs gnomeui
```

The string it produces looks like this:

```
-rdynamic -L/usr/lib -L/usr/X11R6/lib -lgnomeui -lart_lgpl
-lgdk_imlib -lSM -lICE -lgtk -lgdk -lgmodule -lXext -lX11
-lgnome -lgnomesupport -lesd -laudiofile -lm -ldb -lglib -ldl
```

As you can see, there are a lot of libraries. Without the gnome-config script, maintaining this list could be very frustrating.

There are valid names other than gnomeui. For example, to compile an applet, LDLIBS can be set with this command:

```
gnome-config --libs applets
```

The result looks like this:

```
-rdynamic -L/usr/lib -L/usr/X11R6/lib -lpanel_applet -lgnorba
-lORBitCosNaming -lORBit -lIIOP -lORBitutil -lgnomeui -lart_lgpl
-lgdk_imlib -lSM -lICE -lgtk -lgdk -lgmodule -lXext -lX11
-lgnome -lgnomesupport -lesd -laudiofile -lm -ldb -lglib -ldl
```

There are a number of other valid names. The name gtk can be used to call the gtk-config script described earlier. Also, the name glib can be used to invoke the glib-config script. To see all of the available names, enter this:

```
gnome-config --help
```

The information comes from two sources. Some of the names, such as gnomeui, are inside the body of the script itself. Others, such as applets, are stored on disk in the directory /usr/lib. The file names begin with the name used on the command line and end with "Config.sh". For example, the file holding the applets settings is:

```
/usr/lib/appletsConfig.sh
```

Whenever the script doesn't already know the name on the command line, it looks in the /usr/lib directory for a file with the right name. Here, you can create your own environment settings. For example, if your project includes libraries and has its own include files, you can set all of those up as config files. The contents of these config files are very straightforward. Here is an example for a project named "fred." The file named /usr/lib/fredConf.sh contains this:

```
FRED_LIBDIR="-L/home/fred/lib"
FRED_LIBS="-lfredout -lmrk"
FRED_INCLUDEDIR="-I/home/fred/include"
```

Once this file is in place, it can be used in your make files just like the others:

```
CFLAGS=`gnome-config --cflags fred`
LDFLAGS=`gnome-config --libs fred`
```

The Beginning of a GNOME Application

This example brings together some things from the previous examples and creates a small main application window with a menu. This is a do-nothing GNOME application that just displays its window and waits for instructions to shutdown cleanly. It was written with the intention of being used as the seed source code when starting a new application.

```
 1 /** gnomebase.c **/
 2 #include <gnome.h>
 3
 4 static void shutdown();
 5 static void showhelp();
 6 gint eventDelete(GtkWidget *widget,
 7         GdkEvent *event,gpointer data);
 8 gint eventDestroy(GtkWidget *widget,
 9         GdkEvent *event,gpointer data);
10
11 GnomeUIInfo fileMenu[] = {
12     {   GNOME_APP_UI_ITEM,
13         N_("Exit"),N_("Close all files and exit"),
14         shutdown,NULL,NULL,
15         GNOME_APP_PIXMAP_STOCK,GNOME_STOCK_MENU_ABOUT,
16         0,0,NULL
17     },
18     GNOMEUIINFO_SEPARATOR,
19     GNOMEUIINFO_END
20 };
21
22 GnomeUIInfo helpMenu[] = {
23     {   GNOME_APP_UI_ITEM,
24         N_("Help"),N_("Display help information"),
```

```
25              showhelp,NULL,NULL,
26              GNOME_APP_PIXMAP_STOCK,GNOME_STOCK_MENU_ABOUT,
27              0,0,NULL
28          },
29      GNOMEUIINFO_SEPARATOR,
30      GNOMEUIINFO_END
31 };
32
33 GnomeUIInfo mainMenu[] = {
34      GNOMEUIINFO_SUBTREE(N_("File"),fileMenu),
35      GNOMEUIINFO_SUBTREE(N_("Help"),helpMenu),
36      GNOMEUIINFO_END
37 };
38
39 int main(int argc,char *argv[])
40 {
41      GtkWidget *appWindow;
42
43      gnome_init("gnomebase","1.0",argc,argv);
44      appWindow = gnome_app_new("gnomebase","Gnome Base");
45      gtk_widget_show(appWindow);
46      gnome_app_create_menus(GNOME_APP(appWindow),mainMenu);
47
48      gtk_signal_connect(GTK_OBJECT(appWindow),
49              "delete_event",
50              GTK_SIGNAL_FUNC(eventDelete),
51              NULL);
52      gtk_signal_connect(GTK_OBJECT(appWindow),
53              "destroy",
54              GTK_SIGNAL_FUNC(eventDestroy),
55              NULL);
56
57      gtk_main();
58      exit(0);
59 }
60 void showhelp() {
61      g_print("Show the help window\n");
62 }
63 gint eventDelete(GtkWidget *widget,
64          GdkEvent *event,gpointer data) {
65      return(FALSE);
66 }
67 gint eventDestroy(GtkWidget *widget,
68          GdkEvent *event,gpointer data) {
69      shutdown();
70      return(0);
71 }
72 void shutdown() {
73      gtk_main_quit();
74 }
```

The menus are defined as arrays of structures. Each item on the menu (button, separator, and so on) is a single entry in an array. There is one array that is the menu bar across the top. Each new menu level is stored in its own array. In the previous example, the menu bar itself is on line 33 as the `mainMenu` array. It contains two submenus that are defined by the macro `GNOMEUIINFO_SUBTREE` using the name of the submenu and the name of the submenu's defining array. The end of the array is marked by a `GNOMEUIINFO_END` entry.

The two submenus, defined on lines 11 and 22, have one entry each. Each member of the array is a specific type, meaning that it does a specific job for the menu system. The submenus both have `GNOME_APP_UI_ITEM` as their types, and this means, when selected, there is a call made to a function. The first string is the name that appears on the menu, and the second string is the help tip that pops up when the menu item is used as a selection on a toolbar. Next comes the name of the function that is called when the menu item is selected. There are plenty of other options and settings; all of them are explained in Chapter 6.

The code that actually creates the menu and sets it up for management consists of a single function call to `gnome_app_create_menus()`. As its first argument, the function requires a pointer to a `GnomeApp` struct, so the macro `GNOME_APP` is used to get one from the `GtkWidget`, which is used to define the top-level window. The window displayed for this program is shown in Figure 2-4. The menu bar across the top shows the two selections defined in the program.

Figure 2-4: A simple application with a menu bar

There is a new way to exit the program. As in the previous examples, closing signals from the window manager can be caught causing the program to exit. But now there is also a menu selection, as defined on line 14, that calls the `shutdown()` function, as defined on line 72, to exit the program. With the idea that it is best to have a single exit point, `eventDestroy()` function calls `shutdown()`.

There is nothing really new in the make file. It looks like this:

```
CC=gcc
LDLIBS=`gnome-config --libs gnomeui`
```

```
CFLAGS=-Wall -g `gnome-config --cflags gnomeui`

gnomebase: gnomebase.o
    $(CC) $(LDLIBS) gnomebase.o -o gnomebase

gnomebase.o: gnomebase.c
    $(CC) $(CFLAGS) -c gnomebase.c

clean:
    rm -f gnomebase
    rm -f *.o
```

Summary

With GNOME on top of GTK, and GTK on top of Xlib, you can get a lot done by making one function call. A GNOME application does not spend any time with low-level configuration - it just goes straight for the window. If you successfully compiled and ran the examples in this chapter, you now have your GNOME and GTK software development environment set up and ready to go, and should be somewhat familiar with the following:

✦ The make utility, which runs and generates executables from source

✦ The configuration script gnome-config, which generates make-file options

✦ The relationship of GNOME to GTK

✦ The form of a GNOME application

In the next chapter, more windows are introduced. An application normally has one main window and other windows that pop up and down for special purpose. You also are introduced to events that must be retrieved from a window, and different ways to handle the mouse in the GNOME environment.

✦　　✦　　✦

Displaying a Popup Dialog

A program normally has one main window and can have
several other windows that pop up and down under
control of the mouse. This chapter is about the mechanism
required to create, display, and destroy these transient
windows.

Some transient windows occur so often that they are supplied
as a standard part of GNOME. For example, there is a box that
displays text and is closed with an OK button. Most applications
also require some specialized windows of their own. The first
half of this chapter demonstrates the use of the predefined
transient windows; the second half shows the mechanism for
creating and displaying temporary windows of your own.

The Popup, the Dialog, and the Widget

The terms *popup* and *dialog* are general computer terms and
tend to be used interchangeably. They have distinct meanings,
but they are similar enough that in many cases the use of either
term is appropriate. A *popup* is a window that suddenly appears
to give information to the user, accept input from the user, or
both. When the popup is no longer needed, it disappears
(sometimes said to *pop down*). A *dialog* is any window that
contains widgets, which display data and/or accept data input
from the user.

The GTK+ toolkit assigned special meanings to these terms.
A *popup* is a displayed window that has no decoration —
meaning that the window manager does not put a title bar
with the system menus on its top. A *dialog* is a displayed
window to which the window manager adds the title bar and
system menus.

A popup or a dialog is made up of one or more widgets. A *widget* is a single-purpose software object that usually displays a window. The window is used for input, output, or both. A widget can be quite simple (such as a push button) or quite complicated (such as a dynamically sized, pull-down selection list). There is an exception here and there, but most widgets are intended for inclusion in a window, along with other widgets, to define the interface for a popup or dialog window.

Dialogs Are on Their Own

There are all kinds of popup windows. The simple ones have a single statement and an OK button, and others have multiple labels and other widgets for data input. Normally a program has one main window and everything else is done by dialogs that appear and disappear under the control of the user's mouse.

When your program creates and displays a dialog, the dialog immediately goes off on its own. This architecture is part of the basics of the X Window System. Once a dialog is running, the function that created it returns so your program can continue to run. The only way your program can hear from a dialog is if it calls the optional callback function you specified. Of course, it can grab the mouse to prevent access to any other windows in your application, but your program won't know about that. It just waits patiently for input from the mouse or keyboard.

Every program uses the same function for its main loop:

```
gtk_main()
```

This function call waits for events to come from the mouse or the keyboard. Whenever an event arrives, the information is dispatched to the correct window, which, in turn, may invoke a callback function. If you write a callback function that uses a lot of time (for instance, sorting a huge file) the entire time your function is running, the mouse has no effect whatsoever because there are no events being read. There are ways to run time-consuming tasks while leaving the mouse active, as discussed in Chapter 5, but the point I want to make here is that a dialog box disassociates itself from your program so the event-grabbing loop in gtk_main() can continue to function.

The GNOME Defined Dialogs

There is a collection of dialog boxes that are predefined and ready to be displayed. They are the traditional information and question boxes that inform the user of things such as, "File not found!" and ask things such as, "Are you sure?"

Make a Simple Statement

This program demonstrates that a dialog box can be displayed using very little code:

```
/** okdialog.c **/
#include <gnome.h>

int main(int argc,char *argv[])
{
    gnome_init("okdialog","1.0",argc,argv);
    gnome_ok_dialog("A simple information window");
    gtk_main();
    exit(0);
}
```

Before the dialog can be displayed, it is only necessary to call gnome_init(). The function call to gnome_ok_dialog() creates and displays the dialog box as shown in Figure 3-1. The call to gtk_main() waits for you to click the OK button; when that happens, the dialog is closed.

Figure 3-1: A simple message popup

There is no information fed back to the program from this dialog. In fact, the program continues on just as if the dialog had not been displayed—it remains on the screen until the OK button is clicked and then it silently disappears.

The dialog box automatically adjusts its size to accommodate the size of the text. If the text is too long to fit on a single line, it can continue on the next line with the insertion of a newline character, like the ones in this example:

```
/** okmultiple.c **/
#include <gnome.h>

gchar message[] =
    "To display a message on\nmore than one line\n"
    "it is only necessary to insert\na newline character\n"
    "wherever you would like the line to break.";

int main(int argc,char *argv[])
```

```
{
    gnome_init("okmultiple","1.0",argc,argv);
    gnome_ok_dialog(message);
    gtk_main();
    exit(0);
}
```

The multiline dialog produced by this example is shown in Figure 3-2.

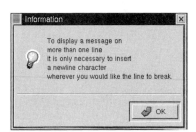

Figure 3-2: A simple message popup with multiple lines

A dialog box also can be made *modal*, which means that no other window in the application will accept mouse or keyboard input. This program demonstrates how that works:

```
 1 /** okmdialog.c **/
 2 #include <gnome.h>
 3
 4 int main(int argc,char *argv[])
 5 {
 6     GtkWidget *app;
 7     GtkWidget *dialog;
 8     GtkWidget *button;
 9
10     gnome_init("okmdialog","1.0",argc,argv);
11     app = gnome_app_new("okmdialog","Okay Dialog");
12     button = gtk_button_new_with_label("Button");
13     gtk_container_set_border_width(GTK_CONTAINER(app),30);
14     gnome_app_set_contents(GNOME_APP(app),button);
15     gtk_widget_show(button);
16     gtk_widget_show(app);
17
18     dialog = gnome_ok_dialog(
19             "A simple information window");
20     gtk_window_set_modal(GTK_WINDOW(dialog),TRUE);
21
22     gtk_main();
23     exit(0);
24 }
```

This program displays the dialog box previously shown in Figure 3-1, and also displays the window shown in Figure 3-3. Lines 10 through 20 create and display the main window and its button. While both the main window and the dialog are being displayed, only the button in the dialog box responds to the mouse because of the call to `gtk_window_set_modal()` on line 20. The button in the main window ignores the mouse until the OK button of the dialog box is clicked and the dialog closes. After that, the main window button works normally.

Figure 3-3: The button of the main window

Lines 15 and 16 display the `button` and `app` widgets. In this example, the `button` widget is displayed before its parent, the `app` widget. If the order of the calls to `gtk_widget_show()` is reversed, the end result is the same — but the process of painting the widgets on the screen is different. I discuss more about this later in the chapter.

The code on lines 18 through 20 that creates and displays the dialog does not require the `app` window as an argument. This means that a dialog easily can be created from any point in your program and can halt all window activity within the application until the dialog is acknowledged.

The calls to `gtk_widget_show()` on lines 15 and 16 can be in any order. The fact is that the `button` widget does not display at all if the `app` widget is not being displayed also, because the call to `gnome_app_set_contents()` on line 14 places the `button` inside the `app` widget. Generally speaking, it is better to display the widgets from the inside out this way because the entire window and all its widgets will appear at once. In a large window — one that contains lots of widgets — if the outer window is displayed first, the widgets can all appear one at a time after the containing window first appears.

Up until now, the dialog window has been a free agent and the mouse could place it either in front or behind any of the other windows on the display. This example shows that if the dialog has a parent window, it always remains in front of the parent. This seems to make especially good sense when using modal dialogs, because the parent window is inactive anyway and hiding the dialog could cause confusion. You can alter the program by changing lines 18 and 19 to this:

```
dialog = gnome_ok_dialog_parented(
        "A simple information window",
        GTK_WINDOW(app));
```

This causes the app window to be the parent of the dialog. Any window can be the parent of one or more child windows, so you can use this same technique for popping up dialogs for any window in an application.

There are two other dialog windows that work the same way as the OK dialog window. The warning and error dialog windows both have parented and non-parented modes, and they both can be modal or non-modal. To display the error window shown in Figure 3-4, change lines 18 and 19 to this:

```
dialog = gnome_error_dialog_parented(
        "A simple error window",
        GTK_WINDOW(app));
```

Figure 3-4: A simple error popup

The third form of the simple OK popups is the warning, as shown in Figure 3-5. The display code follows the same form as the others:

```
dialog = gnome_warning_dialog_parented(
        "A simple warning window",
        GTK_WINDOW(app));
```

Figure 3-5: A simple warning popup

Ask a Simple Question

To get a yes or no answer from a dialog box, it is necessary to find out which of the two choices the user made. The response is captured with a callback function. Here is an example of a program that displays a question dialog box and captures the response:

```
1 /** questiondialog.c **/
2 #include <gnome.h>
3
4 void cbfunction(gint reply,gpointer data);
5
6 int main(int argc,char *argv[])
7 {
8     gnome_init("questiondialog","1.0",argc,argv);
9
10    gnome_question_dialog("A simple question window",
11        (GnomeReplyCallback)cbfunction,
12        NULL);
13
14    gtk_main();
15    exit(0);
16 }
17 void cbfunction(gint reply,gpointer data) {
18    if(reply == GNOME_YES)
19        g_print("The answer is YES\n");
20    else
21        g_print("The answer is NO\n");
22 }
```

The window that this program displays is shown in Figure 3-6. The function call
on line 10 creates and displays the dialog box. The name of the callback function
cbfunction() is passed to the dialog so that, when the user selects either the
YES or NO button, the function is called to notify your program of the choice. The
cbfunction() function on line 17 is called from the dialog with an integer value
holding the reply and a copy of the data pointer that was passed in on line 12.
There is a reason for this data pointer — sometimes a callback function performs
an action that requires access to data and, instead of making the data global, it
can be passed in.

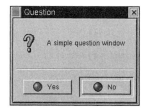

Figure 3-6: A simple question popup

When the question is answered, the value of the reply argument is either
GNOME_YES or GNOME_NO. An important point: you <u>must</u> use the named constants
for testing the reply value because the actual values are the reverse of those in the
standard C numeric true and false tests. This will give you an unexpected answer:

```
if(reply) . . .         /** wrong **/
```

There are four of these constant values. The constant value of GNOME_OK is the same as GNOME_YES, and GNOME_CANCEL is the same as GNOME_NO.

Here is another example that asks the same question previously shown in Figure 3-6, but this time the dialog is modal and is related to a parent window:

```
1 /** qmpdialog.c **/
2 #include <gnome.h>
3
4 void yes_or_no(gint reply,gpointer data);
5
6 int main(int argc,char *argv[])
7 {
8     GtkWidget *app;
9     GtkWidget *dialog;
10    GtkWidget *button;
11
12    gnome_init("qmpdialog","1.0",argc,argv);
13    app - gnome_app_new("qmpdialog","Question Dialog");
14    button = gtk_button_new_with_label("Button");
15    gtk_container_set_border_width(GTK_CONTAINER(app),30);
16    gnome_app_set_contents(GNOME_APP(app),button);
17    gtk_widget_show(button);
18    gtk_widget_show(app);
19
20    dialog = gnome_question_dialog_modal_parented(
21            "A simple question window",
22            (GnomeReplyCallback)yes_or_no,
23            NULL,
24            GTK_WINDOW(app));
25
26    gtk_main();
27    exit(0);
28 }
29 void yes_or_no(gint reply,gpointer data) {
30     if(reply == GNOME_YES)
31         g_print("The answer is YES\n");
32     else
33         g_print("The answer is NO\n");
34 }
```

This example displays a main window with a button, and pops up the question dialog box. The function call on line 20 creates the dialog with the main window of the application as its parent, and displays the dialog as modal. Because the dialog is parented, the main window (and its parent windows, if any) can never obscure the dialog. It also means that when the main window is moved from one place to another, the dialog moves with it. Being modal, the dialog prevents the button on the main window of the application from being sensitive. In other words, the question must be answered before the user can proceed with anything else. The modality only applies to the one application and no windows displayed by concurrently running applications are affected.

There are two other function calls that you can use to create the question dialog window. There are circumstances in which you may want to have a modal window, but not attached to a parent. To do this, change lines 20 through 24 to this:

```
dialog = gnome_question_dialog_modal(
        "A simple question window",
        (GnomeReplyCallback)yes_or_no,
        NULL);
```

As a result, the rest of the windows become inactive and don't respond to the mouse. Use this with care because the dialog can be hidden from view while the application windows are inactive, leading to confusion on the part of the user. To create a question dialog that stays on top of its parent window, but does not disable any windows in the application, change lines 20 through 24 to this:

```
dialog = gnome_question_dialog_parented(
        "A simple question window",
        (GnomeReplyCallback)yes_or_no,
        NULL,
        GTK_WINDOW(app));
```

Are You Sure?

A very common question asked by a program of a user is whether some requested action should take place. This type of question has its own dialog box, with OK and CANCEL buttons, as shown in Figure 3-7.

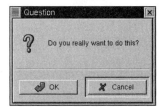

Figure 3-7: The last chance to cancel

The function called to do this is very similar to the question function of the previous example:

```
1 /** canmpdialog.c **/
2 #include <gnome.h>
3
4 void cancel_or_ok(gint reply,gpointer data);
5
6 int main(int argc,char *argv[])
7 {
8     GtkWidget *app;
```

```
 9      GtkWidget *dialog;
10      GtkWidget *button;
11
12      gnome_init("canmpdialog","1.0",argc,argv);
13      app = gnome_app_new("canmpdialog","Question Dialog");
14      button = gtk_button_new_with_label("Button");
15      gtk_container_set_border_width(GTK_CONTAINER(app),30);
16      gnome_app_set_contents(GNOME_APP(app),button);
17      gtk_widget_show(button);
18      gtk_widget_show(app);
19
20      dialog = gnome_ok_cancel_dialog_modal_parented(
21              "Do you really want to do this?",
22              (GnomeReplyCallback)cancel_or_ok,
23              NULL,
24              GTK_WINDOW(app));
25
26      gtk_main();
27      exit(0);
28 }
29 void cancel_or_ok(gint reply,gpointer data) {
30      if(reply == GNOME_CANCEL)
31          g_print("Action cancelled\n");
32      else
33          g_print("Action okayed\n");
34 }
```

The main window has a button that is disabled while the dialog is being displayed because the function call on line 20 that creates the dialog specifies a modal dialog. Also, the main window cannot hide the dialog because the dialog created is parented. However, there are other function calls that can be used to create non-modal and/or non-parented dialogs. It is a simple matter of replacing lines 20 through 24 with one of the following. To create a dialog that is parented but not modal, use this form:

```
dialog = gnome_ok_cancel_dialog_parented(
        "Do you really want to do this?",
        (GnomeReplyCallback)cancel_or_ok,
        NULL,
        GTK_WINDOW(app));
```

To create a dialog that is modal but not parented, use this form:

```
dialog = gnome_ok_cancel_dialog_modal(
        "Do you really want to do this?",
        (GnomeReplyCallback)cancel_or_ok,
        NULL,
        GTK_WINDOW(app));
```

To create a dialog that is neither parented nor modal, use this form:

```
dialog = gnome_ok_cancel_dialog(
        "Do you really want to do this?",
        (GnomeReplyCallback)cancel_or_ok,
        NULL,
        GTK_WINDOW(app));
```

Keyboard Input

There is a dialog box that you can use to get input directly from the keyboard. It prompts for the input of a single string, such as the name of a file or the URL of a web site. This program demonstrates the string dialog:

```
 1 /** stringdialog.c **/
 2 #include <gnome.h>
 3
 4 void stringCallback(gchar *string,gpointer data);
 5
 6 int main(int argc,char *argv[])
 7 {
 8     GtkWidget *app;
 9     GtkWidget *dialog;
10     GtkWidget *button;
11
12     gnome_init("stringdialog","1.0",argc,argv);
13     app = gnome_app_new("stringdialog","String Dialog");
14     button = gtk_button_new_with_label("Button");
15     gtk_container_set_border_width(GTK_CONTAINER(app),30);
16     gnome_app_set_contents(GNOME_APP(app),button);
17     gtk_widget_show(button);
18     gtk_widget_show(app);
19
20     dialog = gnome_request_string_dialog(
21             "File name",
22             (GnomeStringCallback)stringCallback,
23             NULL);
24     gtk_window_set_modal(GTK_WINDOW(dialog),TRUE);
25
26     gtk_main();
27     exit(0);
28 }
29 void stringCallback(gchar *string,gpointer data)
30 {
31     if(string == NULL)
32         g_print("Called back with a NULL string\n");
33     else if(strlen(string) == 0)
34         g_print("Called back with a zero-length string\n");
35     else
36         g_print("GOT: %s\n",string);
37 }
```

The call to gnome_request_string_dialog() on line 20 creates the dialog and displays it, as shown in Figure 3-8. When created, the dialog is assigned the callback function stringCallback() which is defined on line 29. Table 3-1 describes the four possible actions a user can take, and the result of each action.

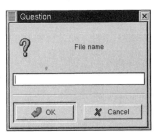

Figure 3-8: Prompt for user input

Table 3-1	
Results of User Responses	
Action	*Result in Callback*
Enter a string and select OK	The entered string is passed to the callback
Leave the string blank and select OK	A zero-length string is passed to the callback
Leave the string blank and select Cancel	A NULL string pointer is passed to the callback
Enter a string and select Cancel	A NULL string pointer is passed to the callback

There is no function to create a modal string dialog, but you may find it more convenient to have a modal string request. The dialog in the example program is modal because of the call to gtk_window_set_modal() on line 24. There is a function call that you can use to create a parented dialog—just change lines 20 through 23 to this:

```
dialog = gnome_request_string_dialog_parented(
        "File name",
        (GnomeStringCallback)stringCallback,
        NULL,
        GTK_WINDOW(app));
```

There are two other functions that create dialogs that accept string input, but with one difference. The entered text is not echoed to the screen. The window displays an asterisk for each character entered, as shown in Figure 3-9. You can modify the program that prompts for visible string input to prompt for obscured string by changing lines 20 through 23 to the following:

```
dialog = gnome_request_password_dialog(
        "Password",
```

```
        (GnomeStringCallback)stringCallback,
        NULL);
```

And you can create a parented version this way:

```
dialog = gnome_request_password_dialog_parented(
        "Password",
        (GnomeStringCallback)stringCallback,
        NULL,
        GTK_WINDOW(app));
```

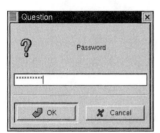

Figure 3-9: The password dialog

There are times when you need a little more control over the input string dialog box. You may want to specify the maximum length of the input string or initialize the dialog input with a default value. Do this using the function call in this example:

```
 1  /** requestdialog.c **/
 2  #include <gnome.h>
 3
 4  void requestCallback(gchar *string,gpointer data);
 5
 6  int main(int argc,char *argv[])
 7  {
 8      GtkWidget *app;
 9      GtkWidget *dialog;
10      GtkWidget *button;
11
12      gnome_init("requestdialog","1.0",argc,argv);
13      app = gnome_app_new("requestdialog","Request Dialog");
14      button = gtk_button_new_with_label("Button");
15      gtk_container_set_border_width(GTK_CONTAINER(app),30);
16      gnome_app_set_contents(GNOME_APP(app),button);
17      gtk_widget_show(button);
18      gtk_widget_show(app);
19
20      dialog = gnome_request_dialog(FALSE,
21              "File name",
22              "/var/tmp/workfile.dat",
23              36,
24              (GnomeStringCallback)requestCallback,
25              NULL,
```

```
26                    GTK_WINDOW(app));
27         gtk_window_set_modal(GTK_WINDOW(dialog),TRUE);
28
29         gtk_main();
30         exit(0);
31 }
32 void requestCallback(gchar *string,gpointer data)
33 {
34     if(string == NULL)
35         g_print("Called back with a NULL string\n");
36     else if(strlen(string) == 0)
37         g_print("Called back with a zero-length string\n");
38     else
39         g_print("GOT: %s\n",string);
40 }
```

The call to gnome_request_dialog() on line 20 creates the dialog box shown in Figure 3-10.

Figure 3-10: A string prompt with a default value

The first argument is either TRUE or FALSE to indicate whether or not the input string is to be obscured, as with a password. If the value is TRUE, both the initial value and any characters typed by the user are displayed as a string of asterisks. The second argument is the displayed prompt and the third is the default string value that is inserted into the text field as the dialog first appears. If no initial value is needed, you either can pass the function a NULL or a zero-length string.

The next parameter, on line 23 in this example, is the maximum number of characters that are allowed in the input string. Use 0 for the maximum if you don't want to limit the number of characters. The number of characters can be more than will fit in the data entry window because the window can be scrolled back and forth as necessary to allow data entry.

The last two arguments are the same as in the previous examples. Line 25 is the data pointer that is passed to the callback routine and, the last parameter, is the window that will be the parent of this one. If you don't want the dialog parented, pass a NULL pointer as the parent's window.

Data to the Callback

As shown in the previous examples, there is a provision for passing a data pointer to the GNOME function that is passed on to the callback function. This data pointer is completely ignored by GNOME and GTK+, which means you can pass the address of anything you like. The ability to pass this pointer can be very useful in a program in which you make several related decisions in different locations.

For example, if a program responds to a Save As menu selection by popping up a dialog asking for the name of a file, the callback function may need to have access to the current file name as well as the one the user selects. This could be done by storing all the information in global variables, of course, but it is generally considered better for control and design to pass the data as arguments. But because you do not call the callback functions directly from your program, it is necessary to pass the arguments indirectly, as in this example:

```
 1 /** datacallback.c **/
 2 #include <gnome.h>
 3
 4 typedef struct {
 5     GtkWidget *app;
 6     gchar defaultFilename[40];
 7     gchar currentFilename[40];
 8 } pgmContext;
 9
10 gint eventDelete(GtkWidget *widget,
11         GdkEvent *event,gpointer data);
12 gint eventDestroy(GtkWidget *widget,
13         GdkEvent *event,gpointer data);
14 void saveAsButton(GtkWidget *widget,pgmContext *pc);
15 void setTermination(GtkWidget *app);
16 void fileSaveCallback(gchar *filename,pgmContext *pc);
17
18 int main(int argc,char *argv[])
19 {
20     GtkWidget *button;
21     pgmContext pc;
22
23     strcpy(pc.defaultFilename,"/var/dcall/sqlim.dat");
24
25     gnome_init("datacallback","1.0",argc,argv);
26     pc.app = gnome_app_new("datacallback","Data Passing");
27     setTermination(pc.app);
28
29     button = gtk_button_new_with_label(
30             "Save As");
31     gtk_signal_connect(GTK_OBJECT(button),
32             "clicked",
33             GTK_SIGNAL_FUNC(saveAsButton),
```

```
34                 &pc);
35         gnome_app_set_contents(GNOME_APP(pc.app),button);
36
37         gtk_container_set_border_width(
38                 GTK_CONTAINER(pc.app),30);
39         gtk_widget_show(button);
40         gtk_widget_show(pc.app);
41         gtk_main();
42         exit(0);
43 }
44 void saveAsButton(GtkWidget *widget,pgmContext *pc) {
45         GtkWidget *dialog;
46
47         dialog = gnome_request_dialog(FALSE,
48                 "File name",
49                 pc->defaultFilename,
50                 40,
51                 (GnomeStringCallback)fileSaveCallback,
52                 pc,
53                 GTK_WINDOW(pc->app));
54         gtk_window_set_modal(GTK_WINDOW(dialog),TRUE);
55 }
56 void fileSaveCallback(gchar *filename,pgmContext *pc) {
57         if((filename == NULL) || (strlen(filename) == 0))
58                 return;
59         strcpy(pc->currentFilename,filename);
60         g_print("Save file as %s\n",pc->currentFilename);
61 }
62
63 void setTermination(GtkWidget *app) {
64         gtk_signal_connect(GTK_OBJECT(app),
65                 "delete_event",
66                 GTK_SIGNAL_FUNC(eventDelete),
67                 NULL);
68         gtk_signal_connect(GTK_OBJECT(app),
69                 "destroy",
70                 GTK_SIGNAL_FUNC(eventDestroy),
71                 NULL);
72 }
73 gint eventDelete(GtkWidget *widget,
74         GdkEvent *event,gpointer data) {
75     return(FALSE);
76 }
77 gint eventDestroy(GtkWidget *widget,
78         GdkEvent *event,gpointer data) {
79     gtk_main_quit();
80     return(0);
81 }
```

This program displays a window with a single push button, as shown in Figure 3-11.

Figure 3-11: A Save As button

Passing data to a callback function is achieved by passing a single pointer. If you need to pass more than one piece of data, you can define a structure to contain the data and then pass a pointer to the structure. In this example, a structure for this purpose is defined as pgmContext on line 4 and, on line 21, a structure of this type is created. Line 23 inserts the default file name and line 26 stores a GtkWidget pointer to the application's main window. On line 31, the call to gtk_signal_connect() is made to specify the callback function for the button and, as the last argument, the address of the struct is passed as the data pointer. This means that whenever the button is pressed, the address of pc is passed to the callback function.

The callback function for the button is defined on line 44. All this function does is create a dialog window to enable the user to enter the name of the file. On line 49, the default file name from the pgmContext structure is inserted into the dialog and the resulting display is shown in Figure 3-12. Also, on lines 51 and 52, the addresses of the callback function and the pgmContext structure are supplied to the dialog so the function is called and the structure is passed to it. The dialog's callback function is fileSaveCallback(), as defined on line 56.

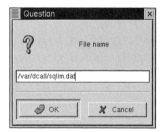

Figure 3-12: Prompt with a default string

The first argument to fileSaveCallback()is the name of the file entered by the user, and the second argument is the pgmContext data structure. The code on line 57 tests whether the user pressed the Cancel button or pressed the OK button with a zero-length file name. If the user entered a file name (or allowed the name to default) and pressed the OK button, the file name is stored in the structure on line 59.

This program simply prints the name of the file; but because the name of the file is stored in the context structure, another popup could be created to verify the name of the file. Or a progress bar could appear while the file is being saved. Or, because the user's selection is stored in the context structure, the structure could be used to create another thread allowing the file to be saved in the background.

Progress Bar

There is a GNOME dialog box that displays a constantly moving progress bar. An application creates the progress bar and then provides it with a constantly updated percentage-of-completion value. Here is a simple example that demonstrates a progress bar constantly updated at a regular interval:

```
1 /** progress.c **/
2 #include <gnome.h>
3
4 gdouble percentCallback(gdouble *pct);
5 void cancelCallback(gdouble *pct);
6 void stringCallback(gchar *string,gpointer data);
7
8 int main(int argc,char *argv[])
9 {
10     GtkWidget *app;
11     gdouble pct = 0.0;
12     GnomeAppProgressKey *kcy;
13
14     gnome_init("progress","1.0",argc,argv);
15     app = gnome_app_new("progress","Progress Dialog");
16
17     key = gnome_app_progress_timeout(GNOME_APP(app),
18             "Label for Progress Bar",
19             250,
20             (GnomeAppProgressFunc)percentCallback,
21             (GnomeAppProgressCancelFunc)cancelCallback,
22             &pct);
23
24     gtk_main();
25     exit(0);
26 }
27 gdouble percentCallback(gdouble *pct) {
28     if((*pct += 0.01) >= 1.0)
29         *pct = 1.0;
30     return(*pct);
31 }
32 void cancelCallback(gdouble *pct) {
33     gtk_main_quit();
34 }
```

There are two kinds of progress bars: those that are manipulated manually by your program and those that operate in an automatic mode. The one in the example is an automatic one that is created by the function call to `gnome_app_progress_timeout()` on line 17. The third argument is the number of milliseconds the program waits between calls to `percentCallback()`. The callback function `percentCallback()` defined on line 27 has the job of returning the percentage-complete value. The number is in the range of 0.0 to 1.0 (0% to 100% complete).

This example displays the progress bar shown in Figure 3-13. The `percentCallback()` function on line 27 is called by the progress bar once every 250 milliseconds, and, every time it is called, the percent value increases by 0.01 (the numeric equivalent of 1%).

Figure 3-13: A moving progress bar

The value does not need to change every time, as it does in this example. The value may stay the same for several callbacks. It is even possible to have the progress go in the other direction. For example, it reverses the movement of the bar if you initialize `pct` to 1.0 on line 11 and change the code on lines 28 and 29 to this:

```
if((*pct -= 0.01) >= 1.0)
    *pct = 1.0;
```

Notice that in this example the top-level window never appears. It is created because the progress bar needs to have a parent window. Since there is never a call to `gtk_widget_show()`, the top-level window never appears.

Creating a Popup and a Dialog

As shown in Table 3-2, there are three kinds of windows that you can create by making a call to `gtk_window_new()`. In the programs described earlier in this chapter, the main window was created with a call to `gnome_app_new()`, which made a call to `gtk_window_new()` using `GTK_WINDOW_TOPLEVEL` as the argument.

Table 3-2 The Window Types Known to GTK+	
Type	**Description**
`GTK_WINDOW_TOPLEVEL`	Normally used as the only main window for an application, but it is possible for a complicated application to have more than one.
`GTK_WINDOW_DIALOG`	A temporary window with one or more widgets. It has a title bar and system menu buttons just as the top-level window does.
`GTK_WINDOW_POPUP`	A temporary window with one or more widgets. It has no title bar or system menu buttons.

A popup window is under the control of the window manager. However, no application is required to have a top-level window in order to be able to use one or more popup or dialog windows. This example has no top-level window, but is able to use a popup with a button to close the application:

```
 1 /** hellopopup.c **/
 2 #include <gnome.h>
 3
 4 void buttonShutdown(GtkWidget *widget,gpointer data);
 5
 6 int main(int argc,char *argv[])
 7 {
 8     GtkWidget *popup;
 9     GtkWidget *button;
10
11     gnome_init("hellopopup","1.0",argc,argv);
12
13     popup = gtk_window_new(GTK_WINDOW_POPUP);
14     button = gtk_button_new_with_label("Close");
15     gtk_container_set_border_width(
16             GTK_CONTAINER(popup),20);
17     gtk_container_add(GTK_CONTAINER(popup),button);
18     gtk_signal_connect(GTK_OBJECT(button),
19             "clicked",
20             GTK_SIGNAL_FUNC(buttonShutdown),
21             NULL);
22     gtk_widget_show(button);
23     gtk_widget_show(popup);
24
25     gtk_main();
26     exit(0);
27 }
28 void buttonShutdown(GtkWidget *widget,gpointer data)
29 {
30     exit(0);
31 }
```

Line 13 creates a popup widget and line 14 creates the push button that goes into it. The call to gtk_container_add() on line 17 adds the push button to the popup widget, and line 18 assigns a callback method to the push button. Lines 22 and 23 display the popup window and the button as shown in Figure 3-14. The callback function beginning on line 28 simply exits the program with the call to exit() on line 30.

Figure 3-14: A popup window has no window manager frame.

A dialog window can be created with only one change to the code. The only difference between a popup and a dialog is the absence or presence of the window manager's controls. To have the window manager add a title bar and other window controls as shown in Figure 3-15, change line 13 to this:

```
popup = gtk_window_new(GTK_WINDOW_DIALOG);
```

Figure 3-15: A dialog window has a window manager frame.

Destroying After Popping Down

This example program introduces several new things. For one thing, it has a main window with more than one button as shown in Figure 3-16; for another, it introduces the callback function used to pop the window back down again. The top button on the main window brings up the popup window shown in Figure 3-17, and the bottom button brings up the dialog shown in Figure 3-18. This example pops up dialogs and, when a dialog is popped down, it is destroyed so its allocated memory is returned to the system:

```
 1 /** popup_dialog.c **/
 2 #include <gnome.h>
 3
 4 void destroyPopup(GtkWidget *widget,gpointer data);
 5 void destroyDialog(GtkWidget *widget,gpointer data);
 6 void showPopup(GtkWidget *widget,gpointer data);
 7 void showDialog(GtkWidget *widget,gpointer data);
 8 gint eventDestroy(GtkWidget *widget,
 9          GdkEvent *event,gpointer data);
10
11 int main(int argc,char *argv[])
12 {
13     GtkWidget *topLevelWindow;
14     GtkWidget *popupButton;
15     GtkWidget *dialogButton;
16     GtkWidget *box;
17
18     gnome_init("popup_dialog","1.0",argc,argv);
19     topLevelWindow = gtk_window_new(GTK_WINDOW_TOPLEVEL);
20     gtk_signal_connect(GTK_OBJECT(topLevelWindow),
21          "destroy",
22          GTK_SIGNAL_FUNC(eventDestroy),
23          NULL);
24     gtk_container_set_border_width(
```

```
25                 GTK_CONTAINER(topLevelWindow),20);
26      box = gtk_vbox_new(FALSE,0);
27
28      popupButton = gtk_button_new_with_label("Popup");
29      gtk_signal_connect(GTK_OBJECT(popupButton),
30              "clicked",
31              GTK_SIGNAL_FUNC(showPopup),
32              NULL);
33      gtk_box_pack_start(GTK_BOX(box),popupButton,
34              FALSE,FALSE,0);
35      gtk_widget_show(popupButton);
36
37      dialogButton = gtk_button_new_with_label("Dialog");
38      gtk_signal_connect(GTK_OBJECT(dialogButton),
39              "clicked",
40              GTK_SIGNAL_FUNC(showDialog),
41              NULL);
42      gtk_box_pack_start(GTK_BOX(box),dialogButton,
43              FALSE,FALSE,0);
44      gtk_widget_show(dialogButton);
45
46      gtk_container_add(GTK_CONTAINER(topLevelWindow),box);
47      gtk_widget_show(box);
48      gtk_widget_show(topLevelWindow);
49
50      gtk_main();
51      exit(0);
52 }
53 gint eventDestroy(GtkWidget *widget,
54              GdkEvent *event,gpointer data) {
55      gtk_main_quit();
56      return(0);
57 }
58 void showPopup(GtkWidget *widget,gpointer data) {
59      GtkWidget *popup;
60      GtkWidget *button;
61
62      popup = gtk_window_new(GTK_WINDOW_POPUP);
63      button = gtk_button_new_with_label("Close Popup");
64      gtk_container_set_border_width(
65              GTK_CONTAINER(popup),20);
66      gtk_container_add(GTK_CONTAINER(popup),button);
67      gtk_signal_connect(GTK_OBJECT(button),
68              "clicked",
69              GTK_SIGNAL_FUNC(destroyPopup),
70              popup);
71      gtk_widget_show(button);
72      gtk_widget_show(popup);
73 }
74 void showDialog(GtkWidget *widget,gpointer data) {
```

```
75      GtkWidget *dialog;
76      GtkWidget *button;
77
78      dialog = gtk_window_new(GTK_WINDOW_DIALOG);
79      button = gtk_button_new_with_label("Close Dialog");
80      gtk_container_set_border_width(
81              GTK_CONTAINER(dialog),20);
82      gtk_container_add(GTK_CONTAINER(dialog),button);
83      gtk_signal_connect(GTK_OBJECT(button),
84              "clicked",
85              GTK_SIGNAL_FUNC(destroyDialog),
86              dialog);
87      gtk_widget_show(button);
88      gtk_widget_show(dialog);
89 }
90
91 void destroyPopup(GtkWidget *widget,gpointer data)
92 {
93      gtk_widget_destroy(GTK_WIDGET(data));
94 }
95 void destroyDialog(GtkWidget *widget,gpointer data)
96 {
97      gtk_widget_destroy(GTK_WIDGET(data));
98 }
```

Figure 3-16: A main window with two buttons

Figure 3-17: A popup window with a Close button

Figure 3-18: A dialog window with a Close button

Lines 18 through 25 initialize GNOME, set the destroy callback, create a top-level window, and specify the margin around the window to be 20 pixels wide.

Line 26 creates a box widget, which is a special kind of widget called a *container*. A container widget is capable of organizing and displaying several widgets at once. This is necessary because the main window needs to display more than one widget.

Instead of inserting the buttons directly into the main window, they are inserted into the box lines 33 and 42. In turn, the box is inserted into the main window on line 47. There are two basic kinds of boxes (horizontal and vertical) and there are different ways of packing widgets into each of them, which I discuss in detail in Chapter 4. In this example, the function call `gtk_vbox_new()` on line 26 creates a box that organizes the buttons vertically, and the call to `gtk_box_pack_start()` on lines 33 and 42 insert the buttons into the vertical box starting at the top. The box resizes itself to fit snugly around the buttons, and the main window adds a 20-pixel border around the box.

The main window's callback functions, starting on lines 58 and 74, each create a temporary window. The function `showDialog()` creates and displays the dialog window shown in Figure 3-18 and the function `showPopup()` creates and displays the popup window shown in Figure 3-17. These two functions are almost identical except for the type of window specified on lines 62 and 78.

Both the popup and the dialog have callbacks that delete themselves. The call to `gtk_signal_connect()` on line 83 specifies `destroyDialog()` as the callback function for the dialog. The last argument passed to the function, on line 86, is a pointer to the dialog window. This pointer is passed to the callback function on line 95 as the `data` pointer. A call is made to `gtk_widget_destroy()` on line 97, causing the dialog to disappear and returning any allocated memory back to the system.

This program works, but it has a quirk or two that probably needs to be changed (depending on your application). As it stands here, you get a new dialog or popup every time you press one of the buttons in the main window—and you can get as many of them as you like. Each one uses the same callback and can be closed individually in any order, so there may be times when this comes in handy. However, for most programs, it makes more sense to allow only one copy of a dialog to appear.

One way to prevent multiple dialogs from appearing is to set your dialog to modal. The dialog in this example can be made modal by adding this line of code somewhere between lines 78 and 87:

```
gtk_window_set_modal(GTK_WINDOW(dialog),TRUE);
```

In the same way, the popup can be made modal by inserting this line between lines 62 and 71:

```
gtk_window_set_modal(GTK_WINDOW(popup),TRUE);
```

The function `gtk_window_set_modal()` can be used to change any window from non-modal to modal by using `TRUE` as the second argument. Conversely, this function also can be used to change any window from modal to non-modal by using `FALSE` as the second argument.

Popping Down by Hiding

In the previous example, a new dialog was constructed every time it was to be displayed; when it was closed, it was destroyed. This is a valid and especially useful approach if the dialog is to be a little different each time it is displayed. However, if a dialog is going to be used a lot, you may want to build it once and then pop it up and down whenever you want to. This example hides and redisplays a dialog:

```
 1  /** hiding.c **/
 2  #include <gnome.h>
 3
 4  void closeDialog(GtkWidget *widget,gpointer data);
 5  void showDialog(GtkWidget *widget,gpointer data);
 6  gint eventShutdown(GtkWidget *widget,gpointer data);
 7
 8  typedef struct {
 9      GtkWidget *dialog;
10  } hidingContext;
11
12  int main(int argc,char *argv[])
13  {
14      GtkWidget *topLevelWindow;
15      GtkWidget *dialogButton;
16      hidingContext context;
17
18      context.dialog = NULL;
19
20      gnome_init("hiding","1.0",argc,argv);
21      topLevelWindow = gtk_window_new(GTK_WINDOW_TOPLEVEL);
22      gtk_signal_connect(GTK_OBJECT(topLevelWindow),
23              "destroy",
24              GTK_SIGNAL_FUNC(eventShutdown),
25              &context);
26      gtk_container_set_border_width(
27              GTK_CONTAINER(topLevelWindow),20);
28
29      dialogButton = gtk_button_new_with_label("Dialog");
30      gtk_signal_connect(GTK_OBJECT(dialogButton),
31              "clicked",
32              GTK_SIGNAL_FUNC(showDialog),
33              &context);
34      gtk_container_add(GTK_CONTAINER(topLevelWindow),
35              dialogButton);
36
37      gtk_widget_show(dialogButton);
38      gtk_widget_show(topLevelWindow);
39
40      gtk_main();
41      exit(0);
```

```
42 }
43 gint eventShutdown(GtkWidget *widget,gpointer data) {
44     hidingContext *context;
45
46     context = (hidingContext *)data;
47     if(context->dialog != NULL)
48         gtk_widget_destroy(GTK_WIDGET(context->dialog));
49     gtk_main_quit();
50     return(0);
51 }
52 void showDialog(GtkWidget *widget,gpointer data) {
53     GtkWidget *button;
54     hidingContext *context;
55
56     context = (hidingContext *)data;
57
58     if(context->dialog == NULL) {
59         context->dialog =
60                 gtk_window_new(GTK_WINDOW_DIALOG);
61         button = gtk_button_new_with_label("Close Dialog");
62         gtk_container_set_border_width(
63                 GTK_CONTAINER(context->dialog),20);
64         gtk_container_add(GTK_CONTAINER(context->dialog),
65                 button);
66         gtk_signal_connect(GTK_OBJECT(button),
67                 "clicked",
68                 GTK_SIGNAL_FUNC(closeDialog),
69                 context->dialog);
70         gtk_window_set_modal(GTK_WINDOW(context->dialog),
71                 TRUE);
72         gtk_widget_show(button);
73     }
74     gtk_widget_show(context->dialog);
75 }
76
77 void closeDialog(GtkWidget *widget,gpointer data)
78 {
79     gtk_widget_hide(GTK_WIDGET(data));
80 }
```

The top-level window contains the button defined on lines 29 through 33. The callback function for the button is showDialog() defined on line 52. The data passed to the callback is the hidingContext struct defined on line 8. In a larger application, the struct could be expanded to hold more information; but in this example, it holds only a pointer to the dialog widget. The first call to hidingContext(), line 58, determines that the dialog doesn't exist, so it creates the dialog widget and stores its address in the struct. Once the dialog is created, it remains in existence and subsequent calls to hidingContext() simply makes sure it is displayed with the call to gtk_widget_show() on line 74.

The button in the dialog window, defined on line 61, uses the callback function closeDialog() defined on line 77. The data argument passed to the callback is the pointer to the dialog. In the callback, a call is made to gtk_widget_hide(), causing the dialog box — along with everything it contains — to disappear from the display.

Line 70 sets the dialog to modal. In this small, single-dialog example, this really doesn't matter because the only button on the main window is the one that displays the dialog, and there is only one copy of the dialog. This is unlike some of the previous examples where a new dialog was created each time, allowing the creation of any number of displayed dialogs. Multiple calls to gtk_widget_show() don't have any effect and the dialog continues to display and operate normally.

The callback function eventShutdown() closes the application, and there is a special situation because of the persistence of the dialog. If the dialog is on the display at the time the application is shut down, and it is not specifically destroyed, the dialog continues to display itself. This can be particularly bothersome. For example, if after the application has been halted the user makes a selection in the dialog (pressing the button), then there is no program there to receive the call to the callback function and an error is issued. The dialog continues to remain on the display because it has not been told to do otherwise. To prevent this, the eventShutdown() function, on lines 47 and 48, checks whether the dialog exists and calls gtk_widget_destroy() if it does.

Data Out and Data In

From the point of view of the program, dialogs and popups only exist to display data to the user, get data from the user, or both. There can be a number of widgets in a window that enable the user to enter data. The program must be able to insert data values into the widgets and, later, to retrieve data entered by the user.

The following is a simple program that sets up a dialog and retrieves the user input:

```
 1 /** dataoutin.c **/
 2 #include <gnome.h>
 3
 4 void closeDialog(GtkWidget *widget,gpointer data);
 5 void showDialog(GtkWidget *widget,gpointer data);
 6 gint eventShutdown(GtkWidget *widget,gpointer data);
 7
 8 typedef struct {
 9     GtkWidget *dialog;
10     GtkEntry *nameEntry;
11 } dataoutinContext;
12
```

```
13 int main(int argc,char *argv[])
14 {
15     GtkWidget *topLevelWindow;
16     GtkWidget *dialogButton;
17     dataoutinContext context;
18
19     context.dialog = NULL;
20     context.nameEntry = NULL;
21
22     gnome_init("dataoutin","1.0",argc,argv);
23     topLevelWindow = gtk_window_new(GTK_WINDOW_TOPLEVEL);
24     gtk_signal_connect(GTK_OBJECT(topLevelWindow),
25             "destroy",
26             GTK_SIGNAL_FUNC(eventShutdown),
27             &context);
28     gtk_container_set_border_width(
29             GTK_CONTAINER(topLevelWindow),20);
30
31     dialogButton = gtk_button_new_with_label("Dialog");
32     gtk_signal_connect(GTK_OBJECT(dialogButton),
33             "clicked",
34             GTK_SIGNAL_FUNC(showDialog),
35             &context);
36     gtk_container_add(GTK_CONTAINER(topLevelWindow),
37             dialogButton);
38
39     gtk_widget_show(dialogButton);
40     gtk_widget_show(topLevelWindow);
41
42     gtk_main();
43     exit(0);
44 }
45 gint eventShutdown(GtkWidget *widget,gpointer data) {
46     dataoutinContext *context;
47
48     context = (dataoutinContext *)data;
49     if(context->dialog != NULL)
50         gtk_widget_destroy(GTK_WIDGET(context->dialog));
51     gtk_main_quit();
52     return(0);
53 }
54 void showDialog(GtkWidget *widget,gpointer data) {
55     GtkWidget *box;
56     GtkWidget *okButton;
57     dataoutinContext *context;
58
59     context = (dataoutinContext *)data;
60
61     if(context->dialog == NULL) {
62         context->dialog =
63                 gtk_window_new(GTK_WINDOW_DIALOG);
```

```
64            gtk_container_set_border_width(
65                    GTK_CONTAINER(context->dialog),20);
66            box = gtk_vbox_new(FALSE,0);
67            gtk_container_add(
68                    GTK_CONTAINER(context->dialog),box);
69            gtk_widget_show(GTK_WIDGET(box));
70
71            context->nameEntry = (GtkEntry *)gtk_entry_new();
72            gtk_entry_set_text(context->nameEntry,
73                    "Initial String");
74            gtk_box_pack_start(GTK_BOX(box),
75                    GTK_WIDGET(context->nameEntry),
76                    FALSE,FALSE,0);
77            gtk_widget_show(GTK_WIDGET(context->nameEntry));
78
79            okButton = gtk_button_new_with_label("OK");
80            gtk_signal_connect(GTK_OBJECT(okButton),
81                    "clicked",
82                    GTK_SIGNAL_FUNC(closeDialog),
83                    context);
84            gtk_box_pack_start(GTK_BOX(box),
85                    okButton,FALSE,FALSE,0);
86            gtk_widget_show(okButton);
87
88            gtk_window_set_modal(
89                    GTK_WINDOW(context->dialog),TRUE);
90        }
91        gtk_widget_show(context->dialog);
92 }
93
94 void closeDialog(GtkWidget *widget,gpointer data)
95 {
96        dataoutinContext *context;
97        gchar *gotName;
98
99        context = (dataoutinContext *)data;
100
101        gotName = gtk_entry_get_text(context->nameEntry);
102        g_print("GOT: %s\n",gotName);
103
104        gtk_widget_hide(GTK_WIDGET(context->dialog));
105 }
```

The top-level window shown in Figure 3-19 has a single button that is used to pop up the dialog box shown in Figure 3-20. The dialog box here contains two widgets: a window allowing text entry and an OK button. When the OK button is pressed, the dialog disappears and the program displays the entered string on the command line. The structure of this program is not all that it should be, but it was kept simple to demonstrate the basic method of retrieving user-input data from the screen.

Figure 3-19: The main window contains a button to pop up the dialog.

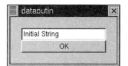

Figure 3-20: A dialog box capable of accepting keyboard input

The structure defined on line 8 is the data passed to the callbacks. It contains a pointer to the dialog widget and a pointer to the text-entry widget that is inside the dialog. With both of them in the structure, the display of the dialog can be controlled and the text can be extracted from the data-entry widget.

The context structure is initialized on lines 19 and 20. On line 35, its address is used as the data pointer passed to the button's callback function showDialog(). The showDialog() function starting on line 54 creates a new dialog if there is not one already installed in the context structure. When the data entry widget is created, on lines 72 and 73, the initial value in the window is set to the string "Initial String". The OK push button is built on lines 79 through 86, and has a callback assigned to it. On line 83, the address of the context struct is used as the data pointer to the callback function. There is no callback function defined for the data entry widget because it accepts and retains the user's input, and there is no need to retrieve the text until the OK button is pressed.

Starting on line 94 is the callback function for the OK button. The context pointer is passed to it, so it has the address of the data-entry widget and the dialog. Line 101 retrieves the character string from the data-entry widget. The return value from gtk_entry_get_text() is a pointer to the string. If you need to save the string, your program should make a copy of it before using it. (In this example, the string is simply printed and then ignored.) Memory for the string is allocated inside the widget, and then deallocated again by the widget.

The data-entry widget keeps track of the current string and displays its internal string whenever the dialog pops up. As the user edits the string, the internal string is modified. This way, the changes are in effect even after the window is popped down and back up again. This may or may not be what you want and there is more about data control in Chapter 4.

Summary

Dialog and popup windows are just like any other window. Once they are put on display, they have a life of their own with the only connection to the main program being one or more callback functions. For example, in this chapter you learned:

✦ There is a collection of built-in dialogs designed for the standard operations of displaying a message to the user or asking the user a yes or no question.

✦ A dialog can grab the mouse, preventing the rest of the application from being accessible.

✦ There are two basic kinds of temporary windows. A dialog pops up with a full frame around it, just as if it were the main window of an application. A popup pops up with no frame and no window manager controls.

✦ Widgets can be assigned a callback function and, when some specific action takes place, the function is called. The first parameter of the call is always the widget itself. The last parameter is the address that your program specified should be passed to the callback. There may or may not be other parameters in between these two.

✦ When a dialog disappears, it can be destroyed or it can be saved for display again.

✦ A dialog is a widget that contains another widget. The other widget it contains can be displayed as the dialog is being displayed. The widget contained in a dialog, or popup, window can be a special container widget. A container widget can organize and display several other widgets.

In the next chapter, you'll learn how to place widgets on windows using boxes and tables.

✦   ✦   ✦

Laying Out Widgets in a Window

✦   ✦   ✦   ✦

In This Chapter

Packing widgets in a box, horizontally and vertically

Varying the configuration settings of a box to change the way it arranges widgets

Packing widgets in a table, horizontally and vertically

Varying the configuration settings and packing commands to change the way a table arranges widgets

Combining tables and boxes

✦   ✦   ✦   ✦

This is the first of two chapters that are concerned with placing widgets on a window. In this chapter, the positioning is achieved using boxes and tables. The process of positioning widgets in a table or box is called *packing* widgets. Using boxes and tables, you can implement complicated windows rapidly. It is just a matter of creating the box or the table, and then stuffing the widgets into it. A box is also a widget and can be packed into other boxes. The same is true of a table. In fact, you can pack tables into boxes and boxes into tables.

Packing Boxes

There are two kinds of boxes. Widgets are displayed stacked one on top of the other packed into a vertical box, or they are displayed side by side packed into a horizontal box. It may be more accurate to refer to a box of widgets as a list of widgets because widgets must be arranged either side by side or one on top of the other. By nesting boxes, however, this process turns out to be very flexible and easy to manage.

A box is a widget designed to contain widgets. This means that a box may contain other boxes. For example, if a horizontal box contains a pair of vertical boxes, and each vertical box contains four widgets, the widgets are displayed in two columns and four rows. Further, because any widget contained in a box can be another box containing widgets, it is possible to create windows filled with widgets in many different patterns.

The sizing is all done automatically by the box "talking" to the widget it contains to find out what the widget can and cannot do. Each widget has its own internal height and width minimums, and the box must take these into account when calculating positions and dimensions of the layout. There are times when the box will request that the widget expand either vertically or horizontally to a size larger than the widget requires.

The Vertical Packing Box

A vertical box is a widget capable of containing several widgets and displaying them vertically like the ones in Figure 4-1.

Figure 4-1: Four buttons in a vertical box

This is an example program that creates the box shown in Figure 4-1 containing the four buttons:

```
 1 /** vertbox.c **/
 2 #include <gnome.h>
 3
 4 GtkWidget *makeBox();
 5 gint eventDelete(GtkWidget *widget,
 6        GdkEvent *event,gpointer data);
 7 gint eventDestroy(GtkWidget *widget,
 8        GdkEvent *event,gpointer data);
 9
10 int main(int argc,char *argv[])
11 {
12     GtkWidget *window;
13     GtkWidget *box;
14
15     gnome_init("vertbox","1.0",argc,argv);
16     window = gtk_window_new(GTK_WINDOW_TOPLEVEL);
17     gtk_container_set_border_width(
18            GTK_CONTAINER(window),25);
19     gtk_signal_connect(GTK_OBJECT(window),
20            "delete_event",
21            GTK_SIGNAL_FUNC(eventDelete),
22            NULL);
23     gtk_signal_connect(GTK_OBJECT(window),
24            "destroy",
25            GTK_SIGNAL_FUNC(eventDestroy),
```

```
26              NULL);
27
28       box = makeBox();
29       gtk_container_add(GTK_CONTAINER(window),box);
30       gtk_widget_show(window);
31       gtk_main();
32       exit(0);
33 }
34 GtkWidget *makeBox() {
35       GtkWidget *box;
36       GtkWidget *button;
37
38       box = gtk_vbox_new(FALSE,0);
39       gtk_widget_show(box);
40
41       button = gtk_button_new_with_label("Start 1");
42       gtk_box_pack_start(GTK_BOX(box),button,FALSE,FALSE,0);
43       gtk_widget_show(button);
44
45       button = gtk_button_new_with_label("End 1");
46       gtk_box_pack_end(GTK_BOX(box),button,FALSE,FALSE,0);
47       gtk_widget_show(button);
48
49       button = gtk_button_new_with_label("Start 2 button");
50       gtk_box_pack_start(GTK_BOX(box),button,FALSE,FALSE,0);
51       gtk_widget_show(button);
52
53       button = gtk_button_new_with_label("End 2 button");
54       gtk_box_pack_end(GTK_BOX(box),button,FALSE,FALSE,0);
55       gtk_widget_show(button);
56
57       return(box);
58 }
59 gint eventDelete(GtkWidget *widget,
60         GdkEvent *event,gpointer data) {
61       return(FALSE);
62 }
63 gint eventDestroy(GtkWidget *widget,
64         GdkEvent *event,gpointer data) {
65       gtk_main_quit();
66       return(0);
67 }
```

The mainline of the program creates a top-level window on line 16 and places a 25-pixel border around its edges on lines 17 and 18. After the shutdown callbacks are initialized, the box of widgets is created on line 28 with a call to makeBox(). The function gtk_container_add() on line 29 places the box widget in the main window, and the call to gtk_widget_show() on line 30 makes the main window visible.

The makeBox() function starting on line 34 constructs and returns a vertical box containing four buttons. The call to gtk_vbox_new() on line 38 constructs the box. The buttons are added in the order in which they will be displayed, but they can be added from the top or bottom. The button constructed on line 41 is added to the start of the box on line 42 — this means that it is inserted at the top of the box. The button constructed on line 45 is added to the end of the box on line 46 — this means that it is inserted at the bottom of the box. Any other widgets added to the top go below the ones that are already there, and any other widgets added to the bottom go above the ones already there.

The default size of the display in Figure 4-1 shows that everything fits. Each of the buttons reported its size to the box. The box wants to line things up along its edges, so it analyzes the height and width of each button to determine the over all size and position of each. All of the buttons are the same height so no vertical adjustment is necessary. The box determines the width of the widest button, which is the Start 2 button, and uses that value to set the width of all the buttons. Along with the width information, the box tells each button its *x* and *y* coordinates on the screen. Each button follows its instructions, centers its text, and displays itself at the requested location and in the requested size. The box is also a widget so when the main window queries the box for its size, the box returns the total area required for it to display all four buttons. The main window uses this size information, adding a pixel margin of 25 around the edges, to give the box its *x* and *y* coordinates.

The default sizes and configurations are optimal. The mouse can be used to resize the window, but it cannot be made smaller than its original size either horizontally or vertically. However, the mouse can be made larger. For example, lengthening the window vertically as shown in Figure 4-2 causes the box to spread things apart by splitting the list of buttons — the ones packed at the top stay at the top, and the ones packed at the bottom stay at the bottom. Stretching the box horizontally as shown in Figure 4-3 also resizes the buttons and they are stretched to fill the box.

Figure 4-2: Vertical resizing separates buttons.

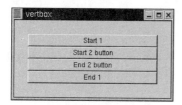

Figure 4-3: Horizontal resizing stretches buttons.

It is apparent that buttons cannot be expanded vertically by a vertical box, but they can be expanded to fill horizontally. Also, the offset of the widgets contained in a box is calculated from either the top or the bottom, depending on how the widget was added to the box. In practice, this turns out to be quite useful. If all the widgets are packed at one end of the box, they remain together on that end of the box no matter how much the box itself is stretched out of shape.

The Horizontal Packing Box

The horizontal and vertical boxes work exactly alike, except that packing a widget at the start puts it on the left and packing a widget at the end puts it on the right. The previous program named vertbox.c can be converted to horizbox.c by changing the name of the program and one line of code. Line 38 looks like this for the vertical box:

```
box = gtk_vbox_new(FALSE,0);
```

Replacing it with this line makes it a horizontal box:

```
box = gtk_hbox_new(FALSE,0);
```

That's all there is to it. The display now looks like the one in Figure 4-4.

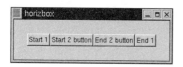

Figure 4-4: Four buttons in a horizontal box

Adjustments made to the size of a horizontal box have the same effect as adjustments to a vertical box, except they are made along the other dimension. Figure 4-5 shows the horizontal box made taller, and the buttons all made taller to fit. Figure 4-6 shows the horizontal box made wider and the buttons, instead of being resized, are positioned to fit against the end to which they originally were added.

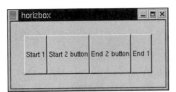

Figure 4-5: Vertical resizing stretches buttons.

Figure 4-6: Horizontal resizing separates buttons.

The Options of the Horizontal Box

There are three option settings that control how widgets are placed in a box. (Well, actually there are four settings, but I discuss spacing later in this chapter.) The three settings are Boolean, so there are a total of eight combinations as shown in Figure 4-7.

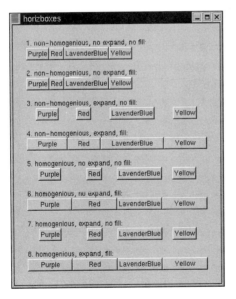

Figure 4-7: Using horizontal boxes to place widgets

In a horizontal box, the widgets are *homogeneous* if they are all assigned display areas of the same width. Each widget is displayed in the horizontal center of the area assigned to it, and the widget may or may not expand to fill the area.

The widgets can be instructed to *expand* so they use the entire box. This doesn't affect the displayed size of the widget. Instead it centers the existing widget in a region that may or may not be larger than the widget's natural width. The areas for each widget are allocated on a percentage basis. If one widget's minimum-size default is half that of another, that same size ratio is maintained after they are expanded to fill the box. For example, if a box is 800 pixels wide and it contains one widget that is 100 pixels wide and another that is 300 pixels wide, the size of both widgets are doubled to 200 and 600 pixels respectively to fill the box.

The widgets can be instructed to *fill* the area assigned to them. By default, the area assigned to a widget is also its minimum width; but if the widget has been commanded to expand, and has a larger area allocated to it, it widens to fill the area.

Figure 4-7 shows all eight of the possible combinations, but there is some duplication. There are actually only six distinct display layouts. The display produced by numbers 5 and 7 are the same, as are the display from numbers 6 and 8. The reason is that if a box is homogeneous, the expand setting has no effect.

The window shown in Figure 4-7 is produced by the following program. It creates a main window containing a single vertical box. In turn, the vertical box is filled with all the horizontal boxes. Button widgets are used to fill the horizontal boxes because they are simple widgets with beveled edges, making it easy to see where each one begins and ends.

```
 1 /** horizboxes.c **/
 2 #include <gnome.h>
 3
 4 GtkWidget *makeBoxes();
 5 gint eventDelete(GtkWidget *widget,
 6         GdkEvent *event,gpointer data);
 7 gint eventDestroy(GtkWidget *widget,
 8         GdkEvent *event,gpointer data);
 9 void buttonFill(GtkWidget *box,gboolean expand,
10         gboolean fill,guint spacing);
11
12 static gchar *buttonLabel[] = {
13     "Purple",
14     "Red",
15     "LavenderBlue",
16     "Yellow"
17 };
18
19 int main(int argc,char *argv[])
20 {
21     GtkWidget *window;
22     GtkWidget *box;
23
24     gnome_init("horizboxes","1.0",argc,argv);
```

```
25      window = gtk_window_new(GTK_WINDOW_TOPLEVEL);
26      gtk_signal_connect(GTK_OBJECT(window),
27              "delete_event",
28              GTK_SIGNAL_FUNC(eventDelete),
29              NULL);
30      gtk_signal_connect(GTK_OBJECT(window),
31              "destroy",
32              GTK_SIGNAL_FUNC(eventDestroy),
33              NULL);
34
35      box = makeBoxes();
36      gtk_container_set_border_width(
37              GTK_CONTAINER(window),25);
38      gtk_container_add(GTK_CONTAINER(window),box);
39      gtk_widget_show(box);
40
41      gtk_widget_show(window);
42      gtk_main();
43      exit(0);
44 }
45 GtkWidget *makeBoxes() {
46      GtkWidget *vbox;
47      GtkWidget *hbox;
48      GtkWidget *label;
49
50      gboolean homogeneous;
51      gboolean expand;
52      gboolean fill;
53      gint hCount;
54      gint eCount;
55      gint fCount;
56      gint count = 0;
57      gchar labelString[80];
58
59      vbox = gtk_vbox_new(FALSE,0);
60
61      for(hCount = 0; hCount <= 1; hCount++) {
62          homogeneous = hCount ? TRUE : FALSE;
63          for(eCount = 0; eCount <= 1; eCount++) {
64              expand = eCount ? TRUE : FALSE;
65              for(fCount = 0; fCount <= 1; fCount++) {
66                  fill = fCount ? TRUE : FALSE;
67                  if(count > 0) {
68                      label = gtk_label_new(" ");
69                      gtk_box_pack_start(GTK_BOX(vbox),
70                              label,FALSE,FALSE,0);
71                      gtk_widget_show(label);
72                  }
73                  sprintf(labelString,"%d. ",++count);
74                  if(homogeneous)
```

```
 75                         strcat(labelString,"homogeneous, ");
 76                     else
 77                         strcat(labelString,"non-homogeneous, ");
 78                     if(expand)
 79                         strcat(labelString,"expand, ");
 80                     else
 81                         strcat(labelString,"no expand, ");
 82                     if(fill)
 83                         strcat(labelString,"fill:");
 84                     else
 85                         strcat(labelString,"no fill:");
 86                     label = gtk_label_new(labelString);
 87                     gtk_misc_set_alignment(
 88                             GTK_MISC(label),0,0);
 89                     gtk_box_pack_start(GTK_BOX(vbox),
 90                             label,FALSE,FALSE,0);
 91                     gtk_widget_show(label);
 92                     hbox = gtk_hbox_new(homogeneous,0);
 93                     buttonFill(hbox,expand,fill,0);
 94                     gtk_box_pack_start(GTK_BOX(vbox),
 95                             hbox,FALSE,FALSE,0);
 96                     gtk_widget_show(hbox);
 97                 }
 98             }
 99         }
100     return(vbox);
101 }
102 void buttonFill(GtkWidget *box,gboolean expand,
103         gboolean fill,guint spacing)
104 {
105     GtkWidget *button;
106     gint i;
107
108     for(i=0; i<4; i++) {
109         button = gtk_button_new_with_label(buttonLabel[i]);
110         gtk_box_pack_start(GTK_BOX(box),button,
111             expand,fill,spacing);
112         gtk_widget_show(button);
113     }
114 }
115 gint eventDelete(GtkWidget *widget,
116         GdkEvent *event,gpointer data) {
117     return(FALSE);
118 }
119 gint eventDestroy(GtkWidget *widget,
120         GdkEvent *event,gpointer data) {
121     gtk_main_quit();
122     return(0);
123 }
```

The call to makeBoxes() on line 35 returns the vertical box that contains all the horizontal boxes. Lines 36 through 39 define the border around the box, add it to the main window, and put it on display.

The function makeBoxes() starting on line 45 builds one box for each of the eight possible configuration settings. For this example, the display is somewhat repetitious and there is no need to assign callbacks to the buttons, so all the boxes and buttons are constructed with the loop beginning on line 61. Actually, this is a nested loop with a for statement for each of the settings. The Boolean values homogeneous, expand, and fill are toggled at the top of each loop and all possible combinations are used to construct a box full of buttons.

Each horizontal box is preceded by a blank label (for spacing), and a label that describes the settings of the box. Lines 67 through 72 insert the blank label. Lines 74 through 85 use the configuration settings to create the descriptive character string that is used to construct the label widget on line 86. The call to gtk_misc_set_alignment() on line 88 left-justifies the text in the label (the default centers it).

The call to gtk_hbox_new() on line 92 creates the horizontal box and the call to buttonFill() on line 93 fills it with buttons. This is where the configuration settings are made. It is up to the box — not the individual widgets — whether the widget placement is to be homogeneous, so the call to gtk_hbox_new() has as its first argument the Boolean homogeneous value. The expand and fill arguments are applied widget by widget, so they are passed to the buttonFill() function to be applied to each new button.

The function buttonFill() starting on line 102 uses the value of the arguments passed to it to pack a box with four button widgets. The button labels are created from an array of strings of different lengths so the differences in position are more apparent. The loop beginning on line 108 builds each button and adds it to the box.

The Options of the Vertical Box

Figure 4-8 shows the results of applying all eight combinations to a sequence of vertical boxes. Comparing the vertical boxes in this figure to the horizontal boxes shown previously in Figure 4-7 should give you a pretty good idea how the placement works. The same size and position rules apply to both horizontal and vertical orientation.

This example is very much like the previous one. The only differences in the program are the statements that are necessary to change the boxes from horizontal to vertical, and to have them display properly.

```
1 /** vertboxes.c **/
2 #include <gnome.h>
3
```

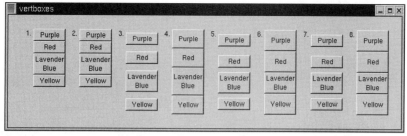

Figure 4-8: Using vertical boxes to place widgets

```
 4 GtkWidget *makeBoxes();
 5 gint eventDelete(GtkWidget *widget,
 6         GdkEvent *event,gpointer data);
 7 gint eventDestroy(GtkWidget *widget,
 8         GdkEvent *event,gpointer data);
 9 void buttonFill(GtkWidget *box,gboolean expand,
10         gboolean fill,guint spacing);
11
12 static gchar *buttonLabel[] = {
13     "Purple",
14     "Red",
15     "Lavender\nBlue",
16     "Yellow"
17 };
18
19 int main(int argc,char *argv[])
20 {
21     GtkWidget *window;
22     GtkWidget *box;
23
24     gnome_init("vertboxes","1.0",argc,argv);
25     window = gtk_window_new(GTK_WINDOW_TOPLEVEL);
26     gtk_signal_connect(GTK_OBJECT(window),
27             "delete_event",
28             GTK_SIGNAL_FUNC(eventDelete),
29             NULL);
30     gtk_signal_connect(GTK_OBJECT(window),
31             "destroy",
32             GTK_SIGNAL_FUNC(eventDestroy),
33             NULL);
34
35     box = makeBoxes();
36     gtk_container_set_border_width(
37             GTK_CONTAINER(window),25);
38     gtk_container_add(GTK_CONTAINER(window),box);
39     gtk_widget_show(box);
40
```

```
41    gtk_widget_show(window);
42    gtk_main();
43    exit(0);
44 }
45 GtkWidget *makeBoxes() {
46    GtkWidget *hbox;
47    GtkWidget *buttonBox;
48    GtkWidget *label;
49
50    gboolean homogeneous;
51    gboolean expand;
52    gboolean fill;
53    gint hCount;
54    gint eCount;
55    gint fCount;
56    gint count = 0;
57    gchar labelString[80];
58
59    hbox = gtk_hbox_new(FALSE,0);
60
61    for(hCount = 0; hCount <= 1; hCount++) {
62        homogeneous = hCount ? TRUE : FALSE;
63        for(eCount = 0; eCount <= 1; eCount++) {
64            expand = eCount ? TRUE : FALSE;
65            for(fCount = 0; fCount <= 1; fCount++) {
66                fill = fCount ? TRUE : FALSE;
67                if(count > 0) {
68                    label = gtk_label_new(" ");
69                    gtk_box_pack_start(GTK_BOX(hbox),
70                            label,FALSE,FALSE,0);
71                    gtk_widget_show(label);
72                }
73                sprintf(labelString," %d. ",++count);
74                label = gtk_label_new(labelString);
75                gtk_misc_set_alignment(
76                        GTK_MISC(label),0,0);
77                gtk_box_pack_start(GTK_BOX(hbox),
78                        label,FALSE,FALSE,0);
79                gtk_widget_show(label);
80                buttonBox = gtk_vbox_new(homogeneous,0);
81                buttonFill(buttonBox,expand,fill,0);
82                gtk_box_pack_start(GTK_BOX(hbox),
83                        buttonBox,FALSE,FALSE,0);
84                gtk_widget_show(buttonBox);
85            }
86        }
87    }
88    return(hbox);
89 }
90 void buttonFill(GtkWidget *box,gboolean expand,
91        gboolean fill,guint spacing)
```

```
 92 {
 93     GtkWidget *button;
 94     gint i;
 95
 96     for(i=0; i<4; i++) {
 97         button = gtk_button_new_with_label(buttonLabel[i]);
 98         gtk_box_pack_start(GTK_BOX(box),button,
 99                 expand,fill,spacing);
100         gtk_widget_show(button);
101     }
102 }
103 gint eventDelete(GtkWidget *widget,
104         GdkEvent *event,gpointer data) {
105     return(FALSE);
106 }
107 gint eventDestroy(GtkWidget *widget,
108         GdkEvent *event,gpointer data) {
109     gtk_main_quit();
110     return(0);
111 }
```

The name of the color defined on line 15 has a newline character in it, which forces the button to have two lines of text instead of just one. Having different numbers of lines makes the buttons vary in size a bit, helping to show how the positioning works.

The call to makeBoxes() on line 35 creates the collection of vertical boxes contained within a horizontal box, and line 38 adds the horizontal box to the main window. The three nested loops beginning on line 61 toggle the value settings to create all eight possible combinations. Lines 73 through 76 create a label for each vertical box. The label contains only a number so things display properly, but the numbers shown previously in Figure 4-8 mean the same thing as the ones shown previously in Figure 4-7.

Spacing Widgets in Boxes

There is more than one way to insert space between the widgets inside a box. You can specify a count of pixels to add to the space around every widget in a box, you can specify the amount of added space widget by widget, or you can do both of these at once. This works the same way with both horizontal and vertical boxes. This example demonstrates how spacing works in a vertical box.

```
1 /** spacebox.c **/
2 #include <gnome.h>
3
4 GtkWidget *makeBox();
5 gint eventDelete(GtkWidget *widget,
6         GdkEvent *event,gpointer data);
7 gint eventDestroy(GtkWidget *widget,
```

```
 8          GdkEvent *event,gpointer data);
 9
10 #define ALL_SPACE 5
11 #define FIRST_SPACE 0
12 #define SECOND_SPACE 0
13 #define THIRD_SPACE 0
14 #define FOURTH_SPACE 0
15
16 int main(int argc,char *argv[])
17 {
18     GtkWidget *window;
19     GtkWidget *box;
20
21     gnome_init("spacebox","1.0",argc,argv);
22     window = gtk_window_new(GTK_WINDOW_TOPLEVEL);
23     gtk_signal_connect(GTK_OBJECT(window),
24             "delete_event",
25             GTK_SIGNAL_FUNC(eventDelete),
26             NULL);
27     gtk_signal_connect(GTK_OBJECT(window),
28             "destroy",
29             GTK_SIGNAL_FUNC(eventDestroy),
30             NULL);
31
32     box = makeBox();
33     gtk_container_add(GTK_CONTAINER(window),box);
34     gtk_widget_show(window);
35     gtk_main();
36     exit(0);
37 }
38 GtkWidget *makeBox() {
39     GtkWidget *box;
40     GtkWidget *btn;
41
42     box = gtk_vbox_new(FALSE,ALL_SPACE);
43     gtk_widget_show(box);
44
45
46     btn = gtk_button_new_with_label("The First Widget");
47     gtk_box_pack_start(GTK_BOX(box),btn,
48             FALSE,FALSE,FIRST_SPACE);
49     gtk_widget_show(btn);
50
51     btn = gtk_button_new_with_label("The Second Widget");
52     gtk_box_pack_start(GTK_BOX(box),btn,
53             FALSE,FALSE,SECOND_SPACE);
54     gtk_widget show(btn);
55
56     btn = gtk_button_new_with_label("The Third Widget");
57     gtk_box_pack_start(GTK_BOX(box),btn,
58             FALSE,FALSE,THIRD_SPACE);
```

```
59        gtk_widget_show(btn);
60
61        btn = gtk_button_new_with_label("The Fourth Widget");
62        gtk_box_pack_start(GTK_BOX(box),btn,
63                FALSE,FALSE,FOURTH_SPACE);
64        gtk_widget_show(btn);
65
66        return(box);
67 }
68 gint eventDelete(GtkWidget *widget,
69          GdkEvent *event,gpointer data) {
70        return(FALSE);
71 }
72 gint eventDestroy(GtkWidget *widget,
73          GdkEvent *event,gpointer data) {
74        gtk_main_quit();
75        return(0);
76 }
```

The defined constants on lines 10 through 14 are the spacing values used to position the widgets in the vertical box. The value ALL_SPACE is applied to every widget in the box by being used as an argument to gtk_box_vbox_new() when creating the box on line 44. The other four values are applied to each widget by being used as arguments to each of widget insertion calls to gtk_box_pack_start() on lines 49, 54, 59, and 64.

The spacing values in the example program — a value of 5 for the box and 0 for each specific widget — results in the window shown in Figure 4-9. When the box does the spacing, it only inserts spaces between the widgets. There is no space inserted above the top widget or below the bottom one, but there is a five-pixel space inserted between each pair of widgets.

Figure 4-9: Vertical spacing is the same for all widgets

The spacing can be specified for each individual widget. You can create the display in Figure 4-10 by changing lines 10 through 14 to this:

```
#define ALL_SPACE 0
#define FIRST_SPACE 5
#define SECOND_SPACE 10
#define THIRD_SPACE 20
#define FOURTH_SPACE 40
```

Figure 4-10: Different spacing for each widget

There are 5 pixel spaces inserted on top of the first widget because the widget itself requests the margin. The box, when laying out the widgets, asks each widget how much space it needs. Because the first widget's spacing value is set to 5, it actually gets 10 extra pixels — 5 above and 5 below the body of the widget. The second widget then requests a spacing of 10, so there is actually a total of 15 pixels inserted between the first and second widgets. Similarly, there are 30 pixels (10 + 20) inserted between the second and third widgets, and 60 (20 + 40) pixels between the third and fourth. There are 40 pixels inserted below the fourth widget.

You can specify the spacing simultaneously for the box as a whole and for each individual widget. For instance, you can create the display in Figure 4-11 by changing lines 10 through 14 to:

```
#define ALL_SPACE 5
#define FIRST_SPACE 2
#define SECOND_SPACE 10
#define THIRD_SPACE 10
#define FOURTH_SPACE 2
```

Figure 4-11: Combining box and widget spacing

The actual spacing applied in each case is the sum of all the spacings that normally apply. The first widget is placed 2 pixels from the top of the window because the box only inserts the ALL_SPACE value between widgets. The spacing between the first and second widgets is a total of 17 pixels — the box specifies 5 pixels, the first widget adds 2, and the second widget adds 10. The space between the second and third widgets is 25 pixels, which is the sum of the overall spacing of 5 and the two individual widget's spacing of 10 each. Between the third and fourth widgets there are 17 pixels, and there are 2 pixels below the fourth widget.

Because the spacing value assigned to a widget is added both above and below it, there are combinations of spacing that you cannot achieve using this method. There is no direct way to have three widgets placed together with spaces inserted above and below them, without inserting another box to hold them (as demonstrated in the next section). But many special layouts can be defined by using spacing within a single box. For example, the layout in Figure 4-12 is achieved by changing the constants to this:

```
#define ALL_SPACE 0
#define FIRST_SPACE 0
#define SECOND_SPACE 30
#define THIRD_SPACE 0
#define FOURTH_SPACE 5
```

Figure 4-12: Varied widget spacing

This demonstrates that the distance between widgets can vary quite a bit. The first widget has no spacing defined, so it is placed against the top of its containing box. The second widget has 30 pixels inserted both above and below it. The fourth widget has 5 pixels inserted between it and the third widget, and between it and the bottom of the box.

Boxes within Boxes

You can achieve any combination of spacing and positioning you like by placing boxes inside other boxes. Boxes are designed to contain widgets, and boxes also *are* widgets, so you can pack boxes within boxes to your heart's content. I demonstrate this in some of the examples earlier in this chapter, but the following example shows how boxes within boxes can be used to lay out some complicated positioning. Let's say you want to have a window with one button at the top, three more clustered together in the middle, and two more side by side at the bottom like shown in Figure 4-13.

Figure 4-13: Using boxes within boxes
to position widgets

This layout is achieved by using a vertical box containing a single button at its
top, a nested vertical box in the center, and a horizontal box at the bottom. This
program creates the layout:

```
 1 /** boxnest.c **/
 2 #include <gnome.h>
 3
 4 GtkWidget *makeBox();
 5 GtkWidget *makeMiddleBox();
 6 GtkWidget *makeBottomBox();
 7 gint eventDelete(GtkWidget *widget,
 8         GdkEvent *event,gpointer data);
 9 gint eventDestroy(GtkWidget *widget,
10         GdkEvent *event,gpointer data);
11
12 int main(int argc,char *argv[])
13 {
14     GtkWidget *window;
15     GtkWidget *box;
16
17     gnome_init("boxnest","1.0",argc,argv);
18     window = gtk_window_new(GTK_WINDOW_TOPLEVEL);
19     gtk_signal_connect(GTK_OBJECT(window),
20             "delete_event",
21             GTK_SIGNAL_FUNC(eventDelete),
22             NULL);
23     gtk_signal_connect(GTK_OBJECT(window),
24             "destroy",
25             GTK_SIGNAL_FUNC(eventDestroy),
26             NULL);
27
28     box = makeBox();
29     gtk_container_add(GTK_CONTAINER(window),box);
30     gtk_widget_show(box);
31
32     gtk_widget_show(window);
33     gtk_main();
34     exit(0);
35 }
36 GtkWidget *makeBox() {
37     GtkWidget *box;
38     GtkWidget *button;
```

```
39        GtkWidget *middleBox;
40        GtkWidget *bottomBox;
41
42        box = gtk_vbox_new(FALSE,30);
43
44        button = gtk_button_new_with_label("Alone at Top");
45        gtk_box_pack_start(GTK_BOX(box),button,
46                FALSE,FALSE,0);
47        gtk_widget_show(button);
48
49        middleBox = makeMiddleBox();
50        gtk_box_pack_start(GTK_BOX(box),middleBox,
51                FALSE,FALSE,0);
52        gtk_widget_show(middleBox);
53
54        bottomBox = makeBottomBox();
55        gtk_box_pack_start(GTK_BOX(box),bottomBox,
56                FALSE,FALSE,0);
57        gtk_widget_show(bottomBox);
58
59        return(box);
60 }
61 GtkWidget *makeMiddleBox() {
62        GtkWidget *box;
63        GtkWidget *button;
64
65        box = gtk_vbox_new(FALSE,0);
66
67        button = gtk_button_new_with_label(
68                "First of Three in Middle");
69        gtk_box_pack_start(GTK_BOX(box),button,FALSE,FALSE,0);
70        gtk_widget_show(button);
71
72        button = gtk_button_new_with_label(
73                "Second of Three in Middle");
74        gtk_box_pack_start(GTK_BOX(box),button,FALSE,FALSE,0);
75        gtk_widget_show(button);
76
77        button = gtk_button_new_with_label(
78                "Third of Three in Middle");
79        gtk_box_pack_start(GTK_BOX(box),button,FALSE,FALSE,0);
80        gtk_widget_show(button);
81
82        return(box);
83 }
84 GtkWidget *makeBottomBox() {
85        GtkWidget *box;
86        GtkWidget *button;
87
88        box = gtk_hbox_new(FALSE,0);
89
90        button = gtk_button_new_with_label("Left");
91        gtk_box_pack_start(GTK_BOX(box),button,TRUE,TRUE,5);
92        gtk_widget_show(button);
```

```
 93
 94      button = gtk_button_new_with_label("Right");
 95      gtk_box_pack_end(GTK_BOX(box),button,TRUE,TRUE,5);
 96      gtk_widget_show(button);
 97
 98      return(box);
 99 }
100 gint eventDelete(GtkWidget *widget,
101         GdkEvent *event,gpointer data) {
102      return(FALSE);
103 }
104 gint eventDestroy(GtkWidget *widget,
105         GdkEvent *event,gpointer data) {
106      gtk_main_quit();
107      return(0);
108 }
```

The call to makeBox() on line 28 creates the box and all its contents. The box is given to the container of the main window on line 29.

The makeBox() function beginning on line 36 creates a vertical box and inserts three widgets into it. On line 42, the box is created with the spacing between its contained widgets set to 30 pixels. The first widget is a button created and inserted into the box on lines 44 through 47. The second widget is a box returned from the call to makeMiddleBox() on line 49, and the third is the box returned from the call to makeBottomBox() on line 54. When displayed, the main window adjusts itself to fit the height and width of the box it contains. The height of the box, and thus the height of the window, is the sum of the height of each of these three widgets — plus two spaces of 30 pixels each.

The function makeMiddleBox() starting on line 61 creates a vertical box containing three buttons. This box is created with zero separation between the widgets, so its overall size is the width of the widest button and its height is the sum of all the button heights.

The function makeBottomBox() starting on line 84 creates a horizontal box that contains two buttons. The buttons are placed in the box as homogeneous (so they both are the same width) and instructed to expand (so they fill all the space available to them). Also, they both are given a 5-pixel spacing from its neighbor. The result is that, when the window is stretched horizontally, the buttons resize themselves and move to maintain the distances and ratios.

When you lay out a complicated window by packing boxes, you first need to figure out what your boxes are. It is not uncommon to have boxes nested three, four, or even five deep to get the exact layout you are after.

Packing Tables

You can place widgets in a window by using *x* and *y* coordinate values, and you can define the size of the grid. To place a widget on the grid, simply tell the widget where to go and how many grid squares to cover. This grid is called a *table* and is a container widget very much like a box, except it uses a different set of rules for positioning the widgets it holds.

Packing a Small Table

The widget layout shown in Figure 4-14 is based on a table that is two cells wide and three cells high. The edges of the widgets are attached to the edges of the cells. Figure 4-15 layout shows the 2x3 grid used to create the layout.

Figure 4-14: Positioning buttons by using a table

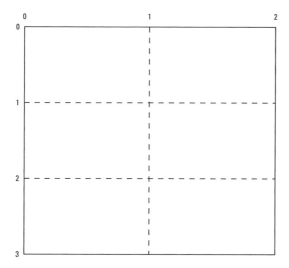

Figure 4-15: A 2x3 table grid

A widget is positioned in the grid by having its edges attached to the grid lines. All four edges of the widget must be attached to a grid line. For example, in Figure 4-14, the button labeled "Mid Left" is attached on its left to the vertical grid line 0 and on its right to the vertical grid line 1. Its top is attached to the horizontal grid line 1 and its bottom is attached to the horizontal grid line 2.

A single widget can cover any number of grids. For example, in Figure 4-14, the button labeled "Bottom" is attached to horizontal grids 2 at the top and 3 on the bottom, and vertical grids 0 on the left and 2 on the right. The horizontal attachment causes the button to stretch to cover two cells of the table.

The following program creates the display shown in Figure 4-14. The buttons are laid out on a table that is two columns wide and three rows high. The four buttons at the top of the window are each placed in a single cell within the table, and the button at the bottom covers two cells.

```
 1 /** fiver.c **/
 2 #include <gnome.h>
 3
 4 GtkWidget *makeTable();
 5 gint eventDelete(GtkWidget *widget,
 6         GdkEvent *event,gpointer data);
 7 gint eventDestroy(GtkWidget *widget,
 8         GdkEvent *event,gpointer data);
 9
10 int main(int argc,char *argv[])
11 {
12     GtkWidget *window;
13     GtkWidget *table;
14
15     gnome_init("fiver","1.0",argc,argv);
16     window = gtk_window_new(GTK_WINDOW_TOPLEVEL);
17     gtk_signal_connect(GTK_OBJECT(window),
18             "delete_event",
19             GTK_SIGNAL_FUNC(eventDelete),
20             NULL);
21     gtk_signal_connect(GTK_OBJECT(window),
22             "destroy",
23             GTK_SIGNAL_FUNC(eventDestroy),
24             NULL);
25
26     table = makeTable();
27     gtk_container_add(GTK_CONTAINER(window),table);
28     gtk_widget_show(window);
29     gtk_main();
30     exit(0);
31 }
32 GtkWidget *makeTable() {
33     GtkWidget *table;
```

```
34      GtkWidget *button;
35
36      table = gtk_table_new(3,2,TRUE);
37      gtk_widget_show(table);
38
39
40      button = gtk_button_new_with_label("Top Left");
41      gtk_table_attach_defaults(GTK_TABLE(table),button,
42              0,1,0,1);
43      gtk_widget_show(button);
44
45      button = gtk_button_new_with_label("Top Right");
46      gtk_table_attach_defaults(GTK_TABLE(table),button,
47              1,2,0,1);
48      gtk_widget_show(button);
49
50      button = gtk_button_new_with_label("Mid Left");
51      gtk_table_attach_defaults(GTK_TABLE(table),button,
52              0,1,1,2);
53      gtk_widget_show(button);
54
55      button = gtk_button_new_with_label("Mid Right");
56      gtk_table_attach_defaults(GTK_TABLE(table),button,
57              1,2,1,2);
58      gtk_widget_show(button);
59
60      button = gtk_button_new_with_label("Bottom");
61      gtk_table_attach_defaults(GTK_TABLE(table),button,
62              0,2,2,3);
63      gtk_widget_show(button);
64
65      return(table);
66 }
67 gint eventDelete(GtkWidget *widget,
68         GdkEvent *event,gpointer data) {
69      return(FALSE);
70 }
71 gint eventDestroy(GtkWidget *widget,
72         GdkEvent *event,gpointer data) {
73      gtk_main_quit();
74      return(0);
75 }
```

The call to the function makeTable() on line 26 returns the table widget and the buttons it contains. The table is added to the main window on line 27. The table is a widget, so it can be included in another window just the same as a box, a button, or any other widget.

The table itself is created on line 36 of the makeTable() function. The first argument is the number of rows and the second argument is the number of columns. The third argument specifies whether the table cells are to be homogeneous — in other words, whether to force all the cells to be the same size. In this example, the cells are homogeneous. A table sizes itself to fit whatever widget it contains. If a table is homogeneous, all cells are exactly the same size because they are set to the height of the tallest cell and the width of the widest cell.

If a table is not homogeneous, the cells in each row are all the same height and the cells in each column are all the same width. The height of a row of widgets is the height of the tallest widget in the row, and the width is determined by the widest widget in a column. If there are no widgets in a column, the entire column has zero width.

Each widget is responsible for displaying itself. The table asks for the minimum widget heights and widths to achieve the sizing of each widget. It then figures out the minimum size for each row and column, and passes the adjusted height and width numbers back to each widget. One of the characteristics of a widget is that it has a standard set of function calls used to give instructions and return data.

 Cross-Reference   For more on the internals of widgetry, see Chapter 18.

The displayable widgets — in this example, a group of buttons — are created and added to the table on lines 40 through 63. The button created on line 40 is attached by the call to `gtk_table_attach_defaults ()` in line 41. The positional parameters are "0,1,0,1", which means attach the left to grid line zero, attach the right to grid line 1, attach the top to grid line zero, and attach the bottom to grid line 1. The positional arguments on line 52 are "0,1,1,2", which means attach the left to grid line 0, attach the right to grid line 1, attach the top to grid line 1, and attach the bottom to grid line 2.

To stretch a widget across two or more cells, you only need to specify the starting and ending grid lines. The "Bottom" button, which is positioned on line 61, has the positional values "0,2,2,3", which attaches it to grid line 0 on the left and grid line 3 on the right — grid line 2 is skipped and is covered by the widget.

Three Buttons on the Table

This program lays out three widgets on a table. Each widget displays, as its text, the numbers used to define its position in the table.

```
1 /** thrice.c **/
2 #include <gnome.h>
3
4 GtkWidget *makeTable();
5 gint eventDelete(GtkWidget *widget,
6          GdkEvent *event,gpointer data);
7 gint eventDestroy(GtkWidget *widget,
8          GdkEvent *event,gpointer data);
9
```

```
10 #define HOMOGENEOUS FALSE
11
12 #define ROWS 3
13 #define COLS 3
14
15 #define LOCATE_1N  0,1,0,1
16 #define LOCATE_2N  1,2,1,2
17 #define LOCATE_3N  2,3,2,3
18
19 #define LOCATE_1S "0,1,0,1"
20 #define LOCATE_2S "1,2,1,2"
21 #define LOCATE_3S "2,3,2,3"
22
23 int main(int argc,char *argv[])
24 {
25     GtkWidget *window;
26     GtkWidget *table;
27
28     gnome_init("thrice","1.0",argc,argv);
29     window = gtk_window_new(GTK_WINDOW_TOPLEVEL);
30     gtk_signal_connect(GTK_OBJECT(window),
31             "delete_event",
32             GTK_SIGNAL_FUNC(eventDelete),
33             NULL);
34     gtk_signal_connect(GTK_OBJECT(window),
35             "destroy",
36             GTK_SIGNAL_FUNC(eventDestroy),
37             NULL);
38
39     table = makeTable();
40     gtk_container_add(GTK_CONTAINER(window),table);
41     gtk_widget_show(window);
42     gtk_main();
43     exit(0);
44 }
45 GtkWidget *makeTable() {
46     GtkWidget *table;
47     GtkWidget *button;
48
49     table = gtk_table_new(ROWS,COLS,HOMOGENEOUS);
50     gtk_widget_show(table);
51
52
53     button = gtk_button_new_with_label(LOCATE_1S);
54     gtk_table_attach_defaults(GTK_TABLE(table),button,
55             LOCATE_1N);
56     gtk_widget_show(button);
57
58     button = gtk_button_new_with_label(LOCATE_2S);
59     gtk_table_attach_defaults(GTK_TABLE(table),button,
60             LOCATE_2N);
61     gtk_widget_show(button);
62
```

```
63      button = gtk_button_new_with_label(LOCATE_3S);
64      gtk_table_attach_defaults(GTK_TABLE(table),button,
65              LOCATE_3N);
66      gtk_widget_show(button);
67
68      return(table);
69 }
70 gint eventDelete(GtkWidget *widget,
71          GdkEvent *event,gpointer data) {
72      return(FALSE);
73 }
74 gint eventDestroy(GtkWidget *widget,
75          GdkEvent *event,gpointer data) {
76      gtk_main_quit();
77      return(0);
78 }
```

The constant definitions on lines 10 through 21 determine the size of the table, the placement, and the text of the button labels. In this example, the text of each button label displays the button's position in the table. The constant on lines 10 through 13 are used on the call to gtk_table_new() on line 49 to specify a 3x3 grid, and to specify that this table is not homogeneous. The definitions on lines 15 through 17 are used as the last four arguments to gtk_table_attach_default() on lines 54, 59, and 65.

The layout from this program is shown in Figure 4-16. The table is nonhomogeneous, so the width of the columns and heights of the rows can vary—but the buttons are all the same size forcing the rows and columns to be uniform.

Figure 4-16: Three widgets positioned on a table

The same program can be used to add space between the widgets, but a table must be homogeneous to insert spacing. To demonstrate this, the defined constants on lines 10 through 21 in the previous program are changed to this:

```
#define HOMOGENEOUS TRUE

#define ROWS 5
#define COLS 5

#define LOCATE_1N   0,1,0,1
#define LOCATE_2N   1,2,1,2
#define LOCATE_3N   4,5,4,5
```

```
#define LOCATE_1S "0,1,0,1"
#define LOCATE_2S "1,2,1,2"
#define LOCATE_3S "4,5,4,5"
```

This enlargens the grid to 5x5 and makes the table homogeneous. The last button is positioned in the lower-right corner of the table. Because the table is homogeneous, all cells are the same size and the display is like that shown in Figure 4-17.

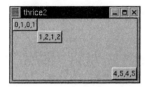

Figure 4-17: Blank area inserted by a homogeneous table

Changing the setting of HOMOGENEOUS from TRUE to FALSE changes the appearance of the window to that shown in Figure 4-18. Every cell in the table is set to its minimum size. There is nothing between vertical grid lines 2 and 4, so the minimum width of zero is used. Also, there is nothing between horizontal grid lines 2 and 4, so the minimum height of zero is used.

Figure 4-18: Blanks suppressed by a nonhomogeneous table

Remembering the correct order of the positioning parameters can be a problem. In the middle of positioning a bunch of widgets, you can find yourself in a which-number-goes-where quandary. If you get some of them in the wrong place, the resulting display can be very confusing. In fact, just a couple of misplaced numbers can cause the display to look so different, you may be inclined to start all over. I find it handy to sketch a little diagram, on a notepad or something, that looks like this:

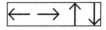

Each arrow points in the direction of the attachment. The first number specifies the grid line on the left; the second number specifies the grid line on the right, then the top, and finally the bottom.

Optional Settings

In all the previous examples, the function `gtk_table_attach_defaults()` was used to insert a widget into a table. If you need more control, make the call to `gtk_table_attach()` and override the default settings. These functions both use the same arguments, in the same order, except `gtk_table_attach()` requires four more arguments. The fact is that there is only one function. The function `gtk_table_attach_defaults()` calls `gtk_table_attach()` this way:

```
gtk_table_attach(table,
        widget,
        left_attach,
        right_attach,
        top_attach,
        bottom_attach,
        GTK_EXPAND | GTK_FILL, /* xoptions */
        GTK_EXPAND | GTK_FILL, /* yoptions */
        0,                     /* xpadding */
        0);                    /* ypadding */
```

The last two arguments are the horizontal and vertical *padding values*—the number pixels that specify either the width or height of a margin around the widget. The specified number pixels are added to both sides of the widget. For example, if you specify a padding value of 5, the overall size is increased by 10.

The `xoptions` and `yoptions` are flags that give instructions to the widget about how to place and size itself within the table cell. The values for this option are listed in Table 4-1. As you can see from the above argument list, the options can cause the widget to act one way vertically and another horizontally. When you mix these options with the *padding*, a table's grid positioning and homogeneous setting, there are a lot of possible combinations you can use to configure a widget's display.

Table 4-1 Values of the Table Attach Options	
Value	*Description*
0	The widget is not resized. It appears at its minimum size. If the containing cell, or cells, is larger than the widget, the widget is centered.
GTK_FILL	The widget expands to completely fill the cell, or cells, to which it is assigned. Resizing the table resizes the widget.
GTK_SHRINK	If the cell, or cells, containing the widget is smaller than its minimum size, it compresses itself further to fit.
GTK_EXPAND	This instructs the table itself to expand to fill any unused space in the window around it.

The following program demonstrates how these settings work:

```
 1 /** opset.c **/
 2 #include <gnome.h>
 3
 4 GtkWidget *makeTable();
 5 gint eventDelete(GtkWidget *widget,
 6         GdkEvent *event,gpointer data);
 7 gint eventDestroy(GtkWidget *widget,
 8         GdkEvent *event,gpointer data);
 9
10 #define HOMOGENEOUS FALSE
11 #define X_MARGIN 0
12 #define Y_MARGIN 0
13
14 struct {
15     gint setting;
16     gchar *text;
17 } op[] = {
18     { 0, "0" },
19     { GTK_EXPAND, "Ex" },
20     { GTK_FILL, "Fi" },
21     { GTK_SHRINK, "Sh" },
22     { GTK_FILL | GTK_EXPAND, "FiEx" },
23     { GTK_SHRINK | GTK_EXPAND, "ShEx" },
24     { GTK_FILL | GTK_SHRINK, "FiSh" },
25     { GTK_SHRINK | GTK_FILL | GTK_EXPAND, "ShFiEx" }
26 };
27
28 int main(int argc,char *argv[])
29 {
30     GtkWidget *window;
31     GtkWidget *table;
32
33     gnome_init("opset","1.0",argc,argv);
34     window = gtk_window_new(GTK_WINDOW_TOPLEVEL);
35     gtk_signal_connect(GTK_OBJECT(window),
36             "delete_event",
37             GTK_SIGNAL_FUNC(eventDelete),
38             NULL);
39     gtk_signal_connect(GTK_OBJECT(window),
40             "destroy",
41             GTK_SIGNAL_FUNC(eventDestroy),
42             NULL);
43
44     table = makeTable();
45     gtk_container_add(GTK_CONTAINER(window),table);
46     gtk_widget_show(window);
47     gtk_main();
48     exit(0);
```

```
49 }
50 GtkWidget *makeTable() {
51     int r;
52     int c;
53     int index;
54     GtkWidget *table;
55     GtkWidget *button;
56
57     table = gtk_table_new(2,4,HOMOGENEOUS);
58     gtk_widget_show(table);
59
60     for(r=0; r<2; r++) {
61         for(c=0; c<4; c++) {
62             index = (r * 4) + c;
63             button = gtk_button_new_with_label(
64                     op[index].text);
65             gtk_table_attach(GTK_TABLE(table),button,
66                     c,c+1,r,r+1,
67                     op[index].setting,
68                     op[index].setting,
69                     X_MARGIN,
70                     Y_MARGIN);
71             gtk_widget_show(button);
72         }
73     }
74     return(table);
75 }
76 gint eventDelete(GtkWidget *widget,
77         GdkEvent *event,gpointer data) {
78     return(FALSE);
79 }
80 gint eventDestroy(GtkWidget *widget,
81         GdkEvent *event,gpointer data) {
82     gtk_main_quit();
83     return(0);
84 }
```

Lines 10 through 11 define whether the table is homogeneous and how much padding to add around the widgets. The struct array defined on lines 14 through 25 contains all the possible combinations for the options, along with a text label for each one. Line 57 creates a 2x4 table to hold all the widgets, and the loop beginning on lines 60 and 61 creates and inserts buttons into all the cells. Figure 4-19 shows the window as it first appears when the program is run. Figure 4-20 shows the window after using the mouse to expand it.

Figure 4-19: A nonhomogeneous window at its minimum size

Figure 4-20: A nonhomogeneous window expanded

All of the widgets with the GTK_FILLER (designated by "Fi" on the display) increased their size until they covered the entire cell. The option GTK_EXPAND ("Ex" on the display) did not cause its widgets to expand because GTK_EXPAND is really an instruction to the table, not to the widget.

All of these examples apply the same rules to both the vertical and horizontal components of widget space and size. However, with the two arguments, it is possible to set the options in each direction independently of one another. The window can be made homogeneous by changing line 10 to this:

```
#define HOMOGENEOUS TRUE
```

The resulting display, with every cell exactly the same size, is shown in Figure 4-21. When the mouse is used to resize the window, all the cells increase in size by the same amount as shown in Figure 4-22.

Figure 4-21: A homogeneous window at its minimum size

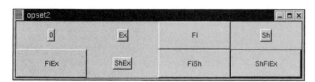

Figure 4-22: A homogeneous window expanded

The final two arguments are used for padding around a widget. You can create the window in Figure 4-23 by changing lines 10 through 12 to:

```
#define HOMOGENEOUS FALSE
#define X_MARGIN 5
#define Y_MARGIN 10
```

Every widget has 5 pixels added to both its right and left sides, and 10 pixels added to both its top and bottom. This means that the widgets are separated from one another vertically by 20 pixels (10 from each widget) and separated from the top or bottom by 10 pixels. The resulting window is shown in Figure 4-23 and, when expanded, looks like the one in Figure 4-24. Through expansion and contraction, the widgets always keep their distance.

Figure 4-23: A nonhomogeneous window with spacing

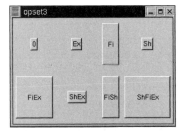

Figure 4-24: An expanded nonhomogeneous window with spacing

Overlapping Widgets

If one widget is positioned at the same location as another, the one in front obscures the one behind it. The order of adding widgets to the table determines which one ends up on top—the first widget added remains on top. This characteristic may not be very valuable as a software development technique, but you should be aware of it so, if a widget is missing, you can figure out where it went. This program demonstrates overlapping:

```
 1  /** overlap.c **/
 2  #include <gnome.h>
 3
 4  GtkWidget *makeTable();
 5  gint eventDelete(GtkWidget *widget,
 6          GdkEvent *event,gpointer data);
 7  gint eventDestroy(GtkWidget *widget,
 8          GdkEvent *event,gpointer data);
 9
10  int main(int argc,char *argv[])
11  {
12      GtkWidget *window;
13      GtkWidget *table;
14
15      gnome_init("overlap","1.0",argc,argv);
16      window = gtk_window_new(GTK_WINDOW_TOPLEVEL);
17      gtk_signal_connect(GTK_OBJECT(window),
```

```
18                    "delete_event",
19                    GTK_SIGNAL_FUNC(eventDelete),
20                    NULL);
21        gtk_signal_connect(GTK_OBJECT(window),
22                    "destroy",
23                    GTK_SIGNAL_FUNC(eventDestroy),
24                    NULL);
25
26        table = makeTable();
27        gtk_container_add(GTK_CONTAINER(window),table);
28        gtk_widget_show(window);
29        gtk_main();
30        exit(0);
31 }
32 GtkWidget *makeTable() {
33        GtkWidget *table;
34        GtkWidget *button;
35
36        table = gtk_table_new(5,4,TRUE);
37        gtk_widget_show(table);
38
39        button = gtk_button_new_with_label("1,2,1,2");
40        gtk_table_attach_defaults(GTK_TABLE(table),button,
41                1,2,1,2);
42        gtk_widget_show(button);
43
44        button = gtk_button_new_with_label("0,2,0,2");
45        gtk_table_attach_defaults(GTK_TABLE(table),button,
46                0,2,0,2);
47        gtk_widget_show(button);
48
49        button = gtk_button_new_with_label("1,5,3,4");
50        gtk_table_attach_defaults(GTK_TABLE(table),button,
51                1,5,3,4);
52        gtk_widget_show(button);
53
54        button = gtk_button_new_with_label("3,4,0,5");
55        gtk_table_attach_defaults(GTK_TABLE(table),button,
56                3,4,0,5);
57        gtk_widget_show(button);
58
59        return(table);
60 }
61 gint eventDelete(GtkWidget *widget,
62        GdkEvent *event,gpointer data) {
63        return(FALSE);
64 }
65 gint eventDestroy(GtkWidget *widget,
66        GdkEvent *event,gpointer data) {
67        gtk_main_quit();
68        return(0);
69 }
```

This program creates the 5x4 table and places four buttons on it as shown in Figure 4-25. In the upper lefthand corner, a smaller button is sitting on top of a larger one. The smaller one is on top because it was added to the table first. If they were added in the opposite order, the smaller button would be completely invisible. The two buttons in the lower right criss-cross one another, but the wide button was added to the table first, so it is on top.

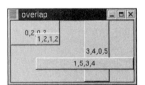

Figure 4-25: Buttons obscuring parts of other buttons

Combining Boxes and Tables

Boxes, tables, and other widgets can be combined freely. You can have boxes of widgets stored inside tables, which in turn can be stored in other boxes and widgets. The advantage of combining boxes and tables is that the resulting layer of storage can have its own positioning and resizing rules, giving you the freedom to lay things out just about any way you like.

This program shows how you can nest boxes and tables to create a window containing multiple widgets:

```
1 /** collection.c **/
2 #include <gnome.h>
3
4 GtkWidget *makeTable();
5 GtkWidget *makeCheckButtons();
6 GtkWidget *makeTextEntry();
7 GtkWidget *makeButtonBox();
8 gint eventDelete(GtkWidget *widget,
9         GdkEvent *event,gpointer data);
10 gint eventDestroy(GtkWidget *widget,
11         GdkEvent *event,gpointer data);
12
13 int main(int argc,char *argv[])
14 {
15     GtkWidget *window;
16     GtkWidget *table;
17
18     gnome_init("collection","1.0",argc,argv);
19     window = gtk_window_new(GTK_WINDOW_TOPLEVEL);
20     gtk_signal_connect(GTK_OBJECT(window),
21             "delete_event",
22             GTK_SIGNAL_FUNC(eventDelete),
23             NULL);
```

```
24      gtk_signal_connect(GTK_OBJECT(window),
25              "destroy",
26              GTK_SIGNAL_FUNC(eventDestroy),
27              NULL);
28
29      table = makeTable();
30      gtk_container_add(GTK_CONTAINER(window),table);
31      gtk_widget_show(window);
32      gtk_main();
33      exit(0);
34 }
35 GtkWidget *makeTable() {
36      GtkWidget *table;
37      GtkWidget *checkButtons;
38      GtkWidget *textEntry;
39      GtkWidget *buttonBox;
40
41      table = gtk_table_new(2,2,FALSE);
42      gtk_widget_show(table);
43
44      textEntry = makeTextEntry();
45      gtk_table_attach(GTK_TABLE(table),textEntry,
46              0,1,0,1,
47              0,
48              0,
49              5,
50              5);
51      gtk_widget_show(textEntry);
52
53      checkButtons = makeCheckButtons();
54      gtk_table_attach(GTK_TABLE(table),checkButtons,
55              1,2,0,1,
56              GTK_EXPAND | GTK_FILL,
57              GTK_EXPAND | GTK_FILL,
58              10,
59              0);
60      gtk_widget_show(checkButtons);
61
62      buttonBox = makeButtonBox();
63      gtk_table_attach(GTK_TABLE(table),buttonBox,
64              0,2,1,2,
65              GTK_EXPAND | GTK_FILL,
66              0,
67              0,
68              8);
69      gtk_widget_show(buttonBox);
70
71      return(table);
72 }
73 GtkWidget *makeCheckButtons()
74 {
75      GtkWidget *vbox;
76      GtkWidget *check;
```

```
77
78      vbox = gtk_vbox_new(FALSE,0);
79
80      check = gtk_check_button_new_with_label("Get Mad");
81      gtk_box_pack_start(GTK_BOX(vbox),check,FALSE,FALSE,0);
82      gtk_widget_show(check);
83
84      check = gtk_check_button_new_with_label("Get Even");
85      gtk_box_pack_start(GTK_BOX(vbox),check,FALSE,FALSE,0);
86      gtk_widget_show(check);
87
88      check = gtk_check_button_new_with_label("Get Down");
89      gtk_box_pack_start(GTK_BOX(vbox),check,FALSE,FALSE,0);
90      gtk_widget_show(check);
91
92      check = gtk_check_button_new_with_label(
93              "Reverse Neutron Polarity");
94      gtk_box_pack_start(GTK_BOX(vbox),check,FALSE,FALSE,0);
95      gtk_widget_show(check);
96
97      return(vbox);
98 }
99 GtkWidget *makeTextEntry()
100 {
101     GtkWidget *vbox;
102     GtkWidget *label;
103     GtkWidget *text;
104
105     vbox = gtk_vbox_new(FALSE,0);
106
107     label = gtk_label_new("Enter destination planet");
108     gtk_box_pack_start(GTK_BOX(vbox),label,FALSE,FALSE,0);
109     gtk_widget_show(label);
110
111     text = gtk_entry_new_with_max_length(32);
112     gtk_box_pack_start(GTK_BOX(vbox),text,FALSE,FALSE,0);
113     gtk_widget_show(text);
114
115     return(vbox);
116 }
117 GtkWidget *makeButtonBox()
118 {
119     GtkWidget *hbox;
120     GtkWidget *button;
121
122     hbox = gtk_hbox_new(TRUE,0);
123
124     button = gtk_button_new_with_label("OK");
125     gtk_box_pack_start(GTK_BOX(hbox),button,FALSE,FALSE,0);
126     gtk_widget_show(button);
127
128     button = gtk_button_new_with_label("Apply");
129     gtk_box_pack_start(GTK_BOX(hbox),button,FALSE,FALSE,0);
```

```
130        gtk_widget_show(button);
131
132        button = gtk_button_new_with_label("Cancel");
133        gtk_box_pack_start(GTK_BOX(hbox),button,FALSE,FALSE,0);
134        gtk_widget_show(button);
135
136        return(hbox);
137 }
138 gint eventDelete(GtkWidget *widget,
139            GdkEvent *event,gpointer data) {
140        return(FALSE);
141 }
142 gint eventDestroy(GtkWidget *widget,
143            GdkEvent *event,gpointer data) {
144        gtk_main_quit();
145        return(0);
146 }
```

The entire window is laid on the table created on line 41. It is a 2x2 table that contains three widgets. The window is shown in Figure 4-26. Three widgets are attached to the table, and there are three functions to build the widgets.

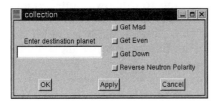

Figure 4-26: Widgets, tables, and boxes inside tables and boxes

The function makeCheckButtons() beginning on line 73 creates a vertical box and packs three checkbuttons into it. The function makeTextEntry() beginning on line 99 creates a vertical box and packs a label and a text-entry widget into it. The function makeButtonBox() creates a horizontal box and attaches three buttons to it. This last box is created to be homogeneous, so the buttons space themselves evenly across the bottom of the window.

Lines 44 through 51 create the text-entry widget and attach it to the cell at the upper left. The widget is created by the call to makeTextEntry(). The attachment options are set for no expansion and no filling, so the widget remains the same size no matter what happens to the table that holds it. There is also a 5-pixel margin placed all the way around it.

Lines 53 through 60 create the widgets with the check boxes, and then attach the widgets to the upper right. The widgets are constructed by the call to makeCheckButtons(). The widget is attached using GTK_EXPAND and GTK_FILL options, which produces the same result as with gtk_table_attach_defaults(), but there is a 10-pixel margin added to the left and right.

Lines 62 through 69 create a widget holding the three buttons, and attach it to the table so it covers the two cells at the bottom of the table. It is set to expand and fill along the *x*-axis, but not to do so along the *y*-axis. There is also an 8-pixel margin inserted above and below it.

The fact that everything is a widget makes life very nice for the programmer. Notice that the declarations on lines 37, 38, and 39 define each of the objects to be contained in the table as a `GtkWidget`. This way, the function `makeTable()` doesn't have to know exactly what kind of widget is to be contained. Instead, it just retrieves a `GtkWidget` pointer from a function and adds it to the table. The widget can be another table, a box, a button, a label, or any of the other dozens of widgets available. This is a very important characteristic. Not only does it simplify coding, but it also enables you to make changes to one part of the layout without being concerned about the impact it will have on other parts. Of course, if you make some size changes, you may need to make some positional adjustments — but you won't have to rewrite portions of the program because of type incompatibilities.

Summary

In this chapter, we've reviewed ways to add widgets to windows. You learned that tables and boxes can be packed with widgets to lay out a dialog window very quickly. In addition, the widget's automation of positioning and spacing within the dialog box frees up the hands of the programmer to tackle more important details.

In this chapter, you also learned:

✦ There are two kinds of boxes — vertical and horizontal.

✦ Widgets can be added to a box from either end.

✦ A table is a grid onto which widgets can be hung.

✦ The cells of a table can be fixed or variable size.

✦ Any widget can be packed into boxes or tables — including other boxes or tables.

However, this is just the beginning of widgets. For instance, there are several more ways to pack widgets. There are also special requests that you can make of widgets, such as complete pixel-by-pixel control over placement. Chapter 5 reviews some specialized widget containers that can be used in conjunction with, or in place of, tables and boxes.

✦   ✦   ✦

Widgets to Contain Widgets

◆ ◆ ◆ ◆

In This Chapter

Positioning widgets
at specific *x* and *y*
coordinates

Attaching moveable
scrollbars to a large
window

Setting a widget so
it follows its own
resizing rules instead
of that of its container

Configuring widgets
so that they maintain
the same aspect ratio
of height to width if
their container is
resized

Grouping widgets by
position and by a
surrounding frame

◆ ◆ ◆ ◆

This chapter deals with detailed control of a widget's
location, size, and how it reacts when the window is
resized. To do all of this, there are several widgets that are
used to contain other widgets and influence their actions.
Each has its own peculiarities and special capabilities, and
can be used to create decorative and detailed layouts.

The Fixed Container

You can use a fixed container to place widgets at a specific
location by specifying x and y coordinates. The following
example program creates three buttons and places them on
a fixed container widget. The buttons initially are placed at
(100,100), which means the upper-left corner of each button is
100 pixels over and 100 pixels down from the upper-left corner
of the container. The button label contains the x and y values
of its location. Each button, when clicked, moves to another
location by having its x and y values changed.

```
 1 /** fixed.c **/
 2 #include <gnome.h>
 3
 4 typedef struct {
 5     GtkWidget *fixed;
 6     GtkWidget *button;
 7 } ButtonMover;
 8
 9 GtkWidget *makeFixedContainer();
10 gint eventDelete(GtkWidget *widget,
11         GdkEvent *event,gpointer data);
12 gint eventDestroy(GtkWidget *widget,
13         GdkEvent *event,gpointer data);
14 void buttonClick(GtkWidget
*widget,ButtonMover *bm);
15
```

```
16 #define WIDTH 400
17 #define HEIGHT 300
18
19 int main(int argc,char *argv[])
20 {
21     GtkWidget *window;
22     GtkWidget *fixed;
23
24     gnome_init("fixed","1.0",argc,argv);
25     window = gtk_window_new(GTK_WINDOW_TOPLEVEL);
26     gtk_window_set_default_size(GTK_WINDOW(window),
27             WIDTH,HEIGHT);
28     gtk_signal_connect(GTK_OBJECT(window),
29             "delete_event",
30             GTK_SIGNAL_FUNC(eventDelete),
31             NULL);
32     gtk_signal_connect(GTK_OBJECT(window),
33             "destroy",
34             GTK_SIGNAL_FUNC(eventDestroy),
35             NULL);
36
37     fixed = makeFixedContainer();
38
39     gtk_container_add(GTK_CONTAINER(window),fixed);
40     gtk_widget_show(window);
41     gtk_main();
42     exit(0);
43 }
44 GtkWidget *makeFixedContainer() {
45     int i;
46     GtkWidget *fixed;
47     static ButtonMover bm[3];
48
49     fixed = gtk_fixed_new();
50     gtk_widget_show(fixed);
51
52     for(i=0; i<3; i++) {
53         bm[i].fixed = fixed;
54         bm[i].button = gtk_button_new_with_label(
55             "(100,100)");
56         gtk_signal_connect(GTK_OBJECT(bm[i].button),
57             "clicked",
58             GTK_SIGNAL_FUNC(buttonClick),
59             &bm[i]);
60         gtk_widget_show(bm[i].button);
61         gtk_fixed_put(GTK_FIXED(fixed),bm[i].button,
62             100,100);
63     }
64     return(fixed);
65 }
66 void buttonClick(GtkWidget *widget,ButtonMover *bm)
```

```
67 {
68     gchar labelString[80];
69     GtkWidget *label;
70
71     gint x = (int)(random() % WIDTH);
72     gint y = (int)(random() % HEIGHT);
73     sprintf(labelString,"(%d,%d)",x,y);
74     label = GTK_WIDGET(GTK_BUTTON(bm->button)->child);
75     gtk_label_set_text(GTK_LABEL(label),labelString);
76     gtk_fixed_move(GTK_FIXED(bm->fixed),bm->button,x,y);
77 }
78 gint eventDelete(GtkWidget *widget,
79         GdkEvent *event,gpointer data) {
80     return(FALSE);
81 }
82 gint eventDestroy(GtkWidget *widget,
83         GdkEvent *event,gpointer data) {
84     gtk_main_quit();
85     return(0);
86 }
```

The function makeFixedContainter() starting on line 44 creates a fixed container and adds the three buttons to it. The container itself is created by the call to gtk_fixed_new() on line 49.

The fixed container has no predefined size. Instead, it automatically resizes itself to hold all of the widget positions that are added to it. In the previous example, the window holding the container was set to a fixed size by the call to gtk_window_set_ default_size() on line 26. This forces the window to stay the same size no matter what. If this function call is taken out of the code, the displayed window starts off small. As the buttons are moved from one place to another, the container expands forcing the window to expand to hold it.

The loop beginning on line 52 creates the three buttons and adds them to the container. The call to gtk_fixed_put() attaches each button to the container at location (100,100). There is a ButtonMover struct defined on line 4 and declared as an array — one for each button — on line 47. Pointers to the button and to the fixed container are stored in the struct so they can be passed to the callback function. The callback function buttonClick() is used for all three buttons.

The callback function buttonClick() beginning on line 66 moves the selected button from one place to another. Lines 71 and 72 use a random number generator to establish a new set of *x* and *y* coordinates. Lines 73 and 74 set up the ASCII representation of the values as the label for the button. A button contains a label widget for the purpose of displaying text, so line 75 calls gtk_label_set_text() to change the string displayed by the button. On line 76, a call is made to gtk_fixed_move() with the new coordinates to reposition the button. After a few clicks on the buttons, the display looks something like the one in Figure 5-1.

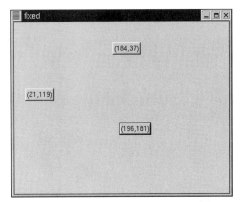

Figure 5-1: Buttons being positioned in a fixed container

The minimum size of a fixed widget is fairly easy to calculate. The width is the maximum distance from the left side of the container to the right side of each widget. Likewise, the height is the maximum distance from the top of the container to the bottom of each widget.

Widgets can be moved from one place to another. You can do this whether or not the window is actively displayed. The call to `gtk_fixed_move()` to reposition a widget has the same arguments as `gtk_fixed_put()` but does to add a widget. For example, if the widget `button` is already added to the fixed container, this call moves it to a new location:

```
gtk_fixed_move(GTK_FIXED(fixed),button,25,25);
```

The Alignment Container

This container can be used to hold a single widget and to impose some control over the widget's size and position. The contained widget changes and positions to fit inside the current size and shape of the alignment container. The widget is positioned in the container a certain percentage of the distance from the top, and a certain percentage of the distance from the left side. Also, the widget is sized as a certain percentage of the width and height of the container.

This example program centers a `GtkButton` widget in an alignment container:

```
 1 /** alignment.c **/
 2 #include <gnome.h>
 3
 4 GtkWidget *makeAlignment();
 5 gint eventDelete(GtkWidget *widget,
 6        GdkEvent *event,gpointer data);
```

```
 7 gint eventDestroy(GtkWidget *widget,
 8         GdkEvent *event,gpointer data);
 9
10 int main(int argc,char *argv[])
11 {
12     GtkWidget *window;
13     GtkWidget *alignment;
14
15     gnome_init("alignment","1.0",argc,argv);
16     window = gtk_window_new(GTK_WINDOW_TOPLEVEL);
17     gtk_window_set_default_size(GTK_WINDOW(window),
18             200,200);
19     gtk_signal_connect(GTK_OBJECT(window),
20             "delete_event",
21             GTK_SIGNAL_FUNC(eventDelete),
22             NULL);
23     gtk_signal_connect(GTK_OBJECT(window),
24             "destroy",
25             GTK_SIGNAL_FUNC(eventDestroy),
26             NULL);
27
28     alignment = makeAlignment();
29
30     gtk_container_add(GTK_CONTAINER(window),alignment);
31     gtk_widget_show(window);
32     gtk_main();
33     exit(0);
34 }
35 GtkWidget *makeAlignment() {
36     GtkWidget *alignment;
37     GtkWidget *button;
38     gfloat xalign = 0.5;
39     gfloat yalign = 0.5;
40     gfloat xscale = 0.8;
41     gfloat yscale = 0.8;
42
43     alignment = gtk_alignment_new(xalign,yalign,
44             xscale,yscale);
45     gtk_widget_show(alignment);
46     button = gtk_button_new_with_label("Button");
47     gtk_widget_show(button);
48     gtk_container_add(GTK_CONTAINER(alignment),button);
49
50     return(alignment);
51 }
52 gint eventDelete(GtkWidget *widget,
53         GdkEvent *event,gpointer data) {
54     return(FALSE);
55 }
56 gint eventDestroy(GtkWidget *widget,
57         GdkEvent *event,gpointer data) {
58     gtk_main_quit();
59     return(0);
60 }
```

The function `makeAlignment()` beginning on line 35 creates an alignment container holding a `GtkButton` widget. The alignment widget is created with the call to `gtk_alignment_new()` on line 43. The alignment container can contain only one widget, and the values that control its size and positioning are set when the container is constructed. The values `xalign` and `yalign` specify the position of the widget relative to the size and shape of the container. The values `xscale` and `yscale` specify the size of the widget relative to the size of the container.

The values shown on lines 38 through 41, along with the initial window size specification on line 17, cause the window in Figure 5-2 to appear. The button resizes itself to fit its container. Figure 5-3 shows the same window after the mouse was used to change its size.

Figure 5-2: A button being centered by a GtkAlignment container

Figure 5-3: Resizing a GtkAlignment container resizes its widget

The two sizing numbers `xscale` and `yscale` are floating point values from 0.0 to 1.0. They size the widget to a percentage of the total height and width of the container. In the example, both values are set to 0.8, so the button covers 80 percent of the height and the width of the container. Using 1.0 for these numbers expands the button to completely fill the alignment container.

The two alignment numbers, `xalign` and `yalign`, are floating point values from 0.0 to 1.0 that represent a percentage of the distance across the container. In Figure 5-2, the button is centered because the value of both `xalign` and `yalign` is 0.5. Setting both `xalign` and `yalign` to 0.0 causes the window to look like the one in Figure 5-4. Setting both `xalign` and `yalign` to 1.0 causes the window to look like the one in Figure 5-5.

Figure 5-4: A button in the top left corner of a GtkAlignment container

Figure 5-5: A button in the bottom right corner of a GtkAlignment container

The algorithm used to calculate the actual widget position, from the relative values xalign and yalign, never positions any part of the widget outside the container. To do this, the size of the widget is calculated first so the height and width can be accounted for during positioning. Figure 5-6 shows how to accomplish vertical positioning. The dashed line represents all of the possible vertical positions of the center of the widget. The extreme positions are at the center of the widget if it were flush against the top or bottom. The extreme positions are used as end points of the line used to position the widget. The actual vertical position, then, is a percentage of the distance from the top of the line. The same method is used for horizontal positioning with the percentage being measured from 0.0 on the left to 1.0 on the right.

You are not stuck with the alignment you used when you created the alignment container. You can change it with a call to this function:

```
gtk_alignment_new(GTK_ALIGNMENT(alignment),
        xalign,yalign,
        xscale,yscale);
```

The first argument is the alignment container to receive the new values, and the four floating point values are the same ones that were used on gtk_alignment_new() in the example program.

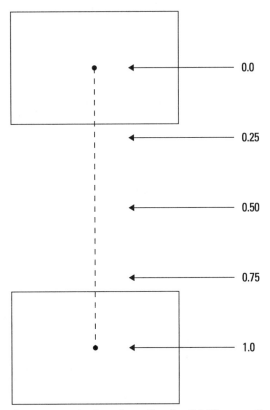

Figure 5-6: The imaginary line for GtkAlignment's
method of positioning widgets

The Frame Container

A *frame container* is capable of containing a single widget and adding a rectangular
box around it. The drawn box also can include a label at the top. There are different
line types that you can use to draw the rectangle — there are five if you count
the case where nothing is drawn. The following example uses frames around a
sequence of labels to demonstrate the line-drawing options. The output is shown
in Figure 5-7.

```
1 /** frame1.c **/
2 #include <gnome.h>
3
4 GtkWidget *makeFrames();
5 gint eventDelete(GtkWidget *widget,
```

```
 6            GdkEvent *event,gpointer data);
 7 gint eventDestroy(GtkWidget *widget,
 8            GdkEvent *event,gpointer data);
 9
10 struct {
11     gchar *typeName;
12     GtkShadowType type;
13 } shadow[] = {
14     { "GTK_SHADOW_NONE", GTK_SHADOW_NONE },
15     { "GTK_SHADOW_IN", GTK_SHADOW_IN },
16     { "GTK_SHADOW_OUT", GTK_SHADOW_OUT },
17     { "GTK_SHADOW_ETCHED_IN", GTK_SHADOW_ETCHED_IN },
18     { "GTK_SHADOW_ETCHED_OUT", GTK_SHADOW_ETCHED_OUT }
19 };
20
21 int main(int argc,char *argv[])
22 {
23     GtkWidget *window;
24     GtkWidget *frame;
25
26     gnome_init("frame1","1.0",argc,argv);
27     window = gtk_window_new(GTK_WINDOW_TOPLEVEL);
28     gtk_container_set_border_width(
29            GTK_CONTAINER(window),25);
30     gtk_signal_connect(GTK_OBJECT(window),
31            "delete_event",
32            GTK_SIGNAL_FUNC(eventDelete),
33            NULL);
34     gtk_signal_connect(GTK_OBJECT(window),
35            "destroy",
36            GTK_SIGNAL_FUNC(eventDestroy),
37            NULL);
38
39     frame = makeFrames();
40     gtk_container_add(GTK_CONTAINER(window),frame);
41     gtk_widget_show(window);
42     gtk_main();
43     exit(0);
44 }
45 GtkWidget *makeFrames() {
46     int i;
47     GtkWidget *box;
48     GtkWidget *frame;
49     GtkWidget *label;
50
51     box = gtk_vbox_new(FALSE,10);
52     gtk_widget_show(box);
53
54     for(i=0; i<5; i++) {
55         frame = gtk_frame_new(NULL);
56         gtk_widget_show(frame);
```

```
57          gtk_frame_set_shadow_type(GTK_FRAME(frame),
58                  shadow[i].type);
59          gtk_container_add(GTK_CONTAINER(box),frame);
60          label = gtk_label_new(shadow[i].typeName);
61          gtk_widget_show(label);
62          gtk_container_add(GTK_CONTAINER(frame),label);
63      }
64
65      return(box);
66 }
67 gint eventDelete(GtkWidget *widget,
68          GdkEvent *event,gpointer data) {
69      return(FALSE);
70 }
71 gint eventDestroy(GtkWidget *widget,
72          GdkEvent *event,gpointer data) {
73      gtk_main_quit();
74      return(0);
75 }
```

The array `shadow` defined on lines 10 through 18 contains the names and numeric values representing each of the methods of drawing the rectangle. The struct is used in a loop to create the set of framed labels.

The function that creates the set of frames is `makeFrames()` and it starts on line 45. Because there is more than one widget to be included in the list, a box container widget is created on line 51 and is packed with the labels inside the loop on line 62. The loop, beginning on line 54, has one notation for each type of line the frame uses. A frame is created and configured on lines 55 and 57, and the call to `gtk_frame_set_shadow_type()` specifies the kind of frame to draw — the default is `GTK_SHADOW_ETCHED_IN`. The frame is added to the vertical box on line 59. Lines 60 through 61 create the label and insert it into the frame.

Figure 5-7: There are five different appearances to frame

Frames can be used simply for decoration, but they often are used to group related items on a dialog window. The following program displays the window shown in Figure 5-8.

```
 1 /** frame2.c **/
 2 #include <gnome.h>
 3
 4 GtkWidget *makeFrame();
 5 gint eventDelete(GtkWidget *widget,
 6         GdkEvent *event,gpointer data);
 7 gint eventDestroy(GtkWidget *widget,
 8         GdkEvent *event,gpointer data);
 9
10 int main(int argc,char *argv[])
11 {
12     GtkWidget *window;
13     GtkWidget *frame;
14
15     gnome_init("frame2","1.0",argc,argv);
16     window = gtk_window_new(GTK_WINDOW_TOPLEVEL);
17     gtk_signal_connect(GTK_OBJECT(window),
18             "delete_event",
19             GTK_SIGNAL_FUNC(eventDelete),
20             NULL);
21     gtk_signal_connect(GTK_OBJECT(window),
22             "destroy",
23             GTK_SIGNAL_FUNC(eventDestroy),
24             NULL);
25
26     frame = makeFrame();
27     gtk_container_add(GTK_CONTAINER(window),frame);
28     gtk_widget_show(window);
29     gtk_main();
30     exit(0);
31 }
32 GtkWidget *makeFrame() {
33     GtkWidget *box;
34     GtkWidget *frame;
35     GtkWidget *button;
36
37     box = gtk_vbox_new(FALSE,0);
38     gtk_widget_show(box);
39
40     button = gtk_check_button_new_with_label(
41             "Calculate new average");
42     gtk_widget_show(button);
43     gtk_container_add(GTK_CONTAINER(box),button);
44
45     button = gtk_check_button_new_with_label(
46             "Calculate new median");
47     gtk_widget_show(button);
48     gtk_container_add(GTK_CONTAINER(box),button);
49
50     button = gtk_check_button_new_with_label(
51             "Calculate new maximum");
```

```
52      gtk_widget_show(button);
53      gtk_container_add(GTK_CONTAINER(box),button);
54
55      frame = gtk_frame_new("Calculations");
56      gtk_widget_show(frame);
57      gtk_container_set_border_width(GTK_CONTAINER(frame),
58              15);
59      gtk_container_add(GTK_CONTAINER(frame),box);
60
61      return(frame);
62 }
63 gint eventDelete(GtkWidget *widget,
64         GdkEvent *event,gpointer data) {
65      return(FALSE);
66 }
67 gint eventDestroy(GtkWidget *widget,
68         GdkEvent *event,gpointer data) {
69      gtk_main_quit();
70      return(0);
71 }
```

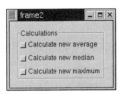

Figure 5-8: A default shadow with a default label position

The function makeFrame() beginning on line 32 creates a box, fills the box with checkbuttons, and then puts a frame around the box. The buttons are created on lines 40 through 53. The frame with its label text is created on line 55. The default position of the label is on top and left justified. Line 57 specifies that there should be a 15-pixel margin between the box and its container, the frame.

You can set the position of the label on the frame by calling gtk_frame_set_label_align(). The label appearing at the top of the frame can be justified to the left (the default), justified to the right, or placed in the center. The placement is a floating-point number with a value of 0.0 for a left justified label and 1.0 for a right justified label. By using values between 0.0 and 1.0, the label can be positioned between the two extremes. For example, using 0.5 centers the label. To shift the label to the right, as shown in Figure 5-9, add this line of code following the call on line 55 to gtk_frame_new() to create the frame:

```
gtk_frame_set_label_align(GTK_FRAME(frame),1.0,0.0);
```

The first argument is the frame widget. The second argument of xalign is 1.0 to shift the label to the right. The third argument is called yalign, but it has no effect on the display.

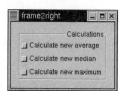

Figure 5-9: Repositioning a frame label

The Aspect Frame Container

The *aspect frame container* holds one widget, and forces the widget to maintain the same aspect ratio no matter how the window gets resized. The aspect frame container combines some of the capabilities of the previous two containers. Like the frame container, it surrounds the contained widget with a frame and a label. And, like the alignment container, you have control over the placement of the widget within the container.

The shadowing used to create the frame always appears as GTK_SHADOW_ETCHED_IN, and the label is always positioned starting in the upper-left corner of the frame. The following example program displays the window shown in Figure 5-10.

```
 1 /** aspect.c **/
 2 #include <gnome.h>
 3
 4 GtkWidget *makeAspectFrame();
 5 gint eventDelete(GtkWidget *widget,
 6         GdkEvent *event,gpointer data);
 7 gint eventDestroy(GtkWidget *widget,
 8         GdkEvent *event,gpointer data);
 9
10 int main(int argc,char *argv[])
11 {
12     GtkWidget *window;
13     GtkWidget *aspect;
14
15     gnome_init("aspect","1.0",argc,argv);
16     window = gtk_window_new(GTK_WINDOW_TOPLEVEL);
17     gtk_window_set_default_size(GTK_WINDOW(window),
18             200,200);
19     gtk_signal_connect(GTK_OBJECT(window),
20             "delete_event",
21             GTK_SIGNAL_FUNC(eventDelete),
22             NULL);
23     gtk_signal_connect(GTK_OBJECT(window),
```

```
24              "destroy",
25              GTK_SIGNAL_FUNC(eventDestroy),
26              NULL);
27
28     aspect = makeAspectFrame();
29
30     gtk_container_add(GTK_CONTAINER(window),aspect);
31     gtk_widget_show(window);
32     gtk_main();
33     exit(0);
34 }
35 GtkWidget *makeAspectFrame() {
36     GtkWidget *aspect;
37     GtkWidget *button;
38     gfloat xalign = 0.5;
39     gfloat yalign = 0.5;
40     gfloat ratio = 2;
41
42     aspect = gtk_aspect_frame_new("AspectFrame",
43              xalign,yalign,
44              ratio,
45              FALSE);
46     gtk_widget_show(aspect);
47     gtk_container_set_border_width(GTK_CONTAINER(aspect),
48              10);
49     button = gtk_button_new_with_label("Button");
50     gtk_widget_show(button);
51     gtk_container_set_border_width(GTK_CONTAINER(button),
52              10);
53     gtk_container_add(GTK_CONTAINER(aspect),button);
54
55     return(aspect);
56 }
57 gint eventDelete(GtkWidget *widget,
58          GdkEvent *event,gpointer data) {
59     return(FALSE);
60 }
61 gint eventDestroy(GtkWidget *widget,
62          GdkEvent *event,gpointer data) {
63     gtk_main_quit();
64     return(0);
65 }
```

Figure 5-10: A button in an aspect frame at a 2:1 ratio

The aspect frame container is created in the function `makeAspectFrame()`, which begins on line 35. The frame widget is constructed on line 42. The first argument is the label that goes at the top of the frame. The second and third arguments are the values `xalign` and `yalign` used to position the contained widget — they work here exactly the same as they do for the alignment widget described earlier. In this example, both alignment values are 0.5, which places the contained widget in the middle both horizontally and vertically.

The ratio on line 44 is the ratio resulting from dividing the width by the height. If you want a widget to be four times as wide as it is tall, use the ratio 4/1. If you want the widget to be four times as tall as it is wide, use the ratio 1/4. A ratio number of 1 produces a square widget. Numbers larger than 1 are wide; numbers smaller than 1 are tall.

The last argument, on line 45, is `TRUE` if the ratio is to be derived from the contained widget or `FALSE` if the ratio is to be taken from the value passed to it. That is, if you specify `TRUE`, the ratio value you specify as an argument is ignored and the value from the contained widget is taken. Every widget has a preferred height and width, which implies a preferred aspect ratio.

There are two calls to `gtk_container_set_border_width()`: the one on line 47 inserts 10 pixels around the outside of the frame and the one on line 51 inserts 10 pixels between the button and the frame.

Figure 5-10 shows the window as it first appears. The overall window size and shape is determined by the aspect ratio, minimum size requirements of the button, and the thickness of the surrounding borders. If the same window is stretched wider while being shrunk vertically, it looks like the window in Figure 5-11. And, if the window is made narrow but longer, it looks like the window in Figure 5-12. The size changes but the aspect remains the same.

Figure 5-11: Stretching horizontally maintains widget aspect

You can alter the alignment and ratio information dynamically. To change any or all of the sizing parameters that were established when the aspect frame was created, use a function call like this:

```
gtk_aspect_frame_set(GTK_ASPECT_FRAME(aspect),
        xalign,yalign,
        ratio,
        FALSE);
```

Figure 5-12: Stretching vertically maintains widget aspect

This changes all of the initial settings except the text of the label, but that also can change. Because the aspect frame is an extension of the frame container, this call can be made to change the label:

```
gtk_frame_set_label(GTK_FRAME(aspect),"New Label Text");
```

The Paned Container

The *paned container* holds two widgets, either side by side or one above the other, and displays them with a divider between them. The mouse can be used to move the divider back and forth to resize each of the contained widgets. The divider bar is called the *gutter*. The button on the gutter that is used to drag it back and forth is called the *handle*.

The following example demonstrates a horizontal paned container with a text widget on each side, as shown in Figure 5-13. The text widgets each contain a single line of text that is automatically wrapped to fill the widget — the automatic wrapping is indicated by the circular arrows at the end of each line. Using the mouse to drag the handle moves the gutter and resizes both widgets, as shown in Figure 5-14.

```
 1 /** hpaned.c **/
 2 #include <gnome.h>
 3
 4 GtkWidget *makeHorizontalPane();
 5 gint eventDelete(GtkWidget *widget,
 6         GdkEvent *event,gpointer data);
 7 gint eventDestroy(GtkWidget *widget,
 8         GdkEvent *event,gpointer data);
 9
10 int main(int argc,char *argv[])
11 {
12     GtkWidget *window;
```

```
13      GtkWidget *pane;
14
15      gnome_init("hpaned","1.0",argc,argv);
16      window = gtk_window_new(GTK_WINDOW_TOPLEVEL);
17      gtk_window_set_default_size(GTK_WINDOW(window),
18              200,200);
19      gtk_signal_connect(GTK_OBJECT(window),
20              "delete_event",
21              GTK_SIGNAL_FUNC(eventDelete),
22              NULL);
23      gtk_signal_connect(GTK_OBJECT(window),
24              "destroy",
25              GTK_SIGNAL_FUNC(eventDestroy),
26              NULL);
27
28      pane = makeHorizontalPane();
29
30      gtk_container_add(GTK_CONTAINER(window),pane);
31      gtk_widget_show(window);
32      gtk_main();
33      exit(0);
34 }
35 GtkWidget *makeHorizontalPane() {
36      int i;
37      GtkWidget *leftText;
38      GtkWidget *rightText;
39      GtkWidget *paned;
40
41      leftText = gtk_text_new(NULL,NULL);
42      gtk_widget_show(leftText);
43      rightText = gtk_text_new(NULL,NULL);
44      gtk_widget_show(rightText);
45      for(i=0; i<15; i++) {
46          gtk_text_insert(GTK_TEXT(leftText),NULL,NULL,NULL,
47            "The quick brown fox jumped on the leftovers. ",
48            -1);
49          gtk_text_insert(GTK_TEXT(rightText),NULL,NULL,NULL,
50            "The lazy gray dog slept by the leftovers. ",
51            -1);
52      }
53
54      paned = gtk_hpaned_new();
55      gtk_widget_show(paned);
56      gtk_paned_add1(GTK_PANED(paned),leftText);
57      gtk_paned_add2(GTK_PANED(paned),rightText);
58
59      return(paned);
60 }
61 gint eventDelete(GtkWidget *widget,
62          GdkEvent *event,gpointer data) {
63      return(FALSE);
64 }
```

```
65 gint eventDestroy(GtkWidget *widget,
66        GdkEvent *event,gpointer data) {
67    gtk_main_quit();
68    return(0);
69 }
```

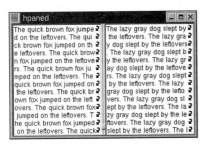

Figure 5-13: A horizontal pane with two text widgets

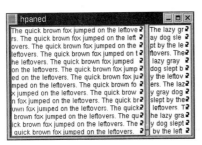

Figure 5-14: A horizontal pane with two text widgets

The function `makeHorizontalPane()` beginning on line 35 creates the paned container and inserts the two text widgets into it. The text widgets are created and filled with text on lines 41 through 52.

The call to `gtk_hpaned_new()` on line 54 creates a horizontal paned widget like the one shown in Figures 5-13 and 5-14.

The call to the function `gtk_hpaned_new()` on line 52 creates a new horizontal pane widget. On lines 56 and 57, the function `gtk_paned_add1()` adds the text widget on the left and `gtk_paned_add2()` adds the text widget to the right.

That's all there is to it. The paned widget and its two contained widgets communicate with one another about positioning and resizing. The overall window can be resized and the gutter can be shifted back and forth to make all the widgets resize together. The minimum widget size does not limit gutter movement, and it is possible to move the gutter all the way to one side or the other completely obscuring one widget and allocating the whole window to the other.

A vertical paned container is shown in Figures 5-15 and 5-16. You can achieve this configuration by changing one line of code in the example. Line 54 should look like this:

```
paned = gtk_vpaned_new();
```

Everything else can stay the same. The same functions are used to add widgets to a vertical paned container. The gtk_paned_add1() function adds a widget at the top and gtk_paned_add2() adds a widget at the bottom.

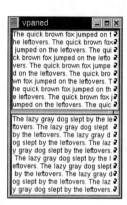

Figure 5-15: A vertical pane with two text widgets

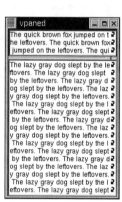

Figure 5-16: A vertical pane with two text widgets

It is possible to adjust the thickness of the gutter and size of the button. For example, to produce the configuration shown in Figure 5-17, insert the following two function calls after line 54 in the above example:

```
gtk_paned_set_handle_size(GTK_PANED(paned),30);
gtk_paned_set_gutter_size(GTK_PANED(paned),20);
```

This makes the handle into a square that is 30 pixels on a side, and sets the gutter width to 20 pixels. However, the width of the handle is limited to the width of the gutter, so the handle ends up being a rectangle of 20x30 pixels. The default handle size is 10 and the default gutter size is 6.

Figure 5-17: A paned container with custom button and gutter sizes

The Layout Container

The *layout container* can hold any number of widgets. The widgets are positioned by *x* and *y* pixel offsets. There is no limit to the size of this container. It can be as tall and as wide as you like. There is also a pair of special adjustment objects, one for each axis, that can be set to specify which portions of the container are available. In effect, you are looking at a section of the container window through a porthole; the window can be moved around making different portions of it visible.

This example program creates a layout container covered with buttons and uses the positional values from a pair of scrollbars to determine which buttons are visible.

```
 1 /** layout.c **/
 2 #include <gnome.h>
 3
 4 GtkWidget *makeLayout();
 5 void addButtons(GtkWidget *layout);
 6 gint eventDelete(GtkWidget *widget,
 7        GdkEvent *event,gpointer data);
 8 gint eventDestroy(GtkWidget *widget,
 9        GdkEvent *event,gpointer data);
10
11 int main(int argc,char *argv[])
12 {
13     GtkWidget *window;
14     GtkWidget *layout;
15
16     gnome_init("layout","1.0",argc,argv);
17     window = gtk_window_new(GTK_WINDOW_TOPLEVEL);
```

```
18      gtk_window_set_default_size(GTK_WINDOW(window),
19              200,200);
20      gtk_signal_connect(GTK_OBJECT(window),
21              "delete_event",
22              GTK_SIGNAL_FUNC(eventDelete),
23              NULL);
24      gtk_signal_connect(GTK_OBJECT(window),
25              "destroy",
26              GTK_SIGNAL_FUNC(eventDestroy),
27              NULL);
28
29      layout = makeLayout();
30
31      gtk_container_add(GTK_CONTAINER(window),layout);
32      gtk_widget_show_all(window);
33      gtk_main();
34      exit(0);
35  }
36  GtkWidget *makeLayout()
37  {
38      GtkWidget *layout;
39      GtkWidget *vscroll;
40      GtkWidget *hscroll;
41      GtkWidget *table;
42      GtkAdjustment *horizAdj;
43      GtkAdjustment *vertAdj;
44
45      vertAdj = (GtkAdjustment *)gtk_adjustment_new(
46              0.0,
47              0.0,
48              1000.0,
49              1.0,
50              10.0,
51              20.0);
52      horizAdj = (GtkAdjustment *)gtk_adjustment_new(
53              0.0,
54              0.0,
55              1000.0,
56              1.0,
57              10.0,
58              20.0);
59
60      layout = gtk_layout_new(horizAdj,vertAdj);
61      gtk_layout_set_size(GTK_LAYOUT(layout),1000,1000);
62      addButtons(layout);
63
64      vscroll = gtk_vscrollbar_new(vertAdj);
65      hscroll = gtk_hscrollbar_new(horizAdj);
66
67      table = gtk_table_new(2,2,FALSE);
68
```

```
69      gtk_table_attach_defaults(GTK_TABLE(table),layout,
70           0,1,0,1);
71      gtk_table_attach(GTK_TABLE(table),vscroll,
72           1,2,0,1,
73           GTK_FILL,GTK_FILL,0,0);
74      gtk_table_attach(GTK_TABLE(table),hscroll,
75           0,1,1,2,
76           GTK_FILL,GTK_FILL,0,0);
77
78      return(table);
79 }
80 void addButtons(GtkWidget *layout)
81 {
82      gint i;
83      gint j;
84      GtkWidget *button;
85      gchar label[20];
86
87      for(i=100; i<1000; i += 100) {
88          for(j=100; j<1000; j+= 50) {
89              sprintf(label,"(%d,%d)",i,j);
90              button = gtk_button_new_with_label(label);
91              gtk_layout_put(GTK_LAYOUT(layout),button,i,j);
92          }
93      }
94 }
95 gint eventDelete(GtkWidget *widget,
96          GdkEvent *event,gpointer data) {
97      return(FALSE);
98 }
99 gint eventDestroy(GtkWidget *widget,
100         GdkEvent *event,gpointer data) {
101     gtk_main_quit();
102     return(0);
103 }
```

This example creates a 2x2 table that holds a layout widget in the upper-left corner, and holds scrollbars on the right and on the bottom — as shown in Figure 5-18. The layout has buttons placed at regular intervals across it. The label of each button is the values of its *x* and *y* coordinates within the layout container. So you are able to move the layout around and see all the buttons, the GtkAdjustment objects used by the layout are the same ones used by the scrollbar.

The makeLayout() function beginning on line 36 creates a table and inserts the various widgets into it. The table is a 2x2 grid with the layout in the upper left, a vertical scrollbar in the upper right, and a horizontal scrollbar in the lower left. There is nothing in the cell at the lower right.

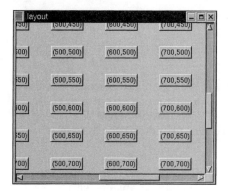

Figure 5-18: A layout container makes part of its window visible

Lines 45 through 58 create a pair of GtkAdjustment objects that are used to control the position of the layout container. There is one adjustment object for horizontal positioning and one for vertical. The function gtk_adjustment_new() requires six floating-point values. The first argument is the initial value, and it must be some value between the values of the second and third arguments. The second and third ones are the beginning and ending values of the position of the layout container. In this example, both the vertical and horizontal sizes are set so the values can range from 0 to 1000.

The last three arguments to gtk_adjustment_new() are instructions to any software elements (such as scrollbars) that will update the current GtkAdjustment value. The argument 1.0 is the step increment. It is the minimum amount the window can be shifted. (In this example, the value 1.0 just happens to correspond with 1 pixel.) The argument 10.0 is the number of units the layout is to move when it jumps (that is, when you select the trough of the scrollbar with the mouse). The last value is the size of a page in case you want the software to be capable of shifting up or down by a whole page.

The layout container is created on line 60. It is passed the two adjustment objects. To change the position of the layout container in the displayable porthole, you only need to adjust the current value of the adjustment object. Line 62 sets the size of the layout object, and line 62 calls addButton() to fill it with buttons. The addButtons() function beginning on line 80 is a simple loop creating buttons and placing them on the layout container in a large rectangle. The buttons are hung onto the face of the layout by gtk_layout_put() on line 91.

Note   Notice the call to gtk_widget_show_all() on line 32. This causes the named widget (in this case, the main window) and all of its child widgets to be displayed. This has the same effect as calling gtk_widget_show() for each individual widget.

You can move a widget to another location on the layout with a call to
`gtk_layout_move()` like this:

```
gtk_layout_move(GTK_LAYOUT(layout),button,5,10);
```

This moves the widget named `button` to the position 5 pixels from the left and
10 down from the top. The visible portion of a layout can be sized by calling
`gtk_layout_set_size()` and specifying the width and height. For example,
this call makes the visible window 200 pixels high and 350 pixels wide:

```
gtk_layout_set_size(GTK_LAYOUT(layout),200,350);
```

You can retrieve the horizontal and vertical adjustment objects with these two
function calls:

```
vertAdj = gtk_layout_get_vadjustment(GTK_LAYOUT(layout));
horizAdj = gtk_layout_get_hadjustment(GTK_LAYOUT(layout));
```

Sometimes, you may need to retrieve the adjustment settings because they have
been changed internally. The functions used to set the adjustments have some
built-in constraints on numeric values. Invalid numbers are corrected silently. Also,
it is normal for the current position to be reflected by the `GtkAdjustment` object.
These functions can assign new adjustment values:

```
gtk_layout_set_hadjustment(GTK_LAYOUT(layout),horizAdj);
gtk_layout_set_vadjustment(GTK_LAYOUT(layout),vertAdj);
```

Using a group of the above functions to make multiple changes can cause a flurry of
motion to appear on the display as the widgets appear, disappear, and move from
one place to another with each function call. If, instead, you want to suppress the
automatic repainting of the windows that occurs with each function call, you can
freeze the display before making any changes and thaw it out afterward causing all
the changes to appear simultaneously:

```
gtk_layout_freeze(GTK_LAYOUT(layout));
    /*  The code to make the changes goes here. */
gtk_layout_thaw(GTK_LAYOUT(layout));
```

The Scrolled Window Container

A *scrolled window container* displays a portion of a larger window through a view
port. It also attaches a vertical scrollbar on the right and a horizontal scrollbar on
the left. This example uses a fixed container widget to create a large window
containing a 30x30 grid of buttons (shown in Figure 5-19).

```
1 /** scrolled.c **/
2 #include <gnome.h>
```

```
 3
 4  GtkWidget *makeScrolledWindow();
 5  gint eventDelete(GtkWidget *widget,
 6          GdkEvent *event,gpointer data);
 7  gint eventDestroy(GtkWidget *widget,
 8          GdkEvent *event,gpointer data);
 9
10  int main(int argc,char *argv[])
11  {
12      GtkWidget *window;
13      GtkWidget *scrolled;
14
15      gnome_init("scrolled","1.0",argc,argv);
16      window = gtk_window_new(GTK_WINDOW_TOPLEVEL);
17      gtk_window_set_default_size(GTK_WINDOW(window),
18              200,200);
19      gtk_signal_connect(GTK_OBJECT(window),
20              "delete_event",
21              GTK_SIGNAL_FUNC(eventDelete),
22              NULL);
23      gtk_signal_connect(GTK_OBJECT(window),
24              "destroy",
25              GTK_SIGNAL_FUNC(eventDestroy),
26              NULL);
27
28      scrolled = makeScrolledWindow();
29
30      gtk_container_add(GTK_CONTAINER(window),scrolled);
31      gtk_widget_show_all(window);
32      gtk_main();
33      exit(0);
34  }
35  GtkWidget *makeScrolledWindow()
36  {
37      gint i;
38      gint j;
39      gchar label[40];
40      GtkWidget *scrolled;
41      GtkWidget *button;
42      GtkWidget *fixed;
43
44      scrolled = gtk_scrolled_window_new(NULL,NULL);
45      gtk_scrolled_window_set_policy(
46              GTK_SCROLLED_WINDOW(scrolled),
47              GTK_POLICY_ALWAYS,
48              GTK_POLICY_ALWAYS);
49
50      fixed = gtk_fixed_new();
51      for(i=30; i<300; i += 30) {
52          for(j=30; j<300; j += 30) {
53              sprintf(label,"(%3d,%3d)",2*i,j);
54              button = gtk_button_new_with_label(label);
```

```
55                  gtk_fixed_put(GTK_FIXED(fixed),button,2*i,j);
56          }
57      }
58
59      gtk_scrolled_window_add_with_viewport(
60              GTK_SCROLLED_WINDOW(scrolled),
61              fixed);
62
63      return(scrolled);
64 }
65 gint eventDelete(GtkWidget *widget,
66         GdkEvent *event,gpointer data) {
67      return(FALSE);
68 }
69 gint eventDestroy(GtkWidget *widget,
70         GdkEvent *event,gpointer data) {
71      gtk_main_quit();
72      return(0);
73 }
```

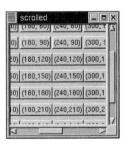

Figure 5-19: A scrolled window with a view port

The scrolled window container is constructed on line 44. The call to gtk_scrolled_window_new() is passed NULL pointers for both of its arguments. The first argument is the GtkAdjustment object that controls horizontal positioning, and the second argument is the GtkAdjustment object that controls vertical adjustments. If you pass NULL pointers for either of these, the adjustment objects are created automatically. It is normal to let the container create the adjustment objects. However, you need access to them if you want to reposition the window using something besides the scrollbars, or if you want to set the incremental values used by the scrollbar to move the window.

The call to gtk_scrolled_window_set_policy() on line 45 instructs both scrollbars to always be present. The first policy setting is for the scrollbar at the bottom, and second setting is for the one on the right. The value GTK_POLICY_ALWAYS instructs the scrolled window to always display a scrollbar, whether or not it is really needed. Specifying the setting GTK_POLICY_AUTOMATIC causes scrollbars to appear only if the window is larger than the view port. Both scrollbars can be made automatic by replacing lines 45 through 48 with this:

```
gtk_scrolled_window_set_policy(
        GTK_SCROLLED_WINDOW(scrolled),
        GTK_POLICY_AUTOMATIC,
        GTK_POLICY_AUTOMATIC);
```

With the scrollbars set to automatic, Figure 5-20 shows the window after it is resized vertically so it is large enough to display the entire column of buttons. There is no scrolling necessary, so the scrollbar disappears. Figure 5-21 shows the window expanded horizontally, causing the unnecessary horizontal scrollbar to disappear.

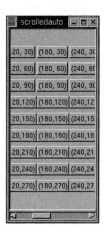

Figure 5-20: Vertical scrollbar disappears automatically

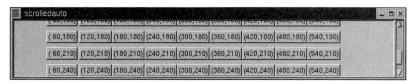

Figure 5-21: Horizontal scrollbar disappears automatically

The Notebook Container

The *notebook container* stacks widgets one on top of the other and supplies a row of tabs that can be used to switch from one to another. The tabs can be placed on the top, bottom, or on either side. The contained widgets can consist of any kind of displayable widgets, including other notebook widgets.

Each widget contained by the notebook is called a *page* because, similar to a book, all the other *pages* are hidden by the visible one. The one that is currently visible is called the *active* page.

There are a couple of size constraints. If the tabs are on the top or bottom, the notebook is at least as wide as the button. Likewise, if the tabs are on the left or right, the notebook is at least as tall as the buttons are. Also, the notebook's window is always large enough to display the largest widget it contains.

The following example displays the window shown in Figure 5-22.

```
 1 /** notebook.c **/
 2 #include <gnome.h>
 3
 4 GtkWidget *makeNotebook();
 5 GtkWidget *makeButtonPage(gchar *str);
 6 GtkWidget *makeTextPage(gchar *str);
 7 gint eventDelete(GtkWidget *widget,
 8        GdkEvent *event,gpointer data);
 9 gint eventDestroy(GtkWidget *widget,
10        GdkEvent *event,gpointer data);
11
12 int main(int argc,char *argv[])
13 {
14     GtkWidget *window;
15     GtkWidget *notebook;
16
17     gnome_init("notebook","1.0",argc,argv);
18     window = gtk_window_new(GTK_WINDOW TOPLEVEL);
19     gtk_window_set_default_size(GTK_WINDOW(window),
20           200,200);
21     gtk_signal_connect(GTK_OBJECT(window),
22           "delete_event",
23           GTK_SIGNAL_FUNC(eventDelete),
24           NULL);
25     gtk_signal_connect(GTK_OBJECT(window),
26           "destroy",
27           GTK_SIGNAL_FUNC(eventDestroy),
28           NULL);
29
30     notebook = makeNotebook();
31
32     gtk_container_add(GTK_CONTAINER(window),notebook);
33     gtk_widget_show_all(window);
34     gtk_main();
35     exit(0);
36 }
37 GtkWidget *makeNotebook() {
38     GtkWidget *notebook;
39     GtkWidget *page;
```

```
40      GtkWidget *label;
41
42      notebook = gtk_notebook_new();
43      gtk_notebook_set_tab_pos(GTK_NOTEBOOK(notebook),
44              GTK_POS_TOP);
45
46      page = makeButtonPage("First Button Page");
47      label = gtk_label_new("Front");
48      gtk_notebook_append_page(GTK_NOTEBOOK(notebook),
49              page,label);
50
51      page = makeTextPage("first");
52      label = gtk_label_new("Second");
53      gtk_notebook_append_page(GTK_NOTEBOOK(notebook),
54              page,label);
55
56      page = makeButtonPage("Second Button Page");
57      label = gtk_label_new("Third");
58      gtk_notebook_append_page(GTK_NOTEBOOK(notebook),
59              page,label);
60
61      page = makeTextPage("second");
62      label = gtk_label_new("Fourth");
63      gtk_notebook_append_page(GTK_NOTEBOOK(notebook),
64              page,label);
65
66      page = makeButtonPage("Third Button Page");
67      label = gtk_label_new("Back");
68      gtk_notebook_append_page(GTK_NOTEBOOK(notebook),
69              page,label);
70
71      return(notebook);
72 }
73 GtkWidget *makeButtonPage(gchar *str)
74 {
75      GtkWidget *alignment;
76      GtkWidget *button;
77
78      alignment = gtk_alignment_new(0.5,0.5,0.5,0.5);
79      button = gtk_button_new_with_label(str);
80      gtk_container_add(GTK_CONTAINER(alignment),button);
81
82      return(alignment);
83 }
84 GtkWidget *makeTextPage(gchar *str)
85 {
86      int i;
87      GtkWidget *text;
88      gchar string[80];
89
90      text = gtk_text_new(NULL,NULL);
```

```
91      sprintf(string,
92          "This is the text of the %s text page. ",str);
93      for(i=0; i<80; i++) {
94          gtk_text_insert(GTK_TEXT(text),NULL,NULL,NULL,
95              string,-1);
96      }
97
98      return(text);
99  }
100 gint eventDelete(GtkWidget *widget,
101         GdkEvent *event,gpointer data) {
102     return(FALSE);
103 }
104 gint eventDestroy(GtkWidget *widget,
105         GdkEvent *event,gpointer data) {
106     gtk_main_quit();
107     return(0);
108 }
```

Figure 5-22: A notebook containing five pages

The function makeNotebook(), starting on line 37, creates the notebook and stores several pages into it. The notebook is created and configured on lines 42 through 44. The pages are created and inserted into the notebook container on lines 46 through 69. (The actual pages are created by the makeButtonPage() and makeTextPage() functions starting on lines 73 and 84.)

The notebook container can position the row of tabs against any one of its four sides. The call to gtk_notebook_set_tab_pos() is used to set the position of the tabs. The value GTK_POS_TOP places the buttons on top (as shown in Figure 5-22). Using the value GTK_POS_BOTTOM places the tabs on bottom as they are in Figure 5-23. Using GTK_POS_LEFT places the tabs on the left, producing a window like the one shown in Figure 5-24. The value GTK_POS_RIGHT places the tabs on the right. The default, and probably the most used position, is GTK_POS_TOP.

Figure 5-23: A notebook with the tabs on bottom

Figure 5-24: A notebook with the tabs on the left

Each page widget is installed in the notebook by the function `gtk_notebook_append_page()`. This function adds a new page behind any other pages that already are in the notebook. In other words, the newly added page becomes the last one in the notebook. A page, added this way, positions its tab at the bottom or on the far right, depending on tab orientation.

The call to `gtk_notebook_append_page()` has a third parameter. When adding a new page to the notebook, you need to specify the widget that is to be used as the label on the tab. Normally, and in this example, a label widget is used to display text on the tab. However, there is nothing that prevents a graphic widget from being used; this widget causes the tabs to look and work like icons.

There is also a function named `gtk_notebook_prepend_page()` — with the same set of parameters as `gtk_notebook_append_page()` — that does the same thing, except the inserted page becomes the first page instead of the last page.

The pages are held inside the notebook in an ordered list, and each one has a position number: the first is 0, the second is 1, and so on. A position number can be used to insert a page in between two pages already in the notebook. For example, if a notebook already contains four pages (numbered 0, 1, 2, and 3), a new page can be stored in the center of the list with this function call:

```
gtk_notebook_insert_page(GTK_NOTEBOOK(notebook),
        page,
        label,
        2);
```

After this function is called, the page that was number 3 is now number 4, and the one that was number 2 moves to number 3. The newly added page is number 2. You can remove a page by using its position number. For example, use this to remove page number two:

```
gtk_notebook_remove_page(GTK_NOTEBOOK(notebook),2);
```

If you want more control over the display — if you want to select the tab from inside your program — you can call `gtk_notebook_set_page()` to select any of the active pages as the active one. For example, the following makes page 2 active:

```
gtk_notebook_set_page(GTK_NOTEBOOK(notebook),2);
```

This function call can be used in the previous example to determine which page is currently active:

```
gint loc;
. . .
loc = gtk_notebook_get_current_page(GTK_NOTEBOOK(notebook));
```

The tabs can be omitted. This means the user will not have the option of using the tabs to switch from one page to another. However, the capability to switch is still available inside the program, so there are situations where this makes sense. For instance, if you can operate your program in more than one mode, the option windows can be maintained as notebooks and the active pages switched each time the mode changes. By default, the tabs are visible. This function call omits the tabs:

```
gtk_notebook_set_show_tabs(GTK_NOTEBOOK(notebook),FALSE);
```

The tabs can be made visible by specifying TRUE instead of FALSE.

The Button Box

Almost every window has at least one button and most of them have more than one. Because it is needed so often, there is a special container widget designed for the purpose of grouping buttons. One advantage of using a *button box* is that spacing and layout controls can be set globally. In other words, you can control the layout of all the buttons in your entire application with a single setting. And if you want even more control, you can specify the layout for individual button boxes and let some of the others follow your default settings.

This example demonstrates how simple it is to use a button box to create a group of buttons:

```
1 /** hbuttonbox.c **/
2 #include <gnome.h>
```

```
 3
 4 GtkWidget *makeButtonBox();
 5 gint eventDelete(GtkWidget *widget,
 6         GdkEvent *event,gpointer data);
 7 gint eventDestroy(GtkWidget *widget,
 8         GdkEvent *event,gpointer data);
 9
10 int main(int argc,char *argv[])
11 {
12     GtkWidget *window;
13     GtkWidget *buttonbox;
14
15     gnome_init("hbuttonbox","1.0",argc,argv);
16     window = gtk_window_new(GTK_WINDOW_TOPLEVEL);
17     gtk_signal_connect(GTK_OBJECT(window),
18             "delete_event",
19             GTK_SIGNAL_FUNC(eventDelete),
20             NULL);
21     gtk_signal_connect(GTK_OBJECT(window),
22             "destroy",
23             GTK_SIGNAL_FUNC(eventDestroy),
24             NULL);
25
26     buttonbox = makeButtonBox();
27
28     gtk_container_add(GTK_CONTAINER(window),buttonbox);
29     gtk_widget_show_all(window);
30     gtk_main();
31     exit(0);
32 }
33 GtkWidget *makeButtonBox() {
34     GtkWidget *buttonbox;
35     GtkWidget *button;
36
37     buttonbox = gtk_hbutton_box_new();
38     gtk_container_set_border_width(
39             GTK_CONTAINER(buttonbox),10);
40
41     button = gtk_button_new_with_label("OK");
42     gtk_container_add(GTK_CONTAINER(buttonbox),button);
43
44     button = gtk_button_new_with_label("Refresh");
45     gtk_container_add(GTK_CONTAINER(buttonbox),button);
46
47     button = gtk_button_new_with_label("Clear");
48     gtk_container_add(GTK_CONTAINER(buttonbox),button);
49
50     button = gtk_button_new_with_label("Cancel");
51     gtk_container_add(GTK_CONTAINER(buttonbox),button);
52
53     return(buttonbox);
```

```
54 }
55 gint eventDelete(GtkWidget *widget,
56          GdkEvent *event,gpointer data) {
57     return(FALSE);
58 }
59 gint eventDestroy(GtkWidget *widget,
60          GdkEvent *event,gpointer data) {
61     gtk_main_quit();
62     return(0);
63 }
```

The function makeButtonBox() beginning on line 33 creates a horizontal button box and fills it with buttons. The box is created on line 37 by the call to gtk_hbutton _box_new(), which requires no parameters. Each button is added to the box with the calls to gtk_container_add() on lines 41 through 51. The call to gtk_container_ set_border_width() on line 38 adds a 10-pixel boundary around the set of buttons—resulting in the window shown in Figure 5-25.

Figure 5-25: A horizontal button box

You can create a vertical button box by changing one letter. To create the display shown in Figure 5-26, change line 37 to this:

```
buttonbox = gtk_vbutton_box_new();
```

Figure 5-26: A vertical button box

A button box has four different layout options that can be set by using these five values:

```
GTK_BUTTONBOX_DEFAULT_STYLE
GTK_BUTTONBOX_SPREAD
GTK_BUTTONBOX_EDGE
GTK_BUTTONBOX_START
GTK_BUTTONBOX_END
```

The following program demonstrates the results of setting each of the options for a button box. The four button boxes produced by this program — one with each layout option set — are shown in Figure 5-27.

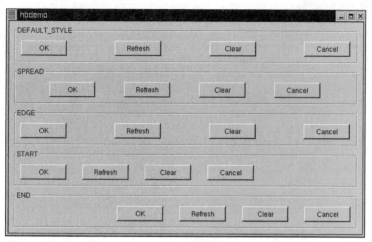

Figure 5-27: Horizontal button boxes with different layouts

The layout options all deal with positioning buttons when the button box is larger than the minimum size. The GTK_BUTTONBOX_SPREAD option distributes the buttons evenly across the button box, and also inserts some space at each end of the row of buttons. The GTK_BUTTONBOX_EDGE option also spaces the buttons evenly, but does not add space at the beginning or end. The GTK_BUTTONBOX_START option maintains the default spacing and moves all buttons to the left. The GTK_BUTTONBOX_END option also maintains the default spacing, but moves the buttons to the right.

The GTK_BUTTONBOX_DEFAULT_STYLE specifies that the button box be configured using the default value. Unless you change it, the default is GTK_BUTTON_EDGE.

```
1 /** hbdemo.c **/
2 #include <gnome.h>
3
4 typedef struct {
5     gchar *name;
6     GtkButtonBoxStyle value;
7 } layoutOption;
8
9 GtkWidget *makeButtonFrame(layoutOption *option);
10 GtkWidget *makeButtonBox(layoutOption *option);
11 GtkWidget *makeDisplay();
12 gint eventDelete(GtkWidget *widget,
```

```
13            GdkEvent *event,gpointer data);
14 gint eventDestroy(GtkWidget *widget,
15            GdkEvent *event,gpointer data);
16
17 layoutOption option[] = {
18     { "DEFAULT_STYLE", GTK_BUTTONBOX_DEFAULT_STYLE },
19     { "SPREAD", GTK_BUTTONBOX_SPREAD },
20     { "EDGE", GTK_BUTTONBOX_EDGE },
21     { "START", GTK_BUTTONBOX_START },
22     { "END", GTK_BUTTONBOX_END }
23 };
24
25 int main(int argc,char *argv[])
26 {
27     GtkWidget *window;
28     GtkWidget *demoDisplay;
29
30     gnome_init("hbdemo","1.0",argc,argv);
31     window = gtk_window_new(GTK_WINDOW_TOPLEVEL);
32     gtk_signal_connect(GTK_OBJECT(window),
33             "delete_event",
34             GTK_SIGNAL_FUNC(eventDelete),
35             NULL);
36     gtk_signal_connect(GTK_OBJECT(window),
37             "destroy",
38             GTK_SIGNAL_FUNC(eventDestroy),
39             NULL);
40
41     demoDisplay = makeDisplay();
42
43     gtk_container_add(GTK_CONTAINER(window),demoDisplay);
44     gtk_widget_show_all(window);
45     gtk_main();
46     exit(0);
47 }
48 GtkWidget *makeDisplay()
49 {
50     int i;
51     GtkWidget *vbox;
52     GtkWidget *frame;
53
54     vbox = gtk_vbox_new(FALSE,10);
55     gtk_container_set_border_width(GTK_CONTAINER(vbox),10);
56     for(i=0; i<5; i++) {
57         frame = makeButtonFrame(&option[i]);
58         gtk_box_pack_start(GTK_BOX(vbox),frame,
59                 FALSE,FALSE,0);
60     }
61     return(vbox);
62 }
63 GtkWidget *makeButtonFrame(layoutOption *option)
```

```
 64 {
 65      GtkWidget *frame;
 66      GtkWidget *buttonbox;
 67
 68      frame = gtk_frame_new(option->name);
 69      buttonbox = makeButtonBox(option);
 70      gtk_container_add(GTK_CONTAINER(frame),buttonbox);
 71      return(frame);
 72 }
 73 GtkWidget *makeButtonBox(layoutOption *option)
 74 {
 75      GtkWidget *buttonbox;
 76      GtkWidget *button;
 77
 78      buttonbox = gtk_hbutton_box_new();
 79      gtk_button_box_set_layout(GTK_BUTTON_BOX(buttonbox),
 80              option->value);
 81      gtk_container_set_border_width(
 82              GTK_CONTAINER(buttonbox),10);
 83
 84      button = gtk_button_new_with_label("OK");
 85      gtk_container_add(GTK_CONTAINER(buttonbox),button);
 86
 87      button = gtk_button_new_with_label("Refresh");
 88      gtk_container_add(GTK_CONTAINER(buttonbox),button);
 89
 90      button = gtk_button_new_with_label("Clear");
 91      gtk_container_add(GTK_CONTAINER(buttonbox),button);
 92
 93      button = gtk_button_new_with_label("Cancel");
 94      gtk_container_add(GTK_CONTAINER(buttonbox),button);
 95
 96      return(buttonbox);
 97 }
 98 gint eventDelete(GtkWidget *widget,
 99          GdkEvent *event,gpointer data) {
100      return(FALSE);
101 }
102 gint eventDestroy(GtkWidget *widget,
103          GdkEvent *event,gpointer data) {
104      gtk_main_quit();
105      return(0);
106 }
```

The function makeDisplay() beginning on line 48 creates the vertical box to hold all of the displayable widgets. The loop beginning on line 56 creates five button frames — one for each layout option — by using the text and the values stored in the array defined on line 17. For each of the layouts, a frame holding a button box is created on line 57 and stored into the vertical box on line 58.

The function `makeButtonFrame()` beginning on line 63 creates a frame that has the name of the layout option as its label. The button box is created on line 69 with a call to `makeButtonBox()`, and is inserted into the frame on line 70.

The function `makeButtonBox()` starting on line 73 creates a button box and puts four buttons into it. The call to `gtk_button_box_set_layout()` on line 79 uses the layout value passed in as an argument to set the layout option.

The same layout options apply to vertical button boxes (as shown in Figure 5-28). The program that created the vertical buttons is almost the same as the previous example, except that vertical is used for horizontal, and vice versa.

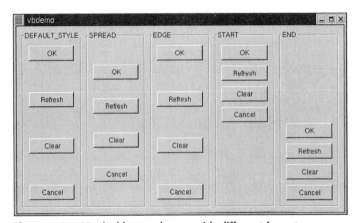

Figure 5-28: Vertical button boxes with different layouts

As mentioned earlier, the default layout style is `GTK_BUTTONBOX_EDGE`. You can change the default; your new default value applies to all buttons that are not assigned specific layout values. There are two functions to do this, one for each orientation. For example, to set vertical button boxes to `START` and horizontal boxes to `SPREAD`:

```
gtk_vbutton_box_set_layout_default(GTK_BUTTONBOX_START);
gtk_hbutton_box_set_layout_default(GTK_BUTTONBOX_SPREAD);
```

You can retrieve the current layout option for each orientation of the button boxes this way:

```
gint vLayout;
gint hLayout;
. . .
vLayout = gtk_vbutton_box_get_layout_default();
hLayout = gtk_hbutton_box_get_layout_default();
```

In both the vertical and horizontal button boxes, there is a default space that is inserted between the buttons. The horizontal default is 30 pixels and the vertical default is 10 pixels, but you can change the default settings. For example, to set the vertical separation to 3 pixels and the horizontal separation to 15 pixels:

```
gtk_vbutton_box_set_spacing_default(3);
gtk_hbutton_box_set_spacing_default(15);
```

You can retrieve the current default spacing values this way:

```
gint vSpacing;
gint hSpacing;
. . .
vSpacing = gtk_vbutton_box_get_spacing_default();
hSpacing = gtk_hbutton_box_get_spacing_default();
```

Summary

All of the containers are built to contain one or more widgets, and all of the containers *are* widgets. This means that one container can be contained inside another. For example, you can place some fixed containers inside a table, then insert the table into a scrolled window so the user can move around the table, and then put the whole thing inside a notebook so you have several other windows available on a row of tabs. This chapter explored the types of containers, and these facts:

✦ Widgets can be positioned and grouped in almost any configuration. This makes it possible for you to create windows that are clear and easy to understand.

✦ So much of the work of positioning widgets is automated inside the containers that it makes it very easy to place your widgets where you want them. For most containers, it is simply a matter of inserting the widgets, checking the result, and tweaking the options until you have it looking the way you want.

✦ The functions used to place widgets on display are consistent from one container to the next and are given descriptive easy-to-read names.

The examples and explanations explored in this chapter — along with the ones in Chapter 4 — provide you with information on all the tools you need to create any window layout you can think of. Chapter 6 explains how you can make your widgets useful by sending messages from the user to your application.

✦   ✦   ✦

Events, Signals, and Callbacks

This chapter deals with some of the problems that arise from using the event model. If the program constantly remains blocked waiting for input from the event queue, there is no opportunity to read data from files or over a communication link. Another problem comes from the fact that whenever your program is processing data, it is ignoring the event queue and it also ignores any mouse and keyboard input.

Events come in through the event queue, they are translated into signals, and the signals cause callback functions to be called. But because there are so many signals defined in so many different places in the code, it can become very confusing for a programmer trying to keep track of them all. And it is hard to keep track of which arguments are being passed to which callback functions.

Reading the Event Queue

The *event queue* is the center of every application. Not only does the event queue supply the information from the user's mouse and keyboard, it also can be used as a timer and as a method of inter-process communications.

Your application initializes itself and then calls the function `gtk_main()`, which does not return until it is time for your process to halt. You can verify this by surrounding the call to `gtk_main()` with two print statements like this:

```
g_print("The call to gtk_main()\n");
gtk_main();
g_print("The return from gtk_main()\n");
```

When the program is run, the first line displays immediately (well, as soon as the program finishes initializing itself and is ready to open a window). The second line only displays when you exit the program. Of course, if your program crashes or ceases operation in some other abrupt fashion, the second line never displays.

External processes or devices use the event queue to send information to your program. The queue is read-only, so if your program needs to talk to other programs or to devices it has to use some other method.

There are several different types of events. A number of them are of no real consequence to an application because the underlying GTK+ event handler does most of the work. For example, if a window becomes unobscured, an event arrives specifying that window must be redrawn completely or partially. But there normally is no need for the application to bother with it because GTK+ takes care of it. However, there are circumstances in which you may want to have more information about the incoming events. For example, if your application uses input from the mouse to draw lines on the screen, you need to know where the mouse is located and whether a button is being held down. This information is all included with the event and is passed to your callback functions.

The Sequence of Dispatching Events

An event happens (such as a key being pressed on the keyboard) and your program reacts. There may be several programs running at the same time, so a process needs to decide which process is to receive information about the event and a mechanism needs to get it there. The following steps are a high-level overview of the process.

Step 1:   The mouse pointer is moved around the display and a button is pressed. This causes a hardware interrupt.

Step 2:   The software driver for the mouse fields the interrupt and packages the information in the standard form for the system. The information includes the x and y location of the mouse click and which button was pressed. The driver then passes the information on to the process that registered with it — in the case of X, it is the window manager.

Step 3:   The window manager has the job of positioning all the windows on the display and determining the stacking order (which windows are obscured by other windows). Using this geographic information, the window manager determines which window just received the mouse click. With the keyboard, the process is a little different because there is no on-screen location information. There is one window that has the focus, and that window receives all keystrokes.

Step 4:   Every time an application program opens a window, it does so by sending the information to the window manager. This way, the window manager has the address of the event queue for every window. The window manager packages the data in the standard format for X and writes it to the event queue associated with the chosen window.

Step 5:   The main loop of the application uses a low-level X function to read the event from its queue. The software then determines which widget is to receive the signal by looking up the window ID that comes with the message. GTK+ then passes the information to a function, such as gtk_signal_emit(), which reformats the information as a signal and passes it on to the widget.

Step 6:   Part of the definition of a widget is the function that is to receive all incoming signals. The information is included in the struct that defines each object.

Step 7:   The widget looks at the list of callback functions that have been connected with this particular signal, and calls them all. The fact that the mouse button has been pressed means that it has reached its final destination.

Issuing Your Own Signal

There are ways to simulate an event, by generating a signal, without going through the actual event queue. You can use the function gtk_signal_emit() to create a signal, but to do so requires that you know the internal signal ID number. It is probably easier to use gtk_signal_emit_by_name() because all that is required is the textual name of the signal and a pointer to the object to receive the signal. This example shows how to send your own signal:

```
 1 /** simsignal.c **/
 2 #include <gnome.h>
 3
 4 GtkWidget *makeButtonBox();
 5 gint eventDelete(GtkWidget *widget,
 6        GdkEvent *event,gpointer data);
 7 gint eventDestroy(GtkWidget *widget,
 8        GdkEvent *event,gpointer data);
 9 void buttonFirstCallback(GtkWidget *widget,
10        GdkEvent *event,gpointer data);
11 void buttonSecondCallback(GtkWidget *widget,
12        GdkEvent *event,gpointer data);
13
14 GtkWidget *buttonFirst;
15 GtkWidget *buttonSecond;
16
```

```
17 int main(int argc,char *argv[])
18 {
19     GtkWidget *window;
20     GtkWidget *buttonbox;
21
22     gnome_init("simsignal","1.0",argc,argv);
23     window = gtk_window_new(GTK_WINDOW_TOPLEVEL);
24     gtk_signal_connect(GTK_OBJECT(window),"delete_event",
25             GTK_SIGNAL_FUNC(eventDelete),NULL);
26     gtk_signal_connect(GTK_OBJECT(window),"destroy",
27             GTK_SIGNAL_FUNC(eventDestroy),NULL);
28
29     buttonbox = makeButtonBox();
30
31     gtk_container_add(GTK_CONTAINER(window),buttonbox);
32     gtk_widget_show_all(window);
33     gtk_main();
34     exit(0);
35 }
36 GtkWidget *makeButtonBox() {
37     GtkWidget *buttonbox;
38
39     buttonbox = gtk_hbutton_box_new();
40     gtk_container_set_border_width(
41             GTK_CONTAINER(buttonbox),10);
42
43     buttonFirst = gtk_button_new_with_label("First");
44     gtk_container_add(GTK_CONTAINER(buttonbox),
45             buttonFirst);
46     gtk_signal_connect(GTK_OBJECT(buttonFirst),
47             "clicked",
48             GTK_SIGNAL_FUNC(buttonFirstCallback),
49             NULL);
50
51     buttonSecond = gtk_button_new_with_label("Second");
52     gtk_container_add(GTK_CONTAINER(buttonbox),
53             buttonSecond);
54     gtk_signal_connect(GTK_OBJECT(buttonSecond),
55             "clicked",
56             GTK_SIGNAL_FUNC(buttonSecondCallback),
57             NULL);
58
59     return(buttonbox);
60 }
61 void buttonFirstCallback(GtkWidget *widget,
62         GdkEvent *event,gpointer data) {
63     g_print("Clicked: First\n");
64 }
65 void buttonSecondCallback(GtkWidget *widget,
66         GdkEvent *event,gpointer data) {
67     gtk_signal_emit_by_name(GTK_OBJECT(buttonFirst),
```

```
68              "clicked");
69      g_print("Clicked: Second\n");
70 }
71
72 gint eventDelete(GtkWidget *widget,
73          GdkEvent *event,gpointer data) {
74      return(FALSE);
75 }
76 gint eventDestroy(GtkWidget *widget,
77          GdkEvent *event,gpointer data) {
78      gtk_main_quit();
79      return(0);
80 }
```

The function makeButtonBox() beginning on line 36 creates a window with two
buttons. They both have "clicked" callback functions defined for them — the button
labeled "First" uses buttonFirstCallback() and the button labeled "Second"
uses buttonSecondCallback().

The function buttonFirstCallback() beginning on line 61 responds to the signal
by displaying a string identifying the button. The buttonSecondCallback()
function on line 65 also displays a string identifying itself, but there is a call to
gtk_signal_emit_by_name() on line 67 that creates a "clicked" signal that goes
to buttonFirst. This means that whenever the second button is pressed, the first
button acts just as if it had been pressed.

When this program runs, each mouse click displays one or two lines. Clicking the
second button causes the first button to display before the second one does. This
is because you are causing the callback functions to be called directly (instead of
asynchronously through some sort of queuing system). Any code following the call
to gtk_signal_emit_by_name() has to wait until the entire signal is processed
before the function returns.

Signals and callback functions can be used to tie things together without requiring
you to add some special code to the widget. If a widget has an action defined as a
callback, just emit a signal, which has the effect of a direct call to the callback
function. And if there is any change in the widget (such as deleting or adding
callback functions) things will continue to work correctly.

Note

Be careful if you are going to emit signals to connect things together inside a program. A callback function emitting its own signal is recursive — that is, it effectively
calls itself. Also, if callback function A emits a signal to execute callback function
B — which, in turn, emits a signal executing callback function A — an unbreakable
infinite loop exists and the program crashes. An infinite loop occurs no matter how
many callbacks are involved. In essence, if callback function A invokes callback
function B, B invokes C, and C invokes A again, the program inevitably crashes.

Names and IDs of the Signals

To be able to use signals in an application, you must write callback functions with the return value and set of arguments that match the ones defined for the signal. Unfortunately, there is no overall standard definition of a callback function, so it can be difficult to determine exactly what is required. Because the calls to the callback functions are generated at runtime, there is no way the compiler can check to make sure your function has the correct return type and number of parameters.

Each widget class defines its own set of signals, and each widget also inherits the signals of its parent class. For example, the GtkButton widget defines its own clicked, pressed, released, enter, and leave signals. The GtkButton widget inherits from GtkBin, GtkContainer, GtkWidget, and GtkObject. The GtkBin class has no signals, the GtkContainer class has 5, the GtkWidget class has 54, and the GtkObject class has 1. This is a total of 65 signals—all of which are available inside a GtkButton widget.

Signals are defined dynamically at runtime. Whenever the first object of a certain class is created, all of the signals that possibly could be used by the class are added to the internal tables.

Forms of the Callback Functions

Every callback function has the same two parameters, but many of them have added parameters of their own. The prototype of the simplest possible callback function looks like this:

```
void cb(GtkWidget *,gpointer);
```

There are signal callbacks that have added parameters, and they are always inserted between the two standard parameters. Here is an example prototype for a callback that includes the GdkEvent as a parameter:

```
void cb(GtkWidget *,GdkEvent *,gpointer);
```

Also, a callback can return void, gint, or gboolean. Here is a prototype for the "drag-drop" callback function defined in the GtkWidget class:

```
gboolean cb(GtkWidget *,GdkDragContext *,
        gint,gint,guint,gpointer);
```

It's hard to keep up with the definitions of the formats of all the callback functions. For one thing, in the source code, the callbacks are not all defined in one place because each widget carries its own set of signal and callback function definitions.

These definitions are found inside GTK+ objects, inside the GNOME objects (and sometimes inside things other than graphical widgets), and inside other utility functions throughout that define signals of their own. Also, if you write a widget or two, you will be adding your own, and you can expect libraries to come with their own sets of objects with callbacks.

You can run the following program to determine the class inheritance and format of the callback functions for any set of objects you choose. To do this, each of the object types is created (causing the signal information to be registered) and this program reads the information from the internal table and prints a sorted list of the object names, the object inheritance, the signal names, and a prototype of the callback function.

```
1  /** signames.c **/
2  #include <gnome.h>
3
4  typedef struct SigDescStruct {
5      struct SigDescStruct *left;
6      struct SigDescStruct *right;
7      gchar *signal_name;
8      gchar *type_name;
9      gchar *parent_type_name;
10     gchar *fn;
11 } SigDesc;
12
13 static SigDesc *sigdesc = NULL;
14 static gchar last_name_printed[100] = "";
15
16 static void load_signals();
17 static void add_siglist(const gchar *signal_name,
18         const gchar *type_name,
19         const gchar *parent_type_name,const gchar *fn);
20 static void add_sigdesc_to_tree(SigDesc *new,
21         SigDesc *node);
22 static void print_signals(SigDesc *sd,FILE *file);
23 static gchar *inheritance(GtkType type);
24
25 void signames(FILE *file)
26 {
27     load_signals();
28     print_signals(sigdesc,file);
29 }
30 static void widget_list()
31 {
32     gtk_button_new();
33     gtk_calendar_new();
34 }
35 int main(int argc,char *argv[])
36 {
```

```
37      gnome_init("signames","1.0",argc,argv);
38      widget_list();
39      signames(stdout);
40      exit(0);
41  }
42  static void load_signals()
43  {
44      gint i = 0;
45      gint j;
46      gchar *type_name;
47      gchar *parent_type_name;
48      gchar *return_type_name;
49      gchar *param_name;
50      gchar fn[256];
51      GtkSignalQuery *q;
52
53      while((q = gtk_signal_query(++i)) != NULL) {
54          type_name = gtk_type_name(q->object_type);
55          return_type_name = gtk_type_name(q->return_val);
56          parent_type_name = inheritance(q->object_type);
57          sprintf(fn,"%s cb(GtkWidget *",return_type_name);
58          for(j=0; j<q->nparams; j++) {
59              param_name = gtk_type_name(q->params[j]);
60              strcat(fn,",");
61              strcat(fn,param_name);
62          }
63          strcat(fn,",gpointer)");
64          add_siglist(q->signal_name,type_name,
65                  parent_type_name,fn);
66      }
67  }
68  static void add_siglist(const gchar *signal_name,
69          const gchar *type_name,
70          const gchar *parent_type_name,const gchar *fn)
71  {
72      SigDesc *new_sigdesc;
73
74      new_sigdesc = g_malloc(sizeof(SigDesc));
75      new_sigdesc->signal_name =
76              g_malloc(strlen(signal_name)+1);
77      strcpy(new_sigdesc->signal_name,signal_name);
78      new_sigdesc->type_name = g_malloc(strlen(type_name)+1);
79      strcpy(new_sigdesc->type_name,type_name);
80      new_sigdesc->fn = g_malloc(strlen(fn)+1);
81      strcpy(new_sigdesc->fn,fn);
82      if(parent_type_name == NULL) {
83          new_sigdesc->parent_type_name = NULL;
84      } else {
85          new_sigdesc->parent_type_name =
86                  g_malloc(strlen(parent_type_name)+1);
87          strcpy(new_sigdesc->parent_type_name,
```

```
 88                     parent_type_name);
 89      }
 90      new_sigdesc->left = NULL;
 91      new_sigdesc->right = NULL;
 92
 93      if(sigdesc == NULL) {
 94          sigdesc = new_sigdesc;
 95      } else {
 96          add_sigdesc_to_tree(new_sigdesc,sigdesc);
 97      }
 98 }
 99 static void add_sigdesc_to_tree(SigDesc *new,SigDesc *node)
100 {
101      int cond;
102
103      if((cond = strcmp(new->type_name,
104                      node->type_name)) < 0) {
105          if(node->left == NULL)
106              node->left = new;
107          else
108              add_sigdesc_to_tree(new,node->left);
109      } else if(cond > 0) {
110          if(node->right == NULL)
111              node->right = new;
112          else
113              add_sigdesc_to_tree(new,node->right);
114      } else if((cond = strcmp(new->signal_name,
115                      node->signal_name)) < 0) {
116          if(node->left == NULL)
117              node->left = new;
118          else
119              add_sigdesc_to_tree(new,node->left);
120      } else if(cond > 0) {
121          if(node->right == NULL)
122              node->right = new;
123          else
124              add_sigdesc_to_tree(new,node->right);
125      }
126 }
127 static void print_signals(SigDesc *sd,FILE *file)
128 {
129      int i;
130      int j;
131      gchar string[256];
132
133      if(sd != NULL) {
134          print_signals(sd->left,file);
135          if(strcmp(last_name_printed,sd->type_name)) {
136              fprintf(file,"\n%s   (->%s)\n",
137                      sd->type_name,sd->parent_type_name);
138              strcpy(last_name_printed,sd->type_name);
```

```
139              }
140          sprintf(string,"   \"%s\" %s",
141                  sd->signal_name,sd->fn);
142          if(strlen(string) > 63) {
143              for(i=63; i>0; i--) {
144                  if(string[i] == ',') {
145                      for(j = strlen(string); j > i; j--)
146                          string[j+9] = string[j];
147                      string[i+1] = '\n';
148                      for(j=2; j<10; j++)
149                          string[j+i] = ' ';
150                      break;
151                  }
152              }
153          }
154          fprintf(file,"%s\n",string);
155          print_signals(sd->right,file);
156      }
157 }
158
159 static gchar *inheritance(GtkType type)
160 {
161      GtkType parent_type;
162      gchar *parent_type_name;
163      static gchar string[256];
164
165      string[0] = '\0';
166      while(1) {
167          parent_type = gtk_type_parent(type);
168          parent_type_name = gtk_type_name(parent_type);
169          if(parent_type_name == NULL)
170              break;
171          if(strlen(string) > 1) {
172              strcat(string,"->");
173              strcat(string,parent_type_name);
174          } else {
175              strcpy(string,parent_type_name);
176          }
177          type = parent_type;
178      }
179      if(strlen(string) > 1)
180          return(string);
181      return("none");
182 }
```

The main() function beginning on line 35 calls gnome_init(), as usual for any GNOME application, to initialize both GNOME and GTK+. Next it calls widget_list() to initialize the signal information by creating instances of objects. The signames() function is called to generate the output. In the signames() function on line 25, the function load_signals() is called to retrieve the signal

information and store it into a sorted list. Finally, a call is made to print_signals()
to write signal information from the sorted list to standard output.

You can add and remove the widgets included in the output listing by adding and
removing widget creation calls in the widget_list() function on line 30. In this
example, there are two calls: one to create a button widget and one to create a
calendar widget. There is no need to save the returned widget because it is only
necessary for the class to initialize itself, causing the list of callbacks to become
defined in the internal tables.

Note   This program was written to run as a standalone, but with a simple modification it
can be compiled and linked to run from inside your application. To do this, delete
the main() and widget_list() functions, then compile it and link it with your
program. Just before you enter the main loop of your application — after you have
created all of your objects — add code to open a file and call signames() to output the callback information. For example:

```
FILE *file;
file = fopen("cbfile","w");
signames(file);
fclose(file);
gtk_main();
```

The function load_signals() beginning on line 42 reads the signal and callback
information from the internal tables. Each new signal is assigned an ID number, with
the first number being 1, the second 2, and so on. This means that the loop beginning
on line 53 will get them all by starting with number 1 and incrementing through the
loop until an unassigned ID number is found. The call to gtk_signal_query() at the
top of the loop returns the GtkSignalQuery struct that contains information about
the callback.

Quite a bit of information is available in the GtkSignalQuery struct. The call to
gtk_type_name() on line 54 uses the object type ID to retrieve the name of the
object. The call to gtk_type_name() on line 55 retrieves the type-name of the return
value from the callback function. On line 56, the call to inheritance() returns a
string containing the list of inherited objects all the way back to GtkObject.

The function inheritance() beginning on line 159 walks through the parental links of
the object to determine its entire heritage. The object type is passed in as an argument
and is used as the starting point of the walk. The call to gtk_type_parent() on line
167 returns the type ID of the parent object, and the call to gtk_type_name() on line
168 retrieves its name. As each name is retrieved, it is added to the string of names
that represent the entire heritage.

Line 57 begins construction of the prototype function call by printing the return
value and the first parameter to a string. If there are any parameters other than the
two default ones, the loop on lines 58 through 62 adds them to the string. The call

to gtk_type_name() on line 59 is used to extract the type of each parameter, but there is one piece of information missing. You cannot determine from the contents of the GtkSignalQuery struct whether the parameter is a pointer. This information exists, but is held inside the static array named gtk_signals in the GTK source file gtksignals.c. There is no way to extract the information without modifying gtksignals.c. There is a version of this program (named signames2.c) supplied with the source code, and there are comments in it that describe the GTK code changes necessary to make it work.

The function add_siglist(), beginning on line 68, creates a new node for a signal and adds it to the tree. Lines 74 through 91 create the node and fill it with values. Lines 93 through 97 add it to the tree by calling add_sigdesc_to_tree().

The function add_sigdesc_to_tree(), starting on line 99, walks the binary tree and appends the new member in the correct location. The tree is sorted first by name of the type of object that emits the signal, and then by the name of the signal itself. This way, the signals are in alphabetical order grouped by their object type.

The output is generated by the function print_signals(), beginning on line 127. It is a recursive routing expecting a tree node as an argument. It does three things: looks to the left, prints the current node, and then looks to the right. It looks to the left by calling itself with the left pointer on line 134. The printing is done on lines 135 through 153. On line 135, it compares the last object name printed against the current object name and prints it only if it is different — this creates an object name header for each group of signals. If a line is too long (in this example, 64 characters is considered too long) it is broken at the first comma to the left of the 63rd character. Finally, it looks to the left by calling itself on line 155.

The output of the example program looks like this:

```
GnomeClient    (->GtkObject)
  "connect" void cb(GtkWidget *,gboolean,gpointer)
  "die" void cb(GtkWidget *,gpointer)
  "disconnect" void cb(GtkWidget *,gpointer)
  "save-complete" void cb(GtkWidget *,gpointer)
  "save-yourself" gboolean cb(GtkWidget *,gint,GtkEnum,
        gboolean,GtkEnum,gboolean,gpointer)
  "shutdown-cancelled" void cb(GtkWidget *,gpointer)

GtkButton    (->GtkBin->GtkContainer->GtkWidget->GtkObject)
  "clicked" void cb(GtkWidget *,gpointer)
  "enter" void cb(GtkWidget *,gpointer)
  "leave" void cb(GtkWidget *,gpointer)
  "pressed" void cb(GtkWidget *,gpointer)
  "released" void cb(GtkWidget *,gpointer)

GtkCalendar    (->GtkWidget->GtkObject)
  "day-selected" void cb(GtkWidget *,gpointer)
```

```
  "day-selected-double-click" void cb(GtkWidget *,gpointer)
  "month-changed" void cb(GtkWidget *,gpointer)
  "next-month" void cb(GtkWidget *,gpointer)
  "next-year" void cb(GtkWidget *,gpointer)
  "prev-month" void cb(GtkWidget *,gpointer)
  "prev-year" void cb(GtkWidget *,gpointer)

GtkContainer   (->GtkWidget->GtkObject)
  "add" void cb(GtkWidget *,GtkWidget,gpointer)
  "check-resize" void cb(GtkWidget *,gpointer)
  "focus" GtkDirectionType cb(GtkWidget *,GtkDirectionType,
       gpointer)
  "remove" void cb(GtkWidget *,GtkWidget,gpointer)
  "set-focus-child" void cb(GtkWidget *,GtkWidget,gpointer)

GtkObject   (->none)
  "destroy" void cb(GtkWidget *,gpointer)

GtkWidget   (->GtkObject)
  "add-accelerator" void cb(GtkWidget *,guint,GtkAccelGroup,
       guint,GdkModifierType,GtkAccelFlags,gpointer)
  "button-press-event" gboolean cb(GtkWidget *,GdkEvent,
       gpointer)
  "button-release-event" gboolean cb(GtkWidget *,GdkEvent,
       gpointer)
  "client-event" gboolean cb(GtkWidget *,GdkEvent,gpointer)
  "configure-event" gboolean cb(GtkWidget *,GdkEvent,gpointer)
  "debug-msg" void cb(GtkWidget *,GtkString,gpointer)
  "delete-event" gboolean cb(GtkWidget *,GdkEvent,gpointer)
  "destroy-event" gboolean cb(GtkWidget *,GdkEvent,gpointer)
  "drag-begin" void cb(GtkWidget *,GdkDragContext,gpointer)
  "drag-data-delete" void cb(GtkWidget *,GdkDragContext,
       gpointer)
  "drag-data-get" void cb(GtkWidget *,GdkDragContext,
       GtkSelectionData,guint,guint,gpointer)
  "drag-data-received" void cb(GtkWidget *,GdkDragContext,gint,
       gint,GtkSelectionData,guint,guint,gpointer)
  "drag-drop" gboolean cb(GtkWidget *,GdkDragContext,gint,gint,
       guint,gpointer)
  "drag-end" void cb(GtkWidget *,GdkDragContext,gpointer)
  "drag-leave" void cb(GtkWidget *,GdkDragContext,guint,
       gpointer)
  "drag-motion" gboolean cb(GtkWidget *,GdkDragContext,gint,
       gint,guint,gpointer)
  "draw" void cb(GtkWidget *,gpointer,gpointer)
  "draw-default" void cb(GtkWidget *,gpointer)
  "draw-focus" void cb(GtkWidget *,gpointer)
  "enter-notify-event" gboolean cb(GtkWidget *,GdkEvent,
       gpointer)
  "event" gboolean cb(GtkWidget *,GdkEvent,gpointer)
  "expose-event" gboolean cb(GtkWidget *,GdkEvent,gpointer)
```

```
"focus-in-event" gboolean cb(GtkWidget *,GdkEvent,gpointer)
"focus-out-event" gboolean cb(GtkWidget *,GdkEvent,gpointer)
"grab-focus" void cb(GtkWidget *,gpointer)
"hide" void cb(GtkWidget *,gpointer)
"key-press-event" gboolean cb(GtkWidget *,GdkEvent,gpointer)
"key-release-event" gboolean cb(GtkWidget *,GdkEvent,
      gpointer)
"leave-notify-event" gboolean cb(GtkWidget *,GdkEvent,
      gpointer)
"map" void cb(GtkWidget *,gpointer)
"map-event" gboolean cb(GtkWidget *,GdkEvent,gpointer)
"motion-notify-event" gboolean cb(GtkWidget *,GdkEvent,
      gpointer)
"no-expose-event" gboolean cb(GtkWidget *,GdkEvent,gpointer)
"parent-set" void cb(GtkWidget *,GtkObject,gpointer)
"property-notify-event" gboolean cb(GtkWidget *,GdkEvent,
      gpointer)
"proximity-in-event" gboolean cb(GtkWidget *,GdkEvent,
      gpointer)
"proximity-out-event" gboolean cb(GtkWidget *,GdkEvent,
      gpointer)
"realize" void cb(GtkWidget *,gpointer)
"remove-accelerator" void cb(GtkWidget *,GtkAccelGroup,guint,
      GdkModifierType,gpointer)
"selection-clear-event" gboolean cb(GtkWidget *,GdkEvent,
      gpointer)
"selection-get" void cb(GtkWidget *,GtkSelectionData,guint,
      guint,gpointer)
"selection-notify-event" gboolean cb(GtkWidget *,GdkEvent,
      gpointer)
"selection-received" void cb(GtkWidget *,GtkSelectionData,
      guint,gpointer)
"selection-request-event" gboolean cb(GtkWidget *,GdkEvent,
      gpointer)
"show" void cb(GtkWidget *,gpointer)
"size-allocate" void cb(GtkWidget *,gpointer,gpointer)
"size-request" void cb(GtkWidget *,gpointer,gpointer)
"state-changed" void cb(GtkWidget *,GtkStateType,gpointer)
"style-set" void cb(GtkWidget *,GtkStyle,gpointer)
"unmap" void cb(GtkWidget *,gpointer)
"unmap-event" gboolean cb(GtkWidget *,GdkEvent,gpointer)
"unrealize" void cb(GtkWidget *,gpointer)
"visibility-notify-event" gboolean cb(GtkWidget *,GdkEvent,
      gpointer)
```

This list contains an entry for GtkButton and GtkCalendar—as expected—because those two objects are initialized before the listing is generated. Also, the inheritance is shown for each of the objects. For example, GtkButton is derived from GtkBin, which, in turn, is derived from GtkWidget, which is derived from GtkObject. This means that your program can cast a GtkButton to any of these

types and use its signals to set up callbacks. That is, the valid castings for a
GtkButton **object are:**

```
GTK_BUTTON(button)
GTK_BIN(button)
GTK_WIDGET(button)
GTK_OBJECT(button)
```

There are five signals defined for a button. The "enter" and "leave" signals generate
callbacks whenever the mouse pointer enters or leaves the button's rectangle, and
the other callbacks are generated by the mouse button being pressed while the
mouse pointer is inside the button. The callback functions for GtkButton have no
return values, and they use only the two default arguments.

Because GtkButton and GtkCalendar are derived from other objects, the signals
for all of them are initialized and they are also listed. The object GnomeClient is
not found in the inheritance of the objects we initialized — these are some special
GNOME callbacks that are initialized by the call to gnome_init(). Also notice that
every chain of inheritance goes back to GtkObject, which means that all widgets
can be addressed by this set of callbacks. GtkObject is the only object without a
parent.

Background Processing during Idle Time

If you have a lot of processing to do and, at the same time, need to continue to
respond to the mouse, you do the processing in the background running what is
known as an *idle function*. It is called idle because it is executed whenever the event
queue is idle and the application is just waiting for events.

The problem with running a background process is that your application is busy
being blocked waiting for an event. The solution is a function that enables you
to register your idle function and have it called from GTK+ whenever there is a
slack moment (that is, an empty input queue). This is fine as long as you allow
for the fact that as long as your function is executing, no incoming events can be
processed. However, there is a way to have your function relinquish control from
time to time to check for, and process, incoming events.

This program shows how to register an idle function and have the idle function
relinquish control back to event processing.

```
1 /** idle.c **/
2 #include <gnome.h>
3
4 gint eventDelete(GtkWidget *widget,
5           GdkEvent *event,gpointer data);
```

```
 6 gint eventDestroy(GtkWidget *widget,
 7         GdkEvent *event,gpointer data);
 8 void eventButton(GtkWidget *widget,
 9         GdkEvent *event,gpointer data);
10 gint idleFunction(gpointer data);
11
12 int main(int argc,char *argv[])
13 {
14     GtkWidget *window;
15     GtkWidget *button;
16
17     gnome_init("idle","1.0",argc,argv);
18     window = gtk_window_new(GTK_WINDOW_TOPLEVEL);
19     gtk_signal_connect(GTK_OBJECT(window),
20             "delete_event",
21             GTK_SIGNAL_FUNC(eventDelete),
22             NULL);
23     gtk_signal_connect(GTK_OBJECT(window),
24             "destroy",
25             GTK_SIGNAL_FUNC(eventDestroy),
26             NULL);
27     button = gtk_button_new_with_label("Button");
28     gtk_signal_connect(GTK_OBJECT(button),
29             "clicked",
30             GTK_SIGNAL_FUNC(eventButton),
31             NULL);
32     gtk_container_add(GTK_CONTAINER(window),button);
33     gtk_container_set_border_width(GTK_CONTAINER(window),
34             25);
35     gtk_widget_show_all(window);
36
37     gtk_idle_add(idleFunction,NULL);
38
39     gtk_main();
40     exit(0);
41 }
42 void eventButton(GtkWidget *widget,
43         GdkEvent *event,gpointer data)
44 {
45     g_print("Button pressed!\n");
46 }
47 gint idleFunction(gpointer data)
48 {
49     gint i;
50     static gint counter = 1;
51
52     for(i=0; i<5; i++) {
53         g_print("Counter %d in loop number %d\n",
54                 counter,i+1);
55         sleep(1);
56     }
```

```
57      if(counter++ < 5)
58          return(TRUE);
59      return(FALSE);
60 }
61 gint eventDelete(GtkWidget *widget,
62          GdkEvent *event,gpointer data) {
63      return(FALSE);
64 }
65 gint eventDestroy(GtkWidget *widget,
66          GdkEvent *event,gpointer data) {
67      gtk_main_quit();
68      return(0);
69 }
```

The displayed window contains a single button. On line 28, the call to gtk_signal_connect() assigns the function eventButton() on line 42 as the one to be called each time the button is clicked. All this callback function does is send a message string to standard output.

An idle function is added with the call to gtk_idle_add() on line 37. The first argument is the name of the idle function, and the second argument is a data pointer that will be passed to the idle function when it is called.

The idle function is named idleFunction() and it begins on line 47. To simulate extensive processing, the idle function repeatedly calls sleep() for one-second intervals. This achieves the same effect as it would for the program to process database records, perform a large sort-merge operation, or any number of other things that take a lot of time. There is the static invocation counter variable that keeps track of the number of times the function is called, and there is a loop counter i that prints out a line just before each one-second wait.

The idle function is called over and over again as long as it returns TRUE. Once the function returns FALSE, it is never called again. This way, the function can be designed to perform its task in incremental steps because, after returning to the system, it is called again.

Running this program shows that no events are processed while the idle function is being executed. The function gtk_main() looks at the event queue and, finding nothing there, calls the idle function and waits for its return. If the return is FALSE, the function is removed from the list of idle functions and is never called again. If the function return is TRUE, it is called again as soon as the event queue is empty. If you click the button several times while the idle function is running, nothing seems to happen. The fact is that the mouse events are queued and are all processed when the idle function releases control back to the event loop. This blockage not only affects the button, but it also affects mouse access to the control buttons and menu at the top of the window.

Timers

By setting *timers*, it is possible to generate callbacks that will occur at some specific time in the future. This works by placing an event in the incoming queue that will not be pulled out by the main loop until a certain amount of time has passed. This way, you can have several timers running at once and they don't interfere with the current processing in any way.

The following program demonstrates the mechanism used to start and stop timers. There are two timers: a one-second timer and a ten-second timer. The results shown in Figure 6-1 are created by having each callback display the current time whenever its timer expires. The one-second timer updates the text on top and the ten-second timer updates the text on bottom. Whenever the ten-second timer is triggered, it toggles the one-second timer on or off. When the program starts running, nothing happens for 10 seconds, and then the ten-second timer updates the display and starts the one-second timer. The one-second timer continuously updates the display until the ten-second timer stops it from running.

```
 1 /** timing.c **/
 2 #include <gnome.h>
 3
 4 GtkWidget *makeDisplay();
 5 gint eventDelete(GtkWidget *widget,
 6         GdkEvent *event,gpointer data);
 7 gint eventDestroy(GtkWidget *widget,
 8         GdkEvent *event,gpointer data);
 9
10 gint oneSecondCallback(gpointer data);
11 gint tenSecondCallback(gpointer data);
12
13 static gint oneSecondTag;
14 static gint tenSecondTag;
15 static GtkWidget *oneSecondLabel;
16 static GtkWidget *tenSecondLabel;
17
18 static gboolean oneSecondRunning = FALSE;
19
20 int main(int argc,char *argv[])
21 {
22     GtkWidget *window;
23     GtkWidget *display;
24
25     gnome_init("timing","1.0",argc,argv);
26     window = gtk_window_new(GTK_WINDOW_TOPLEVEL);
27     gtk_container_set_border_width(GTK_CONTAINER(window),
28             20);
29     gtk_signal_connect(GTK_OBJECT(window),"delete_event",
30             GTK_SIGNAL_FUNC(eventDelete),NULL);
```

```
31      gtk_signal_connect(GTK_OBJECT(window),"destroy",
32              GTK_SIGNAL_FUNC(eventDestroy),NULL);
33      display = makeDisplay();
34      gtk_container_add(GTK_CONTAINER(window),display);
35      gtk_widget_show_all(window);
36      gtk_main();
37      exit(0);
38 }
39 GtkWidget *makeDisplay() {
40      GtkWidget *box;
41
42      box = gtk_vbox_new(FALSE,0);
43
44      oneSecondLabel = gtk_label_new("One Second Timer");
45      gtk_box_pack_start(GTK_BOX(box),oneSecondLabel,
46              FALSE,FALSE,0);
47
48      tenSecondLabel = gtk_label_new("Ten Second Timer");
49      gtk_box_pack_start(GTK_BOX(box),tenSecondLabel,
50              FALSE,FALSE,0);
51      tenSecondTag = gtk_timeout_add(10000,
52              (GtkFunction)tenSecondCallback,NULL);
53
54      return(box);
55 }
56 gchar *getTimeString()
57 {
58      struct tm *t;
59      time_t tt;
60      gchar *string;
61
62      tt = time(NULL);
63      t = localtime(&tt);
64      string = asctime(t);
65      string[strlen(string)-1] = '\0';
66      return(string);
67 }
68 gint oneSecondCallback(gpointer data)
69 {
70      gtk_label_set_text(GTK_LABEL(oneSecondLabel),
71              getTimeString());
72      return(TRUE);
73 }
74 gint tenSecondCallback(gpointer data)
75 {
76      gtk_label_set_text(GTK_LABEL(tenSecondLabel),
77              getTimeString());
78      if(oneSecondRunning) {
79          gtk_timeout_remove(oneSecondTag);
80          oneSecondRunning = FALSE;
81      } else {
```

```
82          oneSecondTag = gtk_timeout_add(1000,
83              (GtkFunction)oneSecondCallback,NULL);
84          oneSecondRunning = TRUE;
85      }
86      return(TRUE);
87 }
88
89 gint eventDelete(GtkWidget *widget,
90      GdkEvent *event,gpointer data) {
91      return(FALSE);
92 }
93 gint eventDestroy(GtkWidget *widget,
94      GdkEvent *event,gpointer data) {
95      gtk_main_quit();
96      return(0);
97 }
```

Figure 6-1: Interval timers starting and stopping

The window, constructed by the function makeDisplay() on line 39, consists of two labels in a vertical box. The call to gtk_timeout_add() on line 51 sets a timer that triggers every 10,000 milliseconds (10 seconds). When it triggers, it calls the callback function named tenSecondCallback(). The last argument (the NULL value) is the optional data pointer that is standard for all callback functions.

The function getTimeString() on line 56 is simply a convenience function to create a character string holding the current date and time without the traditional '\n' on the end.

The callback function oneSecondCallback() on line 68 updates the text of its label by calling gtk_label_set_text() using a date and time string. The return value of TRUE tells the system that the timer that called this function should restart the timer and, after another interval has expired, call the function again. A return value of FALSE here causes the timer to stop and the callback is not executed again unless it is specifically scheduled to do so.

The callback function tenSecondCallback() on line 74 does all the things that the oneSecondCallback() function does, but it also starts and stops the one-second timer. If the one-second timer is running (as indicated by the Boolean value oneSecondRunning) it is stopped; if it is not running, it is started. The timer is stopped on line 79 by the call to gtk_timeout_remove(), using the tag that was returned from the call to gtk_timeout_add() on line 82 that started the timer running.

Reading Input from a File or Socket

There are a number of ways of getting data from another location into a Linux program. It is not uncommon to have a Linux program read from a file as another process is writing to it. It is also possible to create a socket and use it to establish a TCP/IP link to communicate over an Internet link. There are also FIFO (first-in first-out) files and pipes. For your program to read input from any of these sources, your program must either block itself and read the input constantly, or check the input status from time to time for the arrival of data.

One of the problems with having an event queue is that your process cannot block and wait for input from other locations. If you need to read data from a socket or a file as it becomes available, you can't simply block and wait for the input because the program cannot process events. Thus, it will appear to be dead because it no longer responds to the mouse or the keyboard. You can use a timing callback, as described in the previous section, but this has a double disadvantage. First, it adds process overhead by constantly calling functions. Secondly, your process cannot detect new input until the timer expires.

There is a facility in the GDK library that can be used to generate a callback whenever input becomes available at a socket or in a file. The mechanism is identical for files and sockets — they both operate using an int value as a file descriptor.

The following program shows how this can be used. To simplify the example code, the standard input that is already open is used. This program displays a window with a single button. It also is set to respond to the button and, simultaneously, read input from standard input.

```
 1 /** inputadd.c **/
 2 #include <fcntl.h>
 3 #include <gnome.h>
 4
 5 gint eventDelete(GtkWidget *widget,
 6         GdkEvent *event,gpointer data);
 7 gint eventDestroy(GtkWidget *widget,
 8         GdkEvent *event,gpointer data);
 9 void inputSetup();
10 void inputCallback(gpointer data,gint fd,
11         GdkInputCondition in);
12
13 GtkWidget *button;
14
15 int main(int argc,char *argv[])
16 {
17     GtkWidget *window;
18
```

```
19      gnome_init("inputadd","1.0",argc,argv);
20      window = gtk_window_new(GTK_WINDOW_TOPLEVEL);
21      gtk_window_set_default_size(GTK_WINDOW(window),
22              200,200);
23      gtk_container_set_border_width(GTK_CONTAINER(window),
24              40);
25      gtk_signal_connect(GTK_OBJECT(window),"delete_event",
26              GTK_SIGNAL_FUNC(eventDelete),NULL);
27      gtk_signal_connect(GTK_OBJECT(window),"destroy",
28              GTK_SIGNAL_FUNC(eventDestroy),NULL);
29      button = gtk_button_new_with_label("Button");
30      gtk_container_add(GTK_CONTAINER(window),button);
31      gtk_widget_show_all(window);
32
33      inputSetup();
34
35      gtk_main();
36
37      exit(0);
38 }
39 void inputSetup()
40 {
41      int fd;
42
43      fd = 0;
44      fcntl(fd,F_SETFL,O_NONBLOCK);
45      gdk_input_add(fd,GDK_INPUT_READ,
46              (GdkInputFunction)inputCallback,NULL);
47 }
48 void inputCallback(gpointer data,gint fd,
49          GdkInputCondition in)
50 {
51      int i;
52      gint count;
53      gchar string[20];
54
55      while((count = read(fd,string,20)) > 0) {
56          for(i=0; i<count; i++)
57              putchar(string[i]);
58      }
59 }
60 gint eventDelete(GtkWidget *widget,
61          GdkEvent *event,gpointer data) {
62      return(FALSE);
63 }
64 gint eventDestroy(GtkWidget *widget,
65          GdkEvent *event,gpointer data) {
66      gtk_main_quit();
67      return(0);
68 }
```

The function `inputSetup()` beginning on line 39 initializes the input by calling `gtk_input_add()`. The first argument is the internal file descriptor number (0 being the file descriptor number for Linux `stdin`, which reads from the keyboard).

The second argument to `gtk_input_add()` is a `GtkInputCondition` object. It has the value `GTK_INPUT_READ`, which causes the callback to be executed whenever input data is ready. It can be `GTK_INPUT_WRITE` if your program wants to execute the callback whenever it is possible to output data to the file, and this can have relevance when an output socket fills up and can't accept more data until it flushes what it already has. A third option is setting it to `GTK_INPUT_EXCEPTION` to cause the callback to execute whenever some exception or other occurs with the file.

The call to `fcntl()` on line 44 sets the file descriptor to nonblocking mode so a `read()` executed on it simply returns if there is no data available. If the callback function reads the file in blocking mode, the function never returns and the program effectively shuts down.

The function `inputCallback()` on line 48 is called each time data becomes available on the file descriptor. The first argument is the data pointer that was passed to the call to `gtk_input_add()`. The second argument is the file descriptor. The third argument is the value of the `GtkInputCondition`. The loop beginning on line 55 reads up to 20 characters at a time until all the characters are read and echoed to the standard output. Everything that is typed in on the keyboard is echoed to standard output.

> **Note**
>
> You may not be able to use this technique with regular files. If you want to have some other program write to a file and simultaneously read from the file into your program, you probably will be better served to use a timer rather than this data detection technique. It works, but it may cause your callback function to be called several times a second. The code that detects the status of the input file descriptor apparently becomes confused and believes there is always data available. Anyway, this facility is mainly intended for use with sockets and works very well that way—both reading and writing.

Summary

The heart of a GNOME application is its event queue. A program does not have to block on the event queue and ignore everything else—there are some things that can be done to implement background processing. No matter what method is used, however, all processing must take the event queue into consideration. This chapter demonstrated the following:

✦ The data coming in from the event queue is ignored completely unless the application calls functions to specify a callback that should be used for it. If so, the callback function is called with the appropriate set of arguments.

✦ A utility program named `signames` displays a list of the available signal names and the arguments that will be passed to the callback functions. It has the advantage of listing only the signal information for objects that already exist. It can be used as a standalone program, or it can be linked to your application.

✦ It is possible to process data while waiting on the event queue by using the idle time. That is, you can specify a function to be called every time the main loop discovers that the event queue is empty.

✦ You also can process data while waiting on the event queue by setting a timer that will, at regular intervals, call a function to do the processing.

✦ It is possible to wait for input from an incoming socket or file while also waiting on the event queue. The same mechanism can be used for output so data being written to a slow socket does not halt your application.

The GNOME/GTK+ software is a graphical user interface, so there must be some way of storing and displaying graphics. The next chapter describes the two basic formats of graphic storage and has some examples that display the graphics in different ways.

✦   ✦   ✦

Bitmaps, Pixmaps, and Cursors

CHAPTER

7

This chapter is an introduction to simple graphics and cursors. Small graphics can be used as icons, labels for toolbar buttons, menu buttons, and decorative logos for things such as the GNOME About box. Most graphics are displayed in multiple colors, but cursors can only be displayed in two colors. There are a lot of things to consider when you are going to include graphics in your program, and there are a number of different ways to do it. The graphics can be stored in files that your program loads dynamically when it needs to display a picture. Also, you can compile the graphic information as part of your program. This results in a program that can execute without other files. You can even display pixel values generated in your program.

Two Kinds of Graphics

The two basic kinds of graphics are *bitmaps* and *pixmaps*:

✦ A *pixmap* is a rectangular array of pixel values. Each value in the array represents a color for one pixel. A pixmap can contain as many colors as you can load into your palette at any one time.

✦ A *bitmap* is a rectangular array of bits in which each bit corresponds to one pixel. A bitmap only has two colors — that is, each pixel is either "on" or "off." Normally, this is displayed as black and white, but GTK+ enables you to display a bitmap using any two colors. A bitmap is really just a special case of a pixmap, but it is used often enough that it has its own special file format.

There seems to be no end to graphic file formats. Fortunately, almost any graphics file format can be used inside a GNOME application because of a "universal" conversion utility. The `convert` utility (described in more detail later in this chapter) can convert a graphics file from some external format into a format that can be displayed. For example, the following command shows how to convert a JPEG file into a pixmap — a form that can be compiled directly into your program.

```
convert rickrack.jpeg rickrack.xpm
```

If you want to include a bitmap (no color) in your program, you can make the conversion this way:

```
convert rickrack.jpeg rickrack.xbm
```

The `convert` utility looks at the contents of the input file to determine what kind of file it is (it doesn't trust the file suffix on input) and looks at the suffix of the output file name to determine what kind of graphics file to produce.

The XPM Format

The *XPM (XPixMap)* graphics format is a standard in X for storing graphics as ASCII text. This format enables you to use your text editor to create or modify simple color graphics. Not only is an XPM definition ASCII, but its format is C source code that you can compile directly into your program.

The following is an example of an XPM graphic with four colors:

```
 1 /* XPM */
 2 /** essPixmap.xpm **/
 3 static char *essPixmap[] = {
 4 "12 14 4 1",
 5 "  c None",
 6 "X c #FFFFFF",
 7 "R c Red",
 8 "B c #0000FF",
 9 "    RRBB    ",
10 "XXXXXXXXXXXX",
11 "XXXXXXXXXXXX",
12 "XX  RRBB    ",
13 "XX  RRBB    ",
14 "XX  RRBB    ",
15 "XXXXXXXXXXXX",
16 "XXXXXXXXXXXX",
17 "    RRBB  XX",
18 "    RRBB  XX",
19 "    RRBB  XX",
20 "XXXXXXXXXXXX",
21 "XXXXXXXXXXXX",
22 "    RRBB    ",
23 };
```

The syntax of this XPM file is defined as an array of character strings. The comment on the first line must be present because it is used by utilities to determine the file type.

Line 4 contains four numbers that are used to describe the data that follows. The first number specifies that the pixmap is 12 pixels wide, and the second number specifies it is 14 pixels high. The next number specifies that four colors are used in drawing the graphic. The last digit specifies one letter is used as the tag for each of the colors (more about this a little further on).

Lines 5 through 9 are the color definitions. Each string begins with a character being assigned a color. Any ASCII character can be used. Line 5 defines the space character as the color named None. This specifies that no pixel is to be painted and produces transparency because the background is not overwritten. Line 6 assigns the value of white to the letter X. The hexadecimal value FFFFFF is the red-green-blue (RGB) value for white (in base 10, the values are 255 255 255). Line 8 uses the hexadecimal value 0000FF to assign the color green to the letter G. Line 7 uses a name to define a color for the letter R — the name must be assigned one of the RGB values found in the file /usr/X11R6/lib/X11/rgb.txt.

The graphic itself begins on line 9 and continues through to line 22. Each string is 12 characters long because the graphic is 12 pixels wide and only one character is used to represent a pixel. There are 14 of these strings because the graphic is 14 pixels high. Every pixel is assigned a value by containing one of the four-color characters defined earlier.

An XPM file can be used to contain large, high-resolution image with a large number of colors. For example, with the Linux distribution, there is a file named logo.gif that contains the Linux penguin. You can convert the GIF file to an XPM file with this command:

```
convert logo.gif logo.xpm
```

There is more than 24-bit color information includes, and there are more colors than can be represented by single characters. The entire XPM file is 560 lines long. Here is an excerpt:

```
/* XPM */
static char *magick[] = {
"257 303 251 2",
"   c Gray0",
".  c #080800000404",
"X  c #080808080000",
"o  c Gray3",
"O  c #101004040404",
"+  c #101010100404",
    . . .
"{. c #f0f0b8b80808",
"}. c #f8f8b0b00808",
"|. c #f8f8b8b80808",
```

```
" X  c #f0f0b0b01010",
".X  c #f0f0b8b81010",
"XX  c #f8f8b8b81010",
"BX  c #d8d8d8d8e8e8",
"VX  c #e0e0e0e0d8d8",
"CX  c #f0f0e8e8d8d8",
"ZX  c Gray88",
"AX  c Gray91",
"SX  c #e8e8e8e8f0f0",
"DX  c #f0f0e8e8ecec",
"FX  c #f0f0f0f0e8e8",
"GX  c Gray94",
"HX  c #f8f8f8f8f8f8",
"JX  c None",
         . . .
```

This XPM graphic is 257 pixels wide and 303 pixels tall. It contains a total of 251
colors and uses 2 characters to represent each color. The first few characters may
appear to be defined by a single character, but in fact, two characters are used
because the blank serves as the second character. As you can see further down in
the file, the period and X characters are used. Because 2 characters are required to
specify a color, each string defining a row of pixel values has to be 514 characters
long (twice 257).

Also, notice that the hexadecimal numbers for the colors have 12 digits instead
of 6. This is still an RGB format but each color is 16 bits (four hexadecimal digits).
Either length is valid for an XPM file — the software that reads it counts the digits to
determine the format. The colors in the file /usr/X11R6/lib/X11/rgb.txt, and
many colors found in other places, are defined as three 8-bit values. This simple
program converts three 8-bit values into both the long and short hexadecimal
strings required by XPM:

```c
/* hexcolor */
#include <stdio.h>
#include <stdlib.h>
char *usage[] = {
"           Usage: hexcolor r g b",
" Enter the three RBG color values in the",
" range of 0 to 256. The output is both a",
" 24-bit and 48-bit hexadecimal number of the",
" color that can be used in an XPM file."
};
int main(int argc,char *argv[])
{
    int i;
    int r,g,b;

    if(argc < 4) {
        for(i=0; i<5; i++)
            printf("%s\n",usage[i]);
        exit(1);
    }
```

```
    r = atoi(argv[1]);
    g = atoi(argv[2]);
    b = atoi(argv[3]);
    printf("#%02X%02X%02X\n",r,g,b);
    printf("#%02X00%02X00%02X00\n",r,g,b);
    exit(0);
}
```

Show XPM from Data

Because the `convert` utility can convert virtually any graphics file into an XPM file, and because the XPM format is C source code, almost any graphic can be compiled directly into your program. This is mostly used for icons, button labels, list bullets, and other decorative items. The following program is an example of compiling an XPM file directly into the code and displaying it:

```
 1 /** show_xpm_data.c **/
 2 #include <gnome.h>
 3
 4 gint eventDelete(GtkWidget *widget,
 5         GdkEvent *event,gpointer data);
 6 gint eventDestroy(GtkWidget *widget,
 7         GdkEvent *event,gpointer data);
 8
 9 #include "essPixmap.xpm"
10
11 int main(int argc,char *argv[])
12 {
13     GtkWidget *topLevel;
14     GdkBitmap *mask;
15     GdkPixmap *pixmap;
16     GtkWidget *pixmapWidget;
17     GtkStyle *style;
18
19     gnome_init("show_xpm_data","1.0",argc,argv);
20     topLevel = gtk_window_new(GTK_WINDOW_TOPLEVEL);
21     gtk_window_set_default_size(GTK_WINDOW(topLevel),
22             200,50);
23     gtk_widget_show(topLevel);
24
25     gtk_signal_connect(GTK_OBJECT(topLevel),"delete_event",
26             GTK_SIGNAL_FUNC(eventDelete),NULL);
27     gtk_signal_connect(GTK_OBJECT(topLevel),"destroy",
28             GTK_SIGNAL_FUNC(eventDestroy),NULL);
29
30     style = gtk_widget_get_style(topLevel);
31     pixmap = gdk_pixmap_create_from_xpm_d(topLevel->window,
32             &mask,&style->bg[GTK_STATE_NORMAL],
33             (gchar **)essPixmap);
34     pixmapWidget = gtk_pixmap_new(pixmap,mask);
35     gtk_container_add(GTK_CONTAINER(topLevel),
```

```
36              pixmapWidget);
37
38     gtk_widget_show_all(topLevel);
39     gtk_main();
40     exit(0);
41 }
42 gint eventDelete(GtkWidget *widget,
43         GdkEvent *event,gpointer data) {
44     return(FALSE);
45 }
46 gint eventDestroy(GtkWidget *widget,
47         GdkEvent *event,gpointer data) {
48     gtk_main_quit();
49     return(0);
50 }
```

The #include statement on line 9 causes the XPM data to be compiled directly into the program.

Line 30 retrieves the GtkStyle object from the window. All that is needed from the GtkStyle is a graphics context object (a GtkGC object) that can be used to render the pixels. There is more than one graphics context in a GtkStyle object, but for this example, the one that is used to draw the window in its normal state appears on line 32.

Note   The GtkStyle object is designed to contain all the information required to draw the window of a widget. Many widgets have multiple modes, and each mode can have its own style. For example, a GtkButton can show up as being pressed or released, or even grayed-out as disabled. A GtkStyle object is capable of containing all the colors, the graphic contexts, and even a set of pixmaps that can render the widget. Refer to Chapter 11 for examples of this.

Line 31 is a call to gdk_pixmap_create_from_xpm_d() that uses the XPM data compiled into the program to create a GdkPixmap. The function creates the pixmap according to the characteristics of a window, so topLevel->window inside the topLevel widget is referenced. The mask is a return value that contains one bit for each pixel that specifies which pixels are to be drawn and which are to be left transparent. The last argument, on line 33, is the XPM data.

A GtkWidget object can be added to a container and displayed so, on line 34, a call is made to gtk_pixmap_new() to create the widget. The function call requires the pixmap and its mask to create a pixmap widget. Lines 35 and 36 add the new widget to the top-level window. The resulting display is shown in Figure 7-1.

Figure 7-1: Displaying XPM data in the top-level window

Show XPM from File

You can load the XPM graphic from a file, instead of compiling it as part of the program, by making a slight change to the previous example. All that is needed is a different function to create the pixmap. Delete the `include` statement on line 9. Change line 31 to the new function name (the one that does not end with _d) and then change line 33, the last argument, to the name of the file instead of a reference to the data. The new function call looks like this:

```
31      pixmap = gdk_pixmap_create_from_xpm(topLevel->window,
32          &mask,&style->bg[GTK_STATE_NORMAL],
33          "essPixel.xmp");
```

You can use absolute or relative addressing for the file name. The display is identical to the one previously shown in Figure 7-1.The sxpm utility can be used to view graphics in an XPM file. It also can read old XPM files in versions 1 or 2, and convert them to the current version 3 format.

If the software complains about an invalid XPM file, it may be in an older format. The file must be in version 3 for you to use it. Make the conversion with a command like the following:

```
sxpm -nod infile -o outfile
```

Using XPM to Decorate a Button

A button contains a window just like any other, so it can display a picture as well as text. The following program uses an XPM file to paint the face of a button:

```
1 /** show_xpm_button.c **/
2 #include <gnome.h>
3
4 gint eventDelete(GtkWidget *widget,
5         GdkEvent *event,gpointer data);
6 gint eventDestroy(GtkWidget *widget,
7         GdkEvent *event,gpointer data);
8
9 int main(int argc,char *argv[])
10 {
11     GtkWidget *topLevel;
12     GdkBitmap *mask;
13     GdkPixmap *pixmap;
14     GtkStyle *style;
15     GtkWidget *button;
16     GtkWidget *pixmapWidget;
```

```
17
18      gnome_init("show_xpm_button","1.0",argc,argv);
19      topLevel = gtk_window_new(GTK_WINDOW_TOPLEVEL);
20      gtk_container_set_border_width(GTK_CONTAINER(topLevel),
21              10);
22      gtk_widget_show(topLevel);
23
24      gtk_signal_connect(GTK_OBJECT(topLevel),"delete_event",
25              GTK_SIGNAL_FUNC(eventDelete),NULL);
26      gtk_signal_connect(GTK_OBJECT(topLevel),"destroy",
27              GTK_SIGNAL_FUNC(eventDestroy),NULL);
28
29      style = gtk_widget_get_style(topLevel);
30      pixmap = gdk_pixmap_create_from_xpm(topLevel->window,
31              &mask,&style->bg[GTK_STATE_NORMAL],
32              "island.xpm");
33      pixmapWidget = gtk_pixmap_new(pixmap,mask);
34
35      button = gtk_button_new();
36      gtk_container_add(GTK_CONTAINER(button),pixmapWidget);
37      gtk_container_add(GTK_CONTAINER(topLevel),button);
38
39      gtk_widget_show_all(topLevel);
40      gtk_main();
41      exit(0);
42 }
43 gint eventDelete(GtkWidget *widget,
44         GdkEvent *event,gpointer data) {
45      return(FALSE);
46 }
47 gint eventDestroy(GtkWidget *widget,
48         GdkEvent *event,gpointer data) {
49      gtk_main_quit();
50      return(0);
51 }
```

Using the same method as in the previous examples, lines 29 through 33 construct a pixmap widget from the XPM file island.xpm. An empty button is created on line 35. The pixmap widget is inserted into the button on line 36 and the button is inserted into the top-level window on line 37. To display the window, the call is made to gtk_window_display_all() on line 39 and produces the window shown in Figure 7-2. You can see that there is a border around the picture — this is the edge of the button that changes its appearance whenever the mouse selects the button.

Figure 7-2: A button with a graphic instead of text

The XBM Format

If there are only two colors (usually black and white) it is more efficient to store a picture with a single pixel for each bit as is done in *XBM (XBitMap)* format. The XBM format is most often used to define mouse and keyboard cursors, but it also has other purposes. Like the XPM format, an XBM file is an ASCII file that can be compiled directly into a C program. The following is an example of a XBM file:

```
#define arrow_width 16
#define arrow_height 16
#define arrow_x_hot 15
#define arrow_y_hot 7
static unsigned char arrow_bits[] = {
    0x00, 0x00, 0x00, 0x00, 0xc0, 0x07, 0x80, 0x0f, 0x80,
    0x1f, 0xfc, 0x3f, 0xfc, 0x7f, 0xfc, 0xff, 0xfc, 0x7f,
    0xfc, 0x3f, 0x80, 0x1f, 0x80, 0x0f, 0xc0, 0x07, 0x00,
    0x00, 0x00, 0x00, 0x00};
```

The first two lines determine the height and width in pixels. The next two lines specify the coordinates of the hot spot. The *hot spot* is the exact *x* and *y* pixel location inside the bitmap that is considered to be the mouse location whenever the bitmap is used as a mouse cursor. The specification of the hot spot is optional, so the two lines can be omitted. Figure 7-3 shows the appearance of this bitmap. The hot spot is at the point of the arrow on the right.

 Figure 7-3: A bitmap defines graphics in black and white

In the file, the bit settings are written as byte values and each number specifies the on-or-off status of eight pixels. The pixels are mapped from left to right, and then from top to bottom. The pixel is in a single array, so the software that uses it must have the height and width information.

The bitmap Utility

There is a utility that you can use to create bitmap files, and to modify them once they are created. To create a new bitmap with the default size of 16x16, just enter the command name with no arguments. If you want to create a bitmap that is 24 pixels wide and 32 pixels high, enter the command this way:

```
bitmap -size 24x32
```

Once a bitmap is created and written to disk, it can be loaded again for editing by being named on the command line this way:

```
bitmap arrow.xbm
```

The window used to edit the arrow is shown in Figure 7-4. As you can see from the array of controlling buttons, you can edit the figure in a number of ways. The figure layout is displayed in the grid on the right, enabling you to use the left mouse button to set pixel values to 0 and the right mouse button to set them to 1. The diamond-shaped pixel on the right indicates the hot spot — there can be only one hot spot. To set the hot spot, select the "Set Hot Spot" button and then select a pixel.

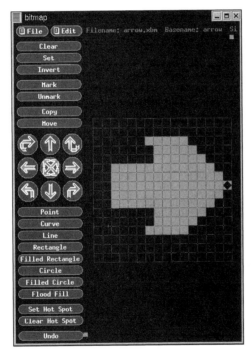

Figure 7-4: The bitmap editor with arrow.xbm loaded

Note   This program is part of the standard X distribution. It has buttons and menu labels that look very different from the ones in GNOME. The reason is that this program was developed using a completely different set of widgets and utilities. However, even with these differences, the underlying X standards and protocols allow programs based on completely different software to all execute simultaneously on the same display.

Show XBM Cursor

There are a number of standard cursors supplied by X. Whenever the mouse
pointer enters a window, the cursor automatically is changed to the cursor image
specified for that window. If you create a window and do not specify a cursor, the
cursor of the parent window is assumed. This means that you can set the cursor to
a top-level window and the cursor change will take effect on all of the windows and
widgets you include in it.

It is quite simple to do this with any window. The following code snippet shows
how to set the cursor for the top-level window:

```
    . . .
GdkCursor *cursor
    . . .
gtk_widget_show(topLevel);
cursor = gdk_cursor_new(GDK_FLEUR);
gdk_window_set_cursor(topLevel->window,cursor);
    . . .
```

The cursor named GDK_FLEUR is selected and is set for the top-level window. It
requires a call to the gtk_widget_show() function first because the window must
be realized before it can accept the cursor definition.

Besides the convenience, using a predefined cursor can help standardize the look
and feel of your application. There are a lot of predefined cursors and, unless you
are doing something out of the ordinary, you should be able to find what you are
looking for. To help you search through the various cursors, the following program
can be used to switch from one to the other:

```
 1 /** cursall.c **/
 2 #include <gnome.h>
 3
 4 void setCursor();
 5 GtkWidget *makeBox();
 6 gint eventDelete(GtkWidget *widget,
 7         GdkEvent *event,gpointer data);
 8 gint eventDestroy(GtkWidget *widget,
 9         GdkEvent *event,gpointer data);
10
11 GtkWidget *topLevel;
12 GtkWidget *nameLabel;
13 GdkCursor *cur = NULL;
14
15 gint cursorIndex = 0;
16 struct cursorStruct {
17     gchar *name;
18     GdkCursorType type;
```

```
19  } cursor[] = {
20      { "GDK_X_CURSOR", GDK_X_CURSOR },
21      { "GDK_ARROW", GDK_ARROW },
22      { "GDK_BASED_ARROW_DOWN", GDK_BASED_ARROW_DOWN },
23      { "GDK_BASED_ARROW_UP", GDK_BASED_ARROW_UP },
24      { "GDK_BOAT", GDK_BOAT },
25      { "GDK_BOGOSITY", GDK_BOGOSITY },
26      { "GDK_BOTTOM_LEFT_CORNER", GDK_BOTTOM_LEFT_CORNER },
27      { "GDK_BOTTOM_RIGHT_CORNER",GDK_BOTTOM_RIGHT_CORNER },
28      { "GDK_BOTTOM_SIDE", GDK_BOTTOM_SIDE },
29      { "GDK_BOTTOM_TEE", GDK_BOTTOM_TEE },
30      { "GDK_BOX_SPIRAL", GDK_BOX_SPIRAL },
31      { "GDK_CENTER_PTR", GDK_CENTER_PTR },
32      { "GDK_CIRCLE", GDK_CIRCLE },
33      { "GDK_CLOCK", GDK_CLOCK },
34      { "GDK_COFFEE_MUG", GDK_COFFEE_MUG },
35      { "GDK_CROSS", GDK_CROSS },
36      { "GDK_CROSS_REVERSE", GDK_CROSS_REVERSE },
37      { "GDK_CROSSHAIR", GDK_CROSSHAIR },
38      { "GDK_DIAMOND_CROSS", GDK_DIAMOND_CROSS },
39      { "GDK_DOT", GDK_DOT },
40      { "GDK_DOTBOX", GDK_DOTBOX },
41      { "GDK_DOUBLE_ARROW", GDK_DOUBLE_ARROW },
42      { "GDK_DRAFT_LARGE", GDK_DRAFT_LARGE },
43      { "GDK_DRAFT_SMALL", GDK_DRAFT_SMALL },
44      { "GDK_DRAPED_BOX", GDK_DRAPED_BOX },
45      { "GDK_EXCHANGE", GDK_EXCHANGE },
46      { "GDK_FLEUR", GDK_FLEUR },
47      { "GDK_GOBBLER", GDK_GOBBLER },
48      { "GDK_GUMBY", GDK_GUMBY },
49      { "GDK_HAND1", GDK_HAND1 },
50      { "GDK_HAND2", GDK_HAND2 },
51      { "GDK_HEART", GDK_HEART },
52      { "GDK_ICON", GDK_ICON },
53      { "GDK_IRON_CROSS", GDK_IRON_CROSS },
54      { "GDK_LEFT_PTR", GDK_LEFT_PTR },
55      { "GDK_LEFT_SIDE", GDK_LEFT_SIDE },
56      { "GDK_LEFT_TEE", GDK_LEFT_TEE },
57      { "GDK_LEFTBUTTON", GDK_LEFTBUTTON },
58      { "GDK_LL_ANGLE", GDK_LL_ANGLE },
59      { "GDK_LR_ANGLE", GDK_LR_ANGLE },
60      { "GDK_MAN", GDK_MAN },
61      { "GDK_MIDDLEBUTTON", GDK_MIDDLEBUTTON },
62      { "GDK_MOUSE", GDK_MOUSE },
63      { "GDK_PENCIL", GDK_PENCIL },
64      { "GDK_PIRATE", GDK_PIRATE },
65      { "GDK_PLUS", GDK_PLUS },
66      { "GDK_QUESTION_ARROW", GDK_QUESTION_ARROW },
67      { "GDK_RIGHT_PTR", GDK_RIGHT_PTR },
68      { "GDK_RIGHT_SIDE", GDK_RIGHT_SIDE },
69      { "GDK_RIGHT_TEE", GDK_RIGHT_TEE },
```

```
 70       { "GDK_RIGHTBUTTON", GDK_RIGHTBUTTON },
 71       { "GDK_RTL_LOGO", GDK_RTL_LOGO },
 72       { "GDK_SAILBOAT", GDK_SAILBOAT },
 73       { "GDK_SB_DOWN_ARROW", GDK_SB_DOWN_ARROW },
 74       { "GDK_SB_H_DOUBLE_ARROW", GDK_SB_H_DOUBLE_ARROW },
 75       { "GDK_SB_LEFT_ARROW", GDK_SB_LEFT_ARROW },
 76       { "GDK_SB_RIGHT_ARROW", GDK_SB_RIGHT_ARROW },
 77       { "GDK_SB_UP_ARROW", GDK_SB_UP_ARROW },
 78       { "GDK_SB_V_DOUBLE_ARROW", GDK_SB_V_DOUBLE_ARROW },
 79       { "GDK_SHUTTLE", GDK_SHUTTLE },
 80       { "GDK_SIZING", GDK_SIZING },
 81       { "GDK_SPIDER", GDK_SPIDER },
 82       { "GDK_SPRAYCAN", GDK_SPRAYCAN },
 83       { "GDK_STAR", GDK_STAR },
 84       { "GDK_TARGET", GDK_TARGET },
 85       { "GDK_TCROSS", GDK_TCROSS },
 86       { "GDK_TOP_LEFT_ARROW", GDK_TOP_LEFT_ARROW },
 87       { "GDK_TOP_LEFT_CORNER", GDK_TOP_LEFT_CORNER },
 88       { "GDK_TOP_RIGHT_CORNER", GDK_TOP_RIGHT_CORNER },
 89       { "GDK_TOP_SIDE", GDK_TOP_SIDE },
 90       { "GDK_TOP_TEE", GDK_TOP_TEE },
 91       { "GDK_TREK", GDK_TREK },
 92       { "GDK_UL_ANGLE", GDK_UL_ANGLE },
 93       { "GDK_UMBRELLA", GDK_UMBRELLA },
 94       { "GDK_UR_ANGLE", GDK_UR_ANGLE },
 95       { "GDK_WATCH", GDK_WATCH },
 96       { "GDK_XTERM", GDK_XTERM },
 97 };
 98
 99 int main(int argc,char *argv[])
100 {
101     GtkWidget *box;
102
103     gnome_init("cursall","1.0",argc,argv);
104     topLevel = gtk_window_new(GTK_WINDOW_TOPLEVEL);
105     gtk_container_set_border_width(GTK_CONTAINER(topLevel),
106           50);
107     gtk_window_set_default_size(GTK_WINDOW(topLevel),
108           400,0);
109
110     gtk_signal_connect(GTK_OBJECT(topLevel),"delete_event",
111           GTK_SIGNAL_FUNC(eventDelete),NULL);
112     gtk_signal_connect(GTK_OBJECT(topLevel),"destroy",
113           GTK_SIGNAL_FUNC(eventDestroy),NULL);
114
115     box = makeBox();
116     gtk_container_add(GTK_CONTAINER(topLevel),box);
117     gtk_widget_show_all(topLevel);
118
119     setCursor();
120
```

```
121     gtk_main();
122     exit(0);
123 }
124
125 void next(GtkWidget *widget,gpointer data )
126 {
127     int size = sizeof(cursor)/sizeof(struct cursorStruct);
128     if(++cursorIndex < size)
129         setCursor();
130     else
131         cursorIndex--;
132 }
133 void previous(GtkWidget *widget,gpointer data )
134 {
135     if(--cursorIndex >= 0)
136         setCursor();
137     else
138         cursorIndex++;
139 }
140 void setCursor()
141 {
142     if(cur != NULL)
143         gdk_cursor_destroy(cur);
144     cur = gdk_cursor_new(cursor[cursorIndex].type);
145     gdk_window_set_cursor(topLevel->window,cur);
146     gtk_label_set_text(GTK_LABEL(nameLabel),
147             cursor[cursorIndex].name);
148 }
149
150 GtkWidget *makeBox()
151 {
152     GtkWidget *buttonBox;
153     GtkWidget *box;
154     GtkWidget *button;
155
156     buttonBox = gtk_hbox_new(TRUE,10);
157
158     button = gtk_button_new_with_label("Previous");
159     gtk_box_pack_start(GTK_BOX(buttonBox),button,
160             FALSE,FALSE,0);
161     gtk_signal_connect(GTK_OBJECT(button),"clicked",
162             GTK_SIGNAL_FUNC(previous),NULL);
163
164     button = gtk_button_new_with_label("Next");
165     gtk_box_pack_start(GTK_BOX(buttonBox),button,
166             FALSE,FALSE,0);
167     gtk_signal_connect(GTK_OBJECT(button),"clicked",
168             GTK_SIGNAL_FUNC(next),NULL);
169
170     box = gtk_vbox_new(FALSE,0);
171
```

```
172        nameLabel = gtk_label_new("");
173        gtk_box_pack_start(GTK_BOX(box),nameLabel,
174            FALSE,FALSE,0);
175        gtk_box_pack_start(GTK_BOX(box),buttonBox,
176            FALSE,FALSE,0);
177
178        return(box);
179 }
180
181 gint eventDelete(GtkWidget *widget,
182        GdkEvent *event,gpointer data) {
183    return(FALSE);
184 }
185 gint eventDestroy(GtkWidget *widget,
186        GdkEvent *event,gpointer data) {
187    gtk_main_quit();
188    return(0);
189 }
```

This program displays the window shown in Figure 7-5. The window displays
the name of a cursor and the cursor itself. It has two buttons that can be used
to move back and forth through the list changing both the displayed name and
cursor. The name displayed is the one that can be used to create a cursor by
calling gdk_cursor_new().

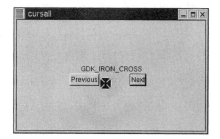

Figure 7-5: The name and appearance of
one of the built-in cursors

Lines 16 through 97 define an array of structs holding the names and numeric
values of the cursors. In the struct, the character string name is used to display
the name for use in your call to gdk_cursor_new(), and the type is the enum
value used to identify the cursor to the system.

Lines 117 through 119 create the window to be displayed, add it to the top-level
window, then call setCursor() to set the cursor to the current one in the table.
(The default index is 0.) Remember, the cursor cannot be modified for a window
until after gtk_widget_show() is called.

The function makeBox() beginning on line 150 uses boxes to construct the layout. A horizontal box is used to hold the two buttons, and a vertical box is used to hold the label and the horizontal box. Each button is assigned a callback function — the "Previous" button calls previous() and the "Next" button calls next().

The callback function next() beginning on line 125 increments the cursor index value by one — if it is not already at the end of the array. The count of the number of members in the array is calculated by dividing the size of the entire array by the size of one member. The callback function previous() reduces the index by one if the index is larger than zero. In both functions, if the index value is incremented, a call is made to setCursor() to change the current cursor.

The setCursor() function beginning on line 140 changes the current cursor to the one in the array addressed by the index. If a cursor is already created, it is destroyed before a new one is created. If your program uses several cursors, you can create them once and reuse them as needed. A call is made to gdk_cursor_new() to create a GdkCursor object. Using this new cursor in a call to gtk_label_set_cursor() makes the new cursor become the one used by the top-level window and its descendants. (The cursor is also changed for the buttons and the label.) Finally, the text of the label is updated by a call to gtk_label_set_text() so the name of the cursor is displayed.

Note The built-in cursors are all defined by the list of named values in the file gtk/gdk/gdkcursors.h, which is included by gtk/gdk/gtktypes.h where it is used as the body of an enum. The list of cursors is quite stable — most of them have been a part of X for several years. However, it is possible that some new entries will be made and, if so, you will need to update the list of names and values compiled into this program.

Create Cursor

It is a simple matter to create your own cursor. The bitmap utility can be used to create both the cursor and the mask to go with it. Then, these two bitmaps can be converted directly into the current cursor.

A cursor is normally black and white. It either has a black body with white trim surrounding it, or it has a white body with black trim. This way, the cursor can be placed on top of any color (including black or white) and still be visible. Also, cursors usually are kept small to be less intrusive. However, there is nothing that limits you to black and white cursors, and you can choose any two colors you like. The following example creates a large, x-shaped cursor that is red with black trim.

There are three ways that a pixel can be rendered in a cursor. It can be drawn in one of two colors, or it can be left transparent (not drawing a pixel lets the background pixel show through). This transparency option is the reason for the masking bitmap.

The two bitmaps are the same size. If the mask bit relating to the pixel is 0, then the pixel is not drawn — it is transparent. If the mask bit is 1, the pixel is drawn in one of two colors (depending on the value of the bit in the other bitmap).

The `bitmap` utility described earlier can be used to create a cursor. Both the cursor design and its mask are bitmaps. For this following example, the cursor design is the one shown in Figure 7-6 and its mask is shown in Figure 7-7. The cursor design is very much like the default root window cursor with the hot spot in its center.

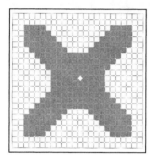

Figure 7-6: The black and white pixels of a cursor

Figure 7-7: The mask defining the outline of the cursor

The two bitmaps produced by the utility look like this:

```
/* xbitmap.xbm */
#define xbitmap_width 24
#define xbitmap_height 24
#define xbitmap_x_hot 12
#define xbitmap_y_hot 11
static unsigned char xbitmap_bits[] = {
    0x00, 0x00, 0x00, 0x00, 0x00, 0x00, 0x3c, 0x00,
    0x3c, 0x7c, 0x00, 0x3e, 0xfc, 0x00, 0x3f, 0xfc,
    0x81, 0x3f, 0xf8, 0xc3, 0x1f, 0xf0, 0xff, 0x0f,
    0xe0, 0xff, 0x07, 0xc0, 0xff, 0x03, 0x80, 0xff,
    0x01, 0x80, 0xff, 0x01, 0x80, 0xff, 0x01, 0x80,
```

```
    0xff, 0x01, 0xc0, 0xff, 0x03, 0xe0, 0xff, 0x07,
    0xf0, 0xff, 0x0f, 0xf8, 0xc3, 0x1f, 0xfc, 0x81,
    0x3f, 0xfc, 0x00, 0x3f, 0x7c, 0x00, 0x3e, 0x3c,
    0x00, 0x3c, 0x00, 0x00, 0x00, 0x00, 0x00, 0x00};

/* xmask.xbm */
#define xmask_width 24
#define xmask_height 24
static unsigned char xmask_bits[] = {
    0x00, 0x00, 0x00, 0x3e, 0x00, 0x7c, 0x7e, 0x00,
    0x7e, 0xfe, 0x00, 0x7f, 0xfe, 0x81, 0x7f, 0xfe,
    0xc3, 0x7f, 0xfc, 0xe7, 0x3f, 0xf8, 0xff, 0x1f,
    0xf0, 0xff, 0x0f, 0xe0, 0xff, 0x07, 0xc0, 0xff,
    0x03, 0x80, 0xff, 0x01, 0x80, 0xff, 0x01, 0xc0,
    0xff, 0x03, 0xe0, 0xff, 0x07, 0xf0, 0xff, 0x0f,
    0xf8, 0xff, 0x1f, 0xfc, 0xe7, 0x3f, 0xfe, 0xc3,
    0x7f, 0xfe, 0x81, 0x7f, 0xfe, 0x00, 0x7f, 0x7e,
    0x00, 0x7e, 0x3e, 0x00, 0x7c, 0x00, 0x00, 0x00};
```

The following example program uses these bitmaps to create a cursor and assign it as the cursor to appear any time the mouse is over the top-level window of the application:

```
 1 /** xbmcursor.c **/
 2 #include <gnome.h>
 3
 4 gint eventDelete(GtkWidget *widget,
 5         GdkEvent *event,gpointer data);
 6 gint eventDestroy(GtkWidget *widget,
 7         GdkEvent *event,gpointer data);
 8
 9 #include "xbitmap.xbm"
10 #include "xmask.xbm"
11
12 static GdkColor oneColor = {0,0xFFFF,0x0000,0x0000};
13 static GdkColor zeroColor = {0,0x0000,0x0000,0x0000};
14
15 int main(int argc,char *argv[])
16 {
17     GtkWidget *topLevel;
18     GdkCursor *cursor;
19     GdkBitmap *bitmap;
20     GdkBitmap *mask;
21
22     gnome_init("xbmcursor","1.0",argc,argv);
23     topLevel = gtk_window_new(GTK_WINDOW_TOPLEVEL);
24     gtk_window_set_default_size(GTK_WINDOW(topLevel),
25             150,150);
26
27     gtk_signal_connect(GTK_OBJECT(topLevel),"delete_event",
```

```
28                    GTK_SIGNAL_FUNC(eventDelete),NULL);
29         gtk_signal_connect(GTK_OBJECT(topLevel),"destroy",
30                    GTK_SIGNAL_FUNC(eventDestroy),NULL);
31
32         gtk_widget_show_all(topLevel);
33
34         bitmap = gdk_bitmap_create_from_data(NULL,xbitmap_bits,
35                    xbitmap_width,xbitmap_height);
36         mask = gdk_bitmap_create_from_data(NULL,xmask_bits,
37                    xmask_width,xmask_height);
38         cursor = gdk_cursor_new_from_pixmap(
39                    bitmap,mask,
40                    &oneColor,&zeroColor,
41                    xbitmap_x_hot,xbitmap_y_hot);
42         gdk_window_set_cursor(topLevel->window,cursor);
43
44         gtk_main();
45         exit(0);
46  }
47  gint eventDelete(GtkWidget *widget,
48         GdkEvent *event,gpointer data) {
49         return(FALSE);
50  }
51  gint eventDestroy(GtkWidget *widget,
52         GdkEvent *event,gpointer data) {
53         gtk_main_quit();
54         return(0);
55  }
```

To be used in the program, the two bitmaps must be converted to GtkBitmap
objects. You do this with calls to gdk_bitmap_create_from_data() on lines 34
through 37. The first argument to this function can be the GdkWindow object, but
it is not necessary in this case because the default is the root window. The other
three arguments are the values that define the layout of the bitmap.

The GdkCursor object is created by the call to gdk_cursor_new_from_pixmap()
on line 38. The first two arguments are the two GdkBitmap objects created from the
ram-resident bitmaps. The second and third arguments are the two colors to be
used in drawing the cursor. The colors in the example, defined on lines 12 and 13,
are red and black. The oneColor is defined as red and the zeroColor is black.
Where the mask is 1 and the bitmap is 0, the pixel is black. Where the mask is 1 and
the bitmap is 1, the color is red. The last two arguments are the *x* and *y* coordinates
of the hot spot.

The call to gdk_window_set_cursor() on line 42 makes the newly created cursor
the one that is displayed whenever the mouse pointer is in the window.

Create Cursor from XPM

A cursor also can be created from XPM data, but you must leave out the color information. The following example does this by choosing one of the XPM letters to represent the "black" color and another to represent the "white" color. Cursors usually are painted as black and white, but as this example shows, you can pick any two colors you like. All pixels that are neither black nor white are transparent.

The contents of the file `sancha.xpm` look like this:

```
/* XPM */
/** sancha.xpm **/
static char *sancha[] = {
"24 24 5 1",
"  c none",
"B c Black",
"W c White",
"r c Red",
"y c Yellow",
"rrWWWWWWW        WWWWWWWrr",
"rrWBBBBBW        WBBBBBWrr",
"rrWBBBBBW        WBBBBBWrr",
"rrWBBBBBW        WBBBBBWrr",
"rrWBBBBBW        WBBBBBWrr",
"rrWBBBBBBW      WBBBBBBWrr",
"rrrWBBBBBBW    WBBBBBBWrrr",
"rrrrWBBBBBBWWBBBBBBWrrrr",
"rrrrrWBBBBBBBBBBBBWrrrrr",
"rrrrrrWBBBBBBBBBBWrrrrrr",
"rrrrrrrWBBBBBBBBWrrrrrrr",
"rrrrrrrrWBBBBBBWrrrrrrrr",
"rrrrrrrrrWBBBBWrrrrrrrrr",
"yyyyyyyyyWBBWyyyyyyyyy",
"yyyyyyyyyWBBBBWyyyyyyyy",
"yyyyyyyyWBBBBBBWyyyyyyy",
"yyyyyyyWBBBBBBBBWyyyyyy",
"yyyyyyWBBBBBBBBBBWyyyyy",
"yyyyyWBBBBBBBBBBBBWyyyy",
"yyyyWBBBBBBBBBBBBBBWyyy",
"yyyWBBBBBBBBBBBBBBBBWyy",
"WWWBBBBBBBBBBBBBBBBBWWW",
"WBBBBBBBBBBBBBBBBBBBBBW",
"WBBBBBBBBBBBBBBBBBBBBBW",
"WWWWWWWWWWWWWWWWWWWWWW",
};
```

This XPM definition contains five colors. It is made up of a central black area outlined in white; the background on each side is red and yellow. There is a transparent area at the top. It is shown in Figure 7-8.

 **Figure 7-8:** The XPM figure to be converted to a cursor

In the following example, two of the XMP colors (B and W) are selected to represent the visible pixel locations. The other colors (r, y, and blank) all become transparent. The window with its cursor is shown in Figure 7-9.

Figure 7-9: A cursor constructed from XPM graphics data

```
1 /** xpmcursor.c **/
2 #include <gnome.h>
3
4 gint eventDelete(GtkWidget *widget,
5         GdkEvent *event,gpointer data);
6 gint eventDestroy(GtkWidget *widget,
7         GdkEvent *event,gpointer data);
8 GdkCursor *newCursorFromXPM(gchar *xpm[],
9         gchar blackLetter,GdkColor *blackColor,
10         gchar whiteLetter,GdkColor *whiteColor,
11         gint xHot,gint yHot);
12
13 #include "sancha.xpm"
14
15 GdkColor green = {0,0x0000,0xFFFF,0x0000};
16 GdkColor black = {0,0x0000,0x0000,0x0000};
17
18 int main(int argc,char *argv[])
19 {
20     GtkWidget *topLevel;
21     GdkCursor *cursor;
22
23     gnome_init("xpmcursor","1.0",argc,argv);
24     topLevel = gtk_window_new(GTK_WINDOW_TOPLEVEL);
25     gtk_window_set_default_size(GTK_WINDOW(topLevel),
26             150,150);
27
28     gtk_signal_connect(GTK_OBJECT(topLevel),"delete_event",
29             GTK_SIGNAL_FUNC(eventDelete),NULL);
30     gtk_signal_connect(GTK_OBJECT(topLevel),"destroy",
31             GTK_SIGNAL_FUNC(eventDestroy),NULL);
32
33     gtk_widget_show_all(topLevel);
```

```
34
35      cursor = newCursorFromXPM(sancha,
36            'B',&black,'W',&green,
37            12,13);
38      gdk_window_set_cursor(topLevel->window,cursor);
39
40      gtk_main();
41      exit(0);
42  }
43  GdkCursor *newCursorFromXPM(gchar *xpm[],
44          gchar blackLetter,GdkColor *blackColor,
45          gchar whiteLetter,GdkColor *whiteColor,
46          gint xHot,gint yHot)
47  {
48      gint height;
49      gint width;
50      gint colors;
51      gint pchars;
52      gint x;
53      gint y;
54      GdkBitmap *bitmap;
55      GdkBitmap *mask;
56      GdkCursor *cursor;
57
58      guchar *bitmapData;
59      guchar *maskData;
60      gint byteIndex = 0;
61      gint bitCount = 0;
62
63      sscanf(xpm[0],"%d %d %d %d",
64            &height,&width,&colors,&pchars);
65      g_assert(pchars == 1);
66
67      bitmapData = (guchar *)g_malloc((width * height) / 8);
68      maskData = (guchar *)g_malloc((width * height) / 8);
69
70      for(y=(colors+4); y < (height+4); y++) {
71          for(x=0; x<width; x++) {
72              if(xpm[y][x] == whiteLetter) {
73                  maskData[byteIndex] |= 0x80;
74                  bitmapData[byteIndex] |= 0x80;
75              } else if(xpm[y][x] == blackLetter) {
76                  maskData[byteIndex] |= 0x80;
77              }
78              if(++bitCount == 8) {
79                  byteIndex++;
80                  bitCount = 0;
81              } else {
82                  maskData[byteIndex] >= 1;
83                  bitmapData[byteIndex] >= 1;
84              }
85          }
```

```
 86        }
 87        bitmap = gdk_bitmap_create_from_data(NULL,bitmapData,
 88              width,height);
 89        mask = gdk_bitmap_create_from_data(NULL,maskData,
 90              width,height);
 91        cursor = gdk_cursor_new_from_pixmap(bitmap,mask,
 92              whiteColor,blackColor,
 93              xHot,yHot);
 94        g_free(bitmapData);
 95        g_free(maskData);
 96        return(cursor);
 97 }
 98 gint eventDelete(GtkWidget *widget,
 99        GdkEvent *event,gpointer data) {
100        return(FALSE);
101 }
102 gint eventDestroy(GtkWidget *widget,
103        GdkEvent *event,gpointer data) {
104        gtk_main_quit();
105        return(0);
106 }
```

The XPM data is included on line 13. The two colors that are to be used for the cursor are defined on lines 15 and 16. For this example, the cursor is green outlined in black. The cursor object is created by a function call on line 35. The first argument to the function is the XPM data. The next two arguments specify the letter and actual color that are to become the "black" color. And the next two arguments specify the letter and the actual color that is to become the "white" color. The last two arguments are the *x* and *y* coordinates of the cursor hot spot.

The conversion from XPM to GtkCursor is made by the function newCursorFromXPM() starting on line 43. The first character string in the XPM array contains a set of numbers describing the data that follows, and is read on line 63. Line 65 makes certain that each color is represented by a single color because this function cannot handle more than one letter per color. Locations to hold the bitmaps are allocated on lines 67 and 68. The function g_malloc() makes a call to calloc() to actually allocate memory, so the returned data is initialized to zero.

The loop starting on line 70 uses the value of *y* as the index for each of the strings in the input array. The inner loop, starting on line 71, iterates once for each character in the string. On line 72, if the pixel is to be painted by the "white" color, the high-order bit of both the bitmap and the mask are set. On line 75, if the pixel is to be painted by the "black" color, the high-order bit of the mask is set. Lines 78 through 84 use a bit counter to determine whether or not the current byte is already full. If the byte is full, the index is incremented to the next byte—if not, the bits within the byte are shifted over to make room for the next bit.

The bitmaps are created on lines 87 and 89. The bitmaps are used to create the cursor on line 91. Lines 94 through 96 release the allocated memory and return the GdkCursor to the caller.

Note The name of the function that creates the cursor from a pair of bitmaps is named as if it were using a pixmap instead of a bitmap. While these two are distinctly different formats, the same software can be used to operate on both of them and there is an occasional bit of carelessness about the names of things.

Summary

There is a lot more to graphics, but this chapter presented enough of an introduction so you can create picture buttons for toolbars and change the cursor appearance to reflect the state of your application. This chapter explained the following:

✦ The two basic types of graphics of a GNOME application are the bitmap and the pixmap. A bitmap contains no color information — it just specifies either 1 or 0 for each pixel. A pixmap can be any number of colors.

✦ Both the pixmap (known as the XPM format) and the bitmap (known as the XBM format) can be compiled directly into your program or dynamically loaded at runtime.

✦ Many widgets have the capability of displaying pixmaps instead of solid colors for their background.

✦ You need two bitmaps to define a cursor because, while a bitmap has two colors, a cursor requires a third to represent the transparent pixels.

✦ There is a large selection of built-in cursors that you can use to standardize the appearance of your application.

The pixmaps introduced in this chapter will be used to decorate the menus and toolbars introduced in the next chapter. One of the basic tenets of a graphical user interface is to have graphics that enable the user to instantly recognize the purpose of a button, a menu selection, or toolbar selection.

✦　　✦　　✦

Menus and Toolbars

◆ ◆ ◆ ◆

In This Chapter

Using the GNOME mechanism to quickly construct menus and toolbars

Using the recommended standard menu layout to help standardize GNOME applications

Using push buttons, toggle buttons, radio buttons, sub-menus and -toolbars, icons, text, and popup dialog boxes

◆ ◆ ◆ ◆

A *menu* is a hierarchical grouping of buttons that can be used to issue commands to the program. So is a toolbar (well, almost). One difference between the two is that a menu uses text as a button label and a toolbar uses a graphic for the label. Also, a menu keeps some of its parts hidden, while a toolbar generally keeps everything visible. They both can be oriented horizontally or vertically. Because toolbars and menus are basically the same, GNOME has chosen to use the same technique for defining both of them. There are some differences here and there, but in many cases, if you code the definition used to create a menu, you also can use it to create a toolbar.

This area of programming traditionally has been one of the less elegant areas in the development of X applications. While the menu system has worked quite well from the early days of X, there is no way it could be called intuitive on the part of the programmer. GNOME simplifies this process by providing the programmer with a way to define everything in arrays that are organized in the same way as the menu produced on the display.

The Mechanics of a Menu Creation

A menu is made up of a row or column of buttons. We are accustomed to seeing a menu bar appear as a horizontal row of buttons across the top of a window. Selecting one of these buttons causes a vertical column of buttons to appear. Each button in a menu either causes another column of menu buttons to pop up or invokes a callback function inside the program. There are a few other things that can be done with menu buttons (such as creating toggle buttons and a group of radio buttons), but the two basic actions of using a button for selection provides the basis of all menu operations.

A menu has a hierarchical form — submenus within submenus within a main menu. GNOME provides a struct named GnomeUIInfo that you can use to create menu items. A member of an array of GnomeUIInfo structs defines a button, or other item, on the menu. The items are connected in a sequence that matches the order of their appearance in the array. If a menu has a submenu, it contains the address of the array that contains the definition of the submenu's items.

The following program produces a window with a menu as shown in Figure 8-1. It is a normal hierarchical menu positioned at the top of the window and, as shown in the figure, is capable of displaying submenus, sub-submenus, and so on. The menu created by this example is a *tear-off menu* (the default). The button at the left end of the menu can be dragged, using the left mouse button, to any location on the desktop as shown in Figure 8-2. Use the button to freely move the menu around the display. To return the menu to the window, simply drag it back to either the top or bottom of the window where it docks itself. When you close an application, GNOME keeps track of the location of the menu for each login, so the next time the application starts, the menu is wherever you put it.

Figure 8-1: A simple menu constructed from tables

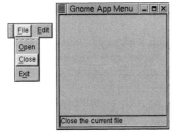

Figure 8-2: A simple menu torn off of its parent

The GnomeApp status bar displayed at the bottom of the window is optional. The text that appears in the status bar is defined in the array of GnomeUIInfo structs and is displayed whenever the mouse moves over the top of one of the buttons. The status bar can be used by an application to continuously display the current status of a program — it uses a push/pop architecture so it can be used simultaneously by different elements of your program.

```
 1 /** gnomeappmenu.c **/
 2 #include <gnome.h>
 3
 4 static void fileOpen(GtkObject *,gpointer);
 5 static void fileClose(GtkObject *,gpointer);
 6 static void fileExit(GtkObject *,gpointer);
 7 static void editCut(GtkObject *,gpointer);
 8 static void editPaste(GtkObject *,gpointer);
 9 static void editCopy(GtkObject *,gpointer);
10 static void editDelete(GtkObject *,gpointer);
11 static void editMoveUp(GtkObject *,gpointer);
12 static void editMoveDown(GtkObject *,gpointer);
13
14 gint eventDelete(GtkWidget *widget,
15         GdkEvent *event,gpointer data);
16 gint eventDestroy(GtkWidget *widget,
17         GdkEvent *event,gpointer data);
18
19 GnomeUIInfo fileMenu[] = {
20     { GNOME_APP_UI_ITEM,"_Open",
21       "Open an existing file",
22       fileOpen,NULL,NULL,
23       GNOME_APP_PIXMAP_NONE,
24       NULL,0,0,NULL },
25     { GNOME_APP_UI_ITEM,"_Close",
26       "Close the current file",
27       fileClose,NULL,NULL,
28       GNOME_APP_PIXMAP_NONE,
29       NULL,0,0,NULL },
30     GNOMEUIINFO_SEPARATOR,
31     { GNOME_APP_UI_ITEM,"E_xit",
32       "Close the window and cease",
33       fileExit,NULL,NULL,
34       GNOME_APP_PIXMAP_NONE,
35       NULL,0,0,NULL },
36
37     GNOMEUIINFO_END
38 };
39
40 GnomeUIInfo editMoveMenu[] = {
41     { GNOME_APP_UI_ITEM,"_Up",
42       "Move selection up",
43       editMoveUp,NULL,NULL,
44       GNOME_APP_PIXMAP_NONE,
45       NULL,0,0,NULL },
46     { GNOME_APP_UI_ITEM,"D_own",
47       "Move selection down",
48       editMoveDown,NULL,NULL,
49       GNOME_APP_PIXMAP_NONE,
50       NULL,0,0,NULL },
51     GNOMEUIINFO_END
```

```
52  };
53
54  GnomeUIInfo editMenu[] = {
55      { GNOME_APP_UI_ITEM,"_Cut",
56        "Delete and copy selection to clipboard",
57        editCut,NULL,NULL,
58        GNOME_APP_PIXMAP_NONE,
59        NULL,0,0,NULL },
60      { GNOME_APP_UI_ITEM,"Cop_y",
61        "Copy selection to clipboard",
62        editCopy,NULL,NULL,
63        GNOME_APP_PIXMAP_NONE,
64        NULL,0,0,NULL },
65      { GNOME_APP_UI_ITEM,"_Paste",
66        "Paste selection from clipboard",
67        editPaste,NULL,NULL,
68        GNOME_APP_PIXMAP_NONE,
69        NULL,0,0,NULL },
70      GNOMEUIINFO_SUBTREE("_Move",editMoveMenu),
71      { GNOME_APP_UI_ITEM,"_Delete",
72        "Delete the current selection",
73        editDelete,NULL,NULL,
74        GNOME_APP_PIXMAP_NONE,
75        NULL,0,0,NULL },
76      GNOMEUIINFO_END
77  };
78
79  GnomeUIInfo mainMenu[] = {
80      GNOMEUIINFO_SUBTREE("_File",fileMenu),
81      GNOMEUIINFO_SUBTREE("_Edit",editMenu),
82      GNOMEUIINFO_END
83  };
84
85  int main(int argc,char *argv[])
86  {
87      GtkWidget *app;
88      GtkWidget *statusbar;
89
90      gnome_init("gnomeappmenu","1.0",argc,argv);
91      app = gnome_app_new("appmenu","Gnome App Menu");
92      gtk_window_set_default_size(GTK_WINDOW(app),200,200);
93      gtk_signal_connect(GTK_OBJECT(app),"delete_event",
94              GTK_SIGNAL_FUNC(eventDelete),NULL);
95      gtk_signal_connect(GTK_OBJECT(app),"destroy",
96              GTK_SIGNAL_FUNC(eventDestroy),NULL);
97
98      gnome_app_create_menus(GNOME_APP(app),mainMenu);
99
100     statusbar = gtk_statusbar_new();
101     gnome_app_install_statusbar_menu_hints(
102             GTK_STATUSBAR(statusbar),mainMenu);
103     gnome_app_set_statusbar(GNOME_APP(app),statusbar);
```

```
104
105      gtk_widget_show_all(app);
106
107      gtk_main();
108      exit(0);
109 }
110 static void fileOpen(GtkObject *object,gpointer data) {
111      gnome_ok_dialog("\"File/Open\" selected.");
112 }
113 static void fileClose(GtkObject *object,gpointer data) {
114      gnome_ok_dialog("\"File/Close\" selected.");
115 }
116 static void fileExit(GtkObject *object,gpointer data) {
117      gtk_main_quit();
118 }
119 static void editCut(GtkObject *object,gpointer data) {
120      gnome_ok_dialog("\"Edit/Cut\" selected.");
121 }
122 static void editCopy(GtkObject *object,gpointer data) {
123      gnome_ok_dialog("\"Edit/Copy\" selected.");
124 }
125 static void editPaste(GtkObject *object,gpointer data) {
126      gnome_ok_dialog("\"Edit/Paste\" selected.");
127 }
128 static void editDelete(GtkObject *object,gpointer data) {
129      gnome_ok_dialog("\"Edit/Delete\" selected.");
130 }
131 static void editMoveUp(GtkObject *object,gpointer data) {
132      gnome_ok_dialog("\"Edit/Move/Up\" selected.");
133 }
134 static void editMoveDown(GtkObject *object,gpointer data) {
135      gnome_ok_dialog("\"Edit/Move/Down\" selected.");
136 }
137 gint eventDelete(GtkWidget *widget,
138          GdkEvent *event,gpointer data) {
139      return(FALSE);
140 }
141 gint eventDestroy(GtkWidget *widget,
142          GdkEvent *event,gpointer data) {
143      gtk_main_quit();
144      return(0);
145 }
```

The main menu definitions begin on line 79 with an array of three GnomeUIInfo structs. There is a type field at the beginning of the struct that is used to define the struct contents. The data for each member of the array can be specified field by field or in a macro, as in this example. Table 8-1, in the next section, describes all of the fields in the struct. The first and second entries found in the array each refer to a submenu. (The submenus must come before their parent menus in the source code so the references are resolved — the C language has no look-ahead.)

The macro GNOMEUIINFO_SUBTREE used on lines 80 and 81 supply all the values for the struct except for the name displayed on the menu and the address of the submenu that the button pops up. Using the macro is the same as the following:

```
    . . .
{   GNOME_APP_UI_SUBTREE,"_File",
    NULL,
    fileMenu,NULL,NULL,
    GNOME_APP_PIXMAP_NONE,
    NULL,0,0,NULL },
    . . .
```

The third entry in the array, on line 82, is a GNOMEUIINFO_END macro that is required as an array terminator by the software that constructs the menu.

The items in the column of the File menu are defined in the array beginning on line 19. There are five members of the array. The first member of the array is a GNOME_APP_UI_ITEM type defining an Open button that, when selected, causes the function fileOpen() to be called. The second member of the array is a Close button configured to call fileClose(). The third member is the separator that was shown in Figure 8-2. The last two members are the Exit button that calls fileExit() and the GNOMEUIINFO_END required terminator.

The Edit menu defined in the array beginning on line 54 contains buttons that execute callback functions, and one button that invokes a submenu. The submenu is defined exactly the same way it is in the main menu. This submenuing can continue for as many levels as you like. Figure 8-1 showed the appearance of the window with the submenu selected.

The prototypes for the callback functions are defined on lines 4 through 12, and the functions themselves are defined on lines 103 through 130. Just like the signal callback functions discussed in previous chapters, there are two default arguments passed to the callback functions. The first one is the GtkObject that causes the function to be called and the second is a data pointer that is specified as part of the GnomeUIInfo struct.

These menus require a GNOME application window. The function call on line 90 to gnome_app_new() creates a window that is an extension of the GTK top-level window. These extensions are for items such as the menu system and the status bar, as well as some other things that I will discuss later. The menus are created with the call to gnome_app_create_menus() on line 97. This one function call creates the entire menu tree and attaches it to the application window.

The names of the menu items have accclerator keys defined for them by preceding the key letter with an underscore character. Then these letters can be used with the meta or alt key to go directly to a menu item. For example, line 41 defines the name of a menu button as "_Up", causing the Meta-U (or Alt-U, depending on the system) to be its accelerator key. Using the accelerator key causes the immediate selection of the menu item just as if you had used the mouse to find and select it.

Accelerator keys must be unique. Whenever an accelerator key is pressed, the menu tree searches for a match; if one is found, that is the menu item that is selected. If there are two or more menu items using the same letter for acceleration, the menu tree concludes the search with the first one it finds and completely ignores any others.

Menu Types and Macros

As you can see from the previous example, GNOME provides a fill-in-the-blanks approach to creating menus. The same technique, and the same structures, can be used to create toolbars. (I cover toolbars in Chapter 9.) All you need to know is what blanks need to be filled, what values can be used to fill them, and what function you need to call to cause the menu or toolbar to be constructed and activated.

A menu is made up of a set of `GnomeUIInfo` arrays. Each member of each array is a standalone item — there is no relationship with its neighboring members other than the coincidence of position. The values stored in the fields determine the item's type and how it is configured. Table 8-1 lists the fields and describes the values that can be stored in each one. As you can see, some fields serve multiple purposes — the contents can change depending on the type of item being defined.

Table 8-1
The Fields of GnomeUIInfo

#	Data Type	Valid For	Description
1	`GnomeUIInfoType` `type`	all	This determines the type of item being defined. (You can find a list of the type names in Table 8-2.)
2	`gchar *label`	all	The character string to use for the label.
3	`gchar *hint`	menu	The character string to appear as the status bar message.
3		toolbar	The tooltip to pop up as the mouse passes over the button.
4	`gpointer` `moreinfo`	item toggle item radio item	A pointer to the callback function to be called when the item is activated.

Continued

Table 8-1 *(continued)*

#	Data Type	Valid For	Description
4		radio item lead	A pointer to an array of `GnomeUIInfo` structs to be used as members of the radio item group.
4		subtree	A pointer to a subtree, which is another array of `GnomeUIInfo` structs.
4		help item	Specifies the name of the help node to be loaded. If it is `NULL`, the application's identifier is assumed.
4		builder data	Address of the `GnomeUIBuilderData` struct.
5	`gpointer user_data`	all	The user-supplied pointer to be passed to callback functions as the second argument.
6	`gpointer unused_data`	-	Reserved.
7	`GnomeUIPixmapType pixmap_type`	all	The type of pixmap. It is `GNOME_APP_PIXMAP_NONE`, `GNOME_APP_PIXMAP_STOCK`, `GNOME_APP_PIXMAP_DATA`, or `GNOME_APP_PIXMAP_FILENAME`.
8	`gpointer pixmap_info`	all	A pointer to the pixmap information. If field 7 defines the pointer as `DATA`, it is the address of XPM data inside the program. If it is `FILENAME`, it is a pointer to the character string form of the file name. If `STOCK`, it is a pointer to name of the stock icon.
9	`guint accelerator_key`		The accelerator key. Zero implies no accelerator key.
10	`GtkModifierType ac_mods`		Mask of modifier keys for the accelerator.
11	`GtkWidget *widget`	all	The creation function stores the widget here so your program can get to it to modify its appearance and actions.

Each `GnomeUIInfo` struct is defined as being a specific type. Table 8-2 lists the possible values for the type field.

Table 8-2	
The Types of GnomeUIInfo Entries	
Type	**Description**
GNOME_APP_UI_ENDOFINFO	A special entry that is used at the end of each array as a terminator.
GNOME_APP_UI_ITEM	A normal menu item — or a radio item, if it is inside a radio item group.
GNOME_APP_UI_TOGGLEITEM	A check box.
GNOME_APP_UI_RADIOITEMS	A group of radio buttons.
GNOME_APP_UI_SUBTREE	A subtree. Includes a pointer to another array of `GnomeUIInfo` structs.
GNOME_APP_UI_SEPARATOR	For a menu, this is a separator line. For a toolbar, it is a blank space.
GNOME_APP_UI_HELP	The list of help topics for the help menu.
GNOME_APP_UI_BUILDER_DATA	At the time the menu is created, the creation function reads information from this array member to configure the ones that follow.
GNOME_APP_UI_ITEM_CONFIGURABLE	A menu item that can be configured. This type completely ignores any value settings made previously by a GNOME_APP_UI_BUILDER_DATA entry.
GNOME_APP_UI_SUBTREE_STOCK	The same as GNOME_APP_UI_SUBTREE, except the label and hint strings are to be looked up in the `gnome-libs` catalog.

Table 8-3 lists the macros defined in `gnome-app-helper.h` that can be used to create menus. There is nothing particularly magic about these macros — they simply expand into a set of values formatted properly to initialize a `GnomeUIInfo` struct — but using them can make your program easier to write and easier to read. With the number of fields in the struct, there are thousands of possible macros; if your application needs something that isn't here, you can certainly write one.

Table 8-3
The Macros Used to Construct Menus and Toolbars

Macro Name	Description
GNOMEUIINFO_END	The type is GNOME_APP_UI_ENDOFINFO. Terminates the array of GnomeUIInfo structs. It must be present in every array.
GNOMEUIINFO_HELP (app_name)	The type is GNOME_APP_UI_HELP. This inserts the help topics indicated by the application's name.
GNOMEUIINFO_ITEM (label, tooltip, callback, xpm_data)	The type is GNOME_APP_UI_ITEM. The item is drawn using xpm_data as the icon. The label, tooltip, and callback functions must be specified.
GNOMEUIINFO_ITEM_DATA (label, tooltip, callback, user_data, xpm_data)	The type is GNOME_APP_UI_ITEM. The item is drawn using xpm_data as the icon. The label, tooltip, callback, and user_data functions must be specified.
GNOMEUIINFO_ITEM_STOCK (label, tooltip, callback)	The type is GNOME_APP_UI_ITEM. The item is drawnwithout an icon. The label, tooltip, and callback functions must be specified.
GNOMEUIINFO_ITEM_STOCK (label, tooltip, callback, stock_id)	The type is GNOME_APP_UI_ITEM. The item is drawn using a stock icon specified by stock_id. The label, tooltip, and callback functions must be specified.
GNOMEUIINFO_RADIOITEM (label, tooltip, callback, xpm_data)	The type is GNOME_APP_UI_ITEM. Inserts a radio item that uses xpm_data as its icon. The label, tooltip, and callback functions must be specified.
GNOMEUIINFO_RADIOITEM_DATA (label, tooltip, callback, user_data, xpm_data)	The type is GNOME_APP_UI_ITEM. Inserts a radio item that uses xpm_data as its icon. The label, tooltip, callback, and user data functions must be specified.
GNOMEUIINFO_SEPARATOR	The type is GNOME_APP_UI_SEPARATOR. For a menu, this inserts a blank line. For a toolbar, it inserts a blank space.
GNOMEUIINFO_SUBTREE (label, tree)	The type is GNOME_APP_UI_SUBTREE. The tree is the address of the first member of an array of GnomeUIInfo structs. The label function must be specified.

Macro Name	Description
GNOMEUIINFO_SUBTREE_HINT (label, tooltip, tree)	The type is GNOME_APP_UI_SUBTREE. The tree is the address of the first member of an array of GnomeUIInfo structs. The label and the tooltip functions must be specified.
GNOMEUIINFO_SUBTREE_STOCK (label, tree, stock_id)	The type is GNOME_APP_UI_SUBTREE. The tree the address of the first member of an array of is GnomeUIInfo structs. The label is for the item and the hint is the text used on the status bar. The stock_id is the stock icon used to draw the item.
GNOMEUIINFO_TOGGLEITEM (label, tooltip, callback, xpm_data)	The type is GNOME_APP_UI_TOGGLEITEM. This is a check box drawn with xpm_data as the icon. The label, tooltip, and callback functions must be specified.
GNOMEUIINFO_TOGGLEITEM_DATA (label, tooltip, callback, user_data, xpm_data)	The type is GNOME_APP_UI_TOGGLEITEM. This is a check box drawn with xpm_data as the icon. The label, tooltip, user_data, and callback functions must be specified.

The Standard GNOME Menu Layout

Using a standard menu organization has some advantages. Because the layout is familiar, users that are new to your application can find what they need quickly — and experienced users don't have to recall multiple menu layouts. Much of the standard layout has evolved over time. We all have come to expect to find the File menu on the left, and the Edit menu next to it. Also, we expect Save and Exit to be in the File menu. Additionally, we expect to find the Help menu on the right, and an About popup window in the Help menu.

It would be a very rare application that needed all of the standard menu selections, just as it would be rare to have an application that would not need to add menu selections of its own. However, starting with the standard layout should simplify the task of overall menu organization.

The following program is the mainline of a program that does nothing more than define a set of menus that has selections in the standard locations.

```
1 /** stdmain.c **/
2 #include <gnome.h>
3
4 GtkWidget *createMenus(GtkWidget *app);
5
```

```
 6 gint eventDelete(GtkWidget *widget,
 7         GdkEvent *event,gpointer data);
 8 gint eventDestroy(GtkWidget *widget,
 9         GdkEvent *event,gpointer data);
10
11 int main(int argc,char *argv[])
12 {
13     GtkWidget *app;
14     GtkWidget *statusbar;
15
16     gnome_init("stdmain","1.0",argc,argv);
17     app = gnome_app_new("stdmain",
18             "Gnome Menu Layout");
19     gtk_window_set_default_size(GTK_WINDOW(app),200,300);
20     gtk_signal_connect(GTK_OBJECT(app),"delete_event",
21             GTK_SIGNAL_FUNC(eventDelete),NULL);
22     gtk_signal_connect(GTK_OBJECT(app),"destroy",
23             GTK_SIGNAL_FUNC(eventDestroy),NULL);
24
25     statusbar = createMenus(app);
26
27     gtk_widget_show_all(app);
28
29     gtk_main();
30     exit(0);
31 }
32 gint eventDelete(GtkWidget *widget,
33         GdkEvent *event,gpointer data) {
34     return(FALSE);
35 }
36 gint eventDestroy(GtkWidget *widget,
37         GdkEvent *event,gpointer data) {
38     gtk_main_quit();
39     return(0);
40 }
```

The call to `createMenus()` on line 25 creates all of the menus and installs a status
bar at the bottom of the window. The status bar displays the *hint* (or tooltip) *text*
whenever the mouse is inside a menu item. The status bar widget is returned, so it
is available if other parts of the application wish to use it.

The following defines the menu layout, and provides a function that can be used
to create the menu and attach it to a `GnomeApp` window. Some special macros were
devised to create these menu items, so they not only are located in the same position
as other applications, but also have the same icons decorating them.

```
1 /** stdmenu.c **/
2 #include <gnome.h>
3
4 const gchar data[] = "Dummy callback data";
```

```
 5
 6 static void helpAbout(GtkWidget *widget,gpointer data)
 7 {
 8     GtkWidget *aboutBox;
 9
10     const gchar *writtenBy[] = {
11         "Arthur Griffith",
12         "Lance Peterson",
13         NULL
14     };
15     aboutBox = gnome_about_new("Gnome Menu Layout",
16             "0.0",
17             "(C) 1999 the Free Software Foundation",
18             writtenBy,
19             "This source code can be used as a starting "
20             "point to create a Gnome application.",
21             NULL);
22     gtk_widget_show(aboutBox);
23 }
24 static void dummyCallback(GtkObject *object,
25         gpointer data) {
26     gnome_ok_dialog("Not implemented...");
27 }
28
29 GnomeUIInfo dummyMenu[] = {
30     { GNOME_APP_UI_ITEM,"Dummy",
31       "A placeholder menu entry",
32       dummyCallback,NULL,NULL,
33       GNOME_APP_PIXMAP_NONE,
34       NULL,0,0,NULL },
35     GNOMEUIINFO_END
36 };
37
38 GnomeUIInfo fileMenu[] = {
39     GNOMEUIINFO_MENU_NEW_ITEM("New Window",
40         "Open a new application window",
41         dummyCallback,data),
42     GNOMEUIINFO_MENU_NEW_SUBTREE(dummyMenu),
43     GNOMEUIINFO_SEPARATOR,
44     GNOMEUIINFO_MENU_OPEN_ITEM(dummyCallback,data),
45     GNOMEUIINFO_MENU_SAVE_ITEM(dummyCallback,data),
46     GNOMEUIINFO_MENU_SAVE_AS_ITEM(dummyCallback,data),
47     GNOMEUIINFO_MENU_REVERT_ITEM(dummyCallback,data),
48     GNOMEUIINFO_MENU_PRINT_ITEM(dummyCallback,data),
49     GNOMEUIINFO_MENU_PRINT_SETUP_ITEM(dummyCallback,data),
50     GNOMEUIINFO_SEPARATOR,
51     GNOMEUIINFO_MENU_CLOSE_ITEM(dummyCallback,data),
52     GNOMEUIINFO_MENU_EXIT_ITEM(dummyCallback,data),
53     GNOMEUIINFO_END
54 };
55
```

```
56 GnomeUIInfo editMenu[] = {
57     GNOMEUIINFO_MENU_UNDO_ITEM(dummyCallback,data),
58     GNOMEUIINFO_MENU_REDO_ITEM(dummyCallback,data),
59     GNOMEUIINFO_SEPARATOR,
60     GNOMEUIINFO_MENU_CUT_ITEM(dummyCallback,data),
61     GNOMEUIINFO_MENU_COPY_ITEM(dummyCallback,data),
62     GNOMEUIINFO_MENU_PASTE_ITEM(dummyCallback,data),
63     GNOMEUIINFO_MENU_CLEAR_ITEM(dummyCallback,data),
64     GNOMEUIINFO_MENU_SELECT_ALL_ITEM(dummyCallback,data),
65     GNOMEUIINFO_SEPARATOR,
66     GNOMEUIINFO_MENU_FIND_ITEM(dummyCallback,data),
67     GNOMEUIINFO_MENU_FIND_AGAIN_ITEM(dummyCallback,data),
68     GNOMEUIINFO_MENU_REPLACE_ITEM(dummyCallback,data),
69     GNOMEUIINFO_MENU_PROPERTIES_ITEM(dummyCallback,data),
70     GNOMEUIINFO_END
71 };
72
73 GnomeUIInfo gameMenu[] = {
74     GNOMEUIINFO_MENU_NEW_GAME_ITEM(dummyCallback,data),
75     GNOMEUIINFO_MENU_PAUSE_GAME_ITEM(dummyCallback,data),
76     GNOMEUIINFO_MENU_RESTART_GAME_ITEM(dummyCallback,data),
77     GNOMEUIINFO_MENU_UNDO_MOVE_ITEM(dummyCallback,data),
78     GNOMEUIINFO_MENU_HINT_ITEM(dummyCallback,data),
79     GNOMEUIINFO_MENU_SCORES_ITEM(dummyCallback,data),
80     GNOMEUIINFO_MENU_END_GAME_ITEM(dummyCallback,data),
81     GNOMEUIINFO_END
82 };
83
84 GnomeUIInfo settingsMenu[] = {
85     GNOMEUIINFO_MENU_PREFERENCES_ITEM(dummyCallback,data),
86     GNOMEUIINFO_END
87 };
88
89 GnomeUIInfo windowsMenu[] = {
90     GNOMEUIINFO_MENU_NEW_WINDOW_ITEM(dummyCallback,data),
91     GNOMEUIINFO_MENU_CLOSE_WINDOW_ITEM(dummyCallback,data),
92     GNOMEUIINFO_END
93 };
94
95 GnomeUIInfo helpMenu[] = {
96     GNOMEUIINFO_HELP("stdmain"),
97     GNOMEUIINFO_MENU_ABOUT_ITEM(helpAbout,data),
98     GNOMEUIINFO_END
99 };
100
101 GnomeUIInfo mainMenu[] = {
102     GNOMEUIINFO_SUBTREE("_File",fileMenu),
103     GNOMEUIINFO_SUBTREE("_Edit",editMenu),
104     GNOMEUIINFO_SUBTREE("_View",dummyMenu),
105     GNOMEUIINFO_SUBTREE("_Game",gameMenu),
106     GNOMEUIINFO_SUBTREE("[custom]",dummyMenu),
```

```
107        GNOMEUIINFO_SUBTREE("_Settings",settingsMenu),
108        GNOMEUIINFO_SUBTREE("_Windows",windowsMenu),
109        GNOMEUIINFO_SUBTREE("_Help",helpMenu),
110        GNOMEUIINFO_END
111 };
112
113 GtkWidget *createMenus(GtkWidget *app)
114 {
115        GtkWidget *statusbar;
116
117        gnome_app_create_menus(GNOME_APP(app),mainMenu);
118
119        statusbar = gtk_statusbar_new();
120        gnome_app_install_statusbar_menu_hints(
121                GTK_STATUSBAR(statusbar),mainMenu);
122        gnome_app_set_statusbar(GNOME_APP(app),statusbar);
123
124        return(statusbar);
125 }
```

Line 4 contains the dummy data that is to be passed to all the callback functions. Instead of this format, you can change the program to simply pass a NULL pointer.

To avoid the necessity of writing prototypes for the callback functions, they are placed at the top of the file. The function helpAbout() that begins on line 6 creates a standard GNOME About box. The other callback function, starting on line 24, is named dummyCallback() and is used as a placeholder for all of the menu items that require callbacks — it pops up the announcement that the chosen menu item has not been implemented.

The submenu defined on lines 29 through 36 is a dummy to be used in places where a submenu is needed. There is no standard definition of what it should contain.

The entire menu is defined on lines 38 through 111. Lines 101 through 111 determine the order of appearance of the top-level menu items. The File and Edit menus should be familiar. The View menu is application-specific and should be used to switch among different ways to view data (such as zooming, changing colors, or modifying the sort order). The Game menu is present only for game software. The menu labeled [custom] marks the spot where applications should add its own menu (or menus). The Settings menu is used to configure the application — it may have some toggle buttons on it, but it should have a Preferences selection, and the Windows menu controls which window is being displayed currently.

The entries in the menu are defined by macros that were designed especially for the purpose. For example, the macro GNOMEUIINFO_MENU_COPY_ITEM() on line 61 was designed to create a menu selection with the word Copy and use the standard copy icon. Three of these menus are shown in Figures 8-3 through 8-5.

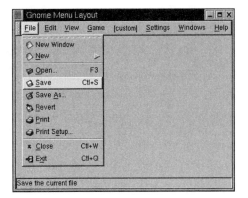

Figure 8-3: The appearance of the standard File menu

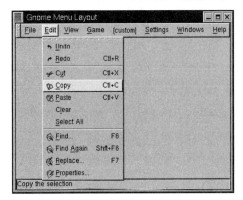

Figure 8-4: The appearance of the standard Edit menu

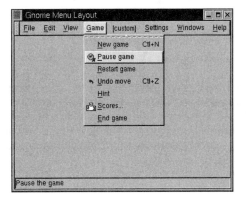

Figure 8-5: The appearance of the standard Game menu

Lines 39 through 43 define menu items that allow for the New option or options. This is commonly used (as in Netscape) to open a new application window. If there is only one New option, the macro beginning on line 39 should be used. If there is more than one New option, you should put them on a submenu, as on line 42. In an actual application, only one of these two options should be used.

There is a special menu item defined on line 96. This macro generates the code necessary to create a Help menu, listing the various help topics available for this application. The list of actual topics available is derived from the help files themselves, as described later in this chapter. Figure 8-6 shows the appearance of the menu for an application that has two topics defined in the help files.

Figure 8-6: Help is available under two topics

Beginning on line 113 is the function that creates the set of menus along with the application's status bar. The menus are created, and attached to the window, on line 117. The status bar is created on line 119, and the call to `gnome_app_install_menu_hints()` on line 120 prepares the status bar to display the message found in the menu definitions. The status bar is attached to the application window with the call to `gnome_app_set_statusbar()` on line 122.

The Help Files

The help files are written in HTML and a browser displays them. To make this work, you place the HTML files — along with an index — into a specific directory. When your application starts running, it reads the topic index file and creates the menu from it.

Note   In the current version of GNOME, the Netscape Web browser is spawned to display the help text. Future plans are for GNOME to have its own HTML display mechanism designed to work specifically with the help system.

In the previous example, this is achieved on line 96 by using the `GNOMEUIINFO_HELP()` macro as part of the help-menu definition. You should include this macro in the help menu always because a menu selection is created only if there is help text defined for the application. Also, the name used is usually the name of the application because these names usually are unique and, hopefully, easy to remember.

Both the program and help file names are `stdmain` in the previous example. This means the program looks in the following directory for help files:

```
/usr/share/gnome/help/stdmain/C
```

The C directory is the default, but there can be help text written in a number of languages, and each one with its own directory. For example, a set of help-menu definitions and files for the German language would be stored in this directory:

```
/usr/share/gnome/help/stdmain/de
```

The language used is determined by the current locale settings, as discussed in Chapter 23. The file used by your application to create the menu is in this directory and is named `topic.dat`. There is one line in this file for each menu member. The `topic.dat` file for the previous example program looks like this:

```
helpshow.html _Overview
helpshow.html#topicfile The _Topic File
```

Each line begins with the URL of a local help file and ends with the name to be displayed on the menu. The names can be written the same ways as they are for any menu entry. Blanks are allowed and the underscore character is used to specify the shortcut character. In this example, both of the URLs point to different places in the same help file — but you also can have entries that address other files.

You can see how simple it is to modify the help information because the application itself is not involved. Not only can you do this with your applications, but you also can add a special "My Notes" entry on the help menu and use it to annotate any application. In the previous example, when a selection is made from the menu, the Netscape browser produces the display shown in Figure 8-7.

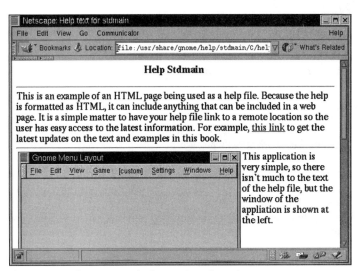

Figure 8-7: The GNOME help text is written in HTML

A Popup Menu

A popup menu is one that normally is not visible but, by using the right mouse button anywhere in the window, the menu appears. The menu from the following example is shown in Figure 8-8.

```
1  /** gnomepopup.c **/
2  #include <gnome.h>
3
4  static void dummyCallback(GtkObject *,gpointer);
5
6  gint eventDelete(GtkWidget *widget,
7          GdkEvent *event,gpointer data);
8  gint eventDestroy(GtkWidget *widget,
9          GdkEvent *event,gpointer data);
10
11 GnomeUIInfo showMenu[] = {
12     GNOMEUIINFO_ITEM("Next",NULL,dummyCallback,NULL),
13     GNOMEUIINFO_ITEM("Previous",NULL,dummyCallback,NULL),
14     GNOMEUIINFO_ITEM("Zoom In",NULL,dummyCallback,NULL),
15     GNOMEUIINFO_ITEM("Zoom Out",NULL,dummyCallback,NULL),
16     GNOMEUIINFO_END
17 };
18
19 GnomeUIInfo editMenu[] = {
20     GNOMEUIINFO_MENU_CUT_ITEM(dummyCallback,NULL),
21     GNOMEUIINFO_MENU_COPY_ITEM(dummyCallback,NULL),
22     GNOMEUIINFO_MENU_PASTE_ITEM(dummyCallback,NULL),
23     GNOMEUIINFO_ITEM("Delete",NULL,dummyCallback,NULL),
24     GNOMEUIINFO_END
25 };
26
27 GnomeUIInfo mainMenu[] = {
28     GNOMEUIINFO_SUBTREE("Show",showMenu),
29     GNOMEUIINFO_ITEM("Reduce",NULL,
30       dummyCallback,NULL),
31     GNOMEUIINFO_ITEM("Expand",NULL,
32       dummyCallback,NULL),
33     GNOMEUIINFO_SUBTREE("Edit",editMenu),
34     GNOMEUIINFO_END
35 };
36
37 int main(int argc,char *argv[])
38 {
39     GtkWidget *window;
40     GtkWidget *menu;
41
42     gnome_init("gnomepopup","1.0",argc,argv);
43     window = gnome_app_new("gnomepopup","Popup");
```

```
44     gtk_container_set_border_width(GTK_CONTAINER(window),
45             80);
46     gtk_signal_connect(GTK_OBJECT(window),"delete_event",
47             GTK_SIGNAL_FUNC(eventDelete),NULL);
48     gtk_signal_connect(GTK_OBJECT(window),"destroy",
49             GTK_SIGNAL_FUNC(eventDestroy),NULL);
50
51     menu = gnome_popup_menu_new(mainMenu);
52     gnome_popup_menu_attach(menu,window,NULL);
53     gtk_widget_show_all(window);
54
55     gtk_main();
56     exit(0);
57 }
58 static void dummyCallback(GtkObject *object,gpointer data)
59 {
60     gnome_ok_dialog("Not implemented");
61 }
62 gint eventDelete(GtkWidget *widget,
63         GdkEvent *event,gpointer data) {
64     return(FALSE);
65 }
66 gint eventDestroy(GtkWidget *widget,
67         GdkEvent *event,gpointer data) {
68     gtk_main_quit();
69     return(0);
70 }
```

Figure 8-8: A popup menu

The menu definitions on lines 11 through 35 use the same macros and initializers as the previous examples. The difference comes on line 51 with a call to gnome_popup_ menu_new() where the menu is created. The call to gnome_popup_menu_attach() on line 52 makes an association between the menu and the right mouse button of the window. As you can see in Figure 8-8, the menu appears the same as it does for a visible menu. One exception: the main menu portion is displayed vertically instead of horizontally.

Creating a Toolbar

The following example creates and displays a toolbar. The technique for creating a toolbar is basically the same as creating a menu. An array of GnomeUIInfo structures are all filled with the information required for each toolbar button and a function is called to create the toolbar and attach it to the window. A toolbar acts like a menu in that it displays itself as a list of mouse-sensitive rectangles and waits for a mouse click to execute a callback function.

```
1 /** toolbar.c **/
2 #include <gnome.h>
3
4 gint eventDelete(GtkWidget *widget,
5          GdkEvent *event,gpointer data);
6 gint eventDestroy(GtkWidget *widget,
7          GdkEvent *event,gpointer data);
8
9 static void toolbarNew(GtkObject *,gpointer);
10 static void toolbarOpen(GtkObject *,gpointer);
11 static void toolbarSave(GtkObject *,gpointer);
12 static void toolbarSaveAs(GtkObject *,gpointer);
13
14 static GnomeUIInfo toolbarFile[] = {
15     { GNOME_APP_UI_ITEM,"New",
16       "Create a new file",toolbarNew,NULL,NULL,
17       GNOME_APP_PIXMAP_STOCK,GNOME_STOCK_PIXMAP_NEW,
18       0,0,NULL },
19     { GNOME_APP_UI_ITEM,"Open",
20       "Open an existing file",toolbarOpen,NULL,NULL,
21       GNOME_APP_PIXMAP_STOCK,GNOME_STOCK_PIXMAP_OPEN,
22       0,0,NULL },
23     { GNOME_APP_UI_ITEM,"Save",
24       "Save the current file",toolbarSave,NULL,NULL,
25       GNOME_APP_PIXMAP_STOCK,GNOME_STOCK_PIXMAP_SAVE,
26       0,0,NULL },
27     { GNOME_APP_UI_ITEM,"Save as",
28       "Save to a new file",toolbarSaveAs,NULL,NULL,
29       GNOME_APP_PIXMAP_STOCK,GNOME_STOCK_PIXMAP_SAVE_AS,
30       0,0,NULL },
31     GNOMEUIINFO_END
32 };
33
34 int main(int argc,char *argv[])
35 {
36     GtkWidget *app;
37
38     gnome_init("toolbar","1.0",argc,argv);
39     app = gnome_app_new("toolbar",
40            "Gnome Toolbar Layout");
```

```
41      gtk_window_set_default_size(GTK_WINDOW(app),300,200);
42      gtk_signal_connect(GTK_OBJECT(app),"delete_event",
43              GTK_SIGNAL_FUNC(eventDelete),NULL);
44      gtk_signal_connect(GTK_OBJECT(app),"destroy",
45              GTK_SIGNAL_FUNC(eventDestroy),NULL);
46
47      gnome_app_create_toolbar(GNOME_APP(app),toolbarFile);
48
49      gtk_widget_show_all(app);
50      gtk_main();
51      exit(0);
52 }
53 static void toolbarNew(GtkObject *object,gpointer data)
54 {
55      gnome_ok_dialog("New");
56 }
57 static void toolbarOpen(GtkObject *object,gpointer data)
58 {
59      gnome_ok_dialog("Open");
60 }
61 static void toolbarSave(GtkObject *object,gpointer data)
62 {
63      gnome_ok_dialog("Save");
64 }
65 static void toolbarSaveAs(GtkObject *object,gpointer data)
66 {
67      gnome_ok_dialog("Save as");
68 }
69 gint eventDelete(GtkWidget *widget,
70          GdkEvent *event,gpointer data) {
71      return(FALSE);
72 }
73 gint eventDestroy(GtkWidget *widget,
74          GdkEvent *event,gpointer data) {
75      gtk_main_quit();
76      return(0);
77 }
```

The toolbar is defined by the array on lines 14 through 32. The tag names and callbacks all work the same as they do for a menu. Each entry in this array uses a GNOME stock pixmap icon, and both annotation and tooltip text. You can find a discussion of the stock icons in the section following this one.

The call to the function gnome_app_create_toolbar() on line 47 uses the array to create the toolbar and attach it to the window.

Figure 8-9 shows the toolbar in its default configuration at the top of the window. The tooltip, or hint, is displayed whenever the mouse pointer is inside the toolbar button. The toolbar can be torn off and placed anywhere on the screen as shown in Figure 8-10. Also, the toolbar can be docked at the top, bottom, left, or right side of the window (unlike a menu, which can be docked only at the top and bottom).

Figure 8-11 shows the toolbar in its vertical configuration, docked on the left side of the window.

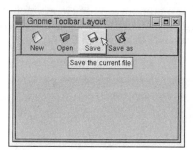

Figure 8-9: The default toolbar configuration

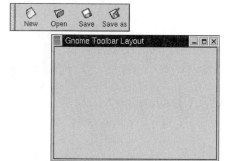

Figure 8-10: A toolbar can be moved to any location on the screen

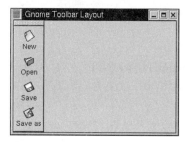

Figure 8-11: Docking a toolbar on the side converts it to a vertical layout

If you prefer not to have the text included as part of the displayed toolbar, just use NULL where you normally specify the string. Making this change to the above program creates a window with a thinner toolbar, like the one shown in Figure 8-12.

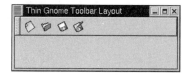

Figure 8-12: A toolbar without identifying text

The Stock Icons

Using stock icons is another way to standardize your application so it works very much like other GNOME applications. There are a number of stock icons included with GNOME. Figure 8-13 displays the standard set of icons. The icons are stored on disk as PNG files that have the same name as the labels shown in the figure.

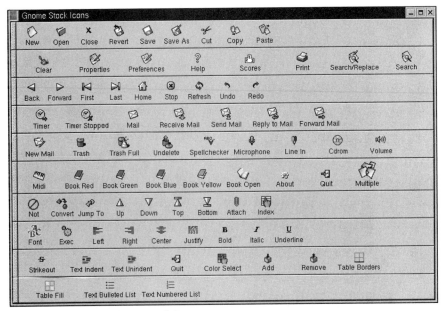

Figure 8-13: The GNOME stock icons

The following program creates the display shown in Figure 8-13.

```
1 /** showstock.c **/
2 #include <gnome.h>
3
4 gint eventDelete(GtkWidget *widget,
5       GdkEvent *event,gpointer data);
6 gint eventDestroy(GtkWidget *widget,
7       GdkEvent *event,gpointer data);
8
9 gchar *stock[] = {
10    GNOME_STOCK_PIXMAP_NEW,
11    GNOME_STOCK_PIXMAP_OPEN,
12    GNOME_STOCK_PIXMAP_CLOSE,
```

```
13      GNOME_STOCK_PIXMAP_REVERT,
14      GNOME_STOCK_PIXMAP_SAVE,
15      GNOME_STOCK_PIXMAP_SAVE_AS,
16      GNOME_STOCK_PIXMAP_CUT,
17      GNOME_STOCK_PIXMAP_COPY,
18      GNOME_STOCK_PIXMAP_PASTE,
19      GNOME_STOCK_PIXMAP_CLEAR,
20      GNOME_STOCK_PIXMAP_PROPERTIES,
21      GNOME_STOCK_PIXMAP_PREFERENCES,
22      GNOME_STOCK_PIXMAP_HELP,
23      GNOME_STOCK_PIXMAP_SCORES,
24      GNOME_STOCK_PIXMAP_PRINT,
25      GNOME_STOCK_PIXMAP_SRCHRPL,
26      GNOME_STOCK_PIXMAP_SEARCH,
27      GNOME_STOCK_PIXMAP_BACK,
28      GNOME_STOCK_PIXMAP_FORWARD,
29      GNOME_STOCK_PIXMAP_FIRST,
30      GNOME_STOCK_PIXMAP_LAST,
31      GNOME_STOCK_PIXMAP_HOME,
32      GNOME_STOCK_PIXMAP_STOP,
33      GNOME_STOCK_PIXMAP_REFRESH,
34      GNOME_STOCK_PIXMAP_UNDO,
35      GNOME_STOCK_PIXMAP_REDO,
36      GNOME_STOCK_PIXMAP_TIMER,
37      GNOME_STOCK_PIXMAP_TIMER_STOP,
38      GNOME_STOCK_PIXMAP_MAIL  ,
39      GNOME_STOCK_PIXMAP_MAIL_RCV,
40      GNOME_STOCK_PIXMAP_MAIL_SND,
41      GNOME_STOCK_PIXMAP_MAIL_RPL,
42      GNOME_STOCK_PIXMAP_MAIL_FWD,
43      GNOME_STOCK_PIXMAP_MAIL_NEW,
44      GNOME_STOCK_PIXMAP_TRASH,
45      GNOME_STOCK_PIXMAP_TRASH_FULL,
46      GNOME_STOCK_PIXMAP_UNDELETE,
47      GNOME_STOCK_PIXMAP_SPELLCHECK,
48      GNOME_STOCK_PIXMAP_MIC,
49      GNOME_STOCK_PIXMAP_LINE_IN,
50      GNOME_STOCK_PIXMAP_CDROM,
51      GNOME_STOCK_PIXMAP_VOLUME,
52      GNOME_STOCK_PIXMAP_MIDI,
53      GNOME_STOCK_PIXMAP_BOOK_RED,
54      GNOME_STOCK_PIXMAP_BOOK_GREEN,
55      GNOME_STOCK_PIXMAP_BOOK_BLUE,
56      GNOME_STOCK_PIXMAP_BOOK_YELLOW,
57      GNOME_STOCK_PIXMAP_BOOK_OPEN,
58      GNOME_STOCK_PIXMAP_ABOUT,
59      GNOME_STOCK_PIXMAP_QUIT,
60      GNOME_STOCK_PIXMAP_MULTIPLE,
61      GNOME_STOCK_PIXMAP_NOT,
62      GNOME_STOCK_PIXMAP_CONVERT,
```

```
63          GNOME_STOCK_PIXMAP_JUMP_TO,
64          GNOME_STOCK_PIXMAP_UP,
65          GNOME_STOCK_PIXMAP_DOWN,
66          GNOME_STOCK_PIXMAP_TOP,
67          GNOME_STOCK_PIXMAP_BOTTOM,
68          GNOME_STOCK_PIXMAP_ATTACH,
69          GNOME_STOCK_PIXMAP_INDEX,
70          GNOME_STOCK_PIXMAP_FONT,
71          GNOME_STOCK_PIXMAP_EXEC,
72          GNOME_STOCK_PIXMAP_ALIGN_LEFT,
73          GNOME_STOCK_PIXMAP_ALIGN_RIGHT,
74          GNOME_STOCK_PIXMAP_ALIGN_CENTER,
75          GNOME_STOCK_PIXMAP_ALIGN_JUSTIFY,
76          GNOME_STOCK_PIXMAP_TEXT_BOLD,
77          GNOME_STOCK_PIXMAP_TEXT_ITALIC,
78          GNOME_STOCK_PIXMAP_TEXT_UNDERLINE,
79          GNOME_STOCK_PIXMAP_TEXT_STRIKEOUT,
80          GNOME_STOCK_PIXMAP_TEXT_INDENT,
81          GNOME_STOCK_PIXMAP_TEXT_UNINDENT,
82          GNOME_STOCK_PIXMAP_EXIT,
83          GNOME_STOCK_PIXMAP_COLORSELECTOR,
84          GNOME_STOCK_PIXMAP_ADD,
85          GNOME_STOCK_PIXMAP_REMOVE,
86          GNOME_STOCK_PIXMAP_TABLE_BORDERS,
87          GNOME_STOCK_PIXMAP_TABLE_FILL,
88          GNOME_STOCK_PIXMAP_TEXT_BULLETED_LIST,
89          GNOME_STOCK_PIXMAP_TEXT_NUMBERED_LIST
90  };
91
92  static GnomeUIInfo iconInfo = {
93          GNOME_APP_UI_ITEM,NULL,NULL,NULL,NULL,NULL,
94          GNOME_APP_PIXMAP_STOCK,NULL,0,0,NULL
95  };
96  static GnomeUIInfo endInfo = GNOMEUIINFO_END;
97  static GnomeUIInfo toolbarInfo[10];
98
99  int main(int argc,char *argv[])
100 {
101     int s;
102     int t;
103     int count;
104     int total_size;
105     GtkWidget *app;
106
107     gnome_init("showstock","1.0",argc,argv);
108     app = gnome_app_new("showstock",
109             "Gnome Stock Icons");
110     gtk_signal_connect(GTK_OBJECT(app),"delete_event",
111             GTK_SIGNAL_FUNC(eventDelete),NULL);
```

```
112        gtk_signal_connect(GTK_OBJECT(app),"destroy",
113                GTK_SIGNAL_FUNC(eventDestroy),NULL);
114
115
116        total_size = sizeof(stock)/sizeof(gchar *);
117        s = 0;
118        while(s < total_size) {
119            for(t=0, count=0; count<9; t++, count++) {
120                memcpy(&toolbarInfo[t],
121                        &iconInfo,sizeof(iconInfo));
122                toolbarInfo[t].label = stock[s];
123                toolbarInfo[t].pixmap_info = stock[s];
124                memcpy(&toolbarInfo[t+1],
125                        &endInfo,sizeof(endInfo));
126                if(strlen(stock[s]) > 12)
127                    count++;
128                if(++s >= total_size)
129                    break;
130            }
131            gnome_app_create_toolbar(GNOME_APP(app),
132                    toolbarInfo);
133            gtk_widget_show_all(app);
134        }
135
136        gtk_main();
137        exit(0);
138 }
139 gint eventDelete(GtkWidget *widget,
140        GdkEvent *event,gpointer data) {
141        return(FALSE);
142 }
143 gint eventDestroy(GtkWidget *widget,
144        GdkEvent *event,gpointer data) {
145        gtk_main_quit();
146        return(0);
147 }
```

A character string, in the array of strings beginning on line 9, identifies each icon. The GNOME header file gnome-stock.h has definitions for each character string that names an icon. You simply can insert the quoted string directly but that prevents the compiler from detecting a typo. The definitions of the names look like this:

```
#define GNOME_STOCK_PIXMAP_NEW          "New"
#define GNOME_STOCK_PIXMAP_OPEN         "Open"
#define GNOME_STOCK_PIXMAP_CLOSE        "Close"
   . . .
```

All of the icon names are included in the single array beginning on line 96. The array of names is used to insert icons into the toolbars to be displayed. The GnomeUIInfo array on line 97 is used as a construction location for the toolbar definitions. The GnomeUIInfo struct on line 92 is an entry for an icon item, but it is missing the label and the item name. The GnomeUIInfo struct on line 96 is the standard array terminator.

The while loop beginning on line 118 is executed once for each toolbar created. The inner loop on line 119 is executed once for each icon being inserted into the current toolbar. The call to memcpy() on line 120 copies an icon entry into the array. Then the icon-identifier strings are inserted on lines 122 and 123 (it isn't required, but in this example, the name of the icon and the label text are the same). The call to memcpy() on line 124 copies the terminator to the next position in the array, making it a valid toolbar definition.

The display sizes of toolbar icons are all the same—that is, every icon on a toolbar expands both horizontally and vertically to match whichever size is the largest. As you can see in Figure 8-13, it is the text of the label that makes some of the icons very wide. To make the display better fit the window, the count of the number of icons added to the toolbar is adjusted on line 127 whenever a name exceeds 12 characters.

Removing the text annotation beneath the icons results in a much smaller display. Figure 8-14 shows the results of removing line 123 of the program, resulting in icons with no text. The figure also shows that every toolbar can be positioned and oriented separately—a toolbar can be docked horizontally on the top or bottom, docked vertically on the left or right, or placed anywhere on the screen in either horizontal or vertical orientation.

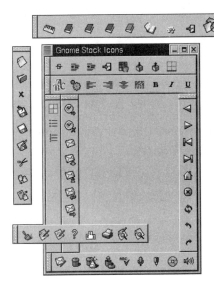

Figure 8-14: Toolbars can be repositioned independently

Non-Standard Icons

You can get your icons from anywhere. Just about any graphic you have can be used as a toolbar icon. Once you convert it to an XPM file, you can compile it directly into the program or load it at runtime. The toolbar in the following program mixes the three different methods of generating the icons in a toolbar.

```
 1 /** toolbarcustom.c **/
 2 #include <gnome.h>
 3
 4 static char *modulate[] = {
 5     "25 24 2 1",
 6     "  c None",
 7     "B c Black",
 8     "                        ",
 9     "                 B      ",
10     "                 B      ",
11     " B               B      ",
12     " B             B B      ",
13     " B     B     B B B      ",
14     " B B   B B   B B B   B  ",
15     " B B   B B   B B B   B  ",
16     " B B   B B   B B B B B  ",
17     " B B   B B   B B B B B  ",
18     " B B B B B   B B B B B B ",
19     " B B B B B B B B B B B B ",
20     " B B B B B B B B B B B B ",
21     " B B B B B   B B B B B B ",
22     " B B   B B   B B B B B  ",
23     " B B   B B   B B B B B  ",
24     " B B   B B   B B B B B  ",
25     " B B   B B   B B B   B  ",
26     " B B   B     B B B   B  ",
27     " B     B     B B B      ",
28     " B             B B      ",
29     " B               B      ",
30     "                 B      ",
31     "                 B      "
32 };
33
34 gint eventDelete(GtkWidget *widget,
35         GdkEvent *event,gpointer data);
36 gint eventDestroy(GtkWidget *widget,
37         GdkEvent *event,gpointer data);
38
39 static GnomeUIInfo toolbarFile[] = {
40     { GNOME_APP_UI_ITEM,"Redeks",
41       "Create a new file",NULL,NULL,NULL,
42       GNOME_APP_PIXMAP_FILENAME,"redeks.xpm",
43       0,0,NULL },
44     { GNOME_APP_UI_ITEM,"Open",
45       "Open an existing file",NULL,NULL,NULL,
```

```
46        GNOME_APP_PIXMAP_STOCK,GNOME_STOCK_PIXMAP_OPEN,
47        0,0,NULL },
48      { GNOME_APP_UI_ITEM,"Modulate",
49        "Create a new file",NULL,NULL,NULL,
50        GNOME_APP_PIXMAP_DATA,&modulate,
51        0,0,NULL },
52      { GNOME_APP_UI_ITEM,"Save",
53        "Save the current file",NULL,NULL,NULL,
54        GNOME_APP_PIXMAP_STOCK,GNOME_STOCK_PIXMAP_SAVE,
55        0,0,NULL },
56      GNOMEUIINFO_END
57 };
58
59 int main(int argc,char *argv[])
60 {
61      GtkWidget *app;
62
63      gnome_init("toolbarcustom","1.0",argc,argv);
64      app = gnome_app new("toolbarcustom",
65              "Custom Toolbar Icons");
66      gtk_window_set_default_size(GTK_WINDOW(app),300,200);
67      gtk_signal_connect(GTK_OBJECT(app),"delete_event",
68              GTK_SIGNAL_FUNC(eventDelete),NULL);
69      gtk_signal_connect(GTK_OBJECT(app),"destroy",
70              GTK_SIGNAL_FUNC(eventDestroy),NULL);
71
72      gnome_app_create_toolbar(GNOME_APP(app),toolbarFile);
73
74      gtk_widget_show_all(app);
75      gtk_main();
76      exit(0);
77 }
78 gint eventDelete(GtkWidget *widget,
79          GdkEvent *event,gpointer data) {
80      return(FALSE);
81 }
82 gint eventDestroy(GtkWidget *widget,
83          GdkEvent *event,gpointer data) {
84      gtk_main_quit();
85      return(0);
86 }
```

The toolbar definition beginning on line 39 is made up of two custom icons and two
GNOME stock icons. The Open and Save icons defined on lines 44 and 52 are the
two stock icons. The window displayed is shown in Figure 8-15.

Figure 8-15: Toolbars mix
custom and stock icons

Line 48 is the toolbar definition of the Modulate icon. Its pixmap type is GNOME_APP_ PIXMAP_DATA, which means the graphic for the icon either is compiled as a part of the program (as in this example) or is defined as an array of character strings. With the data included in the program this way, it is even possible for you to define pixel values in your program. The data is held in the XPM format (as described in Chapter 7) and is declared in this program as the array of strings beginning on line 4. It is 25 pixels wide and 24 pixels high, and only has two colors—the transparent background and the black vertical lines.

Line 40 is the toolbar definition of the Redeks icon. Just as with the Modulate icon, it uses XPM data. But its type is specified as GNOME_APP_PIXMAP_FILENAME, so it reads the graphics data from the named disk file. In this example, the file is named redeks.xpm and has the following contents. This is the definition of an icon that is 25 pixels wide, 24 pixels high, and has three colors (red, black, and transparent):

```
/* XPM */
static char *redeks[] = {
"25 24 3 1",
"  c None",
"B c Black",
"R c Red",
"                         ",
"                         ",
"                         ",
" BBB                 BBB ",
" BRRB               BRRB ",
" BRRRBB           BBRRRB ",
" BRRRRRBB       BBRRRRRB ",
" BRRRRRRRBB   BBRRRRRRRB ",
"   BBRRRRRRRBBBRRRRRRRBB ",
"     BBRRRRRRRRRRRRRRBB   ",
"       BBRRRRRRRRRRRBB    ",
"         BBRRRRRRRRBB     ",
"           BBRRRRBB       ",
"         BBRRRRRRRRBB     ",
"       BBRRRRRRRRRRRBB    ",
"     BBRRRRRRRRRRRRRRBB   ",
"   BBRRRRRRRBBBRRRRRRRBB ",
" BRRRRRRRBB   BBRRRRRRRB ",
" BRRRRRBB       BBRRRRRB ",
" BRRRBB           BBRRRB ",
" BRRB               BRRB ",
" BBB                 BBB ",
"                         ",
"                         ",
};
```

Disabling and Enabling Menu Items

A menu item can be disabled and enabled dynamically. When it is disabled, it appears grayed-out and does not respond to the mouse. This technique often is used to prevent user access to functions that have no meaning under the current circumstances. For example, the Save button can be disabled if there is no data available to be written to disk.

The following program has a simple three-button menu. The top and bottom buttons can be used to enable and disable the one in the middle.

```
1  /** mdisable.c **/
2  #include <gnome.h>
3
4  static void dummyCallback(GtkObject *,gpointer);
5  static void enableProperties(GtkObject *,gpointer);
6  static void disableProperties(GtkObject *,gpointer);
7  gint eventDelete(GtkWidget *widget,
8          GdkEvent *event,gpointer data);
9  gint eventDestroy(GtkWidget *widget,
10         GdkEvent *event,gpointer data);
11
12 #define PROP_INDEX 1
13 GnomeUIInfo enableMenu[] = {
14     GNOMEUIINFO_MENU_NEW_ITEM("Enable Properties",
15         "Enable the Properties menu selection",
16         enableProperties,NULL),
17     GNOMEUIINFO_MENU_PROPERTIES ITEM(dummyCallback,NULL),
18     GNOMEUIINFO_MENU_NEW_ITEM("Disable Properties",
19         "Disable the Properties menu selection",
20         disableProperties,NULL),
21     GNOMEUIINFO_END
22 };
23
24 GnomeUIInfo mainMenu[] = {
25     GNOMEUIINFO_SUBTREE("Enable/Disable",enableMenu),
26     GNOMEUIINFO_END
27 };
28
29 int main(int argc,char *argv[])
30 {
31     GtkWidget *app;
32
33     gnome_init("mdisable","1.0",argc,argv);
34     app = gnome_app_new("mdisable","Menu Disable");
35     gtk_window_set_default_size(GTK_WINDOW(app),200,100);
36     gtk_signal_connect(GTK_OBJECT(app),"delete_event",
37             GTK_SIGNAL_FUNC(eventDelete),NULL);
38     gtk_signal_connect(GTK_OBJECT(app),"destroy",
```

```
39                  GTK_SIGNAL_FUNC(eventDestroy),NULL);
40
41      gnome_app_create_menus(GNOME_APP(app),mainMenu);
42
43      gtk_widget_show_all(app);
44      gtk_main();
45      exit(0);
46 }
47 static void dummyCallback(GtkObject *object,gpointer data)
48 {
49      gnome_ok_dialog("The dummy callback executed.");
50 }
51 static void disableProperties(GtkObject *object,
52              gpointer data) {
53      gtk_widget_set_sensitive(
54              GTK_WIDGET(enableMenu[PROP_INDEX].widget),
55              FALSE);
56 }
57 static void enableProperties(GtkObject *object,
58              gpointer data) {
59      gtk_widget_set_sensitive(
60              GTK_WIDGET(enableMenu[PROP_INDEX].widget),
61              TRUE);
62 }
63 gint eventDelete(GtkWidget *widget,
64          GdkEvent *event,gpointer data) {
65      return(FALSE);
66 }
67 gint eventDestroy(GtkWidget *widget,
68          GdkEvent *event,gpointer data) {
69      gtk_main_quit();
70      return(0);
71 }
```

The array declared on lines 13 through 21 defines the three-button menu shown in Figure 8-16. The first button has the callback function enableProperties() and the third button has the callback function disableProperties().

Figure 8-16: A three-button menu fully enabled

The callback function disableProperties() defined starting on line 51 disables the second button on the menu. The function gtk_widget_set_sensitive() is called with two arguments. The first argument is the widget that is inserted into the menu array during the call to gnome_app_create_menus(). The second argument is the

Boolean value FALSE that turns the sensitivity off, causing the menu to appear as it does in Figure 8-17. The callback function of the third button—enableProperties() defined starting on line 57—also calls gtk_widget_set_sensitive(), but with the Boolean value set to TRUE, which restores the button to its original active state.

Figure 8-17: A three-button menu with one button disabled

Note The index value of the menu item to be addressed is defined as a named constant on line 12. If the menu is modified later, by inserting new items or deleting old ones, the defined constant that appears right there with the array should remind you to update its value. This is a self-defense move that could save some future problems caused by seemingly random menu items becoming disabled.

Disabling and Enabling Toolbar Items

A toolbar item can be disabled and enabled dynamically. When an item is disabled, it appears grayed-out and does not respond to the mouse. The following program creates a simple, three-button toolbar in which the button in the center can be enabled and disabled by the buttons on each side of it.

```
 1 /** tbdisable.c **/
 2 #include <gnome.h>
 3
 4 static void dummyCallback(GtkObject *,gpointer);
 5 static void enableProperties(GtkObject *,gpointer);
 6 static void disableProperties(GtkObject *,gpointer);
 7
 8 gint eventDelete(GtkWidget *widget,
 9         GdkEvent *event,gpointer data);
10 gint eventDestroy(GtkWidget *widget,
11         GdkEvent *event,gpointer data);
12
13 #define DISPROP_INDEX 1
14 static GnomeUIInfo enableToolbar[] = {
15     { GNOME_APP_UI_ITEM,"Enable Properties",
16       "Enable the Properties toolbar selection",
17       enableProperties,NULL,NULL,
18       GNOME_APP_PIXMAP_STOCK,GNOME_STOCK_PIXMAP_NEW,
19       0,0,NULL },
20     { GNOME_APP_UI_ITEM,"Properties",
21       "Configure application properties",
22       dummyCallback,NULL,NULL,
23       GNOME_APP_PIXMAP_STOCK,GNOME_STOCK_PIXMAP_PROPERTIES,
```

```
24        0,0,NULL },
25      { GNOME_APP_UI_ITEM,"Disable Properties",
26        "Disable the Properties toolbar selection",
27        disableProperties,NULL,NULL,
28        GNOME_APP_PIXMAP_STOCK,GNOME_STOCK_PIXMAP_SAVE_AS,
29        0,0,NULL },
30      GNOMEUIINFO_END
31 };
32
33 int main(int argc,char *argv[])
34 {
35     GtkWidget *app;
36
37     gnome_init("tbdisable","1.0",argc,argv);
38     app = gnome_app_new("tbdisable","Toolbar Disable");
39     gtk_signal_connect(GTK_OBJECT(app),"delete_event",
40             GTK_SIGNAL_FUNC(eventDelete),NULL);
41     gtk_signal_connect(GTK_OBJECT(app),"destroy",
42             GTK_SIGNAL_FUNC(eventDestroy),NULL);
43
44     gnome_app_create_toolbar(GNOME_APP(app),enableToolbar);
45     gtk_widget_show_all(app);
46
47     gtk_main();
48     exit(0);
49 }
50 static void dummyCallback(GtkObject *object,gpointer data)
51 {
52     gnome_ok_dialog("The dummy callback executed.");
53 }
54 static void disableProperties(GtkObject *object,
55                 gpointer data) {
56     gtk_widget_set_sensitive(
57         GTK_WIDGET(enableToolbar[DISPROP_INDEX].widget),
58         FALSE);
59 }
60 static void enableProperties(GtkObject *object,
61                 gpointer data) {
62     gtk_widget_set_sensitive(
63         GTK_WIDGET(enableToolbar[DISPROP_INDEX].widget),
64         TRUE);
65 }
66 gint eventDelete(GtkWidget *widget,
67         GdkEvent *event,gpointer data) {
68     return(FALSE);
69 }
70 gint eventDestroy(GtkWidget *widget,
71         GdkEvent *event,gpointer data) {
72     gtk_main_quit();
73     return(0);
74 }
```

The array declared on lines 14 through 30 defines the toolbar shown in Figure 8-18. The left button has the callback function enableProperties() and the button on the right has the callback function disableProperties().

Figure 8-18: A toolbar with all selections enabled

The enabling and disabling code for a toolbar item is the same as it is for a menu item. The callback function disableProperties() defined starting on line 54 disables the middle button on the toolbar. The function gtk_widget_set_sensitive() is called with two arguments. The first argument is the widget that is inserted into the menu array during the call to gnome_app_create_menus(). The second argument is the Boolean value FALSE that turns the sensitivity off, causing the toolbar to appear as it does in Figure 8-19. The callback function of the left button — enableProperties() defined starting on line 60 — also calls gtk_widget_set_sensitive(), but with the Boolean value set to TRUE, which restores the toolbar item to its original active state.

Figure 8-19: A toolbar with one selection disabled

Hiding and Showing Menu Items

The fact that a menu is defined by a statically defined array of GnomeUIInfo structs prevents your program from dynamically inserting and deleting menu selections. A hidden menu item is not displayed and the rest of the menu looks just as it would if the hidden item were not in the array. This way, to modify a menu, you simply hide and show the individual menu items.

The following example creates a menu with three buttons. The top button causes the middle button to disappear from the menu, and the bottom button causes the middle button to reappear.

```
 1 /** mhide.c **/
 2 #include <gnome.h>
 3
 4 static void dummyCallback(GtkObject *,gpointer);
 5 static void showProperties(GtkObject *,gpointer);
 6 static void hideProperties(GtkObject *,gpointer);
 7
 8 gint eventDelete(GtkWidget *widget,
 9         GdkEvent *event,gpointer data);
10 gint eventDestroy(GtkWidget *widget,
11         GdkEvent *event,gpointer data);
```

```
12
13 #define PROPERTIES_INDEX 1
14 GnomeUIInfo showMenu[] = {
15     GNOMEUIINFO_MENU_NEW_ITEM("Show Properties",
16         "Show the Properties menu selection",
17         showProperties,NULL),
18     GNOMEUIINFO_MENU_PROPERTIES_ITEM(dummyCallback,NULL),
19     GNOMEUIINFO_MENU_NEW_ITEM("Hide Properties",
20         "Hide the Properties menu selection",
21         hideProperties,NULL),
22     GNOMEUIINFO_END
23 };
24
25 GnomeUIInfo mainMenu[] = {
26     GNOMEUIINFO_SUBTREE("Show/Hide",showMenu),
27     GNOMEUIINFO_END
28 };
29
30 int main(int argc,char *argv[])
31 {
32     GtkWidget *app;
33
34     gnome_init("mhide","1.0",argc,argv);
35     app = gnome_app_new("mhide","Menu Hide");
36     gtk_window_set_default_size(GTK_WINDOW(app),200,100);
37     gtk_signal_connect(GTK_OBJECT(app),"delete_event",
38             GTK_SIGNAL_FUNC(eventDelete),NULL);
39     gtk_signal_connect(GTK_OBJECT(app),"destroy",
40             GTK_SIGNAL_FUNC(eventDestroy),NULL);
41
42     gnome_app_create_menus(GNOME_APP(app),mainMenu);
43
44     gtk_widget_show_all(app);
45     gtk_main();
46     exit(0);
47 }
48 static void dummyCallback(GtkObject *object,
49             gpointer data) {
50     gnome_ok_dialog("The dummy callback executed.");
51 }
52 static void showProperties(GtkObject *object,
53             gpointer data) {
54     gtk_widget_show(
55             GTK_WIDGET(showMenu[PROPERTIES_INDEX].widget));
56 }
57 static void hideProperties(GtkObject *object,
58             gpointer data) {
59     gtk_widget_hide(
60             GTK_WIDGET(showMenu[PROPERTIES_INDEX].widget));
61 }
62 gint eventDelete(GtkWidget *widget,
63         GdkEvent *event,gpointer data) {
64     return(FALSE);
```

```
65 }
66 gint eventDestroy(GtkWidget *widget,
67         GdkEvent *event,gpointer data) {
68     gtk_main_quit();
69     return(0);
70 }
```

The three-button menu is defined by the array on lines 14 through 23. The menu is created and attached to the main window by the call to gnome_app_create_menus() on line 42. When the menu first appears, it has all three buttons visible and looks like the one in Figure 8-20.

Figure 8-20: A three-button menu with all items showing

Selecting the bottom menu button executes the callback function hideProperties() beginning on line 57. The call to gtk_widget_hide() on line 59 makes the second button invisible. The menu closes up to fill the empty space and the new configuration looks like the one in Figure 8-21. Selecting the top menu button executes the callback function showProperties() beginning on line 52 that calls gtk_widget_show(), causing the second button to become visible again. Showing a button that is being shown already (or hiding one that already is hidden) has no effect.

Figure 8-21: A three-button menu with one button hidden

Hiding and Showing Toolbar Items

While a toolbar is defined statically as an array of GnomeUIInfo structs, it is possible to select which ones are displayed and which ones are not. When a toolbar item is not displayed, the toolbar configures itself just as it would if the hidden item were not included in the defining array.

The following example creates a toolbar with three buttons. The right button causes the middle button to disappear, and the left button causes the middle button to reappear.

```
1 /** tbhide.c **/
2 #include <gnome.h>
3
```

```
 4 static void dummyCallback(GtkObject *,gpointer);
 5 static void showProperties(GtkObject *,gpointer);
 6 static void hideProperties(GtkObject *,gpointer);
 7
 8 gint eventDelete(GtkWidget *widget,
 9        GdkEvent *event,gpointer data);
10 gint eventDestroy(GtkWidget *widget,
11        GdkEvent *event,gpointer data);
12
13 #define PROPERTIES_INDEX 1
14 static GnomeUIInfo showToolbar[] = {
15     { GNOME_APP_UI_ITEM,"Show Properties",
16       "Enable the Properties toolbar selection",
17       showProperties,NULL,NULL,
18       GNOME_APP_PIXMAP_STOCK,GNOME_STOCK_PIXMAP_NEW,
19       0,0,NULL },
20     { GNOME_APP_UI_ITEM,"Properties",
21       "Configure application properties",
22       dummyCallback,NULL,NULL,
23       GNOME_APP_PIXMAP_STOCK,GNOME_STOCK_PIXMAP_PROPERTIES,
24       0,0,NULL },
25     { GNOME_APP_UI_ITEM,"Hide Properties",
26       "Hide the Properties toolbar selection",
27       hideProperties,NULL,NULL,
28       GNOME_APP_PIXMAP_STOCK,GNOME_STOCK_PIXMAP_SAVE_AS,
29       0,0,NULL },
30     GNOMEUIINFO_END
31 };
32
33 int main(int argc,char *argv[])
34 {
35     GtkWidget *app;
36
37     gnome_init("tbhide","1.0",argc,argv);
38     app = gnome_app_new("tbhide","Toolbar Hide");
39     gtk_signal_connect(GTK_OBJECT(app),"delete_event",
40         GTK_SIGNAL_FUNC(eventDelete),NULL);
41     gtk_signal_connect(GTK_OBJECT(app),"destroy",
42         GTK_SIGNAL_FUNC(eventDestroy),NULL);
43
44     gnome_app_create_toolbar(GNOME_APP(app),showToolbar);
45     gtk_widget_show_all(app);
46
47     gtk_main();
48     exit(0);
49 }
50 static void dummyCallback(GtkObject *object,gpointer data)
51 {
52     gnome_ok_dialog("The dummy callback executed.");
53 }
54 static void showProperties(GtkObject *object,gpointer data)
```

```
55 {
56     gtk_widget_show(
57         GTK_WIDGET(showToolbar[PROPERTIES_INDEX].widget));
58 }
59 static void hideProperties(GtkObject *object,gpointer data)
60 {
61     gtk_widget_hide(
62         GTK_WIDGET(showToolbar[PROPERTIES_INDEX].widget));
63 }
64 gint eventDelete(GtkWidget *widget,
65         GdkEvent *event,gpointer data) {
66     return(FALSE);
67 }
68 gint eventDestroy(GtkWidget *widget,
69         GdkEvent *event,gpointer data) {
70     gtk_main_quit();
71     return(0);
72 }
```

The three-button toolbar is defined by the array on lines 14 through 31. The toolbar is created and attached to the main window by the call to gnome_app_create_ toolbar() on line 42. When the toolbar first appears, it has all three buttons visible and looks like the one in Figure 8-22.

Figure 8-22: A three-button toolbar with all items showing

Selecting the button on the right executes the callback function hideProperties() beginning on line 59. The call to gtk_widget_hide() on line 61 makes the middle button disappear from the display—the toolbar immediately closes up to fill the empty space and the new configuration looks like that of Figure 8-23. Selecting the left button executes the callback function showProperties() beginning on line 54 that calls gtk_widget_show(), causing the middle button to become visible again. Showing a button that already is being shown (or hiding one that already is hidden) has no effect.

Figure 8-23: A three-button toolbar with one item hidden

Radio Buttons in a Menu

You can include a set of radio buttons directly on a menu. One, and only one, of the radio buttons is selected at any one time. The following program creates a menu containing three radio buttons.

```
1  /** mradio.c **/
2  #include <gnome.h>
3
4  static void dummyCallback(GtkObject *,gpointer);
5  static void radioOne(GtkObject *,gpointer);
6  static void radioTwo(GtkObject *,gpointer);
7  static void radioThree(GtkObject *,gpointer);
8
9  gint eventDelete(GtkWidget *widget,
10         GdkEvent *event,gpointer data);
11 gint eventDestroy(GtkWidget *widget,
12         GdkEvent *event,gpointer data);
13
14 GnomeUIInfo menuRadioList[] = {
15     GNOMEUIINFO_RADIOITEM("Radio One",
16         "The first radio button",
17         radioOne,NULL),
18     GNOMEUIINFO_RADIOITEM("Radio Two",
19         "The second radio button",
20         radioTwo,NULL),
21     GNOMEUIINFO_RADIOITEM("Radio Three",
22         "The third radio button",
23         radioThree,NULL),
24     GNOMEUIINFO_END
25 };
26
27 GnomeUIInfo radioMenu[] = {
28     GNOMEUIINFO_MENU_REDO_ITEM(dummyCallback,NULL),
29     GNOMEUIINFO_SEPARATOR,
30     GNOMEUIINFO_RADIOLIST(menuRadioList),
31     GNOMEUIINFO_SEPARATOR,
32     GNOMEUIINFO_MENU_CUT_ITEM(dummyCallback,NULL),
33     GNOMEUIINFO_END
34 };
35
36 GnomeUIInfo mainMenu[] = {
37     GNOMEUIINFO_SUBTREE("RadioButtons",radioMenu),
38     GNOMEUIINFO_END
39 };
40
41 int main(int argc,char *argv[])
42 {
43     GtkWidget *app;
```

```
44
45      gnome_init("mradio","1.0",argc,argv);
46      app = gnome_app_new("mradio","Menu Radio Buttons");
47      gtk_window_set_default_size(GTK_WINDOW(app),200,100);
48      gtk_signal_connect(GTK_OBJECT(app),"delete_event",
49             GTK_SIGNAL_FUNC(eventDelete),NULL);
50      gtk_signal_connect(GTK_OBJECT(app),"destroy",
51             GTK_SIGNAL_FUNC(eventDestroy),NULL);
52
53      gnome_app_create_menus(GNOME_APP(app),mainMenu);
54
55      gtk_widget_show_all(app);
56      gtk_main();
57      exit(0);
58 }
59 static void dummyCallback(GtkObject *object,gpointer data)
60 {
61      gnome_ok_dialog("The dummy callback executed.");
62 }
63 static void radioOne(GtkObject *object,gpointer data)
64 {
65      if(GTK_CHECK_MENU_ITEM(object)->active)
66          gnome_ok_dialog("The radio one button is on.");
67      else
68          gnome_ok_dialog("The radio one button is off.");
69 }
70 static void radioTwo(GtkObject *object,gpointer data)
71 {
72      if(GTK_CHECK_MENU_ITEM(object)->active)
73          gnome_ok_dialog("The radio two button is on.");
74      else
75          gnome_ok_dialog("The radio two button is off.");
76 }
77 static void radioThree(GtkObject *object,gpointer data)
78 {
79      if(GTK_CHECK_MENU_ITEM(object)->active)
80          gnome_ok_dialog("The radio three button is on.");
81      else
82          gnome_ok_dialog("The radio three button is off.");
83 }
84 gint eventDelete(GtkWidget *widget,
85         GdkEvent *event,gpointer data) {
86      return(FALSE);
87 }
88 gint eventDestroy(GtkWidget *widget,
89         GdkEvent *event,gpointer data) {
90      gtk_main_quit();
91      return(0);
92 }
```

The pull-down portion of the menu is defined in the array radiomen on lines 27 through 34. The set of radio buttons is included using the macro GNOMEUIINFO_ RADIOLIST() on line 30. The radio buttons need to be defined as a single unit because of the way that they interact with one another. Whenever one of them is selected, the others are deselected.

The individual buttons are defined in the `GnomeUIInfo` array on lines 14 through 25. Each one is defined by the macro `GNOMEUIINFO_RADIOITEM()`. Other than the terminating `GNOME_APP_UI_ENDOF_INFO` type, all of the members of the array must be of the type `GNOME_APP_UI_ITEM`—which is the type used by the `GNOMEUIINFO_RADIOITEM()` macro.

Everything needed to create the radio buttons is included in the defining arrays, so the menu is constructed as usual with the call to `gnome_app_create_menus()` on line 53. The resulting menu is shown in Figure 8-24.

Figure 8-24: A set of radio buttons in a menu

Each menu button has its own callback function (defined on lines 63, 70, and 77) and each callback function has two possible choices. Whenever a callback is made, the function must test to see whether the button is being selected or deselected. When a button is selected, the `active` value in the widget is nonzero and there are two callbacks. The newly selected button issues a callback with its `active` value set to a nonzero value. The button that was toggled becomes deselected issues a callback with the `active` value set to zero. If the user selects the button that already is active, there is only one callback, and the active value is nonzero.

Radio Buttons in a Toolbar

You also can include a set of radio buttons as part of a toolbar. They look the same as regular buttons, except that one—and only one—of the radio buttons can be selected at any one time. It remains selected until another is chosen. The following program creates a toolbar containing three radio buttons.

```
 1 /** tbradio.c **/
 2 #include <gnome.h>
 3
 4 #include "tbxpm.h"
 5
 6 static void dummyCallback(GtkObject *,gpointer);
 7 static void radioOneToolbar(GtkObject *,gpointer);
 8 static void radioTwoToolbar(GtkObject *,gpointer);
 9 static void radioThreeToolbar(GtkObject *,gpointer);
10
```

```
11 gint eventDelete(GtkWidget *widget,
12        GdkEvent *event,gpointer data);
13 gint eventDestroy(GtkWidget *widget,
14        GdkEvent *event,gpointer data);
15
16 GnomeUIInfo radioList[] = {
17     GNOMEUIINFO_RADIOITEM("Radio One",
18         "The first radio button",
19         radioOneToolbar,downXPM),
20     GNOMEUIINFO_RADIOITEM("Radio Two",
21         "The second radio button",
22         radioTwoToolbar,attachXPM),
23     GNOMEUIINFO_RADIOITEM("Radio Three",
24         "The third radio button",
25         radioThreeToolbar,propertiesXPM),
26     GNOMEUIINFO_END
27 };
28
29 static GnomeUIInfo radioToolbar[] = {
30     { GNOME_APP_UI_ITEM,"New",
31       "Create a new file",dummyCallback,NULL,NULL,
32       GNOME_APP_PIXMAP_STOCK,GNOME_STOCK_PIXMAP_NEW,
33       0,0,NULL },
34     GNOMEUIINFO_SEPARATOR,
35     GNOMEUIINFO_RADIOLIST(radioList),
36     GNOMEUIINFO_SEPARATOR,
37     { GNOME_APP_UI_ITEM,"Save as",
38       "Save to a new file",dummyCallback,NULL,NULL,
39       GNOME_APP_PIXMAP_STOCK,GNOME_STOCK_PIXMAP_SAVE_AS,
40       0,0,NULL },
41     GNOMEUIINFO_END
42 };
43
44 int main(int argc,char *argv[])
45 {
46     GtkWidget *app;
47
48     gnome_init("tbradio","1.0",argc,argv);
49     app = gnome_app_new("tbradio","Toolbar Radio Buttons");
50     gtk_signal_connect(GTK_OBJECT(app),"delete_event",
51             GTK_SIGNAL_FUNC(eventDelete),NULL);
52     gtk_signal_connect(GTK_OBJECT(app),"destroy",
53             GTK_SIGNAL_FUNC(eventDestroy),NULL);
54
55     gnome_app_create_toolbar(GNOME_APP(app),radioToolbar);
56     gtk_widget_show_all(app);
57
58     gtk_main();
59     exit(0);
60 }
61 static void dummyCallback(GtkObject *object,gpointer data)
```

```
62 {
63     gnome_ok_dialog("The dummy callback executed.");
64 }
65 static void radioOneToolbar(GtkObject *object,
66                 gpointer data) {
67     if(gtk_toggle_button_get_active(
68                         GTK_TOGGLE_BUTTON(object)))
69         gnome_ok_dialog("The radio one button is on.");
70     else
71         gnome_ok_dialog("The radio one button is off.");
72 }
73 static void radioTwoToolbar(GtkObject *object,
74                 gpointer data) {
75     if(gtk_toggle_button_get_active(
76                         GTK_TOGGLE_BUTTON(object)))
77         gnome_ok_dialog("The radio one button is on.");
78     else
79         gnome_ok_dialog("The radio one button is off.");
80 }
81 static void radioThreeToolbar(GtkObject *object,
82                 gpointer data) {
83     if(gtk_toggle_button_get_active(
84                         GTK_TOGGLE_BUTTON(object)))
85         gnome_ok_dialog("The radio one button is on.");
86     else
87         gnome_ok_dialog("The radio one button is off.");
88 }
89 gint eventDelete(GtkWidget *widget,
90         GdkEvent *event,gpointer data) {
91     return(FALSE);
92 }
93 gint eventDestroy(GtkWidget *widget,
94         GdkEvent *event,gpointer data) {
95     gtk_main_quit();
96     return(0);
97 }
```

The toolbar is defined in the array radioToolbar on lines 29 through 42. The set of radio buttons is included using the macro GNOMEUIINFO_RADIOLIST() on line 35. The radio buttons (as in the menu) need to be defined as a single unit this way because of the way that they interact with one another. Whenever one of them is selected, the others are deselected.

The individual buttons are defined in the GnomeUIInfo array on lines 16 through 27. The three graphic icons for the buttons (attachXPM, downXPM, and propertiesXPM) are in XPM format and are in the header file tbxpm.h included on line 4. Each button is defined by the macro GNOMEUIINFO_RADIOITEM(). Other than the terminating GNOME_APP_UI_ENDOF_INFO type, all of the members of the array must be of the type GNOME_APP_UI_ITEM, which is the type used by the GNOMEUIINFO_RADIOITEM() macro.

Everything needed to create the radio buttons is included in the defining arrays, so the menu is constructed as usual with the call to `gnome_app_create_toolbar()` on line 55. The resulting toolbar is shown with the first button selected in Figure 8-25, and the second button selected in Figure 8-26.

Figure 8-25: The first button selected in a set of toolbar radio buttons

Figure 8-26: The second button selected in a set of toolbar radio buttons

Each menu button has its own callback function (defined on lines 65, 73, and 81) and each callback function has two possible choices. Whenever a callback is made, it must be determined whether this is the button being selected, or whether the selection of another button is causing this one to be deselected. When a button is selected, the return value from `gtk_toggle_button_get_active()` indicates that it is active by returning a nonzero value. Whenever a radio button is selected, there are two callbacks. The newly selected button issues one callback, and the button that previously was selected (and is becoming deselected) issues another callback. If the user selects a button that already is active, there is only one callback, and the button remains active.

Toggle Buttons in a Menu

A toggle button changes state each time the mouse is used to select it. If it is on, a mouse click turns it off; if it is off, the mouse turns it on. The following example demonstrates how to include toggle buttons as part of a menu.

```
1 /** mtoggle.c **/
2 #include <gnome.h>
3
4 static void dummyCallback(GtkObject *,gpointer);
5 static void toggleOne(GtkObject *,gpointer);
6 static void toggleTwo(GtkObject *,gpointer);
7 static void toggleThree(GtkObject *,gpointer);
```

```
 8
 9 gint eventDelete(GtkWidget *widget,
10        GdkEvent *event,gpointer data);
11 gint eventDestroy(GtkWidget *widget,
12        GdkEvent *event,gpointer data);
13
14 GnomeUIInfo toggleMenu[] = {
15     GNOMEUIINFO_MENU_NEW_GAME_ITEM(dummyCallback,NULL),
16     GNOMEUIINFO_SEPARATOR,
17     GNOMEUIINFO_TOGGLEITEM("Toggle One",
18        "The first toggle button",
19        toggleOne,NULL),
20     GNOMEUIINFO_TOGGLEITEM("Toggle Two",
21        "The second toggle button",
22        toggleTwo,NULL),
23     GNOMEUIINFO_TOGGLEITEM("Toggle Three",
24        "The third toggle button",
25        toggleThree,NULL),
26     GNOMEUIINFO_SEPARATOR,
27     GNOMEUIINFO_MENU_PAUSE_GAME_ITEM(dummyCallback,NULL),
28     GNOMEUIINFO_END
29 };
30
31 GnomeUIInfo mainMenu[] = {
32     GNOMEUIINFO_SUBTREE("Toggle Buttons",toggleMenu),
33     GNOMEUIINFO_END
34 };
35
36 int main(int argc,char *argv[])
37 {
38     GtkWidget *app;
39
40     gnome_init("mtoggle","1.0",argc,argv);
41     app = gnome_app_new("mtoggle","Menu Toggles");
42     gtk_window_set_default_size(GTK_WINDOW(app),200,100);
43     gtk_signal_connect(GTK_OBJECT(app),"delete_event",
44            GTK_SIGNAL_FUNC(eventDelete),NULL);
45     gtk_signal_connect(GTK_OBJECT(app),"destroy",
46            GTK_SIGNAL_FUNC(eventDestroy),NULL);
47
48     gnome_app_create_menus(GNOME_APP(app),mainMenu);
49
50     gtk_widget_show_all(app);
51     gtk_main();
52     exit(0);
53 }
54 static void dummyCallback(GtkObject *object,gpointer data)
55 {
56     gnome_ok_dialog("The dummy callback executed.");
57 }
58 static void toggleOne(GtkObject *object,
```

```
59              gpointer data) {
60      if(GTK_CHECK_MENU_ITEM(object)->active)
61          gnome_ok_dialog("The toggle one button is on.");
62      else
63          gnome_ok_dialog("The toggle one button is off.");
64 }
65 static void toggleTwo(GtkObject *object,
66              gpointer data) {
67      if(GTK_CHECK_MENU_ITEM(object)->active)
68          gnome_ok_dialog("The toggle two button is on.");
69      else
70          gnome_ok_dialog("The toggle two button is off.");
71 }
72 static void toggleThree(GtkObject *object,
73              gpointer data) {
74      if(GTK_CHECK_MENU_ITEM(object)->active)
75          gnome_ok_dialog("The toggle three button is on.");
76      else
77          gnome_ok_dialog("The toggle three button is off.");
78 }
79 gint eventDelete(GtkWidget *widget,
80          GdkEvent *event,gpointer data) {
81      return(FALSE);
82 }
83 gint eventDestroy(GtkWidget *widget,
84          GdkEvent *event,gpointer data) {
85      gtk_main_quit();
86      return(0);
87 }
```

The pull-down portion of the menu is defined by the array on lines 14 through 29. Each toggle button is defined by using a GNOMEUIINFO_TOGGLEITEM() macro. The toggle buttons are grouped together in this example, but there is no need to do so. There is no interaction between them, as there is with radio buttons.

The menu is created from the set of GnomeUIInfo arrays by the call to gnome_app_ create_menus() on line 48. The resulting menu is shown in Figure 8-27.

Figure 8-27: Toggle buttons on a menu

The same callback function is called by a toggle button whether it is being toggled on or off. For example, the callback function for the first toggle button is named toggleOne() and is defined on line 58. If the button is being toggled on, the value of `active` (being tested on line 60) is nonzero. If the button is being toggled off, the value of `active` is zero.

Toggle Buttons in a Toolbar

A toggle button changes its state each time a mouse button is used to select it. If it is on, a mouse click switches it off; if it is off, the mouse switches it on. The following example demonstrates how you can include toggle buttons as part of a toolbar.

```
1 /** tbtoggle.c **/
2 #include <gnome.h>
3
4 #include "tbxpm.h"
5
6 static void dummyCallback(GtkObject *,gpointer);
7 static void toggleOne(GtkObject *,gpointer);
8 static void toggleTwo(GtkObject *,gpointer);
9 static void toggleThree(GtkObject *,gpointer);
10
11 gint eventDelete(GtkWidget *widget,
12        GdkEvent *event,gpointer data);
13 gint eventDestroy(GtkWidget *widget,
14        GdkEvent *event,gpointer data);
15
16 static GnomeUIInfo toggleToolbar[] = {
17     { GNOME_APP_UI_ITEM,"New",
18       "Create a new file",dummyCallback,NULL,NULL,
19       GNOME_APP_PIXMAP_STOCK,GNOME_STOCK_PIXMAP_NEW,
20       0,0,NULL },
21     GNOMEUIINFO_SEPARATOR,
22     GNOMEUIINFO_TOGGLEITEM("Toggle One",
23         "The first toggle button",
24         toggleOne,downXPM),
25     GNOMEUIINFO_TOGGLEITEM("Toggle Two",
26         "The second toggle button",
27         toggleTwo,attachXPM),
28     GNOMEUIINFO_TOGGLEITEM("Toggle Three",
29         "The third toggle button",
30         toggleThree,propertiesXPM),
31     GNOMEUIINFO_SEPARATOR,
32     { GNOME_APP_UI_ITEM,"Save as",
33       "Save to a new file",dummyCallback,NULL,NULL,
34       GNOME_APP_PIXMAP_STOCK,GNOME_STOCK_PIXMAP_SAVE_AS,
35       0,0,NULL },
36     GNOMEUIINFO_END
37 };
38
39 int main(int argc,char *argv[])
```

```
40 {
41     GtkWidget *app;
42
43     gnome_init("tbtoggle","1.0",argc,argv);
44     app = gnome_app_new("tbtoggle","Toolbar Toggles");
45     gtk_signal_connect(GTK_OBJECT(app),"delete_event",
46             GTK_SIGNAL_FUNC(eventDelete),NULL);
47     gtk_signal_connect(GTK_OBJECT(app),"destroy",
48             GTK_SIGNAL_FUNC(eventDestroy),NULL);
49
50     gnome_app_create_toolbar(GNOME_APP(app),toggleToolbar);
51     gtk_widget_show_all(app);
52
53     gtk_main();
54     exit(0);
55 }
56 static void dummyCallback(GtkObject *object,gpointer data)
57 {
58     gnome_ok_dialog("The dummy callback executed.");
59 }
60 static void toggleOne(GtkObject *object,
61             gpointer data) {
62     if(gtk_toggle_button_get_active(
63                 GTK_TOGGLE_BUTTON(object)))
64         gnome_ok_dialog("The toggle one button is on.");
65     else
66         gnome_ok_dialog("The toggle one button is off.");
67 }
68 static void toggleTwo(GtkObject *object,
69             gpointer data) {
70     if(gtk_toggle_button_get_active(
71                 GTK_TOGGLE_BUTTON(object)))
72         gnome_ok_dialog("The toggle two button is on.");
73     else
74         gnome_ok_dialog("The toggle two button is off.");
75 }
76 static void toggleThree(GtkObject *object,
77             gpointer data) {
78     if(gtk_toggle_button_get_active(
79                 GTK_TOGGLE_BUTTON(object)))
80         gnome_ok_dialog("The toggle three button is on.");
81     else
82         gnome_ok_dialog("The toggle three button is off.");
83 }
84 gint eventDelete(GtkWidget *widget,
85         GdkEvent *event,gpointer data) {
86     return(FALSE);
87 }
88 gint eventDestroy(GtkWidget *widget,
89         GdkEvent *event,gpointer data) {
90     gtk_main_quit();
```

```
91      return(0);
92 }
```

The toolbar is defined by the array on lines 16 through 37. Each toggle button is defined by using a GNOMEUIINFO_TOGGLEITEM() macro, and each toggle button is assigned a graphics icon in the form of XPM data contained in the header file tbxpm.h. The toggle buttons are grouped together between a pair of separators in this example, but there is no need to do so since there is no interaction between them, as there is with radio buttons.

The toolbar is created from the GnomeUIInfo array by the call to gnome_app_ create_toolbar() on line 50. The resulting toolbar is shown in Figure 8-28.

Figure 8-28: Toggle buttons on a toolbar

The same callback function is called by a toggle button whether it is being switched on or off. For example, the callback function for the first toggle button is named toggleOne() and is defined on line 60. If the button is being toggled on, the returned value from gtk_toggle_button_get_active() is nonzero. If the button is being toggled off, the returned value is zero.

Summary

In a GUI interface, the user interacts with the applications by selecting items with the mouse. A menu bar enables the user to find and select things by name (with an optional icon) and a toolbar enables the user to find things by an icon (with optional text). This chapter showed you how to create menus and toolbars:

✦ Menus and toolbars are defined by arrays of structures. The array members specify everything needed by the menu or toolbar item, including callback functions and graphics. Most of the members of these structures can be generated from macros supplied as a part of GNOME.

✦ GNOME includes a set of predefined menu macros, and a suggested menu layout, that you can use to promote consistent interfaces among GNOME applications.

✦ A toolbar can be docked on any one of the four sides of the application window. A menu can be docked at the top or bottom of the window. Both the toolbar and the menu can be "torn off" of the application window and placed anywhere on the display. You can create a popup menu that appears whenever the application window is selected by the mouse.

✦ Both menus and toolbars can have their members dynamically enabled and disabled.

✦ Both menus and toolbars can include toggle buttons and sets of radio buttons.

This chapter concludes the first section of the book that contains all the basic and structural knowledge you will need to program a complete application. The second section of the book is primarily designed to go into detail on various aspects of programming an application, but some new things will also be introduced. For example, the next chapter discusses the GnomeCanvas — a special kind of container widget that can contain certain types of displayable objects.

✦   ✦   ✦

Step by Step

✦   ✦   ✦   ✦

In This Chapter

✦   ✦   ✦   ✦

The GnomeCanvas Widget

◆ ◆ ◆ ◆

In This Chapter

Using the
GnomeCanvas
as a high-level
widget with low-
level capabilities

Sorting out the
mouse information
so it is directed to
the appropriate
GnomeCanvas item

Organizing the
display of items of
different types and
sizes

Drawing polygons
and installing them
among the other
GnomeCanvas items

Reshaping display-
able objects using
affine transforms

◆ ◆ ◆ ◆

T he GnomeCanvas can be used to draw figures, display graphics, position widgets, and more. If you wish to create windows that change dynamically, or if you want detailed control over the position and size of the widgets on a window, the GnomeCanvas can do that for you.

A GnomeCanvas is a window with a container widget called a *group*. By specifying the coordinates and the size, you can add any number of *items* to the group. An item can be some other widget, such as a button, or even another container, such as a horizontal box containing widgets of its own. A group can even contain other groups. There are some special items that are designed to be included in the canvas. This chapter has an example of each of the different item types.

When working with items in a canvas, you may need to access the fields inside the GdkEvent issued by an item. Also, GdkEvents are used throughout the rest of this book. The last part of this chapter lists all the GdkEvent types and explains their purpose and the data included by each one.

The GnomeCanvas Widget

The GnomeCanvas is a high-level widget that can be used to display a collection of graphic structures. It is high level in the sense that it was devised for use in the creation of interactive or dynamic graphic displays. It can display lines, rectangles, circles, and text.

Each graphic item is constructed as an independent object and can be moved from one place to another, resized, and otherwise modified independently. There are a collection of affine transform functions that can be used to modify the shape, size, and location of the graphic items. Also, each item can be set to receive events from the mouse and keyboard.

You can organize canvas items into groups. When a GnomeCanvas is created, it has a single root group and all items added to the canvas are added to that group. If your graphic becomes complicated—you have a lot of graphic items to manipulate—you may find it more convenient to organize them into separate groups. All of the groups are organized into a hierarchical tree. The members of a group (whether individual items or other groups) have a stacking order. There is one member that is at the bottom and is drawn first, then the next-to-bottom member is drawn, and on up until the top member is drawn last. This draws the top member over the top of all the others on the display.

The following program creates a window containing a GnomeCanvas and uses it to display a rectangle and a line with two segments. The window produced by this program is shown in Figure 9-1.

```
 1 /** canvas.c **/
 2 #include <gnome.h>
 3
 4 gint eventDelete(GtkWidget *widget,
 5         GdkEvent *event,gpointer data);
 6 gint eventDestroy(GtkWidget *widget,
 7         GdkEvent *event,gpointer data);
 8
 9 #define WIDTH 400
10 #define HEIGHT 200
11
12 int main(int argc,char *argv[])
13 {
14     GtkWidget *app;
15     GtkWidget *canvas;
16     GnomeCanvasPoints *points;
17     GnomeCanvasGroup *rootGroup;
18
19     gnome_init("canvas","1.0",argc,argv);
20     app = gnome_app_new("canvas","Gnome Canvas");
21     gtk_signal_connect(GTK_OBJECT(app),"delete_event",
22             GTK_SIGNAL_FUNC(eventDelete),NULL);
23     gtk_signal_connect(GTK_OBJECT(app),"destroy",
24             GTK_SIGNAL_FUNC(eventDestroy),NULL);
25
26     canvas = gnome_canvas_new();
27     gtk_widget_set_usize(canvas,WIDTH,HEIGHT);
28     gnome_canvas_set_scroll_region(GNOME_CANVAS(canvas),
29             0.0,0.0,WIDTH,HEIGHT);
30     rootGroup = gnome_canvas_root(GNOME_CANVAS(canvas));
```

```
31        gnome_app_set_contents(GNOME_APP(app),canvas);
32
33        gnome_canvas_item_new(rootGroup,
34                         gnome_canvas_rect_get_type(),
35                         "x1",(double)10,
36                         "y1",(double)10,
37                         "x2",(double)(WIDTH - 10),
38                         "y2",(double)(HEIGHT - 10),
39                         "fill_color","white",
40                         "outline_color","black",
41                         NULL);
42
43        points = gnome_canvas_points_new(3);
44        points->coords[0] = 20;
45        points->coords[1] = 20;
46        points->coords[2] = WIDTH - 20;
47        points->coords[3] = HEIGHT / 2;
48        points->coords[4] = 20;
49        points->coords[5] = HEIGHT - 20;
50        gnome_canvas_item_new(rootGroup,
51                         gnome_canvas_line_get_type(),
52                         "points",points,
53                         "fill_color","black",
54                         "width_pixels",2,
55                         NULL);
56        gnome_canvas_points_free(points);
57
58        gtk_widget_show_all(app);
59        gtk_main();
60        exit(0);
61 }
62 gint eventDelete(GtkWidget *widget,
63         GdkEvent *event,gpointer data) {
64        return(FALSE);
65 }
66 gint eventDestroy(GtkWidget *widget,
67         GdkEvent *event,gpointer data) {
68        gtk_main_quit();
69        return(0);
70 }
```

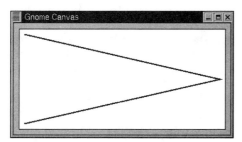

Figure 9-1: Using a GnomeCanvas to display shapes and lines

An empty and uninitialized GnomeCanvas object is created on line 26 by the call to gnome_canvas_new(). Line 27 calls gtk_widget_set_usize() to specify the height and width of the canvas. Once the overall size is determined, it is necessary to specify a rectangle within the canvas that is to be the displayed area. The size of the viewable area is specified by the call to gnome_canvas_set_scroll_region() on line 28. In simple cases, such as this one, the displayed area is set to fill the entire canvas. But in an application that needs to display regions of a larger graphic, you can use this positioning technique to specify both the size and location of the displayed area.

The origin of the coordinate system is in the upper-left corner of the canvas — that is, the upper-left corner of both x and y equal zero. The value of y increases downward and x increases to the right. The origin is always measured in terms of the entire canvas no matter what the current setting is for the scroll region. For example, if the upper-left corner of the scroll region begins with the x value defined at 10 — and you want to display an item at the left of the displayed area — then you need to set x to 10 because setting x to 0 would place it 10 pixels beyond the displayed area. However, as we shall see later in this chapter, it is possible to translate the coordinates of each item to a more convenient set of values.

The call to gnome_canvas_root() on line 30 retrieves the root GnomeCanvasGroup. The purpose of a GnomeCanvas object is to display graphical items, so it must contain all the positioning and other information necessary to draw the items on its window. To do this, the canvas uses the root GnomeCanvasGroup object as a container for these items. Items are not added directly to the canvas — instead, they are added to the root group contained in the canvas. Because a GnomeCanvasGroup object can contain other GnomeCanvasGroup objects, you are able to create groups within groups in a hierarchical tree. Each group can contain multiple graphic items and keep them in such a way that they are drawn in a specific order. This order determines which graphic object is drawn later and thus on top of the ones already there. Also, by creating subgroups, you are able to manipulate a group of graphic items as a single unit.

The call to gnome_app_set_contents() on line 31 adds the canvas as the only widget to be displayed in the application window. If the main window were a GtkWindow instead of a GnomeApp, a call to gtk_container_add() would have been used to insert the canvas.

The call to gnome_canvas_item_new() on line 33 is used to create a rectangle and add it to the root group. The first argument is the group and the second specifies the type of object being created. The rest of the arguments are used to pass configuration information. Notice that the arguments on lines 35 through 40 are in pairs. The first member of each pair is the name of the parameter and the second is the value that is associated with that name. In this case, the parameter names "x1", "y1", "x2", and "y2" specify the coordinates of the four corners of the rectangle. The parameter named "fill_color" specifies the fill color for the rectangle. The parameter named "outline_color" specifies the color of the border that surrounds the rectangle. The last argument, on line 41, is NULL so the called routine can recognize the end of the variable length array of arguments.

The call to gnome_canvas_item_new() on line 50 creates and adds a line with two segments. The first two arguments specify the group and the type of the object being created. There are three named arguments. The parameter named "width_pixels" has an argument value of 2, specifying the width of the line. The "fill_color" specifies "black" as the color of the line. The parameter named "points" passes the address of a GnomeCanvasPoints object containing an array of x and y points. Each point in the array is a vertex of the segmented line.

The GnomeCanvasPoints object is created by the call to gnome_canvas_points_ new() on line 43. The total number of points (in this example, there are 3) is passed to the function so an array of the proper size is created. There is only one array, and each point requires two values, so the even-numbered members of the coord array contain the x values and the odd numbered members contains the y values. If you need to iterate through the complete list of points, you can do it like this:

```
points = gnome_canvas_points_new(19);
for(i=0; i<19; i++) {
    /**  calculate x and y **/
    points->coords[i*2] = x;
    points->coords[(i*2)+1] = y;
}
```

Because the list of points is in allocated memory, and it normally serves no purpose there once the graphic object is constructed, the memory is freed in the call to gnome_canvas_points_free() on line 56.

The Mouse, the Event, and the Stacking Order

Whenever a new item is added to a group, it is added to the top of the list. That means, when the group is drawn in the window, the last item added is the last one drawn and the last to appear on top of any others in the same group. This stacking order can be changed at any time. The following program overlaps three graphic items, as shown in Figure 9-2, and attaches a callback function to them so the one with the mouse pointer inside it pops up to the top of the stack.

```
 1 /** canvasorder.c **/
 2 #include <gnome.h>
 3
 4 gint eventDelete(GtkWidget *widget,
 5         GdkEvent *event,gpointer data);
 6 gint eventDestroy(GtkWidget *widget,
 7         GdkEvent *event,gpointer data);
 8 static gint itemEvent(GnomeCanvasItem *item,
 9         GdkEvent *event,gpointer data);
10
```

```
11 #define HORIZ 100
12 #define VERT 60
13 #define WIDTH (HORIZ * 6)
14 #define HEIGHT (VERT * 6)
15
16 int main(int argc,char *argv[])
17 {
18     GtkWidget *app;
19     GtkWidget *canvas;
20     GnomeCanvasGroup *rootGroup;
21     GnomeCanvasItem *item;
22
23     gnome_init("canvasorder","1.0",argc,argv);
24     app = gnome_app_new("canvasorder",
25             "Gnome Canvas Order");
26     gtk_signal_connect(GTK_OBJECT(app),"delete_event",
27             GTK_SIGNAL_FUNC(eventDelete),NULL);
28     gtk_signal_connect(GTK_OBJECT(app),"destroy",
29             GTK_SIGNAL_FUNC(eventDestroy),NULL);
30
31     canvas = gnome_canvas_new();
32     gtk_widget_set_usize(canvas,WIDTH,HEIGHT);
33     gnome_canvas_set_scroll_region(GNOME_CANVAS(canvas),
34             0.0,0.0,WIDTH,HEIGHT);
35     rootGroup = gnome_canvas_root(GNOME_CANVAS(canvas));
36     gnome_app_set_contents(GNOME_APP(app),canvas);
37
38     item = gnome_canvas_item_new(rootGroup,
39                     gnome_canvas_rect_get_type(),
40                     "x1",(double)(HORIZ * 1),
41                     "y1",(double)(VERT * 1),
42                     "x2",(double)(HORIZ * 3),
43                     "y2",(double)(VERT * 3),
44                     "fill_color","white",
45                     "outline_color","black",
46                     NULL);
47     gtk_signal_connect(GTK_OBJECT(item),"event",
48             (GtkSignalFunc)itemEvent,NULL);
49
50     item = gnome_canvas_item_new(rootGroup,
51                     gnome_canvas_ellipse_get_type(),
52                     "x1",(double)(HORIZ * 2),
53                     "y1",(double)(VERT * 2),
54                     "x2",(double)(HORIZ * 4),
55                     "y2",(double)(VERT * 4),
56                     "fill_color","blue",
57                     "outline_color","black",
58                     NULL);
59     gtk_signal_connect(GTK_OBJECT(item),"event",
60             (GtkSignalFunc)itemEvent,NULL);
61
```

```
62      item = gnome_canvas_item_new(rootGroup,
63                      gnome_canvas_rect_get_type(),
64                      "x1",(double)(HORIZ * 3),
65                      "y1",(double)(VERT * 3),
66                      "x2",(double)(HORIZ * 5),
67                      "y2",(double)(VERT * 5),
68                      "fill_color","black",
69                      "outline_color","white",
70                      NULL);
71      gtk_signal_connect(GTK_OBJECT(item),"event",
72              (GtkSignalFunc)itemEvent,NULL);
73
74      gtk_widget_show_all(app);
75      gtk_main();
76      exit(0);
77 }
78 static gint itemEvent(GnomeCanvasItem *item,
79        GdkEvent *event,gpointer data) {
80      if(event->type == GDK_ENTER_NOTIFY)
81          gnome_canvas_item_raise_to_top(item);
82      return(0);
83 }
84 gint eventDelete(GtkWidget *widget,
85        GdkEvent *event,gpointer data) {
86      return(FALSE);
87 }
88 gint eventDestroy(GtkWidget *widget,
89        GdkEvent *event,gpointer data) {
90      gtk_main_quit();
91      return(0);
92 }
```

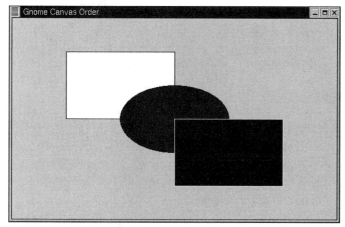

Figure 9-2: Three overlapped canvas items showing their stacking order

The constant value defined on lines 11 through 14 are used to define the layout of the canvas items. The values of HORIZ and VERT are used to position and size each of the figures, and the values of WIDTH and HEIGHT are the overall size of the canvas.

The canvas is created and configured on lines 31 through 34. By a call to gnome_canvas_root() on line 35, the root group is retrieved. The canvas is set as the contents of the GNOME application window with the call to gnome_app_set_contents() on line 36.

The first of the three shapes is a rectangle created by the call to gnome_canvas_item_new() on lines 38 through 46. The first argument is the group to which the item is to be attached, while the second argument defines the type of the object. The next four arguments specify the coordinates of the four corners of the rectangle, the outline color, and the fill color. On line 47, the call to the function gtk_signal_connect() specifies that the callback function itemEvent() be called for every event relating to the item.

Two more items — an ellipse and another rectangle — are created on lines 50 through 72. These items are assigned the same callback function as the first shape. The window this displays was shown in Figure 9-2.

The callback function itemEvent() on line 78 is called once for every event of any kind that is reported to the item. As you can see from the parameter list, the first parameter is the item causing the callback and the second is the event itself. There are several types of events that can be contained in a GdkEvent struct, as shown in Table 9-2 later in this chapter. The callback function, on lines 80 and 81, responds to the GDK_ENTER_NOTIFY (issued whenever the mouse pointer is moved from outside to inside the item) and moves the item to the top with a call to gnome_canvas_item_raise_to_top().

There is a family of functions that you can use to reposition the items in the stack. The opposite of the function used in this example is one that pushes an item down to the bottom of the stack:

```
gnome_canvas_item_lower_to_bottom(item);
```

You can move items relative to one another by moving an item up or down a certain number of places. For example, if you have an item at position 7 in the stack and you want to move it to position 5, you can move it up those two positions like this:

```
gnome_canvas_item_raise(item,2);
```

You also can move items down in the stack. For example, the following function moves an item at position 3 down to position 8:

```
gnome_canvas_item_lower(item,5);
```

Events Passing Down to Canvas Items

The GnomeCanvas is a single window used to display the various items attached to
it. Whenever a mouse event arrives and the location of the event shows it is within
the exposed boundary of one of the items, the event is passed on to the item. Not
all events are forwarded—just those having to deal with mouse positions and
movements.

Note
There is a more detailed description of the different kinds of GdkEvents at the
end of this chapter. Items in a GnomeCanvas window receive *only* mouse
events—the other events are fielded and processed by the GnomeCanvas or its
parent window.

The following program is a variation on the previous example, with event information
listed for one of the items on display.

```
 1 /** canvascall.c **/
 2 #include <gnome.h>
 3
 4 gint eventDelete(GtkWidget *widget,
 5         GdkEvent *event,gpointer data);
 6 gint eventDestroy(GtkWidget *widget,
 7         GdkEvent *event,gpointer data);
 8 static gint itemEvent(GnomeCanvasItem *item,
 9         GdkEvent *event,gpointer data);
10 static gint rectangleEvent(GnomeCanvasItem *item,
11         GdkEvent *event,gpointer data);
12 void describeEventButton(gchar *name,GdkEvent *event);
13 void describeEventMotion(gchar *name,GdkEvent *event);
14 void describeEventCrossing(gchar *name,GdkEvent *event);
15
16 #define HORIZ 100
17 #define VERT 60
18 #define WIDTH (HORIZ * 6)
19 #define HEIGHT (VERT * 6)
20
21 int main(int argc,char *argv[])
22 {
23     GtkWidget *app;
24     GtkWidget *canvas;
25     GnomeCanvasGroup *rootGroup;
26     GnomeCanvasItem *item;
27
28     gnome_init("canvascall","1.0",argc,argv);
29     app = gnome_app_new("canvascall",
30             "Gnome Canvas Order");
31     gtk_signal_connect(GTK_OBJECT(app),"delete_event",
32             GTK_SIGNAL_FUNC(eventDelete),NULL);
```

```
33      gtk_signal_connect(GTK_OBJECT(app),"destroy",
34              GTK_SIGNAL_FUNC(eventDestroy),NULL);
35
36      canvas = gnome_canvas_new();
37      gtk_widget_set_usize(canvas,WIDTH,HEIGHT);
38      gnome_canvas_set_scroll_region(GNOME_CANVAS(canvas),
39              0.0,0.0,WIDTH,HEIGHT);
40      rootGroup = gnome_canvas_root(GNOME_CANVAS(canvas));
41      gnome_app_set_contents(GNOME_APP(app),canvas);
42
43      item = gnome_canvas_item_new(rootGroup,
44                      gnome_canvas_ellipse_get_type(),
45                      "x1",(double)(HORIZ * 1),
46                      "y1",(double)(VERT * 1),
47                      "x2",(double)(HORIZ * 3),
48                      "y2",(double)(VERT * 3),
49                      "fill_color","white",
50                      "outline_color","black",
51                      NULL);
52      gtk_signal_connect(GTK_OBJECT(item),"event",
53              (GtkSignalFunc)itemEvent,NULL);
54
55      item = gnome_canvas_item_new(rootGroup,
56                      gnome_canvas_rect_get_type(),
57                      "x1",(double)(HORIZ * 2),
58                      "y1",(double)(VERT * 2),
59                      "x2",(double)(HORIZ * 4),
60                      "y2",(double)(VERT * 4),
61                      "fill_color","blue",
62                      "outline_color","black",
63                      NULL);
64      gtk_signal_connect(GTK_OBJECT(item),"event",
65              (GtkSignalFunc)itemEvent,NULL);
66      gtk_signal_connect(GTK_OBJECT(item),"event",
67              (GtkSignalFunc)rectangleEvent,NULL);
68
69      item = gnome_canvas_item_new(rootGroup,
70                      gnome_canvas_ellipse_get_type(),
71                      "x1",(double)(HORIZ * 3),
72                      "y1",(double)(VERT * 3),
73                      "x2",(double)(HORIZ * 5),
74                      "y2",(double)(VERT * 5),
75                      "fill_color","black",
76                      "outline_color","white",
77                      NULL);
78      gtk_signal_connect(GTK_OBJECT(item),"event",
79              (GtkSignalFunc)itemEvent,NULL);
80
81      gtk_widget_show_all(app);
82      gtk_main();
83      exit(0);
```

```
 84 }
 85 static gint itemEvent(GnomeCanvasItem *item,
 86         GdkEvent *event,gpointer data) {
 87     if(event->type == GDK_BUTTON_PRESS)
 88         gnome_canvas_item_raise_to_top(item);
 89     return(0);
 90 }
 91 static gint rectangleEvent(GnomeCanvasItem *item,
 92         GdkEvent *event,gpointer data) {
 93     switch(event->any.type) {
 94     case GDK_ENTER_NOTIFY:
 95         describeEventCrossing("GDK_ENTER_NOTIFY",event);
 96         break;
 97     case GDK_LEAVE_NOTIFY:
 98         describeEventCrossing("GDK_LEAVE_NOTIFY",event);
 99         break;
100     case GDK_MOTION_NOTIFY:
101         describeEventMotion("GDK_MOTION_NOTIFY",event);
102         break;
103     case GDK_BUTTON_PRESS:
104         describeEventButton("GDK_BUTTON_PRESS",event);
105         break;
106     case GDK_2BUTTON_PRESS:
107         describeEventButton("GDK_2BUTTON_PRESS",event);
108         break;
109     case GDK_3BUTTON_PRESS:
110         describeEventButton("GDK_3BUTTON_PRESS",event);
111         break;
112     case GDK_BUTTON_RELEASE:
113         describeEventButton("GDK_BUTTON_RELEASE",event);
114         break;
115     default:
116         g_print("An unexpected event......\n");
117         break;
118     }
119     g_print("    GdkEvent #%d",event->type);
120     if(event->any.send_event)
121         g_print(" (from another client,");
122     else
123         g_print(" (from server,");
124     if(event->any.window != NULL) {
125         if(data == NULL)
126             g_print(" with no data)\n");
127         else
128             g_print(" with data %p)\n",data);
129     }
130     return(0);
131 }
132 void describeEventButton(gchar *name,GdkEvent *event)
133 {
134     g_print("%s -- GdkEventButton\n",name);
```

```
135      g_print("    x=%g y=%g xtilt=%g ytilt=%g"
136                   " pressure=%g button=%d\n",
137           event->button.x,event->button.y,
138           event->button.xtilt,event->button.ytilt,
139           event->button.pressure,event->button.button);
140      g_print("    x_root=%g y_root=%g  time=%u"
141                   " state=0x%08X\n",
142           event->button.x_root,event->button.y_root,
143           event->button.time,event->button.state);
144 }
145 void describeEventMotion(gchar *name,GdkEvent *event)
146 {
147      g_print("%s -- GdkEventMotion\n",name);
148      g_print("    x=%g y=%g xtilt=%g ytilt=%g"
149                   " pressure=%g is_hint=%s\n",
150           event->motion.x,event->motion.y,
151           event->motion.xtilt,event->motion.ytilt,
152           event->motion.pressure,
153           event->motion.is_hint ? "TRUE" : "FALSE");
154      g_print("    x_root=%g y_root=%g  time=%u"
155                   " state=0x%08X\n",
156           event->motion.x_root,event->motion.y_root,
157           event->motion.time,event->motion.state);
158 }
159 void describeEventCrossing(gchar *name,GdkEvent *event)
160 {
161      gchar *mode =
162       event->crossing.mode == GDK_CROSSING_NORMAL
163       ? "Normal" : event->crossing.mode == GDK_CROSSING_GRAB
164       ? "Grab" : "Ungrab";
165
166      g_print("%s -- GdkEventCrossing\n",name);
167      g_print("    x=%g y=%g x_root=%g y_root=%g focus=%s\n",
168           event->crossing.x,event->crossing.y,
169           event->crossing.x_root,event->crossing.y_root,
170           event->crossing.focus ? "TRUE" : "FALSE");
171      g_print("    mode=%s time=%u detail=%d state=0x%08X\n",
172           mode,event->crossing.time,
173           event->crossing.detail,event->crossing.state);
174 }
175 gint eventDelete(GtkWidget *widget,
176         GdkEvent *event,gpointer data) {
177      return(FALSE);
178 }
179 gint eventDestroy(GtkWidget *widget,
180         GdkEvent *event,gpointer data) {
181      gtk_main_quit();
182      return(0);
183 }
```

Lines 36 through 41 create and initialize a GnomeCanvas, get the address of the root group, and attach the canvas to the application window.

Three items are created and added to the root group on lines 43 through 79. On lines 52, 64, and 78, the three items are connected to the callback function itemEvent(). The second item, the rectangle (shown in Figure 9-3), is also connected to the callback function rectangleEvent() by the call to gtk_signal_connect() on line 66. An item can be connected to any number of callback functions, and each one is called for every event. In this program, it is convenient to have one callback respond to mouse clicks and move the selected item.

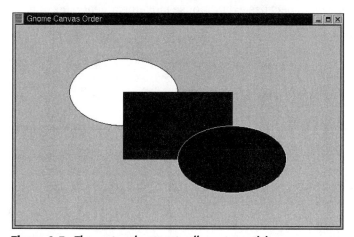

Figure 9-3: The rectangle reports all mouse activity

The callback function itemEvent() on line 85 is called for every mouse click on each item in the window. The call to gnome_canvas_item_raise_to_top() on line 88 places the item in front of all the other items in the canvas window.

The callback function rectangleEvent() is called only when some kind of event occurs on the rectangle in the center. The function doesn't take any action involved with displaying the item. Instead, it lists information contained in the event. There are different kinds of events, with a different data layout for each one, but they all arrive as a GdkEvent — a union of all of the event types. The first data field for all of the event structs is a type field, which can be checked to determine the actual format of the data. Beginning on line 104, there is a switch/case statement that detects the type of event and calls a function that lists data for that type. There are more types of events than there are event formats. (For example, all button clicks share the same data layout, whether they are single, double, or more.)

There is a callback function that displays the data supplied with each of the seven types of mouse events. The function `describeEventButton()` on line 132 is called with a `GdkEventButton` struct whenever a mouse button is pressed. The function `describeEventMotion()` on line 145 is called with a `GdkEventMotion` struct whenever the mouse pointer moves from one location to another within an item. The function `describeEventCrossing()` on line 159 is called with a `GdkEventCrossing` struct whenever the mouse pointer crosses the boundary at the edge of an item.

The following is an example output from the program with the mouse pointer entering the item, having the first button pressed, moving the mouse within the item, releasing the button, and then moving again to exit the item. There are a lot of `GdkEventMotion` events because every mouse movement generates one, so I deleted a number of them from the list:

```
GDK_ENTER_NOTIFY  --   GdkEventCrossing
     x=345 y=120 x_root=445 y_root=248 focus=FALSE
     mode=Normal time=4027445079 detail=0 state=0x00000000
     GdkEvent #10 (from server, with no data)
GDK_MOTION_NOTIFY  --   GdkEventMotion
     x=345 y=120 xtilt=0 ytilt=0 pressure=0.5 is_hint=FALSE
     x_root=445 y_root=248   time=4027449171 state=0x00000000
     GdkEvent #3 (from server, with no data)
GDK_MOTION_NOTIFY  --   GdkEventMotion
     x=345 y=121 xtilt=0 ytilt=0 pressure=0.5 is_hint=FALSE
     x_root=445 y_root=249   time=4027449192 state=0x00000000
     GdkEvent #3 (from server, with no data)
             . . .
GDK_MOTION NOTIFY  --   GdkEventMotion
     x=345 y=135 xtilt=0 ytilt=0 pressure=0.5 is_hint=FALSE
     x_root=445 y_root=263   time=4027449457 state=0x00000000
     GdkEvent #3 (from server, with no data)
GDK_BUTTON_PRESS  -- GdkEventButton
     x=345 y=135 xtilt=0 ytilt=0 pressure=0.5 button=1
     x_root=445 y_root=263   time=4027449967 state=0x00000000
     GdkEvent #4 (from server, with no data)
GDK_MOTION_NOTIFY  --   GdkEventMotion
     x=346 y=135 xtilt=0 ytilt=0 pressure=0.5 is_hint=FALSE
     x_root=446 y_root=263   time=4027450007 state=0x00000100
     GdkEvent #3 (from server, with no data)
GDK_MOTION_NOTIFY  --   GdkEventMotion
     x=346 y=136 xtilt=0 ytilt=0 pressure=0.5 is_hint=FALSE
     x_root=446 y_root=264   time=4027450038 state=0x00000100
     GdkEvent #3 (from server, with no data)
             . . .
GDK_MOTION_NOTIFY  --   GdkEventMotion
     x=363 y=149 xtilt=0 ytilt=0 pressure=0.5 is_hint=FALSE
     x_root=463 y_root=277   time=4027451089 state=0x00000100
     GdkEvent #3 (from server, with no data)
GDK_MOTION_NOTIFY  --   GdkEventMotion
```

```
        x=364 y=149 xtilt=0 ytilt=0 pressure=0.5 is_hint=FALSE
        x_root=464 y_root=277  time=4027451282 state=0x00000100
        GdkEvent #3 (from server, with no data)
GDK_BUTTON_RELEASE -- GdkEventButton
        x=364 y=149 xtilt=0 ytilt=0 pressure=0.5 button=1
        x_root=464 y_root=277  time=4027451619 state=0x00000100
        GdkEvent #7 (from server, with no data)
GDK_MOTION_NOTIFY --  GdkEventMotion
        x=364 y=150 xtilt=0 ytilt=0 pressure=0.5 is_hint=FALSE
        x_root=464 y_root=278  time=4027451925 state=0x00000000
        GdkEvent #3 (from server, with no data)
GDK_MOTION_NOTIFY --  GdkEventMotion
        x=365 y=150 xtilt=0 ytilt=0 pressure=0.5 is_hint=FALSE
        x_root=465 y_root=278  time=4027452159 state=0x00000000
        GdkEvent #3 (from server, with no data)
        . . .
GDK_MOTION_NOTIFY --  GdkEventMotion
        x=396 y=152 xtilt=0 ytilt=0 pressure=0.5 is_hint=FALSE
        x_root=496 y_root=280  time=4027452333 state=0x00000000
        GdkEvent #3 (from server, with no data)
GDK_MOTION_NOTIFY --  GdkEventMotion
        x=398 y=151 xtilt=0 ytilt=0 pressure=0.5 is_hint=FALSE
        x_root=498 y_root=279  time=4027452343 state=0x00000000
        GdkEvent #3 (from server, with no data)
GDK_LEAVE_NOTIFY --  GdkEventCrossing
        x=401 y=151 x_root=501 y_root=279 focus=FALSE
        mode=Normal time=0 detail=0 state=0x00000000
        GdkEvent #11 (from server, with no data)
```

Moving a Canvas Item

You can move the items in a GnomeCanvas window from one place to another by supplying the distance you want the items moved in both the *x* and *y* directions. The following program is basically the same as the preceding examples, except there is a callback function that detects whether a key is held down when the mouse is moved and, if it is, moves the item to a new location.

```
1 /** canvasdrag.c **/
2 #include <gnome.h>
3
4 gint eventDelete(GtkWidget *widget,
5         GdkEvent *event,gpointer data);
6 gint eventDestroy(GtkWidget *widget,
7         GdkEvent *event,gpointer data);
8 static gint dragEvent(GnomeCanvasItem *item,
9         GdkEvent *event,gpointer data);
10
```

```
11 #define HORIZ 100
12 #define VERT 60
13 #define WIDTH (HORIZ * 6)
14 #define HEIGHT (VERT * 6)
15
16 int main(int argc,char *argv[])
17 {
18     GtkWidget *app;
19     GtkWidget *canvas;
20     GnomeCanvasGroup *rootGroup;
21     GnomeCanvasItem *item;
22
23     gnome_init("canvasdrag","1.0",argc,argv);
24     app = gnome_app_new("canvasdrag",
25             "Gnome Canvas Dragging");
26     gtk_signal_connect(GTK_OBJECT(app),"delete_event",
27             GTK_SIGNAL_FUNC(eventDelete),NULL);
28     gtk_signal_connect(GTK_OBJECT(app),"destroy",
29             GTK_SIGNAL_FUNC(eventDestroy),NULL);
30
31     canvas = gnome_canvas_new();
32     gtk_widget_set_usize(canvas,WIDTH,HEIGHT);
33     gnome_canvas_set_scroll_region(GNOME_CANVAS(canvas),
34             0.0,0.0,WIDTH,HEIGHT);
35     rootGroup = gnome_canvas_root(GNOME_CANVAS(canvas));
36     gnome_app_set_contents(GNOME_APP(app),canvas);
37
38     item = gnome_canvas_item_new(rootGroup,
39                     gnome_canvas_rect_get_type(),
40                     "x1",(double)(HORIZ * 1),
41                     "y1",(double)(VERT * 1),
42                     "x2",(double)(HORIZ * 3),
43                     "y2",(double)(VERT * 3),
44                     "fill_color","white",
45                     "outline_color","black",
46                     NULL);
47     gtk_signal_connect(GTK_OBJECT(item),"event",
48             (GtkSignalFunc)dragEvent,NULL);
49
50     item = gnome_canvas_item_new(rootGroup,
51                     gnome_canvas_ellipse_get_type(),
52                     "x1",(double)(HORIZ * 2),
53                     "y1",(double)(VERT * 2),
54                     "x2",(double)(HORIZ * 4),
55                     "y2",(double)(VERT * 4),
56                     "fill_color","blue",
57                     "outline_color","black",
58                     NULL);
59     gtk_signal_connect(GTK_OBJECT(item),"event",
60             (GtkSignalFunc)dragEvent,NULL);
```

```
61
62      item = gnome_canvas_item_new(rootGroup,
63                      gnome_canvas_rect_get_type(),
64                      "x1",(double)(HORIZ * 3),
65                      "y1",(double)(VERT * 3),
66                      "x2",(double)(HORIZ * 5),
67                      "y2",(double)(VERT * 5),
68                      "fill_color","black",
69                      "outline_color","white",
70                      NULL);
71      gtk_signal_connect(GTK_OBJECT(item),"event",
72              (GtkSignalFunc)dragEvent,NULL);
73
74      gtk_widget_show_all(app);
75      gtk_main();
76      exit(0);
77  }
78  static gint dragEvent(GnomeCanvasItem *item,
79          GdkEvent *event,gpointer data) {
80      static gint x;
81      static gint y;
82      gint new_x;
83      gint new_y;
84
85      switch(event->type) {
86      case GDK_MOTION_NOTIFY:
87          if(event->button.state & 0x00000400) {
88              new_x = event->button.x;
89              new_y = event->button.y;
90              gnome_canvas_item_move(item,
91                  (double)(new_x - x),
92                  (double)(new_y - y));
93              x = new_x;
94              y = new_y;
95          }
96          break;
97      case GDK_BUTTON_PRESS:
98          if(event->button.button == 1)
99              gnome_canvas_item_raise_to_top(item);
100         x = event->button.x;
101         y = event->button.y;
102         break;
103     default:
104         break;
105     }
106     return(0);
107 }
108 gint eventDelete(GtkWidget *widget,
109         GdkEvent *event,gpointer data) {
110     return(FALSE);
111 }
```

```
112 gint eventDestroy(GtkWidget *widget,
113         GdkEvent *event,gpointer data) {
114     gtk_main_quit();
115     return(0);
116 }
```

As shown in Figure 9-4, there are three items in the canvas. Each of these items can be moved freely from one place to another because they all use the callback function dragEvent() on line 78.

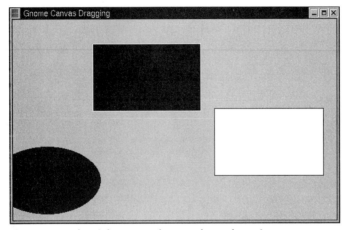

Figure 9-4: The right mouse button drags these items

Lines 80 and 81 define x and y values as static so they retain their values from one callback to the next. These values are needed because an item's move is made according to the *distance* of the move, not the absolute location, and the only way to determine the distance is to find the difference between the old and new locations. This turns out to be very handy for using the mouse pointer to move an item because it is only necessary to track the mouse pointer to generate the distance values required—the actual position of the item being moved doesn't matter.

The case statement on line 86 is executed with every movement of the mouse. Nothing is done unless the right mouse button is held down during the mouse movement. Later in this chapter, with the description of the GdkEvent, Table 9-2 lists the bits to be tested for each of the mouse buttons. To actually move the item, a call is made to gnome_canvas_item_move() with the difference between the previous and current mouse positions. After the move, the stored values of x and y are updated to reflect the new position so the next move distance can be calculated.

The case statement on line 97 is executed with every press of a mouse button. If it is the left button (button number 1), the item is raised to the top of the stack. The values of x and y are set in case this is the beginning of a drag operation.

Canvas Images

An image can be displayed on a GnomeCanvas by converting it to a GdkImlibImage
and then adding it to the canvas as an item. The following example uses XPM
images that were created using the techniques described in Chapter 7.

```
1 /** canvasimage.c **/
2 #include <gnome.h>
3
4 #include "logo.xpm"
5 #include "foot.xpm"
6
7 gint eventDelete(GtkWidget *widget,
8         GdkEvent *event,gpointer data);
9 gint eventDestroy(GtkWidget *widget,
10         GdkEvent *event,gpointer data);
11 static gint dragEvent(GnomeCanvasItem *item,
12         GdkEvent *event,gpointer data);
13
14 int main(int argc,char *argv[])
15 {
16     GtkWidget *app;
17     GtkWidget *canvas;
18     GnomeCanvasGroup *rootGroup;
19     GnomeCanvasItem *item;
20     GdkImlibImage *image;
21
22     gnome_init("canvasimage","1.0",argc,argv);
23     app = gnome_app_new("canvasimage",
24             "Gnome Canvas Image");
25     gtk_signal_connect(GTK_OBJECT(app),"delete_event",
26             GTK_SIGNAL_FUNC(eventDelete),NULL);
27     gtk_signal_connect(GTK_OBJECT(app),"destroy",
28             GTK_SIGNAL_FUNC(eventDestroy),NULL);
29
30     canvas = gnome_canvas_new();
31     gtk_widget_set_usize(canvas,600,360);
32     gnome_canvas_set_scroll_region(GNOME_CANVAS(canvas),
33             0.0,0.0,600,360);
34     rootGroup = gnome_canvas_root(GNOME_CANVAS(canvas));
35     gnome_app_set_contents(GNOME_APP(app),canvas);
36
37     image = gdk_imlib_create_image_from_xpm_data(logo);
38     item = gnome_canvas_item_new(rootGroup,
39                 gnome_canvas_image_get_type(),
40                 "image",image,
41                 "x",(double)100,
42                 "y",(double)100,
43                 "width",(double)257,
44                 "height",(double)303,
45                 "anchor",GTK_ANCHOR_CENTER,
```

```
46                          NULL);
47      gtk_signal_connect(GTK_OBJECT(item),"event",
48              (GtkSignalFunc)dragEvent,NULL);
49      gdk_imlib_destroy_image(image);
50
51      image = gdk_imlib_create_image_from_xpm_data(foot);
52      item = gnome_canvas_item_new(rootGroup,
53                      gnome_canvas_image_get_type(),
54                      "image",image,
55                      "x",(double)300,
56                      "y",(double)100,
57                      "width",(double)172,
58                      "height",(double)51,
59                      "anchor",GTK_ANCHOR_CENTER,
60                      NULL);
61      gtk_signal_connect(GTK_OBJECT(item),"event",
62              (GtkSignalFunc)dragEvent,NULL);
63
64      item = gnome_canvas_item_new(rootGroup,
65                      gnome_canvas_image_get_type(),
66                      "image",image,
67                      "x",(double)200,
68                      "y",(double)150,
69                      "width",(double)200,
70                      "height",(double)200,
71                      "anchor",GTK_ANCHOR_CENTER,
72                      NULL);
73      gtk_signal_connect(GTK_OBJECT(item),"event",
74              (GtkSignalFunc)dragEvent,NULL);
75      gdk_imlib_destroy_image(image);
76
77      gtk_widget_show_all(app);
78      gtk_main();
79      exit(0);
80 }
81 static gint dragEvent(GnomeCanvasItem *item,
82          GdkEvent *event,gpointer data) {
83      static gint x;
84      static gint y;
85      gint new_x;
86      gint new_y;
87
88      switch(event->type) {
89      case GDK_MOTION_NOTIFY:
90          if(event->button.state & 0x00000100) {
91              new_x = event->button.x;
92              new_y = event->button.y;
93              gnome_canvas_item_move(item,
94                  (double)(new_x - x),
95                  (double)(new_y - y));
96              x = new_x;
```

```
 97                    y = new_y;
 98              }
 99         break;
100      case GDK_BUTTON_PRESS:
101           if(event->button.button == 1)
102                gnome_canvas_item_raise_to_top(item);
103           x = event->button.x;
104           y = event->button.y;
105           break;
106      default:
107           break;
108      }
109      return(0);
110 }
111 gint eventDelete(GtkWidget *widget,
112           GdkEvent *event,gpointer data) {
113      return(FALSE);
114 }
115 gint eventDestroy(GtkWidget *widget,
116           GdkEvent *event,gpointer data) {
117      gtk_main_quit();
118      return(0);
119 }
```

Lines 4 and 5 include the files that hold the definition of the two images to be displayed. As described in Chapter 7, you can create XPM formatted images from another form for the purpose of compiling them directly inside your program.

Line 37 creates a GdkImlibImage by calling gdk_imlib_create_image_from_xpm(). The image is added to the canvas with the call to gnome_canvas_item_new() on line 38. The GdkImlibImage is passed as the "image" argument. The values for x and y specify the anchor point for the image within the canvas window, and the value of anchor determines which part of the image is placed at that point. The example uses GTK_ANCHOR_CENTER to place the center of the image at the anchor point. You can have it anchored at the center of one of its sides, or at one of the corners, by using one of the values from Table 9-1. There is a longer form for each of the names in the table—for example, the name GTK_ANCHOR_NORTH_EAST is the same as GTK_ANCHOR_NE.

Even though the image itself has a built-in size, it is required that you supply both height and width values. The image is scaled to fit the dimensions you specify; so if you don't want it to scale the image automatically, you need to pass the same dimension values as those defined in the original image. Two of the three images in this example are displayed in their "actual" size, but the image that has its height and width values set on lines 69 and 70 is rescaled to the larger size automatically, as shown in Figure 9-5.

Table 9-1	
Anchor Points that Attach an Image to a Canvas	
Name	*Anchor the Image by...*
GTK_ANCHOR_CENTER	...its center
GTK_ANCHOR_E	...the middle of its right edge
GTK_ANCHOR_N	...the middle of its top edge
GTK_ANCHOR_NE	...its upper-right corner
GTK_ANCHOR_NW	...its upper-left corner
GTK_ANCHOR_S	...the middle of its bottom edge
GTK_ANCHOR_SE	...its lower-right corner
GTK_ANCHOR_SW	...its lower-left corner
GIK_ANCHOR_W	...the middle of its left edge

Figure 9-5: Displayed images can be set to respond to the mouse

Once your image is added to the canvas, you can delete it if you wish because
GnomeCanvasItem creates its own (possibly rescaled) copy. The image created
on line 37 is deleted on line 49. The other image, the one created on line 51, is not
deleted until it is used in the creation of two GnomeCanvasItems. It is deleted with
the call to gdk_imlib_destroy_image() on line 75.

The callback function `dragEvent()` essentially is the same as the one in the previous example. In this version, the left button is selected to raise an item to the top of the display stack (by checking the button number on line 101). The left button is also the selected button for moving the item around the canvas (by checking the `state` bit on line 90).

Canvas Text

Text can be used as an item displayed on a canvas. A text item has much of the same capabilities as any other item. The following example creates three text items and positions them on a canvas.

```
1 /** canvastext.c **/
2 #include <gnome.h>
3
4 gint eventDelete(GtkWidget *widget,
5         GdkEvent *event,gpointer data);
6 gint eventDestroy(GtkWidget *widget,
7         GdkEvent *event,gpointer data);
8 static gint dragEvent(GnomeCanvasItem *item,
9         GdkEvent *event,gpointer data);
10
11 #define WIDTH 600
12 #define HEIGHT 75
13
14 int main(int argc,char *argv[])
15 {
16     GtkWidget *app;
17     GtkWidget *canvas;
18     GnomeCanvasGroup *rootGroup;
19     GnomeCanvasItem *item;
20
21     gnome_init("canvastext","1.0",argc,argv);
22     app = gnome_app_new("canvastext",
23             "Gnome Canvas Text");
24     gtk_signal_connect(GTK_OBJECT(app),"delete_event",
25             GTK_SIGNAL_FUNC(eventDelete),NULL);
26     gtk_signal_connect(GTK_OBJECT(app),"destroy",
27             GTK_SIGNAL_FUNC(eventDestroy),NULL);
28
29     canvas = gnome_canvas_new();
30     gtk_widget_set_usize(canvas,WIDTH,HEIGHT);
31     gnome_canvas_set_scroll_region(GNOME_CANVAS(canvas),
32             0.0,0.0,WIDTH,HEIGHT);
33     rootGroup = gnome_canvas_root(GNOME_CANVAS(canvas));
34     gnome_app_set_contents(GNOME_APP(app),canvas);
35
```

```
36      item = gnome_canvas_item_new(rootGroup,
37                      gnome_canvas_text_get_type(),
38                      "text","This is on the left-",
39                      "x",(double)(WIDTH / 2),
40                      "y",(double)25,
41                      "anchor",GTK_ANCHOR_E,
42                      NULL);
43      gtk_signal_connect(GTK_OBJECT(item),"event",
44              (GtkSignalFunc)dragEvent,NULL);
45
46      item = gnome_canvas_item_new(rootGroup,
47                      gnome_canvas_text_get_type(),
48                      "text","-and this is on the right.",
49                      "x",(double)(WIDTH / 2),
50                      "y",(double)25,
51                      "anchor",GTK_ANCHOR_W,
52                      NULL);
53      gtk_signal_connect(GTK_OBJECT(item),"event",
54              (GtkSignalFunc)dragEvent,NULL);
55
56      item = gnome_canvas_item_new(rootGroup,
57                      gnome_canvas_text_get_type(),
58                      "text","These larger red letters"
59                          " go all the way across.",
60                      "font","12x24",
61                      "x",(double)(WIDTH / 2),
62                      "y",(double)50,
63                      "fill_color","red",
64                      "anchor",GTK_ANCHOR_CENTER,
65                      NULL);
66      gtk_signal_connect(GTK_OBJECT(item),"event",
67              (GtkSignalFunc)dragEvent,NULL);
68
69      gtk_widget_show_all(app);
70      gtk_main();
71      exit(0);
72 }
73 static gint dragEvent(GnomeCanvasItem *item,
74          GdkEvent *event,gpointer data) {
75      static gint x;
76      static gint y;
77      gint new_x;
78      gint new_y;
79
80      switch(event->type) {
81      case GDK_MOTION_NOTIFY:
82          if(event->button.state & 0x00000100) {
83              new_x = event->button.x;
84              new_y = event->button.y;
85              gnome_canvas_item_move(item,
86                  (double)(new_x - x),
```

```
 87                     (double)(new_y - y));
 88              x = new_x;
 89              y = new_y;
 90          }
 91          break;
 92      case GDK_BUTTON_PRESS:
 93          if(event->button.button == 1)
 94              gnome_canvas_item_raise_to_top(item);
 95          x = event->button.x;
 96          y = event->button.y;
 97          break;
 98      default:
 99          break;
100      }
101      return(0);
102 }
103 gint eventDelete(GtkWidget *widget,
104         GdkEvent *event,gpointer data) {
105     return(FALSE);
106 }
107 gint eventDestroy(GtkWidget *widget,
108         GdkEvent *event,gpointer data) {
109     gtk_main_quit();
110     return(0);
111 }
```

The first of the three text items is created by the call to gnome_canvas_item_new()
on line 36. The text itself is specified as a character string. You specify x and y
coordinates and use an anchor to specify how the text is to be positioned in relation
to the point used to define the text item's location. The possible anchor positions
are listed in Table 9-1 (in the previous section). The first text item is attached to the
point by its right side (that is, the East end).

Defined on line 46, the second text item uses the same anchor point as the first one,
but it is attached to the point by its left side (that is, its West end). The two lines of
text are thus joined together to look like a single line, as shown in Figure 9-6.

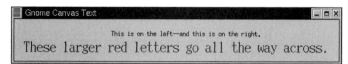

Figure 9-6: Text appearing as an item on a canvas

The third text item is defined on line 56. The text is to a point that is 50 pixels from
the top of the canvas and in the horizontal center of the window. Using the anchor
to attach the text to the point by its center results in centered text. The color of the
text and the name of the font are specified.

These text items act just like any other item on a canvas. All three are connected to the callback function dragEvent( ) on lines 43, 53, and 66. The callback function enables you to use the left mouse button to drag the text from one location to another. The layout shown in Figure 9-7 is made by dragging the text around the canvas.

Figure 9-7: Canvas text items can be manipulated the same as any other item

Grouping Items in a Canvas

When a canvas is created, there is also a canvas group created, which is responsible for handling the various items that are placed on display. Because a canvas group is also an item, it is possible to insert one canvas group into another. This enables you to manipulate an entire group just as you would any other single item. The following program creates a subgroup containing four ellipses.

```
1 /** grouping.c **/
2 #include <gnome.h>
3
4 gint eventDelete(GtkWidget *widget,
5         GdkEvent *event,gpointer data);
6 gint eventDestroy(GtkWidget *widget,
7         GdkEvent *event,gpointer data);
8 static gint dragEvent(GnomeCanvasItem *item,
9         GdkEvent *event,gpointer data);
10
11 #define HORIZ 50
12 #define VERT 50
13 #define WIDTH (HORIZ * 6)
14 #define HEIGHT (VERT * 6)
15
16 int main(int argc,char *argv[])
17 {
18     int i;
19     GtkWidget *app;
20     GtkWidget *canvas;
21     GnomeCanvasGroup *rootGroup;
22     GnomeCanvasItem *item;
23     GnomeCanvasItem *innerGroup;
24
```

```
25        gnome_init("grouping","1.0",argc,argv);
26        app = gnome_app_new("grouping",
27              "Canvas Grouping");
28        gtk_signal_connect(GTK_OBJECT(app),"delete_event",
29              GTK_SIGNAL_FUNC(eventDelete),NULL);
30        gtk_signal_connect(GTK_OBJECT(app),"destroy",
31              GTK_SIGNAL_FUNC(eventDestroy),NULL);
32
33        canvas = gnome_canvas_new();
34        gtk_widget_set_usize(canvas,WIDTH,HEIGHT);
35        gnome_canvas_set_scroll_region(GNOME_CANVAS(canvas),
36              0.0,0.0,WIDTH,HEIGHT);
37        rootGroup = gnome_canvas_root(GNOME_CANVAS(canvas));
38        gnome_app_set_contents(GNOME_APP(app),canvas);
39
40        innerGroup = gnome_canvas_item_new(rootGroup,
41                        gnome_canvas_group_get_type(),
42                        "x",(double)(HORIZ),
43                        "y",(double)(VERT),
44                        NULL);
45        gtk_signal_connect(GTK_OBJECT(innerGroup),"event",
46              (GtkSignalFunc)dragEvent,NULL);
47
48        for(i=0; i<4; i++) {
49            item = gnome_canvas_item_new(
50                        GNOME_CANVAS_GROUP(innerGroup),
51                            gnome_canvas_ellipse_get_type(),
52                            "x1",(double)(0),
53                            "y1",(double)(VERT * i),
54                            "x2",(double)(HORIZ),
55                            "y2",(double)(VERT * (i+1)),
56                            "fill_color","white",
57                            "outline_color","black",
58                            NULL);
59            if(i == 2)
60                gtk_signal_connect(GTK_OBJECT(item),"event",
61                        (GtkSignalFunc)dragEvent,NULL);
62        }
63
64        item = gnome_canvas_item_new(rootGroup,
65                        gnome_canvas_ellipse_get_type(),
66                        "x1",(double)(HORIZ * 3),
67                        "y1",(double)(VERT * 2),
68                        "x2",(double)(HORIZ * 5),
69                        "y2",(double)(VERT * 4),
70                        "fill_color","green",
71                        "outline_color","white",
72                        NULL);
73        gtk_signal_connect(GTK_OBJECT(item),"event",
74              (GtkSignalFunc)dragEvent,NULL);
75
```

```
76      gtk_widget_show_all(app);
77      gtk_main();
78      exit(0);
79 }
80 static gint dragEvent(GnomeCanvasItem *item,
81          GdkEvent *event,gpointer data) {
82      static gint x;
83      static gint y;
84      gint new_x;
85      gint new_y;
86
87      switch(event->type) {
88      case GDK_MOTION_NOTIFY:
89          if(event->button.state & 0x00000100) {
90              new_x = event->button.x;
91              new_y = event->button.y;
92              gnome_canvas_item_move(item,
93                  (double)(new_x - x),
94                  (double)(new_y - y));
95              x = new_x;
96              y = new_y;
97          }
98          break;
99      case GDK_BUTTON_PRESS:
100         if(event->button.button == 1)
101             gnome_canvas_item_raise_to_top(item);
102         x = event->button.x;
103         y = event->button.y;
104         break;
105     default:
106         break;
107     }
108     return(0);
109 }
110 gint eventDelete(GtkWidget *widget,
111         GdkEvent *event,gpointer data) {
112     return(FALSE);
113 }
114 gint eventDestroy(GtkWidget *widget,
115         GdkEvent *event,gpointer data) {
116     gtk_main_quit();
117     return(0);
118 }
```

The canvas is created and a pointer to its root group is retrieved on lines 33 through 38.

Another group—the one that will be added to the main group—is created by the call to gnome_canvas_item_new() on line 40. The inner group is simply laid right over the root group, but it makes no visual difference because they are both completely transparent on the display and to the mouse. The x and y values supplied to it are the coordinates of the upper-left corner of the inner group. The coordinate settings are a matter of convenience for programming because a group item has no boundaries — the defining coordinates simply specify the origin from which all distances are measured. In this example, the coordinates (the values of x and y) are (50,50) so attaching something to the point (0,0) on the inner group places it at (50,50) on the root group.

Four circles (created from four ellipses with the same height and width) are added to the inner group in the loop beginning on line 48. All of the circles are the same except for their locations in the inner group. The item defined on line 64 is a larger circle on the right, as shown in Figure 9-8, and is attached to the root group.

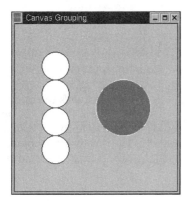

Figure 9-8: A number of individual items can be grouped as one

The callback function dragEvent(), beginning on line 80, enables the mouse to be used to drag an item from one place to another. The callback function is connected to the inner group on line 45. It also is connected to the third circle of the inner group on lines 59 through 61. The callback function is connected to the larger circle on line 73.

You can drag the larger circle to any position, just as you saw in previous examples. By dragging any one of them (except the third one), you drag the group of circles to a new position. The third circle in the inner group can be moved on its own because it has its own callback. The inner group also has a callback, but it is transparent to the mouse, so the only time the callback is executed occurs when the mouse pointer is inside one of the objects attached to the inner group. When any circle (except the third one) is dragged, every circle (including the third one) is dragged along with it. The circles can be repositioned to look like Figure 9-9.

Briefly, if there is an item that does not have a callback function, the mouse event is passed on to the group containing the object. When a group is moved, all of the items attached to the group move with it. If an item has its own callback function, no events from it are passed on to its group object.

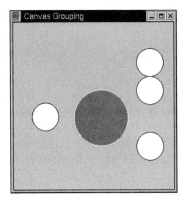

Figure 9-9: Callbacks allow for both individual and group access

Adding Widgets to a Canvas

Any widget can be placed on a canvas. In this way, you can use a canvas to configure the layout of a window if the generalized containers (as described in Chapter 5) do not have the flexibility to lay things out the way you would like them. Another advantage is the ability to mix graphic objects in among the widgets. The disadvantage of using canvas as a container is that your program is responsible for the exact placement and size of everything.

The following program creates three-button widgets and uses the canvas to position and size them.

```
 1 /** canvaswidget.c **/
 2 #include <gnome.h>
 3
 4 gint eventDelete(GtkWidget *widget,
 5        GdkEvent *event,gpointer data);
 6 gint eventDestroy(GtkWidget *widget,
 7        GdkEvent *event,gpointer data);
 8
 9 #define HORIZ 50
10 #define VERT 30
11 #define WIDTH (HORIZ * 5)
12 #define HEIGHT (VERT * 5)
13
14 int main(int argc,char *argv[])
15 {
16     GtkWidget *app;
17     GtkWidget *canvas;
18     GtkWidget *button;
19     GnomeCanvasGroup *rootGroup;
```

```
20      GnomeCanvasItem *item;
21
22      gnome_init("canvaswidget","1.0",argc,argv);
23      app = gnome_app_new("canvaswidget",
24              "Gnome Canvas Widget");
25      gtk_signal_connect(GTK_OBJECT(app),"delete_event",
26              GTK_SIGNAL_FUNC(eventDelete),NULL);
27      gtk_signal_connect(GTK_OBJECT(app),"destroy",
28              GTK_SIGNAL_FUNC(eventDestroy),NULL);
29
30      canvas = gnome_canvas_new();
31      gtk_widget_set_usize(canvas,WIDTH,HEIGHT);
32      gnome_canvas_set_scroll_region(GNOME_CANVAS(canvas),
33              0.0,0.0,WIDTH,HEIGHT);
34      rootGroup = gnome_canvas_root(GNOME_CANVAS(canvas));
35      gnome_app_set_contents(GNOME_APP(app),canvas);
36
37      button = gtk_button_new_with_label("Button 1");
38      item = gnome_canvas_item_new(rootGroup,
39                      gnome_canvas_widget_get_type(),
40                      "widget",button,
41                      "x",(double)(HORIZ),
42                      "y",(double)(VERT),
43                      "width",(double)(HORIZ),
44                      "height",(double)(VERT),
45                      "anchor",GTK_ANCHOR_NW,
46                      NULL);
47
48      button = gtk_button_new_with_label("Button 2");
49      item = gnome_canvas_item_new(rootGroup,
50                      gnome_canvas_widget_get_type(),
51                      "widget",button,
52                      "x",(double)(HORIZ * 3),
53                      "y",(double)(VERT),
54                      "width",(double)(HORIZ),
55                      "height",(double)(VERT),
56                      "anchor",GTK_ANCHOR_NW,
57                      NULL);
58      button = gtk_button_new_with_label("Button Three");
59      item = gnome_canvas_item_new(rootGroup,
60                      gnome_canvas_widget_get_type(),
61                      "widget",button,
62                      "x",(double)(HORIZ),
63                      "y",(double)(VERT * 3),
64                      "width",(double)(HORIZ * 3),
65                      "height",(double)(VERT),
66                      "anchor",GTK_ANCHOR_NW,
67                      NULL);
68
69      gtk_widget_show_all(app);
```

```
70     gtk_main();
71     exit(0);
72 }
73 gint eventDelete(GtkWidget *widget,
74         GdkEvent *event,gpointer data) {
75     return(FALSE);
76 }
77 gint eventDestroy(GtkWidget *widget,
78         GdkEvent *event,gpointer data) {
79     gtk_main_quit();
80     return(0);
81 }
```

Lines 30 through 35 create and configure the canvas and attach it to the application's main window.

The call to gtk_button_new_with_label() on line 37 creates a button with the label "Button 1". The button is configured as a canvas item and placed on the root group by the function call gnome_canvas_item_new() on line 38. The widget (specified on line 40) is added to the canvas using the anchoring point specified as x and y. The button is attached to the anchoring point by its upper-left corner because GTK_ANCHOR_NW is specified. You can find a complete list of the anchoring options in Table 9-1 earlier in this chapter. The height and width of the button can be allowed to default, but in this example, the height and width are specified.

In similar fashion, "Button 2" and "Button Three" are created and added to the canvas on lines 48 through 67. Figure 9-10 shows the results.

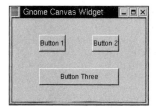

Figure 9-10: Widgets positioned in a window by using a canvas

Note   There are no callbacks added to the canvas widget items as in the previous examples of canvas items. This is because a button widget has its own set of callback functions available and traps some of the mouse events — some come through to the item containing the button, and some do not. Anyway, you can define normal button callbacks to do anything you like.

Drawing Polygons on a Canvas

A *polygon* (a figure of any shape with any number of sides) can be made into an item and displayed on a canvas. The following example program creates a simple arrow item and displays it on a canvas.

```
 1 /** canvaspolygon.c **/
 2 #include <gnome.h>
 3
 4 gint eventDelete(GtkWidget *widget,
 5         GdkEvent *event,gpointer data);
 6 gint eventDestroy(GtkWidget *widget,
 7         GdkEvent *event,gpointer data);
 8 GnomeCanvasPoints *makeArrow(gint h,gint v,
 9         gint h_off,gint v_off);
10
11 #define HORIZ 30
12 #define VERT 30
13 #define WIDTH (HORIZ * 6)
14 #define HEIGHT (VERT * 6)
15
16 int main(int argc,char *argv[])
17 {
18     GtkWidget *app;
19     GtkWidget *canvas;
20     GnomeCanvasGroup *rootGroup;
21     GnomeCanvasItem *item;
22
23     gnome_init("canvaspolygon","1.0",argc,argv);
24     app = gnome_app_new("canvaspolygon",
25             "Polygon Item");
26     gtk_signal_connect(GTK_OBJECT(app),"delete_event",
27             GTK_SIGNAL_FUNC(eventDelete),NULL);
28     gtk_signal_connect(GTK_OBJECT(app),"destroy",
29             GTK_SIGNAL_FUNC(eventDestroy),NULL);
30
31     canvas = gnome_canvas_new();
32     gtk_widget_set_usize(canvas,WIDTH,HEIGHT);
33     gnome_canvas_set_scroll_region(GNOME_CANVAS(canvas),
34             0.0,0.0,WIDTH,HEIGHT);
35     rootGroup = gnome_canvas_root(GNOME_CANVAS(canvas));
36     gnome_app_set_contents(GNOME_APP(app),canvas);
37
38     item = gnome_canvas_item_new(rootGroup,
39             gnome_canvas_polygon_get_type(),
40             "points",makeArrow(HORIZ,VERT,HORIZ,VERT),
41             "fill_color","white",
42             "outline_color","black",
43             NULL);
```

```
44
45      gtk_widget_show_all(app);
46      gtk_main();
47      exit(0);
48 }
49
50 GnomeCanvasPoints *makeArrow(gint h,gint v,
51            gint h_off,gint v_off) {
52      int i;
53      GnomeCanvasPoints *points;
54      static const gint xy[16] = {
55          2,0, 0,2, 1,2, 1,4, 3,4, 3,2, 4,2, 2,0
56      };
57
58      points = gnome_canvas_points_new(8);
59      for(i=0; i<16; i += 2) {
60          points->coords[i] = (xy[i] * h) + h_off;
61          points->coords[i+1] = (xy[i+1] * v) + v_off;
62      }
63      return(points);
64 }
65 gint eventDelete(GtkWidget *widget,
66          GdkEvent *event,gpointer data) {
67      return(FALSE);
68 }
69 gint eventDestroy(GtkWidget *widget,
70          GdkEvent *event,gpointer data) {
71      gtk_main_quit();
72      return(0);
73 }
```

The function makeArrow() starting on line 50 creates the GnomeCanvasPoints object that is used to create the item. The h and v arguments are pixel-count values that determine the size of the arrow. The h_off and v_off arguments are added to each point and determine the placement of the arrow in the canvas. The xy array defined on line 54 contains the list of points in "unit" form — that is, each value in the array is multiplied by the h and v arguments to size each segment of the drawing.

There are a total of 8 points in the arrow, so the xy array has 16 entries. Those with even-numbered subscripts are *x*-axis coordinates, and the odd-numbered ones are *y*-axis coordinates. This organization conforms to the organization of coordinate points inside the GnomeCanvasPoints object, so it is easy to translate from one to the other. The GnomeCanvasPoints object is created on line 58, and the loop to calculate the coordinates for the arrow begins on line 59. Lines 60 and 61 calculate the actual point positions by multiplying the "unit" value of a point by the number of pixels each unit represents; then the offset is added to shift the point to the requested position.

The polygon item is created with the call to gnome_canvas_item_new() on line 38. The makeArrow() function is called to return a pointer to the GnomeCanvasPoints object. The points are all scaled and placed properly, so all that remains is to color the polygon, which is done on lines 41 and 42. The result is shown in Figure 9-11.

Figure 9-11: Different shapes can be defined as a set of points

Canvas Affine Transforms

An *affine transform* can be used to move, scale, rotate, and otherwise manipulate a displayed item. The following example creates three arrows and applies an affine transform to each one of them. This example only demonstrates the basics of using affine transforms on canvas items.

Note If you are not familiar with affine transforms, they can seem mysterious and almost magic. Affine transforms are used to resize, flip, rotate, invert, stretch, skew, or shrink a graphic object. And there are ways to combine a group of affine transforms to perform a series of manipulations in a single step.

```
1 /** canvasaffine.c **/
2 #include <gnome.h>
3
4 gint eventDelete(GtkWidget *widget,
5         GdkEvent *event,gpointer data);
6 gint eventDestroy(GtkWidget *widget,
7         GdkEvent *event,gpointer data);
8 GnomeCanvasPoints *makeOriginArrow(gint h,gint v);
9
10 #define HORIZ 30
11 #define VERT 30
12 #define WIDTH (HORIZ * 6)
13 #define HEIGHT (VERT * 6)
14
15 int main(int argc,char *argv[])
16 {
17     GtkWidget *app;
18     GtkWidget *canvas;
19     GnomeCanvasGroup *rootGroup;
```

```
20      GnomeCanvasItem *item;
21
22      double affine[6];
23
24      gnome_init("canvasaffine","1.0",argc,argv);
25      app = gnome_app_new("canvasaffine",
26              "Canvas Affine");
27      gtk_signal_connect(GTK_OBJECT(app),"delete_event",
28              GTK_SIGNAL_FUNC(eventDelete),NULL);
29      gtk_signal_connect(GTK_OBJECT(app),"destroy",
30              GTK_SIGNAL_FUNC(eventDestroy),NULL);
31
32      canvas = gnome_canvas_new();
33      gtk_widget_set_usize(canvas,WIDTH,HEIGHT);
34      gnome_canvas_set_scroll_region(GNOME_CANVAS(canvas),
35              -WIDTH/2,-HEIGHT/2,WIDTH/2,HEIGHT/2);
36      rootGroup = gnome_canvas_root(GNOME_CANVAS(canvas));
37      gnome_app_set_contents(GNOME_APP(app),canvas);
38
39
40      item = gnome_canvas_item_new(rootGroup,
41              gnome_canvas_polygon_get_type(),
42              "points",makeOriginArrow(HORIZ,VERT),
43              "fill_color","white",
44              "outline_color","black",
45              NULL);
46      art_affine_scale(affine,1.3,1.3);
47      gnome_canvas_item_affine_relative(item,affine);
48
49      item - gnome_canvas_item_new(rootGroup,
50              gnome_canvas_polygon_get_type(),
51              "points",makeOriginArrow(HORIZ/2,VERT/2),
52              "fill_color","black",
53              "outline_color","white",
54              NULL);
55      art_affine_rotate(affine,45.0);
56      gnome_canvas_item_affine_relative(item,affine);
57
58      item = gnome_canvas_item_new(rootGroup,
59              gnome_canvas_polygon_get_type(),
60              "points",makeOriginArrow(HORIZ/2,VERT/2),
61              "fill_color","green",
62              "outline_color","black",
63              NULL);
64      art_affine_translate(affine,60,-50);
65      gnome_canvas_item_affine_relative(item,affine);
66
67      gtk_widget_show_all(app);
68      gtk_main();
69      exit(0);
70  }
```

```
71
72 GnomeCanvasPoints *makeOriginArrow(gint h,gint v)
73 {
74     int i;
75     GnomeCanvasPoints *points;
76     static const gint xy[16] = {
77         0,-2, -2,0, -1,0, -1,2, 1,2, 1,0, 2,0, 0,-2
78     };
79
80     points = gnome_canvas_points_new(8);
81     for(i=0; i<16; i += 2) {
82         points->coords[i] = (xy[i] * h);
83         points->coords[i+1] = (xy[i+1] * v);
84     }
85     return(points);
86 }
87 gint eventDelete(GtkWidget *widget,
88         GdkEvent *event,gpointer data) {
89     return(FALSE);
90 }
91 gint eventDestroy(GtkWidget *widget,
92         GdkEvent *event,gpointer data) {
93     gtk_main_quit();
94     return(0);
95 }
```

This example creates three arrow items and applies an affine transformation to each one. The resulting display is shown in Figure 9-12.

Figure 9-12: Three items manipulated by affine transforms

An affine transform is an array of 6 numbers, as defined on line 22. When an affine is applied to a graphic object, this array of numbers is applied to each point in the object — thus transferring all of its points to another location. There are some GNOME functions that can be used to initialize the array for certain standard affine operations.

The arrows are all created by a call to the function makeOriginArrow() on line 72. This arrow is slightly different from the one in the previous example because this one places the origin — the (0,0) point — at the center of the arrow. To have the arrows appear in the center of the window, the canvas is exposed with the origin at its center. This is done by the call to `gnome_canvas_set_scroll_region()` on line 34. Positioning the origin at the center means the point (0,0) is at the center of the display, which is convenient because certain transform operations (such as rotation) operate relative to the origin. There are other ways to achieve the same thing, but it takes a bit more affine manipulation.

The white arrow that shows up in the background of Figure 9-12 is created by the call to `gnome_canvas_item_new()` on line 40. On line 46, an affine transform is initialized by the call to `art_affine_scale()` to enlarge the arrow 1.3 times its size along both axes. The number is a multiplier, so numbers greater than 1.0 increase the size and numbers less than 1.0 reduce the size. The expansion occurs relative to the origin, which is at the center of the arrow, so it expands equally in all directions.

The black arrow that sits at an angle in the center of the window is created on line 49. The affine transform to rotate it 45 degrees to the right is initialized by the call to `art_affine_rotate()` on line 55. The rotation is applied on line 56.

The arrow in the upper-right corner, created on line 58, starts in exactly the same position as the rotated arrow in the center. By calling `art_affine_translate()` on line 64 an affine transform is created — which translates the arrow to the right by 60 pixels and up by 50 pixels. (Positive numbers move down and to the right; negative numbers move up and to the left).

GdkEvent

At the lowest level, the mouse or keyboard (or whatever) issues an `Xevent` that is sent to your application. This `Xevent` contains a tag identifying the window for which it is intended. Table 9-2 lists the types of events and the names of the structs used to define the contents of each one. Following the table, I describe the contents of each of the event structs.

Table 9-2
The GdkEvent Names, Formats, and Purposes

Defined Event Name	Struct Used	Description
GDK_2BUTTON_PRESS	GdkEventButton	Double-click any mouse button.
GDK_3BUTTON_PRESS	GdkEventButton	Triple-click (or more) any mouse button.
GDK_BUTTON_PRESS	GdkEventButton	Mouse button pressed.
GDK_BUTTON_RELEASE	GdkEventButton	Mouse button released.

Defined Event Name	Struct Used	Description
GDK_CLIENT_EVENT	GdkEventClient	This process, or another process, issued this event.
GDK_CONFIGURE	GdkEventConfigure	A change in the item's configuration.
GDK_DELETE	GdkEventAny	A request has been made to delete the window.
GDK_DESTROY	GdkEventAny	The window has been destroyed.
GDK_DRAG_ENTER	GdkEventDND	A dragging mouse has entered the window.
GDK_DRAG_LEAVE	GdkEventDND	A dragging mouse has left the window.
GDK_DRAG_MOTION	GdkEventDND	A dragging mouse has moved within the window.
GDK_DRAG_STATUS	GdkEventDND	Either the source or destination has modified the status of the drag.
GDK_DROP_FINISHED	GdkEventDND	The drop operation has completed.
GDK_DROP_START	GdkEventDND	The drop operation is about to commence.
GDK_ENTER_NOTIFY	GdkEventCrossing	The mouse pointer has entered the window.
GDK_EXPOSE	GdkEventExpose	All or part of the window has been exposed.
GDK_FOCUS_CHANGE	GdkEventFocus	The focus has been moved either to or away from the window.
GDK_KEY_PRESS	GdkEventKey	A keyboard key has been pressed.
GDK_KEY_RELEASE	GdkEventKey	A keyboard key has been released.
GDK_LEAVE_NOTIFY	GdkEventCrossing	The mouse pointer has moved out of the window.
GDK_MAP	GdkEventAny	The window has been made visible (mapped).
GDK_MOTION_NOTIFY	GdkEventMotion	The mouse has moved.
GDK_NOTHING	GdkEventAny	A non-event.

Continued

Table 9-2 *(continued)*

Defined Event Name	Struct Used	Description
`GDK_NO_EXPOSE`	`GdkEventNoExpose`	In an image copy operation, the source window was available, so it did not require exposure.
`GDK_PROPERTY_NOTIFY`	`GdkEventProperty`	A window property has been changed or deleted.
`GDK_PROXIMITY_IN`	`GdkEventProximity`	A stylus has made physical contact with a graphics tablet.
`GDK_PROXIMITY_OUT`	`GdkEventProximity`	A stylus has broken physical contact with a graphics tablet.
`GDK_SELECTION_CLEAR`	`GdkEventSelection`	During cut-and-paste, the selected object is no longer owned by the receiver of this event.
`GDK_SELECTION_NOTIFY`	`GdkEventSelection`	During cut-and-paste, the new owner of a selection issues this event to indicate success or failure with ownership transfer.
`GDK_SELECTION_REQUEST`	`GdkEventSelection`	During cut-and--paste, another client has requested ownership of a selection.
`GDK_UNMAP`	`GdkEventAny`	The window is no longer being displayed (unmapped).
`GDK_VISIBILITY_NOTIFY`	`GdkEventVisibility`	There has been a change in the visibility of a window.

Most widgets use their entire window as the subject for all events, but the `GnomeCanvas` carries this one step further. If the event has a location associated with it — that is, the *x* and *y* coordinates of a point in the window — the event is passed on to the item for processing. This makes it possible to use callback functions on individual items displayed in a `GnomeCanvas`.

In the header files, each struct is defined in two parts. One is the struct itself and the other is a `typedef` for it. The names differ only in the initial character — the struct begins with an underscore character and the `typedef` does not. For example, the `typedef` for `GdkEventAny` is declared this way:

```
typedef struct _GdkEventAny GdkEventAny;
```

Then the struct is defined this way:

```
struct _GdkEventAny {
    . . .
};
```

The result is that declarations of the event can be done with the same sort of syntax as with any other fundamental type, like this:

```
GdkEventAny any;
```

Some Common Fields

There are several event formats that have some of the same fields. For example, a mouse button-press event and a mouse button-release event both contain the coordinates of the mouse pointer at the time of the event.

X and Y

In the events that have position information, there are two sets of coordinates. The values x and y are the coordinates of the mouse pointer relative to the upper-left corner of the current window. The second set of coordinates — x_root and y_root — are the coordinates of the same point, except the location is relative to the upper-left corner of the root window.

Note   In a GtkCanvas window, the coordinates are not relative to the corner of an item within the canvas. They are relative to the canvas window as a whole.

Time

Many of the GdkEvent structs have time fields. The value is a finely grained time stamp that you can use to determine the order in which events actually occur (under some networking circumstances, the events can arrive out of order) and, more importantly, to determine how close together two events occur. The GDK software uses these time stamps to determine when a mouse button is double-clicked to issue double-click events.

State

Some of the GdkEvent structs (in particular, the ones that deal with the mouse) have a field named state that specifies which buttons are being pressed. Each of the buttons is assigned a single bit because there can be multiple bits held down at any one time. Table 9-3 lists the buttons and the bits that are assigned to them. A state bit is set to 1 while a button is being held down so, if no buttons are being held down, the value of state is all zeroes.

Table 9-3
The state Bits Indicating Button Presses

State	Assigned Bit
The keyboard Shift key is down.	0x00000001
The keyboard Caps Lock key is on.	0x00000002
The keyboard Control key is down.	0x00000004
The keyboard Alt or Meta key is down.	0x00000008
The first (left) mouse button is down.	0x00000100
The second (middle) mouse button is down.	0x00000200
The third (right) mouse button is down.	0x00000400

Source

When the event originates with a hardware device, there is a field named source of the type GdkInputSource that is used to indicate the type of device. This is an *enum*, which can be one of the following values:

```
GDK_SOURCE_MOUSE
GDK_SOURCE_PEN
GDK_SOURCE_ERASER
GDK_SOURCE_CURSOR
```

GdkEvent

The GdkEvent is a union of several event structs. Each of these structs contain the data fields necessary for one or more events. This allows the system to propogate all events as being the same type, but it also means that your software must determine which type it really is. All of the structs have type as their first field to make it easy for a program to identify the type of event, and which struct layout contains the associated data.

```
union _GdkEvent {
    GdkEventType         type;
    GdkEventAny          any;
    GdkEventExpose       expose;
    GdkEventNoExpose     no_expose;
    GdkEventVisibility   visibility;
    GdkEventMotion       motion;
    GdkFventButton       button;
    GdkEventKey          key;
    GdkEventCrossing     crossing;
    GdkEventFocus        focus_change;
    GdkEventConfigure    configure;
    GdkEventProperty     property;
```

```
    GdkEventSelection      selection;
    GdkEventProximity      proximity;
    GdkEventClient         client;
    GdkEventDND            dnd;
};
```

To get access to a field in one of the events, you can cast it to its actual type, or use the name included in the union. For example, if you want to copy the x value from a GdkEventMotion event type, address it this way:

```
GkdEvent *event;
   . . .
if(event->type == GDK_MOTION_NOTIFY) {
    xlocation = event->motion.x;
   . . .
```

It also is possible to cast the union into a struct so the fields can be accessed directly, like this:

```
GdkEvent *event;
GdkEventMotion *motion;
   . . .
if(event->type == GDK_MOTION_NOTIFY) {
    motion = (GdkEventMotion *)event;
    xlocation = motion->x;
   . . .
```

GdkEventAny

Any events that do not require extra information can be passed as "any" events because they contain only the basic fields that appear in all events. An example of an event of this type is GDK_DESTROY, which indicates the window has been destroyed.

```
struct _GdkEventAny {
  GdkEventType type;
  GdkWindow *window;
  gint8 send_event;
};
```

GdkEventButton

The value of button is a number indicating which button was used. A value of 1 indicates the left button, a value of 2 the middle button, and a value of 3 for the right button.

The value of pressure is always 0.5. The values of xtilt and ytilt are always 0.0. The possible values of state are listed in Table 9-3 (in the "State" section earlier in this chapter).

The value of `source` is the ID of the input device. It normally is `GDK_CORE_POINTER`, which is the constant value `0xFEDC`.

```
struct _GdkEventButton {
  GdkEventType type;
  GdkWindow *window;
  gint8 send_event;
  guint32 time;
  gdouble x;
  gdouble y;
  gdouble pressure;
  gdouble xtilt;
  gdouble ytilt;
  guint state;
  guint button;
  GdkInputSource source;
  guint32 deviceid;
  gdouble x_root, y_root;
};
```

GdkEventClient

You can use this event for *interprocess* (or inter-window) *communication*. For this event, the value of `sent_event` will always be `TRUE`, because events of this type are always originated in a process. To hold the communcations data, a block of up to 20 bytes is included inside the event struct.

The `message_type` is used to specify the actual type of the event. It is a character string transmitted in the form of a `GdkAtom`.

The value of `data_format` is the number of bits in each member of the data array. If it is 8, the array named `b` contains 20 bytes of data. If it is 16, the `s` array contains ten 16-bit binary values. If it is 32, the `l` array contains five 32-bit values.

```
struct _GdkEventClient {
  GdkEventType type;
  GdkWindow *window;
  gint8 send_event;
  GdkAtom message_type;
  gushort data_format;
  union {
    char b[20];
    short s[10];
    long l[5];
  } data;
};
```

GdkEventConfigure

This event is issued when there is some change in the size and/or position of the window. The values of x and y indicate the position, and the values of width and height indicate the size.

```
struct _GdkEventConfigure {
  GdkEventType type;
  GdkWindow *window;
  gint8 send_event;
  gint16 x, y;
  gint16 width;
  gint16 height;
};
```

GdkEventCrossing

This event is issued whenever the mouse pointer crosses the boundary at the edge of the window.

```
struct _GdkEventCrossing {
  GdkEventType type;
  GdkWindow *window;
  gint8 send_event;
  GdkWindow *subwindow;
  guint32 time;
  gdouble x;
  gdouble y;
  gdouble x_root;
  gdouble y_root;
  GdkCrossingMode mode;
  GdkNotifyType detail;
  gboolean focus;
  guint state;
};
```

The mode is usually GDK_CROSSING_NORMAL. However, if the crossing occurs at the start of a grab operation, the value is GDK_CROSSING_GRAB; if it is at the end of a grab operation, the value is GDK_CROSSING_UNGRAB.

If the destination window (the one the mouse is moving into) has the focus, or one of its ancestors has the focus, the value of focus is TRUE.

The window field is a pointer to this window, and the subwindow is the window that the mouse is being moved from or to. The detail field contains one of the values in Table 9-4 to supply more information about the subwindow.

Table 9-4	
Detail Codes Specifying the Other Window in a Crossing	

Name	*Description*
GDK_NOTIFY_ANCESTOR	The other window is a parent (or some grandparent) of this window.
GDK_NOTIFY_INFERIOR	The other window is a child (or some grandchild) of this window.
GDK_NOTIFY_NONLINEAR	The other window is neither a child nor a parent of this one—the two are in separate hierarchies.
GDK_NOTIFY_VIRTUAL	The pointer is passing between two windows in the same hierarchy as this one; one of them is a child (or some grandchild) and the other is a parent (or some grandparent) of this window.
GDK_NOTIFY_NONLINEAR_VIRTUAL	The pointer is moving between a child (or some grandchild) of this window and a window that is not in the same hierarchy as this window.

GdkEventDND

All drag-and-drop operations use this event type to communicate the status of the operation. The context field contains the drag-and-drop information. Refer to Chapter 16 for examples of using this event.

```
struct _GdkEventDND {
   GdkEventType type;
   GdkWindow *window;
   gint8 send_event;
   GdkDragContext *context;
   guint32 time;
   gshort x_root, y_root;
};
```

GdkEventExpose

The internal utilities that copy a rectangle of pixels from a window—to another location on the same window or to another drawable—issues this event if the source is unavailable because it currently is not visible. It could be obscured by another window or it could simply be scrolled completely or partially out of view. If the source of the copy is available, a GdkEventNoExpose is sent instead.

The `area` specifies what portion of the window is in question. There are circumstances in which more than one rectangular area is used as the source, so there can be a series of these events that you can join together to describe the entire area. If there are other `GdkEventExpose` events to follow, the value of `count` specifies how many.

```
struct _GdkEventExpose {
  GdkEventType type;
  GdkWindow *window;
  gint8 send_event;
  GdkRectangle area;
  gint count;
};
```

GdkEventFocus

This event specifies a focus change for the current window. If the value of `in` is nonzero, the window is gaining focus. If `in` is zero, the window is in focus but is losing focus.

```
struct _GdkEventFocus {
  GdkEventType type;
  GdkWindow *window;
  gint8 send_event;
  gint16 in;
};
```

GdkEventKey

This event specifies that a keyboard key has been either pressed or released. The value of `keyval` identifies the key. The `state` can be used to determine whether the Control, Shift, Alt, or Meta key is being held down.

The `string` is an ASCII description of the key. The length is the number of characters in the `string`.

```
struct _GdkEventKey {
  GdkEventType type;
  GdkWindow *window;
  gint8 send_event;
  guint32 time;
  guint state;
  guint keyval;
  gint length;
  gchar *string;
};
```

GdkEventMotion

An event of this type is received whenever the mouse pointer moves from one location to another within a window.

The values of x, y, x_root, and y_root reflect the new location.

```
struct _GdkEventMotion {
  GdkEventType type;
  GdkWindow *window;
  gint8 send_event;
  guint32 time;
  gdouble x;
  gdouble y;
  gdouble pressure;
  gdouble xtilt;
  gdouble ytilt;
  guint state;
  gint16 is_hint;
  GdkInputSource source;
  guint32 deviceid;
  gdouble x_root, y_root;
};
```

The is_hint field is used to warn you that, although this event is showing the correct motion information for the specified time stamp, there are other events following this one that can change the values. This allows the application, for the sake of efficiency, to skip processing the current position information and wait for the next one. Under normal circumstances, this field does not have any effect — it mostly happens when there is a relatively slow link causing events to back up in the server.

GdkEventNoExpose

The internal utilities that copy a rectangle of pixels from a window — to another location on the same window or to another drawable — issues this event if the source was mapped and available for copying. A GdkEventExpose is sent instead if the source or the copy operation is obscured by another window or is scrolled completely or partially out of view.

```
struct _GdkEventNoExpose {
  GdkEventType type;
  GdkWindow *window;
  gint8 send_event;
};
```

GdkEventProperty

This event indicates that a window property has changed.

The `atom` is the key value used to locate the property value. The `state` is 0 if this is a change to an existing property, and 1 if the property is being deleted.

```
struct _GdkEventProperty {
  GdkEventType type;
  GdkWindow *window;
  gint8 send_event;
  GdkAtom atom;
  guint32 time;
  guint state;
};
```

GdkEventProximity

This event notifies the program when the mouse pointer is inside or outside the area in which the application window should draw its own cursor. This event is almost never used in an application program because GNOME provides much simpler ways to handle cursor changes.

```
struct _GdkEventProximity {
  GdkEventType type;
  GdkWindow *window;
  gint8 send_event;
  guint32 time;
  GdkInputSource source;
  guint32 deviceid;
};
```

GdkEventSelection

Events of this type are sent from one application to another to indicate change of ownership as the result of a drag-and-drop or cut-and-paste operation.

```
struct _GdkEventSelection {
  GdkEventType type;
  GdkWindow *window;
  gint8 send_event;
  GdkAtom selection;
  GdkAtom target;
  GdkAtom property;
  guint32 requestor;
  guint32 time;
};
```

The selection atom identifies the item that is being transferred from one owner to another.

The target is the format into which the data is to be converted to complete the transfer. If the value of target is zero, the data cannot be converted.

The requestor is the ID of the window requesting the transfer of ownership.

GdkEventVisibility

This event is sent whenever there is a change in the state of the visibility of a window. Visibility changes when all or part of the window becomes obscured or visible due to iconization, deiconization, or a change in the window stacking order.

```
struct _GdkEventVisibility {
    GdkEventType type;
    GdkWindow *window;
    gint8 send_event;
    GdkVisibilityState state;
};
```

The value of state indicates the current visibility status of the window. It is one of the following:

```
GDK_VISIBILITY_UNOBSCURED
GDK_VISIBILITY_PARTIAL
GDK_VISIBILITY_FULLY_OBSCURED
```

Summary

If none of the containers described in Chapters 4 and 5 are flexible enough for the layout you wish to achieve, a GnomeCanvas widget may be the solution. Not only do you have absolute control of the size and position of each item, but you also can use affine transforms to modify their appearance. The description of the GnomeCanvas in this chapter included:

✦ A GnomeCanvas maintains its own internal stacking order and relays mouse events to the item currently containing the mouse pointer. The only events propagated this way are the mouse events.

✦ An item on a canvas can be moved from one location to another. In fact, the canvas has no limitation on its width and height, so you can move an item anywhere.

✦ Items are kept in a group, and a group is also an item. This means any group can contain any number of subgroups.

✦ There are special graphical primitive items that you can use to render drawings. You can further modify them by applying affine transforms.

✦ Mouse, keyboard, and other events can be directed to the individual items being managed by a GnomeCanvas.

Where the GnomeCanvas widget of this chapter allows you great flexibility in widget placement, the GtkDrawingArea widget of the next chapter allows you to draw pixels directly to the window. Besides just pixels, there are a number of functions that make it possible for you to draw and/or fill rectangles, polygons, circles, ellipses, arcs, text, and pixmaps.

✦   ✦   ✦

The Drawing Area and Graphic Primitives

CHAPTER

In This Chapter

Drawing individual pixels on a display window

Drawing squares, rectangles, and polygons

Drawing curves, circles, ellipses, and arcs

Mixing text and other renderings inside the same window

Painting a pixmap on the surface of a window

Animating in a window by drawing multiple frames

◆   ◆   ◆   ◆

There is a widget named `GtkDrawingArea` that displays a blank window. This window can be used to draw graphics. You can draw them one pixel at a time, one line at a time, or you can draw simple geometric shapes, polygons, pixmap images, or any combination of these.

This chapter contains a collection of examples that draw graphic shapes to a drawing area. Because the application program assumes the responsibility for drawing the graphics and placing them on the window, it also must assume the responsibility of refreshing the window each time it is exposed. It also may need to monitor the size and shape of the window to make any necessary adjustments to the drawing.

In a way, every displayable widget contains a drawing area because it is simply a window. The `GtkDrawingArea` widget is best for this purpose because it doesn't do any drawing itself. You could perform the same operations on, say, a button widget, but you would be competing with the natural button actions of updating the status coloring and writing the text — the results would be unpredictable. With a drawing area, you have complete control.

Drawing Area Basics

A GtkDrawingArea widget is not much more than a basic X window — it is simply a window as a widget. There is a set of function calls that you can use to paint the pixels in a variety of ways. But the process is a little different than that of other widgets. Your program must take more responsibility for the details because this is all done at a level below some of the GTK+ (and the entire GNOME) automation.

Most GNOME and GTK+ widgets assume the responsibility of keeping their display updated. This is not so with a GdkDrawingArea. You need to set up a callback function that draws the window whenever it becomes visible. Also, since you have pixel-by-pixel control of what gets drawn, you need to use GdkGC (graphics context) objects to do the drawing. There are a number of GdkGC objects that are supplied as a part of the GTK+ widget but, for special situations, you may need to create your own.

The following example demonstrates the basics of setting up a drawing area. This program fills the application window with a GdkDrawingArea and draws two lines on it.

```
1 /** simpleline.c **/
2 #include <gnome.h>
3
4 gint eventDelete(GtkWidget *widget,
5         GdkEvent *event,gpointer data);
6 gint eventDestroy(GtkWidget *widget,
7         GdkEvent *event,gpointer data);
8 gboolean eventDraw(GtkWidget *widget,
9         GdkEvent *event,gpointer data);
10
11 #define WIDTH 200
12 #define HEIGHT 100
13
14 int main(int argc,char *argv[])
15 {
16     GtkWidget *app;
17     GtkWidget *area;
18
19     gnome_init("simpleline","1.0",argc,argv);
20     app = gnome_app_new("simpleline","Drawing Area");
21     gtk_signal_connect(GTK_OBJECT(app),"delete_event",
22         GTK_SIGNAL_FUNC(eventDelete),NULL);
23     gtk_signal_connect(GTK_OBJECT(app),"destroy",
24         GTK_SIGNAL_FUNC(eventDestroy),NULL);
25
26     area = gtk_drawing_area_new();
27     gtk_widget_set_usize(area,WIDTH,HEIGHT);
28     gnome_app_set_contents(GNOME_APP(app),area);
29
30     gtk_signal_connect(GTK_OBJECT(area),"event",
31         GTK_SIGNAL_FUNC(eventDraw),NULL);
```

```
32
33      gtk_widget_show_all(app);
34      gtk_main();
35      exit(0);
36 }
37 gboolean eventDraw(GtkWidget *widget,
38          GdkEvent *event,gpointer data) {
39      gdk_draw_line(widget->window,
40              widget->style->black_gc,
41              10,
42              10,
43              WIDTH - 10,
44              HEIGHT - 10);
45      gdk_draw_line(widget->window,
46              widget->style->white_gc,
47              10,
48              HEIGHT - 10,
49              WIDTH - 10,
50              10);
51      return(TRUE);
52 }
53 gint eventDelete(GtkWidget *widget,
54          GdkEvent *event,gpointer data) {
55      return(FALSE);
56 }
57 gint eventDestroy(GtkWidget *widget,
58          GdkEvent *event,gpointer data) {
59      gtk_main_quit();
60      return(0);
61 }
```

The drawing area is created by the call to gtk_drawing_area_new() on line 26, and its size is set on line 27. The call to gnome_app_set_contents() attaches the drawing area as the only displayable content of the application window. The application window adjusts its size to contain the drawing area.

The call to gtk_signal_connect() on line 30 assigns a callback function to the *event* signal. This signal (available from all widgets) is particularly appropriate for a drawing area because it not only signals window configuration and mapping events, it also signals when the window is exposed and needs to be drawn. An exposure event occurs whenever there is any kind of exposure to any part of the window — by deiconization, being uncovered by another window, or even a disappearing tooltip that partially obscured the window.

The callback function eventDraw() begins on line 37. This is a simple callback that ignores the type of the event and draws the entire window whenever an event occurs. The function gtk_draw_line() is used with two different graphics contexts to draw lines of two different colors. A graphics context object — a GdkGC object — defines the color for each. As you can see from lines 40 and 46, there are some standard graphics contexts included as part of a widget. The result is shown in Figure 10-1.

Figure 10-1: A pair of lines
drawn on a drawing area

One Pixel at a Time

If you want to have ultimate control over your graphics, you can write to the window
one pixel at a time. There are two basic ways of doing this — a *single-point function*
draws a single pixel, and a *multiple-point function* enables you to store the pixel
locations in an array. The following example demonstrates both of these methods.

```
 1 /** pixels.c **/
 2 #include <gnome.h>
 3
 4 gint eventDelete(GtkWidget *widget,
 5        GdkEvent *event,gpointer data);
 6 gint eventDestroy(GtkWidget *widget,
 7        GdkEvent *event,gpointer data);
 8 gboolean eventDraw(GtkWidget *widget,
 9        GdkEvent *event,gpointer data);
10
11 #define WIDTH 400
12 #define HEIGHT 200
13
14 int main(int argc,char *argv[])
15 {
16     GtkWidget *app;
17     GtkWidget *area;
18
19     gnome_init("pixels","1.0",argc,argv);
20     app = gnome_app_new("pixels","Drawing Pixels");
21     gtk_signal_connect(GTK_OBJECT(app),"delete_event",
22             GTK_SIGNAL_FUNC(eventDelete),NULL);
23     gtk_signal_connect(GTK_OBJECT(app),"destroy",
24             GTK_SIGNAL_FUNC(eventDestroy),NULL);
25
26     area = gtk_drawing_area_new();
27     gtk_widget_set_usize(area,WIDTH,HEIGHT);
28     gnome_app_set_contents(GNOME_APP(app),area);
29
30     gtk_signal_connect(GTK_OBJECT(area),"event",
31             GTK_SIGNAL_FUNC(eventDraw),NULL);
32
33     gtk_widget_show_all(app);
34     gtk_main();
35     exit(0);
36 }
37 gboolean eventDraw(GtkWidget *widget,
```

```
38              GdkEvent *event,gpointer data) {
39      static GdkPoint points[] = {
40          { 50,100 }, { 51,100 }, { 50,101 }, { 51,101 },
41          { 60,100 }, { 61,100 }, { 60,101 }, { 61,101 },
42          { 55,105 }, { 56,105 }, { 55,106 }, { 56,106 },
43          { 50,110 }, { 51,111 }, { 52,112 }, { 53,112 },
44          { 54,113 }, { 55,113 }, { 56,113 }, { 57,113 },
45          { 58,112 }, { 59,112 }, { 60,111 }, { 61,110 },
46      };
47      gint x = WIDTH/4;
48      gint y = 0;
49      gint i;
50
51      while(y < HEIGHT) {
52          for(i=0; i<10; i++) {
53              gdk_draw_point(widget->window,
54                      widget->style->black_gc,
55                      x++,
56                      y);
57          }
58          for(i=0; i<10; i++) {
59              gdk_draw_point(widget->window,
60                      widget->style->white_gc,
61                      x,
62                      y++);
63          }
64      }
65
66      srand(1);
67      for(i=0; i<2000; i++) {
68          x = (int)((((double)rand()*WIDTH)/RAND_MAX);
69          y = (int)((((double)rand()*HEIGHT)/RAND_MAX);
70          gdk_draw_point(widget->window,
71                  widget->style->white_gc,
72                  x,
73                  y);
74      }
75
76      gdk_draw_points(widget->window,
77                  widget->style->black_gc,
78                  points,
79                  sizeof(points)/sizeof(GdkPoint));
80
81      return(TRUE);
82 }
83 gint eventDelete(GtkWidget *widget,
84          GdkEvent *event,gpointer data) {
85      return(FALSE);
86 }
87 gint eventDestroy(GtkWidget *widget,
88          GdkEvent *event,gpointer data) {
89      gtk_main_quit();
90      return(0);
91 }
```

Lines 26 through 31 create the drawing area, attach it to the application window, and assign to it the callback function eventDraw(). The pixels are painted to the window in the callback function.

The loop beginning on line 51 draws a zigzag line diagonally across the window as shown in Figure 10-2. The call to gdk_draw_point() on line 53 draws a black pixel. Because it is in a loop (beginning on line 52) and the x coordinate is incremented with each pixel drawing, the result is the horizontal line portion of the zigzag. The second loop, beginning on line 58, calls gdk_draw_point() to draw a white pixel while incrementing the y coordinate — which is the vertical portion of the zigzag.

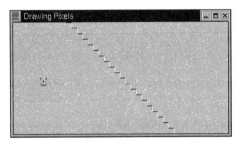

Figure 10-2: Individual pixels drawn to a window

Lines 66 through 73 scatter white pixels randomly around the window. Using a constant value to seed the random number generator, as done in the call to srand() on line 66, the same sequence of pseudo-random numbers is generated. In this case, the ability to reproduce the same sequence is an advantage because the window can draw itself in exactly the same way every time it is exposed. Lines 68 and 69 call rand() to generate new values for both x and y. The function rand() returns a number from 0 to RAND_MAX, so it is necessary to scale the number to the range of possible pixel locations. The call to gdk_draw_point() draws the pixel using the white GdkGC. You can see the white spots scattered around the window in Figure 10-2.

Lines 76 through 79 use a different method of drawing pixels. Instead of calculating each pixel position and looping to draw each one, the pixel locations are stored in the array of GtkPoint structs defined on line 39. When drawn as black pixels, it appears as the smiley face on the left side of Figure 10-2. The GdkPoint struct contains nothing more than an x and a y value:

```
struct _GdkPoint {
    gint16 x;
    gint16 y;
};
```

The call to gdk_draw_points() on line 76 requires the address of the array of points and the number of members of the array. Line 79 determines the number of members of the array by dividing the size of the array by the size of one of its members.

There is a standard X utility that you can use to make it easier to inspect the pixels. To run it, enter **xmag** from the command line and then select the upper-left corner of a region on the display — it is not limited to a single window. Figure 10-3 displays the details of the pixels written by this example.

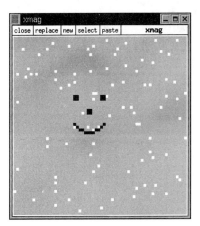

Figure 10-3: A close-up of pixels: drawn one at a time

Drawing and Filling Rectangles

Rectangles can be drawn as either a block of color or as an outline. By combining the two, you can have a rectangle with an outline.

```
 1 /** rectangles.c **/
 2 #include <gnome.h>
 3
 4 gint eventDelete(GtkWidget *widget,
 5        GdkEvent *event,gpointer data);
 6 gint eventDestroy(GtkWidget *widget,
 7        GdkEvent *event,gpointer data);
 8 gboolean eventDraw(GtkWidget *widget,
 9        GdkEvent *event,gpointer data);
10
11 #define HORIZ 50
12 #define VERT 60
13 #define WIDTH (HORIZ * 10)
14 #define HEIGHT (VERT * 3)
15
```

```
16 int main(int argc,char *argv[])
17 {
18     GtkWidget *app;
19     GtkWidget *area;
20
21     gnome_init("rectangles","1.0",argc,argv);
22     app = gnome_app_new("rectangles","Drawing Rectangles");
23     gtk_signal_connect(GTK_OBJECT(app),"delete_event",
24             GTK_SIGNAL_FUNC(eventDelete),NULL);
25     gtk_signal_connect(GTK_OBJECT(app),"destroy",
26             GTK_SIGNAL_FUNC(eventDestroy),NULL);
27
28     area = gtk_drawing_area_new();
29     gtk_widget_set_usize(area,WIDTH,HEIGHT);
30     gnome_app_set_contents(GNOME_APP(app),area);
31
32     gtk_signal_connect(GTK_OBJECT(area),"event",
33             GTK_SIGNAL_FUNC(eventDraw),NULL);
34
35     gtk_widget_show_all(app);
36     gtk_main();
37     exit(0);
38 }
39 gboolean eventDraw(GtkWidget *widget,
40         GdkEvent *event,gpointer data) {
41     gint x;
42     gint y;
43     gint width = HORIZ * 2;
44     gint height = VERT;
45
46     x = HORIZ;
47     y = VERT;
48     gdk_draw_rectangle(widget->window,
49             widget->style->black_gc,
50             FALSE,
51             x,y,
52             width,height);
53
54     x = HORIZ * 4;
55     gdk_draw_rectangle(widget->window,
56             widget->style->white_gc,
57             TRUE,
58             x,y,
59             width,height);
60
61     x = HORIZ * 7;
62     gdk_draw_rectangle(widget->window,
63             widget->style->white_gc,
64             TRUE,
65             x,y,
66             width,height);
67     gdk_draw_rectangle(widget->window,
```

```
68                  widget->style->black_gc,
69                  FALSE,
70                  x,y,
71                  width,height);
72
73      return(TRUE);
74 }
75 gint eventDelete(GtkWidget *widget,
76          GdkEvent *event,gpointer data) {
77      return(FALSE);
78 }
79 gint eventDestroy(GtkWidget *widget,
80          GdkEvent *event,gpointer data) {
81      gtk_main_quit();
82      return(0);
83 }
```

Figure 10-4 shows the rectangles drawn by this program. They all are drawn by calling gdk_draw_rectangle() with the *x* and *y* coordinates of the upper-left corner and the height and width of the rectangle.

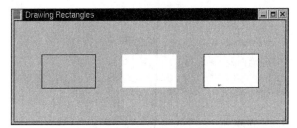

Figure 10-4: Rectangles can be filled or outlined

The rectangle on the left is drawn by the call to gdk_draw_rectangle() on line 48. The built-in black GdkGC is used and the third parameter is set to FALSE, which specifies that the rectangle not be filled — just the outline is drawn. The rectangle in the center is drawn the same as the one on the left, except the built-in white GdkGC object is used and the fill option is set to TRUE.

The third rectangle shown in the window is really the same rectangle drawn twice. The call to gdk_draw_rectangle() on line 62 draws the white-filled rectangle, and the function call on line 67 draws the black line surrounding it.

There is something a little odd about drawing rectangles in X. Outlines of rectangles are one pixel wider and taller than filled-in rectangles. The top and left are in the same place, but the bottom and the right are extended by one pixel. If you want to draw an outline around a filled rectangle, you need to draw the outline last. If you draw the outline first, the filled rectangle covers the top and left portion of the outline, but it leaves the bottom and right portion visible.

Note   As a bit of legacy built into X at its very beginning, outlined rectangles are larger than filled rectangles. The drawing concept used is that a coordinate specifies a point *between* the pixels, and all drawing at that point occurs to the pixel below and to the right of the coordinate. For the most part this works the way we expect, but this one-pixel difference in size results from using these rules to determine which pixels are bound by the coordinates when filling, and which pixels are drawn when outlining.

Drawing and Filling Polygons

A polygon can be drawn from a set of points. The points are stored as an array of GdkPoint struct—the same as for pixel-by-pixel drawing described earlier in this chapter. The function gdk_draw_polygon() draws a line segment from the first point to the second one, then to the third, and so on until a line is drawn to the last point. Then, to close the polygon, a line is drawn from the last point back to the first one. The following example draws the same polygon in different ways to show the results of filling and outlining.

```
 1 /** polygons.c **/
 2 #include <gnome.h>
 3
 4 gint eventDelete(GtkWidget *widget,
 5         GdkEvent *event,gpointer data);
 6 gint eventDestroy(GtkWidget *widget,
 7         GdkEvent *event,gpointer data);
 8 gboolean eventDraw(GtkWidget *widget,
 9         GdkEvent *event,gpointer data);
10
11 #define HORIZ 20
12 #define VERT 20
13 #define WIDTH (HORIZ * 29)
14 #define HEIGHT (VERT * 9)
15
16 static GdkPoint points[] = {
17         { 80, 20 },
18         { 20, 80 },
19         { 40, 80 },
20         { 60, 120 },
21         { 20, 160 },
22         { 80, 140 },
23         { 140, 160 },
24         { 100, 120 },
25         { 120, 80 },
26         { 140, 80 },
27 };
28
29 int main(int argc,char *argv[])
```

```
30 {
31     GtkWidget *app;
32     GtkWidget *area;
33
34     gnome_init("polygons","1.0",argc,argv);
35     app = gnome_app_new("polygons","Drawing Polygons");
36     gtk_signal_connect(GTK_OBJECT(app),"delete_event",
37             GTK_SIGNAL_FUNC(eventDelete),NULL);
38     gtk_signal_connect(GTK_OBJECT(app),"destroy",
39             GTK_SIGNAL_FUNC(eventDestroy),NULL);
40
41     area = gtk_drawing_area_new();
42     gtk_widget_set_usize(area,WIDTH,HEIGHT);
43     gnome_app_set_contents(GNOME_APP(app),area);
44
45     gtk_signal_connect(GTK_OBJECT(area),"event",
46             GTK_SIGNAL_FUNC(eventDraw),NULL);
47
48     gtk_widget_show_all(app);
49     gtk_main();
50     exit(0);
51 }
52 gboolean eventDraw(GtkWidget *widget,
53         GdkEvent *event,gpointer data) {
54     gint i;
55     GdkPoint *p = malloc(sizeof(points));
56     gint pointCount = sizeof(points)/sizeof(GdkPoint);
57
58     for(i=0; i<pointCount; i++) {
59         p[i].x = points[i].x;
60         p[i].y = points[i].y;
61     }
62     gdk_draw_polygon(widget->window,
63             widget->style->black_gc,
64             FALSE,
65             p,
66             pointCount);
67
68     for(i=0; i<pointCount; i++)
69         p[i].x += 140;
70     gdk_draw_polygon(widget->window,
71             widget->style->white_gc,
72             TRUE,
73             p,
74             pointCount);
75
76     for(i=0; i<pointCount; i++)
77         p[i].x += 140;
78     gdk_draw_polygon(widget->window,
79             widget->style->black_gc,
80             FALSE,
81             p,
```

```
82                  pointCount);
83         gdk_draw_polygon(widget->window,
84                  widget->style->white_gc,
85                  TRUE,
86                  p,
87                  pointCount);
88
89         for(i=0; i<pointCount; i++)
90             p[i].x += 140;
91         gdk_draw_polygon(widget->window,
92                  widget->style->white_gc,
93                  TRUE,
94                  p,
95                  pointCount);
96         gdk_draw_polygon(widget->window,
97                  widget->style->black_gc,
98                  FALSE,
99                  p,
100                 pointCount);
101
102        free(p);
103        return(TRUE);
104 }
105 gint eventDelete(GtkWidget *widget,
106        GdkEvent *event,gpointer data) {
107        return(FALSE);
108 }
109 gint eventDestroy(GtkWidget *widget,
110        GdkEvent *event,gpointer data) {
111        gtk_main_quit();
112        return(0);
113 }
```

The polygon itself is defined in the points array on line 16. This same shape is used to draw all of polygons, so it is necessary for the routine doing the actual drawing—the one named eventDraw() on line 52—to make a copy of the array and adjust the coordinates to move the polygon from one place to another. A working copy of the array is constructed on line 55, and a count of the total number of points in the array is calculated on line 56. The original array is duplicated in the loop beginning one line 58. The eventDraw() function can be called any number of times, so it is important to return allocated memory back to the system—as is done with a call to free() on line 102.

The polygon on the left in Figure 10-5 is drawn by the call to gdk_draw_polygon() on line 62. The built-in black GdkGC is used. The fill parameter is set to FALSE, which causes only the outline to be drawn.

The loop on line 68 moves the working polygon to the right by 140 pixels by simply adding 140 to all the x values in the array. The call to gdk_draw_polygon() on line 70 draws a filled polygon using the built-in white GdkGC.

Figure 10-5: Polygons being filled and outlined

Lines 76 through 87 move the array coordinates to the right and draw two polygons. The first drawing is a black outline and the second is a white-filled shape. The same situation that applies to rectangles applies to polygons — the outline is slightly larger than the filled form. As with a rectangle, vertical right sides are one pixel further to the right and horizontal bottom sides are one pixel further down. As you can see from the patterns along the edges of the third polygon in the figure, the filled polygon covers some of the pixels and leaves others.

The polygon on the right, drawn by lines 89 to 100, has the filler drawn first and then the outline drawn on top of it. This way, the outline around the polygon is complete.

Drawing Circles, Ellipses, and Arcs

The following program demonstrates the drawing and filling of curved shapes. The same function is used to draw both circles and ellipses (a circle is simply an ellipse with the same height and width). This function also has the ability to limit the drawing to only a portion of the circle or ellipse. Additionally, there is an option to draw the figure as an outline, or to fill the region created by the shape.

```
 1 /** arcs.c **/
 2 #include <gnome.h>
 3
 4 gint eventDelete(GtkWidget *widget,
 5         GdkEvent *event,gpointer data);
 6 gint eventDestroy(GtkWidget *widget,
 7         GdkEvent *event,gpointer data);
 8 gboolean eventDraw(GtkWidget *widget,
 9         GdkEvent *event,gpointer data);
10 static void drawArcs(GtkWidget *widget,gint y,gint fill);
11
12 #define WIDTH 455
13 #define HEIGHT 140
14
15 int main(int argc,char *argv[])
16 {
17     GtkWidget *app;
```

```
18      GtkWidget *area;
19
20      gnome_init("arcs","1.0",argc,argv);
21      app = gnome_app_new("arcs",
22              "Drawing Circles and Ellipses");
23      gtk_container_set_border_width(GTK_CONTAINER(app),20);
24      gtk_signal_connect(GTK_OBJECT(app),"delete_event",
25              GTK_SIGNAL_FUNC(eventDelete),NULL);
26      gtk_signal_connect(GTK_OBJECT(app),"destroy",
27              GTK_SIGNAL_FUNC(eventDestroy),NULL);
28
29      area = gtk_drawing_area_new();
30      gtk_widget_set_usize(area,WIDTH,HEIGHT);
31      gnome_app_set_contents(GNOME_APP(app),area);
32
33      gtk_signal_connect(GTK_OBJECT(area),"event",
34              GTK_SIGNAL_FUNC(eventDraw),NULL);
35
36      gtk_widget_show_all(app);
37      gtk_main();
38      exit(0);
39 }
40 gboolean eventDraw(GtkWidget *widget,
41          GdkEvent *event,gpointer data) {
42
43      drawArcs(widget,0,FALSE);
44      drawArcs(widget,80,TRUE);
45      return(TRUE);
46 }
47 static void drawArcs(GtkWidget *widget,gint y,gint fill)
48 {
49      gdk_draw_arc(widget->window,
50              widget->style->black_gc,
51              fill,
52              0,y,
53              60,60,
54              0,360 * 64);
55      gdk_draw_arc(widget->window,
56              widget->style->black_gc,
57              fill,
58              80,y,
59              60,60,
60              135 * 64,90 * 64);
61      gdk_draw_arc(widget->window,
62              widget->style->black_gc,
63              fill,
64              110,y,
65              60,60,
66              135 * 64,-270 * 64);
67
68      gdk_draw_arc(widget->window,
69              widget->style->black_gc,
70              fill,
71              190,y,
```

```
72                100,60,
73                0,360 * 64);
74      gdk_draw_arc(widget->window,
75              widget->style->black_gc,
76              fill,
77              310,y,
78              100,60,
79              135 * 64,90 * 64);
80      gdk_draw_arc(widget->window,
81              widget->style->black_gc,
82              fill,
83              350,y,
84              100,60,
85              135 * 64,-270 * 64);
86 }
87 gint eventDelete(GtkWidget *widget,
88          GdkEvent *event,gpointer data) {
89      return(FALSE);
90 }
91 gint eventDestroy(GtkWidget *widget,
92          GdkEvent *event,gpointer data) {
93      gtk_main_quit();
94      return(0);
95 }
```

The function eventDraw() on line 40 is called whenever the drawing area is exposed. It calls drawArcs() to do the actual drawing. The top row shown in Figure 10-6 is drawn by the call to drawArcs() on line 43, and the second row is drawn by the call on line 44. The first argument is the drawing area widget. The second argument is the offset along the *y*-axis. The third argument determines whether or not the drawn figures are filled.

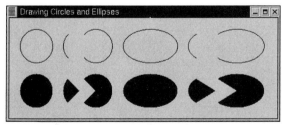

Figure 10-6: Draw and fill both complete and incomplete arcs

The call to gdk_draw_arcs() on line 49 draws a complete circle in the upper-left corner of the drawing area. The first and second arguments are the window and the graphics context. The next argument is TRUE if the figure is to be filled, and FALSE if otherwise. The next two arguments are the *x* and *y* coordinates of the circle. These coordinates determine the location of the upper-left corner of the box bounding the circle or ellipse. The next two arguments are the width and height of the bounding box.

The next-to-last argument to gdk_draw_arcs() is the angle at which the drawing of the arc should begin. The last argument determines how far around the circle the drawing should proceed. The angles are integer values; the units are 1/64th of a degree. The angles are set up in the Cartesian coordinate system with zero degrees to the right and positive angles counter-clockwise.

The mechanics involved with drawing an arc are shown in Figure 10-7. In the figure, the drawing begins at the 45-degree point and proceeds counter-clockwise for a total of 270 degrees — which, after adding the original 45 degrees to it, brings the end of the circle to an angle of 315 degrees. You can specify a negative value for either or both of the angles. A negative starting angle positions itself clockwise from the 0-degree location on the left. Also, a negative angle value for the second angle causes drawing to take place from the starting angle in a clockwise manner. For example, another way to draw the same arc as in Figure 10-7 is to use -(45 * 64) as the starting angle and -(270 * 64) as the number of degrees to draw. The resulting curve looks like the one in the figure, but the curve is drawn in the opposite direction.

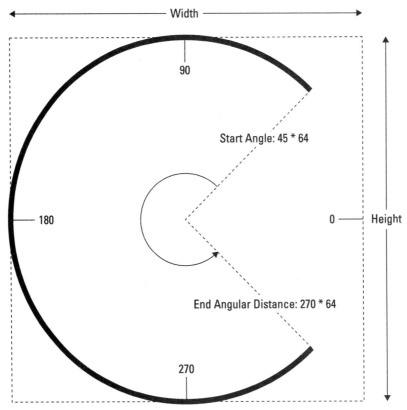

Figure 10-7: Two angles define the portion of the arc drawn

Figure 10-6 showed the same set of figures being drawn and filled. With a closed circle or ellipse, the outline inscribes the same shape as the fill. When the circle or ellipse is not closed, the outline simply leaves a portion blank, while the fill function assumes boundary lines from each end of the curve to the center of the figure.

Drawing Text

There are two functions that draw strings of characters to a drawing area. They both require an array of character values as input, but one draws the entire string while the other draws a selected subset.

```
 1 /** text.c **/
 2 #include <gnome.h>
 3
 4 gint eventDelete(GtkWidget *widget,
 5         GdkEvent *event,gpointer data);
 6 gint eventDestroy(GtkWidget *widget,
 7         GdkEvent *event,gpointer data);
 8 gboolean eventDraw(GtkWidget *widget,
 9         GdkEvent *event,gpointer data);
10 static void mark(GtkWidget *widget,gint x,gint y);
11
12 #define WIDTH 420
13 #define HEIGHT 140
14
15 int main(int argc,char *argv[])
16 {
17     GtkWidget *app;
18     GtkWidget *area;
19
20     gnome_init("text","1.0",argc,argv);
21     app = gnome_app_new("text","Drawing Text");
22     gtk_signal_connect(GTK_OBJECT(app),"delete_event",
23         GTK_SIGNAL_FUNC(eventDelete),NULL);
24     gtk_signal_connect(GTK_OBJECT(app),"destroy",
25         GTK_SIGNAL_FUNC(eventDestroy),NULL);
26
27     area = gtk_drawing_area_new();
28     gtk_widget_set_usize(area,WIDTH,HEIGHT);
29     gnome_app_set_contents(GNOME_APP(app),area);
30
31     gtk_signal_connect(GTK_OBJECT(area),"event",
32         GTK_SIGNAL_FUNC(eventDraw),NULL);
33
34     gtk_widget_show_all(app);
35     gtk_main();
36     exit(0);
```

```
37 }
38 gboolean eventDraw(GtkWidget *widget,
39         GdkEvent *event,gpointer data) {
40     static gchar outString[] =
41        "every character in the string is displayed";
42     GdkFont *font;
43
44     font = gdk_font_load("vga");
45     gdk_draw_string(widget->window,
46             font,
47             widget->style->black_gc,
48             50,50,
49             outString);
50     gdk_font_unref(font);
51     mark(widget,50,50);
52
53     font = gdk_font_load("10x20");
54     gdk_draw_text(widget->window,
55             font,
56             widget->style->black_gc,
57             50,80,
58             &outString[19],
59             23);
60     gdk_font_unref(font);
61     mark(widget,50,80);
62
63     font = gdk_font_load("12x24");
64     gdk_draw_text(widget->window,
65             font,
66             widget->style->black_gc,
67             50,110,
68             &outString[6],
69             9);
70     gdk_font_unref(font);
71     mark(widget,50,110);
72
73     return(TRUE);
74 }
75 static void mark(GtkWidget *widget,gint x,gint y)
76 {
77     gdk_draw_line(widget->window,
78             widget->style->white_gc,
79             x - 5,y,
80             x + 5,y);
81     gdk_draw_line(widget->window,
82             widget->style->white_gc,
83             x,y-5,
84             x,y+5);
85 }
86 gint eventDelete(GtkWidget *widget,
87         GdkEvent *event,gpointer data) {
```

```
88     return(FALSE);
89 }
90 gint eventDestroy(GtkWidget *widget,
91          GdkEvent *event,gpointer data) {
92     gtk_main_quit();
93     return(0);
94 }
```

Lines 27 through 32 create the drawing area window and connect a callback function to it. The text is displayed in the callback function eventDraw() beginning on line 38. The character string outString is defined on line 40 as a null-terminated array of ASCII characters. As shown in Figure 10-8, the string — and parts of the string — are displayed using three different fonts.

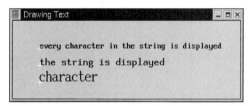

Figure 10-8: Strings and substrings displayed on a drawing area

Lines 44 through 50 draw the top string in the figure. The font named vga is selected on line 44. There are hundreds of fonts available, and there are a number of things that you can do with font size, color, style, and so on. The fonts are explained in Chapter 13.

The font objects are dereferenced after they are used to make sure there is no memory leak. The first GdkFont object is created by the call to gdk_font_load() on line 44. Like all new objects, it assumes an internal reference count of one. Then the font is passed to the gdk_draw_string() on line 45. From this viewpoint — the viewpoint of the application program — exactly what happens to the font object inside the drawing routine is completely unknown. It can create a new object by making a clone of this one. It can keep a pointer to the one you passed to it. It also can use it to do the drawing and not keep any reference to it at all. But, thanks to the reference counter, it doesn't matter what the drawing routine does. By calling gdk_font_unref() on line 50, the internal reference counter is decremented and the font object is deleted — but only if the count goes to zero. That is, the font object persists only if the drawing function adds its own reference to the count.

The function gdk_draw_string() uses the font to draw each character of the string, until it encounters the null string terminator. The location of the string is determined by the *x* and *y* coordinates on line 48.

The function `gdk_draw_text()` on line 54 doesn't necessarily begin at the start of the array, and it doesn't use the null terminator to end the string. The arguments on lines 58 and 59 cause the display to begin with the 19th character of the array and continue for a maximum of 23 characters. The function `gdk_draw_text()` on line 64 draws a substring from the middle of the character array. On lines 68 and 69, the starting point is at the sixth character and only nine characters are displayed.

After each line of text is drawn, the function `mark()` on line 75 is called to mark the position of the *x* and *y* values used to draw the text (the little white crosses mark the beginning of each line of text). This is so you can see how the point relates to the actual drawn text. The origin of drawing text is quite different from the geometric figures drawn earlier (they all use the point as their upper-left corner). For text, the point appears at the bottom-left of the text — almost. Most characters line up with their bottoms on the line, but there are descenders on some characters (such as y and g) that go below the line. Also, in some special fonts, the first character can be extended to the left of the point — that is, the point may be inside the character instead of to its left. This, along with the varying point size and a range of height and width ratios, can make text very difficult to place. Chapter 13 has methods for calculating sizes and positions that enable you to align text properly.

Drawing a Pixmap

As shown in earlier chapters, it is possible to draw a pixmap without using a drawing area; but with a drawing area, a pixmap easily can be intermixed with other graphics types. The following example draws a pixmap and then uses other drawing area types to annotate it.

```
 1 /** pixmap.c **/
 2 #include <gnome.h>
 3
 4 #include "logo.xpm"
 5
 6 gint eventDelete(GtkWidget *widget,
 7       GdkEvent *event,gpointer data);
 8 gint eventDestroy(GtkWidget *widget,
 9       GdkEvent *event,gpointer data);
10 gboolean eventDraw(GtkWidget *widget,
11       GdkEvent *event,gpointer data);
12
13 #define WIDTH 500
14 #define HEIGHT 300
15
16 int main(int argc,char *argv[])
17 {
18     GtkWidget *app;
19     GtkWidget *area;
```

```
20
21        gnome_init("pixmap","1.0",argc,argv);
22        app = gnome_app_new("pixmap","Pixmaps Etcetera");
23        gtk_signal_connect(GTK_OBJECT(app),"delete_event",
24                GTK_SIGNAL_FUNC(eventDelete),NULL);
25        gtk_signal_connect(GTK_OBJECT(app),"destroy",
26                GTK_SIGNAL_FUNC(eventDestroy),NULL);
27
28        area = gtk_drawing_area_new();
29        gtk_widget_set_usize(area,WIDTH,HEIGHT);
30        gnome_app_set_contents(GNOME_APP(app),area);
31
32        gtk_signal_connect(GTK_OBJECT(area),"event",
33                GTK_SIGNAL_FUNC(eventDraw),NULL);
34
35        gtk_widget_show_all(app);
36        gtk_main();
37        exit(0);
38 }
39 gboolean eventDraw(GtkWidget *widget,
40         GdkEvent *event,gpointer data) {
41     GdkBitmap *mask;
42     GdkPixmap *pixmap;
43     GtkStyle *style;
44     GdkFont *font = gdk_font_load("10x20");
45     static GdkPoint points[] = {
46         { 210, 253 },
47         { 220, 245 },
48         { 220, 252 },
49         { 295, 252 },
50         { 295, 254 },
51         { 220, 254 },
52         { 220, 260 },
53     };
54
55     style = gtk_widget_get_style(widget);
56     pixmap = gdk_pixmap_create_from_xpm_d(widget->window,
57             &mask,&style->bg[GTK_STATE_NORMAL],
58             (gchar **)logo);
59
60     gdk_draw_pixmap(widget->window,
61             widget->style->black_gc,
62             pixmap,
63             0,0,
64             0,0,
65             257,303);
66
67     gdk_draw_pixmap(widget->window,
68             widget->style->black_gc,
69             pixmap,
70             70,60,
```

```
 71                     210,50,
 72                     90,50);
 73          gdk_draw_string(widget->window,
 74                  font,
 75                  widget->style->white_gc,
 76                  240,75,
 77                  "Beak");
 78
 79          gdk_draw_pixmap(widget->window,
 80                  widget->style->black_gc,
 81                  pixmap,
 82                  0,200,
 83                  350,105,
 84                  100,100);
 85          gdk_draw_string(widget->window,
 86                  font,
 87                  widget->style->black_gc,
 88                  350,210,
 89                  "Right.");
 90
 91          gdk_draw_string(widget->window,
 92                  font,
 93                  widget->style->black_gc,
 94                  300,260,
 95                  "Left");
 96          gdk_draw_polygon(widget->window,
 97                  widget->style->black_gc,
 98                  TRUE,
 99                  points,
100                  sizeof(points) / sizeof(GdkPoint));
101
102          gdk_pixmap_unref(pixmap);
103          gdk_font_unref(font);
104          return(TRUE);
105   }
106   gint eventDelete(GtkWidget *widget,
107          GdkEvent *event,gpointer data) {
108          return(FALSE);
109   }
110   gint eventDestroy(GtkWidget *widget,
111          GdkEvent *event,gpointer data) {
112          gtk_main_quit();
113          return(0);
114   }
```

Lines 28 through 33 create the drawing area window and attach the callback
function eventDraw(). All of the drawing is done by the callback so the window
correctly redraws itself whenever it is exposed. The display, shown in Figure 10-9, is
made by drawing three areas of a pixmap, three text strings, and one filled polygon.

Figure 10-9: Trimmed pixmaps with strings and a polygon

The pixmap starts out as XPM-formatted data in the file logo.xpm and is included in the program on line 4. The call to gdk_pixmap_create_from_xpm_d() on line 56 converts the XPM data into a GdkPixmap.

The call to gdk_draw_pixmap() on line 60 draws the entire pixmap to the drawing area. The first three arguments specify the window of the drawing area, the GdkGC to be used for drawing, and the GdkPixmap to be drawn. Inside the function, the actual drawing is achieved by copying a rectangle of pixels from the pixmap to the window, so the last six arguments are the x and y source location, the x and y destination location, and the height and width of the rectangular area to be copied. On line 60, the objective is to draw the entire pixmap, so the source coordinates are (0,0). To place it in the upper-left corner of the drawing area, the destination coordinates are also (0,0). The height and width values are the ones defined in the XPM data.

Note   It may seem odd to you that the call to gdk_draw_pixmap() requires a graphics context, because all the sizes and colors are defined by the pixmap and the other arguments. It turns out that there is some hidden information inside the GdkGC object that is needed by the low-level function XCopyArea(), which copies pixels from one place to another.

The call to gdk_draw_pixmap() on line 67 uses the same pixmap as input, but only copies a small section of it. On line 70, the upper-left corner of the rectangle to be copied is set to (70,60). The upper-left corner of the destination rectangle is defined on line 71 to be (210,50). Line 72 sets the width of the rectangle to 90 pixels and the height to 50 pixels. As a result, only the area immediately surrounding the beak is copied to the window.

In a drawing area, you can draw right over the top of things that are there already. On line 73, there is a call to gdk_draw_string() that places the "Beak" text directly on top of the pixmap placed there earlier.

Lines 79 through 89 copy the right-foot section of the source bitmap to the drawing area, and then, using another string, adds a tag noting that it is the right foot. Lines 91 through 100 add an annotation to the left foot. The call to `gkd_draw_string()` draws the text. The call to `gdk_draw_polygon()` uses the set of points defined on line 45 to draw a filled arrow pointing from the text to the foot.

Lines 102 and 103 return the pixmap and the font to the system. The callback routine builds them from scratch each time it is called, so there is no need to keep it — besides, failure to return it can cause memory leaks. In a real application, it makes more sense to store both of these in static variables so they can be used again without requiring a complete rebuild.

Resizing the Drawing Area

The drawing area may be resized, depending on the rules applied to it by its containing widget. If you ignore the size change, your drawing can leave spaces or be clipped on the right and bottom. However, you can have your drawing resize itself to fit the new window configuration.

Note   It may not be worth the effort to write the code that resizes the drawing. To make a drawing resizable, you need to calculate all the coordinates as a ratio of width and height of the window. Some things, such as XPM image data and text fonts, don't rescale easily. Also, a change in the aspect ratio changes circles to ellipses and squares to rectangles.

The following example draws rectangles based on the height and width of the window, and allows for these values to change.

```
 1 /** configure.c **/
 2 #include <gnome.h>
 3
 4 gint eventDelete(GtkWidget *widget,
 5         GdkEvent *event,gpointer data);
 6 gint eventDestroy(GtkWidget *widget,
 7         GdkEvent *event,gpointer data);
 8 gboolean eventDraw(GtkWidget *widget,
 9         GdkEvent *event,gpointer data);
10 gboolean eventConfigure(GtkWidget *widget,
11         GdkEventConfigure *event,gpointer data);
12
13 static int width = 20;
14 static int height = 20;
15
16 int main(int argc,char *argv[])
17 {
18     GtkWidget *app;
```

```
19      GtkWidget *area;
20
21      gnome_init("configure","1.0",argc,argv);
22      app = gnome_app_new("configure","Resizing Rectangles");
23      gtk_signal_connect(GTK_OBJECT(app),"delete_event",
24              GTK_SIGNAL_FUNC(eventDelete),NULL);
25      gtk_signal_connect(GTK_OBJECT(app),"destroy",
26              GTK_SIGNAL_FUNC(eventDestroy),NULL);
27
28      area = gtk_drawing_area_new();
29      gtk_widget_set_usize(area,width,height);
30      gnome_app_set_contents(GNOME_APP(app),area);
31
32      gtk_signal_connect(GTK_OBJECT(area),"expose-event",
33              GTK_SIGNAL_FUNC(eventDraw),NULL);
34      gtk_signal_connect(GTK_OBJECT(area),"configure-event",
35              GTK_SIGNAL_FUNC(eventConfigure),NULL);
36
37      gtk_widget_show_all(app);
38      gtk_main();
39      exit(0);
40 }
41 gboolean eventDraw(GtkWidget *widget,
42          GdkEvent *event,gpointer data) {
43      gint xDelta = width / 5;
44      gint yDelta = height / 5;
45
46      gdk_draw_rectangle(widget->window,
47              widget->style->white_gc,
48              TRUE,
49              0,0,
50              width,height);
51
52      gdk_draw_rectangle(widget->window,
53              widget->style->black_gc,
54              TRUE,
55              xDelta,yDelta,
56              width - (2 * xDelta),height - (2 * yDelta));
57
58      xDelta *= 2;
59      yDelta *= 2;
60      gdk_draw_rectangle(widget->window,
61              widget->style->white_gc,
62              TRUE,
63              xDelta,yDelta,
64              width - (2 * xDelta),height - (2 * yDelta));
65
66      return(TRUE);
67 }
68 gboolean eventConfigure(GtkWidget *widget,
69          GdkEventConfigure *event,gpointer data) {
```

```
70
71      width = event->width;
72      height = event->height;
73
74      return(TRUE);
75 }
76 gint eventDelete(GtkWidget *widget,
77           GdkEvent *event,gpointer data) {
78      return(FALSE);
79 }
80 gint eventDestroy(GtkWidget *widget,
81           GdkEvent *event,gpointer data) {
82      gtk_main_quit();
83      return(0);
84 }
```

Lines 28 through 30 create a drawing area and insert it into the main window of the application. Whenever this main window is resized, the drawing area also is resized. The callback routines are connected to the drawing area on lines 32 through 35. The `"expose-event"` calls `eventDraw()` whenever the figure needs to be drawn. The `"configure-event"` calls `eventConfigure()` whenever the drawing area changes its height or width.

The rectangles are drawn by the callback function `eventDraw()` beginning on line 41. The values of `xDelta` and `yDelta`, used to size and position the rectangles, are calculated as fractional values of the height and width. The call to `gdk_draw_rectangle()` on line 46 uses the width and height values to clear the entire drawing area to a white background. Using the fractional values, a black rectangle is drawn on line 52 and a white one is drawn inside it on line 60. Because all dimensions are calculated from the size of the window itself, the figure is drawn to fit. Figure 10-10 shows the appearance of the window in four different sizes and shapes.

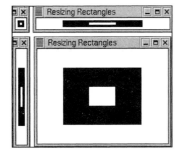

Figure 10-10: Rectangles reshaped to fit the window

The callback function `eventConfigure()` on line 68 is called whenever the window configuration changes. Lines 71 and 73 retrieve the new height and width values and store them until the next time the window is drawn. There is no need to do anything else because an `"expose-event"` always follows a `"configure-event"`, and `eventDraw()` is called to render the figure.

Drawing to Memory and Animation

There are times when it is convenient to write graphics to a location in memory instead of directly to a window. One such example is when doing animation because the first step in creating a new frame is to clear the old frame. If this is done directly on the window, the animation flickers with each frame. Fortunately, it is possible to draw to a pixmap and then use it to update the entire window all at once.

The following program performs the simple animation of dropping balls from the top of the window and bouncing them off the bottom. Each ball continues to bounce lower and lower until it finally disappears off the left or right side of the window.

```
 1 /** animation.c **/
 2 #include <gnome.h>
 3 #include <math.h>
 4
 5 static struct ballStruct {
 6     double x;
 7     double y;
 8     double xVelocity;
 9     double yVelocity;
10 } ball[5];
11
12 gint eventDelete(GtkWidget *widget,
13         GdkEvent *event,gpointer data);
14 gint eventDestroy(GtkWidget *widget,
15         GdkEvent *event,gpointer data);
16 gint nextFrame(gpointer data);
17 void newBall(struct ballStruct *b);
18 void nextBall(struct ballStruct *b);
19 gint nextFrame(gpointer data);
20
21 #define WIDTH 400
22 #define HEIGHT 300
23 #define GRAVITY 0.8
24 #define RADIUS 5
25 #define DIAMETER (RADIUS * 2)
26 #define INTERVAL 30
27
28 int main(int argc,char *argv[])
29 {
30     int i;
31     GtkWidget *app;
32     GtkWidget *area;
33
34     gnome_init("animation","1.0",argc,argv);
35     app = gnome_app_new("animation",
36             "Drawing Area Animation");
37     gtk_container_set_border_width(GTK_CONTAINER(app),20);
```

```
38      gtk_signal_connect(GTK_OBJECT(app),"delete_event",
39              GTK_SIGNAL_FUNC(eventDelete),NULL);
40      gtk_signal_connect(GTK_OBJECT(app),"destroy",
41              GTK_SIGNAL_FUNC(eventDestroy),NULL);
42
43      area = gtk_drawing_area_new();
44      gtk_widget_set_usize(area,WIDTH,HEIGHT);
45      gnome_app_set_contents(GNOME_APP(app),area);
46
47      gtk_timeout_add(INTERVAL,nextFrame,area);
48      for(i=0; i<5; i++)
49          newBall(&ball[i]);
50
51      gtk_widget_show_all(app);
52      gtk_main();
53      exit(0);
54 }
55 gint nextFrame(gpointer data)
56 {
57      int i;
58      static GdkPixmap *pixmap = NULL;
59      GtkWidget *widget = (GtkWidget *)data;
60
61      if(pixmap == NULL) {
62          pixmap = gdk_pixmap_new(widget->window,
63                  WIDTH,HEIGHT,-1);
64      }
65
66      gdk_draw_rectangle(pixmap,
67              widget->style->white_gc,
68              TRUE,
69              0,0,
70              WIDTH,HEIGHT);
71
72      for(i=0; i<5; i++) {
73          nextBall(&ball[i]);
74          gdk_draw_arc(pixmap,
75                  widget->style->black_gc,
76                  TRUE,
77                  (int)ball[i].x,(int)ball[i].y,
78                  DIAMETER,DIAMETER,
79                  0,360*64);
80      }
81
82      gdk_draw_pixmap(widget->window,
83              widget->style->black_gc,
84              pixmap,
85              0,0,
86              0,0,
87              WIDTH,HEIGHT);
88
```

```
 89      return(TRUE);
 90 }
 91 void newBall(struct ballStruct *b)
 92 {
 93      b->x = (((double)rand()*WIDTH)/RAND_MAX);
 94      b->y = (((double)rand()*HEIGHT)/RAND_MAX) - HEIGHT;
 95      do {
 96          b->xVelocity = (((double)rand()*10)/RAND_MAX) - 5;
 97          b->yVelocity = (((double)rand()*10)/RAND_MAX) - 5;
 98      } while(fabs(b->xVelocity) < 0.5);
 99 }
100 void nextBall(struct ballStruct *b)
101 {
102      if((b->x < -DIAMETER) || (b->x > WIDTH)) {
103          newBall(b);
104          return;
105      }
106      if((b->y + DIAMETER) >= HEIGHT) {
107          if(b->yVelocity > 0)
108              b->yVelocity = -b->yVelocity;
109          b->yVelocity *= 0.9;
110      } else {
111          b->yVelocity += GRAVITY;
112      }
113      b->x += b->xVelocity;
114      b->y += b->yVelocity;
115 }
116 gint eventDelete(GtkWidget *widget,
117          GdkEvent *event,gpointer data) {
118      return(FALSE);
119 }
120 gint eventDestroy(GtkWidget *widget,
121          GdkEvent *event,gpointer data) {
122      gtk_main_quit();
123      return(0);
124 }
```

On lines 43 through 45, the drawing area is constructed and attached to the main window of the application. There is no callback function connected to the window because there are no events to be processed. Instead, the call to gtk_timeout_add() on line 47 sets up an interval timer that calls the function named nextFrame() every 30 milliseconds. A pointer to the drawing area widget is passed to function nextFrame(). The loop on line 48 sets the initial values (position and velocity) for each of the five balls.

The function nextFrame() beginning on line 55 has the job of updating the display to the next frame of the animation sequence. To do its work, it needs a location to accomplish the piece-by-piece construction of the new frame; therefore, a pixmap is created on line 61. The pixmap itself is declared as static on line 58, so it only needs to be created the first time this function exits — it repeatedly uses the same pixmap to draw each frame. Before the frame can be drawn, it is necessary to clear the pixmap of the previous frame. The call to `gdk_draw_rectangle()` on line 66 uses the white graphics context and the entire width and height, which clears the entire pixmap to white.

The loop beginning on line 72 executes once for each of the five balls. The function `nextBall()` is called to reposition each one to its next position on the display, and a call is made to `gdk_draw_arc()` to draw a filled circle to the pixmap. The balls are moved and drawn one at a time until the pixmap holds a frame that has all the balls one step ahead of their position in the displayed window. The call to `gdk_draw_pixmap()` on line 82 draws the entire pixmap to the window, which — because the two are the same size — completely redraws the window in a single operation. The next screen update changes the entire frame at once.

The function `newBall()` beginning on line 91 stores a random set of initial values for a ball. The random number generator is used to place the ball on the window somewhere between the left and right sides and somewhere above the top. It is okay to draw outside the defined area enclosed by the pixmap or window — but the drawing has no effect — and it usually is easier to draw things that won't show rather than calculate whether or not all or part of your graphic will show. Each ball, as defined by the struct on line 5, has four settings. The values of x and y are the coordinates of its position in the window, with the origin at the upper-left. The values `xVelocity` and `yVelocity` specify how fast the ball is moving — they are the values that are added to the x and y values the next time the ball moves. A falling ball has a positive `yVelocity` and a rising ball has a negative `yVelocity`. A ball moving to the right has a positive `xVelocity` and a ball moving to the left has a negative `xVelocity`.

The function `nextBall()` on line 100 moves a ball from one position to the next. Recall that the *x* and *y* coordinates are at the upper-left corner of the drawn figures, so the `DIAMETER` value must be added to find the locations of the right and bottom sides. If the horizontal range tested on line 102 shows that the ball has moved to the left or right until it is outside the window, it is abandoned and a new ball is created in its place by the call to `newBall()`. The text on line 106 determines whether a descending ball has reached the bottom of the window and, if so, its velocity is reversed by being negated on line 108. There is friction in the bounce; so on line 109, the velocity is reduced in magnitude by 10 percent. If the ball is at any location other than the bottom, the velocity is adjusted on line 111 by adding the `GRAVITY` factor — this slows a rising ball and speeds a falling one. Finally, on lines 113 and 114, the current velocity values are used to update the x and y position of the ball.

Summary

There are a number of fundamental operations that give your application low-level access to the pixels that make up a window. Some of these operations are at such a low level that they are only wrappers for the underlying Xlib function. Other operations, such as the GTK+ functions described in this chapter, operate at a higher level and demonstrate how:

✦ Your program can draw one pixel at a time to the window. Each pixel has its own position and color.

✦ You can draw an individual line, or you can draw a series of joined lines by drawing them in segments.

✦ There is a collection of shape-drawing routines that you can use to create rectangles, squares, circles, ellipses, and arcs. There is also a generalized polygon function that you can use to draw any other shape. All of these shapes can be outlined or filled.

✦ You can use the same set of drawing primitives to draw to a pixmap — a drawable that is resident in RAM instead of on the display. Then the pixmap can be used to make up all or part of the final window display. The pixmap is particularly useful in animation because the detailed drawing occurs in the background and the entire window updates at once.

✦ If the user changes the size of the drawing area, then you can have your program respond by resizing the drawings to fit the new size.

This chapter rendered all of the graphics in black and white. The next chapter shows how you can use colors for everything from filling polygons to drawing text. Your program can specify and install an exact color, or it can choose the already-installed color that is the closest to the one you want.

✦   ✦   ✦

Color and the Graphics Context

This chapter deals with color and other drawing configuration settings. The colors are stored in a graphics context that is used to draw pixels to the window of a widget. Also, inside this graphics context, are settings that control the kind and shape of lines that get drawn. It is possible to fill a region on a window with a solid color, a transparent stippled color, or even a full-color pixmap.

Coloring widgets is very simple, but you need to understand the color model and how to manipulate the colors. That's what this chapter is about. There is a wide range of color capabilities with the various hardware options available, but the X color model scales easily across them all. When you work with color, you decide what color you want and pass it on to the system — the system then either uses your exact color, or selects another one that is close to it.

The Architecture of Color

The X Window System uses a color system with each of the three primary colors represented by a binary value. The intensity of each color is the ratio of the color value to the maximum value possible. For example, to get 50 percent red on a system with 8 bits per color, the value would be 127. To get 50 percent on a system with 16 bits per color, the value would be 32767. Colors also can be represented by floating-point values, usually in the range of 0.0 to 1.0, so a 50 percent color level would be 0.5.

There are a number of different kinds of display architectures. The X Window System has devised a method of dealing with them in a standard way. The GNOME/GTK+ software is built on top of this generalized system so you probably will never need to know all the low-level details (unless you need to do something very special). However, some of the operations your program needs to perform make a lot more sense if you have some idea of what's going on in the basement.

A display has a storage location for each pixel it displays on the screen. The contents of the items in storage determine the color and brightness of their associated pixels — to change a pixel, change the contents of its storage location. Hardware uses different methods of converting the stored value into a color — while some use the numeric value and directly convert it into a color, others use the stored value as an index into a table of colors. The table of colors is known as a *color map*. Different hardware requires different kinds of color maps. Table 11-1 lists the various types.

Table 11-1
The Classes of Displays

Name	Description
Pseudo Color	The pixel value indexes a color map containing RGB values. The color map can be modified dynamically.
Direct Color	The pixel value is split into three values and used to index three separate color maps: one for the red component, one for blue, and one for green. The color maps can be modified dynamically.
Gray Scale	The pixel value indexes a color map containing displayable gray scale values. The color map can be modified dynamically.
Static Color	The pixel value indexes a color map containing RGB values. The color map is static in the hardware and cannot be changed.
True Color	The pixel value is split into three values and used to index three separate color maps: one for the red component, one for blue, and one for green. Each of the color maps is an even (or near-even) gradient from no color to full saturation and cannot be altered.
Static Gray	The pixel value indexes a color map containing displayable gray scale values. The color map is static and cannot be modified.

The color map is used by the display hardware to paint all pixels in all windows, so changing the color map changes the appearance of everything. Some color maps allow this sort of change, and some don't. There is seldom a need to make a color map change, but if your application does change the color map, it would be polite to put the original one back when you lose focus to another application.

The following program tells you what kind of display you have, the number of bits per pixel, the size of the color map, and some other related items.

```
1 /** visual.c **/
2 #include <gnome.h>
3
4 gint eventDelete(GtkWidget *widget,
5         GdkEvent *event,gpointer data);
6 gint eventDestroy(GtkWidget *widget,
7         GdkEvent *event,gpointer data);
8
9 int main(int argc,char *argv[])
10 {
11      GtkWidget *app;
12      GtkWidget *label;
13      GdkVisual *visual;
14      gchar work[80];
15      gchar text[4096];
16
17      gnome_init("visual","1.0",argc,argv);
18      app = gnome_app_new("visual","GdkVisual");
19      gtk_container_set_border_width(GTK_CONTAINER(app),30);
20      gtk_signal_connect(GTK_OBJECT(app),"delete_event",
21              GTK_SIGNAL_FUNC(eventDelete),NULL);
22      gtk_signal_connect(GTK_OBJECT(app),"destroy",
23              GTK_SIGNAL_FUNC(eventDestroy),NULL);
24
25      visual = gdk_visual_get_system();
26
27      sprintf(text,"Type: ");
28      switch(visual->type) {
29      case GDK_VISUAL_STATIC_GRAY:
30          strcat(text,"Static Gray\n");
31          break;
32      case GDK_VISUAL_GRAYSCALE:
33          strcat(text,"Grayscale\n");
34          break;
35      case GDK_VISUAL_STATIC_COLOR:
36          strcat(text,"Static Color\n");
37          break;
38      case GDK_VISUAL_PSEUDO_COLOR:
39          strcat(text,"Pseudo Color\n");
40          break;
41      case GDK_VISUAL_TRUE_COLOR:
42          strcat(text,"True Color\n");
43          break;
```

```
44      case GDK_VISUAL_DIRECT_COLOR:
45          strcat(text,"Direct Color\n");
46          break;
47      }
48      sprintf(work,"Depth (number of bits per pixel): %d\n",
49              visual->depth);
50      strcat(text,work);
51      strcat(text,"Byte order: ");
52      switch(visual->byte_order) {
53      case GDK_LSB_FIRST:
54          strcat(text,"LSB first\n");
55          break;
56      case GDK_MSB_FIRST:
57          strcat(text,"MSB first\n");
58          break;
59      }
60      sprintf(work,"\nSize of colormap array: %d\n",
61              visual->colormap_size);
62      strcat(text,work);
63      sprintf(work,"Colormap bits per RGB: %d\n",
64              visual->bits_per_rgb);
65      strcat(text,work);
66
67      strcat(text,
68              "\nColor       Mask        Shift    Bits\n");
69      sprintf(work," red    0x%08X    %2d      %2d\n",
70              visual->red_mask,visual->red_shift,
71              visual->red_prec);
72      strcat(text,work);
73      sprintf(work,"green   0x%08X    %2d      %2d\n",
74              visual->green_mask,visual->green_shift,
75              visual->green_prec);
76      strcat(text,work);
77      sprintf(work," blue   0x%08X    %2d      %2d\n",
78              visual->blue_mask,visual->blue_shift,
79              visual->blue_prec);
80      strcat(text,work);
81
82      label = gtk_label_new(text);
83      gtk_label_set_justify(GTK_LABEL(label),
84              GTK_JUSTIFY_LEFT);
85      gtk_misc_set_padding(GTK_MISC(label),GNOME_PAD,0);
86
87      gnome_app_set_contents(GNOME_APP(app),label);
88
89      gtk_widget_show_all(app);
90      gtk_main();
91      exit(0);
92  }
```

```
 93 gint eventDelete(GtkWidget *widget,
 94        GdkEvent *event,gpointer data) {
 95     return(FALSE);
 96 }
 97 gint eventDestroy(GtkWidget *widget,
 98        GdkEvent *event,gpointer data) {
 99     gtk_main_quit();
100     return(0);
101 }
```

The call to gdk_visual_get_system() on line 25 returns a GdkVisual struct containing information on the system display. The data from the display is formatted as text on lines 27 through 80. On lines 82 through 87, the text is inserted into a label and the label is inserted into the application window.

The resulting display from one system is shown in Figure 11-1. This system has a true color display with 15 bits per pixel. There are 32 red values, 32 blue values, and 32 green values in the three color map arrays. This means there are 32,768 colors available. To determine, for example, the red component of a color, the bits of the red mask are anded with the bits of the pixel value and the result is shifted 10 bits to the right. The resulting 5-bit number is the index into the red color map.

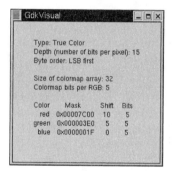

Figure 11-1: Characteristics and capabilities of the display

The Graphics Context

All pixel-painting is done according to the values stored in a GdkGC object — a *graphics context*. There are two colors in the graphics context: one for painting the foreground and one for the background (along with several other items). There are settings that determine the width of drawn lines, the style for drawing lines, the types of corners made by joining line segments, the clipping region, tiling and stippling masks, fill rules, and more.

There are some special exceptions (such as foreground and background colors) but for the most part, the contents of a graphics context cannot be addressed directly. However, they can be copied in and out using a GdkGCValues struct:

```
struct _GdkGCValues {
    GdkColor foreground;
    GdkColor background;
    GdkFont *font;
    GdkFunction function;
    GdkFill fill;
    GdkPixmap *tile;
    GdkPixmap *stipple;
    GdkPixmap *clip_mask;
    GdkSubwindowMode subwindow_mode;
    gint ts_x_origin;
    gint ts_y_origin;
    gint clip_x_origin;
    gint clip_y_origin;
    gint graphics_exposures;
    gint line_width;
    GdkLineStyle line_style;
    GdkCapStyle cap_style;
    GdkJoinStyle join_style;
};
```

The following example retrieves the graphics context from a window and displays information about its contents. It not only displays the values stored in a GdkGC, it also demonstrates which values are available for each field.

```
 1 /** showgc.c **/
 2 #include <gnome.h>
 3
 4 gint eventDelete(GtkWidget *widget,
 5         GdkEvent *event,gpointer data);
 6 gint eventDestroy(GtkWidget *widget,
 7         GdkEvent *event,gpointer data);
 8 gint listValues(gpointer data);
 9 static char *functionString(GdkFunction function);
10 static char *fillString(GdkFill fill);
11 static char *subwindowString(GdkSubwindowMode mode);
12 static char *lineStyleString(gint style);
13 static char *capStyleString(gint style);
14 static char *joinStyleString(gint style);
15
16 #define WIDTH 40
17 #define HEIGHT 30
18
19 int main(int argc,char *argv[])
20 {
21     GtkWidget *app;
22     GtkWidget *area;
23
```

```
24      gnome_init("showgc","1.0",argc,argv);
25      app = gnome_app_new("flasher","Listing GC");
26      gtk_signal_connect(GTK_OBJECT(app),"delete_event",
27              GTK_SIGNAL_FUNC(eventDelete),NULL);
28      gtk_signal_connect(GTK_OBJECT(app),"destroy",
29              GTK_SIGNAL_FUNC(eventDestroy),NULL);
30
31      area = gtk_drawing_area_new();
32      gtk_widget_set_usize(area,WIDTH,HEIGHT);
33      gnome_app_set_contents(GNOME_APP(app),area);
34      gtk_signal_connect(GTK_OBJECT(app),"realize",
35              GTK_SIGNAL_FUNC(listValues),area);
36
37      gtk_widget_show_all(app);
38      gtk_main();
39      exit(0);
40 }
41 gint listValues(gpointer data)
42 {
43      GtkWidget *widget = GTK_WIDGET(data);
44      GdkGC *gc;
45      GdkGCValues gcv;
46
47      gc = widget->style->white_gc;
48      gdk_gc_get_values(gc,&gcv);
49
50      printf("foreground RGB: %u %u %u (0x%08X)\n",
51          gcv.foreground.red,gcv.foreground.green,
52          gcv.foreground.blue,(guint)gcv.foreground.pixel);
53      printf("background RGB: %u %u %u (0x%08X)\n",
54          gcv.background.red,gcv.background.green,
55          gcv.background.blue,(guint)gcv.background.pixel);
56      printf("font id: %d   ascent: %d   descent: %d\n",
57          gdk_font_id(gcv.font),
58          gcv.font->ascent,gcv.font->descent);
59      printf("pixel drawing function: %s\n",
60          functionString(gcv.function));
61      printf("fill method: %s\n",fillString(gcv.fill));
62      printf("subwindow mode: %s\n",
63          subwindowString(gcv.subwindow_mode));
64      printf("tiling/stippling origin: (%d,%d)\n",
65          gcv.ts_x_origin,gcv.ts_y_origin);
66      printf("clipping origin: (%d,%d)\n",
67          gcv.clip_x_origin,gcv.clip_y_origin);
68      printf("graphic exposures: %d\n",
69          gcv.graphics_exposures);
70      printf("line width: %d\n",gcv.line_width);
71      printf("line style: %s\n",
72          lineStyleString(gcv.line_style));
73      printf("cap style: %s\n",
74          capStyleString(gcv.line_style));
75      printf("join style: %s\n",
```

```
76              joinStyleString(gcv.line_style));
77
78      return(TRUE);
79 }
80 static char *functionString(GdkFunction function)
81 {
82      switch(function) {
83      case GDK_COPY: return("copy");
84      case GDK_INVERT: return("invert");
85      case GDK_XOR: return("xor");
86      case GDK_CLEAR: return("clear");
87      case GDK_AND: return("and");
88      case GDK_AND_REVERSE: return("and reverse");
89      case GDK_AND_INVERT: return("and invert");
90      case GDK_NOOP: return("noop");
91      case GDK_OR: return("or");
92      case GDK_EQUIV: return("equiv");
93      case GDK_OR_REVERSE: return("or reverse");
94      case GDK_COPY_INVERT: return("copy invert");
95      case GDK_OR_INVERT: return("or invert");
96      case GDK_NAND: return("nand");
97      case GDK_SET: return("set");
98      default: return("");
99          }
100 }
101 static char *fillString(GdkFill fill)
102 {
103      switch(fill) {
104      case GDK_SOLID: return("solid");
105      case GDK_TILED: return("tiled");
106      case GDK_STIPPLED: return("stippled");
107      case GDK_OPAQUE_STIPPLED: return("opaque stippled");
108      default: return("");
109          }
110 }
111 static char *subwindowString(GdkSubwindowMode mode)
112 {
113      if(mode == GDK_CLIP_BY_CHILDREN)
114          return("clip by children");
115      else if(mode == GDK_INCLUDE_INFERIORS)
116          return("include inferiors");
117      return("");
118 }
119 static char *lineStyleString(gint style)
120 {
121      switch(style) {
122      case GDK_LINE_SOLID: return("solid");
123      case GDK_LINE_ON_OFF_DASH: return("on off dash");
124      case GDK_LINE_DOUBLE_DASH: return("double dash");
125      default: return("");
126          }
127 }
128 static char *capStyleString(gint style)
```

```
129 {
130     switch(style) {
131     case GDK_CAP_NOT_LAST: return("not last");
132     case GDK_CAP_BUTT: return("butt");
133     case GDK_CAP_ROUND: return("round");
134     case GDK_CAP_PROJECTING: return("projecting");
135     default: return("");
136     }
137 }
138 static char *joinStyleString(gint style)
139 {
140     switch(style) {
141     case GDK_JOIN_MITER: return("miter");
142     case GDK_JOIN_ROUND: return("round");
143     case GDK_JOIN_BEVEL: return("bevel");
144     default: return("");
145     }
146 }
147
148 gint eventDelete(GtkWidget *widget,
149         GdkEvent *event,gpointer data) {
150     return(FALSE);
151 }
152 gint eventDestroy(GtkWidget *widget,
153         GdkEvent *event,gpointer data) {
154     gtk_main_quit();
155     return(0);
156 }
```

Lines 31 through 35 create a drawing area, insert it into the main window, and connect the callback function listValues() to the area. The callback is triggered by the "realize" signal, which means the callback is called just once—when the window is fully constructed and capable of being displayed. It is necessary to wait until the window is realized because there are GdkGC values available until then.

The callback function listValues(), beginning on line 41, prints every value from a graphics context found in the widget. There are a number of graphics contexts in the widget, which I describe later in this chapter, but this program gets the one named white_gc on line 47. The values in a GdkGC object are not accessible directly, so, on line 48, the call to gdk_gc_get_values() fills a GdkGCValues struct with information in the GdkGC. The rest of this function prints the values.

Lines 50 through 55 display information about the colors. There are two colors stored in a graphics context: one for the foreground and one for the background. All painting and drawing is done using the foreground color, while clearing and erasing is performed using the background color.

Line 56 lists information about the font. About all that is known about it is an internal ID number, the maximum number of pixels a character may ascend above the base line, and the maximum number of pixels a character may descend below the base line. Adding these two figures together gives you the height of the tallest character. There is other size information available, but it only has meaning when applied to a specific string, as described in Chapter 13.

Line 59 calls the function functionString(), defined on line 80, to display the method (the function) that will be used to draw a pixel. There are several methods available as shown in Table 11-2. The default, and the most common of these, is GDK_COPY, which simply overwrites the old pixel value with the new value. The functions are bit-by-bit operations, so they work exactly the same for any number of bits per pixel.

Table 11-2
Functions Used to Write Pixels

Function	Bitwise Operation Description
GDK_AND	Each destination bit is the result of an *and* between source and destination bits.
GDK_AND_INVERT	The bits in the source are *inverted*. Then, each destination bit is the result of an *and* between source and destination bits.
GDK_AND_REVERSE	The bits in the destination are *inverted*. Then, each destination bit is the result of an *and* between source and destination bits.
GDK_CLEAR	All the bits in the destination pixel are set to 0. The source pixels are ignored.
GDK_COPY	The destination pixel is *copied* from the source pixel.
GDK_COPY_INVERT	The source is *copied* to the destination and then it is *inverted*.
GDK_EQUIV	The bits in the source are *inverted*. Then, each destination bit is the result of an *exclusive or* operation between the source and destination bits.
GDK_INVERT	The bits in the destination pixel are *inverted* (zeroes become ones and ones become zeroes). The source pixels are ignored.
GDK_NAND	Both the source and destination are *inverted*. Then, the destination is the result of the *and* between the source and destination bits.
GDK_NOOP	The destination is unchanged.
GDK_OR	Each destination bit is the result of an *or* between source and destination bits.
GDK_OR_REVERSE	The bits in the destination are *inverted*. Then, each destination is the result of the *or* between source and destination bits.
GDK_SET	All destination pixels are set to 1.
GDK_XOR	Each destination pixel bit is the result of an *exclusive or* between the source and destination pixel bit.

Line 61 calls the function `fillString()`, defined on line 101, to list the method used for filling regions of the window. Table 11-3 lists the fill functions, in terms of the fields in the `_GdkGCValues` struct, and describes how each uses the pixmaps. The default is `GDK_SOLID` to fill the region with a solid color.

Table 11-3
Functions Used for Filling Regions

Function	Description
GDK_SOLID	Every pixel in the area is painted the `foreground` color. The pixmaps have no effect.
GDK_TILED	The `tile` pixmap is copied to the destination in such a way that it fills the entire area. The upper-left corner of the `tile` pixmap is positioned at the upper-left corner of the area to be filled. If the pixmap is too small, it is repeated both vertically and horizontally until the entire area is filled.
GDK_STIPPLED	The `stipple` pixmap is used as a mask to paint the area. The `stipple` pixmap must have a depth of one—that is, one bit per pixel. Where a stipple bit is set to 1, the `foreground` color is drawn. Where a stipple bit is set to 0, the pixel is left unchanged.
GDK_OPAQUE_STIPPLED	The `stipple` pixmap is used as a mask to paint the area. The `stipple` pixmap must have a depth of one—that is, one bit per pixel. Where a stipple bit is set to 1, the `foreground` color is drawn. Where a stipple bit is set to 0, the `background` color is drawn.

Line 62 displays the subwindow mode by calling the function `subwindowString()`, defined on line 111. If the setting is `GDK_CLIP_BY_CHILDREN`, any drawing to the window does not occur in the regions covered by any child windows. (In other words, this window cannot cover a child window.) The other option is `GDK_INCLUDE_INFERIORS`, which directs the drawing to ignore any child windows and simply draw right over them. (In other words, this window covers its child windows).

Lines 64 through 67 display the *x* and *y* origin points for tiling, stippling, and clipping. The default for all of these values is zero. The default has tiling begin by laying the first tile in the upper-left corner of the window—at coordinate point (0,0) of the drawable (not of a figure being drawn on it). The settings can be used to position the first tile to fit with the figure being drawn, as in the examples later in this chapter. Another reason you might want to do this is for symmetry. For example, if you have a window that is 200 pixels wide and you are using a tile that is 75 pixels wide, you may want to set the horizontal origin of tiling to -25 causing the tile trimming to be the same on both sides of the window. The origin of the clip mask can be repositioned the same way.

Line 68 displays whether or not pixel-copying failure (due to an obscured window) should generate an interrupt. When copying pixels from a window onto the screen, the copy may fail partially or completely if the originating window is partially or completely obscured. This is a consequence of the application being responsible for updating the window—the server is not required to keep a copy of obscured pixels. An GdkEventExpose event is issued when the copy fails, and a GdkEventNoExpose event is issued if it succeeds.

Lines 70 through 76 display the settings that control line drawing. The line width is measured as the number of pixels, with zero being the default of a single-pixel width. While a line of width 0 and 1 show up alike on the display, a line defined as a width of 0 can be displayed only as a solid line. A nonzero width line can be drawn as a solid line, or it can be in one of several dashed forms, as shown in the function lineStyleString() on line 119. A line that is wider than one pixel can have one of four different styles at its end, and one of three different styles where two lines join at an angle. I provide examples of these styles later in this chapter.

The output from this program varies from one system to another because of differences in graphic capabilities. Also the default black color, white color, font size, and line styles may differ. The following is an example of typical output:

```
foreground RGB: 62900 49151 35864 (0x00007FFF)
background RGB: 24744 2055 0 (0x00000001)
font id: 33554437    ascent: 11    descent: 3
pixel drawing function: copy
fill method: solid
subwindow mode: clip by children
tiling/stippling origin: (0,0)
clipping origin: (0,0)
graphics exposures: False
line width: 0
line style: solid
cap style: not last
join style: miter
```

Setting the Color of a Widget

The following program uses numeric values for red, green, and blue to create a color in the form of a GdkColor object. Then the color is inserted as the foreground into a graphics context (a GdkGC object). The graphics context is used to fill a rectangular area. A timer causes rectangles of different colors to be painted continuously to the window. Please note that the color, size, and location of each rectangle are random.

```
 1 /** flasher.c **/
 2 #include <gnome.h>
 3
 4 gint eventDelete(GtkWidget *widget,
 5         GdkEvent *event,gpointer data);
 6 gint eventDestroy(GtkWidget *widget,
 7         GdkEvent *event,gpointer data);
 8 gint drawRandomRectangle(gpointer data);
 9
10 #define WIDTH 400
11 #define HEIGHT 300
12 #define INTERVAL 30
13
14 int main(int argc,char *argv[])
15 {
16     GtkWidget *app;
17     GtkWidget *area;
18
19     gnome_init("flasher","1.0",argc,argv);
20     app = gnome_app_new("flasher","Creating Colors");
21     gtk_signal_connect(GTK_OBJECT(app),"delete_event",
22             GTK_SIGNAL_FUNC(eventDelete),NULL);
23     gtk_signal_connect(GTK_OBJECT(app),"destroy",
24             GTK_SIGNAL_FUNC(eventDestroy),NULL);
25
26     area = gtk_drawing_area_new();
27     gtk_widget_set_usize(area,WIDTH,HEIGHT);
28     gnome_app_set_contents(GNOME_APP(app),area);
29     gtk_timeout_add(INTERVAL,drawRandomRectangle,area);
30
31     gtk_widget_show_all(app);
32     gtk_main();
33     exit(0);
34 }
35 gint drawRandomRectangle(gpointer data)
36 {
37     static GdkColormap *colormap = NULL;
38     static GdkGC *gc = NULL;
39     GdkColor color;
40     GtkWidget *widget = GTK_WIDGET(data);
41     gint x = 20;
42     gint y = 20;
43     gint width = 40;
44     gint height = 40;
45
46     if(colormap == NULL) {
47         colormap = gdk_colormap_get_system();
```

```
48            gc = gdk_gc_new(widget->window);
49        }
50
51        color.red += (((double)rand()*0xFFFF)/RAND_MAX);
52        color.green += (((double)rand()*0xFFFF)/RAND_MAX);
53        color.blue += (((double)rand()*0xFFFF)/RAND_MAX);
54        gdk_color_alloc(colormap,&color);
55
56        gdk_gc_set_foreground(gc,&color);
57
58        x = (((double)rand()*WIDTH)/RAND_MAX) - (WIDTH/4);
59        y = (((double)rand()*HEIGHT)/RAND_MAX) - (HEIGHT/4);
60        width = (((double)rand()*(WIDTH/2))/RAND_MAX);
61        height = (((double)rand()*(HEIGHT/2))/RAND_MAX);
62
63        gdk_draw_rectangle(widget->window,
64                gc,
65                TRUE,
66                x,y,
67                width,height);
68        return(TRUE);
69  }
70
71  gint eventDelete(GtkWidget *widget,
72          GdkEvent *event,gpointer data) {
73        return(FALSE);
74  }
75  gint eventDestroy(GtkWidget *widget,
76          GdkEvent *event,gpointer data) {
77        gtk_main_quit();
78        return(0);
79  }
```

Lines 26 through 29 create the drawing area that is used to display the rectangles, and attaches the function drawRandomRectangle() to a timer. The interval value, defined on line 12, is set to 30 milliseconds. The area widget is passed to the callback function as the data. The function drawRandomRectangle(), beginning on line 35, uses the random number generator in the creation of a color and draws one rectangle.

The system color map is retrieved by the call to gdk_colormap_get_system() on line 47. The local variable color map is defined as static, so it is only necessary for the color map to be retrieved the first time the function is called. The call to gdk_gc_new() on line 48 creates a new graphics context that is suitable for drawing to that particular window.

Note There is a reason that a specific window is used in the call to gdk_gc_new() that creates a new graphics context. There are constraints of sizes, pixel depths, and so on that can vary from one window to the next. This happens quite often in X because any one program may have windows open simultaneously on two or more workstations.

The program creates a color object and places it in the graphics context, and then uses the graphics context to draw the rectangle. A color is defined in the following struct:

```
struct _GdkColor {
    gulong pixel;
    gushort red;
    gushort green;
    gushort blue;
};
```

Lines 51 through 54 create a new color. The GdkColor object is assigned random numbers from 0 to 65535 into each of its red, green, and blue fields. The call to gdk_color_alloc() does whatever necessary to make the color available for use — exactly what it does depends on the system. If there is room in a writeable color map, it just adds the color. If the color map is not writeable, or if it is full, it looks through the color map and finds the closest color to the one requested. If an exact match for the color is not found, it adjusts the GdkColor's red, blue, and green values to the values closest to ones in the color map. Whichever method is used to locate the color, the GdkColor's pixel field is updated with the actual pixel value. Now the color is ready to be used.

Line 56 calls gdk_gc_set_foreground() to insert the GdkColor object into the GdkGC object as the foreground color.

Lines 58 through 61 define the triangle's size and location. The range of values is scaled according to the size of the window in an attempt to have as much of the drawing as possible inside the window, and have the rectangles small enough so several are showing at all times. The call to gdk_draw_rectangle() on line 63 draws the rectangle to the window using the graphics context that holds the recently created color.

Line Styles in a Graphics Context

To manipulate the style of the lines that are drawn, it is necessary to manipulate the values inside a graphics context. Because each drawing operation requires its own GdkGC object, it is quite simple to create one and manipulate it to work any way you want. The following example creates a graphics context and uses it to draw lines in several different styles.

```
1 /** linestyle.c **/
2 #include <gnome.h>
3
4 gint eventDelete(GtkWidget *widget,
5         GdkEvent *event,gpointer data);
6 gint eventDestroy(GtkWidget *widget,
```

```
 7             GdkEvent *event,gpointer data);
 8 gboolean eventDraw(GtkWidget *widget,
 9             GdkEvent *event,gpointer data);
10
11 #define WIDTH 300
12 #define HEIGHT 350
13
14 int main(int argc,char *argv[])
15 {
16     GtkWidget *app;
17     GtkWidget *area;
18
19     gnome_init("linestyle","1.0",argc,argv);
20     app = gnome_app_new("linestyle","Line Styles");
21     gtk_signal_connect(GTK_OBJECT(app),"delete_event",
22             GTK_SIGNAL_FUNC(eventDelete),NULL);
23     gtk_signal_connect(GTK_OBJECT(app),"destroy",
24             GTK_SIGNAL_FUNC(eventDestroy),NULL);
25
26     area = gtk_drawing_area_new();
27     gtk_widget_set_usize(area,WIDTH,HEIGHT);
28     gnome_app_set_contents(GNOME_APP(app),area);
29
30     gtk_signal_connect(GTK_OBJECT(area),"event",
31             GTK_SIGNAL_FUNC(eventDraw),NULL);
32
33     gtk_widget_show_all(app);
34     gtk_main();
35     exit(0);
36 }
37 gboolean eventDraw(GtkWidget *widget,
38             GdkEvent *event,gpointer data) {
39     int i;
40     int x = 40;
41     int y = 180;
42     char dashList[4] = { 5, 15, 20, 30 };
43     GdkGC *gc;
44     GdkColormap *colormap;
45     GdkColor foreground;
46     GdkColor background;
47     GdkFont *font;
48     GdkPoint points[3] = {
49         { 80, 40 },
50         { 40, 120 },
51         { 80, 120 }
52     };
53
54     font = gdk_font_load("vga");
55     gc = gdk_gc_new(widget->window);
56     colormap = gdk_colormap_get_system();
57     if(gdk_color_parse("blue",&foreground)) {
```

```
58              gdk_color_alloc(colormap,&foreground);
59              gdk_gc_set_foreground(gc,&foreground);
60          }
61          if(gdk_color_parse("yellow",&background)) {
62              gdk_color_alloc(colormap,&background);
63              gdk_gc_set_background(gc,&background);
64          }
65
66          /*- The MITER join -*/
67          gdk_gc_set_line_attributes(gc,
68                  10,
69                  GDK_LINE_SOLID,
70                  GDK_CAP_BUTT,
71                  GDK_JOIN_MITER);
72          gdk_draw_polygon(widget->window,
73                  gc,
74                  FALSE,
75                  points,
76                  (int)(sizeof(points)/sizeof(GdkPoint)));
77          gdk_draw_string(widget->window,
78                  font,
79                  gc,
80                  points[1].x,points[1].y + 20,
81                  "Miter");
82
83          /*- The ROUND join -*/
84          for(i=0; i<3; i++)
85              points[i].x += 80;
86          gdk_gc_set_line_attributes(gc,
87                  10,
88                  GDK_LINE_SOLID,
89                  GDK_CAP_BUTT,
90                  GDK_JOIN_ROUND);
91          gdk_draw_polygon(widget->window,
92                  gc,
93                  FALSE,
94                  points,
95                  (int)(sizeof(points)/sizeof(GdkPoint)));
96          gdk_draw_string(widget->window,
97                  font,
98                  gc,
99                  points[1].x,points[1].y + 20,
100                 "Round");
101
102         /*- The BEVEL join -*/
103         for(i=0; i<3; i++)
104             points[i].x += 80;
105         gdk_gc_set_line_attributes(gc,
106                 10,
107                 GDK_LINE_SOLID,
108                 GDK_CAP_BUTT,
```

```
109                     GDK_JOIN_BEVEL);
110         gdk_draw_polygon(widget->window,
111                 gc,
112                 FALSE,
113                 points,
114                 (int)(sizeof(points)/sizeof(GdkPoint)));
115         gdk_draw_string(widget->window,
116                 font,
117                 gc,
118                 points[1].x,points[1].y + 20,
119                 "Bevel");
120
121         /*- Cap BUTT -*/
122         gdk_gc_set_line_attributes(gc,
123                 10,
124                 GDK_LINE_SOLID,
125                 GDK_CAP_BUTT,
126                 GDK_JOIN_MITER);
127         gdk_draw_line(widget->window,
128                 gc,
129                 x,y,
130                 x + 120,y);
131         gdk_draw_string(widget->window,
132                 font,
133                 gc,
134                 x + 130,y + 5,
135                 "Butt");
136
137         /*- Cap NOT LAST -*/
138         y += 20;
139         gdk_gc_set_line_attributes(gc,
140                 10,
141                 GDK_LINE_SOLID,
142                 GDK_CAP_NOT_LAST,
143                 GDK_JOIN_MITER);
144         gdk_draw_line(widget->window,
145                 gc,
146                 x,y,
147                 x + 120,y);
148         gdk_draw_string(widget->window,
149                 font,
150                 gc,
151                 x + 130,y + 5,
152                 "Not last");
153
154         /*- Cap ROUND -*/
155         y += 20;
156         gdk_gc_set_line_attributes(gc,
157                 10,
158                 GDK_LINE_SOLID,
159                 GDK_CAP_ROUND,
```

```
160                  GDK_JOIN_MITER);
161    gdk_draw_line(widget->window,
162            gc,
163            x,y,
164            x + 120,y);
165    gdk_draw_string(widget->window,
166            font,
167            gc,
168            x + 130,y + 5,
169            "Round");
170
171    /*- Cap PROJECTING -*/
172    y += 20;
173    gdk_gc_set_line_attributes(gc,
174            10,
175            GDK_LINE_SOLID,
176            GDK_CAP_PROJECTING,
177            GDK_JOIN_MITER);
178    gdk_draw_line(widget->window,
179            gc,
180            x,y,
181            x + 120,y);
182    gdk_draw_string(widget->window,
183            font,
184            gc,
185            x + 130,y + 5,
186            "Projecting");
187
188    /*- Style SOLID -*/
189    y += 40;
190    gdk_gc_set_line_attributes(gc,
191            10,
192            GDK_LINE_SOLID,
193            GDK_CAP_BUTT,
194            GDK_JOIN_MITER);
195    gdk_draw_line(widget->window,
196            gc,
197            x,y,
198            x + 120,y);
199    gdk_draw_string(widget->window,
200            font,
201            gc,
202            x + 130,y + 5,
203            "Solid");
204
205    /*- Style ON_OFF_DASH -*/
206    y += 20;
207    gdk_gc_set_dashes(gc,
208            0,
209            dashList,
210            4);
```

```
211        gdk_gc_set_line_attributes(gc,
212             10,
213             GDK_LINE_ON_OFF_DASH,
214             GDK_CAP_BUTT,
215             GDK_JOIN_MITER);
216        gdk_draw_line(widget->window,
217             gc,
218             x,y,
219             x + 120,y);
220        gdk_draw_string(widget->window,
221             font,
222             gc,
223             x + 130,y + 5,
224             "On off dash");
225
226        /*- Style DOUBLE DASH -*/
227        y += 20;
228        gdk_gc_set_line_attributes(gc,
229             10,
230             GDK_LINE_DOUBLE_DASH,
231             GDK_CAP_BUTT,
232             GDK_JOIN_MITER);
233        gdk_draw_line(widget->window,
234             gc,
235             x,y,
236             x + 120,y);
237        gdk_draw_string(widget->window,
238             font,
239             gc,
240             x + 130,y + 5,
241             "Double dash");
242
243        gdk_font_unref(font);
244        gdk_gc_unref(gc);
245        return(TRUE);
246 }
247 gint eventDelete(GtkWidget *widget,
248        GdkEvent *event,gpointer data) {
249        return(FALSE);
250 }
251 gint eventDestroy(GtkWidget *widget,
252        GdkEvent *event,gpointer data) {
253        gtk_main_quit();
254        return(0);
255 }
```

Lines 26 through 31 create a GtkDrawingArea widget and attach it to the main window. The callback function eventDraw() is connected to the drawing area. All of the drawing is done in the callback function eventDraw() defined on line 37. The window produced by this program is shown in Figure 11-2.

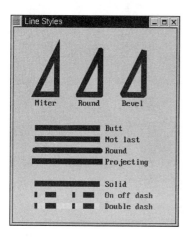

Figure 11-2: Wide lines drawn to demonstrate the line styles

Line 54 calls gdk_font_load() to load the font that is used later to draw the text to the window. This is needed later because a font specification is required to draw strings onto a drawing area.

A new graphics context is constructed on line 55 by calling gdk_gc_new() with the window of the drawing area. The new graphics context is set to the default values for colors, lines, and such and it has its internal values set correctly to draw to the window that is used as the argument.

Lines 55 through 64 set both the foreground and background colors. Colors are constructed and assigned according to a color map, so the system color map is retrieved by the call to gdk_colormap_get_system() on line 56. The call to gdk_color_parse() on line 57 is given the name of a color, and returns TRUE only if the name is recognized and the color values are retrieved.

There are two ways to specify the name of a color in the call to gdk_color_parse(). You can specify the name of the color, as in this example, if the name appears in the file /usr/lib/X11/rgb.txt. This is a text file that is used to map each color name to its set of three RGB numbers. If you add a color name to this file, your program will find it and use it, but your program needs to have some alternative action because the color name may be missing on another system, or even missing in an upgrade of this one. If you want your own color, it is better to specify the RGB values. You can use the method described earlier in this chapter, or you can use the RGB values for the name of the color. Any of the following formats work:

```
"#RGB"
"#RRGGBB"
"#RRRGGGBBB"
"#RRRRGGGGBBBB"
```

Each letter is a hexadecimal digit. The `gdk_color_parse()` function determines which digits are which by counting the total number of digits in the string (the total must be a multiple of 3). For example, to use two digits per color and specify no red, maximum green, and a little blue:

```
"#00FF3C"
```

On line 57, the `gdk_color_parse()` function returns TRUE if the color name is valid. The function `gdk_color_alloc()` is called on line 58 to initialize the color information so it can be used in a graphics context, and the call to `gdk_gc_set_foreground()` on line 59 installs the color into the graphics context as the foreground color. In similar manner, the function calls on lines 61 through 64 establish the background color.

The call to `gdk_gc_set_line_attributes()` on line 67 specifies a *miter joint* on a line that is 10 pixels wide. Wide lines are drawn so the details of the line construction can be seen easily. A miter joint is one where the outside edges of the lines are extended until they meet. This can work well for shallow angles but, as angles get narrow, the point moves further out and can distort the image you are trying to draw. The call to `gdk_polygon()` on line 72 draws the triangle defined in the array of points defined on line 48. Because we are using the new graphics context, the lines are drawn in blue and are 10 pixels wide. The call to `gdk_draw_string()` on line 77 labels the figure as shown in the upper-left corner of Figure 11-2.

The loop on line 84 moves the triangle points to the next position on the window. The following function calls, on lines 86 through 100, draw another triangle. This time, however, the join style is rounded. This is achieved by having the drawing stop when the line reaches the end point, and then drawing a circle around the end point with a diameter that matches with the edges of the line.

On lines 105 through 119, the triangle is moved to the right once again and drawn with a bevel join. You make a *bevel join* by drawing a straight line between the outer edges of the two lines. This probably is best demonstrated by the 90-degree angle at the bottom — both lines end at the same point and the joint is beveled by filling the little triangle that is left over.

Lines 121 through 186 draw four lines with different ending styles. The *butt ending* draws a square end that includes the pixel at the end points. The *not-last ending* is the same as a butt ending, except the last pixel is not drawn. The not-last ending can be used when drawing lines that construct some sort of framework and, because of color differences, the line should not overwrite the pixels of a line already on the display. The round ending is simply a circle drawn around the end points. This extends the line beyond each end point by half the width of the line. The projecting ending extends the length by half of its width — the same amount as the round ending — and draws a butt ending.

Normally, solid lines are drawn but there are two ways to draw dashed lines. Lines 205 through 224 draw *on-off dashed lines*. That is, the foreground color is used to draw every other segment and the other segments are skipped. Lines 226 through 241 draw a double-dash line by using the foreground and background colors alternately.

You can create dashed lines in any pattern you wish. In this program, the dashed line pattern is defined by the `dashList` array on line 42. Each member of the array specifies a number of pixels to be drawn as the foreground or background. The line drawing routine uses `dashList` to draw 5 pixels, then skip 15 pixels, draw 20 pixels, then skip 30 pixels, and go back to the beginning and skip 5 pixels again, and so on until the end of the line is reached. If you have an odd number of members in the array, the on-off selection is reversed with each pass through the array. For example:

```
char dashList[3] = { 5, 10, 15 };
```

The line begins with 5 drawn pixels, then 10 skipped ones, then 15 drawn, then 5 skipped, then 10 drawn, and so on. It's just as if the array had six members with the same values duplicated for the last three.

The call to `gdk_gc_set_dashes()` is made on line 207 and has, as its second argument, an index into the array that specifies the starting member — the first line segment to be drawn. The last argument is the number of values in the array.

Stipple

Using a stippling bitmap gives you bit-by-bit control over which pixels are drawn and which are not. A bitmap is a pixmap with a depth of one — a sort of mask with one bit per pixels that determines which pixels are drawn. A bitmap can be created by using the bitmap utility described in Chapter 7. The bitmap used in the following example is named `stipple.xbm` and, when loaded into the bitmap editor, looks like Figure 11-3.

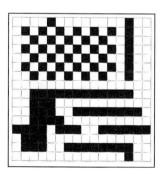

Figure 11-3: A bitmap used as a stippling mask

The bitmap is stored as C source code in the file stipple.xbm. It contains height and width information along with an array of bits with one bit per pixel:

```
#define stipple_width 16
#define stipple_height 16
static unsigned char stipple_bits[] = {
   0x00, 0x20, 0xaa, 0x2a, 0x54, 0x25, 0xaa, 0x2a,
   0x54, 0x25, 0xaa, 0x2a, 0x54, 0x25, 0x00, 0x00,
   0xfc, 0x3f, 0x1c, 0x00, 0x9c, 0x7f, 0x3c, 0x00,
   0xef, 0xfc, 0x0e, 0x00, 0xce, 0x3f, 0x00, 0x20};
```

The following program uses stippling to draw two rectangles. One rectangle is drawn so that it is transparent—that is, the pixels corresponding to the 1 bits are drawn in the foreground color, while the ones corresponding to the 0 bits are not drawn. The second rectangle is drawn with the 1 bits being the foreground color and the 0 bits being the background color—all pixels are drawn so it is opaque.

```
 1 /** stipple.c **/
 2 #include <gnome.h>
 3
 4 #include "stipple.xbm"
 5 #include "terminal.xpm"
 6
 7 gint eventDelete(GtkWidget *widget,
 8         GdkEvent *event,gpointer data);
 9 gint eventDestroy(GtkWidget *widget,
10         GdkEvent *event,gpointer data);
11 gboolean eventDraw(GtkWidget *widget,
12         GdkEvent *event,gpointer data);
13
14 #define WIDTH 250
15 #define HEIGHT 420
16
17 int main(int argc,char *argv[])
18 {
19     GtkWidget *app;
20     GtkWidget *area;
21
22     gnome_init("stipple","1.0",argc,argv);
23     app = gnome_app_new("stipple","Stipple and Tile");
24     gtk_signal_connect(GTK_OBJECT(app),"delete_event",
25         GTK_SIGNAL_FUNC(eventDelete),NULL);
26     gtk_signal_connect(GTK_OBJECT(app),"destroy",
27         GTK_SIGNAL_FUNC(eventDestroy),NULL);
28
29     area = gtk_drawing_area_new();
30     gtk_widget_set_usize(area,WIDTH,HEIGHT);
31     gnome_app_set_contents(GNOME_APP(app),area);
32     gtk_signal_connect(GTK_OBJECT(area),"event",
33         GTK_SIGNAL_FUNC(eventDraw),NULL);
34
35     gtk_widget_show_all(app);
```

```
36      gtk_main();
37      exit(0);
38  }
39  gboolean eventDraw(GtkWidget *widget,
40          GdkEvent *event,gpointer data) {
41      GdkGC *gc;
42      GdkBitmap *mask;
43      GtkStyle *style;
44      GdkPixmap *stipple;
45      GdkPixmap *terminal;
46      GdkColormap *colormap;
47      GdkColor foreground;
48      GdkColor background;
49
50      colormap = gdk_colormap_get_system();
51      gc = gdk_gc_new(widget->window);
52      if(gdk_color_parse("blue",&foreground)) {
53          gdk_color_alloc(colormap,&foreground);
54          gdk_gc_set_foreground(gc,&foreground);
55      }
56      if(gdk_color_parse("yellow",&background)) {
57          gdk_color_alloc(colormap,&background);
58          gdk_gc_set_background(gc,&background);
59      }
60
61      stipple = gdk_bitmap_create_from_data(widget->window,
62              stipple_bits,
63              stipple_width,
64              stipple_height);
65      gdk_gc_set_stipple(gc,stipple);
66
67      style = gtk_widget_get_style(widget);
68      terminal = gdk_pixmap_create_from_xpm_d(widget->window,
69              &mask,
70              &style->bg[GTK_STATE_NORMAL],
71              (gchar **)terminal_sun_xpm);
72      gdk_gc_set_tile(gc,terminal);
73
74      gdk_gc_set_ts_origin(gc,30,30);
75      gdk_gc_set_fill(gc,GDK_STIPPLED);
76      gdk_draw_rectangle(widget->window,
77              gc,
78              TRUE,
79              30,30,
80              200,100);
81
82      gdk_gc_set_ts_origin(gc,30,160);
83      gdk_gc_set_fill(gc,GDK_OPAQUE_STIPPLED);
84      gdk_draw_rectangle(widget->window,
85              gc,
86              TRUE,
87              30,160,
```

```
 88                200,100);
 89
 90      gdk_gc_set_ts_origin(gc,30,280);
 91      gdk_gc_set_fill(gc,GDK_TILED);
 92      gdk_draw_rectangle(widget->window,
 93             gc,
 94             TRUE,
 95             30,280,
 96             200,100);
 97
 98      return(TRUE);
 99 }
100 gint eventDelete(GtkWidget *widget,
101         GdkEvent *event,gpointer data) {
102      return(FALSE);
103 }
104 gint eventDestroy(GtkWidget *widget,
105         GdkEvent *event,gpointer data) {
106      gtk_main_quit();
107      return(0);
108 }
```

The bitmap file for stippling is included on line 4, and the pixmap used for tiling is included on line 5. Lines 29 through 33 create a drawing area, attach it to the application window, and connect the callback function `eventDraw()`.

The call to `gdk_colormap_get_system()` on line 50 retrieves the address of the system color map, and the call to `gdk_gc_new()` on line 51 creates a new graphics context. Lines 52 through 59 define and install the foreground and background colors.

The function `gtk_bitmap_create_from_data()` is called on line 61 to create a pixmap from the bitmap data that is compiled into the program. This result is a pixmap with one bit per pixel. The `stipple_bits` argument is the array of bits used as the values in the pixmap. The `stipple_height` and `stipple_width` values define the rectangular size of the pixmap. Once the pixmap is constructed, the call to `gdk_gc_set_stipple()` on line 65 inserts it into the graphics context as the pixmap to be used for stippling.

Lines 67 through 72 create a tiling pixmap and install it into the graphics context. The call to `gdk_pixmap_create_from_xpm_d()` on line 68 converts the XPM data compiled into the program into a pixmap. There is more information on this process in Chapter 7. The call to `gdk_gc_set_tile()` on line 72 installs the pixmap into the graphics context.

Lines 74 through 80 create the rectangular area displayed at the top of the window shown in Figure 11-4. The call to `gdk_gc_set_ts_origin()` sets the origin of the stipple pattern to the same x and y values used to draw the rectangle. The stipple pattern begins at the upper-left corner of rectangle (instead of the default (0,0), which is the upper-left corner of the drawing area). The stipple pattern is repeated as often as necessary to fill the rectangle. The function gdk_gc_set_fill() is called to set the mode for filling to GDK_STIPPLED, so only the pixels with corresponding 1 bits in the stipple bitmap are drawn. The other pixels are left as they are, resulting in a transparent drawing.

Lines 82 through 88 create the rectangular area in the center of Figure 11-4. As with the previous rectangle, the origin is set to the same as that of the rectangle by a call to gdk_gc_set_ts_origin(). The function gdk_gc_set_fill() is called to set the filling mode to GDK_OPAQUE_STIPPLED. As the name implies, the result is that all pixels are painted, thus covering completely any pixels already in the window. The pixels that correspond to a 1 bit in the stippling bitmap are drawn with the foreground color, and the ones that correspond to a 0 bit are drawn with the background color.

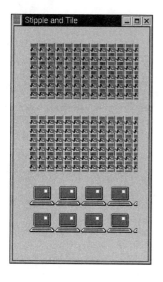

Figure 11-4: Two kinds of stippling and one kind of tiling

Lines 90 through 96 fill the rectangular area at the bottom of Figure 11-4 by tiling a pixmap over its entire area. The call to gdk_gc_set_ts_origin() sets the tiling origin to the same location as the origin of the rectangle being tiled, so the tile in the upper-left corner is complete. The fill mode is set to GDK_TILED by the call to gdk_gc_set_fill(), so the call to gdk_draw_rectangle() fills the region by painting the tiling pixmap—defined on lines 67 through 72—repeatedly until the rectangle is filled.

Note

There are many more ways that you can do tiling and stippling. These examples use the default drawing function GDK_COPY to draw the pixels—that is, the pixel of the source simply overwrites the pixel of the destination. As shown earlier in the chapter in Table 11-2, there are a number of other ways to paint pixels. By combining different bitmaps with different painting functions, you can generate an almost infinite variety of combinations.

Functions that Set Values in a GtkGC

There are two ways to insert values into a GdkGC. The previous examples all use a function call to set each individual value. Alternatively, you can use a GdkGCValues struct to set several values at the time the graphics context is created. The following example demonstrates the two different methods.

```
1  /** setgc.c **/
2  #include <gnome.h>
3
4  gint eventDelete(GtkWidget *widget,
5          GdkEvent *event,gpointer data);
6  gint eventDestroy(GtkWidget *widget,
7          GdkEvent *event,gpointer data);
8  gboolean eventDraw(GtkWidget *widget,
9          GdkEvent *event,gpointer data);
10 static GdkGC *functionCreateGC(GdkWindow *window);
11 static GdkGC *valueCreateGC(GdkWindow *window);
12
13 #define WIDTH 300
14 #define HEIGHT 100
15
16 int main(int argc,char *argv[])
17 {
18     GtkWidget *app;
19     GtkWidget *area;
20
21     gnome_init("setgc","1.0",argc,argv);
22     app = gnome_app_new("setgc","Setting GdkGC Values");
23     gtk_signal_connect(GTK_OBJECT(app),"delete_event",
24             GTK_SIGNAL_FUNC(eventDelete),NULL);
25     gtk_signal_connect(GTK_OBJECT(app),"destroy",
26             GTK_SIGNAL_FUNC(eventDestroy),NULL);
27
28     area = gtk_drawing_area_new();
29     gtk_widget_set_usize(area,WIDTH,HEIGHT);
30     gnome_app_set_contents(GNOME_APP(app),area);
31     gtk_signal_connect(GTK_OBJECT(area),"event",
32             GTK_SIGNAL_FUNC(eventDraw),area);
33
34     gtk_widget_show_all(app);
35     gtk_main();
36     exit(0);
37 }
38 gboolean eventDraw(GtkWidget *widget,
39         GdkEvent *event,gpointer data) {
40     GdkGC *gc;
41     GtkWidget *area;
42
43     area = GTK_WIDGET(data);
```

```
44
45       gc = functionCreateGC(area->window);
46       /****
47       gc = valueCreateGC(area->window);
48       ****/
49
50       gdk_draw_line(area->window,
51               gc,
52               20,HEIGHT/2,
53               WIDTH-20,HEIGHT/2);
54       return(TRUE);
55   }
56   static GdkGC *functionCreateGC(GdkWindow *window)
57   {
58       GdkGC *gc;
59       GdkColormap *colormap;
60       GdkColor foreground;
61       gchar dash[2] = { 1, 20 };
62
63       gc = gdk_gc_new(window);
64
65       colormap = gdk_colormap_get_system();
66       if(gdk_color_parse("white",&foreground)) {
67           gdk_color_alloc(colormap,&foreground);
68           gdk_gc_set_foreground(gc,&foreground);
69       }
70       gdk_gc_set_line_attributes(gc,
71               15,
72               GDK_LINE_ON_OFF_DASH,
73               GDK_CAP_ROUND,
74               GDK_JOIN_MITER);
75       gdk_gc_set_dashes(gc,0,dash,2);
76
77       return(gc);
78   }
79   static GdkGC *valueCreateGC(GdkWindow *window)
80   {
81       GdkGC *gc;
82       GdkColormap *colormap;
83       GdkColor foreground;
84       gchar dash[2] = { 1, 20 };
85       GdkGCValues values;
86
87       colormap = gdk_colormap_get_system();
88       if(gdk_color_parse("white",&foreground))
89           gdk_color_alloc(colormap,&foreground);
90       values.foreground = foreground;
91       values.line_width = 15;
92       values.line_style = GDK_LINE_ON_OFF_DASH;
93       values.cap_style = GDK_CAP_ROUND;
94       values.join_style = GDK_JOIN_MITER;
```

```
 95
 96      gc = gdk_gc_new_with_values(window,&values,
 97              GDK_GC_FOREGROUND | GDK_GC_LINE_WIDTH |
 98              GDK_GC_LINE_STYLE | GDK_GC_CAP_STYLE |
 99              GDK_GC_JOIN_STYLE);
100      gdk_gc_set_dashes(gc,0,dash,2);
101
102      return(gc);
103 }
104 gint eventDelete(GtkWidget *widget,
105          GdkEvent *event,gpointer data) {
106      return(FALSE);
107 }
108 gint eventDestroy(GtkWidget *widget,
109          GdkEvent *event,gpointer data) {
110      gtk_main_quit();
111      return(0);
112 }
```

On lines 28 through 32, a drawing area is constructed and it has the callback function eventDraw() connected to it.

The callback function eventDraw(), starting on line 38, calls a function to create a graphics context and then uses the context to draw a line across the center of the area. The result is shown in Figure 11-5. Either functionCreateGC() on line 45 or valueCreateGC() on line 47 can be used to create the graphics context—the result is the same for whichever one is used. The only difference is in the way the GdkGC object is created.

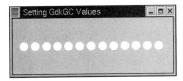

Figure 11-5: A wide-dashed rounded Line

The function functionCreateGC() beginning on line 56 creates a "default" graphics context and then calls a series of functions to set the values. The call to gdk_gc_set_foreground() on line 68 sets the foreground color (the color used to draw the line). On line 70, the call to gdk_gc_set_line_attributes() defines the size and style of the line. The call to gdk_gc_set_dashes() specifies the dash pattern to be used in drawing the line.

Beginning on line 79, the function valueCreateGC() fills a GdkGCValues struct with initializing data and uses it to create the graphics context. On lines 87 through 94, the various values are inserted into the GdkGCValues struct. The GdkGC object is created by the call to gdk_gc_new_with_values() on line 96. The first argument is the window on which the graphics context is to be based. The second argument is a pointer to the struct holding the values, and the third is a collection of flag bits specifying which values are included in the struct. Only those arguments that have flags set for them are included in the GdkGC. The call to the function gdk_gc_set_dashes() on line 100 is necessary because there is no setting for dash patterns in GdkGCValues.

In this example, there doesn't seem to be much advantage of using one method over the other. However, if you are going to construct several GdkGC objects having the same basic set of values, you can create a GdkGCValues struct once and use it over and over. Also, if you want to extract some values from one graphics context and insert them into another, you can do this with successive calls to gdk_gc_get_values() (to retrieve the values from the source GdkGC) and gdk_gc_new_with_value() (to create a new GdkGC containing selected values).

Table 11-4 is designed as a quick reference of the values that you can set, and how to set them. The first column lists the function calls that can be used to set a value (or values) directly into a GdkGC. The second column lists the names of the GdkGCValues field and the third column lists the masks that you can use in setting the value.

Table 11-4
GtkGC Values Set by Function or by GdkGCValues

Function Call	GdkGCValues Field	GdkGCValues Mask
gdk_gc_set_background (GdkGC *gc, GdkColor *color)	Background	GDK_GC_BACKGROUND
gdk_gc_set_clip_mask (GdkGC *gc, GdkBitmap *mask)	Clip_mask	GDK_GC_CLIP_MASK
gdk_gc_set_clip_origin (GdkGC *gc, gint x, gint y)	Clip_x_origin Clip_y_origin	GDK_GC_CLIP_X_ORIGIN GDK_GC_CLIP_Y_ORIGIN
gdk_gc_set_clip_rectangle (GdkGC *gc, GdkRectangle *rectangle)		
gdk_gc_set_clip_region (GdkGC *gc, GdkRegion *region)		

Continued

Table 11-4 *(continued)*

Function Call	GdkGCValues Field	GdkGCValues Mask
gdk_gc_set_dashes(GdkGC *gc, gint dash_offset, gchar dash_list[], gint list_length)		
gdk_gc_set_exposures (GdkGC *gc, gint exposures)	Graphics_ exposures	GDK_GC_EXPOSURES
gdk_gc_set_fill (GdkGC *gc, GdkFill fill)	Fill	GDK_GC_FILL
gdk_gc_set_font(GdkGC *gc, GdkFont *font)	Font	GDK_GC_FONT
gdk_gc_set_foreground (GdkGC *gc, GdkColor *color)	Foreground	GDK_GC_FOREGROUND
gdk_gc_set_fucntion (GdkGC *gc, GdkFunction function)	Function	GDK_GC_FUNCTION
gdk_gc_set_line_ attributes(GdkGC *gc, gint line_width, GdkLineStyle line_style, GdkCapStyle cap_style, GdkJoinStyle join_style)	Line_width Line style Cap_style Join_style	GDK_GC_LINE_WIDTH GDK_GC_LINE_STYLE GDK_GC_CAP_STYLE GDK_GC_JOIN_STYLE
gdk_gc_set_stipple (GdkGC *gc, GdkPixmap *stipple)	Stipple	GDK_GC_STIPPLE
gdk_gc_set_subwindow (GdkGC *gc, GdkSubwindowMode mode)	Subwindow_mode	GDK_GC_SUBWINDOW
gdk_gc_set_tile(GdkGC *gc, GdkPixmap *tile)	Tile	GDK_GC_TILE
gdk_gc_set_ts_origin (GdkGC *gc, gint x, gint y)	tx_x_origin ts_y_origin	GDK_GC_TS_X_ORIGIN GDK_GC_TS_Y_ORIGIN

A Dialog to Select Colors

There is a color-selection dialog box that enables the user to select a color. The following example program displays the dialog box and continuously updates its window to match the current setting in the dialog box.

```
 1 /** selection.c **/
 2 #include <gnome.h>
 3
 4 GtkWidget *makeColorBox();
 5 void showColorsel(GtkWidget *widget,gpointer data);
 6 void changeColor(GtkWidget *widget,
 7         GtkColorSelection *colorSel);
 8 void destroyColorsel(GtkWidget *widget,
 9         gpointer data);
10 void helpColorsel(GtkWidget *widget,gpointer data);
11
12 gint eventDelete(GtkWidget *widget,
13         GdkEvent *event,gpointer data);
14 gint eventDestroy(GtkWidget *widget,
15         GdkEvent *event,gpointer data);
16
17 static GtkWidget *csDialog = NULL;
18 static GtkWidget *area;
19
20 int main(int argc,char *argv[])
21 {
22     GtkWidget *app;
23     GtkWidget *colorBox;
24
25     gnome_init("selection","1.0",argc,argv);
26     app = gnome_app_new("selection","Color Selection");
27     gtk_signal_connect(GTK_OBJECT(app),"delete_event",
28             GTK_SIGNAL_FUNC(eventDelete),NULL);
29     gtk_signal_connect(GTK_OBJECT(app),"destroy",
30             GTK_SIGNAL_FUNC(eventDestroy),NULL);
31
32     colorBox = makeColorBox();
33
34     gnome_app_set_contents(GNOME_APP(app),colorBox);
35     gtk_widget_show_all(app);
36     gtk_main();
37     exit(0);
38 }
39 GtkWidget *makeColorBox()
40 {
41     GtkWidget *colorbox;
42     GtkWidget *button;
43
```

```
44      colorbox = gtk_vbox_new(FALSE,0);
45      gtk_container_set_border_width(
46              GTK_CONTAINER(colorbox),10);
47
48      area = gtk_drawing_area_new();
49      gtk_widget_set_usize(area,300,200);
50      gtk_box_pack_start(GTK_BOX(colorbox),
51              area,FALSE,FALSE,0);
52
53      button = gtk_button_new_with_label("Select");
54      gtk_box_pack_start(GTK_BOX(colorbox),
55              button,FALSE,FALSE,0);
56      gtk_signal_connect(GTK_OBJECT(button),"clicked",
57              GTK_SIGNAL_FUNC(showColorsel),NULL);
58
59      return(colorbox);
60 }
61 void showColorsel(GtkWidget *widget,gpointer data) {
62     GtkWidget *colorSel;
63     GtkWidget *button;
64
65     if(csDialog == NULL) {
66         csDialog = gtk_color_selection_dialog_new(
67              "Selected color fills the rectangle");
68         gtk_signal_connect(GTK_OBJECT(csDialog),
69              "destroy",
70              GTK_SIGNAL_FUNC(destroyColorsel),NULL);
71
72         colorSel =
73              GTK_COLOR_SELECTION_DIALOG(csDialog)->colorsel;
74         gtk_signal_connect(GTK_OBJECT(colorSel),
75              "color_changed",
76              GTK_SIGNAL_FUNC(changeColor),colorSel);
77
78         button = GTK_COLOR_SELECTION_DIALOG(
79                  csDialog)->ok_button;
80         gtk_signal_connect(GTK_OBJECT(button),"clicked",
81              GTK_SIGNAL_FUNC(destroyColorsel),NULL);
82         button = GTK_COLOR_SELECTION_DIALOG(
83                  csDialog)->cancel_button;
84         gtk_signal_connect(GTK_OBJECT(button),"clicked",
85              GTK_SIGNAL_FUNC(destroyColorsel),NULL);
86         button = GTK_COLOR_SELECTION_DIALOG(
87                  csDialog)->help_button;
88         gtk_signal_connect(GTK_OBJECT(button),"clicked",
89              GTK_SIGNAL_FUNC(helpColorsel),NULL);
90     }
91     gtk_widget_show(csDialog);
92 }
93 void changeColor(GtkWidget *widget,
94         GtkColorSelection *colorSel) {
```

```
 95     gdouble colorArray[4];
 96     GdkColor color;
 97     GdkColormap *colormap;
 98
 99     gtk_color_selection_get_color(colorSel,colorArray);
100     color.red = (gushort)(0xFFFFF * colorArray[0]);
101     color.green = (gushort)(0xFFFFF * colorArray[1]);
102     color.blue = (gushort)(0xFFFFF * colorArray[2]);
103     colormap = gdk_colormap_get_system();
104     gdk_color_alloc(colormap,&color);
105     gdk_window_set_background(area->window,&color);
106     gdk_window_clear(area->window);
107 }
108 void destroyColorsel(GtkWidget *widget,gpointer data) {
109     if(csDialog != NULL) {
110         gtk_widget_destroy(csDialog);
111         csDialog = NULL;
112     }
113 }
114 void helpColorsel(GtkWidget *widget,gpointer data) {
115     gnome_ok_dialog("Sorry.\nNo help available");
116 }
117 gint eventDelete(GtkWidget *widget,
118         GdkEvent *event,gpointer data) {
119     return(FALSE);
120 }
121 gint eventDestroy(GtkWidget *widget,
122         GdkEvent *event,gpointer data) {
123     gtk_main_quit();
124     return(0);
125 }
```

Lines 25 through 30 initialize the program. The call to makeColorBox() on line 32 creates a widget that is inserted into the main window by the call to gnome_app_ set_contents() on line 34.

The main application window is created in the function makeColorBox() beginning on line 39. A vertical box container is constructed on line 44 through 46. There are two widgets inserted into the box. On lines 48 through 51, a drawing area is created and inserted as the topmost widget in the vertical box. On lines 53 through 55, a button is created and inserted below the drawing area. On line 56, the button is assigned the callback function showColorsel().

The callback function showColorsel() beginning on line 61 is called to pop up a color selection window. A pointer to the widget, defined as csDialog on line 17, is declared as static so the window need only be created once. If the test on line 65 shows csDialog to be NULL, this must be the first call to this function and the dialog box needs to be constructed. The dialog window itself is constructed completely by the call to gtk_color_selection_dialog_new() on line 66. All that is left to do is set the callback functions. The call to gtk_signal_connect() on line 68 causes the function destroyColorsel() whenever the window is closed by the window manager (such as the user selecting the kill button in the upper-right corner). At the bottom of the showColorsel() function on line 91 is a call to gtk_widget_show() to pop up the dialog window. If the window is being displayed already, this function call has no effect. This way, you can press the Select button on the main window more than once, but only one dialog box will appear. The result is shown in Figure 11-6.

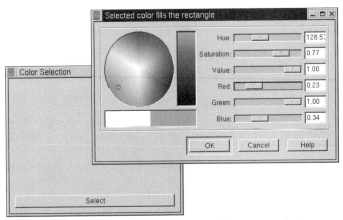

Figure 11-6: A color selection widget and its parent window

The callback defined on lines 72 through 76 causes the function changeColor() to be called each time the user changes the color settings in the dialog window. Also, there are three buttons in the window and, to make the window fully functional, it is necessary to assign callbacks to them. Lines 78 through 85 set both the OK and Cancel buttons to call the function destroyColorsel(). On lines 86 through 89, the Help button is assigned the callback function helpColorsel().

The changeColor() callback beginning on line 93 is called every time the user changes the color in the dialog box. This function extracts the color and uses it to paint the drawing area of the main window. The call to gtk_color_selection_get_color() on line 99 retrieves the current color information in an array of floating-point values. Each of the three color values (the fourth member of the array is the 'alpha,' or transparency, setting) in the array range from 0.0 to 1.0, so they are scaled to the correct range for a GdkColor object on lines 100 through 102. The color map retrieved on line 103 is used to allocate the color by the call to gdk_color_alloc() on line 104. Lines 105 and 106 call gdk_window_set_background() to insert the new color as the background color and then call gdk_window_clear() to paint the entire window with the background color.

The callback function `destroyColorsel()` on line 108 is called to pop down the dialog box. The dialog box is destroyed and its pointer set to `NULL`, so if there is another call to `showColorsel()` a new dialog box will be created.

The help callback function defined on line 114 is called whenever the Help button on the dialog box is pressed. It just pops up an OK dialog box stating that no help is available.

Explanation of GtkStyle

Inside every widget, there is a `GtkStyle` struct that contains the graphics contexts and colors used to draw the widget in each of its states. There are multiple graphics contexts because a widget may have more than one appearance. For example, a button changes color when it is pressed. Also, the shading around the button changes colors to give it the appearance of being indented. A button also looks different when it is disabled, as often happens with menu buttons. Buttons can be decorated with pixmaps instead of text. Widgets that are more complicated than buttons can require even more settings.

To extract a copy of the `GtkStyle` struct from any widget, use the function `gtk_widget_get_style()` like this:

```
GtkWidget *widget;
GtkStyle *style;
style = gtk_widget_get_style(widget);
```

The returned value is a pointer to the struct used internally by the widget. The data is fairly low level and should be treated with care. You probably should not use the fields listed below the `/* private */` tag because they are for internal operations and could be changed in a way that would cause your program to fail. The struct looks like this:

```
struct _GtkStyle {
    GtkStyleClass *klass;
    GdkColor fg[5];
    GdkColor bg[5];
    GdkColor light[5];
    GdkColor dark[5];
    GdkColor mid[5];
    GdkColor text[5];
    GdkColor base[5];
    GdkColor black;
    GdkColor white;
    GdkFont *font;
    GdkGC *fg_gc[5];
    GdkGC *bg_gc[5];
```

```
        GdkGC *light_gc[5];
        GdkGC *dark_gc[5];
        GdkGC *mid_gc[5];
        GdkGC *text_gc[5];
        GdkGC *base_gc[5];
        GdkGC *black_gc;
        GdkGC *white_gc;
        GdkPixmap *bg_pixmap[5];

        /* private */
        gint ref_count;
        gint attach_count;
        gint depth;
        GdkColormap *colormap;
        GtkThemeEngine *engine;
        gpointer engine_data;
        GtkRcStyle *rc_style;
        GSList *styles;
    };
```

There are a large number of graphics context and colors defined in this structure. Probably the most common reason to access this structure is to retrieve the default black and white colors, or the black and white graphics contexts. There are arrays of colors and graphics contexts that are used by the widget to draw itself in different states. The five states are defined by the enum GtkStateType:

```
    typedef enum {
        GTK_STATE_NORMAL,
        GTK_STATE_ACTIVE,
        GTK_STATE_PRELIGHT,
        GTK_STATE_INSENSITIVE
    } GtkStateType;
```

Exactly what is meant by each of these states depends on the widget. The GTK_STATE_NORMAL state is the widget at rest awaiting instructions (such as a button that the mouse hasn't touched). The GTK_STATE_ACTIVE state is used when the widget is activated (such as a button being pushed). The GTK_STATE_PRELIGHT state is used when the mouse pointer is inside the widget, but no mouse button is pressed. The GTK_STATE_INSENSITIVE state is used when the widget is disabled (such as a menu button being grayed-out).

Summary

Using graphics contexts and color objects can simplify fundamental drawing and painting onto a window. Using various options, you can create a window to look any way you like. This chapter explained how:

✦ All pixel painting is done using a GdkGC object (called a graphics context).

✦ The color information is stored in a GdkColor object. This, in turn, may be stored in a GdkGC object as either the foreground or background color. A widget contains a large number of both GdkColor objects and GdkGC objects and uses different ones at different times.

✦ You can select the pixels to be painted by using a bitmap as a rectangular set of flags that determines which pixels are painted already.

✦ A full-color PixMap can be loaded into memory, included in a graphics context, and painted directly onto a window.

✦ There are three separate options that can be configured for line drawing. The line width can be set to some value other than the default of one pixel wide. The default draws a solid continuous line, but there are functions that are capable of changing it to any pattern of dashes. A line also can be drawn with rounded, pointed, or blunt ends and joints.

This chapter explained some of the requirements for creating colorful displays. The information in the following chapter can be used to bring the display to life by having it respond to the mouse and keyboard. Also, many display settings and characteristics can be controlled by arguments on the command line of a GNOME application.

✦   ✦   ✦

The Mouse and the Keyboard

In its simplest form, the mouse information consists of a location on the screen and the click of a button—but there is a bit more to it. To start with, the X server figures out which window (if any) contains the mouse pointer and reports the event to the owner of that window. If, however, the owner of a window *grabs* the mouse, then all events are set to the grabber regardless of the location of the mouse. Even more complicated, the grabber can claim the mouse events for some windows, but not for others. Add to that the fact that you may need to know which button (or buttons) have been pressed, whether or not a button is being held down, whether there has been a double-click, or even which keyboard keys were down when the mouse action was taken.

Then there is a keyboard. Some keys are displayable and some are not. Some are used simply to modify the meanings of other keys (such as the Shift key generating uppercase letters). For most applications, the text widgets can handle this, but there are times when you need to have every keystroke come into your program.

Fortunately, all of this information is available, from any window you choose, in the form of mouse and keyboard events.

Responding to Mouse Events

The following program uses a GNOME canvas to implement a scribble drawing program with some special capabilities.

```
1 /** mousefollow.c **/
2 #include <gnome.h>
3
4 struct stateStruct {
5     gboolean havePoints;
6     gboolean drawing;
7     gint x;
```

```
 8      gint y;
 9      GdkGC *lineGC;
10 };
11
12 gint eventDelete(GtkWidget *widget,
13         GdkEvent *event,gpointer data);
14 gint eventDestroy(GtkWidget *widget,
15         GdkEvent *event,gpointer data);
16 gboolean canvasEvent(GtkWidget *widget,
17         GdkEvent *event,struct stateStruct *state);
18
19 #define WIDTH 400
20 #define HEIGHT 300
21 #define INTERVAL 30
22 #define RADIUS 20
23
24 int main(int argc,char *argv[])
25 {
26     GtkWidgct *app;
27     GtkWidget *canvas;
28     struct stateStruct state;
29
30     gnome_init("mousefollow","1.0",argc,argv);
31     app = gnome_app_new("mousefollow",
32             "Following Mouse Events");
33     gtk_signal_connect(GTK_OBJECT(app),"delete_event",
34             GTK_SIGNAL_FUNC(eventDelete),NULL);
35     gtk_signal_connect(GTK_OBJECT(app),"destroy",
36             GTK_SIGNAL_FUNC(eventDestroy),NULL);
37
38     canvas = gnome_canvas_new();
39     gtk_widget_set_usize(canvas,WIDTH,HEIGHT);
40     gnome_app_set_contents(GNOME_APP(app),canvas);
41     gtk_signal_connect(GTK_OBJECT(canvas),"event",
42             GTK_SIGNAL_FUNC(canvasEvent),&state);
43
44     gtk_widget_show_all(app);
45     gtk_main();
46     exit(0);
47 }
48 gboolean canvasEvent(GtkWidget *widget,
49         GdkEvent *event,struct stateStruct *state) {
50     GdkColor color;
51     GdkEventMotion *eventMotion;
52     GdkEventCrossing *eventCrossing;
53     GdkEventButton *eventButton;
54     GdkEventExpose *eventExpose;
55
56     static gint counter = 1;
57     static GdkColormap *colormap;
58
59     switch(event->type) {
60     case GDK_MAP:
61         g_print("%4d MAP\n",counter++);
```

```
62          colormap = gdk_colormap_get_system();
63          state->lineGC = gdk_gc_new(widget->window);
64          state->havePoints = FALSE;
65          state->drawing = FALSE;
66          break;
67      case GDK_ENTER_NOTIFY:
68          g_print("%4d ENTER_NOTIFY\n",counter++);
69          eventCrossing = (GdkEventCrossing *)event;
70          state->x = eventCrossing->x;
71          state->y = eventCrossing->y;
72          state->havePoints = TRUE;
73          break;
74      case GDK_LEAVE_NOTIFY:
75          g_print("%4d LEAVE_NOTIFY\n",counter++);
76          break;
77      case GDK_BUTTON_PRESS:
78          g_print("%4d BUTTON_PRESS\n",counter++);
79          eventButton = (GdkEventButton *)event;
80          if(eventButton->button == 1) {
81              state->x = eventButton->x;
82              state->y = eventButton->y;
83              state->havePoints = TRUE;
84              state->drawing = TRUE;
85          } else if(eventButton->button == 3) {
86              color.red=(((double)rand()*0xFFFF)/RAND_MAX);
87              color.green=(((double)rand()*0xFFFF)/RAND_MAX);
88              color.blue=(((double)rand()*0xFFFF)/RAND_MAX);
89              gdk_color_alloc(colormap,&color);
90              gdk_gc_set_foreground(state->lineGC,&color);
91          }
92          break;
93      case GDK_BUTTON_RELEASE:
94          g_print("%4d BUTTON_RELEASE\n",counter++);
95          eventButton = (GdkEventButton *)event;
96          if(eventButton->button == 1) {
97              state->drawing = FALSE;
98              state->havePoints = FALSE;
99          }
100         break;
101     case GDK_2BUTTON_PRESS:
102         g_print("%4d 2BUTTON_PRESS\n",counter++);
103         eventButton = (GdkEventButton *)event;
104         if(eventButton->button == 1) {
105             gdk_draw_arc(eventButton->window,state->lineGC,
106                     TRUE,
107                     eventButton->x - RADIUS,
108                     eventButton->y - RADIUS,
109                     2 * RADIUS,2 * RADIUS,
110                     0,360*64);
111         }
112         break;
113     case GDK_3BUTTON_PRESS:
114         g_print("%4d 2BUTTON_PRESS\n",counter++);
115         eventButton = (GdkEventButton *)event;
```

```
116            if(eventButton->button == 2)
117                exit(0);
118            break;
119        case GDK_MOTION_NOTIFY:
120            g_print("%4d MOTION_NOTIFY\n",counter++);
121            eventMotion = (GdkEventMotion *)event;
122            if(state->havePoints && state->drawing) {
123                gdk_draw_line(eventMotion->window,
124                    state->lineGC,
125                    state->x,state->y,
126                    (gint)(eventMotion->x),
127                    (gint)(eventMotion->y));
128            }
129            state->x = (gint)(eventMotion->x);
130            state->y = (gint)(eventMotion->y);
131            state->havePoints = TRUE;
132            break;
133        case GDK_EXPOSE:
134            eventExpose = (GdkEventExpose *)event;
135            g_print("%4d EXPOSE\n",counter++);
136            state->drawing = FALSE;
137            state->havePoints = FALSE;
138            gdk_window_clear(eventExpose->window);
139            break;
140        default:
141            g_print("%4d Other: %d\n",counter++,event->type);
142            break;
143        }
144        return(TRUE);
145 }
146 gint eventDelete(GtkWidget *widget,
147        GdkEvent *event,gpointer data) {
148        return(FALSE);
149 }
150 gint eventDestroy(GtkWidget *widget,
151        GdkEvent *event,gpointer data) {
152        gtk_main_quit();
153        return(0);
154 }
```

In this program, certain combinations of the mouse buttons draw circles, change the drawing color, and exit the program:

✦ Dragging with the left mouse button draws a line in the current color.

✦ Double-clicking the left mouse button draws a circle.

✦ Pressing the right mouse button changes the color used to draw lines and circles.

✦ Triple-clicking the middle mouse button exits the program.

✦ Uncovering the window, or any part of the window, clears it.

Lines 38 through 42 create a `GnomeCanvas` widget and connect it to the callback function `canvasEvent()`. The callback function, beginning on line 48, is called when the window is first created and, after that, for every mouse event occurring in the canvas. Everything this program does is in the callback function, and is under the control of the mouse. The details of each event are listed in Chapter 9.

The struct defined on line 4 is a collection of state values that need to live from one invocation of the callback function to another. For example, when the mouse moves to a new location and a line is to be drawn, it is necessary to know the previous location of the mouse so the dots can be connected. An instance of the struct is declared in the mainline of the program on line 28, and, by including it on the call to `gtk_signal_connect()` on line 35, its address is passed to the callback function in the form of the data pointer.

The callback function begins on line 48. Line 56 defines a `counter` that is used to display the number of each event. Each time this function is called, the number and type of event is listed to the standard output. As you run the program, and watch the list of events scroll up, notice that almost all of the events are mouse motion events (one is issued for every movement of the mouse). Also, if you hold down a mouse button while you move the mouse pointer, the motion events continue to be reported to this window even when the mouse pointer is outside of the window.

Line 60 responds to the `GDK_MAP` event. This event is issued whenever the window is first constructed and ready for display. You can be sure that it will arrive before any mouse events. This program takes advantage of this assumption to do some one-time initialization. A `GtkGC` is constructed on lines 62 and 63, and the Boolean values are set to `FALSE` to indicate that the struct does not hold coordinate points and that line drawing is not taking place currently.

Line 67 responds to the `GDK_ENTER_NOTIFY` event. One of these events occurs whenever the mouse enters the window from some place else on the display. This entry can be caused by the window first appearing directly underneath the mouse, the mouse pointer moving across the edge of this window, or being moved into the middle of this window from a partially overlapping window. In any case, there is one of these events every time the mouse comes into the window. Lines 70 through 72 get a copy of the point of entry and change the state to show that there are valid points in the `state` struct.

Line 74 responds to the `GDK_LEAVE_NOTIFY` event. This event arrives every time the mouse leaves the window. This has no effect on this program, so nothing is done.

Line 77 responds to the `GDK_BUTTON_PRESS` event. This event signals that one of the mouse buttons has been pressed. Line 80 tests for it being the left button (button number 1); if it is, the current location in the window is set to the current location of the mouse pointer. The state is updated to reflect that there is a valid point in the `state` struct and that now you are drawing a line. If, on line 85, it is the right button (button number 3) that has been pressed, a new color is created and stored in the graphics context as the new foreground color.

Line 93 responds to the GDK_BUTTON_RELEASE event. For this program, the release event only has meaning if it is the left button (number 1) to indicate the end of drawing. If it is the left button, the state is changed to indicate that there is to be no drawing done.

Note   These events are quite independent of one another. For example, you can hold the left button down and drag it around drawing a line and, at the same time, click the right button to change the line color.

Line 101 responds to the GDK_2BUTTON_PRESS event. This is the double-click. The only one this program responds to is the left button, which executes the call to gdk_draw_arc() on line 105 and draws a filled circle at the location of the mouse.

Line 113 responds to the GDK_3BUTTON_PRESS event. This is the triple-click. The test on line 116 determines whether it is the middle button (button 2); if it is, it exits the program immediately.

Note   Whenever there is a double- or triple-click, the single events also are reported. That is, whenever there is a GDK_2BUTTON_PRESS event, there also is a GDK_BUTTON_PRESS and GDK_BUTTON_RELEASE. The last two are known as *real events* because they represent an actual hardware event, whereas the double-click is known as a *pseudo event* because it is generated by the software — it times the proximity of the two real events. The same situation is true of the triple-click — there are two each of the press and release events.

Line 119 responds to the GDK_MOTION_NOTIFY event. This event is issued whenever the mouse moves. Line 122 checks the current state, and if there are valid points in the state struct and if the program currently is drawing lines, a line is drawn from the old point to the new point. Whether or not a line is drawn, the x and y values in the state are updated to reflect the new mouse position.

Line 133 responds to the GDK_EXPOSE event. This event is issued when any part of the window is uncovered. A real application normally redraws the screen, but because this program hasn't bothered to save the necessary data to do that, the screen is cleared and the mode is set to indicate there are no points and there is no drawing taking place.

An example of the kind of display that you can create with this program is shown in Figure 12-1.

Grabbing and Releasing the Mouse

There comes a time when your program must get some response from the user before continuing. To do this, it is possible to have a window pop up and grab the mouse and not let go until the user responds.

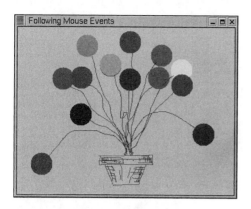

Figure 12-1: The mouse draws circles and lines

To grab a mouse, a window simply grabs all the events coming from the mouse. The second, and optional, part of the grab is to limit the movement of the mouse. The following program is an example of grabbing the mouse, changing the cursor to reflect the grab state, and waiting until a button is clicked before releasing it.

```
1 /** mousegrab.c **/
2 #include <gnome.h>
3
4 gint eventDelete(GtkWidget *widget,
5         GdkEvent *event,gpointer data);
6 gint eventDestroy(GtkWidget *widget,
7         GdkEvent *event,gpointer data);
8 void grabMouse(GtkWidget *widget,GtkWidget *containWidget);
9 void ungrabMouse(GtkWidget *widget,gpointer data);
10
11 int main(int argc,char *argv[])
12 {
13     GtkWidget *window;
14     GtkWidget *box;
15     GtkWidget *button;
16
17     gnome_init("mousegrab","1.0",argc,argv);
18     window = gtk_window_new(GTK_WINDOW_TOPLEVEL);
19     gtk_container_set_border_width(
20             GTK_CONTAINER(window),30);
21     gtk_signal_connect(GTK_OBJECT(window),"delete_event",
22             GTK_SIGNAL_FUNC(eventDelete),NULL);
23     gtk_signal_connect(GTK_OBJECT(window),"destroy",
24             GTK_SIGNAL_FUNC(eventDestroy),NULL);
25
26     box = gtk_vbox_new(FALSE,0);
27
28     button = gtk_button_new_with_label("Grab Mouse");
29     gtk_box_pack_start(GTK_BOX(box),button,FALSE,FALSE,0);
```

```
30      gtk_signal_connect(GTK_OBJECT(button),"clicked",
31              GTK_SIGNAL_FUNC(grabMouse),window);
32
33      button = gtk_button_new_with_label("Ungrab Mouse");
34      gtk_box_pack_end(GTK_BOX(box),button,FALSE,FALSE,0);
35      gtk_signal_connect(GTK_OBJECT(button),"clicked",
36              GTK_SIGNAL_FUNC(ungrabMouse),NULL);
37
38      gtk_container_add(GTK_CONTAINER(window),box);
39      gtk_widget_show_all(window);
40      gtk_main();
41      exit(0);
42 }
43 void grabMouse(GtkWidget *widget,GtkWidget *containWidget)
44 {
45      GdkWindow *window = containWidget->window;
46      GdkCursor *cursor = gdk_cursor_new(GDK_CROSSHAIR);
47      gdk_pointer_grab(window,
48              TRUE,
49              (GdkEventMask)0,
50              window,
51              cursor,
52              GDK_CURRENT_TIME);
53 }
54 void ungrabMouse(GtkWidget *widget,gpointer data) {
55      if(gdk_pointer_is_grabbed())
56          gdk_pointer_ungrab(GDK_CURRENT_TIME);
57 }
58
59 gint eventDelete(GtkWidget *widget,
60          GdkEvent *event,gpointer data) {
61      return(FALSE);
62 }
63 gint eventDestroy(GtkWidget *widget,
64          GdkEvent *event,gpointer data) {
65      if(gdk_pointer_is_grabbed())
66          gdk_pointer_ungrab(GDK_CURRENT_TIME);
67      gtk_main_quit();
68      return(0);
69 }
```

A vertical box container is constructed on line 26. Lines 28 through 36 create a pair of buttons, add them to the vertical box, and assign a callback to each one of them. The callback that grabs the mouse is named grabMouse() and the one that releases it is named ungrabMouse(). The connection to grabMouse() on line 31 uses the main window as the data to be passed to the function.

The callback function grabMouse() beginning on line 43 makes a call to the function gdk_pointer_grab() to limit the movement of the mouse to the rectangular area of a specified window.

Line 45 extracts the GdkWindow from the GtkWidget that was passed to the callback function as the data pointer. This window is used as the first argument, on line 47, and again as the fourth argument on line 50. The first argument specifies the window that is to receive all the mouse events — while the mouse is grabbed, this becomes the only window that can receive mouse events, no matter what the location of the mouse. Using the window again as the fourth argument, as in this example, limits the movement of the mouse to that window. In this example, the same window is used for both, so the mouse pointer cannot leave the window that has grabbed the events.

The second argument, on line 48, is set to TRUE so the incoming events are propagated from the grabbing window to its subwindows. In this example, the subwindows are the two buttons. If it were set to FALSE, the buttons would not receive any mouse events, and there would be no way to ungrab the window.

Note   Always leave yourself a way to get out. If you grab the mouse and your program has no way to release it, you are stuck. Even killing the program to close the window won't release it — the grab remains active on the rectangular area that was the window. The X server actually executes the grab and it hangs on to a mouse grab until it gets a specific command to release it.

Line 49 is the event mask to indicate which events are to be sent to the grabbing window. In this example, there is no need to add any events because the events already scheduled will arrive at the buttons (being child windows of the grabbing window) allowing them to be clicked. If, however, you are going to be fielding your own events, you can use any combination of the event masks shown in Table 12-1. For example, if you want to receive notification whenever a mouse button or keyboard key is pressed, use this for the mask value:

```
GDK_BUTTON_PRESS_MASK | GDK_KEY_PRESS_MASK.
```

Table 12-1
The Bit Masks Used to Request Events

Mask	Event
GDK_EXPOSURE_MASK	GdkEventExpose. The window has been exposed and needs to be drawn.
GDK_POINTER_MOTION_MASK	GdkEventMotion. The mouse has moved.
GDK_POINTER_MOTION_HINT_MASK	Reduces the number of events when used with GDK_POINTER_MOTION_MASK.
GDK_BUTTON_MOTION_MASK	GdkEventMotion. Mouse moved with one or more buttons held down.

Continued

Table 12-1 *(continued)*

Mask	Event
GDK_BUTTON1_MOTION_MASK	GdkEventMotion. **Mouse moved while button 1 (left button) held down.**
GDK_BUTTON2_MOTION_MASK	GdkEventMotion. **Mouse moved while button 2 (middle button) held down.**
GDK_BUTTON3_MOTION_MASK	GdkEventMotion. **Mouse moved while button 3 (right button) held down.**
GDK_BUTTON_PRESS_MASK	GdkEventButton. **A mouse button was pressed.**
GDK_BUTTON_RELEASE_MASK	GdkEventButton. **A button was released.**
GDK_KEY_PRESS_MASK	GdkEventKey. **A keyboard key was pressed.**
GDK_KEY_RELEASE_MASK	GdkEventKey. **A keyboard key was released.**
GDK_ENTER_NOTIFY_MASK	GdkEventCrossing. **The mouse pointer has entered the window.**
GDK_LEAVE_NOTIFY_MASK	GdkEventCrossing. **The mouse pointer has left the window.**
GDK_FOCUS_CHANGE_MASK	GdkEventFocus. **The window has either lost or achieved the keyboard focus.**
GDK_STRUCTURE_MASK	GdkEventStructure. **The size or position of the window has changed.**
GDK_PROPERTY_CHANGE_MASK	GdkEventProperty. **An internal property of the window has changed.**
GDK_VISIBILITY_NOTIFY_MASK	GdkEventVisibility. **The window has been made partially or completely visible, or has been obscured.**
GDK_PROXIMITY_IN_MASK	GdkEventProximity. **A finger has been placed on the touch screen, or a stylus has been placed on a tablet.**
GDK_PROXIMITY_OUT_MASK	GdkEventProximity. **A finger has been taken off the touch screen, or a stylus has been lifted from a tablet.**
GDK_SUBSTRUCTURE_MASK	GdkEventConfigure. **An event is issued for every subwindow of the selected window.**
GDK_ALL_EVENTS_MASK	**Receive all events.**

The fifth argument, on line 51, is the cursor. The mouse pointer changes to the cursor when the mouse is grabbed, and changes back again when it is released. Using a NULL pointer for the cursor causes the cursor to remain unchanged. Figure 12-2 shows the window with the cursor changed to a crosshair.

Figure 12-2: A grabbed mouse with a cursor change

The last argument, on line 52, is the time that the grab is supposed to take place. As a convenience, the constant GDK_CURRENT_TIME automatically is converted to the current time, which is usually what you want.

There are two ways to get out of the grab. Pressing the "Ungrab" button executes the callback function ungrabMouse() on line 54. If the call to gdk_pointer_is_ grabbed() returns TRUE, the mouse has been grabbed and should be released. The call to gdk_pointer_ungrab() releases the pointer. This program doesn't allow the mouse to leave the window, so the mouse cannot close the window while the grab is in effect. However, it is still a good idea to release the grabbed mouse when a program exits. The function eventDestroy() on line 63 is called when the window is destroyed; so if the mouse has been grabbed, it is released by the call to gdk_pointer_ungrab() on line 66.

Reading Characters from the Keyboard

Whenever you type something on the keyboard, the keystroke information goes to only one window; therefore, it all goes to one application. When a window is set to be the recipient of keyboard input, it is said to have the keyboard *focus*. There are a number of things that can happen to cause a window to receive the focus, but the most common is for the mouse to select the window. The title bar at the top of the window changes color on the window with the current focus.

Most of the time, you will want to use text input widgets to read information from the keyboard; but if you find that you need to read the keyboard directly, you can do it. You simply need to establish the correct set of callbacks. There are two basic kinds of keyboard events: one when a key is pressed and another when it is released. If you just want keystrokes, use the key press event. The key release event is necessary if you need to know whether a key is being held down.

The following example reads from the keyboard and displays information about the keys being pressed and released.

```
1 /** keylisten.c **/
2 #include <gnome.h>
3
4 gint eventDelete(GtkWidget *widget,
5         GdkEvent *event,gpointer data);
6 gint eventDestroy(GtkWidget *widget,
7         GdkEvent *event,gpointer data);
8 gint eventFocus(GtkWidget *widget,
9         GdkEvent *event,gpointer data);
10 gint eventPressKey(GtkWidget *widget,
11         GdkEvent *event,gpointer data);
12 gint eventReleaseKey(GtkWidget *widget,
13         GdkEvent *event,gpointer data);
14
15 static GtkWidget *keyLabel;
16 static GtkWidget *scrollLabel;
17 static GtkWidget *focusLabel;
18
19 gboolean altKeyDown = FALSE;
20 gboolean controlKeyDown = FALSE;
21 gboolean metaKeyDown = FALSE;
22 gboolean leftShiftKeyDown = FALSE;
23 gboolean rightShiftKeyDown = FALSE;
24
25 int main(int argc,char *argv[])
26 {
27     GtkWidget *window;
28     GtkWidget *box;
29
30     gnome_init("keylisten","1.0",argc,argv);
31     window = gtk_window_new(GTK_WINDOW_TOPLEVEL);
32     gtk_widget_set_usize(window,500,120);
33     gtk_container_set_border_width(
34         GTK_CONTAINER(window),30);
35     gtk_signal_connect(GTK_OBJECT(window),"delete_event",
36         GTK_SIGNAL_FUNC(eventDelete),NULL);
37     gtk_signal_connect(GTK_OBJECT(window),"destroy",
38         GTK_SIGNAL_FUNC(eventDestroy),NULL);
39     gtk_signal_connect(GTK_OBJECT(window),
40         "focus_in_event",
41         GTK_SIGNAL_FUNC(eventFocus),NULL);
42     gtk_signal_connect(GTK_OBJECT(window),
43         "focus_out_event",
44         GTK_SIGNAL_FUNC(eventFocus),NULL);
45     gtk_signal_connect(GTK_OBJECT(window),
46         "key_press_event",
47         GTK_SIGNAL_FUNC(eventPressKey),NULL);
48     gtk_signal_connect(GTK_OBJECT(window),
49         "key_release_event",
50         GTK_SIGNAL_FUNC(eventReleaseKey),NULL);
```

```
 51        gtk_widget_add_events(window,GDK_KEY_RELEASE_MASK);
 52
 53        box = gtk_vbox_new(FALSE,0);
 54
 55        keyLabel = gtk_label_new(" ");
 56        gtk_box_pack_start(GTK_BOX(box),keyLabel,
 57                FALSE,FALSE,0);
 58
 59        scrollLabel = gtk_label_new(" ");
 60        gtk_box_pack_start(GTK_BOX(box),scrollLabel,
 61                FALSE,FALSE,0);
 62
 63        focusLabel = gtk_label_new("Focus?");
 64        gtk_box_pack_end(GTK_BOX(box),focusLabel,
 65                FALSE,FALSE,0);
 66
 67        gtk_container_add(GTK_CONTAINER(window),box);
 68        gtk_widget_show_all(window);
 69        gtk_main();
 70        exit(0);
 71 }
 72 gint eventFocus(GtkWidget *widget,
 73        GdkEvent *event,gpointer data) {
 74     GdkEventFocus *focus;
 75     if(event->type == GDK_FOCUS_CHANGE) {
 76         focus = (GdkEventFocus *)event;
 77         if(focus->in)
 78             gtk_label_set_text(GTK_LABEL(focusLabel),
 79                     "Focus acquired");
 80         else
 81             gtk_label_set_text(GTK_LABEL(focusLabel),
 82                     "Focus lost");
 83     }
 84     return(TRUE);
 85 }
 86 gint eventPressKey(GtkWidget *widget,
 87        GdkEvent *event,gpointer data) {
 88     static char keyList[80] = " ";
 89     char lastKey[80];
 90     int i;
 91     int shift;
 92     char work[10];
 93     GdkEventKey *key = (GdkEventKey *)event;
 94
 95     switch(key->keyval) {
 96     case GDK_Alt_L:
 97     case GDK_Alt_R:
 98         altKeyDown = TRUE;
 99         break;
100     case GDK_Control_L:
101     case GDK_Control_R:
102         controlKeyDown = TRUE;
103         break;
104     case GDK_Meta_L:
```

```
105        case GDK_Meta_R:
106            metaKeyDown = TRUE;
107            break;
108        case GDK_Shift_L:
109            leftShiftKeyDown = TRUE;
110            break;
111        case GDK_Shift_R:
112            rightShiftKeyDown = TRUE;
113            break;
114        }
115
116        strcpy(work,gdk_keyval_name(key->keyval));
117        strcat(keyList," ");
118        strcat(keyList,work);
119        shift = strlen(keyList) - 60;
120        if(shift > 0) {
121            for(i=shift; keyList[i-1] != '\0'; i++)
122                keyList[i-shift] = keyList[i];
123        }
124        gtk_label_set_text(GTK_LABEL(scrollLabel),keyList);
125
126        sprintf(lastKey,"GDK_%s",work);
127        if((key->keyval >= 0x20) && (key->keyval < 0x7F)) {
128            sprintf(work,"    %c",(gchar)key->keyval);
129            strcat(lastKey,work);
130        }
131        if(gdk_keyval_is_lower(key->keyval))
132            strcat(lastKey,"   (not upper case)");
133        else if(gdk_keyval_is_upper(key->keyval))
134            strcat(lastKey,"   (upper case)");
135        sprintf(work,"    [%02X]",key->keyval);
136        strcat(lastKey,work);
137        if(altKeyDown)
138            strcat(lastKey,"  ALT");
139        if(controlKeyDown)
140            strcat(lastKey,"  CONTROL");
141        if(metaKeyDown)
142            strcat(lastKey,"  META");
143        if(leftShiftKeyDown)
144            strcat(lastKey,"  LeftSHIFT");
145        if(rightShiftKeyDown)
146            strcat(lastKey,"  RightSHIFT");
147        gtk_label_set_text(GTK_LABEL(keyLabel),lastKey);
148
149        return(TRUE);
150 }
151 gint eventReleaseKey(GtkWidget *widget,
152        GdkEvent *event,gpointer data) {
153        GdkEventKey *key = (GdkEventKey *)event;
154
155        switch(key->keyval) {
156        case GDK_Alt_L:
```

```
157       case GDK_Alt_R:
158           altKeyDown = FALSE;
159           break;
160       case GDK_Control_L:
161       case GDK_Control_R:
162           controlKeyDown = FALSE;
163           break;
164       case GDK_Meta_L:
165       case GDK_Meta_R:
166           metaKeyDown = FALSE;
167           break;
168       case GDK_Shift_L:
169           leftShiftKeyDown = FALSE;
170           break;
171       case GDK_Shift_R:
172           rightShiftKeyDown = FALSE;
173           break;
174       }
175       return(TRUE);
176 }
177
178 gint eventDelete(GtkWidget *widget,
179         GdkEvent *event,gpointer data) {
180       return(FALSE);
181 }
182 gint eventDestroy(GtkWidget *widget,
183         GdkEvent *event,gpointer data) {
184       gtk_main_quit();
185       return(0);
186 }
```

The events are connected to the main window of the application on lines 35 through 51. To determine whether or not the window has focus, lines 39 through 44 connect the callback function eventFocus() to the window so it is called every time the focus comes to the window, and when it leaves it. The call to gtk_signal_connect() on line 45 assigns the callback function eventPressKey() to be the one called for every keystroke, and the call to gtk_signal_connect() on line 48 assigns the callback function eventReleaseKey() to be the one called every time a key is released. But that doesn't quite do it. At this point, everything works except for the key release callback. By default, a widget is set up to receive the focus events and the key press events, but not the key release events. The call on line 51 to gtk_widget_add_events(), using the mask GDK_KEY_RELEASE_MASK, registers the window to receive the key release events and pass them on to any registered callback functions.

Lines 53 through 65 create three labels and insert them into a vertical box. The top label is named keyLabel and holds a description of the last keystroke. The second label is named scrollLabel and scrolls from right to left showing the most recent series of keystrokes. The third label is named focusLabel and indicates the current status of the main window's focus.

The function eventFocus() beginning on line 72 is called whenever the window either gains or loses focus. The conditional statement on line 77 checks whether the focus is lost or gained, and sets the text of the label to reflect the current status.

Whenever a key is pressed on the keyboard, the function eventPressKey() on line 86 is called with information about the key. The GdkEventKey event contains a field named keyval that contains an ID number for the key itself. There are separate codes for all the special keys. The ASCII key codes are the same values as the ASCII characters. With the variations in keyboard hardware, and with internationalization, there are over 1,300 key codes. If you want to see the entire list, they are defined in the header file gdkkeysyms.h.

The switch statement on line 95 selects some special keys according to their values. Lines 96 through 99 set to TRUE a Boolean value indicating the Alt key has been pressed. Similarly, on lines 100 through 107, the same indicators are set for the Control and Meta keys. Notice that there are two values for each of these keys (L and R) because there can be two of these keys on a keyboard and an application may need to know which of the two has been pressed. Lines 108 through 113 set separate indicators for the left and right Shift keys.

Lines 116 through 124 adjust the text being displayed in the scrolling window showing the most recent keystrokes. A descriptive name of the key value is copied to a work string from a call to gdk_keyval_name() on line 116. This description is simply the character itself if it is displayable; otherwise, it is a word describing the key. Lines 117 and 118 append a blank and the name of the key to the keyList string used to update the label text. The loop defined on line 120 executes whenever the string reaches a maximum length. The characters on the left are discarded to reduce the string length. On line 124, the new string is put into the label with a call to gtk_label_set_text(). The actual number of keys displayed depends on how many characters it takes to describe each one.

Lines 126 through 147 create a string describing information about this character. Line 126 starts the description by prepending GDK_ to the name acquired from the earlier call to gdk_keyval_name(). This form of the name is the defined constant that can be used to identify the character (for example, the switch statement on line 95). The test on line 127 checks whether the character is an ASCII printable character and, if so, the character itself is added to the description. Lines 131 through 134 determine whether or not the character is an uppercase letter. Note that, unlike the standard C islower() macro, the call to gdk_keyval_is_lower() returns TRUE for *every* character except uppercase letters. On lines 135 and 136, the key value itself is printed as a hexadecimal number and added to the string. Lines 137 through 146 check the Boolean values to determine if any of the special keys are being held down and, if so, adds this information to the description string. The call to gtk_label_set_text() on line 147 inserts the new text into the label.

The callback function eventReleaseKey() on line 151 is called whenever a key is released. The only ones that are of concern here are the ones that the switch statement on line 95 detects as being pressed. If it is one of the keys in question, its associated Boolean is set to FALSE to indicate that it no longer is being held down.

Figure 12-3 shows the information about the last key pressed, and something about the keys right before it. The top line shows the current character as being a lowercase *c*. The hexadecimal value of c is 0x63. Also, when the key was pressed, the Control key was held down. Starting from the right end of the middle line, you can see that the last keystroke was the letter *c*. Just before that, the left Control key was pressed. Directly preceding that, there was an exclamation point.

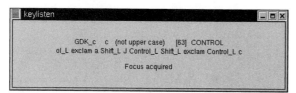

Figure 12-3: Monitoring keystrokes

GNOME's Command-Line Options

Every GNOME application has a set of command-line options available to it. The call to gnome_init() takes argc and argv as arguments and looks for certain options to be present. You can determine the options available in any application by starting it specifying help or -?. You can use the following simple program to demonstrate this.

```
/** showoptions.c **/
#include <gnome.h>

int main(int argc,char *argv[])
{
    gnome_init("showoptions","1.0",argc,argv);
    exit(0);
}
```

This program has no options of its own, but the options for GNOME, GTK+, and X are available. To see them all, run the program like this:

```
showoptions --help | more
```

The output is a complete list of the available options:

```
Usage: showoptions [OPTION...]

GNOME Options
  --disable-sound            Disable sound server usage
  --enable-sound             Enable sound server usage
  --espeaker=HOSTNAME:PORT   Host:port on which the sound
                             server to use is running

Help options
  -?, --help                 Show this help message
  --usage                    Display brief usage message

GTK options
  --gdk-debug=FLAGS          Gdk debugging flags to set
  --gdk-no-debug=FLAGS       Gdk debugging flags to unset
  --display=DISPLAY          X display to use
  --sync                     Make X calls synchronous
  --no-xshm                  Don't use X shared
                             memory extension
  --name=NAME                Program name as used by
                             the window manager
  --class=CLASS              Program class as used by
                             the window manager
  --gxid_host=HOST
  --gxid_port=PORT
  --xim-preedit=STYLE
  --xim-status=STYLE
  --gtk-debug=FLAGS          Gtk+ debugging flags to set
  --gtk-no-debug=FLAGS       Gtk+ debugging flags to unset
  --g-fatal-warnings         Make all warnings fatal
  --gtk-module=MODULE        Load an additional Gtk module

GNOME GUI options
  -V, --version

Help options
  -?, --help                 Show this help message
  --usage                    Display brief usage message

Session management options
  --sm-client-id=ID          Specify session management ID
  --sm-config-prefix=PREFIX  Specify prefix of saved
                             configuration
  --sm-disable               Disable connection to session
                             manager
```

These options are available in every GNOME application. For example, to discover the version number of the program mousefollow in the beginning of this chapter, the command and response looks like this:

```
% mousefollow -V
Gnome mousefollow 1.0
```

A GNOME application can display a brief listing of all the arguments by using the -usage option this way:

```
% showoptions -usage
Usage: showoptions [-?V?] [--disable-sound] [--enable-sound]
    [--espeaker=HOSTNAME:PORT] [--usage] [--gdk-debug=FLAGS]
    [--gdk-no-debug=FLAGS] [--display=DISPLAY] [--sync]
    [--no-xshm] [--name=NAME] [--class=CLASS]
    [--gxid_host=HOST] [--gxid_port=PORT] [--xim-preedit=STYLE]
    [--xim-status=STYLE] [--gtk-debug=FLAGS]
    [--gtk-no-debug=FLAGS] [--g-fatal-warnings]
    [--gtk-module=MODULE] [--usage] [--sm-client-id=ID]
    [- sm-config-prefix=PREFIX] [--sm-disable]
```

Adding Command-Line Options

You can add your own command-line options and have the system treat them the same way it does the built-in options. That is, your options are parsed from the command line and stored for your program to use them later. Also, they are listed on the help and -usage options along with the predefined options. This software is known as *popt*.

You define your options as an array of poptOption structs. Each member of the array is one option. The struct contains all the descriptive information for the option:

```
struct poptOption {
    const char *longName;
    char shortName;
    int argInfo;
    void *arg;
    int val;
    char *descrip;
    char *argDescrip;
};
```

The longName and the shortName hold the characters that are expected on the command line. The long name is the one used with a pair of dashes, and the short name is the character used with a single dash. For example, a long name of "nocolor" and a short name of "n" allows the option to be specified on the command line as either --nocolor or -n.

The string descrip is a brief description of the argument. If it is specified, the string appears as the description when the --help option is used. The argDescrip string also is used in the description to show how the value is to be specified. For example, if an argument with the long name border-color has the argDescrip COLOR, the display in the output from --help is --border-color==COLOR.

The `argInfo` field defines the kind of argument and the data type of the value, if any, expected on the command line. Table 12-2 lists the possible values for `argInfo`. Table 12-3 lists the bit masks that you can use to set options for each of the argument types.

Table 12-2
The Types of Arguments Known to Popt

Argument Type Name	Description
POPT_ARG_NONE	The option is an on-off switch, so it does not require a value on the command line.
POPT_ARG_STRING	The value on the command line is in the form of a quoted string.
POPT_ARG_INT	The value on the command line is limited to the range of values of an `int`.
POPT_ARG_LONG	The value on the command line is limited to the range of values of a `long`.
POPT_ARG_INCLUDE_TABLE	This is not a command-line option. The `arg` pointer in the struct is the address of another `poptOption` array to be included.
POPT_ARG_CALLBACK	This is not a command-line option. The `arg` pointer is the address of a callback function that is to be used to parse the command-line options. This should be included at the beginning of the options array.
POPT_ARG_INTL_DOMAIN	The `arg` value is a pointer to a string defining the translation domain to be used with this table.
POPT_ARG_VAL	This is not a command-line option, although it can be used to set a default value. The location pointed to by `arg` should take on the value of `val`.

Table 12-3
Option Flags to Modify Popt Arguments

Option Name	Description
POPT_ARGFLAG_ONEDASH	Allows a single dash to be used on the long name as well as the short name
POPT_ARGFLAG_DOC_HIDDEN	Suppresses the display of this option with the others by `--help` or `--usage`

Option Name	Description
POPT_CBFLAG_PRE	Used with POPT_ARG_CALLBACK to call the callback before the parse
POPT_CBFLAG_POST	Used with POPT_ARG_CALLBACK to call the callback after the parse

This all may seem to be a bit more complicated than necessary, but the complications are necessary only when you are doing something very special with the arguments. In almost every case, it is simply a matter of creating an array of option descriptions, a place to store the input values, and a single function call. The following program defines and accepts five command-line arguments.

```
 1 /** readparm.c **/
 2 #include <gnome.h>
 3
 4 int toolbarParm = FALSE;
 5 char *titleParm = NULL;
 6 char *backgroundParm = NULL;
 7 int widthParm = 100;
 8 int heightParm = 50;
 9
10 struct poptOption opt[] = {
11     {
12         "title",'t',
13         POPT_ARG_STRING,
14         &titleParm,0,
15         "The text to appear on the title bar",
16         "TITLE"
17     },{
18         "width",'w',
19         POPT_ARG_INT,
20         &widthParm,0,
21         "The width of the window",
22         "WIDTH"
23     },{
24         "height",'h',
25         POPT_ARG_INT,
26         &heightParm,0,
27         "The height of the window",
28         "HEIGHT"
29     },{
30         "toolbar",'T',
31         POPT_ARG_NONE,
32         &toolbarParm,0,
33         "Dislay the toolbar",
34         NULL
```

```
35      },{
36          "background",'\0',
37          POPT_ARG_STRING,
38          &backgroundParm,0,
39          "The background color for the window",
40          "COLORNAME"
41      },{
42          NULL,0,0,NULL,0,NULL,NULL
43      }};
44
45  int main(int argc,char *argv[])
46  {
47      poptContext context;
48
49      gnome_init_with_popt_table("readparm","1.0",argc,argv,
50              opt,0,&context);
51
52      g_print("toolbar: %s\n",
53              toolbarParm ? "TRUE" : "FALSE");
54      g_print("title: %s\n",titleParm ? titleParm : "NULL");
55      g_print("background: %s\n",
56              backgroundParm ? backgroundParm : "NULL");
57      g_print("width: %d\n",widthParm);
58      g_print("height: %d\n",heightParm);
59
60      poptFreeContext(context);
61      exit(0);
62  }
```

The declarations on lines 4 through 8 are the fields that receive the values entered on the command line. If an option does not appear on the command line, its value here is not changed; if you wish, you can store the default values in them, as this program shows with widthParm and heightParm.

Each parameter is defined as a member of the array of poptOption structs beginning on line 10. The first option, starting on line 12, requires a quoted string as its value on the command line and has both a long and short name. The long form can have an equal sign preceding the value. You can enter the argument in any of the following forms:

```
readparm --title "Title Text"
readparm --title="Title Text"
readparm -t "Title Text"
readparm --title TitleText
readparm --title=TitleText
readparm -t TitleText
```

The quotes are necessary only if the string contains blanks or if it begins with a hyphen (in which case, it could be confused with an argument tag). When the string is read from the command line, a pointer to it is stored in `titleParm` on line 5 because its address is specified in the table on line 14.

The height and width parameters defined on lines 18 through 28 are defined to return `int` data. The storage locations for the data are `widthParm` and `heightParm`, defined (with default values) on lines 7 and 8.

The toolbar argument defined on line 30 is a simple on-off switch. That is, there are no values associated with it on the command line. The program treats its presence or absence as a flag. The flag value, defined as `toolbarParm` on line 4, is an `int` with `FALSE` as its initial value. The value is changed to `TRUE` only if either `toolbar` or `-T` is specified on the command line.

The argument defined on line 36 can be used to accept the name of a color as a string. The only way to use this argument is with the long form because the short form letter is the null character. A pointer to the name of the color is stored in `backgroundParm` defined on line 6.

All the arguments are read from the command line, parsed, converted into the appropriate data types, and stored in the specified fields with a single call to `gnome_init_with_popt_table()` on line 49. This call replaces the call to `gnome_init()` by adding three more parameters. The fifth argument is the address of the array of `poptOption` structs defining the parameters. The last argument is the address of a `poptContext` (which is itself a pointer) that receives the address of the descriptive `poptContext`. You can use this context to inquire about the options if more detailed information is required.

Memory is allocated to store the `poptContext`, so it probably should be returned to the system. However, it cannot be returned until you do not need the information stored in it any longer, such as any string arguments that were returned to you as pointers.

The parameters you define in your program are added to the list of those displayed. In this example, enter this command to see the parameters:

```
readparm --help
```

The output is the same list described above, with these added at the bottom:

```
    . . .
  readparm options
    -t, --title=TITLE        The text to appear on the title bar
    -w, --width=WIDTH        The width of the window
    -h, --height=HEIGHT      The height of the window
    -T, --toolbar            Dislay the toolbar
        --background=COLORNAME  The background color for the window
```

Summary

Most widgets respond to the mouse, and many accept keystrokes from the keyboard, but it also is possible to retrieve this information directly without waiting for a widget to react. This chapter explained several non-widget methods for getting input from the user:

✦ Any widget that contains a window can be made sensitive to the mouse movements, mouse buttons, and keystrokes from the keyboard.

✦ A single window can grab the mouse, resulting in all of its events being reported to that window. Optionally, the grab can limit the movement of the mouse to the grabbing window.

✦ Each key press and key release can be read from the keyboard into a window that has the current focus. Every key has an individual ID value — even those that appear more than once on the keyboard (such as the Shift key).

✦ There is a built-in utility in GNOME that reads the command-line arguments and extracts their values and settings.

The next chapter discusses fonts. There are thousands of fonts available — many are included as part of the X11 system, and others are included with other software packages. There is a wide range of variation in the appearance of fonts, but beneath it all, there are standard size and position measurements used by all of them.

✦   ✦   ✦

Fonts

The way that fonts are used by X (and thus by GTK+ and GNOME) may confuse you at first. But once you see what is going on, it becomes quite simple. A method was devised that keeps font handling very flexible and, at the same time, quite straightforward. In your application, you can be specific and use exactly the font you like, or you can leave some leeway in your font selection and allow each system to pick a font that fits with the selection criteria. There is also a widget that enables a user to choose the font.

Fonts vary in size and shape in different ways. There is a special set of metrics applied to fonts. By using the standard values to position characters on the display, you can treat all fonts (no matter how radical) the same way.

The Anatomy of a Font

There are a number of different measurements that can be made on a character, or a string of characters, in a font. The fact that some characters are taller than others, some descend lower than others, and some characters are wider than others makes it a little more complicated. It also is possible to have one character overlap another when they are adjacent to one another in a string—this is quite common in an italic font where the top of a tall character extends above the bottom of the character to its right.

Figure 13-1 shows the measurements that can be made on each character. The origin is the *x*- and *y*-coordinate point that is used to draw the character. In other words, when you draw the letter *t* at a specific coordinate point, it actually appears above and to the right of that point. On the other hand, the letter *p* appears to the right of the point, but both above and below it. The pixel rendering, or graphic design, of a character is called a *glyph*. Every glyph is designed relative to an origin point in such a way that it is only necessary for you to line up the characters—all you need do is line up their origin points.

This string of origin points is called the *baseline*. The *ascent* and *descent values* are the measurements from the base line to the top and bottom of the character — the sum of the ascent and the descent is the height of the character. The width of the character is measured from the origin point to the right side of the character. The *lbearing* (left bearing) is the distance from the origin to the character and the *rbearing* (right bearing) is the width of the graphic part of the character.

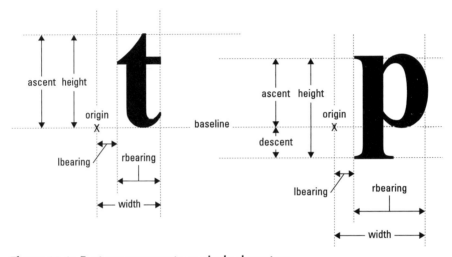

Figure 13-1: Font measurements on single characters

You can see from the ascent, descent, and height measurements in Figure 13-1 that the value of the descent can be zero. It also is possible that the lbearing value be zero. In fact, it can even be negative in the case of the character's glyph being drawn to the left of the origin. (For example, this can happen with the bottom portion of an italic font.)

Figure 13-2 shows the set of measurements that can be made on a string of characters. The ascent, descent, and height can include a leading area that extends outside the maximum extent upward, downward, or both. The same is true of width. The border around the string allows your program to easily place pieces of text, even text in different fonts, next to one another and have the spacing be correct. The origin of the string — the *x* and *y* coordinates used to draw the string — is the origin of the left-most letter in the string. The origins of the other letters are used internally to place each letter next to the other when the string is drawn.

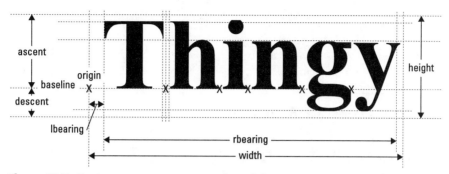

Figure 13-2: Font measurements on a string of characters

The Names of the Fonts

The fonts are stored in disk files. The font files are part of the standard X distribution. When an application requests a font, it is loaded from the file into the X server — not into the application. Because the fonts are in the server, there is no overhead of passing detailed font information from the application to the server for display. This reduction in traffic can save you a lot of time because it is common to open a local X window (with its local server) controlled by an application in another computer. Besides, if more than one application is using the same font, there only has to be one copy loaded.

The font files usually are stored in subdirectories of /usr/lib/X11/fonts. In each subdirectory, the font files have the suffix .pcf or .pcf.gz. In the same directory as the fonts, there is a file named fonts.dir that maps alias names to the actual font file names. There is also a fonts.alias file that you can use to assign alternate names to the fonts defined in fonts.dir. For example, you can use the font file named 10x20.pcf.gz by specifying its name like this:

```
10x20
```

Or you can use the alias name assigned to it, which is:

```
-misc-fixed-medium-r-normal--20-200-75-75-c-100-iso8859-1
```

The short form has the advantage of being easy to remember, but the long form has the advantage of being descriptive. And the software enables you to make selections using wildcards for the various parts of the name. Figure 13-3 shows an example of a long font name with each of the parts labeled, and Table 13-1 describes what each part signifies.

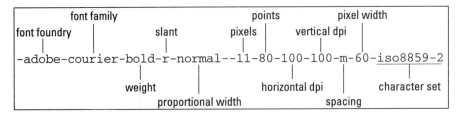

Figure 13-3: A long font name and its parts

Part	Description
	Table 13-1 **The Parts of a Long Font Name**
font foundry	The name of the company or organization that created the font. Some of the more common names are adobe, b&h, bitstream, dec, schumacher, sony, and sun. If no foundry claims the font, the name is misc.
font family	The name of a set of related fonts, of which this font is a member. Possible names are lucida, times, courier, helvetica, and so on.
weight	This is the stroke weight. It is usually either medium or bold, but it also can be black, book, demibold, light, or regular.
slant	The angle of each letter can be italic, oblique, or r (short for *roman*, meaning upright).
proportional width	The relationship between height and width is usually normal, but it can be condensed, semi-condensed, narrow, or double.
pixels	The size of the font in pixels. Normally, font sizes are measured in points (a point is 1/72 of an inch). To arrive at the pixel size value, the point size is translated into the pixel size, which means the point size may have to be rounded up or down to come out on a pixel boundary.
points	The point size of the font in tenths of a point. In the example, the value 80 indicates that this is an 8-point font. The relationship between the point size and the pixel size is determined by the vertical and horizontal *dpi (dots per inch) values*. In this example, at 100 dpi, an 8-point font has a pixel size of 11. At the same dpi, a 12-point font has a pixel size of 17.
horizontal dpi	The number of horizontal pixels per inch of resolution. This value is used to compute the pixel and point sizes. It also is used as a ratio with vertical dpi to determine the horizontal vertical dpi that will cause the font to display properly.

Part	Description
vertical dpi	A number of vertical pixels per inch of resolution.
spacing	This can be m (for monospace), p (for proportional), or c (for character cell). A monospace font is one that has all its characters the same width. A proportional font has characters of various widths (for example, the letter *w* is wider than the letter *i*). A character cell font is a fixed-width font based on the way typewriter fonts are spaced.
pixel width	The average width, in tenths of a pixel, of all the characters in the font.
character set	This is the version of the standard used to define the character set. The *ISO (International Organization for Standardization)* has established standards for the sets of characters that are included in the alphabet of various languages.

Not only are the long-font names descriptive, but they also are in a form that enables you to use wildcard characters in searching for a font. This way, you only need to specify the things you care about and let the rest of it default. For example, you can use the following as the name of a font in a call to gtk_font_load():

    -*-bookman-light-r-normal--14-*-*-*-p-*-iso8859-1

The parts specified in the name must be an exact match with an actual font, while the asterisks can match any value. Of course, several fonts may match, but the first match encountered is the one returned. The above example could select this font:

    -adobe-bookman-light-r-normal--14-135-75-75-p-82-iso8859-1

When specifying a font name, you should be specific only with the parts you need. This way you have a better chance of matching an actual font name. If your specifications do not match the name of a font, the default font named fixed is used, and it is almost never the one you want.

The Font Picker Widget

There is a GNOME widget that enables you to select and display fonts. The widget is placed in your application as a button on a dialog box or in a menu. The following program shows how you can use the widget to select a font, and then how that font can be applied to the text of another widget.

```
1 /** fontpicker.c **/
2 #include <gnome.h>
3
```

```
 4 gint eventDelete(GtkWidget *widget,
 5         GdkEvent *event,gpointer data);
 6 gint eventDestroy(GtkWidget *widget,
 7         GdkEvent *event,gpointer data);
 8 void eventFontSet(GtkWidget *widget,
 9         gchar *string,GtkWidget *label);
10
11 int main(int argc,char *argv[])
12 {
13     GtkWidget *app;
14     GtkWidget *fontpicker;
15     GtkWidget *label;
16     GtkWidget *box;
17
18     gnome_init("fontpicker","1.0",argc,argv);
19     app = gnome_app_new("fontpicker","Font Picker");
20     gtk_container_set_border_width(GTK_CONTAINER(app),30);
21     gtk_signal_connect(GTK_OBJECT(app),"delete_event",
22             GTK_SIGNAL_FUNC(eventDelete),NULL);
23     gtk_signal_connect(GTK_OBJECT(app),"destroy",
24             GTK_SIGNAL_FUNC(eventDestroy),NULL);
25
26     box = gtk_vbox_new(FALSE,0);
27
28     label = gtk_label_new(
29         "Select the button below and the font picker\n"
30         "window will appear.\n"
31         "The font you select will be used to\n"
32         "rewrite this text.");
33     gtk_box_pack_start(GTK_BOX(box),label,
34             FALSE,FALSE,0);
35
36     fontpicker = gnome_font_picker_new();
37     gtk_signal_connect(GTK_OBJECT(fontpicker),"font-set",
38             GTK_SIGNAL_FUNC(eventFontSet),label);
39     gtk_box_pack_start(GTK_BOX(box),fontpicker,
40             FALSE,FALSE,0);
41
42     gnome_app_set_contents(GNOME_APP(app),box);
43     gtk_widget_show_all(app);
44     gtk_main();
45     exit(0);
46 }
47 void eventFontSet(GtkWidget *widget,
48         gchar *string,GtkWidget *label) {
49     GtkStyle *oldStyle;
50     GtkStyle *newStyle;
51     GdkFont *font;
52
53     font = gdk_font_load(string);
54     oldStyle = gtk_widget_get_style(label);
55     newStyle = gtk_style_copy(oldStyle);
56     newStyle->font = font;
57     gtk_widget_set_style(label,newStyle);
```

```
58      gtk_style_unref(oldStyle);
59 }
60 gint eventDelete(GtkWidget *widget,
61         GdkEvent *event,gpointer data) {
62      return(FALSE);
63 }
64 gint eventDestroy(GtkWidget *widget,
65         GdkEvent *event,gpointer data) {
66      gtk_main_quit();
67      return(0);
68 }
```

On line 26, a vertical box is created to contain the text label and the GnomeFont-Picker button. Lines 28 through 34 create the label, with its text, and pack it into the top of the box. The font picker is created on line 36. The callback function eventFontSet() is attached to the font picker on line 37, and the font picker is packed in the box immediately below the label.

The callback function eventFontSet() defined on line 47 is called whenever the OK button is pressed in the font picker dialog box. The call to gdk_font_load() on line 53 uses the name of the selected font to create a GdkFont object. This creation is called "loading" because part of the process is to notify the X server that it should load the font. The returned GtkFont object holds font ID information that is passed to the server whenever the font is to be used. Depending on the currently selected font, the window looks like the one in Figure 13-4.

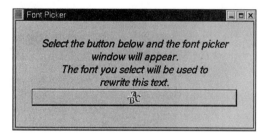

Figure 13-4: A user-selectable font

A widget contains a pointer to a GtkStyle object that contains color and font information (along with some other things). The call to gtk_widget_get_style() on line 54 returns a pointer to the GtkStyle object. This same GtkStyle object can be shared by a number of widgets, so an application should not modify it directly. Instead, a call is made to gtk_style_copy() to create a duplicate of the GtkStyle, then, on line 56, the new font is assigned to the copy. The call to gtk_widget_set_style() on line 54 replaces the original GtkStyle with the copy. Finally, on line 58, a call is made to gtk_style_unref() to drop the reference to the old GtkStyle object. If there are no other references, the memory used by the GtkStyle is returned to the system — otherwise, the reference counter is decremented by one.

Figure 13-5 shows one of the three panels displayed by the font picker dialog box. You can select the three most basic font characteristics — font name, weight and slant, and the font size — from this window. The other two panels can be used to specify the other parts of a font name to refine the search. The preview window at the bottom is updated whenever the selection is changed.

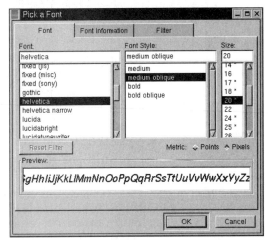

Figure 13-5: The GnomeFontPicker widget

Metrics and Font Placement

The following program positions text on a drawing area. It uses the font metric information for a specific string to determine the top, bottom, middle, right, and left edges of the rectangular area that contains the font. Then these dimensions are used to center the text and place it against the edges.

```
 1 /** fontposition.c **/
 2 #include <gnome.h>
 3
 4 #define HEIGHT 100
 5 #define WIDTH 300
 6
 7 #define STRING_LEFT 1
 8 #define STRING_CENTER 2
 9 #define STRING_RIGHT 3
10 #define STRING_TOP 1
11 #define STRING_MIDDLE 2
12 #define STRING_BOTTOM 3
13
14 typedef struct {
15     GdkFont *font;
16     GtkWidget *drawingArea;
17     gint horizontal;
```

```
18      gint vertical;
19 } Context;
20
21 gint eventDelete(GtkWidget *widget,
22          GdkEvent *event,gpointer data);
23 gint eventDestroy(GtkWidget *widget,
24          GdkEvent *event,gpointer data);
25 void eventFontSet(GtkWidget *widget,
26          gchar *string,Context *context);
27 gboolean eventDraw(GtkWidget *widget,
28          GdkEvent *event,Context *context);
29 void topButton(GtkWidget *widget,Context *context);
30 void middleButton(GtkWidget *widget,Context *context);
31 void bottomButton(GtkWidget *widget,Context *context);
32 void leftButton(GtkWidget *widget,Context *context);
33 void centerButton(GtkWidget *widget,Context *context);
34 void rightButton(GtkWidget *widget,Context *context);
35 static GtkWidget *createPositionWidget(Context *context);
36
37 int main(int argc,char *argv[])
38 {
39      GtkWidget *app;
40      GtkWidget *position;
41      Context context =
42          { NULL, NULL, STRING_RIGHT, STRING_MIDDLE };
43
44      gnome_init("fontposition","1.0",argc,argv);
45      app = gnome_app_new("fontposition","Font Position");
46      gtk_container_set_border_width(GTK_CONTAINER(app),30);
47      gtk_signal_connect(GTK_OBJECT(app),"delete_event",
48              GTK_SIGNAL_FUNC(eventDelete),NULL);
49      gtk_signal_connect(GTK_OBJECT(app),"destroy",
50              GTK_SIGNAL_FUNC(eventDestroy),NULL);
51
52      position = createPositionWidget(&context);
53
54      gnome_app_set_contents(GNOME_APP(app),position);
55      gtk_widget_show_all(app);
56      gtk_main();
57      exit(0);
58 }
59 static GtkWidget *createPositionWidget(Context *context)
60 {
61      GtkWidget *position;
62      GtkWidget *box;
63      GtkWidget *button;
64      GtkWidget *frame;
65      GtkWidget *fontpicker;
66
67      position = gtk_vbox_new(FALSE,0);
68
69      box = gtk_hbox_new(TRUE,10);
70      button = gtk_button_new_with_label("Top");
71      gtk_signal_connect(GTK_OBJECT(button),"clicked",
```

```
72              GTK_SIGNAL_FUNC(topButton),context);
73      gtk_box_pack_start(GTK_BOX(box),button,
74              FALSE,TRUE,0);
75      button = gtk_button_new_with_label("Middle");
76      gtk_signal_connect(GTK_OBJECT(button),"clicked",
77              GTK_SIGNAL_FUNC(middleButton),context);
78      gtk_box_pack_start(GTK_BOX(box),button,
79              FALSE,TRUE,0);
80      button = gtk_button_new_with_label("Bottom");
81      gtk_signal_connect(GTK_OBJECT(button),"clicked",
82              GTK_SIGNAL_FUNC(bottomButton),context);
83      gtk_box_pack_start(GTK_BOX(box),button,
84              FALSE,TRUE,0);
85      gtk_box_pack_start(GTK_BOX(position),box,
86              FALSE,FALSE,0);
87
88      context->drawingArea = gtk_drawing_area_new();
89      gtk_drawing_area_size(
90              GTK_DRAWING_AREA(context->drawingArea),
91              WIDTH,HEIGHT);
92      gtk_signal_connect(GTK_OBJECT(context->drawingArea),
93              "event",GTK_SIGNAL_FUNC(eventDraw),context);
94
95      frame = gtk_frame_new(NULL);
96      gtk_container_add(GTK_CONTAINER(frame),
97              context->drawingArea);
98      gtk_box_pack_start(GTK_BOX(position),frame,
99              FALSE,FALSE,0);
100
101     box = gtk_hbox_new(TRUE,10);
102     button = gtk_button_new_with_label("Left");
103     gtk_signal_connect(GTK_OBJECT(button),"clicked",
104             GTK_SIGNAL_FUNC(leftButton),context);
105     gtk_box_pack_start(GTK_BOX(box),button,
106             FALSE,TRUE,0);
107     button = gtk_button_new_with_label("Center");
108     gtk_signal_connect(GTK_OBJECT(button),"clicked",
109             GTK_SIGNAL_FUNC(centerButton),context);
110     gtk_box_pack_start(GTK_BOX(box),button,
111             FALSE,TRUE,0);
112     button = gtk_button_new_with_label("Right");
113     gtk_signal_connect(GTK_OBJECT(button),"clicked",
114             GTK_SIGNAL_FUNC(rightButton),context);
115     gtk_box_pack_start(GTK_BOX(box),button,
116             FALSE,TRUE,0);
117     gtk_box_pack_start(GTK_BOX(position),box,
118             FALSE,FALSE,0);
119
120     fontpicker = gnome_font_picker_new();
121     gtk_signal_connect(GTK_OBJECT(fontpicker),"font-set",
122             GTK_SIGNAL_FUNC(eventFontSet),context);
123     gtk_box_pack_start(GTK_BOX(position),fontpicker,
124             FALSE,FALSE,0);
125
```

```
126     return(position);
127 }
128 void eventFontSet(GtkWidget *widget,
129         gchar *string,Context *context) {
130
131     if(context->font != NULL)
132         gdk_font_unref(context->font);
133     context->font = gdk_font_load(string);
134     gdk_window_clear_area_e(context->drawingArea->window,
135             0,0,WIDTH,HEIGHT);
136 }
137 gboolean eventDraw(GtkWidget *widget,
138         GdkEvent *event,Context *context) {
139     gchar outstring[40];
140     gint lbearing;
141     gint rbearing;
142     gint width;
143     gint ascent;
144     gint descent;
145     gint x;
146     gint y;
147
148     if(context->font == NULL) {
149         context->font = gdk_font_load(
150       "-*-bookman-light-r-normal--14-*-*-*-p-*-iso8859-1");
151     }
152
153     switch(context->vertical) {
154     case STRING_TOP:
155         strcpy(outstring,"Top");
156         break;
157     case STRING_MIDDLE:
158         strcpy(outstring,"Middle");
159         break;
160     case STRING_BOTTOM:
161         strcpy(outstring,"Bottom");
162         break;
163     }
164     switch(context->horizontal) {
165     case STRING_LEFT:
166         strcat(outstring," Left");
167         break;
168     case STRING_CENTER:
169         strcat(outstring," Center");
170         break;
171     case STRING_RIGHT:
172         strcat(outstring," Right");
173         break;
174     }
175
176     gdk_text_extents(context->font,
177                 outstring,
178                 strlen(outstring),
179                 &lbearing,
```

```
180                        &rbearing,
181                        &width,
182                        &ascent,
183                        &descent);
184
185        switch(context->vertical) {
186        case STRING_TOP:
187            y = ascent;
188            break;
189        case STRING_MIDDLE:
190            y = HEIGHT / 2;
191            y += (ascent - descent) / 2;
192            break;
193        case STRING_BOTTOM:
194            y = HEIGHT - descent;
195            break;
196        }
197        switch(context->horizontal) {
198        case STRING_LEFT:
199            x = 0;
200            break;
201        case STRING_CENTER:
202            x = (WIDTH / 2) - (width / 2);
203            break;
204        case STRING_RIGHT:
205            x = WIDTH - width;
206            break;
207        }
208
209        gdk_draw_string(widget->window,
210                context->font,
211                context->drawingArea->style->black_gc,
212                x,y,
213                outstring);
214
215        return(TRUE);
216 }
217 void topButton(GtkWidget *widget,Context *context) {
218        context->vertical = STRING_TOP;
219        gdk_window_clear_area_e(context->drawingArea->window,
220                0,0,WIDTH,HEIGHT);
221 }
222 void middleButton(GtkWidget *widget,Context *context) {
223        context->vertical = STRING_MIDDLE;
224        gdk_window_clear_area_e(context->drawingArea->window,
225                0,0,WIDTH,HEIGHT);
226 }
227 void bottomButton(GtkWidget *widget,Context *context) {
228        context->vertical = STRING_BOTTOM;
229        gdk_window_clear_area_e(context->drawingArea->window,
230                0,0,WIDTH,HEIGHT);
```

```
231 }
232 void leftButton(GtkWidget *widget,Context *context) {
233     context->horizontal = STRING_LEFT;
234     gdk_window_clear_area_e(context->drawingArea->window,
235         0,0,WIDTH,HEIGHT);
236 }
237 void centerButton(GtkWidget *widget,Context *context) {
238     context->horizontal = STRING_CENTER;
239     gdk_window_clear_area_e(context->drawingArea->window,
240         0,0,WIDTH,HEIGHT);
241 }
242 void rightButton(GtkWidget *widget,Context *context) {
243     context->horizontal = STRING_RIGHT;
244     gdk_window_clear_area_e(context->drawingArea->window,
245         0,0,WIDTH,HEIGHT);
246 }
247 gint eventDelete(GtkWidget *widget,
248         GdkEvent *event,gpointer data) {
249     return(FALSE);
250 }
251 gint eventDestroy(GtkWidget *widget,
252         GdkEvent *event,gpointer data) {
253     gtk_main_quit();
254     return(0);
255 }
```

The mainline of the program, on lines 37 through 58, sets up a GNOME application that has just one window. The call to createPositionWidget() on line 52 creates a widget that is inserted in the main window on line 54 with a call to gnome_app_set_contents().

The application window is shown in Figure 13-6. The row of buttons across the top repositions the string vertically, and the row of buttons toward the bottom repositions it horizontally. The button at the bottom is a font selector that you can use to change the font of the string being positioned.

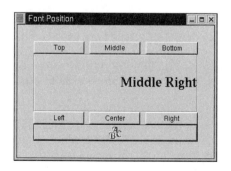

Figure 13-6: Using metrics to position text

The function createPositionWidget() on line 59 creates all the widgets for the display and assigns callback functions to them. A Context struct, defined on line 14, is used to pass information to this function, and to all the callback functions, instead of using global data. All of the widgets are contained in the vertical box created by the call to gtk_vbox_new() on line 67. Lines 69 through 86 create a horizontal box and fill it with buttons. Then the horizontal box is inserted at the top of the vertical box. Each button is assigned its own callback function with the context pointer as the data passed to it.

Lines 88 through 93 create the drawing area that is used to display the text. The call to gtk_drawing_area_size() sets the size of the drawing area to the WIDTH and HEIGHT values defined on lines 4 and 5. The callback function eventDraw() is connected to the drawing area, so whenever there is an exposure event, the function is called to paint the window.

Lines 95 through 118 create the buttons toward the bottom that control the horizontal position of the displayed text. Each button is assigned its own callback function.

A GnomeFontPicker widget is created by the call to gnome_font_picker_new() on lines 120 through 124. Its callback function is eventFontSet(), and it is packed as the last member of the vertical box.

The callback function eventFontSet() on line 128 is called by the font picker whenever a new font is selected. If there is a font already included in the context, the call to gdk_font_unref() on line 132 releases the font allocation both locally and in the X server (unless the same font is in use by some other process). The call to gdk_font_load() on line 133 creates a new font based on the string returned from the font picker. The call to gdk_window_clear_area_e() on line 134 is necessary for the display to be updated. The call does two things—it erases the previously drawn string by filling the drawing area with the background color, and it issues an expose event. The expose event causes the callback function eventDraw() to draw the text using the new font.

The callback function eventDraw() on line 137 is called whenever the string needs to be drawn into the drawing area. Line 148 tests whether a font is loaded already and, if not, loads the default font. The text of the string is determined by its location in the window, so the switch statements on lines 153 and 164 are used to build the string from the two names describing its position. Because both the font and the string are known, a call to gdk_text_extents() on line 176 returns the metrics of the string as it will appear on the display. These values can be used to position the text in the window.

The vertical positioning is set in the switch statement beginning on line 185. If the string is to be at the top of the window, the y value is set to the ascent—that is, the height of the tallest character above the base line. If the string is to be placed at the bottom of the window, the y value is set to the height of the window minus the descent—this puts the bottom of the character with the longest descender directly on the bottom of the window. There is a little bit more involved to calculate the exact vertical center. For most applications, you simply divide the height in half and use the base line at that point. If, however, you want the exact center, you need to take into account the off-center nature of the base line, as is done on line 191.

The horizontal positioning is set in the `switch` statement beginning on line 197. If the string is to be on the left, you simply place the origin at the left margin by setting x to zero. Line 205 positions the string on the right side by setting the value of x to the width of the window — minus the length of the string. Line 202 positions the string in the horizontal center by halving the width of the window and subtracting half of the length of the string.

Each of the buttons has its own callback on lines 217 through 245. Each callback sets the position indicator in the context. Also, each callback calls `gdk_window_ clear_area_e()` to erase the drawing area and issues an "expose" event that causes `eventDraw()` to draw the new string on the window.

Summary

Of all the elements displayed as part of a graphical user interface, the eye is most critical of letters, numbers, and punctuation. We have been reading and writing all of our lives, so our brain instantly recognizes characters and patterns of characters. Some character fonts appear to be nice and friendly, even attractive, while some appear to be clunky or stiff. The actual difference, between one we like and one we don't like, can be very small. Even though characters normally are displayed as very small items in a window, it is easy for us to instantly recognize the details of its shape. This preconceived notion of the appearance of characters is why a font can seem so dramatic to us. In this chapter, the fundamentals of font manipulation were described:

✦ Each font is stored in its own file, so it is easy to add new fonts or delete old ones.

✦ Your application can refer to a specific font by its exact name; or it can select a font by using descriptive terms, such as the font family and point size.

✦ There is a standard set of metrics that you can use to position text in the window, and to determine the size of the displayed text.

✦ The `GnomeFontPicker` widget can be included in your program to enable the user to pick a font.

The next chapter takes a peek inside the widgets. Every widget contains a displayable window and is capable of responding to the mouse and keyboard. But there is much more to a widget. If you know how the widgets work, you will be able to manipulate them into doing what you want them to do. Besides, you may find that some functions of your application can be best written as a widget.

✦　　✦　　✦

Widget Tricks

This chapter deals with widgets. Every displayable object in GNOME has, as its parent or grandparent, a `GtkWidget` object. There are some settings and adjustments that can be made into a widget. A widget is a very sophisticated software object in the way it keeps track of information, passes events forward to the application program, and knows how and when to update itself on the display.

Because all GNOME displayable objects have the same heritage, they are all widgets. Every widget has certain things in common with every other widget. This has the great advantage that any widget-level function that works for one widget works for another. For example, it is possible to make color and font settings at the widget level. There also are standard ways to change the size and position of a widget; the function calls are exactly the same whether the widget is a menu, a label, a drawing area, or something that was made up especially for the application.

Exploring a Widget

Through inheritance, every widget in your program is a combination of parts that include a `GtkObject`, a `GtkWidget`, and, possibly, other widgets. For example, a `GtkButton` widget is built on top of a `GtkBin` widget, which is built on top of a `GtkContainer` widget, which is built on top of a `GtkWidget`, which is built on top of a `GtkObject`. This form of inheritance gives GTK+ its object-oriented characteristics. The GNOME widgets are further extensions of GTK+ widgets, so they also have this same object-oriented form. Chapter 18 describes the internal structure in detail.

Every widget has some internal settings that an application program can read or write. And, because every widget is an *aggregate* — sort of a stack of different widgets — it was necessary to devise an interface that your application can use to address a specific value inside a specific widget found in the inheritance tree. To read or write one of these values, your program needs to know the name of the widget, the name of the value, and the data type.

Note   There are a number of terms used to refer to these program-accessible values stored in a widget. They are known as object arguments, widget parameters, settings, values, options, and so on. However, the term *argument* probably fits best because the three letters "arg" appear internally in GTK+ and GNOME widgets.

The following program displays the list of argument names and types for a widget.

```
1  /** argnames.c **/
2  #include <gnome.h>
3
4  void showArgs(GtkWidget *);
5
6  int main(int argc,char *argv[])
7  {
8      GtkWidget *clist;
9      GtkWidget *window;
10
11     gnome_init("argnames","1.0",argc,argv);
12     window = gtk_window_new(GTK_WINDOW_TOPLEVEL);
13
14     clist = gtk_clist_new(4);
15     showArgs(clist);
16
17     exit(0);
18 }
19 void showArgs(GtkWidget *widget)
20 {
21     GtkType objectType;
22     GtkArg *arg;
23     gint argCount;
24     guint32 *argFlags;
25     GtkArgInfo *argInfo;
26     gint i;
27
28     objectType = GTK_OBJECT_TYPE(widget);
29
30     while(objectType != GTK_TYPE_INVALID) {
31         arg = gtk_object_query_args(objectType,
32                 &argFlags,&argCount);
33         g_print("%s::\n",gtk_type_name(objectType));
34         for(i=0; i<argCount; i++) {
35             gtk_object_arg_get_info(objectType,
36                     arg[i].name,&argInfo);
37             g_print("    \"%s\" %s",
38                     argInfo->name,
39                     gtk_type_name(argInfo->type));
40             if((argInfo->arg_flags & GTK_ARG_READWRITE)
41                     == GTK_ARG_READWRITE)
42                 g_print(" Read/Write");
43             else if(argInfo->arg_flags & GTK_ARG_READABLE)
44                 g_print(" Readonly");
45             else if(argInfo->arg_flags & GTK_ARG_WRITABLE)
46                 g_print(" Writeonly");
```

```
47                        if(argInfo->arg_flags & GTK_ARG_CONSTRUCT_ONLY)
48                            g_print(" (Not writable after realized)");
49                        g_print("\n");
50                    }
51                g_free(arg);
52                g_free(argFlags);
53                objectType = gtk_type_parent(objectType);
54            }
55 }
```

This program has a minimal mainline — all we require is that a widget be created and passed to the showArgs() function to list the available settings. On line 11, a GtkCList widget is created; on line 12, it is used in the call to showArgs(). The showArgs() function, beginning on line 19, contains a nested loop. The outer loop executes once for each widget in the inheritance. The inner loop executes once for each argument found in that widget.

To start things off, you need to get the object type. You do this with the macro GTK_OBJECT_TYPE() on line 28. At the top of the widget loop, on line 31, a call is made to gtk_object_query_args() — using the object type — to retrieve an array of GtkArg structs, a count of the number of members in the array, and a set of flags. The g_print() function call on line 33 calls gtk_type_name() to extract the type name from the object and print it. At the bottom of the outer loop, on lines 51 and 52, the GtkArg array and the flags deallocated because they were dynamically allocated.

The inner loop, beginning on line 34, executes once for each argument found in the widget. On line 35, a call is made to gtk_object_arg_get_info() using the type of the object and the name of the argument. As a return value, the function stores an address in the GtkArgInfo struct pointer defined on line 25. This structure contains all we need to know about the argument.

The test on line 40 determines whether both the GTK_ARG_READABLE and GTK_ARG_WRITABLE flags are set. If both are not set, the code checks to see which one is set. The test on line 47 catches the condition of an argument being writable, but only before a widget has been realized. The output from this program looks like this:

```
GtkCList::
    "n_columns" guint Read/Write (Not writable after realized)
    "shadow_type" GtkShadowType Read/Write
    "selection_mode" GtkSelectionMode Read/Write
    "row_height" guint Read/Write
    "reorderable" gboolean Read/Write
    "titles_active" gboolean Read/Write
    "use_drag_icons" gboolean Read/Write
GtkContainer::
    "border_width" gulong Read/Write
    "resize_mode" GtkResizeMode Read/Write
    "child" GtkWidget Writeonly
GtkWidget::
    "name" GtkString Read/Write
```

```
    "parent" GtkContainer Read/Write
    "x" gint Read/Write
    "y" gint Read/Write
    "width" gint Read/Write
    "height" gint Read/Write
    "visible" gboolean Read/Write
    "sensitive" gboolean Read/Write
    "app_paintable" gboolean Read/Write
    "can_focus" gboolean Read/Write
    "has_focus" gboolean Read/Write
    "can_default" gboolean Read/Write
    "has_default" gboolean Read/Write
    "receives_default" gboolean Read/Write
    "composite_child" gboolean Read/Write
    "style" GtkStyle Read/Write
    "events" GdkEventMask Read/Write
    "extension_events" GdkEventMask Read/Write
GtkObject::
    "user_data" gpointer Read/Write
    "signal" GtkSignal Writeonly
    "signal_after" GtkSignal Writeonly
    "object_signal" GtkSignal Writeonly
    "object_signal_after" GtkSignal Writeonly
```

There are four parts to this widget, as you can see from the output. At the lowest level is GtkObject, which is common to all widgets; it takes on the chore of signaling and passing user data to the callback functions. Extending the GtkObject is GtkWidget. It takes on the responsibility of size, shape, decorations, and other information fundamental to the operation of any widget. The next widget is the GtkContainer widget, which can be used to contain other widgets. The topmost widget—the one that was created in the program—is a GtkCList object. It has settings for information on rows and columns, selection mode, and title display. As a result, all of the arguments in the listing are available if your program has a GtkCList object.

Note Every GNOME and GTK+ widget is based on GtkWidget, which, in turn, is based on GtkObject. This common base gives every widget a common interface, a standard look, and smooth interoperability. For example, you can issue a command to any widget to change its x and y positions because GtkWidget controls those settings.

Each argument has a data type and read/write permissions associated with it. Most arguments are read/write. However, there are some write-only arguments defined in GtkObject, and you also can find this in other widgets. The GtkContainer also has a write-only argument. There are no examples of read-only for this widget, but some widgets do have them. The first argument listed is a special case because it is a read/write argument, but it cannot be written once the widget is realized. That is, once you create and realize the GtkCList object, you can't change the number of columns it contains.

Talking to a Widget

There are two ways to set an argument value inside a widget. You can use a
function dedicated to one or two specific arguments, or you can pass an array of
GtkArg objects. Which one you use depends on your personal preference as well
as which functions are available. (Functions are available for the most commonly
used settings, but not for all of them.)

Many of the widgets have dedicated functions that you can use to set argument
values. For example, the GtkWidget object has an argument called "name" that
can be set by calling the function gtk_widget_set_name(), and retrieved by
calling gtk_widget_get_name().

The following program shows how a function call can be made to set the size
and position of a button. This program creates a GnomeCanvas and places a
GtkButton on it. As discussed in Chapter 9, a canvas has the ability to position
widgets according to a pair of x and y coordinate values. It turns out that the
values of the x and y coordinates are stored in the widget, not in the canvas. The
same is true of height and width, so if you change one of these values, the widget
resizes itself and moves to a new location.

```
 1 /** set1.c **/
 2 #include <gnome.h>
 3
 4 gint eventDelete(GtkWidget *widget,
 5         GdkEvent *event,gpointer data);
 6 gint eventDestroy(GtkWidget *widget,
 7         GdkEvent *event,gpointer data);
 8 void eventChange(GtkWidget *widget,GtkWidget *button);
 9
10 #define WIDTH 300
11 #define HEIGHT 200
12
13 int main(int argc,char *argv[])
14 {
15     GtkWidget *app;
16     GtkWidget *canvas;
17     GtkWidget *button;
18     GnomeCanvasGroup *rootGroup;
19     GnomeCanvasItem *item;
20
21     gnome_init("set1","1.0",argc,argv);
22     app = gnome_app_new("Set 1",
23             "Gnome Canvas Widget");
24     gtk_signal_connect(GTK_OBJECT(app),"delete_event",
25             GTK_SIGNAL_FUNC(eventDelete),NULL);
26     gtk_signal_connect(GTK_OBJECT(app),"destroy",
27             GTK_SIGNAL_FUNC(eventDestroy),NULL);
28
```

```
29        canvas = gnome_canvas_new();
30        gtk_widget_set_usize(canvas,WIDTH,HEIGHT);
31        gnome_canvas_set_scroll_region(GNOME_CANVAS(canvas),
32              0.0,0.0,WIDTH,HEIGHT);
33        rootGroup = gnome_canvas_root(GNOME_CANVAS(canvas));
34        gnome_app_set_contents(GNOME_APP(app),canvas);
35
36        button = gtk_button_new_with_label("Change");
37        gtk_signal_connect(GTK_OBJECT(button),"clicked",
38              GTK_SIGNAL_FUNC(eventChange),button);
39        item = gnome_canvas_item_new(rootGroup,
40                    gnome_canvas_widget_get_type(),
41                    "widget",button,
42                    "x",(double)(5),
43                    "y",(double)(5),
44                    "anchor",GTK_ANCHOR_NW,
45                    NULL);
46
47        gtk_widget_show_all(app);
48        gtk_main();
49        exit(0);
50 }
51 void eventChange(GtkWidget *widget,GtkWidget *button)
52 {
53        gint w;
54        gint h;
55        gint x;
56        gint y;
57
58        w = (gint)((random() % (WIDTH/2))+10);
59        h = (gint)((random() % (HEIGHT/2))+10);
60        gtk_widget_set_usize(GTK_WIDGET(button),w,h);
61
62        x = (gint)((random() % (WIDTH/2))+25);
63        y = (gint)((random() % (HEIGHT/2)))+25;
64        gtk_widget_set_uposition(GTK_WIDGET(button),x,y);
65 }
66 gint eventDelete(GtkWidget *widget,
67        GdkEvent *event,gpointer data) {
68        return(FALSE);
69 }
70 gint eventDestroy(GtkWidget *widget,
71        GdkEvent *event,gpointer data) {
72        gtk_main_quit();
73        return(0);
74 }
```

Lines 29 through 34 create the canvas and assign it as the widget to be displayed by
the main application window. The button is created on line 36, and it is connected
to a callback on line 37. Then the button is attached as a new canvas item with
the call to gnome_canvas_item_new() on line 39. There are four argument values
included with the attachment. The "widget" argument tells the canvas that a widget

is being submitted, and its value is the widget itself. The "anchor" argument tells the canvas what part of the button should be connected to the coordinate locations — I discuss this in more detail in Chapter 9. The x and y argument values are passed on to the button, because it is the button that keeps track of its position on the face of the canvas.

The callback function eventChange() on line 51 is called whenever the button is clicked. The size of the button is adjusted on lines 58 through 60 by creating a couple of random numbers and calling the function gtk_widget_set_usize(). By also using random numbers, the location of the button is changed on lines 62 through 64 with a call to gtk_widget_set_uposition().

Note Automatic updating is one of the nice things about widgets. Whenever you set one of the argument values, the widget immediately changes its characteristics, and redraws the image on the screen if necessary. Your program doesn't have to do anything else once the value is set.

The following function is an alternative way to write the eventChange() function. It does the same thing as the one above, except it calculates all the values first and then calls gtk_object_set() to set them all at once.

```
void eventChange(GtkWidget *widget,GtkWidget *button)
{
    gint w;
    gint h;
    gint x;
    gint y;

    w = (gint)((random() % (WIDTH/2))+10);
    h = (gint)((random() % (HEIGHT/2))+10);
    x = (gint)((random() % (WIDTH/2))+25);
    y = (gint)((random() % (HEIGHT/2)))+25;

    gtk_object_set(GTK_OBJECT(button),
        "x",x,
        "y",y,
        "width",w,
        "height",h,
        NULL);
}
```

The function gtk_object_set() accepts a variable length argument list. Each argument is a pair — the name of the argument and its value. A NULL pointer at the end terminates the list. Because it is a variable length argument list, the NULL is required to determine the last argument in the array.

Note When calling gtk_object_set(), make sure you pass the correct data type for each argument value. Different data types have different amounts of memory on the stack, and a mismatch between what you send and what is expected can cause the stack to get fouled up and crash your program ... mysteriously.

In the above example, the call to `gtk_object_set()` uses the simple name to identify the arguments. The argument name is located by walking up through the widget inheritance until a match is found. For example, in a `GtkCList` object described earlier in this chapter, the search starts in `GtkObject` and, if the argument is not found, the search moves to `GtkWidget`, then to `GtkContainer`, and finally to `GtkCList`. However, there is nothing to prevent two widgets from having the same name for an argument, so it probably is a good idea to specify both the widget and the value. This causes each search to skip all widgets except the one that is named:

```
gtk_object_set(GTK_OBJECT(button),
        "GtkWidget::x",x,
        "GtkWidget::y",y,
        "GtkWidget::width",w,
        "GtkWidget::height",h,
        NULL);
```

Listening to a Widget

Because there are a lot of data types, it is more difficult to retrieve an argument value from a widget than it is to set one. To retrieve a value, you pass in the name of the argument value and a `GtkArg` struct. If the name you pass it is found, and its value is readable, the value is stored in the `GtkArg` struct. To make this work, the `GtkArg` struct must be designed to accept all of the possible data types. There are only three things in the struct. There is a `GtkType` field that specifies the data type, a pointer to a string specifying the argument name, and union containing the various data types:

```
typedef struct _GtkArg GtkArg;

struct _GtkArg {
  GtkType type;
  gchar *name;
  union {
    gchar char_data;
    guchar uchar_data;
    gboolean bool_data;
    gint int_data;
    guint uint_data;
    glong long_data;
    gulong ulong_data;
    gfloat float_data;
    gdouble double_data;
    gchar *string_data;
    gpointer pointer_data;
    GtkObject *object_data;
    struct {
      GtkSignalFunc f;
      gpointer d;
    } signal_data;
```

```
    struct {
      gint n_args;
      GtkArg *args;
    } args_data;
    struct {
      GtkCallbackMarshal marshal;
      gpointer data;
      GtkDestroyNotify notify;
    } callback_data;
    struct {
      GtkFunction func;
      gpointer func_data;
    } c_callback_data;
    struct {
      gpointer data;
      GtkDestroyNotify notify;
    } foreign_data;
  } d;
};
```

The following program creates a GtkCList object, sets some argument values, and — when the widget is displayed — reads back some of the values and displays them.

```
 1 /** get.c **/
 2 #include <gnome.h>
 3
 4 gint eventDelete(GtkWidget *widget,
 5         GdkEvent *event,gpointer data);
 6 gint eventDestroy(GtkWidget *widget,
 7         GdkEvent *event,gpointer data);
 8 void eventShow(GtkWidget *widget,gpointer data);
 9
10 #define WIDTH 300
11 #define HEIGHT 200
12
13 int main(int argc,char *argv[])
14 {
15     GtkWidget *app;
16     GtkWidget *clist;
17     static char *titles[] = {
18         "First",
19         "Second",
20         "Third",
21         "Fourth"
22     };
23
24     gnome_init("get","1.0",argc,argv);
25     app = gnome_app_new("Get","Get Arguments");
26     gtk_signal_connect(GTK_OBJECT(app),"delete_event",
27             GTK_SIGNAL_FUNC(eventDelete),NULL);
28     gtk_signal_connect(GTK_OBJECT(app),"destroy",
29             GTK_SIGNAL_FUNC(eventDestroy),NULL);
30
31     clist = gtk_clist_new_with_titles(4,titles);
```

```
32      gtk_object_set(GTK_OBJECT(clist),
33          "GtkContainer::border_width",(gulong)12,
34          "GtkCList::reorderable",(gboolean)TRUE,
35          "GtkWidget::name","fred",
36          NULL);
37      gtk_signal_connect(GTK_OBJECT(clist),"show",
38          GTK_SIGNAL_FUNC(eventShow),NULL);
39      gnome_app_set_contents(GNOME_APP(app),clist);
40
41      gtk_widget_show_all(app);
42      gtk_main();
43      exit(0);
44  }
45  void eventShow(GtkWidget *widget,gpointer data)
46  {
47      int i;
48      GtkArg arg[5];
49
50      arg[0].name = "GtkCList::reorderable";
51      arg[1].name = "border_width";
52      arg[2].name = "GtkWidget::name";
53      arg[3].name = "GtkCList::n_columns";
54      arg[4].name = "row_height";
55      gtk_object_getv(GTK_OBJECT(widget),5,arg);
56
57      for(i=0; i<5; i++) {
58          switch(arg[i].type) {
59          case GTK_TYPE_UINT:
60              g_print("%s=%u\n",arg[i].name,
61                  GTK_VALUE_UINT(arg[i]));
62              break;
63          case GTK_TYPE_ULONG:
64              g_print("%s=%lu\n",arg[i].name,
65                  GTK_VALUE_ULONG(arg[i]));
66              break;
67          case GTK_TYPE_FLOAT:
68              g_print("%s=%g\n",arg[i].name,
69                  GTK_VALUE_FLOAT(arg[i]));
70              break;
71          case GTK_TYPE_STRING:
72              g_print("%s=\"%s\"\n",arg[i].name,
73                  GTK_VALUE_STRING(arg[i]));
74              break;
75          case GTK_TYPE_BOOL:
76              g_print("%s=%s\n",arg[i].name,
77                  GTK_VALUE_UINT(arg[i]) ? "TRUE" : "FALSE");
78              break;
79          default:
80              g_print("%s is type %d\n",
81                  arg[i].name,arg[i].type);
82              break;
83          }
84      }
85  }
```

```
86 gint eventDelete(GtkWidget *widget,
87       GdkEvent *event,gpointer data) {
88     return(FALSE);
89 }
90 gint eventDestroy(GtkWidget *widget,
91       GdkEvent *event,gpointer data) {
92     gtk_main_quit();
93     return(0);
94 }
```

The `GtkCList` object is created on line 11 with a call to
`gtk_clist_new_with_titles()`. The first argument specifies the number of
columns, and the second specifies the text of the column headings. The call to
`gtk_object_set()` on line 32 sets some of the argument values. The call to
`gtk_signal_connect()` on line 37 causes the callback function `eventShow()` to
be executed whenever the widget is complete and appears on the screen.

The callback function `eventShow()` on line 45 retrieves and displays values from
the widget. A `GtkArg` array is declared, and filled with the names of the desired
arguments, on lines 48 through 54. Notice that some of the name strings specify the
widget and some don't — this doesn't matter unless there is a name conflict
between two widgets in the inheritance. Using this array, and the `GtkCList` cast to
a `GtkObect`, the array is filled with data from the widget. For this call — instead of
being terminated by a `NULL` as in the "set" function on line 36 — the number of
members in the array is passed as the second argument.

The loop beginning on line 57 is executed once for each member of the array. The
switch statement on line 58 is used to separate each argument value by its data type,
and to display the name and the value. The output from this program looks like this:

```
GtkCList::reorderable=TRUE
border_width=12
GtkWidget::name="fred"
GtkCList::n_columns=4
row_height=0
```

There is a set of convenience macros — like the `GTK_VALUE_UINT()` used on line
61 — that you can use to extract the values from the union in `GtkArg`. The macros
are quite simple, but you don't need to deal with the internal structure and they do
return data of the correct type. This is a list of all the macros:

```
GTK_VALUE_ARGS(arg)          GTK_VALUE_FOREIGN(arg)
GTK_VALUE_BOOL(arg)          GTK_VALUE_INT(arg)
GTK_VALUE_BOXED(arg)         GTK_VALUE_LONG(arg)
GTK_VALUE_CALLBACK(arg)      GTK_VALUE_OBJECT(arg)
GTK_VALUE_CHAR(arg)          GTK_VALUE_POINTER(arg)
GTK_VALUE_C_CALLBACK(arg)    GTK_VALUE_SIGNAL(arg)
GTK_VALUE_DOUBLE(arg)        GTK_VALUE_STRING(arg)
GTK_VALUE_ENUM(arg)          GTK_VALUE_UCHAR(arg)
GTK_VALUE_FLAGS(arg)         GTK_VALUE_UINT(arg)
GTK_VALUE_FLOAT(arg)         GTK_VALUE_ULONG(arg)
```

Create, Realize, Map, and Show

The following description is intended to be a conceptual overview of the birth, life, and death of widgets. Widgets can get a bit complicated, and there is a lot going on behind the curtain, so the exact process varies from one widget to another. There is more information on this in Chapter 18.

When a widget is born and works its way up from a pattern of bits in memory to a graphic object appearing on the display, it goes through the process of being created, realized, mapped, and shown. Then, at the end of the widget's life, it is hidden, unmapped, unrealized, and destroyed. But this is not a linear sequence. During the life of a widget, your application can move the widget back and forth between show and hide—causing it to appear and disappear. Also, to move a widget from one parent window to another, it can be unrealized and then realized again.

Create and Destroy

Each widget has at least one _new function that you can use to create new instances of it. For example, `gtk_label_new()` can be used to create `GtkLabel` widgets and `gnome_about_new()` can be used to create new `GnomeAbout` widgets. When a widget is first created, it is an empty shell—its window hasn't been created and it has no parent. Some other things must happen before it can be used.

When a widget is destroyed, all of its allocated memory is returned to the system—it cannot be used again. You can destroy a widget by calling `gtk_widget_destroy()`. If the widget is a type that possibly can have more than one reference, it also can be destroyed by a call to `gtk_widget_unref()`, which reduces a reference counter by one and, if the count reaches zero, destroys the widget. This function makes sure that a window is hidden, unmapped, and unrealized before it is destroyed. Destroying a widget returns all of the allocated memory back to the system.

Show and Hide

When a widget is shown, the window (or windows) of the widget appears on the display. In this state, the window is active and available for mouse and keyboard activity. The window first appears in the area mapped for it by the window manager. A window is shown with a call to `gtk_widget_show()`, which calls `gtk_widget_map()` and `gtk_widget_realize()` if necessary.

When a widget is hidden, its window is no longer visible on the display. A hidden window also is unmapped, allowing the container widget to remap its other child members automatically to update the display. For example, if you hide a button on a menu, the remaining buttons move up so there is no gap left. To hide a window, call `gtk_widget_hide()`, which automatically calls `gtk_widget_unmap()`.

Map and Unmap

You can call the functions `gtk_widget_map()` and `gtk_widget_unmap()` from your application, but it is rarely necessary. The show and hide functions take care of it for you.

A widget window is mapped when the window manager selects a place and size for it on the display. Mapping doesn't apply to widgets that you store in containers, or otherwise include within one of your existing windows, but does apply to every top-level window, popup dialog boxes, and menus. A menu has to be mapped because it is free to extend beyond the edges of its parent window. You can map a window with a call to `gtk_widget_map()`, which calls `gtk_widget_realize()` if necessary.

A widget is unmapped when the window manager is instructed to drop all of the information it is holding about the size and position of its window. A window can be unmapped with a call to `gtk_widget_unmap()`.

Realize and Unrealize

You can call the functions `gtk_widget_realize()` and `gtk_widget_unrealize()` from your application, but it is rarely necessary. The show and hide functions take care of it for you.

A widget is realized if its window, and other internal resources, are allocated. When the window of a widget is realized, it must have been assigned a parent window already, and that parent also must be realized. A widget is realized by calling `gtk_widget_realize()`.

An unrealized widget returns to the form that it took when it was created originally. Its window is deallocated and any events destined for it are removed from the event queue. If necessary, the window is hidden and unmapped before it is unrealized. A widget can be unrealized with a call to `gtk_widget_unrealize()`.

Showing and Hiding a Button

As an applications programmer, you almost certainly will never need to worry about realizing, unrealizing, mapping, or unmapping a widget. You will need to create new widgets and, when you are through with them, you will need to destroy them. Actually, you only need to bother destroying them if your program is going to continue to execute after you are finished with the widgets—when your program stops running, all the memory allocated for widgets is returned to the system.

Hiding and showing isn't needed very often, but there are times when it can be quite useful. The following example shows how to make a button appear and disappear.

```
1 /** hideshow.c **/
2 #include <gnome.h>
3
```

```
 4 gint eventDelete(GtkWidget *widget,
 5        GdkEvent *event,gpointer data);
 6 gint eventDestroy(GtkWidget *widget,
 7        GdkEvent *event,gpointer data);
 8 void eventHideShow(GtkWidget *widget,GtkWidget *button);
 9 GtkWidget *createLayout();
10
11 int main(int argc,char *argv[])
12 {
13     GtkWidget *app;
14     GtkWidget *hideshow;
15     GtkWidget *button;
16     GtkWidget *box;
17
18     gnome_init("hideshow","1.0",argc,argv);
19     app = gnome_app_new("hideshow","Widget Hiding");
20     gtk_container_set_border_width(GTK_CONTAINER(app),30);
21     gtk_signal_connect(GTK_OBJECT(app),"delete_event",
22            GTK_SIGNAL_FUNC(eventDelete),NULL);
23     gtk_signal_connect(GTK_OBJECT(app),"destroy",
24            GTK_SIGNAL_FUNC(eventDestroy),NULL);
25
26
27     box = gtk_hbox_new(FALSE,0);
28     hideshow = gtk_button_new_with_label("Hide/Show");
29     gtk_box_pack_start(GTK_BOX(box),hideshow,
30            FALSE,TRUE,0);
31     button = gtk_button_new_with_label("Button");
32     gtk_signal_connect(GTK_OBJECT(hideshow),"clicked",
33            GTK_SIGNAL_FUNC(eventHideShow),button);
34     gtk_box_pack_start(GTK_BOX(box),button,
35            FALSE,TRUE,0);
36     gnome_app_set_contents(GNOME_APP(app),box);
37     gtk_widget_show_all(app);
38
39     gtk_main();
40     exit(0);
41 }
42 void eventHideShow(GtkWidget *widget,GtkWidget *button) {
43     if(GTK_WIDGET_VISIBLE(button))
44         gtk_widget_hide(button);
45     else
46         gtk_widget_show(button);
47 }
48 gint eventDelete(GtkWidget *widget,
49        GdkEvent *event,gpointer data) {
50     return(FALSE);
51 }
52 gint eventDestroy(GtkWidget *widget,
53        GdkEvent *event,gpointer data) {
54     gtk_main_quit();
55     return(0);
56 }
```

A horizontal box is created on line 27. Lines 28 through 37 create two buttons, attach a callback function to one of them, pack them into the horizontal box, and set the box as the widget to be displayed in the application window. The resulting display looks like that shown in Figure 14-1. Selecting the button on the left executes the callback function eventHideShow() on line 42. The macro GTK_WIDGET_VISIBLE() on line 43 determines whether or not the widget is being shown. If it currently is not visible, it is shown by the call to gtk_widget_show(). If it is being shown, it is hidden by the call to gtk_widget_hide(), and looks like Figure 14-2.

Figure 14-1: Two buttons showing

Figure 14-2: One button showing and one button hidden

While this example uses a simple button to demonstrate showing and hiding, you can use the same technique to show and hide a composite widget. For example, if you have a container filled with other widgets (buttons, labels, and so on), all you have to do is show and hide the container because no widget can be visible unless its parent is visible.

Note   You may find a problem with some containers. Certain containers in certain configurations are not able to handle a widget being hidden and made visible again. If, when the widget is hidden, the container elects to close up the other widgets to fill the space left by the hidden one, it may not be able to open up space for the hidden widget when it reappears. Go ahead and test it to see if it works, but keep an alternate plan in mind.

The Styles of a Widget

The *styles* of a widget are the settings used to specify the way the widget is to display itself. You can set the fonts for widgets that display text. You also can set the widget colors, or use a background pixmap instead of a background color.

There are different settings for each of the five possible display states of a widget. The five states are listed in Table 14-1. Not all widgets have the ability to move into all states (for example, there is no such thing as an active label), but a button widget is a perfect example of a widget that can be in any one of the five states.

Table 14-1
The Five States of a Widget

State Name	Description
GTK_STATE_NORMAL	This is the default state. All widgets first appear in this state, and return to it whenever none of the other states apply.
GTK_STATE_ACTIVE	The widget indicates activity. For example, while a button is pressed it is active. You can set a widget to change its appearance as an indication of a background process becoming active or a file being opened.
GTK_STATE_PRELIGHT	The mouse pointer is inside the widget. Buttons, for example, default to turning a lighter color as the mouse passes over them.
GTK_STATE_SELECTED	The widget is a list (or some other container that allows items to be selected) and currently is selected.
GTK_STATE_INSENSITIVE	The appearance of the widget when it is disabled and does not respond to the mouse. Usually, the text or graphics of the widget is shown in gray or outline form.

All of these settings are stored in a single struct. Each widget contains a pointer to one of these structs. The publicly available part of the struct looks like this:

```
struct _GtkStyle {
    GtkStyleClass *klass;

    GdkColor fg[5];
    GdkColor bg[5];
    GdkColor light[5];
    GdkColor dark[5];
    GdkColor mid[5];
    GdkColor text[5];
    GdkColor base[5];

    GdkColor black;
    GdkColor white;
    GdkFont *font;

    GdkGC *fg_gc[5];
    GdkGC *bg_gc[5];
    GdkGC *light_gc[5];
    GdkGC *dark_gc[5];
    GdkGC *mid_gc[5];
    GdkGC *text_gc[5];
    GdkGC *base_gc[5];
    GdkGC *black_gc;
    GdkGC *white_gc;
```

```
        GdkPixmap *bg_pixmap[5];
            . . .
};
```

There are a few other fields at the bottom of the struct, but they are for internal use only. The following program initializes GNOME and displays the contents of the GtkStyle struct. In an application, each new widget is assigned this same style struct, causing all the widgets in the application to be unified by looking and acting alike.

```
 1  /** examine.c **/
 2  #include <gnome.h>
 3
 4  void showit();
 5
 6  int main(int argc,char *argv[])
 7  {
 8      int i;
 9      GtkStyle *style;
10      GtkWidget *app;
11
12      gnome_init("examine","1.0",argc,argv);
13      app = gnome_app_new("examine","Examine");
14
15      gtk_widget_show(app);
16      style = app->style;
17
18      printf("              Normal     Active      Prelight"
19             "    Selected    Insensitive\n");
20      printf("      fg:");
21      for(i=0; i<5; i++)
22          printf(" 0x%08lX",style->fg[i].pixel);
23      printf("\n      bg:");
24      for(i=0; i<5; i++)
25          printf(" 0x%08lX",style->bg[i].pixel);
26      printf("\n   light:");
27      for(i=0; i<5; i++)
28          printf(" 0x%08lX",style->light[i].pixel);
29      printf("\n    dark:");
30      for(i=0; i<5; i++)
31          printf(" 0x%08lX",style->dark[i].pixel);
32      printf("\n     mid:");
33      for(i=0; i<5; i++)
34          printf(" 0x%08lX",style->mid[i].pixel);
35      printf("\n    text:");
36      for(i=0; i<5; i++)
37          printf(" 0x%08lX",style->text[i].pixel);
38      printf("\n    base:");
39      for(i=0; i<5; i++)
40          printf(" 0x%08lX",style->base[i].pixel);
41      printf("\n\n              black: 0x%08lX\n",
42             style->black.pixel);
43      printf("              white: 0x%08lX\n",
```

```
44                style->white.pixel);
45      printf("\n   fg_gc:");
46      for(i=0; i<5; i++)
47          printf("  %p",style->fg_gc[i]);
48      printf("\n   bg_gc:");
49      for(i=0; i<5; i++)
50          printf("  %p",style->bg_gc[i]);
51      printf("\nlight_gc:");
52      for(i=0; i<5; i++)
53          printf("  %p",style->light_gc[i]);
54      printf("\n dark_gc:");
55      for(i=0; i<5; i++)
56          printf("  %p",style->dark_gc[i]);
57      printf("\n  mid_gc:");
58      for(i=0; i<5; i++)
59          printf("  %p",style->mid_gc[i]);
60      printf("\n text_gc:");
61      for(i=0; i<5; i++)
62          printf("  %p",style->text_gc[i]);
63      printf("\n base_gc:");
64      for(i=0; i<5; i++)
65          printf("  %p",style->base_gc[i]);
66      printf("\n\nbgpixmap:");
67      for(i=0; i<5; i++) {
68          if(style->bg_pixmap[i] == NULL)
69              printf("  0x0000000");
70          else
71              printf("  %p",style->bg_pixmap[i]);
72      }
73      printf("\n");
74
75      exit(0);
76 }
```

Lines 12 and 13 initialize the GNOME environment and create an applications window. The call to gtk_widget_show() on line 15 realizes the window and configures it to be shown—this must be done to make the style available because a widget has to GtkStyle until it is realized. The rest of the program, lines 18 through 73, prints the values from the struct. The output looks like this:

```
        Normal      Active      Prelight    Selected    Insensitive
   fg: 0x00000000 0x00000000 0x00000000 0x00007FFF 0x000039CE
   bg: 0x00006B5A 0x00006318 0x000077BD 0x00000013 0x00006B5A
light: 0x00007FFF 0x00007FFF 0x00007FFF 0x00000019 0x00007FFF
 dark: 0x00004A52 0x00004631 0x00005294 0x0000084B 0x00004A52
  mid: 0x00006739 0x00006318 0x00006B5A 0x00000432 0x00006739
 text: 0x00000000 0x00000000 0x00000000 0x00007FFF 0x00006B5A
 base: 0x00007FFF 0x00007FFF 0x00007FFF 0x00007FFF 0x00006B5A

   black: 0x00000000
   white: 0x00007FFF
```

```
     fg_gc:   0x8075fb0   0x8075fb0   0x8075fb0   0x8076490   0x8076f58
     bg_gc:   0x8076520   0x80766d0   0x80767f0   0x8076910   0x8076520
  light_gc:   0x8076490   0x8076490   0x8076490   0x8076da8   0x8076490
   dark_gc:   0x80765b0   0x8076760   0x8076880   0x8076e38   0x80765b0
    mid_gc:   0x8076640   0x80766d0   0x8076520   0x8076ec8   0x8076640
   text_gc:   0x8075fb0   0x8075fb0   0x8075fb0   0x8076490   0x8076520
   base_gc:   0x8076490   0x8076490   0x8076490   0x8076490   0x8076520

  bgpixmap:   0x0000000   0x0000000   0x0000000   0x0000000   0x0000000
```

There are seven arrays of color settings. The actual pixel values vary from one system to the next. The ones shown here were created on a system using 15 bits for each of the primary colors, so white is 7FFF and black is 0000. You can see how the colors change from one state to another. For example, the normal background (bg) is the gray color 65BA, but becomes the slightly brighter 6318 when it is activated. If the widget responds to the presence of the mouse pointer, as does a button widget, the color changes to the almost white (77BD). When a widget is selected in a list, it changes its foreground color to white (7FFF) and its background color to almost black (0013). The text also reverses color from black to white. The values for light and dark are the ones used to color the frames around the widget window — which edges are painted light and which are painted dark depends on whether the widget's shadows should show up as beveled in or beveled out.

Setting Widget Styles

With all the color and font information held in one place, it is fairly straightforward to customize a widget. The following program sets the appearance of a button by setting the values in its GtkStyle struct.

```
 1 /** stylemod.c **/
 2 #include <gnome.h>
 3
 4 #include "modulate.xpm"
 5
 6 gint eventDelete(GtkWidget *widget,
 7         GdkEvent *event,gpointer data);
 8 gint eventDestroy(GtkWidget *widget,
 9         GdkEvent *event,gpointer data);
10 void eventVisibility(GtkWidget *widget,gpointer data);
11
12 GdkColor red = {0, 0xFFFF, 0x0000, 0x0000 };
13 GdkColor green = {0, 0x0000, 0xFFFF, 0x0000 };
14 GdkColor cyan = {0, 0x0000, 0xFFFF, 0xFFFF };
15
16 int main(int argc,char *argv[])
17 {
18     GtkWidget *app;
19     GtkWidget *button;
```

```
20        GtkStyle *current;
21        GtkStyle *new;
22        GdkBitmap *mask;
23
24        gnome_init("stylemod","1.0",argc,argv);
25        app = gnome_app_new("stylemod","GtkStyle");
26        gtk_container_set_border_width(GTK_CONTAINER(app),40);
27        gtk_signal_connect(GTK_OBJECT(app),"delete_event",
28              GTK_SIGNAL_FUNC(eventDelete),NULL);
29        gtk_signal_connect(GTK_OBJECT(app),"destroy",
30              GTK_SIGNAL_FUNC(eventDestroy),NULL);
31
32        gtk_widget_show(app);
33
34        button = gtk_button_new_with_label("Button");
35        gtk_widget_set_usize(button,100,100);
36
37        current = gtk_widget_get_default_style();
38        new - gtk_style_copy(current);
39
40        new->bg[GTK_STATE_ACTIVE] = green;
41        new->bg[GTK_STATE_PRELIGHT] = red;
42        new->bg[GTK_STATE_NORMAL] = cyan;
43        new->bg_pixmap[GTK_STATE_NORMAL] =
44            gdk_pixmap_create_from_xpm_d(app->window,
45                &mask,&new->bg[GTK_STATE_NORMAL],
46                (gchar **)modulate);
47        gtk_widget_set_style(button,new);
48
49        gnome_app_set_contents(GNOME_APP(app),button);
50        gtk_widget_show_all(app);
51
52        gtk_main();
53        exit(0);
54 }
55 gint eventDelete(GtkWidget *widget,
56        GdkEvent *event,gpointer data) {
57      return(FALSE);
58 }
59 gint eventDestroy(GtkWidget *widget,
60        GdkEvent *event,gpointer data) {
61      gtk_main_quit();
62      return(0);
63 }
```

Immediately after the GNOME environment is initialized on lines 24 through 30, the top-level application window is used in a call to gtk_widget_show() on line 32. This initialization is necessary because it creates a color map and makes information available that is necessary for setting widget styles. The styles can be set later—after the widgets are all displayed—but the initialization enables us to configure the widgets before they are displayed.

Lines 34 and 35 call `gtk_button_new_with_label()` and `gtk_widget_set_usize()` to create a large button.

Line 37 retrieves the current default `GtkStyle`. This is the style that is applied to every widget that does not have a style of its own. It is possible to create a completely new style, but that would mean populating every member of the `GtkStyle` struct — it is more normal to start with the default style and simply make changes. Now, because a pointer is returned from `gtk_widget_get_default_style()`, and the same pointer is used by all of the widgets in the program, making changes directly into the default style changes all of the application's widgets. We need to modify a copy of it, so a call is made to `gtk_style_copy()` on line 38 to create an exact duplicate of the default `GtkStyle`.

In the newly copied `GtkStyle` struct, lines 40 through 42 assign the colors that are to be used to indicate the active, prelight, and normal states. The colors are defined on lines 12 through 14, and it is not necessary to allocate these colors — they are allocated whenever the `GtkStyle` is added to a widget.

Line 43 creates a pixmap and installs it to be used for the button while it is in its normal state. The call to `gdk_pixmap_create_from_xpm_d()` uses the window and color map information from the main application widget, along with the pixmap definition included on line 4. The pixmap is set for the active state, so the background color for that state is supplied to the pixmap creation function on line 45. The resulting button is shown in Figure 14-3. The pixmap is much smaller than the button, but it is tiled repeatedly and fills the entire button area.

Figure 14-3: A button showing a pixmap style

The new style information is set into the widget with a call to `gtk_widget_set_style()` on line 47. Lines 49 and 50 add the button to the main window and the call to `gtk_widget_show_all()` causes the window, now containing the button, to be displayed.

The preceding example shows how to assign a style to a single widget. To apply special styles to a number of widgets, you can call `gtk_widget_set_style()` for each one of them — or you can set the default temporarily. For example, the following code uses a newly created `GtkStyle` object to create more than one widget:

```
        . . .
current = gtk_widget_get_default_style();
new = gtk_style_copy(current);
        /* Make modification to new style */
gtk_widget_push_style(new);
        /* Create new widgets */
gtk_widget_pop_style();
        . . .
```

Calling gtk_widget_push_style() replaces the default style with the new one, and saves the existing one, so a call to gtk_widget_pop_style() restores it. You can use this to make special adjustments to the appearance of groups of widgets. And, because it is a push-pop situation, widgets within the adjusted group can make their own adjustments.

If you have a widget that already has its style modified, and you need to create another widget with the same modifications, do this:

```
style = gtk_widget_get_style(existingWidget);
gtk_widget_set_style(newWidget);
```

Of course, if you want to make further modifications, you need to work with a copy because any changes you make to the original also affects the existing widget.

Summary

At the lowest level, every displayable object is a GtkWidget object, and can be treated as such inside your program. A setting made at the widget level can affect the display and behavior of its descendent — the displayable object (so much so that any object with GtkWidget in its parentage is called a widget). On the subject of configuring widgets, this chapter explored:

✦ There are several states of existence for a widget, ranging from raw allocation to onscreen display. Unless you need to do something special, the movement of a widget from one state to another is completely automatic.

✦ There is information that can be retrieved so your application knows more about a widget. It is especially useful for a container widget to be familiar with the geometry of a contained widget.

✦ The style of a widget — its color patterns and fonts — can be set for any widget at any time. Also, these settings can be copied from one widget to another.

The next chapter discusses a special kind of application. It is called an *applet* and displays its main window as a button on the GNOME panel. It is normally used to start applications, but there are also special-purpose widgets. The GNOME system menu and the clock are two examples of special-purpose applets.

✦   ✦   ✦

Applets

An *applet* is a GNOME application program with one special characteristic — it displays its main window as a member of the GNOME desktop panel. The panel assumes the responsibility for positioning and displaying the window. An applet is no more difficult to write than a GNOME application. The structure is about the same — you call an initialization function, create the widgets to be displayed, and call an event-loop function. The applet widget and the panel do most of the work for you. Once your applet is running, you can do anything with it that you can do with a normal application.

A Simplified Applet

The following example demonstrates the minimum code required to get an applet to work. All this applet does is display a simple button on the panel.

```
1 /** simple_applet.c **/
2 #include <gnome.h>
3 #include <applet-widget.h>
4
5 #define APPLETNAME "simple-applet"
6 #define VERSION "1.0"
7
8 int main(int argc,char *argv[])
9 {
10     GtkWidget *applet;
11     GtkWidget *button;
12
13     applet_widget_init(APPLETNAME,VERSION,
14             argc,argv,
15             NULL,0,NULL);
16
17     applet =
applet_widget_new(APPLETNAME);
18
19     button =
gtk_button_new_with_label("Simple\nApplet");
20     gtk_widget_set_usize(button,48,48);
21
applet_widget_add(APPLET_WIDGET(applet),button
);
```

In This Chapter

Creating an applet with its window inside the panel

Using an applet to launch an application

Displaying data in the panel with an applet window

Adjusting the size and shape of an applet to allow for panel orientation

Adding options to the applet menu

```
22
23        gtk_widget_show_all(applet);
24
25        applet_widget_gtk_main();
26
27        exit(0);
28 }
```

Because the characteristics of an applet normally are not part of a GNOME or GTK+ application, the applet header file is not included by gnome.h. Line 3 includes the header file applet-widget.h, which contains the definition AppletWidget and its associated functions. The inheritance of the applet widget looks very much like the inheritance of any other displayable widget:

```
AppletWidget->GtkPlug->GtkWindow->GtkBin->GtkContainer->
         GtkWidget->GtkObject
```

The call to applet_widget_init() on line 13 initializes the session. This function does for the applet the same thing that gnome_init() does for a GNOME application. The AppletWidget itself is created on line 17 by the call to applet_widget_new(). The AppletWidget inherits from GtkContainer, so it can contain any displayable widget you want to insert into it.

Lines 19 through 22 create a button and add it to the applet widget as the item to be displayed. The button is sized 48x48 to match some of the other applets commonly included on the panel. However, the panel automatically resizes itself to accommodate the largest contained applet, so no matter what size you choose, your applet is visible.

Line 23 calls gtk_show_all() to display the applet and all of its children. Just like any other container widget, the AppletWidget shows itself and all the widgets it contains. The main loop applet_widget_gtk_main() is called on line 25. This is the applet version of gtk_main(). It does not return until the program ceases execution.

Whenever this program is run, it appears as an applet on the panel as shown in Figure 15-1. The button responds to the mouse, but because no callback activity is defined for the button, no action is taken.

Figure 15-1: A simple applet appearing on a panel

The applet modules are not a part of the standard set of GNOME and GTK+ libraries, and need to be included separately. The following is a make file that compiles and links this program.

```
CC=gcc
LDLIBS=`gnome-config --libs gnomeui` -lpanel_applet -lgnorba
CFLAGS=-Wall -g `gnome-config --cflags gnomeui`
```

```
     all: simple_applet

     simple_applet: simple_applet.o
```

The definition of CFLAGS does not change from that of an application, but the definition of LDFLAGS must include the libraries named libpanel_applet and libgnorba.

An Applet That Launches an Application

There are many things that you can do with an applet, but the most basic is to have the applet start a program running. Anything you can enter from the command line, you can enter by clicking an applet. The following program executes an FTP utility program:

```
 1 /** ftp_applet.c **/
 2 #include <gnome.h>
 3 #include <applet-widget.h>
 4
 5 #include "ftp.xpm"
 6
 7 void startCallback(GtkWidget *,gpointer data);
 8
 9 #define APPLETNAME "ftp-applet"
10 #define VERSION "1.0"
11
12 int main(int argc,char *argv[])
13 {
14     GtkWidget *applet;
15     GtkWidget *button;
16     GdkPixmap *pixmap;
17     GtkStyle *style;
18     GdkBitmap *mask;
19     GtkWidget *pixmapWidget;
20
21     applet_widget_init(APPLETNAME,VERSION,
22             argc,argv,
23             NULL,0,NULL);
24
25     applet = applet_widget_new(APPLETNAME);
26     gtk_widget_show(applet);
27
28     style = gtk_widget_get_style(applet);
29     pixmap = gdk_pixmap_create_from_xpm_d(applet->window,
30             &mask,&style->bg[GTK_STATE_NORMAL],
31             (gchar **)ftp_xpm);
32     pixmapWidget = gtk_pixmap_new(pixmap,mask);
33
34     button = gtk_button_new();
35     gtk_signal_connect(GTK_OBJECT(button),"clicked",
36             GTK_SIGNAL_FUNC(startCallback),NULL);
```

```
37       gtk_container_add(GTK_CONTAINER(button),pixmapWidget);
38
39       applet_widget_add(APPLET_WIDGET(applet),button);
40
41       gtk_widget_show_all(applet);
42
43       applet_widget_gtk_main();
44
45       exit(0);
46 }
47 void startCallback(GtkWidget *widget,gpointer data)
48 {
49       system("wxftp &");
50 }
```

Lines 21 through 25 initialize the applet and create the AppletWidget. The call to gtk_widget_show() on line 26 realizes the widget—this is necessary because the program needs the GtkStyle information to create a pixmap to decorate the button.

Lines 28 through 32 use the applet window information to create a pixmap and a pixmap widget. The pixmap is included as the file ftp.xpm on line 5. Lines 34 through 37 create a button, connect it to the callback function startCallback(), and assign the pixmap widget as its decoration.

Whenever the button is selected, the callback startCallback() on line 47 is executed. There is only one command—the system() function call with a command to start the program. This example starts the FTP program wxftp, but you can use this same technique to start any program that uses X as its user interface. Notice that there is an ampersand at the end of the command line to run the program in the background. If the ampersand is left off, the background process respawns itself every time you try to close it.

Displaying Updated Information

The following applet shows the percentage of disk usage. It displays the information from one disk drive at a time, and it constantly updates its information.

```
 1 /** status_applet.c **/
 2 #include <gnome.h>
 3 #include <applet-widget.h>
 4 #include <stdio.h>
 5
 6 gint updateCallback(GtkWidget *label);
 7 void loadStats(void);
 8
 9 static int stIndex;
10 static int stLast;
11 static char stString[40][60];
12
13 #define APPLETNAME "status-applet"
```

```
14 #define VERSION "1.0"
15
16 int main(int argc,char *argv[])
17 {
18     GtkWidget *applet;
19     GtkWidget *label;
20
21     applet_widget_init(APPLETNAME,VERSION,
22             argc,argv,
23             NULL,0,NULL);
24
25     applet = applet_widget_new(APPLETNAME);
26
27     label = gtk_label_new("*\n 0% Used");
28     gtk_widget_set_usize(label,75,47);
29     applet_widget_add(APPLET_WIDGET(applet),label);
30     gtk_widget_show(label);
31
32     loadStats();
33     updateCallback(label);
34     gtk_timeout_add(5000,(GtkFunction)updateCallback,
35             label);
36
37     gtk_widget_show_all(applet);
38     applet_widget_gtk_main();
39     exit(0);
40 }
41 gint updateCallback(GtkWidget *label)
42 {
43     if(stIndex > stLast)
44         loadStats();
45     gtk_label_set_text(GTK_LABEL(label),
46             stString[stIndex++]);
47     return(TRUE);
48 }
49 void loadStats()
50 {
51     int i;
52     FILE *df;
53     char rawInput[80];
54     char fileSystem[40];
55     char percent[40];
56
57     stIndex = 0;
58     stLast = 0;
59     strcpy(stString[0],"No\nStats");
60
61     if((df = popen("df","r")) == NULL)
62         return;
63
64     fgets(rawInput,sizeof(rawInput),df);
65     while(fgets(rawInput,sizeof(rawInput),df) != NULL) {
66         strtok(rawInput," \n");
67         for(i=1; i<4; i++)
```

```
68                strtok(NULL," \n");
69            strcpy(percent,strtok(NULL," \n"));
70            strcpy(fileSystem,strtok(NULL," \n"));
71            stLast = stIndex;
72            sprintf(stString[stIndex++],"%s\n%s Used",
73                fileSystem,percent);
74        }
75        stIndex = 0;
76        pclose(df);
77 }
```

The resulting applet looks like the one shown in Figure 15-2.

Figure 15-2: An applet that constantly updates its status

Lines 21 through 25 create and initialize the applet widget as usual. Lines 27 through 30 create a label and add it to the applet widget as the object to be displayed. Unlike many widgets, this label is not square — it is made wider to accommodate the path names of the disk drives.

The initial text of the label is created and inserted. The call to loadStats() on line 32 creates the array of text strings that display the information. The call to updateCallback() on line 33 uses one of the strings from the array as the text for the label. The call to gtk_timeout_add() starts a five-second interval timer running and assigns updateCallback() as the function to be called.

The function updateCallback() on line 41 checks whether all the strings in the array have been used and, if so, it calls loadStats() to create a new set of strings. The call to gtk_label_set_text() inserts the text. The return value is TRUE to keep the timer running. If the return is FALSE, the timer is deleted and this function is not called again. If your program wished to change the timing interval, the updateCallback() function could start a new timer and then return FALSE to kill the previous one.

The function loadStats() beginning on line 49 reads the disk information and creates an array of label text strings. The strings are stored in the array stString defined on line 11. The value of stLast is set to the last valid index in the array and the value of stIndex is set to zero so updateCallback() displays the first string. The information is gathered by executing the df utility and having the information return through a pipe. Line 64 reads and discards the first line of the df output because it is the column headers. The loop beginning on line 64 is executed once for each line of text coming from df. The values you want — the percentage of the disk in use and the name of the mount point — are the last two tokens on the line, so the program skips over the others and saves the last two in percent and filesystem. The sprintf() function on line 72 is used to format the text string that is used in the label.

The Applet Menu

Selecting an applet with the right mouse button brings up the menu shown in Figure 15-3.

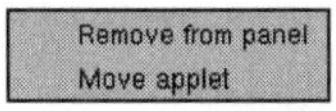

Figure 15-3: The default applet menu

The default menu has two selections — the applet can be removed from the panel or it can be moved to another location. You can add entries to the menu and assign callbacks to them. The following applet adds two entries to its menu, resulting in the menu shown in Figure 15-4.

```
1 /** menu_applet.c **/
2 #include <gnome.h>
3 #include <applet-widget.h>
4
5 #define APPLETNAME "menu-applet"
6 #define VERSION "1.0"
7
8 void changeCallback(AppletWidget *applet,GtkLabel *label);
9 void aboutCallback(AppletWidget *applet,GtkLabel *label);
10
11 int main(int argc,char *argv[])
12 {
13     GtkWidget *applet;
14     GtkWidget *label;
15
16     applet_widget_init(APPLETNAME,VERSION,
17             argc,argv,
18             NULL,0,NULL);
19
20     applet = applet_widget_new(APPLETNAME);
21
22     label = gtk_label_new("Menu\nApplet");
23     gtk_widget_set_usize(label,48,48);
24     applet_widget_add(APPLET_WIDGET(applet),label);
25
26     gtk_widget_show_all(applet);
27
28     applet_widget_register_callback(
29             APPLET_WIDGET(applet),
30             "change","Change",
31             (AppletCallbackFunc)changeCallback,label);
32     applet_widget_register_stock_callback(
33             APPLET_WIDGET(applet),
34             "about",GNOME_STOCK_MENU_ABOUT,
35             "About...",
36             (AppletCallbackFunc)aboutCallback,label);
37
```

```
38      applet_widget_gtk_main();
39
40      exit(0);
41 }
42 void changeCallback(AppletWidget *applet,GtkLabel *label)
43 {
44      int i;
45      static GtkStyle *oldStyle = NULL;
46      static GtkStyle *newStyle = NULL;
47      static int change = TRUE;
48
49      if(oldStyle == NULL) {
50          oldStyle = gtk_widget_get_style(GTK_WIDGET(label));
51          newStyle = gtk_style_copy(oldStyle);
52          for(i=0; i<5; i++) {
53              newStyle->fg[i] = oldStyle->light[i];
54              newStyle->fg_gc[i] = oldStyle->light_gc[i];
55          }
56      }
57
58      if(change)
59          gtk_widget_set_style(GTK_WIDGET(label),newStyle);
60      else
61          gtk_widget_set_style(GTK_WIDGET(label),oldStyle);
62      change = !change;
63 }
64 void aboutCallback(AppletWidget *applet,GtkLabel *label)
65 {
66      GtkWidget *aboutBox;
67
68      const gchar *writtenBy[] = {
69          "Arthur Griffith",
70          "George Spelvin",
71          NULL
72      };
73      aboutBox = gnome_about_new("Menu Applet",
74              "0.0",
75              "(C) 1999 the Free Software Foundation",
76              writtenBy,
77              "This applet demonstrates the code "
78              "necessary to add items to the menu. "
79              "The added menu items can be simple text "
80              "or it can be one of the stock items",
81              NULL);
82      gtk_widget_show(aboutBox);
83 }
```

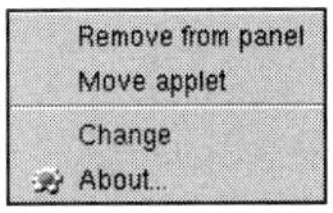

Figure 15-4: An applet menu with two custom selections added

Lines 16 through 26 perform the standard set of tasks necessary to create a widget that displays a `GtkLabel` with text.

A new menu item is added with the call to `applet_widget_register_callback()` on line 28. Of the two name strings on line 30, the first one is the internal widget name and the second is the text that appears on the menu. The last two arguments are the callback function and the data that is to be passed to it (in this case, the address of the label widget).

Another menu item is added — using one of the stock menu definitions — by the call to `applet_widget_register_stock_callback()` on line 32. The quoted string on line 34 is to be the internal name of the widget. Also on line 34 is the defined constant identifying a stock menu item. The quoted string on line 35 is the text that appears on the menu. The last two arguments, on line 36, specify the callback function and the data to be passed to it.

The callback function `changeCallback()` beginning on line 42 changes the color of the text on the applet window. It does this by keeping a copy of the abel's `GtkStyle`, and also making and keeping a copy of the `GtkStyle` with the foreground color changed. The loop starting on line 52 changes the copy of the `GtkStyle` so the foreground settings are the same as the light settings. The Boolean toggle change is tested on line 58; the result of the text determines which `GtkStyle` is used. Line 62 reverses the toggle for the next time this function is called.

The callback function `aboutCallback()` beginning on line 64 displays a standard About box for the applet.

Panel Orientation

Whenever an applet is displayed in a panel, the panel adjusts its size to make sure the entire applet window is displayed. This has the disadvantage that, for large applets, the panel can expand to take up quite a bit of real estate on the desktop. One solution to this is to reshape your applet window smaller, either in the vertical or horizontal position depending on the orientation of the panel. The following applet detects the orientation and position of the panel and adjusts itself accordingly.

```
 1 /** orient_applet.c **/
 2 #include <gnome.h>
 3 #include <applet-widget.h>
 4 #include <stdio.h>
 5
 6 #define APPLETNAME "orient-applet"
 7 #define VERSION "1.0"
 8
 9 void orientEvent(GtkWidget *widget,PanelOrientType orient,
10         GtkWidget *label);
11
```

```
12 int main(int argc,char *argv[])
13 {
14     GtkWidget *applet;
15     GtkWidget *label;
16
17     applet_widget_init(APPLETNAME,VERSION,
18             argc,argv,
19             NULL,0,NULL);
20
21     applet = applet_widget_new(APPLETNAME);
22
23     label = gtk_label_new(" ");
24     gtk_widget_set_usize(label,48,48);
25
26     gtk_signal_connect(GTK_OBJECT(applet),"change_orient",
27         GTK_SIGNAL_FUNC(orientEvent),label);
28
29     applet_widget_add(APPLET_WIDGET(applet),label);
30     gtk_widget_show_all(applet);
31     applet_widget_gtk_main();
32     exit(0);
33 }
34 void orientEvent(GtkWidget *widget,PanelOrientType orient,
35         GtkWidget *label)
36 {
37     gchar *text;
38
39     switch(orient) {
40     case ORIENT_UP:
41         gtk_widget_set_usize(label,100,48);
42         text = "Horizontal Bottom";
43         break;
44     case ORIENT_DOWN:
45         gtk_widget_set_usize(label,90,48);
46         text = "Horizontal Top";
47         break;
48     case ORIENT_LEFT:
49         gtk_widget_set_usize(label,48,48);
50         text = "Vertical\nRight";
51         break;
52     case ORIENT_RIGHT:
53         gtk_widget_set_usize(label,48,48);
54         text = "Vertical\nLeft";
55         break;
56     }
57     gtk_label_set_text(GTK_LABEL(label),text);
58 }
```

The applet is created on lines 17 through 21 and, for its display window, a label is created and sized on lines 23 and 24.

On line 26, a call is made to `gtk_signal_connect()` that connects the signal named `"change_orient"` to the applet widget. This is a special signal defined inside `AppletWidget`. It is set to call the function `orientEvent()` whenever the panel changes its orientation. Lines 29 and 30 insert the label into the applet, and put the applet on display in the panel. The `"change_orient"` callback is made when the applet first appears on the panel.

The callback function `orientEvent()` beginning on line 34 changes the text and resizes the label to reflect the current organization. The second argument, the `PanelOrientType`, is used in the switch statement on line 40 to select the orientation. The orientation names refer to the direction from the applet to the root window. That is, `ORIENT_UP` means the applet is on the bottom of the window with the root window above it. `ORIENT_LEFT` means the applet is on the right with the root window to its left.

The size of the label is modified to fit the orientation. If the applet is in a panel at the top or bottom of the screen, the label is widened to accommodate a single line of text. If the applet is on one of the sides, the label is narrowed and the line of text is split.

Summary

An applet is a program with a small main window, and that window appears inside the GNOME panel. An applet derives its special abilities from the `AppletWidget`, which acts as a presentation layer for the applet's main window.This chapter discussed the parts and options, in building an applet:

✦ The functions that define and control an applet closely resemble the ones that define and control an application. The function `applet_widget_init()` is used in place of `gnome_init()`. The function `applet_widget_new()` is used in place of `gnome_app_new()`. The function `applet_widget_gtk_main()` is used in place of `gtk_main()`.

✦ An applet can be a mouse-sensitive button that serves as the entrance to a much larger program, but it also can be used to display short messages and simple information.

✦ An applet can add any number of members to its menu.

✦ An applet can resize and reorient itself to fit with its current environment.

The following chapter explains how you can make inter-process communications available at the GUI interface. The mouse can be used to drag objects from one location to another. The tricks required to package an object and transfer its ownership from one application to another are all built into the GNOME API.

✦   ✦   ✦

16

Drag, Drop, Copy, Cut, and Paste

◆ ◆ ◆ ◆

In This Chapter

Enabling text to be dragged from one window and dropped onto another

Enabling graphics to be dragged from one window and dropped onto another

Using the drag-and-drop facilities of GNOME to implement the cut-and-paste action

◆ ◆ ◆ ◆

Linux includes a number of ways that one process can communicate with another (through shared memory, pipes, X events, and low-level signals). There are two other methods that are particularly useful for a GUI interface because they work with the actions of the mouse and keyboard. A *drag-and-drop* operation occurs when the mouse selects an item, a button is pressed and held, and the item is dragged to a new location. A *cut-and-paste* (or *copy-and-paste*) operation occurs when selected text is written to the clipboard and, from the clipboard, it is inserted into a text window.

A Simple Text Drag-and-Drop

The following is a bare-bones drag-and-drop program that demonstrates the fundamental parts of the algorithm. The window it displays is shown in Figure 16-1. This program uses the two buttons on each side as sources of the drag, and the button in the center as a destination. The text from the buttons on either side can be dragged and, if dropped on the button in the center, the button label is copied.

Note This program is only a skeleton. It does not have any of the data type checking that normally is required. The intention is to demonstrate only the bare necessities.

```
1 /** simplednd.c **/
2 #include <gnome.h>
3
4 gint eventDelete(GtkWidget *widget,
5         GdkEvent *event,gpointer data);
6 gint eventDestroy(GtkWidget *widget,
7         GdkEvent *event,gpointer data);
8 void sendCallback(GtkWidget *widget,
9         GdkDragContext *context,
```

```
10          GtkSelectionData *selection,guint info,guint time);
11 void receiveCallback(GtkWidget *widget,
12          GdkDragContext *context,
13          gint x,gint y,GtkSelectionData *selection,
14          guint info,guint time);
15 void packSendingButton(GtkWidget *box,gchar *text);
16 void packReceivingButton(GtkWidget *box,gchar *text);
17
18 int main(int argc,char *argv[])
19 {
20     GtkWidget *app;
21     GtkWidget *box;
22
23     gnome_init("simplednd","1.0",argc,argv);
24     app = gnome_app_new("simplednd","Simple DND");
25     gtk_signal_connect(GTK_OBJECT(app),"delete_event",
26          GTK_SIGNAL_FUNC(eventDelete),NULL);
27     gtk_signal_connect(GTK_OBJECT(app),"destroy",
28          GTK_SIGNAL_FUNC(eventDestroy), NULL);
29
30     box = gtk_hbox_new(TRUE,0);
31     gnome_app_set_contents(GNOME_APP(app),box);
32
33     packSendingButton(box,"Left Source Text");
34     packReceivingButton(box,"Destination Window");
35     packSendingButton(box,"Right Source Text");
36
37     gtk_container_set_border_width(GTK_CONTAINER(app),25);
38     gtk_widget_show_all(app);
39     gtk_main();
40     exit(0);
41 }
42 void packSendingButton(GtkWidget *box,gchar *text)
43 {
44     GtkWidget *button;
45     static GtkTargetEntry target = { "text/plain",0,0 };
46
47     button = gtk_button_new_with_label(text);
48     gtk_box_pack_start(GTK_BOX(box),button,TRUE,FALSE,0);
49
50     gtk_signal_connect(GTK_OBJECT(button),"drag_data_get",
51          GTK_SIGNAL_FUNC(sendCallback),NULL);
52     gtk_drag_source_set(button,GDK_BUTTON1_MASK,&target,
53          1,GDK_ACTION_COPY);
54 }
55 void packReceivingButton(GtkWidget *box,gchar *text)
56 {
57     GtkWidget *button;
58     static GtkTargetEntry target = { "text/plain",0,0 };
59
60     button = glk_button_new_with_label(text);
61     gtk_box_pack_start(GTK_BOX(box),button,TRUE,FALSE,0);
62
63     gtk_signal_connect(GTK_OBJECT(button),
```

```
64                  "drag_data_received",
65                  GTK_SIGNAL_FUNC(receiveCallback),NULL);
66      gtk_drag_dest_set(button,
67                  GTK_DEST_DEFAULT_MOTION |
68                  GTK_DEST_DEFAULT_HIGHLIGHT |
69                  GTK_DEST_DEFAULT_DROP,
70                  &target,1,
71                  GDK_ACTION_COPY);
72  }
73  void sendCallback(GtkWidget *widget,
74          GdkDragContext *context,
75          GtkSelectionData *selection,guint info,guint time)
76  {
77      gchar *ascii;
78      GtkWidget *label;
79
80      label = GTK_BUTTON(widget)->child;
81      gtk_label_get(GTK_LABEL(label),&ascii);
82      gtk_selection_data_set(selection,selection->target,
83              8,ascii,strlen(ascii));
84  }
85  void receiveCallback(GtkWidget *widget,
86          GdkDragContext *context,
87          gint x,gint y,GtkSelectionData *selection,
88          guint info,guint time)
89  {
90      GtkWidget *label;
91
92      label = GTK_BUTTON(widget)->child;
93      gtk_label_set_text(GTK_LABEL(label),selection->data);
94  }
95  gint eventDelete(GtkWidget *widget,
96          GdkEvent *event,gpointer data) {
97      return(FALSE);
98  }
99  gint eventDestroy(GtkWidget *widget,
100         GdkEvent *event,gpointer data) {
101     gtk_main_quit();
102     return(0);
103 }
```

Figure 16-1: Drag-and-drop from button to button

Lines 23 through 31 initialize the application, create a horizontal box, and insert the box into the application window. The function calls on lines 33 through 35 create buttons and pack them into the box. Two of the buttons can act as sources and one can act as a destination for ASCII text drag-and-drop.

The function `packSendingButton()` on line 42 creates a button, sets the callback necessary for it to be the source of a drag, and packs the button into the box. The call to `gtk_signal_connect()` on line 50 specifies that the callback function `sendCallback()` is to execute whenever a drag operation originates inside the button. The call to `gtk_drag_source_set()` on line 52 specifies information about the drag (the data type, the mouse button used, and what action should take place to complete the drag-and-drop).

The function `packReceivingButton()` on line 55 creates a button, sets the callback necessary for it to become the destination of a drop, and packs the button into the box. The call to `gtk_signal_connect()` on line 63 specifies that the callback function execute whenever a drop occurs inside the window. The call to `gtk_drag_dest_set()` on line 66 specifies the action to take when this button detects a drag operation.

On line 73, the function `sendCallback()` is called to create the data to be transferred from the source of the drag. Lines 80 and 81 extract the text of the button's label, and the call to `gtk_selection_data_set()` inserts the data into the `GtkSelectionData` struct. This struct is the one sent to the receiving widget.

The function `receiveCallback()` on line 85 is executed whenever a drop operation occurs within the receiving button. The `GtkSelectionData` struct contains a pointer to the ASCII string that becomes the new label.

The callbacks are made only if the data is actually transmitted. If, for example, you use the mouse to start a drag operation, but drop data onto a window that cannot receive it, no callback functions are called. That is, the sender's callback function is executed only when the receiving window is selected. Prior to the drag-and-drop operation, the source calls `gtk_drag_source_set()` and the destination calls `gtk_drag_dest_set()`, and the settings established by these calls are used to determine whether the drag is valid. If the drag-and-drop is valid, the source callback is called, and then the destination callback is called. This way, the sender's callback function does not have to be concerned about whether the receiver has gotten the data — this is particularly important in a `GTK_ACTION_MOVE` operation in which the data is deleted from the source.

Graphic Data Moved among Applications

The drag-and-drop operation can be used with multiple data types. A *MIME (Multipurpose Internet Mail Extensions)* specification determines the type of data. Originally devised as a method for identifying and encoding e-mail attachments, MIME encoding has found many other uses. Each data type is specified by two names: the category and the specific data type within the category. The following are some examples of MIME data type names:

```
text/plain
text/html
```

```
image/jpeg
video/mpeg
```

To see the list of the MIME types known to Linux, select Mime Types in the GNOME
Control Center window. The first column contains the two-word MIME type and the
second column contains the usual file suffix (also called file extension) that contains
the data type. You can use any of these MIME types in a drag-and-drop operation, as
long as the sending and receiving applications understand the same type. Or, if you
wish, you can invent your own type to be used only among your own applications.

You can drag two or more MIME types from the same location. The receiver of the
data determines the actual type selected. The following example demonstrates
the source of a drag operation to be a pixmap widget, but the receiver can elect
to receive either a pixmap or plain text. Figure 16-2 shows the appearance of the
window once a few picture buttons are dragged and dropped on the canvas, and
there is at least one drop on the text button at the bottom (instead of a picture, it
shows the time of the drop). Because standard MIME type names are used, you can
drag-and-drop these items to any application. For example, drag the logo button
from this application to a GNOME terminal and you get the plain text form of the
data (the current date and time).

```
 1 /** typednd.c **/
 2 #include <gnome.h>
 3
 4 #include "minilogo.xpm"
 5
 6 #define HEIGHT 300
 7 #define WIDTH 200
 8
 9 #define TARGET_TYPE_TEXT 80
10 #define TARGET_TYPE_PIXMAP 81
11
12 typedef struct {
13     GtkWidget *app;
14     GnomeCanvasGroup *rootGroup;
15 } tdContext;
16
17 static GtkTargetEntry fromImage[] = {
18     { "text/plain", 0, TARGET_TYPE_TEXT },
19     { "image/x-xpixmap", 0, TARGET_TYPE_PIXMAP }
20 };
21 static GtkTargetEntry toButton =
22     { "text/plain", 0, TARGET_TYPE_TEXT };
23 static GtkTargetEntry toCanvas =
24     { "image/x-xpixmap", 0, TARGET_TYPE_PIXMAP };
25
26 gint eventDelete(GtkWidget *widget,
27         GdkEvent *event,gpointer data);
28 gint eventDestroy(GtkWidget *widget,
29         GdkEvent *event,gpointer data);
30 GtkWidget *makeLayout(tdContext *tdcontext);
31 void addImage(tdContext *tdcontext,char **xpm,
```

```
32          gint x,gint y);
33 void sendCallback(GtkWidget *widget,
34          GdkDragContext *context,
35          GtkSelectionData *selection,guint info,guint time);
36 void receiveCallback(GtkWidget *widget,
37          GdkDragContext *context,
38          gint x,gint y,GtkSelectionData *selection,
39          guint info,guint time,tdContext *tdcontext);
40
41 int main(int argc,char *argv[])
42 {
43     GtkWidget *layout;
44     tdContext *tdcontext = g_malloc0(sizeof(tdContext));
45
46     gnome_init("typednd","1.0",argc,argv);
47     tdcontext->app = gnome_app_new("typednd","Type DND");
48     gtk_signal_connect(GTK_OBJECT(tdcontext->app),
49             "delete_event",
50             GTK_SIGNAL_FUNC(eventDelete),NULL);
51     gtk_signal_connect(GTK_OBJECT(tdcontext->app),
52             "destroy",
53             GTK_SIGNAL_FUNC(eventDestroy), NULL);
54     gtk_widget_show_all(tdcontext->app);
55
56     layout = makeLayout(tdcontext);
57     gnome_app_set_contents(GNOME_APP(tdcontext->app),
58             layout);
59
60     gtk_widget_show_all(tdcontext->app);
61     gtk_main();
62     exit(0);
63 }
64 GtkWidget *makeLayout(tdContext *tdcontext)
65 {
66     GtkWidget *box;
67     GtkWidget *canvas;
68     GtkWidget *button;
69
70     box = gtk_vbox_new(FALSE,0);
71     gtk_widget_show(box);
72
73     canvas = gnome_canvas_new();
74     gtk_widget_set_usize(canvas,WIDTH,HEIGHT);
75     gnome_canvas_set_scroll_region(GNOME_CANVAS(canvas),
76             0.0,0.0,WIDTH,HEIGHT);
77     tdcontext->rootGroup =
78             gnome_canvas_root(GNOME_CANVAS(canvas));
79
80     gtk_signal_connect(GTK_OBJECT(canvas),
81             "drag_data_received",
82             GTK_SIGNAL_FUNC(receiveCallback),tdcontext);
83     gtk_drag_dest_set(canvas,
84             GTK_DEST_DEFAULT_MOTION |
85             GTK_DEST_DEFAULT_HIGHLIGHT |
```

```
 86                         GTK_DEST_DEFAULT_DROP,
 87                         &toCanvas,1,
 88                         GDK_ACTION_COPY);
 89
 90      gtk_box_pack_start(GTK_BOX(box),canvas,TRUE,FALSE,0);
 91
 92      addImage(tdcontext,minilogo,WIDTH/2,HEIGHT/2);
 93
 94      button = gtk_button_new_with_label("Text Target");
 95      gtk_signal_connect(GTK_OBJECT(button),
 96              "drag_data_received",
 97              GTK_SIGNAL_FUNC(receiveCallback),tdcontext);
 98      gtk_drag_dest_set(button,
 99              GTK_DEST_DEFAULT_MOTION |
100              GTK_DEST_DEFAULT_HIGHLIGHT |
101              GTK_DEST_DEFAULT_DROP,
102              &toButton,1,
103              GDK_ACTION_COPY);
104      gtk_box_pack_start(GTK_BOX(box),button,TRUE,FALSE,0);
105
106      return(box);
107 }
108 void addImage(tdContext *tdcontext,char **xpm,
109         gint x,gint y)
110 {
111      int width;
112      int height;
113      GtkStyle *style;
114      GdkBitmap *mask;
115      GdkPixmap *pixmap;
116      GtkWidget *button;
117      GtkWidget *pixmapWidget;
118      GnomeCanvasItem *item;
119
120      style = gtk_widget_get_style(
121              GTK_WIDGET(tdcontext->app));
122      pixmap = gdk_pixmap_create_from_xpm_d(
123              GTK_WIDGET(tdcontext->app)->window,
124              &mask,&style->bg[GTK_STATE_NORMAL],xpm);
125      pixmapWidget = gtk_pixmap_new(pixmap,mask);
126      button = gtk_button_new();
127      gtk_container_add(GTK_CONTAINER(button),pixmapWidget);
128
129      sscanf(xpm[0],"%d %d",&width,&height);
130      item = gnome_canvas_item_new(tdcontext->rootGroup,
131                      gnome_canvas_widget_get_type(),
132                      "widget",button,
133                      "x",(double)x,
134                      "y",(double)y,
135                      "width",(double)width + 10,
136                      "height",(double)height + 10,
137                      "anchor",GTK_ANCHOR_CENTER,
138                      NULL);
139      gtk_signal_connect(GTK_OBJECT(button),"drag_data_get",
```

```
140               GTK_SIGNAL_FUNC(sendCallback),NULL);
141        gtk_drag_source_set(GTK_WIDGET(button),
142               GDK_BUTTON1_MASK,
143               fromImage,2,
144               GDK_ACTION_COPY);
145        gtk_widget_show_all(button);
146 }
147 void sendCallback(GtkWidget *widget,
148        GdkDragContext *context,
149        GtkSelectionData *selection,guint targetType,
150        guint eventTime)
151 {
152     char str[80];
153     time_t now;
154
155     switch(targetType) {
156     case TARGET_TYPE_TEXT:
157         time(&now);
158         strcpy(str,ctime(&now));
159         str[24] = '\0';
160         gtk_selection_data_set(selection,
161             selection->target,8,
162             (guchar *)str,strlen(str));
163         break;
164     case TARGET_TYPE_PIXMAP:
165         gtk_selection_data_set(selection,
166             selection->target,8,
167             (guchar *)minilogo,sizeof(minilogo));
168         break;
169     default:
170         break;
171     }
172 }
173 void receiveCallback(GtkWidget *widget,
174        GdkDragContext *context,
175        gint x,gint y,GtkSelectionData *selection,
176        guint targetType,guint time,tdContext *tdcontext)
177 {
178     GtkWidget *label;
179
180     switch(targetType) {
181     case TARGET_TYPE_TEXT:
182         label = GTK_BUTTON(widget)->child;
183         gtk_label_set_text(GTK_LABEL(label),
184                 selection->data);
185         break;
186     case TARGET_TYPE_PIXMAP:
187         addImage(tdcontext,(gchar **)selection->data,x,y);
188         break;
189     default:
190         break;
191     }
```

```
192 }
193 gint eventDelete(GtkWidget *widget,
194       GdkEvent *event,gpointer data) {
195     return(FALSE);
196 }
197 gint eventDestroy(GtkWidget *widget,
198       GdkEvent *event,gpointer data) {
199     gtk_main_quit();
200     return(0);
201 }
```

Figure 16-2: Drag-and-drop pictures and text

The program's `main()` function begins on line 41. The call to `makeLayout()` on line 56 creates the display and attaches the callback functions. The call to `gnome_app_set_contents()` on line 57 assigns the new layout as the main window of the application.

The `makeLayout()` function beginning on line 64 creates all the widgets and sets up the drag-and-drop callbacks. Lines 70 and 71 create a vertical box to hold the two parts of the window (a canvas at the top and a button at the bottom). Lines 73 through 76 create a `GnomeCanvas`, set its size, and set its scroll region so it always is displayed. When things are added to a canvas, they actually are adding a `GnomeCanvasGroup` already inside the canvas, so lines 77 and 78 retrieve the default. The address of this `GnomeCanvasGroup` is stored in the context structure (defined on line 12) that is passed to the callbacks as data.

The call to `gtk_signal_connect()` on line 80 sets up the canvas as a widget that can receive a drop. Whenever a mouse drag from any application (this one or another one) is released inside the canvas, and a MIME type of the sender matches with a MIME type of the receiver, the callback function `receiveCallback()` is called with the data from the drag operation. If the MIME types do not match, the function is not called.

The call to gtk_drag_dest_set() on line 83 specifies the receivable MIME type and some other characteristics of the canvas as a drop target. The first argument, the canvas, is the widget that receives the drop. The second argument, GtkDestDefault, is a set of flags designating the action to be taken. Setting GTK_DEST_DEFAULT_MOTION causes "drag_motion" signals to be sent to the application so your widget can change its appearance, or take some other action, during a drag operation. Setting GTK_DEST_DEFAULT_ HIGHLIGHT causes the widget to become highlighted. The GTK_DEST_DEFAULT_ DROP flag causes "drag_drop" signals to be sent to your application. To specify all three, simply specify GTK_DEST_DEFAULT_ALL. The next two arguments specify the MIME types — in the form of one or more GtkTargetEntry structs — that this widget is capable of receiving. The canvas accepts only one MIME type; the one defined by toCanvas on line 23. A single callback can receive more than one MIME type by listing them in an array. The number following the address GtkTargetEntry pointer is the number of members in the array. The last argument is a GdkActionType specifying the action to be taken. In this example, we want to copy the data.

The call to addImage() on line 92 uses pixmap information to create a button. The XPM data for the pixmap is named minilogo and is inside the file included on line 4. This call passes the context structure (which now holds all the information necessary to add a pixmap to the canvas), the XPM data, and the coordinates of the center of the canvas.

The code on lines 94 through 104 creates a button, defines it as the target of a drop, and packs it into the box for display. The call to gtk_signal_connect(), on line 95, is the same as the one made earlier for the canvas — they even share the same callback function receiveCallback(). The call to gtk_drag_dest_set() is almost the same as the one used for the canvas — the only difference is a different MIME type is specified. The plain text type defined as toButton on line 21 is used to allow the button to receive plain ASCII text.

The function addImage() on line 108 accepts XPM data, uses it to create a button with a pixmap, places it on the canvas at the specified location, and sets the button as a source for a drag-and-drop operation. Using the XPM data and the style of the GNOME application window, the button is created on lines 120 through 127. The button is added to the canvas by the call to gnome_canvas_item_new() on line 130. The height and width of the button — gotten from the XPM data on line 129 — are used to size the button so it is slightly larger than the pixmap that it holds.

The call to gtk_signal_connect() on line 139 specifies the function sendCallback() as the one to be called whenever a drag operation starts inside the button. The call to gtk_drag_source_set() on line 141 specifies the conditions and actions of a drag operation. The first argument is the widget that is to be the origin of the drag. The second is a set of flags specifying which mouse button to use for the drag — this example uses GTK_BUTTON1_MASK, but it also can be GTK_BUTTON2_MASK and GTK_BUTTON3_MASK, or any combination of the three. One possibility is to use different buttons for slightly different actions. For example, use the left button to create a copy and the middle button to move the object (removing it from its source location).

The array `fromImage`, defined on line 17 and used as an argument on line 143, contains two MIME types that can be used as the source data type for dragging the object. The destination selects the actual type used. When a drag operation performs a drop, the first thing that happens is the MIME types of the target are compared to the MIME types of the destination. If they have one in common, the source callback function is called to package and ship the data. Then the destination callback function is called with the data. If there is no MIME type match, neither function is called. One advantage to this is that you whenever one of these callbacks is made, you know the drag-and-drop operation is confirmed and should complete successfully.

The function `sendCallback()` on line 147 is called whenever the mouse completes defining the connection (including the MIME type) between the source and destination widgets. The `switch` statement on line 155 determines which of the MIME types is selected. These values are arbitrary constants for local use only—in this example, they are defined on lines 9 and 10 and used in the `GtkTargetEntry` arrays on lines 17 through 24. The actual values can change from one program to another because it is the MIME type strings that are used for inter-process comparisons.

In this example, one of two data formats is to be sent. The case statement on line 156 indicates that there is a receiving location that is capable of receiving plain ASCII text. To supply the text, lines 157 through 159 create a string containing the current date and time (being careful to trim the newline character off the end). The call to `gtk_selection_data_set()` on line 160 stores the data in the `GtkSelectionData` struct that is supplied as an argument. The contents of this struct are sent to the drop location. The last two arguments are a pointer to the data and the full size of data to be shipped. The data type is already selected. On line 164, the `case` is executed when the recipient expects pixmap data in the XPM format. The call to `gtk_selection_data_set()` on line 165 is all that is necessary to install the address and size of the XPM data into the structure to have it duplicated and sent to the recipient.

The function `receiveCallback()` on line 173 is called whenever a drop is made. The first argument is the widget that receives the drop. Whenever this function is called, the sender's callback executed already, so the data is installed in the `GtkSelectionData` struct. The switch on line 180 determines which MIME type is received. On line 181, the case statement is executed for a plain text type, so the widget is assumed to be the button and the text is entered into it as the new label. The case on line 186 executes whenever the data is a pixmap. A call is made to `addImage()`, with the x and y coordinates of the drop, to add a new picture button to the canvas.

Cut and Paste

The following program displays a text window that enables you to edit the text. The text also can be copied to a global clipboard, making it available for any application. Additionally, text can be read from the clipboard and inserted in the text. The mouse determines the portion of the text written to the clipboard. As shown in Figure 16-3, the highlighted portion is written to the clipboard. Either a *cut* or *copy* operation writes to the clipboard, while a *paste* operation reads and inserts anything previously stored in the clipboard.

```
1 /** cutnpaste.c **/
2 #include <gnome.h>
3
4 static void fileExit(GtkObject *,gpointer);
5 static void editCut(GtkObject *,gpointer);
6 static void editPaste(GtkObject *,gpointer);
7 static void editCopy(GtkObject *,gpointer);
8
9 static GtkWidget *text;
10
11 gint eventDelete(GtkWidget *widget,
12        GdkEvent *event,gpointer data);
13 gint eventDestroy(GtkWidget *widget,
14        GdkEvent *event,gpointer data);
15
16 GnomeUIInfo fileMenu[] = {
17     { GNOME_APP_UI_ITEM,"E_xit",
18       "Close the window and cease",
19       fileExit,NULL,NULL,
20       GNOME_APP_PIXMAP_NONE,
21       NULL,0,0,NULL },
22
23       GNOMEUIINFO_END
24 };
25
26 GnomeUIInfo editMenu[] = {
27     { GNOME_APP_UI_ITEM,"_Cut",
28       "Delete and copy selection to clipboard",
29       editCut,NULL,NULL,
30       GNOME_APP_PIXMAP_NONE,
31       NULL,0,0,NULL },
32     { GNOME_APP_UI_ITEM,"Cop_y",
33       "Copy selection to clipboard",
34       editCopy,NULL,NULL,
35       GNOME_APP_PIXMAP_NONE,
36       NULL,0,0,NULL },
37     { GNOME_APP_UI_ITEM,"_Paste",
38       "Paste selection from clipboard",
39       editPaste,NULL,NULL,
40       GNOME_APP_PIXMAP_NONE,
41       NULL,0,0,NULL },
```

```
42          GNOMEUIINFO_END
43 };
44
45 GnomeUIInfo mainMenu[] = {
46          GNOMEUIINFO_SUBTREE("_File",fileMenu),
47          GNOMEUIINFO_SUBTREE("_Edit",editMenu),
48          GNOMEUIINFO_END
49 };
50
51 int main(int argc,char *argv[])
52 {
53          GtkWidget *app;
54
55          gnome_init("cutnpaste","1.0",argc,argv);
56          app = gnome_app_new("cutnpaste",
57                  "Cut, Copy, and Paste");
58          gtk_signal_connect(GTK_OBJECT(app),"delete_event",
59                  GTK_SIGNAL_FUNC(eventDelete),NULL);
60          gtk_signal_connect(GTK_OBJECT(app),"destroy",
61                  GTK_SIGNAL_FUNC(eventDestroy),NULL);
62
63          gnome_app_create_menus(GNOME_APP(app),mainMenu);
64
65          text = gtk_text_new(NULL,NULL);
66          gtk_widget_set_usize(text,300,200);
67          gtk_text_set_editable(GTK_TEXT(text),TRUE);
68          gnome_app_set_contents(GNOME_APP(app),text);
69
70          gtk_widget_show_all(app);
71          gtk_main();
72          exit(0);
73 }
74 static void fileExit(GtkObject *object,gpointer data) {
75          gtk_main_quit();
76 }
77 static void editCut(GtkObject *object,gpointer data) {
78          gtk_editable_cut_clipboard(GTK_EDITABLE(text));
79 }
80 static void editCopy(GtkObject *object,gpointer data) {
81          gtk_editable_copy_clipboard(GTK_EDITABLE(text));
82 }
83 static void editPaste(GtkObject *object,gpointer data) {
84          gtk_editable_paste_clipboard(GTK_EDITABLE(text));
85 }
86 gint eventDelete(GtkWidget *widget,
87          GdkEvent *event,gpointer data) {
88      return(FALSE);
89 }
90 gint eventDestroy(GtkWidget *widget,
91          GdkEvent *event,gpointer data) {
92      gtk_main_quit();
93      return(0);
94 }
```

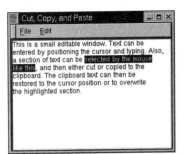

Figure 16-3: An editable text window
that enables you to cut and paste

Cut, copy, and paste operations are part of every widget that has `GtkEditable`
in its parentage. Most notably, this includes `GtkEntry` (allowing a single line of
text to be entered) and `GtkText` (a multiple line, text-editing widget). This example
employs a `GtkText` widget. You can use it to cut and paste within a text window,
or you can run multiple versions of it and cut and paste among them all. You
can even cut or copy text from the edit window and paste it into the window of
another application that accepts text, such as a text editor or a GNOME terminal.

Line 63 calls `gnome_app_create_menus()` to create the menu bar across the top
of the main window. The menus are defined in the arrays on lines 16 through 48 and
consist of only two main headings. The `File` menu has only an `Exit` entry, and the
`Edit` menu contains `Cut`, `Copy`, and `Paste`. Each of the four menu selections is
supplied with its own callback function.

The text widget is created and configured on lines 65 through 68. The call to `gtk_
text_new()` on line 65 pass `NULL` for the horizontal and vertical `GtkAdjustment`
arguments because this sample does not use scrollbars. The call on line 67 to
`gtk_text_set_editable()` specifies that the text is to be accessible from the
keyboard and mouse. (A `GtkText` object that is not editable is a display-only
text window.)

The callback functions on lines 77 through 85 handle all of the cutting and
pasting. The `GtkEdit` widget assumes the responsibility for responding to the
mouse, which selects the text to be cut or copied. The widget then highlights the
text, extracts the text from the highlighted area, writes the extracted text to the
clipboard, reads text from the clipboard, and inserts it into the text window. A
call to `gtk_editable_cut_clipboard()` writes the selected text to the clipboard
and removes it from the text window. A call to `gtk_editable_copy_clipboard()`
does the same, but does not remove it from the text window. A call to
`gtk_editable_paste_clipboard()` reads text from the clipboard and inserts it
at the current cursor location.

Summary

Data can be moved from one application to another under control of the user's mouse. Graphical objects can be dragged from one location to another, and text can be copied to a global clipboard for insertion into another text window, or into another position in the same text window. The following approaches were explored in this chapter:

✦ You can use a drag-and-drop operation to transfer any data type of any size, but the sender and the receiver must agree on the data type. This is accomplished using MIME data type names.

✦ A drag-and-drop operation pre-qualifies a match between the sending and receiving widgets by comparing their respective list of known MIME types.

✦ A fundamental, drag-and-drop operation is quite simple, but as more data types and more options are added, complexity increases.

✦ Any editable widget (`GtkText` or `GtkEntry`) can be used to cut and paste text because the complete procedure is included inside the `GtkEditable` class.

The next chapter is about a very special top-level window that is a container of widgets. It is all about the MDI (Multiple Document Interface), which not only acts as a container of child widgets but also allows the user to select among them, and it allows each of the child widgets to modify the menus and toolbars of the parent MDI window.

✦   ✦   ✦

Multiple Document Interface (MDI)

◆ ◆ ◆ ◆

In This Chapter

Creating and
displaying a simple
MDI window

Causing an MDI
window to display
its child windows in
different modes

Changing the
options on the
menus of an MDI
parent window
by selecting a
child window

Using a toolbar with
an MDI window

◆ ◆ ◆ ◆

A *Multiple Document Interface (MDI)* is a special window
object that has the ability to display one, two, or more
child windows. It can show them one at a time (as if they were
stacked one on top of the other). It also can add tabs to the
side of this stack to allow the mouse to switch from one child
window to another. Finally, the MDI window can split itself
into multiple, top-level windows and display each of the
child windows in its own top-level window.

Because the structure and control of an MDI display differs
from normal windows, the MDI window is not a widget. The
MDI object acts as a broker between one or more top-level
windows and one or more child windows. And, because the
number of top-level windows can vary, the MDI object also
assumes the responsibility of creating and maintaining the
menus and toolbars.

A Simple MDI Window

The following program is a simple MDI application. It creates
and displays four windows and allows the mouse to select
which one is visible at any given time. The collection of
windows is held in a special container — the MDI object — that
allows only one at a time to be visible. In this example, each of
the documents is a label widget. The multiple-document
window is shown in Figure 17-1.

Note   A display object controlled by the MDI software can have several names. It can be called a *document*, which fits with the description of it being part of a multiple-document interface. It also is referred to as a *view*, in that there are different representations of the same, or related, data. Internally, it often is referred to as a *child* because of its relationship with the MDI container. You also can find references to *page* because of the way the software flips from one to the other. No matter what you call it, it simply is a widget with its display controlled by the MDI software.

```
1  /** simplemdi.c **/
2  #include <gnome.h>
3
4  gint eventDelete(GtkWidget *widget,
5          GdkEvent *event,gpointer data);
6  gint eventDestroy(GtkWidget *widget,
7          GdkEvent *event,gpointer data);
8
9  static void addChild(GtkObject *mdi,gchar *name);
10 static GtkWidget *setLabel(GnomeMDIChild *child,
11         GtkWidget *currentLabel,gpointer data);
12 static GtkWidget *createView(GnomeMDIChild *child,
13         gpointer data);
14
15 int main(int argc,char *argv[])
16 {
17     GtkObject *mdi;
18
19     gnome_init("simplemdi","1.0",argc,argv);
20     mdi = gnome_mdi_new("simplemdi","Simple MDI");
21     gtk_signal_connect(mdi,"destroy",
22             GTK_SIGNAL_FUNC(eventDestroy),NULL);
23
24     addChild(mdi,"First");
25     addChild(mdi,"Second");
26     addChild(mdi,"Third");
27     addChild(mdi,"Last");
28
29     gnome_mdi_set_mode(GNOME_MDI(mdi),GNOME_MDI_NOTEBOOK);
30     gnome_mdi_open_toplevel(GNOME_MDI(mdi));
31
32     gtk_main();
33     exit(0);
34 }
35 static void addChild(GtkObject *mdi,gchar *name)
36 {
37     GnomeMDIGenericChild *child;
38
39     child = gnome_mdi_generic_child_new(name);
40     gnome_mdi_add_child(GNOME_MDI(mdi),
41             GNOME_MDI_CHILD(child));
42
```

```
43      gnome_mdi_generic_child_set_view_creator(child,
44              createView,name);
45      gnome_mdi_generic_child_set_label_func(child,setLabel,
46              NULL);
47      gnome_mdi_add_view(GNOME_MDI(mdi),
48              GNOME_MDI_CHILD(child));
49 }
50 static GtkWidget *createView(GnomeMDIChild *child,
51          gpointer data)
52 {
53      char str[80];
54
55      sprintf(str,"View of the\n%s widget",(gchar *)data);
56      return(gtk_label_new(str));
57 }
58 static GtkWidget *setLabel(GnomeMDIChild *child,
59          GtkWidget *currentLabel,gpointer data)
60 {
61      if(currentLabel == NULL)
62          return(gtk_label_new(child->name));
63
64      gtk_label_set_text(GTK_LABEL(currentLabel),
65              child->name);
66      return(currentLabel);
67 }
68 gint eventDestroy(GtkWidget *widget,
69          GdkEvent *event,gpointer data) {
70      gtk_main_quit();
71      return(0);
72 }
```

Figure 17-1: An MDI window displayed in notebook mode

GNOME and GTK+ are initialized by the call to gnome_init() on line 19. Then, instead of an application window, the call to gnome_mdi_new() on line 20 creates a GnomeMDI object. The GnomeMDI object is not a widget — it is a special type of container that has the ability to hold a number of child widgets (or documents, or views) and allows them to be displayed one at a time. When the GnomeMDI object is created, it has nothing to display because it is empty. The application program must call functions to define the displayable contents and make modifications to the option settings.

The call to `gtk_signal_connect()` on line 21 causes the `eventDestroy()` callback to be called immediately to close the application. There is no `"delete_event"` callback (as with other top-level GNOME and GTK+ windows) because that particular signal is not defined for `GnomeMDI`.

Lines 24 through 27 add document widgets to the MDI display. The call to `gnome_mdi_set_mode()` on line 29 sets the display mode so the tabs are available on the left (as shown in Figure 17-1). The call to `gnome_mdi_open_toplevel()` on line 30 creates a top-level window and uses it as a container for the `GnomeMDI` object displaying the document widgets.

The `addChild()` function, beginning on line 35, creates a new document window and adds it to MDI as a child to be displayed. Each displayable object is a `GnomeMDIGenericChild` object, as created by the call to `gnome_mdi_generic_child()` on line 39. This object is added to the `GnomeMDI` object with the call to `gnome_mdi_add_child()` on line 40. Now, the child is added to `GnomeMDI`, but it is not visible until the widget that displays it is defined. The call to `gnome_mdi_generic_child_set_view_creator()` on line 43 specifies that the function `createView()` should be called to return the widget that is the display form of the object. The call to `gnome_mdi_generic_child_set_label_func()` on line 45 specifies that the function `setLabel()` should be called to create a label for the tabs on the page holding the view of the object. Finally, on line 47, the call to `gnome_mdi_add_view()` creates the visible portion of the document by calling the functions that are specified to create the display and the label.

The function `createView()` on line 50 creates a widget that is used to display a view of the object. This example uses the name string that was passed in as the user data (on the call to `gnome_mdi_generic_child_set_view_creator()` on line 43) to create a string that contains the name. Then, the string is used to create and return a `GtkLabel` as the document to be displayed.

The function `setLabel()` on line 58 is called to define a widget that serves as the label on the tab that the mouse uses to flip from one page to another. The second argument is the tab label widget (if any) that was created earlier. Whenever the MDI window first displays in the notebook mode, this function is called to create a label. However, one may exist already from a previous time when the MDI window was shown in the notebook mode.

The notebook mode always supplies the label tabs on the left that you can use to switch from one view to another. If there are more tabs than can be displayed in the window, a pair of up and down arrows are inserted at the bottom so the user can scroll back and forth through the tabs. Figure 17-2 shows the window after reducing the size of the window from the preceding example.

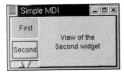

Figure 17-2: Accessing tabs using the up and down arrow buttons

MDI Menus and Display Modes

Because an MDI window is displayed as its own top-level window, there are some special MDI functions that are required to manipulate the menu for it. All of the menu structures and options described in Chapter 8 are valid, but its construction and operation are under control of the MDI functions. The following program creates a menu bar that enables the user to change the mode of the MDI display and toggle among the available views. This program closely resembles the previous example, except a menu bar and its callbacks are added.

```
 1 /** menumdi.c **/
 2 #include <gnome.h>
 3
 4 static GtkObject *mdi;
 5 static GtkWidget *firstView;
 6 static GtkWidget *secondView;
 7 static GtkWidget *thirdView;
 8 static GtkWidget *lastView;
 9
10 gint eventDelete(GtkWidget *widget,
11         GdkEvent *event,gpointer data);
12 gint eventDestroy(GtkWidget *widget,
13         GdkEvent *event,gpointer data);
14
15 static void addChild(gchar *name);
16 static GtkWidget *setLabel(GnomeMDIChild *child,
17         GtkWidget *currentLabel,gpointer data);
18 static GtkWidget *createView(GnomeMDIChild *child,
19         gpointer data);
20
21 static void fileExit(GtkObject *object,gpointer data);
22 static void modeNotebook(GtkObject *object,gpointer data);
23 static void modeToplevel(GtkObject *object,gpointer data);
24 static void modeModal(GtkObject *object,gpointer data);
25 static void modeDefault(GtkObject *object,gpointer data);
26 static void setFirstView(GtkObject *object,gpointer data);
27 static void setSecondView(GtkObject *object,gpointer data);
28 static void setThirdView(GtkObject *object,gpointer data);
29 static void setLastView(GtkObject *object,gpointer data);
30
31 GnomeUIInfo fileMenu[] = {
32     GNOMEUIINFO_SEPARATOR,
33     { GNOME_APP_UI_ITEM,"E_xit",
34       "Close the window and cease",
35       fileExit,NULL,NULL,
36       GNOME_APP_PIXMAP_NONE,
37       NULL,0,0,NULL },
38     GNOMEUIINFO_END
39 };
40
41 GnomeUIInfo modeMenu[] = {
42     { GNOME_APP_UI_ITEM,"Notebook",
43       "Change to notebook display mode",
```

```
44        modeNotebook,NULL,NULL,
45        GNOME_APP_PIXMAP_NONE,
46        NULL,0,0,NULL },
47      { GNOME_APP_UI_ITEM,"Toplevel",
48        "Change to top-level display mode",
49        modeToplevel,NULL,NULL,
50        GNOME_APP_PIXMAP_NONE,
51        NULL,0,0,NULL },
52      { GNOME_APP_UI_ITEM,"Modal",
53        "Change to modal display mode",
54        modeModal,NULL,NULL,
55        GNOME_APP_PIXMAP_NONE,
56        NULL,0,0,NULL },
57      { GNOME_APP_UI_ITEM,"Default",
58        "Change to the default display mode",
59        modeDefault,NULL,NULL,
60        GNOME_APP_PIXMAP_NONE,
61        NULL,0,0,NULL },
62      GNOMEUIINFO_END
63 };
64
65 GnomeUIInfo selectMenu[] = {
66      { GNOME_APP_UI_ITEM,"First",
67        "Switch to the first document",
68        setFirstView,NULL,NULL,
69        GNOME_APP_PIXMAP_NONE,
70        NULL,0,0,NULL },
71      { GNOME_APP_UI_ITEM,"Second",
72        "Switch to the second document",
73        setSecondView,NULL,NULL,
74        GNOME_APP_PIXMAP_NONE,
75        NULL,0,0,NULL },
76      { GNOME_APP_UI_ITEM,"Third",
77        "Switch to the third document",
78        setThirdView,NULL,NULL,
79        GNOME_APP_PIXMAP_NONE,
80        NULL,0,0,NULL },
81      { GNOME_APP_UI_ITEM,"Last",
82        "Switch to the last document",
83        setLastView,NULL,NULL,
84        GNOME_APP_PIXMAP_NONE,
85        NULL,0,0,NULL },
86      GNOMEUIINFO_END
87 };
88
89 GnomeUIInfo mainMenu[] = {
90      GNOMEUIINFO_SUBTREE("_File",fileMenu),
91      GNOMEUIINFO_SUBTREE("_Mode",modeMenu),
92      GNOMEUIINFO_SUBTREE("_Select",selectMenu),
93      GNOMEUIINFO_END
94 };
95
96 int main(int argc,char *argv[])
97 {
```

```
 98        gnome_init("menumdi","1.0",argc,argv);
 99        mdi = gnome_mdi_new("menumdi","Menu MDI");
100        gnome_mdi_set_menubar_template(GNOME_MDI(mdi),
101                mainMenu);
102        gtk_signal_connect(mdi,"destroy",
103                GTK_SIGNAL_FUNC(eventDestroy),NULL);
104
105        addChild("First");
106        addChild("Second");
107        addChild("Third");
108        addChild("Last");
109
110        gnome_mdi_open_toplevel(GNOME_MDI(mdi));
111
112        gtk_main();
113        exit(0);
114 }
115 static void addChild(gchar *name)
116 {
117        GnomeMDIGenericChild *child;
118
119        child = gnome_mdi_generic_child_new(name);
120        gnome_mdi_add_child(GNOME_MDI(mdi),
121                GNOME_MDI_CHILD(child));
122
123        gnome_mdi_generic_child_set_view_creator(child,
124                createView,name);
125        gnome_mdi_generic_child_set_label_func(child,setLabel,
126                NULL);
127        gnome_mdi_add_view(GNOME_MDI(mdi),
128                GNOME_MDI_CHILD(child));
129 }
130 static GtkWidget *createView(GnomeMDIChild *child,
131         gpointer data)
132 {
133        gchar *name;
134        char str[80];
135        GtkWidget *view;
136
137        name = (gchar *)data;
138        sprintf(str,"View of the\n%s widget",name);
139        view = gtk_label_new(str);
140        gtk_widget_set_usize(view,250,100);
141        if(!strcmp(name,"First"))
142            firstView = view;
143        else if(!strcmp(name,"Second"))
144            secondView = view;
145        else if(!strcmp(name,"Third"))
146            thirdView = view;
147        else
148            lastView = view;
149        return(view);
150 }
151 static GtkWidget *setLabel(GnomeMDIChild *child,
```

```
152            GtkWidget *currentLabel,gpointer data)
153 {
154     if(currentLabel == NULL)
155         return(gtk_label_new(child->name));
156
157     gtk_label_set_text(GTK_LABEL(currentLabel),
158             child->name);
159     return(currentLabel);
160 }
161 static void fileExit(GtkObject *object,gpointer data)
162 {
163     gtk_main_quit();
164 }
165 static void modeNotebook(GtkObject *object,gpointer data)
166 {
167     gnome_mdi_set_mode(GNOME_MDI(mdi),GNOME_MDI_NOTEBOOK);
168 }
169 static void modeToplevel(GtkObject *object,gpointer data)
170 {
171     gnome_mdi_set_mode(GNOME_MDI(mdi),GNOME_MDI_TOPLEVEL);
172 }
173 static void modeModal(GtkObject *object,gpointer data)
174 {
175     gnome_mdi_set_mode(GNOME_MDI(mdi),GNOME_MDI_MODAL);
176 }
177 static void modeDefault(GtkObject *object,gpointer data)
178 {
179     gnome_mdi_set_mode(GNOME_MDI(mdi),
180                     GNOME_MDI_DEFAULT_MODE);
181 }
182 static void setFirstView(GtkObject *object,gpointer data)
183 {
184     gnome_mdi_set_active_view(GNOME_MDI(mdi),firstView);
185 }
186 static void setSecondView(GtkObject *object,gpointer data)
187 {
188     gnome_mdi_set_active_view(GNOME_MDI(mdi),secondView);
189 }
190 static void setThirdView(GtkObject *object,gpointer data)
191 {
192     gnome_mdi_set_active_view(GNOME_MDI(mdi),thirdView);
193 }
194 static void setLastView(GtkObject *object,gpointer data)
195 {
196     gnome_mdi_set_active_view(GNOME_MDI(mdi),lastView);
197 }
198 gint eventDestroy(GtkWidget *widget,
199         GdkEvent *event,gpointer data) {
200     gtk_main_quit();
201     return(0);
202 }
```

Lines 21 through 29 are the prototypes of the menu callback functions, and the menu itself is declared on lines 31 through 94. There is much more information on the layout of the menu arrays in Chapter 8. When the MDI software creates the menus from the arrays, the arrays are copied before the menu creation function gnome_app_create_menus_with_data() is called. This means that the menu definition data in your program is not altered.

The main() function begins with a call to gnome_init() on line 98. The call to gnome_mdi_new() on line 99 creates a new, but empty, GnomeMDI object. The call to gnome_mdi_set_menubar_template() on line 100 attaches the menu to the GnomeMDI object. The four calls to the function addChild() on lines 105 through 108 each adds a new document page to the MDI. Finally, on line 110, the MDI window is opened with the call to gnome_mdi_open_toplevel().

The function addChild() beginning on line 115 adds one child document to the MDI window. The call to gnome_mdi_generic_child() creates an empty MDI child, and the call to gnome_mdi_add_child() on line 120 inserts it as a member of the list of child objects that you can use to create views. Lines 123 through 128 use the child to create a view, and add that view to the documents that are displayed in the MDI window.

The functions createVew(), on line 130, and setLabel(), on line 151, are callback functions that are registered with MDI by the function calls on lines 123 and 125. The function createView() is called to create a view of an object. On lines 127 through 140, a label is constructed and sized using text of the name passed in as an argument. Because this program needs access to each of the views later, the address of each one is stored in a global location on lines 141 through 148. Line 149 returns the created view. The function setLabel() on line 151 creates the label that is displayed on the tab when the MDI window is in the notebook mode.

The menu callback function modeNotebook() on line 165 calls gnome_mdi_set_mode(), which changes the MDI display to the notebook mode. In this mode, the documents are stacked in the window with only one visible — but each one has a tab on its left side that the mouse can use to switch from one to another. The resulting window is shown in Figure 17-3. Also shown in the figure, the currently selected child has its name appear on the title bar of the MDI window.

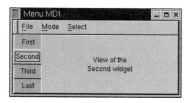

Figure 17-3: Menu bar with the MDI window in notebook mode

The menu callback function `modeModal()` on line 173 changes the mode of the display so it looks like Figure 17-4. The documents are stacked one on top of another and provide no way for the mouse to switch from one to the other. To switch from one document to another, the application program needs to call `gnome_mdi_set_active_view()`. The callback function `modeDefault()` sets the MDI display to its default mode, which happens to be modal.

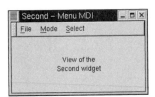

Figure 17-4: Menu bar with the MDI window in modal mode

The callback function `modeToplevel()` on line 169 changes the display to the only form that accommodates the display of more than one page at a time. Each document is assigned its own top-level window and looks like the ones shown in Figure 17-5. Notice that the entire menu bar is duplicated for each window — it is possible to select a mode change on any of the menus and cause the display to collapse back into one window.

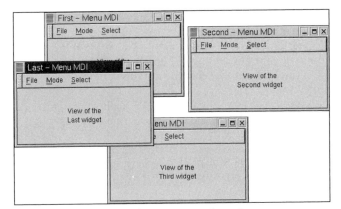

Figure 17-5: Each MDI document can have its own top-level window.

An MDI Window with a Toolbar

The following program demonstrates a method to create a toolbar for an MDI window. The process slightly differs from the one used to create a menu bar in the previous section. The toolbar is created in a special callback function that is executed when the parent window — the `GnomeApp` window — is created. This program has a couple of standard toolbar buttons and a set of radio buttons, but an MDI toolbar can contain any of the toolbar items described in Chapter 8.

```
 1  /** toolbarmdi.c **/
 2  #include <gnome.h>
 3
 4  #include "toolbarxpm.h"
 5
 6  static GtkObject *mdi;
 7
 8  gint eventDestroy(GtkWidget *widget,
 9          GdkEvent *event,gpointer data);
10
11  static void addChild(GtkObject *mdi,gchar *name);
12  static GtkWidget *setLabel(GnomeMDIChild *child,
13          GtkWidget *currentLabel,gpointer data);
14  static GtkWidget *createView(GnomeMDIChild *child,
15          gpointer data);
16
17  static void notebookCallback(GtkObject *object,
18          gpointer data);
19  static void modalCallback(GtkObject *object,
20          gpointer data);
21  static void toplevelCallback(GtkObject *object,
22          gpointer data);
23  static void dummyCallback(GtkObject *object,
24          gpointer data);
25  static void appCreated(GnomeMDI *mdi,GnomeApp *app,
26          gpointer data);
27
28  GnomeUIInfo modeList[] = {
29      GNOMEUIINFO_RADIOITEM("Modal",
30          "Change to the Modal display mode",
31          modalCallback,modalXPM),
32      GNOMEUIINFO_RADIOITEM("Notebook",
33          "Change to the Notebook display mode",
34          notebookCallback,notebookXPM),
35      GNOMEUIINFO_RADIOITEM("Toplevel",
36          "Change to the Toplevel display mode",
37          toplevelCallback,toplevelXPM),
38      GNOMEUIINFO_END
39  };
40
41  static GnomeUIInfo modeToolbar[] = {
42      { GNOME_APP_UI_ITEM,"New",
43        "Create a new file",dummyCallback,NULL,NULL,
44        GNOME_APP_PIXMAP_STOCK,GNOME_STOCK_PIXMAP_NEW,
45        0,0,NULL },
46      GNOMEUIINFO_SEPARATOR,
47      GNOMEUIINFO_RADIOLIST(modeList),
48      GNOMEUIINFO_SEPARATOR,
49      { GNOME_APP_UI_ITEM,"Save as",
50        "Save to a new file",dummyCallback,NULL,NULL,
```

```
51          GNOME_APP_PIXMAP_STOCK,GNOME_STOCK_PIXMAP_SAVE_AS,
52          0,0,NULL },
53      GNOMEUIINFO_END
54  };
55
56  int main(int argc,char *argv[])
57  {
58      gnome_init("toolbarmdi","1.0",argc,argv);
59      mdi = gnome_mdi_new("toolbarmdi","Toolbar MDI");
60      gtk_signal_connect(mdi,"destroy",
61              GTK_SIGNAL_FUNC(eventDestroy),NULL);
62      gtk_signal_connect(mdi,"app_created",
63              GTK_SIGNAL_FUNC(appCreated),NULL);
64
65      addChild(mdi,"First");
66      addChild(mdi,"Second");
67      addChild(mdi,"Third");
68      addChild(mdi,"Last");
69
70      gnome_mdi_open_toplevel(GNOME_MDI(mdi));
71
72      gtk_main();
73      exit(0);
74  }
75  static void addChild(GtkObject *mdi,gchar *name)
76  {
77      GnomeMDIGenericChild *child;
78
79      child = gnome_mdi_generic_child_new(name);
80      gnome_mdi_add_child(GNOME_MDI(mdi),
81              GNOME_MDI_CHILD(child));
82
83      gnome_mdi_generic_child_set_view_creator(child,
84              createView,name);
85      gnome_mdi_generic_child_set_label_func(child,setLabel,
86              NULL);
87      gnome_mdi_add_view(GNOME_MDI(mdi),
88              GNOME_MDI_CHILD(child));
89  }
90  static GtkWidget *createView(GnomeMDIChild *child,
91          gpointer data)
92  {
93      char str[80];
94      GtkWidget *label;
95
96      sprintf(str,"View of the\n%s widget",(gchar *)data);
97      label = gtk_label_new(str);
98      gtk_widget_set_usize(label,200,200);
99      return(label);
100 }
101 static GtkWidget *setLabel(GnomeMDIChild *child,
102         GtkWidget *currentLabel,gpointer data)
103 {
```

```
104     if(currentLabel == NULL)
105         return(gtk_label_new(child->name));
106
107     gtk_label_set_text(GTK_LABEL(currentLabel),
108             child->name);
109     return(currentLabel);
110 }
111 static void appCreated(GnomeMDI *mdi,GnomeApp *app,
112         gpointer data)
113 {
114     gnome_app_create_toolbar(app,modeToolbar);
115 }
116 static void toplevelCallback(GtkObject *object,
117         gpointer data)
118 {
119     GtkToggleButton *button = GTK_TOGGLE_BUTTON(object);
120     if(gtk_toggle_button_get_active(button))
121         gnome_mdi_set_mode(GNOME_MDI(mdi),
122             GNOME_MDI_TOPLEVEL);
123 }
124 static void modalCallback(GtkObject *object,
125         gpointer data)
126 {
127     GtkToggleButton *button = GTK_TOGGLE_BUTTON(object);
128     if(gtk_toggle_button_get_active(button))
129         gnome_mdi_set_mode(GNOME_MDI(mdi),
130             GNOME_MDI_MODAL);
131 }
132 static void notebookCallback(GtkObject *object,
133         gpointer data)
134 {
135     GtkToggleButton *button = GTK_TOGGLE_BUTTON(object);
136     if(gtk_toggle_button_get_active(button))
137         gnome_mdi_set_mode(GNOME_MDI(mdi),
138             GNOME_MDI_NOTEBOOK);
139 }
140 static void dummyCallback(GtkObject *object,gpointer data)
141 {
142     gnome_ok_dialog("The dummy callback.");
143 }
144 gint eventDestroy(GtkWidget *widget,
145         GdkEvent *event,gpointer data) {
146     gtk_main_quit();
147     return(0);
148 }
```

The main() function begins with calls to gnome_init() and gnome_mdi_new(), on lines 58 and 59, to initialize GNOME and create a GnomeMDI object. The call to gtk_signal_connect() on line 62 assigns the callback function appCreated() to the signal named "app_created", which is executed immediately after the GnomeApp window is created. Lines 65 through 68 add four documents to MDI, and line 70 creates the top-level window to contain them.

Lines 75 through 109 are the same as the ones in the previous section's menu example. The function addChild() creates a child document and inserts it into the MDI window, and the function createView() creates the widget that acts as a view of the child object. The function setLabel() is called to create tab labels for each view in the MDI notebook mode.

The callback function appCreated() on line 111 is called whenever the GnomeApp window is created, so the toolbar can be added to it. The menu is created the same way that it is for a normal GNOME application window, as described in Chapter 8. The call to gnome_app_create_toolbar() on line 114 creates the toolbar and attaches it to the window. The toolbar layout is defined in the arrays on lines 28 through 54; for its icons, it uses the XPM data in the file toolbarxpm.h included on line 4. The toolbar and the MDI window are shown in Figure 17-6.

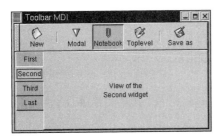

Figure 17-6: An MDI window with a toolbar

The callback functions toplevelCallback(), modalCallback(), and notebookCallback() each are attached to a radio button on the toolbar. This enables the toolbar to switch the display among the three different modes. In each of these functions, before the mode is set, a test determines whether the button is active. If the button is not active, that means it is deselected rather than selected.

The dummyCallback() function on line 140 is called whenever one of the other toolbar buttons is selected.

Summary

An MDI display has the advantage of containing a lot of window real estate in a small area. It does this by stacking the displayable widgets one on top of the other and enabling users to thumb through them to find whatever they desire. This chapter covered the major elements of MDI, which are:

✦ An MDI window displays its child window in one of three modes.

✦ The modal mode of displaying the child windows stacks the windows on top of one another. It can be set up so you can switch from one to the other by using the menu or a toolbar, or through some other technique internal to the application.

✦ The notebook mode is the same as the modal mode, except that there are also tabs on the left side of the window that the mouse can use to switch the view.

✦ The top-level mode displays each of the child windows in its own top-level window.

✦ The top-level window of an MDI object is not a normal GNOME top-level window, but it does have the capabilities of managing a menu and toolbars.

The next chapter contains examples of the ultimate step in customizing your application — the construction of your own custom widgets. There are a number of situations where this can be advantageous, but it is particularly handy when the same interface is to be used in multiple applications. It also encapsulates portions of your application in a way that reduces maintenance difficulties.

✦   ✦   ✦

Creating Your Own Widget

◆ ◆ ◆ ◆

In This Chapter

Exploring the internal organization of a GNOME widget

Designing and constructing a widget that displays bar graphs

Creating the widget's header file for use by other applications

Modifying a widget that is already in use

◆ ◆ ◆ ◆

This chapter shows a method for writing a widget. The art of widgetry can get a bit complex, and there is certainly more than one way to write a widget. The example explained in this chapter should work quite well for constructing widgets you will use in your application.

Widgets are object-oriented. Of course, object orientation is not enforced in the C language; instead, it is achieved by using a set of coding conventions and requesting that everyone follow the same set of rules. While object-oriented languages, such as C++ and Java, have some built-in facilities to simplify programming objects, code can be organized into objects in any language. This chapter contains a description of the internals of a widget, which, at the same time, is also a description of a method of object-oriented programming in C.

The Bar Graph Widget

The widget described in this chapter is very specialized. It has most of the basic structure elements of, say, a GtkButton or a GtkText widget. However, it doesn't bother with issuing signals, counting the number of references, or establishing a collection of values that can be set by ASCII name.

The name of the widget is AgBargraph. Using the widget-naming convention of GTK+ widgets beginning with Gtk, and GNOME widgets beginning with Gnome, this widget is in the hypothetical collection known as the Ag widgets. It displays a multicolored bar graph with a variable number of members. AgBargraph responds to the mouse in two ways — it changes its background color whenever the mouse pointer enters its window, and it responds to the mouse buttons by displaying the name of the selected bar graph. Figure 18-1 shows an example of its output.

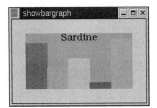

Figure 18-1: The AgBargraph widget ? displaying the name of a bar

The AgBargraph widget has these characteristics:

✦ It is object-oriented. It has special functions that are called to create the widget and, at the end of its life, to destroy it. This way, allocated system resources are released automatically when the widget is deleted. Access to the widget control values is made through function calls.

✦ As with all widgets, AgBargraph is very easy to use as part of your application. It is only necessary to create the widget and attach it to a parent window that displays it.

✦ Your application can create any number of instances of this widget. Each instance operates independently, but uses the same set of functions for configuration and control.

✦ AgBargraph inherits all of the capabilities of GtkWidget. This enables it to select the events to be received simply by asking for them. Because GtkWidget takes care of the underlying structure of AgBargraph, most of the code deals with setting values and drawing the display.

✦ AgBargraph automatically resizes itself to fit the size allocated to it. It redraws itself when it becomes exposed. Additionally, AgBargraph changes its background color when the mouse enters its window. Clicking one of the bars in the graph causes its name to display.

✦ You can add new bar-graph information at any time — either before the widget is realized or while it is being displayed.

Using the AgBargraph Widget

The following program creates and displays an AgBargraph widget.

```
1 /** showbargraph.c **/
2 #include <gnome.h>
3
4 #include "agbargraph.h"
```

```
 5
 6 GtkWidget *makeBox();
 7 gint eventDelete(GtkWidget *widget,
 8         GdkEvent *event,gpointer data);
 9 gint eventDestroy(GtkWidget *widget,
10         GdkEvent *event,gpointer data);
11
12 int main(int argc,char *argv[])
13 {
14     GtkWidget *window;
15     GtkWidget *agbargraph;
16
17     gnome_init("AgBargraph","1.0",argc,argv);
18     window = gtk_window_new(GTK_WINDOW_TOPLEVEL);
19     gtk_container_set_border_width(GTK_CONTAINER(window),
20             25);
21     gtk_signal_connect(GTK_OBJECT(window),"delete_event",
22             GTK_SIGNAL_FUNC(eventDelete),NULL);
23     gtk_signal_connect(GTK_OBJECT(window),"destroy",
24             GTK_SIGNAL_FUNC(eventDestroy),NULL);
25
26     agbargraph = ag_bargraph_new();
27     ag_bargraph_add(AG_BARGRAPH(agbargraph),"Pickle",82);
28     ag_bargraph_add(AG_BARGRAPH(agbargraph),"Onion",39);
29     ag_bargraph_add(AG_BARGRAPH(agbargraph),"Herring",54);
30     ag_bargraph_add(AG_BARGRAPH(agbargraph),"Sardine",12);
31     ag_bargraph_add(AG_BARGRAPH(agbargraph),"Other",90);
32
33     gtk_container_add(GTK_CONTAINER(window),agbargraph);
34     gtk_widget_show_all(window);
35     gtk_main();
36     exit(0);
37 }
38 gint eventDelete(GtkWidget *widget,
39         GdkEvent *event,gpointer data) {
40     return(FALSE);
41 }
42 gint eventDestroy(GtkWidget *widget,
43         GdkEvent *event,gpointer data) {
44     gtk_main_quit();
45     return(0);
46 }
```

This is a very simple GNOME application program. On lines 17 through 24, the system is uninitialized, a window is created, and the callbacks are set up to close the application.

Lines 26 through 31 create the AgBargraph widget and immediately insert five bar graphs into it. The call to ag_bargraph_new() creates a new and empty widget. Each call to ag_bargraph_add() defines a new bar to be displayed by giving it a name and a value from 0 to 100.

Line 33 calls `gtk_container_add()`, which inserts the widget into the window's container. The call to `gtk_widget_show_all()` realizes all the widgets in the tree, including the `AgBargraph` widget.

The AgBargraph Header File

Each widget has its own header file to define the structures, constants, and functions that are included with the widget. The same header file is included by the application program using the widget, and by the C source code of the widget itself. The following is the header file for the `AgBargraph` widget.

```
 1 /* agbargraph.h */
 2
 3 #ifndef __AG_BARGRAPH_H
 4 #define __AG_BARGRAPH_H
 5
 6 #include <gtk/gtk.h>
 7 #include <gtk/gtkwidget.h>
 8
 9 #ifdef __cplusplus
10 extern "C" {
11 #endif
12
13 #define AG_BARGRAPH(obj) \
14     GTK_CHECK_CAST(obj,ag_bargraph_get_type(),AgBargraph)
15 #define AG_BARGRAPH_CLASS(klass) GTK_CHECK_CLASS_CAST( \
16     klass,ag_bargraph_get_type(),AgBargraphClass)
17 #define AG_IS_BARGRAPH(obj) \
18     GTK_CHECK_TYPE(obj,ag_bargraph_get_type())
19
20 typedef struct _AgBargraph AgBargraph;
21 typedef struct _AgBargraphClass AgBargraphClass:
22 typedef struct _AgBargraphBar AgBargraphBar;
23
24 struct _AgBargraph {
25     GtkWidget widget;
26     GdkColor *outside_color;
27     GdkColor *inside_color;
28     gint maximum_value;
29     gint bar_count;
30     gboolean contains_pointer;
31     AgBargraphBar *bars;
32     gchar *show_text;
33     GdkFont *text_font;
34 };
35
36 struct _AgBargraphClass {
```

```
37      GtkWidgetClass parent_class;
38 };
39
40 struct _AgBargraphBar {
41      gchar *name;
42      gint value;
43      GdkGC *gc;
44      gint x_right;
45      gint x_left;
46 };
47
48 #define AG_BARGRAPH_MAXIMUM 100
49
50 GtkWidget *ag_bargraph_new(void);
51 guint ag_bargraph_get_type(void);
52 void ag_bargraph_add(AgBargraph *agbargraph,
53          gchar *name,gint value);
54
55
56 #ifdef __cplusplus
57 }
58 #endif
59
60 #endif /* __AG_BARGRAPH_H */
```

The precompiler conditionals on lines 3, 4, and 60 prevent the header file from inadvertently being included more than once. This widget uses `GtkWidget` as its parent type, so it is necessary to include `gtk.h` and `gtkwidget.h` — as is done on lines 6 and 7. It is possible to use this widget in a C++ program because the compiler is notified that everything between the braces on lines 10 and 57 is to be compiled as C, not C++. A C++ compiler always defines `__cplusplus`.

The macro `AG_BARGRAPH`, defined on line 13, attempts to cast a pointer to an `AgBargraph` widget pointer — if the pointer is of the wrong type, the cast fails and an error message is emitted. In the same manner, the macro `AG_BARGRAPH_CLASS` defined on line 15 casts a pointer to an `AgBargraphClass` pointer. The macro `AG_IS_BARGRAPH` defined on line 17 returns either `TRUE` or `FALSE` depending on whether the object passed to it is an `AgBargraph` widget.

You can see more of the naming convention in the typedef statements on lines 20 through 22. The structs are defined with a leading underscore, and then the typedef is used to assign the name. Using typedef to define the names of the structs has the advantage of allowing declarations of this form:

```
AgBargraph *bargraph;
```

The struct for the AgBargraph is defined on lines 24 through 34. On line 25, the first thing at the top of the AgBargraph struct is a GtkWidget struct. This means that a pointer to an AgBargraph struct also can be treated as a pointer to a GtkWidget struct—both structs begin at the same address. This is why a pointer to an AgBargraph can be cast to a pointer to a GtkWidget. The top of the GtkWidget struct is declared this way:

```
struct _GtkWidget {
    GtkObject object;
    guint16 private_flags;
        . . .
```

Because the first thing in a GtkWidget struct is a GtkObject, all three of these types share the same starting address. This means that an AgBargraph pointer can be cast to a GtkWidget pointer or a GtkObject pointer, and any GtkWidget pointer can be cast to a GtkWidget pointer. This technique is used in all of the objects of GTK+ and GNOME; the parent object of them all is GtkObject. GtkObject is the parent, or grandparent, of all other objects—it inherits from no other object.

The fields defined on lines 26 through 33 are specific to a single instance of the AgBargraph widget. For example, the bar_count value is incremented each time a new bar is added to the widget, so it can be a different value for each instance of AgBargraph. It is this trick of storing all of the variable information in a single struct that makes it so easy to create and manage multiple instances. The class struct _AgBargraphClass on line 36 holds any fields that are defined for the entire class of objects, instead of just for a single instance. For example, the text_font defined on line 33 can be used to set the font independently for each instance of AgBargraph. If the text_font field were included in the class struct instead, changing it once would apply the change to all instances of the widget. In this example, the AgBargraphClass struct contains only the class struct of its parent class.

The struct _AgBargraphBar on line 40 contains the data required to define a single bar. Each time a new bar is added to the widget, a structure of this type is added to the array named bars on line 31.

The function prototypes are defined on lines 50 through 53. These are the nonstatic functions—the ones an application program calls. There is always at least one "new" function so the object can be created, and one "type" function so the object can be identified by a unique type ID number. Normally, there are several other functions that can be used to control the widget. In this example, the only customizing function is ag_bargraph_add(), which adds a new bar to the widget. Some functions can be designed to operate on the entire class, while others operate on one specific instance. A function that operates on a specific instance has a widget pointer as its first argument (so the function knows which instance to operate on), while a class-level function needs no such pointer because it operations apply to the entire class.

The AgBargraph Widget

The following is a description of the C source code of the `AgBargraph` widget.

Although not required, it seems that all widgets are written as a single source-code file. Because this same file is used for both public and private functions, you should declare the private functions as `static` to guard against an application calling them directly. Because static functions can be referenced only from within a single source file, it is probably best to include all the code in one file so the static functions can be called from any of the other functions. The source file begins with the #include files and prototypes of the static functions.

The following listing is a bit larger and more complicated than the others, so I split it into pieces and describe each part separately.

```
 1 /* agbargraph.c */
 2
 3 #include "agbargraph.h"
 4
 5 #include <stdio.h>
 6 #include <stdlib.h>
 7
 8 static void ag_bargraph_class_init(AgBargraphClass *klass);
 9 static void ag_bargraph_init(AgBargraph *bargraph);
10 static void ag_bargraph_realize(GtkWidget *widget);
11 static void ag_bargraph_size_allocate(GtkWidget *widget,
12         GtkAllocation *allocation);
13 static void ag_bargraph_send_configure(
14         AgBargraph *bargraph);
15 static void ag_bargraph_draw(GtkWidget *widget,
16         GdkRectangle *area);
17 static gint ag_bargraph_event(GtkWidget *widget,
18         GdkEvent *event);
19 static void ag_bargraph_size_request(GtkWidget *widget,
20         GtkRequisition *requisition);
21 static void ag_bargraph_destroy(GtkObject *object);
22 static void ag_bargraph_paint(GtkWidget *widget);
23 static void ag_bargraph_add_gc(GtkWidget *widget,
24         AgBargraphBar *bar);
25 static void ag_bargraph_set_text(GtkWidget *widget,
26         GdkEventButton *event);
27 static void ag_bargraph_paint_text(GtkWidget *widget);
28
```

Line 3 includes the header file that defines the widget. There are really two kinds of static functions in a widget. They are the private utility functions, such as `ag_bargraph_paint()`, that are called from other functions inside this same file and the callback functions, such as `ag_bargraph_destroy()`, that are called by the parent or grandparent widgets.

The function `ag_bargraph_get_type()` on line 29 is one of the two required, nonstatic functions. This function is required because every widget must register itself with the system and be assigned a unique ID number. The ID numbers are assigned dynamically, so there is no need for you to invent some kind of unique number. This also means that making a call to this function is the only way to determine the ID number.

```
29 guint ag_bargraph_get_type(void)
30 {
31     static guint ag_bargraph_type = 0;
32
33     if(!ag_bargraph_type) {
34         static const GtkTypeInfo ag_bargraph_info = {
35             "AgBargraph",
36             sizeof(AgBargraph),
37             sizeof(AgBargraphClass),
38             (GtkClassInitFunc)ag_bargraph_class_init,
39             (GtkObjectInitFunc)ag_bargraph_init,
40             NULL,
41             NULL,
42             (GtkClassInitFunc)NULL
43         };
44         ag_bargraph_type = gtk_type_unique(
45             gtk_widget_get_type(),&ag_bargraph_info);
46     }
47     return(ag_bargraph_type);
48 }
```

The type number is stored in the static variable `ag_bargraph_type` declared on line 31 making it present only inside this function. The first time this function is called, a call is made to the function `gtk_type_unique()` on line 44 to register the class and get a unique ID for it. The registration only happens once because later calls simply return the ID number on line 47. If you write your own widget, just insert the function as it is and change the widget names.

The `ag_bargraph_new()` function on line 49 is the second of the two required, nonstatic functions. It is used to create and return a new widget. This example doesn't, but a creation function may require arguments to be used in the creation process. Most widgets have only one creation function, but there are exceptions. For example, to create a button widget, you can call `gtk_button_create()` or `gtk_button_create_with_label()`. The only difference between the two is the arguments that are passed to the function.

```
49 GtkWidget *ag_bargraph_new()
50 {
51     GtkWidget *widget =
52         GTK_WIDGET(gtk_type_new(ag_bargraph_get_type()));
53     return(widget);
54 }
55
```

An application program creates a AgBargraph widget with a call to gtk_type_new()
on line 52. The only argument is the widget type ID number, retrieved by a call to
ag_bargraph_get_type(). You can construct the entire widget this way because
the registration information, on lines 34 through 42, supplies all the information
necessary.

The function ag_bargraph_class_init(), defined on line 56, is specified as the
class initialization function on line 38. It is called once at the beginning of each
widget creation to initialize the class. The primary purpose is to establish the
callback functions. Which of these functions you actually override depends on the
needs of your widget. This widget replaces five functions in the GtkWidget parent
class and one function in the GtkObject grandparent class.

```
56 static void ag_bargraph_class_init(AgBargraphClass *klass)
57 {
58      GtkWidgetClass *widget_class;
59      GtkObjectClass *object_class;
60
61      widget_class = (GtkWidgetClass *)klass;
62      object_class = (GtkObjectClass *)klass;
63
64      widget_class->realize = ag_bargraph_realize;
65      widget_class->draw = ag_bargraph_draw;
66      widget_class->event = ag_bargraph_event;
67      widget_class->size_request = ag_bargraph_size_request;
68      widget_class->size_allocate =
69                              ag_bargraph_size_allocate;
70
71      object_class->destroy = ag_bargraph_destroy;
72 }
```

The callback functions that respond to the callback capabilities of a GtkWidget are
specified on lines 64 through 69. The address of each callback is stored in a class-
level function pointer. The function ag_bargraph_realize() is set to be called only
once—immediately after the widget is first realized. Whenever the widget's window
needs to be drawn, the function ag_bargraph_draw() is called. The function
ag_bargraph_event() is called with each event. The functions ag_bargraph_
size_request() and ag_bargraph_size_allocate() are called by the container
widget to negotiate the widget's window size. On line 71, the assignment causes
ag_bargraph_destroy() to be called to destroy the widget.

The function ag_bargraph_init(), on line 73, is assigned as the widget's
initialization function on line 39. This function sets all of the initial values in the
widget struct.

```
73 static void ag_bargraph_init(AgBargraph *bargraph)
74 {
75      GdkColor *color;
```

```
76
77      color = g_malloc(sizeof(GdkColor));
78      color->red = 45000;
79      color->blue = 15000;
80      color->green = 15000;
81      bargraph->outside_color = color;
82
83      color = g_malloc(sizeof(GdkColor));
84      color->red = 45000;
85      color->blue = 45000;
86      color->green = 45000;
87      bargraph->inside_color = color;
88
89      bargraph->bar_count = 0;
90      bargraph->bars = NULL;
91      bargraph->maximum_value = AG_BARGRAPH_MAXIMUM;
92      bargraph->contains_pointer = FALSE;
93 }
```

When `ag_bargraph_init()` is called, the widget has not been realized so the only initializations you can do are those that don't require window information. In this example, the pair of `GtkColor` structs are created and initialized on lines 77 through 97. While red, green, and blue colors are defined, the color itself is not allocated because there is no color map available yet. Lines 89 through 92 set other default values, and they also ensure that the pointers are set to `NULL`.

The function `ag_bargraph_realize()`, on line 94, is called upon realization of the widget because it will have been assigned this task on line 64. The size and position of the widget's window is determined, and the window should be created and configured.

```
 94 static void ag_bargraph_realize(GtkWidget *widget)
 95 {
 96      AgBargraph *bargraph;
 97      GdkWindowAttr attributes;
 98      guint attributes_mask;
 99
100      g_return_if_fail(widget != NULL);
101      g_return_if_fail(AG_IS_BARGRAPH(widget));
102
103      bargraph = AG_BARGRAPH(widget);
104
105      GTK_WIDGET_SET_FLAGS(widget,GTK_REALIZED);
106
107      attributes.window_type = GDK_WINDOW_CHILD;
108      attributes.x = widget->allocation.x;
109      attributes.y = widget->allocation.y;
110      attributes.width = widget->allocation.width;
111      attributes.height = widget->allocation.height;
```

```
112        attributes.wclass = GDK_INPUT_OUTPUT;
113        attributes.visual = gtk_widget_get_visual(widget);
114        attributes.colormap = gtk_widget_get_colormap(widget);
115        attributes.event_mask = gtk_widget_get_events(widget);
116        attributes.event_mask |= (GDK_EXPOSURE_MASK |
117                                   GDK_BUTTON_PRESS_MASK |
118                                   GDK_BUTTON_RELEASE_MASK |
119                                   GDK_ENTER_NOTIFY_MASK |
120                                   GDK_LEAVE_NOTIFY_MASK);
121
122        attributes_mask = GDK_WA_X | GDK_WA_Y
123               | GDK_WA_VISUAL | GDK_WA_COLORMAP;
124        widget->window = gdk_window_new(
125               gtk_widget_get_parent_window(widget),
126               &attributes,attributes_mask);
127
128        gdk_window_set_user_data(widget->window,widget);
129
130        widget->style = gtk_style_attach(widget->style,
131               widget->window);
132        gtk_style_set_background(widget->style,
133               widget->window,GTK_STATE_NORMAL);
134
135        ag_bargraph_send_configure(AG_BARGRAPH(widget));
136
137        gdk_color_alloc(gtk_widget_get_colormap(widget),
138               bargraph->outside_color);
139        gdk_color_alloc(gtk_widget_get_colormap(widget),
140               bargraph->inside_color);
141 }
```

The `GTK_WIDGET_SET` macro on line 105 is used to set the flag indicating that the widget has been realized. There are a lot of options that can be set when creating a new window, so the arguments are stored in the `GdkWindowAttr` struct defined on line 97 and this struct is used as an argument to the call to `gdk_window_new()` on line 124. Some of the values in the `GdkWindowAttr` struct are required and some are optional—the optional values are ignored unless they have a corresponding flag set, like the ones set in the `attributes_mask` on line 122.

Table 18-1 lists all of the fields of the `GdkWindowAttr` struct and the flag values associated with each one. The flags are used for you to determine which fields contain valid window specification data. If a field has a flag associated with it, the flag bit must be set to 1 in the flag mask passed to the `gdk_window_new()` to cause the supplied value to be used by `gdk_window_new()`. If the flag bit is 0, the default value will be used instead of the one in `GdkWindowAttr`.. Some of the fields have no flags defined for them because the value stored in the `GdkWindowAttr` struct is always used—that is, they are the required arguments. One of the required arguments is the type of window being created. The window type must be one of those listed in Table 18-2.

Table 18-1
The Fields and Flag Settings for GdkWindowAttr

Field	Flag	Description
`gchar *title`	`GDK_WA_TITLE`	The name that appears on the title bar of the window. The default is the name of the program.
`gint event_mask`		The flags determining the events this window receives.
`guint16 x`	`GDK_WA_X`	The horizontal pixel position in relation to the parent window. The default is zero.
`guint16 y`	`GDK_WA_Y`	The vertical pixel position in relation to the parent window. The default is zero.
`guint16 width`		The width of the window in pixels.
`guint16 height`		The height of the window in pixels.
`GdkWindowClass wclass`		A `GDK_INPUT_ONLY` window does not display, but it does accept input events. A `GDK_INPUT_OUTPUT` window both accepts events and displays.
`GdkVisual *visual`	`GDK_WA_VISUAL`	The visual used with this window. If it is not specified, there is a standard default of `GdkVisual` that is used.
`GdkColorMap *colormap`	`GDK_WA_COLORMAP`	The color map used with this window. The default is the system color map (which matches with the default visual).

Field	Flag	Description
`GdkWindowType window_type`		One of the types described in Table 18-2.
`GdkCursor *cursor`	`GDK_WA_CURSOR`	The mouse cursor for this window. The default is the cursor of the parent window.
`gchar *wmclass_name` `gchar *wmclass_class`	`GDK_WA_WMCLASS`	The name and class used for hints. The default is no hints.
`gboolean override_redirect`	`GDK_WA_NOREDIR`	If TRUE, the window manager has no control over the size or position of this window. The default is FALSE (unless the window type is GDK_WINDOW_TEMP).

Table 18-2
The Types of Windows Defined by GdkWindowType

Type	Description
`GDK_WINDOW_ROOT`	The root window covering the entire screen.
`GDK_WINDOW_TOPLEVEL`	The window created by an application as a main window. It normally is framed by a title bar and control menus. It can act as a parent to a number of child windows.
`GDK_WINDOW_CHILD`	A window that is contained inside, and is a child of, a top-level window.
`GDK_WINDOW_DIALOG`	The same as a top-level window, except the window manager is notified that it is a dialog window (and possibly could be treated differently).
`GDK_WINDOW_TEMP`	A window that has a short life, such as a pull-down menu. It is a top-level window without a title bar and control. This window always overrides redirect, which restricts the window manager's control. (For instance, a pull-down menu may extend beyond what otherwise would be its parent window.)

Continued

Table 18-2 *(continued)*

Type	Description
GDK_WINDOW_PIXMAP	The window is stored in memory, and it does not appear on the display. Both a pixmap and a window are considered GdkDrawable objects because the same set of functions can be used to write to either of them.
GDK_WINDOW_FOREIGN	A window not created by GDK+.

The events that are sent to this widget are specified on lines 116 through 120, including the events that are sent to the parent widget. Also, there are five events that are required by this application, so they are set whether or not they also are set in the parent widget.

The call to gdk_window_set_user_data() on line 128 specifies the data to be passed as the first arguments is the widget itself. The call to gtk_style_attach() on line 130 examines the style attached to the window, initializes it, and (if necessary) makes updates and changes to it. It then returns a pointer to a (possibly new) style. The call to gtk_style_set_background() on line 132 initializes the background to display the way it is described in the style, whether a flat color, a pixmap, a stipple, or whatever. Because this is the only state for this widget, there is no need to initialize any other states.

The parent widget needs to be notified of the size and location of the display, so a call is made to ag_bargraph_send_configure() on line 135 to create a GdkEvent Configure event and send it to the parent widget.

The final act of initialization is to allocate the colors from the color map. The calls to gdk_color_alloc() on lines 137 through 140 use the RGB information, stored in the structs on lines 77 through 87, to allocate the colors with the appropriate value for the color map.

The function ag_bargraph_destroy() on line 142 is called whenever the widget is to be destroyed because it is assigned as the "destroy" callback function on line 71. This function's purpose is to free all allocated memory and release any other system resources.

```
142 static void ag_bargraph_destroy(GtkObject *object)
143 {
144     int i;
145     AgBargraph *bargraph;
146     AgBargraphClass *klass;
147
148     g_return_if_fail(object != NULL);
```

```
149        g_return_if_fail(AG_IS_BARGRAPH(object));
150
151        bargraph = AG_BARGRAPH(object);
152        g_free(bargraph->outside_color);
153        g_free(bargraph->inside_color);
154        for(i=0; i<bargraph->bar_count; i++) {
155            g_free(bargraph->bars[i].name);
156            if(bargraph->bars[i].gc != NULL)
157                gdk_gc_destroy(bargraph->bars[i].gc);
158        }
159        g_free(bargraph->bars);
160
161        if(bargraph->text_font != NULL)
162            gdk_font_unref(bargraph->text_font);
163
164        klass = gtk_type_class(gtk_widget_get_type());
165        if(GTK_OBJECT_CLASS(klass)->destroy)
166            (* GTK_OBJECT_CLASS(klass)->destroy)(object);
167 }
```

Lines 151 through 159 free any memory blocks that were allocated by this widget.
Also, on line 157, any existing graphics contexts are destroyed. On line 162, if a font
object is created, its reference count is reduced by one. If the count reduces to
zero, the font deletes itself. If the count does not become zero, the same font is in
use elsewhere in the program.

Lines 164 through 166 call the destroy function of the object. At this point, everything
that your widget allocated has been released, so it is only necessary to call the
destroy function of the parent widget so it can do the same for its allocations. The
call to the destroy() function on line 166 returns all memory to the system—the
widget ceases to exist.

The function ag_bargraph_draw() on line 168 is called whenever the widget needs
to be drawn into a window because it is assigned as the callback on line 65. This
happens when the program first starts running (right after its window is realized). It
also happens when the window is resized.

```
168 static void ag_bargraph_draw(GtkWidget *widget,
169         GdkRectangle *area)
170 {
171     g_return_if_fail(widget != NULL);
172     g_return_if_fail(AG_IS_BARGRAPH(widget));
173
174     ag_bargraph_paint(widget);
175 }
```

The function ag_bargraph_draw() does not do the drawing itself. The actual
drawing is accomplished through the call to ag_bargraph_paint() on line 174. In
a more complex widget (that is, one that takes a while to render), you may want to

consider clipping the output to the rectangular area specified on line 169 by the GtkRectangle object. This rectangle indicates the only area inside the window that needs to be drawn.

The function called whenever an event arrives is ag_bargraph_event() on line 176. The events selected by the flags on lines 115 through 120 all set up a call to this function.

```
176  static gint ag_bargraph_event(GtkWidget *widget,
177          GdkEvent *event)
178  {
179      AgBargraph *bargraph;
180
181      g_return_val_if_fail(widget != NULL,FALSE);
182      g_return_val_if_fail(AG_IS_BARGRAPH(widget),FALSE);
183
184      bargraph = AG_BARGRAPH(widget);
185
186      switch(event->type) {
187      case GDK_ENTER_NOTIFY:
188          bargraph->contains_pointer = TRUE;
189          break;
190      case GDK_LEAVE_NOTIFY:
191          bargraph->contains_pointer = FALSE;
192          break;
193      case GDK_BUTTON_PRESS:
194          ag_bargraph_set_text(widget,
195                  (GdkEventButton *)event);
196          break;
197      case GDK_BUTTON_RELEASE:
198          bargraph->show_text = NULL;
199          break;
200      case GDK_EXPOSE:
201          break;
202      default:
203          return(FALSE);
204      }
205      ag_bargraph_paint(widget);
206      return(TRUE);
207  }
```

The switch statement on line 186 selects actions according to the type of event. The Boolean value contains_pointer is toggled on and off as the mouse pointer enters and exits the window. Whenever a button is pressed, the text to be displayed is determined by a call to ag_bargraph_set_text(). If the event is to have no effect on the display, the default action on line 203 is executed and the function returns having taken no action. Conversely, if it is one of the events that changes the display, the function ag_bargraph_paint() is called on line 205 to update the display.

The function `ag_bargraph_set_text()` on line 208 determines which bar currently is beneath the mouse pointer and stores a pointer to the bar's name in the location that the paint function uses to display the name.

```
208 static void ag_bargraph_set_text(GtkWidget *widget,
209           GdkEventButton *event)
210 {
211     int i;
212
213     AgBargraph *bargraph = AG_BARGRAPH(widget);
214
215     bargraph->show_text = NULL;
216     for(i=0; i<bargraph->bar_count; i++) {
217         if((event->x > bargraph->bars[i].x_left) &&
218           (event->x <= bargraph->bars[i].x_right)) {
219             bargraph->show_text = bargraph->bars[i].name;
220             return;
221         }
222     }
223 }
```

The function `ag_bargraph_paint()` on line 224 draws the complete widget window. Part of its job is to calculate the horizontal and vertical positions of the bars. These calculations are done as floating-point numbers because integer arithmetic tends to accumulate small errors that leave a gap or create an overlap. This also can happen when a floating-point number is converted to an integer pixel, but the error, if any, will be much smaller.

```
224 static void ag_bargraph_paint(GtkWidget *widget)
225 {
226     int i;
227     AgBargraph *bargraph = AG_BARGRAPH(widget);
228     float bar_percent;
229     float bar_width;
230     float bar_height;
231     float bar_x;
232     float bar_y;
233
234     if(bargraph->contains_pointer) {
235         gdk_window_set_background(widget->window,
236                 bargraph->inside_color);
237     } else {
238         gdk_window_set_background(widget->window,
239                 bargraph->outside_color);
240     }
241     gdk_window_clear(widget->window);
242
243     bar_x = 0;
244     bar_width = (float)widget->allocation.width /
```

```
245                (float)bargraph->bar_count;
246        for(i=0; i<bargraph->bar_count; i++) {
247            if(bargraph->bars[i].gc == NULL)
248                ag_bargraph_add_gc(widget,&bargraph->bars[i]);
249            bar_percent = (float)bargraph->bars[i].value /
250                    (float)bargraph->maximum_value;
251            bar_height = bar_percent
252                        * (float)widget->allocation.height;
253            bar_y = (float)widget->allocation.height
254                        * (1.0 - bar_percent);
255            gdk_draw_rectangle(widget->window,
256                    bargraph->bars[i].gc,TRUE,
257                    (gint)bar_x,(gint)bar_y,
258                    (gint)bar_width + 1,(gint)bar_height + 1);
259            bargraph->bars[i].x_left = (gint)bar_x;
260            bar_x += bar_width;
261            bargraph->bars[i].x_right = (gint)bar_x;
262        }
263        ag_bargraph_paint_text(widget);
264 }
```

The if statement on line 234 checks whether the cursor is inside the window
(using the Boolean value set on lines 188 and 191) to select the color for the
background. Then, the window is filled with the background color by the call to
gdk_window_clear() on line 241.

The size and position of each bar is calculated in the loop beginning on line 246. If
this is the first time a particular bar is displayed, a graphics context is constructed
for it by a call to ag_bargraph_add_gc(). The graphics context is constructed at
the last minute to make it simpler to add a new bar to the widget at any time. Once
the size and position of the bar is determined, it is drawn onto the window by a call
to gtk_draw_rectangle() on line 255. At the bottom of the loop, lines 259 through
261, the two x values marking the edges of the bar are saved as part of the bar
information, and the bar_x value is incremented to the start position of the next
bar. Finally, on line 263, a call is made to ag_bargraph_paint_text() so the
selected bar's text can be displayed.

If the show_text pointer for the widget is not NULL, it contains the address of a
string of characters that are to be displayed. Whether or not the pointer is NULL is
determined by the event processing on lines 193 through 199. Only text is present
while a mouse button is held down.

```
265 static void ag_bargraph_paint_text(GtkWidget *widget)
266 {
267     AgBargraph *bargraph = AG_BARGRAPH(widget);
268     gint lbearing;
269     gint rbearing;
270     gint width;
271     gint ascent;
```

```
272        gint descent;
273        gint x;
274        gint y;
275
276        if(bargraph->show_text == NULL)
277            return;
278
279        if(bargraph->text_font == NULL) {
280          bargraph->text_font = gdk_font_load(
281          "-*-bookman-light-r-normal--18-*-*-*-p-*-iso8859-1");
282        }
283        gdk_text_extents(bargraph->text_font,
284                    bargraph->show_text,
285                    strlen(bargraph->show_text),
286                    &lbearing,
287                    &rbearing,
288                    &width,
289                    &ascent,
290                    &descent);
291        y = ascent;
292        x = (widget->allocation.width / 2) - (width / 2);
293
294        gdk_draw_string(widget->window,
295                bargraph->text_font,
296                widget->style->black_gc,
297                x,y,
298                bargraph->show_text);
299 }
```

If this is the first time text is to be displayed, the font is defined by the call to
gdk_font_load() on lines 279 through 282. Then the call to gtk_text_extents()
is made on line 283. The x and y values set from it, on lines 291 and 292, are used to
position the text at the top center of the window. The string is drawn by the call to
gtk_draw_string() on line 294.

Each bar is a different color, and the colors are set by the function ag_bargraph_
add_gc() on line 300. For this example, the color assigned to each bar is selected
randomly. (Actually, it is pseudo-random because it is the same sequence of colors
each time you run the program.)

```
300 static void ag_bargraph_add_gc(GtkWidget *widget,
301         AgBargraphBar *bar)
302 {
303     GdkColor color;
304     GdkColormap *colormap;
305
306     bar->gc = gdk_gc_new(widget->window);
307     color.red += (((double)rand()*0xFFFF)/RAND_MAX);
308     color.green += (((double)rand()*0xFFFF)/RAND_MAX);
309     color.blue += (((double)rand()*0xFFFF)/RAND_MAX);
```

```
310
311     colormap = gtk_widget_get_colormap(widget);
312
313     gdk_color_alloc(colormap,&color);
314     gdk_gc_set_foreground(bar->gc,&color);
315 }
```

The functions `ag_bargraph_size_request()` on line 316 and `ag_bargraph_size_allocate()` on line 325 work together to determine the size and position of the widget. These two functions are set up as sizing callbacks on lines 67 and 68 and they are called by any container widget that has the job of containing an `AgBargraph` **widget.**

```
316 static void ag_bargraph_size_request(GtkWidget *widget,
317         GtkRequisition *requisition)
318 {
319     g_return_if_fail(widget != NULL);
320     g_return_if_fail(AG_IS_BARGRAPH(widget));
321
322     requisition->width = 200;
323     requisition->height = 100;
324 }
325 static void ag_bargraph_size_allocate(GtkWidget *widget,
326         GtkAllocation *allocation)
327 {
328     g_return_if_fail(widget != NULL);
329     g_return_if_fail(AG_IS_BARGRAPH(widgct));
330     g_return_if_fail(allocation != NULL);
331
332     widget->allocation.x = allocation->x;
333     widget->allocation.y = allocation->y;
334     widget->allocation.width = allocation->width;
335     widget->allocation.height = allocation->height;
336
337     if(GTK_WIDGET_REALIZED(widget)) {
338         gdk_window_move_resize(widget->window,
339             allocation->x,allocation->y,
340             allocation->width,allocation->height);
341         ag_bargraph_send_configure(AG_BARGRAPH(widget));
342     }
343 }
```

The process of determining the size of a widget is referred to as *negotiating* the size. But the final say is in the hands of the container. First, the container calls the function `ag_bargraph_size_request()` to retrieve the preferred size of the widget. The container then uses the values returned to it, weighs this against i ts other requirements and constraints to calculate the actual size, and calls `ag_bargraph_size_allocate()` with its final decision on the size and position. The size and location values are stored in the widget on lines 332 through 335. If the widget already is realized then there already is a window. Therefore, on line 338, the existing window is resized and moved to the new location. Additionally, a call to `ag_bargraph_send_configure()` on line 341 issues a reconfigure event that causes the widget to redraw itself to fit the new dimensions.

This widget size negotiation can become quite involved. For example: An `AgBargraph` widget is contained in a frame, which is contained by a vertical box, which, in turn, is contained by the main window. All of these widgets must be involved in the negotiations. The query starts at the very top (the single-widget container of the top-level window) by asking the vertical box how big it should be. The vertical box then asks the same of all the widgets it contains — one of which is the frame. The frame asks the `AgBargraph`. The frame takes the numbers returned to it, adds its own required dimensions to them, and returns the results to the vertical box. The box adds together all of the dimensions from all of its children (perhaps deciding to resize some of them so they fit better) and passes the result on up to the container in the main window. The main window container then decides what the overall size should be and makes the function call telling the vertical box its width and height. In turn, the vertical box divides up the sizes and calls the functions for each of its contained widgets, telling them their sizes. This continues on down until the `AgBargraph` finds out what size it must be, and displays itself that way.

The function `ag_bargraph_send_configure()` on line 344 is not necessary for this widget, but there are cases in which it is needed. For example, if instead of extending `GtkWidget`, this were an extension of `GtkButton`, then the button widget would need to be informed of the change in size, so it could resize the label widget it contains.

```
344 static void ag_bargraph_send_configure(
345         AgBargraph *bargraph)
346 {
347     GtkWidget *widget;
348     GdkEventConfigure event;
349
350     widget = GTK_WIDGET(bargraph);
351
352     event.type = GDK_CONFIGURE;
353     event.window = widget->window;
354     event.x = widget->allocation.x;
355     event.y = widget->allocation.y;
356     event.width = widget->allocation.width;
357     event.height = widget->allocation.height;
358
359     gtk_widget_event(widget,(GdkEvent *)&event);
360 }
```

Lines 352 through 357 store the current size and position values in a `GdkEvent Configure` struct. The call to `gtk_widget_event()` on line 359 issues the event to itself causing any function that is configured to receive the event to be executed.

The function `ag_bargraph_add()` on line 361 is called by the application to add a new bar to the graph.

```
361  void ag_bargraph_add(AgBargraph *bargraph,gchar *name,
362        gint value)
363  {
364      AgBargraphBar *newbars;
365      gint newcount;
366
367      g_return_if_fail(bargraph != NULL);
368      g_return_if_fail(AG_IS_BARGRAPH(bargraph));
369
370      newcount = bargraph->bar_count + 1;
371      newbars = g_malloc(sizeof(AgBargraphBar) * newcount);
372      memcpy(newbars,bargraph->bars,
373          sizeof(AgBargraphBar) * bargraph->bar_count);
374      newbars[bargraph->bar_count].name = g_strdup(name);
375      newbars[bargraph->bar_count].value = value;
376      newbars[bargraph->bar_count].gc = NULL;
377
378      g_free(bargraph->bars);
379      bargraph->bars = newbars;
380      bargraph->bar_count = newcount;
381  }
```

A new bar is created on line 371. The bars are kept in the `bars` array in the `AgBargraph` struct, which extends each time a new bar is added. The extension is achieved by creating a new array, copying the pointers from the old array to the new, and then deleting the old array. The name and value of the bar are stored, but the graphics context is set to `NULL`. The graphics context cannot be created here because this function may be called before any windows are realized, so the `ag_bargraph_paint()` function assumes the responsibility of setting up the graphics context on line 248.

Widget Changes and Upgrades

Because a widget is an object, and because the object is a closed system, it is possible to make additions and modifications without causing a problem in any of the application programs that use it. If the existing API functions — the public ones with their prototypes in `agbargraph.h` — remain and perform the same actions, any number of changes can be made inside the widget, and new functions can be added. You can go ahead and make any changes you like, but be sure to keep the default appearance and action unchanged from the original. That way, any existing software still works while the new capabilities also are available. This is probably the single greatest advantage of object-oriented programming — well, it may be second behind the ability to locate a function quickly that is doing a specific job.

If you need to make basic changes to a widget in such a way that breaks existing applications, it probably is a better idea to write a new widget and use the AgBargraph parent widget (instead of GtkWidget). That way, your new widget can retain the features it likes and change the ones it doesn't. It is not uncommon to have widget inheritance run four or five levels deep.

The AgBargraph widget was left very simple intentionally to demonstrate the structure of a widget. There are a number of things that you can do to add customization control over the widget. For example, you can add the following function to allow the application program to set the maximum value:

```
ag_bargraph_set_maximum(AgBargraph *bargraph,gint value)
{
    bargraph->maximum_value = value;
}
```

You can do the same sort of thing for a minimum value, but some changes need to be made in the size and position calculations. This is because, as the code stands, a minimum value of zero is simply assumed.

You also can make the maximum value dynamic. The default could be to have it work the way it does now (with a fixed maximum) but have the option of allowing the widget itself to determine the maximum value from the bar data added to it. You set this option by adding a creation function that turns it on:

```
GtkWidget *ag_bargraph_new_autoadjust();
```

This function does the same thing as ag_bargraph_new(), but it also sets a flag that causes the maximum value to be adjusted every time a new bar is added. The original functionality is retained, and a new feature is added.

There are a number of things that you can do with this widget to make it more useful and more attractive. For example, you can add a pair of functions to specify the two background colors used when the mouse enters and leaves the widget window. Or you can add color-setting options to the argument list of ag_bargraph_new(). The drawing of the bars also could be made more attractive. You can make them look like three-dimensional blocks. There also can be options to draw the bars horizontally, display the longest first (or last), annotate each one with its name, annotate each one with its numeric value, and so on.

Summary

There are a lot of things to consider when writing a widget, but the basic inheritance struct of GTK+ simplifies things and provides a well-defined structure. If you have a particular displayable item that is repeated (especially if it is duplicated in more than one application), you should consider making it into a widget to standardize the controls and simplify the application program's interface. This chapter included the fundamental mechanics of constructing a widget:

✦ A widget is an object in a hierarchy of objects. Every widget has a `GtkWidget` in its ancestry, and `GtkObject` is the parent of `GtkWidget`. `GtkObject` has no parent.

✦ A custom widget can be contained, controlled, and displayed in exactly the same way as any one of the GTK+ widgets.

✦ A widget is defined in two files — a C source file containing the functions of the widget, and a C header file containing the data definitions and the externally available function prototypes.

✦ There are a number of static functions inside a widget. Many of these functions are assigned the task of responding to callbacks to change the configuration settings, respond to user events, or display the window.

✦ You can extend any widget to create a new widget. If there is already a widget that does something very similar to what you want, it is possible to inherit the capabilities of the existing widget or add your own.

The next chapter — the last chapter in the step-by-step part of the book — discusses how your program can respond to its environment to modify its action. First, your program can store and retrieve environmental settings, which will allow it to adapt to the preferences of a user. Second, it is possible to design your application in such a way that it will automatically translate itself into the local language.

✦   ✦   ✦

Configuration and Internation- alization

◆ ◆ ◆ ◆

In This Chapter

Reading a collection
of environment
settings that can be
used to configure
your application

Writing customized
environment settings
so they will be
available the next
time your appli-
cation runs

Shaping the code of
your program so it
can be translated into
another language
when it is run

◆ ◆ ◆ ◆

This chapter discusses two related subjects. One subject is the configuration settings that your application can save and restore, and the other is the method of having your program automatically translate itself when used in different locales.

By default, the configuration settings are stored in the user's home directory. This means that there can be different settings for each user. Also, the configuration values are stored in plain ASCII, so anyone having access to them can edit or otherwise process them if necessary.

Internationalization (also called *i18n*, because there are 18 letters between i and n) is fairly automated. When the code is written, the strings that are to be translated are marked. Using these marked strings, a human translates them into another language and installs them on disk. When users start the program, and the locale indicates that the text should be translated, the software replaces the strings in the program with their translations.

Environmental Control

A program can have user configuration files to hold settings and values that persist from one invocation of the program to the next. For example, if while running your application, the user changes the font, the size of the window, and some colors, then these values need to be stored so they can be retrieved and used the next time the program is run.

The GNOME API includes a set of functions that can be used to store values so they can be retrieved and used later. When your program starts to run, it can read the configuration settings and use the values found to customize its operation. The program also can read the configuration values and, optionally, change them and write them back. Because the configuration settings are kept in a file on disk, they persist from one invocation of the program to the next.

The Configuration File Format

The configuration is stored in an ASCII text file. The file format includes categories with keys inside each category. The key is associated with a value. This is an example file containing two headings and five keys:

```
[winsize]
width=120
height=80

[colornames]
background=white
edges=blue
lettering=gray42
```

The category named `winsize` contains the keys' width and height. Each key value is an integer. The category `colornames` contains the keys' background, edges, and littering. These three keys all have string values. Note that there is no type information included in the file—the program that reads and writes the values determines the actual data type.

The Configuration File Location

The default is for a file to be located in either the `.gnome` or `.gnome_private` subdirectory of the user's home directory. While the `.gnome` directory normally is used, you may find it desirable to store certain configuration data in the `.gnome_private` directory. The difference is that the `.gnome` directory is accessible to the world, while the `.gnome_private` directory normally restricts access to one user. If you plan to store sensitive items, such as passwords, then consider using `.gnome_private`.

The functions address one key value at a time, so the complete path to the key must be specified with each function call. The path name is comprised of three parts in the following format:

```
/filename/category/keyname
```

The `filename` is the name of the file holding the configuration data. Although it starts with a slash, it is not an absolute path name. The actual file path is constructed—including the user's home directory name—like this:

```
/home/fred/.gnome/filename
```

Or, if you use a function call that handles private values, the file path name looks like this:

```
/home/fred/.gnome_private/filename
```

An address always contains three parts: the file, the category, and the name of the key. That is, each address is the full path name to the key. To complete the two previous addresses, the category and key names must be included like this:

```
/home/fred/.gnome/filename/winsize/width
/home/fred/.gnome_private/filename/winsize/width
```

You have another option. By surrounding the file name with equal signs, you can specify an absolute path and place the configuration file anywhere. This is probably the best way to handle any configuration settings you might have that are to be applied to all users. For example:

```
=/var/maxique/config=/colors/background
```

This stores the file with the absolute path name /var/maxique/config.

Reading and Writing a Configuration File

A configuration file is created when an application first writes to it. Reading from a missing configuration file, or attempting to read a nonexistent key, is not an error — the return indicates that the function has a NULL or zero value. The following file is the one that the following example programs read and write:

```
[geometry]
width=8
height=3
margin=15

[id]
name=Homer
nickname=
show_menu=true
time=931815930
```

This file has two categories: geometry and id. The geometry category defines numeric values for width, height, and margin. The id category specifies a name but has no setting for the nickname. The Boolean key show_menu is true, and the time is the time the configuration file was updated last. The following program was used to create this file:

```
1 /** maxique1.c **/
2 #include <gnome.h>
3
4
5 int main(int argc,char *argv[])
```

```
 6 {
 7     gnome_init("maxique1","1.0",argc,argv);
 8     gnome_config_set_int("/maxique/geometry/width",8);
 9     gnome_config_set_int("/maxique/geometry/height",3);
10     gnome_config_set_int("/maxique/geometry/margin",15);
11     gnome_config_set_string("/maxique/id/name","Homer");
12     gnome_config_set_string("/maxique/id/nickname",NULL);
13     gnome_config_set_bool("/maxique/id/show_menu",TRUE);
14     gnome_config_set_int("/maxique/id/time",time(NULL));
15     gnome_config_sync();
16     exit(0);
17 }
```

A look at the path names shows that the file is named `maxique` and is stored in the user's `.gnome` directory. The 'set' routines are used to store the keys and their associated values in memory (not to disk). Lines 8, 9, and 10 each assign a key to an integer value in the `geometry` category. The `id` category is set with the function calls on lines 11 through 14. In each case, the first argument is the full path to the key and the second argument is the value to be assigned to it. The data remains in memory until the function `gnome_config_sync()` is called to write to the disk file. If this function is never called, the file is never updated.

Writing to the file with a call to `gnome_config_sync()` does not overwrite the values already there. That is, if you specify a file that already contains some keys, and you create just one new key (and do nothing else) before calling `gnome_config_sync()` to write to the file, the new key is simply added to the list — all other keys and values remain unchanged.

The following program reads and displays all of the values stored in this configuration file:

```
 1 /** maxique2.c **/
 2 #include <gnome.h>
 3
 4 int main(int argc,char *argv[])
 5 {
 6     time_t timeval;
 7
 8     gnome_init("maxique2","1.0",argc,argv);
 9     g_print("geometry width=%d\n",
10         gnome_config_get_int("/maxique/geometry/width"));
11     g_print("geometry height=%d\n",
12         gnome_config_get_int("/maxique/geometry/height"));
13     g_print("geometry margin=%d\n",
14         gnome_config_get_int("/maxique/geometry/margin"));
15     g_print("id name=%s\n",
16         gnome_config_get_string("/maxique/id/name"));
17     g_print("id nickname=%s\n",
18         gnome_config_get_string("/maxique/id/nickname"));
```

```
19      g_print("id show_menu=%s\n",
20          gnome_config_get_bool("/maxique/id/show_menu")
21          ? "true" : "false");
22      timeval = gnome_config_get_int("/maxique/id/time");
23      g_print("id time=%s",ctime(&timeval));
24      exit(0);
25 }
```

The functions with names that begin with gnome_config_get_ are used to retrieve data from the configuration file. All the data in the file is stored as character strings, so it is up to your program to know the type and make the appropriate conversion (which is done by calling the corresponding function). The output from this program looks like this:

```
geometry width=8
geometry height=3
geometry margin=15
id name=Homer
id nickname=
id show_menu=true
id time=Mon Jul 12 14:20:44 1999
```

Storing and Retrieving a Vector

You can have more than one value assigned to a key. This collection of values can be called a *list*, an *array*, or a *vector*. The GNOME software normally uses the term *vector*. To assign a list of values to a key, you need to create an array of string pointers. The array of string pointers and the strings to which they point are allocated during the action of reading the array from the configuration file.

The following example contains two functions. One creates an array and writes it to the configuration file; the other reads from the configuration file and displays what it finds.

```
1 /** configvec.c **/
2 #include <gnome.h>
3
4 static void retrieveVector();
5 static void storeVector();
6
7 int main(int argc,char *argv[])
8 {
9     gnome_init("configvec","1.0",argc,argv);
10    storeVector();
11    retrieveVector();
12    exit(0);
13 }
14 static void storeVector()
```

```
15 {
16     gint user_count = 5;
17     const gchar *user_name[] = {
18         "fred",
19         "wilford",
20         "ship worth",
21         "norton",
22         "maglin"
23     };
24
25     gnome_config_set_vector("convec/user/names",
26         user_count,user_name);
27     gnome_config_sync();
28 }
29 static void retrieveVector()
30 {
31     gint i;
32     gint user_count;
33     gchar **user_name;
34
35     gnome_config_get_vector("convec/user/list",
36         &user_count,&user_name);
37     for(i=0; i<user_count; i++)
38         printf("%d:  %s\n",i,user_name[i]);
39     g_strfreev(user_name);
40 }
```

The function `storeVector()` on line 14 stores a list of names in the configuration file named `convec`, in the category named `user`, with the key `list`. One of the five names in the array contains a space. The contents of the file look like this:

```
[user]
names=fred wilford ship\\ worth norton maglin
```

The double slash is used as the escape sequence to indicate the next character is not a space, but is part of the name. The function `retrieveVector()` on line 29 reads the list of names and lists each one. The returned array and its strings are allocated, so it is necessary to return the memory back to the system — as is done by the call to `g_strfreev()` on line 39. This is a convenience function to delete each string in an array, and then delete the array itself.

The Data Types of a Configuration File

Table 19-1 lists the various data types available for use in a configuration file. Because there are so many different ways you can manipulate configuration settings, there are a number of functions designed to work with each type.

Table 19-1
Data Types Stored and Retrieved in the Configuration Files

Type	Description
bool	An integer value with zero representing FALSE and nonzero representing TRUE. It is stored in the file as "true" or "false."
float	A 64-bit floating point number (gdouble). It is stored in the file with a decimal point and, if necessary, an exponent.
int	A 32-bit integer (gint). It is stored in the file as base-10 digits.
string	An ASCII string of characters. It can be empty (the zero-length string). It also can contain spaces.
translated string	A character string that may vary depending on the current language setting.
vector	A list of ASCII string values. The vector can be empty; each value may contain spaces.

The following is a descriptive list of the functions available for communicating with the configuration files. All of these functions include the data type as part of its name.

Functions for bool

These are the functions that store bool values in the configuration file:

```
void gnome_config_set_bool(char *path,gboolean val);
void gnome_config_private_set_bool(char *path,gboolean val);
```

The value of val determines whether the string to be stored in the configuration file is "true" or "false." You can use the following functions to retrieve a bool value from the configuration file:

```
gboolean gnome_config_get_bool(char *path);
gboolean gnome_config_get_bool_with_default(char *path,
        gboolean *def);
gboolean gnome_config_private_get_bool(char *path);
gboolean gnome_config_private_get_bool_with_default(char *path,
        gboolean *def);
```

If the value is not found in the configuration file, the default value of FALSE is returned. If the def argument is specified, the gboolean value it points to is set to TRUE — if the value is found in the file. It is set to FALSE if the default value is returned.

Functions for float

These are the functions that store `float` values in the configuration file:

```
void gnome_config_set_float(char *path,gdouble val);
void gnome_config_private_set_float(char *path,gdouble val);
```

The value of `val` is converted to a character string and stored in the configuration file. You can use the following functions to retrieve a `float` value from the configuration file:

```
gdouble gnome_config_get_float(char *path);
gdouble gnome_config_get_float_with_default(char *path,
        gboolean *def);
gdouble gnome_config_private_get_float(char *path);
gdouble gnome_config_private_get_float_with_default(char *path,
        gboolean *def);
```

If the value is not found in the configuration file, the default value of `0.0` is returned. If the `def` argument is specified, the `gboolean` value it points to is set to `TRUE` — if the value is found in the file. It is set to `FALSE` if the default value is returned.

Functions for int

These are the functions that store `int` values in the configuration file:

```
void gnome_config_set_int(char *path,gint val);
void gnome_config_private_set_int(char *path,gint val);
```

The value of `val` is converted to a character string and stored in the configuration file. You can use the following functions to retrieve an `int` value from the configuration file:

```
gint gnome_config_get_int(char *path);
gint gnome_config_get_int_with_default(char *path,
        gboolean *def);
gint gnome_config_private_get_int(char *path);
gint gnome_config_private_get_int_with_default(char *path,
        gboolean *def);
```

If the value is not found in the configuration file, the default value of `0` is returned. If the `def` argument is specified, the `gboolean` value it points to is set to `TRUE` — if the value is found in the file. It is set to `FALSE` if the default value is returned.

Functions for string

These are the functions that store `string` values in the configuration file:

```
void gnome_config_set_string(char *path,gchar *val);
void gnome_config_private_set_string(char *path,gchar *val);
```

The string pointed to by `val` is stored in the configuration file. You can use the following functions to retrieve a `string` value from the configuration file:

```
gchar *gnome_config_get_string(char *path);
gchar *gnome_config_get_string_with_default(char *path,
    gboolean *def);
gchar *gnome_config_private_get_string(char *path);
gchar *gnome_config_private_get_string_with_default(char *path,
    gboolean *def);
```

If the value is not found in the configuration file, `NULL` is returned. If the `def` argument is specified, the `gboolean` value it points to is set to `TRUE` — if the value is found in the file. It is set to `FALSE` if the default value is returned.

Functions for translated_string

These are the functions that store `translated string` values for the currently selected language:

```
void gnome_config_set_translated_string(char *path,gchar *val);
void gnome_config_private_set_translated_string(char *path,
    gchar *val);
```

The string pointed to by `val` is stored in the configuration file. You can use the following functions to retrieve a `translated string` value from the configuration file:

```
gchar *gnome_config_get_translated_string(char *path);
gchar *gnome_config_get_translated_string_with_default(
    char *path,gboolean *def);
gchar *gnome_config_private_get_translated_string(char *path);
gchar *gnome_config_private_get_translated_string_with_default(
    char *path,gboolean *def);
```

If the value is not found in the configuration file, `NULL` is returned. If the `def` argument is specified, the `gboolean` value it points to is set to `TRUE` — if the value is found in the file. It is set to `FALSE` if the default value is returned.

Functions for vector

These are the functions that store `vector` values in the configuration file:

```
void gnome_config_set_vector(const char *path,int argc,
    const char *const argv[])
void gnome_config_private_set_vector(const char *path,
    int argc,const char *const argv[])
```

The value of `argc` is the number of members of the array. Each member of the `argv` array of pointers holds the address of a character string that is written to the configuration file.

```
void gnome_config_get_vector(const char *path,
    int *argcp, char ***argvp)
void gnome_config_get_vector_with_default(
    const char *path,int *argcp,char ***argvp,
    gboolean *def)
void gnome_config_private_get_vector(const char *path,
    int *argcp,char ***argvp)
void gnome_config_private_get_vector_with_default(
    const char *path,int *argcp,char ***argvp,
    gboolean *def)
```

If the value is not found in the configuration file, an empty array is returned. If the def argument is specified, the gboolean value it points to is set to TRUE — if the value is found in the file. It is set to FALSE if the default value is returned.

Internationalization

If it possible that your application may wind up being translated into another language (and with the Internet being what it is today, it's quite likely), there are some steps you can take to facilitate translation. If, inside your source code, you correctly mark the strings that should be translated, the translation process can be automated. While a human translator is necessary to translate each of your text strings into the other language, your application checks its environment to determine which language to use.

The process is quite simple. The following example shows how to do the initial setup, and how to declare strings so they are available for translation.

```
 1 /** translate.c **/
 2 #include <gnome.h>
 3
 4 #define PACKAGE "translate"
 5 #define GNOMELOCALDIR "/usr/share/locale"
 6
 7 GtkWidget *makeBox();
 8 gint eventDelete(GtkWidget *widget,
 9       GdkEvent *event,gpointer data);
10 gint eventDestroy(GtkWidget *widget,
11       GdkEvent *event,gpointer data);
12
13 static gchar *labelstring = N_("Static string");
14
15 int main(int argc,char *argv[])
16 {
17     GtkWidget *window;
18     GtkWidget *box;
19
20     bindtextdomain(PACKAGE,GNOMELOCALDIR);
```

```
21      textdomain(PACKAGE);
22
23      gnome_init("translate","1.0",argc,argv);
24      window = gtk_window_new(GTK_WINDOW_TOPLEVEL);
25      gtk_container_set_border_width(GTK_CONTAINER(window),
26              25);
27      gtk_signal_connect(GTK_OBJECT(window),"delete_event",
28              GTK_SIGNAL_FUNC(eventDelete), NULL);
29      gtk_signal_connect(GTK_OBJECT(window),"destroy",
30              GTK_SIGNAL_FUNC(eventDestroy),NULL);
31
32      box = makeBox();
33      gtk_container_add(GTK_CONTAINER(window),box);
34      gtk_widget_show(window);
35      gtk_main();
36      exit(0);
37 }
38 GtkWidget *makeBox() {
39      GtkWidget *box;
40      GtkWidget *button;
41
42      box = gtk_vbox_new(FALSE,0);
43      gtk_widget_show(box);
44
45      button = gtk_button_new_with_label(_("Inline string"));
46      gtk_box_pack_start(GTK_BOX(box),button,FALSE,FALSE,0);
47      gtk_widget_show(button);
48
49      button = gtk_button_new_with_label(_(labelstring));
50      gtk_box_pack_start(GTK_BOX(box),button,FALSE,FALSE,0);
51      gtk_widget_show(button);
52
53      return(box);
54 }
55 gint eventDelete(GtkWidget *widget,
56          GdkEvent *event,gpointer data) {
57      return(FALSE);
58 }
59 gint eventDestroy(GtkWidget *widget,
60          GdkEvent *event,gpointer data) {
61      gtk_main_quit();
62      return(0);
63 }
```

The definition of PACKAGE on line 4 assigns a package name to the program. There can be more than one application in a package. Any strings that are shared among applications only need to be translated once because they both use the same lookup tables. The definition of GNOMELOCALDIR on line 5 specifies the directory that will hold the translation files. This directory is where the software will look when it needs to make a translation.

Note   The definitions of PACKAGE and GNOMELOCALDIR normally are defined in a header just for that purpose. This file commonly is named config.h and often holds these and other configuration values. The GTK+ and GNOME software development system has its makefiles automatically generate config.h. Also, it is possible to create the definitions using the -D option on the compiler's command line.

The call to bindtextdomain() on line 20 relates the package name with the directory to be searched so any translation requests know where to look. The call to textdomain() on line 21 assigns the current application to the specified package.

The program creates two buttons, each of which has a text label. The first label is declared as a quoted string on line 45. The label is declared as it normally is, except that it is inside the braces of a macro with the name _( ). The name of the macro is the underscore character; the underscore macro marks the string for translation. Created on line 49, the second button also has a translatable label, but this time a variable name is used. The underscore macro is still required, but because the string is defined elsewhere, there is one more step. The string is declared on line 13 and, because it needs to be marked as translatable, it is enclosed in another macro with a short name—the N_( ) macro.

That's all there is to it. Make sure you mark all the strings that require translation (skipping those that don't, as on lines 23 and 27). If all your strings are marked, and your application is translated into another language, they all are translated and inserted into the tables.

There is a drawback to writing translatable code. Your program is very limited in what it can do to create strings dynamically. If you don't know the contents of a string at compile time, it cannot be translated. There is no way to read a string from a file, or from the user's input, and have it translated for display. You can, however, combine untranslated strings with translated strings by using printf() or sprintf(). For example, say the translator finds this string in need of translation:

```
"The last device in the list is %s\n"
```

This string can be translated, and will work just as you may expect, as long as the %s is left somewhere in the string. Things get a little more difficult if there are two variables in the string. For example:

```
"Device number %d has been set to %s mode\n"
```

It can be translated, but the translator must take care that the %d and %s remain in the same order because that is the order the arguments appear on the function call.

Summary

A wide range of environmental settings and controls can be stored in disk files and used to configure your program. This can include color settings, menu items, toolbars, and even the language. The principal items covered in this chapter were:

✦ Configuration settings can be made for each individual user, and can be made to apply to all users. There also are special provisions for security of configuration data.

✦ There is a standard API for saving and restoring configuration data. The data is stored as ASCII, but is converted to and from C data types inside the application.

✦ You can use the two pre-defined macros to mark text included in an application so it can be translated automatically into another language, depending on the environment in which the program is run.

This chapter completes the second, step-by-step, part of the book. The third part of the book contains information of a more general nature, such as a complete widget reference. The first chapter in the third part, Chapter 20, explains using `automake` and `autoconfig` to automate compiling and linking.

✦   ✦   ✦

References and Mechanics

Configuration and Compilation

This chapter provides a list of steps you can take to set up an applications development environment based on GNOME and GTK+.

There are hundreds of ways to set up a software development environment. The make files used throughout this book are simple and easy to use. However, because of their simplicity, they become unwieldy for a large project. Manually updating the make files can become difficult, and is prone to error. There are any number of ways to automate the compile and link process, but GNOME has a semi-standard form it uses so it makes sense to copy these methods and use them for your GNOME applications.

Using this configuration, you still need to maintain some files by hand. But, once you get set up, there is surprisingly little to do to make changes and additions. For example, to change the version number of the system being compiled, you enter the new version number in one place and it automatically is inserted into the code of a header file. If you add a new source module, you enter its name in one place in one file. Consequently, all of its dependencies are determined and it is compiled in with the rest of the code.

Install GNOME Source Code

For GNOME development, you need access to the GNOME source code. It is supplied as part of GNOME, so if you have GNOME installed, you probably already have the source installed.

One of the great advantages of open source is that you can go and look inside a function to see what it *really* does when you call it. Open-source documentation lags behind open-source programming (sometimes so far behind you can't even see it). And, even when you have the documentation, it may leave out that one little tidbit of information you need. For this reason, you need to have the source tucked away somewhere so you can take a peek at it whenever you get stuck.

Note   One very important reason to have the source code is to prevent memory leaks. For example, if a function returns a pointer to a string, you need to know whether it is returning the address of a static string, or whether the string is allocated. If you don't free an allocated string, that's a *memory leak*. If you attempt to free a static string, you produce a *runtime error*.

The organization described in this chapter follows the organization used by GNOME and GTK+. By exploring the source directories, you can find examples of the things described in this chapter. This should give you a good idea of the structure, as well as the sort of things you are able to do.

Set Up the Development Directory

The first job is to create a directory where all development is to take place. This directory will hold some of the basic configuration files and scripts used to configure and control compilation. It also will have subdirectories that contain some system macros and your source code.

There are some things that you need to do only once. After this initial directory is set up, it is easy to add new projects. This structure gives you the flexibility to add source code for new systems and subsystems as needed. Of course, you don't have to do all of your development in the same directory tree; but because there is a bit of initial configuration and setup to do, it usually is a good idea to do it this way. Adding a new development project to an existing configuration is simply a matter of adding a subdirectory or two, putting the source into the new directory, and setting the configuration settings so the directory is found and the source compiled.

A sort of 'minimal' development root directory contains the following files and directories:

```
AUTHORS      Makefile.am    acconfig.h     helloauto/
ChangeLog    NEWS           autogen.sh*    macros/
IDGBIBLE     README         configure.in
```

All of these files, and the macros directory, are explained in the sections that follow. The `helloauto` directory contains the source code to be compiled and a `Makefile.am` file.

Macros

There are a set of macros that are used in configuration scripts. Some of the macros are quite simple and do things such as test for the presence of the compiler or define an environment variable or two. Others are quite sophisticated and do things such as extract any text to be translated or create a header file that all your applications include. To apply the macros, there is a shell script named `autogen.sh` that does most of the work required to generate the make files.

The macros are found in a subdirectory named `macros` in the GNOME source tree. Look for it as either `gnome/gnome-libs/macros` or `gnome/gnome-core/macros`. You may find it in both places, but if so, they are identical. Also, in future releases, you probably will find them in another location.

Copy the entire `macros` directory into your development directory.

The configure.in File

The contents of the `configure.in` file are processed by `autoconf` to construct a `configure` script. The macros found in the `configure.in` file check for the validity and existence of certain required elements, set up the compiler flags, generate make files, and create the `config.h` file, as well as some other tasks to prepare for compilation.

There are a lot of macros. The ones listed in Table 20-1 are the most useful in setting up a GNOME development environment. If you want to get more information on macros, use one or both of these commands:

```
info autoconf
info automake
```

The macros beginning with AC are for `autoconf`, and the macros beginning with AM are for `automake`.

Table 20-1
The Macros Available for Use in configure.in

Macro	Description
`AC_ARG_PROGRAM`	Provides the capability of changing the name of a program during installation.
`AC_HEADER_STC`	Checks for the presence of standard C header files. (Actually, it checks for a few and assumes the others also are present.)
`AC_INIT` **(file name)**	Always the first macro in the file. It reads the command line and defines some names used in other macros. The file name supplied to it can be any file in the directory — it is only a sanity check to make sure it's running in the right directory.
`AC_OUTPUT`	A list of all the files to be produced.
`AC_PROG_C`	Determines which C compiler to use. If the `CC` environment variable is not set already, search for `gcc`, and then for `cc`, and set `CC` accordingly.
`AC_PROG_CXX`	Determines which C++ compiler to use. If the `CXX` environment variable is not set, the environment variable `CCC` is checked and then the disk is searched for a compiler (likely candidate names are `c++`, `g++`, `gcc`, `CC`, `cxx`, and `c++`). The default is `gcc`.
`AC_SUBST` **(name)**	Create an output variable from a shell variable. The variable name, and its value, is included in each of the produced make files.
`ALL_LINGUAS="l1 l2 l3..."`	This is not a macro. It is an environment variable containing a list of the abbreviations for all the languages to which this application is translated.
`AM_ACLOCAL_INCLUDE` **(directory)**	The name of the directory that contains the m4 macro files. It commonly is in the `macros` subdirectory of the root directory of your development tree. (The utility `m4` is a standard Linux macro processor.)
`AM_CONFIG_HEADER` **(file name)**	The name of the header file to be created. It commonly is named `config.h`.

Macro	*Description*
AM_GNU_GETTEXT	Performs some necessary initializations for internationalization.
AM_INIT_AUTOMAKE (name, version)	Defines PACKAGE using the supplied name, and defines VERSION using the supplied version. The two simply are strings and have no particular format.
AM_MAINTAINER_MODE	Suppresses the generation of files that are intended for software maintenance only.
AM_PROG_LIBTOOL	Required only when the output is to be a shared library created by libtool.
GNOME_COMPILE_WARNINGS	Sets a number of useful compile-time warnings for the gcc compiler.
GNOME_INIT	Defines the set of compiler flags that are specific to GNOME.
GNOME_X_CHECKS	Checks for the presence of X11 and defines the appropriate path variables. It is also capable of setting and clearing the flags used to compile and link the source.

The following is an example showing the contents of a complete configure.in file.

```
AC_INIT(helloauto/helloauto.c)
AM_CONFIG_HEADER(config.h)
AM_INIT_AUTOMAKE(HelloAuto,1.0)
AM_MAINTAINER_MODE
AM_ACLOCAL_INCLUDE(macros)

GNOME_INIT

AC_ISC_POSIX
AC_PROG_CC
AC_HEADER_STDC
AC_ARG_PROGRAM
AC_PROG_CXX
AM_PROG_LIBTOOL

GNOME_COMPILE_WARNINGS

GNOME_X_CHECKS
GNOME_GHTTP_CHECK

ALL_LINGUAS="de en_GB es"
```

```
AM_GNU_GETTEXT

AC_SUBST(CFLAGS)
AC_SUBST(CPPFLAGS)
AC_SUBST(LDFLAGS)

AC_OUTPUT([
Makefile
macros/Makefile
helloauto/Makefile
])
```

The Text Files

Table 20-2 lists a number of text files that are stored in the root directory to document the system. You also can find files by these names in the subdirectories that contain source code.

Table 20-2 Some Usual Documentation Files	
File Name	*Contains*
AUTHORS	The list of names of the software's authors. Quite often the e-mail addresses are listed also.
BUGS	If there is some problem with the code that may cause someone a lot of trouble, it is a good idea to create this file and explain the problem.
COPYING	The copyright information. You can find several of these files throughout the source trees of GNOME and GTK+. There are some slight variations in a few of them, so you can copy the one you like and, if you wish, make your own variation. However, if your changes are such that it no longer is GNU, you cannot say that it is.
DEPENDS	If the compilation depends on the prior existence of something outside this source tree, such as a special library, you can list it in this file.
HACKING	The information listed in this file is for someone that wants to make modifications to the source and compile it. It lists any special utilities or procedures that are required. There often are compile instructions and warnings.

File Name	Contains
INSTALL	This file contains the procedures necessary to install the binary executables.
NEWS	Whenever a change is made, a feature added, or a bug fixed — and the software is tested and a new version number declared — that information is listed at the top of this file. With each new version added at the top of the file, this file becomes a history log of each version.
README	This file contains a description of the software.
TODO	In a system of any complexity, there always are things that you need to do. This file contains a list of the things that you can (or should) do to improve the software.

The scripts are set to check some of these files. They don't look at the contents, so if you have nothing to say at the moment, you simply can create empty files for AUTHORS, ChangeLog, NEWS, and README.

You are not limited to the files named in Table 20-2. For example, you can use a file named DESIGN or ALGORITHM to explain the theory behind the operation of some of the less obvious parts of the software. The files are recognized for what they are because all uppercase files are text files. In the example presented here, there is a text file named IDGBIBLE.

There also is a file named ChangeLog that initially is empty, or simply nonexistent. It stays empty until after the first version of the software is released (or goes to alpha, or whatever). After that, each change is logged according source file, date, and programmer, with a brief description of the change, or changes, made. While a file named NEWS often holds the changes from the user's point of view, the ChangeLog reflects the internal changes that a programmer makes.

The acconfig.h File

In the source directory, create a file named acconfig.h. It is the template used to generate the config.h file. Actually, the program autoheader reads acconfig.h to produce config.h.in. Then the program autoconf uses config.h.in to produce config.h. It is this config.h file that your application's source code should include.

Despite the fact that the acconfig.h file has a .h extension, and its syntax is correct for the C preprocessor, it is not included directly into a source file. All it contains is a sequence of #undef statements. There is one #undef statement for each variable you want defined in config.h.

An `acconfig.h` file, as a minimum, should contain the package and version definitions. It also can include other things to be defined. Each one is named on an `#undef` statement. You will find that some of the other `#undef` definitions must be present for the make file generation to succeed. The following shows the contents of an `acconfig.h` file that is close to the minimal requirements:

```
/* acconfig.h */

#undef ENABLE_NLS
#undef HAVE_CATGETS
#undef HAVE_GETTEXT
#undef HAVE_LC_MESSAGES
#undef HAVE_STPCPY
#undef HAVE_LIBSM

#undef PACKAGE
#undef VERSION
```

The autogen.sh Script

You need to create a script with the name `autogen.sh` in your directory. There is another script by this name in the macros directory, but the two are quite different. The one in the macros directory is quite extensive and does all the detailed work of generating the make files. The one you create in your directory does some simple validation and executes the one that is in the `macros` directory.

```
#!/bin/sh
# Run this to generate all the initial makefiles, etc.

srcdir=`dirname $0`
test -z "$srcdir" && srcdir=.

PKG_NAME="Hello Auto"

(test -f $srcdir/configure.in \
  && test -f $srcdir/IDGBIBLE \
  && test -d $srcdir/helloauto) || {
    echo -n "**Error**: Directory \"\`$srcdir\'\""
    echo -n "does not look like the"
    echo " helloauto development directory"
    exit 1
}

. $srcdir/macros/autogen.sh
```

The environment variable `srcdir` is set to the current directory. The variable `PKG_NAME` is used to assign a name to the entire package — that is, a name for the software that results from compiling all of source in all of the subdirectories. There are two `test` statements that serve no purpose other than verifying that the script is being run in the current directory, and that the current directory contains the right things. In particular, the presence of a file named `IDGBIBLE` and a directory named `helloauto` is assumed to indicate that the script is in the right place.

Your `autogen.sh` finishes by executing the `autogen.sh` in the macros subdirectory. There is a lot of output from this process. Text is output to both `stdout` and `stderr`. I suggest you look at this output so you can get an idea of what is going on; but because there is so much text generated, you need to capture it for later by using this:

```
autogen.sh >fred 2>&1
```

If all goes well (at least, if the script believes all went well) the last line printed is, "Enter 'make' to compile Hello Auto."

The Main Makefile.am File

You need to create a file named `Makefile.am` in the main development directory. This file is used by `autoconf` to create `Makefile.in`. The `Makefile.in` file contains the description of a complete make file. The generated `Makefile.in` contains the information necessary to compile and link the entire system from scratch. It also contains special sets of instructions that undo the act of compiling and linking (`make clean`), install the previously compiled software (`make install`), and create a distribution package (`make dist`). Also, the `autoconf` program scans the source and determines all of the dependencies required for the final make file (such as which header files are included by which other source files).

The exact content of the `Makefile.am` file depends on how many subdirectories there are to include. In the following example, there is one source subdirectory (named `helloauto`) and the `macros` subdirectory containing a local copy of the macros:

```
SUBDIRS=macros helloauto
EXTRA_DIST=IDGBIBLE
```

The `Makefile.am` file is composed of a list of macro definitions that act as input to `automake`. The top-level `Makefile.am` normally is quite simple as compared to those that reside in the directories with the source files. The name `SUBDIRS` is a space-separated list of all of the subdirectory names that contain other `Makefile.am` files. And those `Makefile.am` files can contain the names of other subdirectories containing `Makefile.am` files. While it is possible to specify a directory more than one level down, it is easier to maintain a system that has one `Makefile.am` file in each directory. The name `EXTRA_DIST` is defined as a space-separated list of files in the current directory that are to be included, along with the binary files, as part of the distribution of the software.

The Source Directory

Create a directory to hold your source. If your development environment is to contain source code for more than one program or library, you may want to create a subdirectory to hold the source code for each piece—one for each executable program, one for the source of each library, and so on. The organization of the directory tree should indicate the relationship among the files. These subdirectories can be further subdivided, and each one can be included as part of the automated procedures.

In each of these subdirectories is a `Makefile.am` file that is used to generate a make file.

The Subordinate Makefile.am File

Each source directory needs to contain a `Makefile.am` file that is used to generate a make file. The following is an example `Makefile.am` file that compiles two source code files (`helloauto.c` and `agbargraph.c`) and links them together to create an executable program (`helloauto`).

```
INCLUDES = \
    -I$(top_srcdir) \
    -I$(includedir) \
    -DGNOMELOCALDIR=\""$(datadir)/locale"\" \
    -DG_LOG_DOMAIN=\"HelloAuto\" \
    $(GNOME_INCLUDEDIR)

bin_PROGRAMS = \
    helloauto

helloauto_SOURCES = \
    helloauto.c \
    agbargraph.c \
    agbargraph.h

helloauto_LDADD = \
    $(GNOMEUI_LIBS) \
    $(GNOME_LIBDIR) \
    $(INTLLIBS)
```

The `INCLUDES` variable is used to specify a set of flags to be passed to the compiler. While directories to find include files appear here as `-I` options, you can use any compiler command-line flag. In this example, `-D` is used to define a pair of environment variables.

The variable `bin_PROGRAMS` names the binary output file, or files, that the make file produces.

The variable `helloauto_SOURCES` specifies the source files that are used to build the binary output file named `helloauto`. Using this information, the make file is generated to check all of these files for dependencies.

The variable `helloauto_LDADD` specifies a list of libraries that are searched to resolve external references in the files that make up `helloauto`.

You can add other programs to the same file by adding its name to the list in `bin_PROGRAMS`, and adding a new `SOURCE` and `LDADD` entry for it. Also, if you wish to have subdirectories of source files, you can use a `SUBDIRS` definition to point to the right directory. This means that to add a new directory to your source tree, you simply create a `Makefile.am` file in the new source directory and add a `SUBDIRS` entry in the `Makfile.am` of the parent directory.

Running the autogen.sh Script

There are two steps required to compile everything. First, the script is run from your root development directory like this:

```
autogen.sh
```

This adds a number of files to your root development directory. Exactly what files are added depends largely on the settings and choices you made earlier. For example, if you use `ALL_LINGUAS` to set up some translation, the subdirectories `po` and `intl` are created to hold translation strings.

After the script runs, simply enter:

```
make
```

This command compiles and links everything in the entire directory tree. If you are in any of the source subdirectories, entering `make` only compiles that current directory and those below it.

The make files compare the dates on the source to the dates on the object files, so if you compile again, only the changed files are included. However, you can force a complete recompilation by removing the object files. To delete all the object files, along with any other files that are created during the compile, enter:

```
make clean
```

As you develop your application and add new source files, you will need to update the appropriate `Makefile.am` file and then execute `autogen.sh` to include the new source file.

After you have a successful compile, you can install the executable files with:

```
make install
```

Summary

The setup to get automatic compilation to work is a bit involved, but the rewards come later as you develop your software. All of the dependencies among your source files are tracked automatically, and a correct and complete set of commands is used to compile and link your programs. As explained in detail in this chapter, the following is a list of the steps to take:

✦ Create a development directory containing the appropriate collection of files and directories. It also should include a copy of the macros distributed with the GNOME development software.

✦ Create the `configure.in` file that contains, by using macros, a basic description of your project. Also, create the `acconfig.h` file to be used as a template in creating `config.h`.

✦ Create a simple `autogen.sh` script you can use to find the dependencies and generate the make files.

✦ Create a `Makefile.am` file listing the names of the source files to be used as input, and the names of the object files to be generated. One of these appears in every directory in the development tree.

The next two chapters are for reference. Chapter 21 contains a list of the widgets of GTK+, and Chapter 22 contains a list of the widgets of GNOME. Many of these have been used in programs earlier in the book but, for those that haven't, there are small examples.

✦　　✦　　✦

The Widgets of GTK+

In This Chapter

Listing and explaining the widgets, and other objects, of GTK+

Determining all of the signals and functions that are defined for an object

Determining all of the inherited functions available in an object by examining its inheritance

Determining the enum constants defined for passing configuration settings to the functions

Starting you off by including a simple example of each object

This chapter provides an alphabetical listing of the GTK+ objects. Most of the objects are widgets, but there are a few objects that inherit directly from the base class `GtkObject`. Each entry includes the inheritance and all of the functions that are available to your application.

You can use any widget as the base to create another widget, but not all widgets can be displayed — some are intended for use only as base classes. If a class does not have a function name that ends in _new (or has _new_ somewhere in its name) and returns a pointer to a newly created widget, you can use it only as a base class.

The example code included with each widget is a function that creates the displayable widget and returns a pointer to it. The mainline of all the programs that display the widgets are very much alike. The following example is the one used for the `GtkEntry` widget:

```
/** xgtkentry.c **/
#include <gnome.h>

gint eventDelete(GtkWidget *widget,
        GdkEvent *event,gpointer data);
gint eventDestroy(GtkWidget *widget,
        GdkEvent *event,gpointer data);
static GtkWidget *makeWidget();

int main(int argc,char *argv[])
{
    GtkWidget *app;
    GtkWidget *widget;

    gnome_init("xgtkentry","1.0",argc,argv);
    app =
gnome_app_new("xgtkentry","GtkEntry");

gtk_container_set_border_width(GTK_CONTAINER(a
pp),20);
```

```
        gtk_signal_connect(GTK_OBJECT(app),"delete_event",
            GTK_SIGNAL_FUNC(eventDelete),NULL);
        gtk_signal_connect(GTK_OBJECT(app),"destroy",
            GTK_SIGNAL_FUNC(eventDestroy),NULL);

        widget = makeWidget();

        gnome_app_set_contents(GNOME_APP(app),widget);
        gtk_widget_show_all(app);
        gtk_main();
        exit(0);
    }
gint eventDelete(GtkWidget *widget,
        GdkEvent *event,gpointer data) {
    return(FALSE);
}
gint eventDestroy(GtkWidget *widget,
        GdkEvent *event,gpointer data) {
    gtk_main_quit();
    return(0);
}
static GtkWidget *makeWidget()
{
    GtkWidget *widget;

    widget = gtk_entry_new_with_max_length(40);
    gtk_entry_set_text(GTK_ENTRY(widget),"Edit me!");
    return(widget);
}
```

There may be a minor difference here and there. For example, widgets that wrap themselves in their own top-level window, and thus control their own actions, do not return a pointer. If you examine the source code on the CD, or downloaded from the web site, you see the complete program for each example — not just the snippets shown in this chapter.

GtkAccelLabel

This label widget reads and displays the accelerator key from another widget. It displays the text, if any, used to create it until it is assigned a widget with an accelerator key.

Inheritance
```
GtkAccelLabel->GtkLabel->GtkMisc->GtkWidget->GtkObject
```

Functions
```
guint gtk_accel_label_get_accel_width(
    GtkAccelLabel *accel_label)
GtkType gtk_accel_label_get_type(void)
```

```
GtkWidget *gtk_accel_label_new(const gchar *string)
gboolean gtk_accel_label_refetch(GtkAccelLabel *accel_label)
void gtk_accel_label_set_accel_widget(
    GtkAccelLabel *accel_label, GtkWidget *accel_widget)
```

Signals

```
"changed"              void cb(GtkWidget *, gpointer)
"value_changed"        void cb(GtkWidget *, gpointer)
```

The following example displays the window shown in Figure 21-1.

```
static GtkWidget *makeWidget()
{
    GtkWidget *widget;

    widget = gtk_accel_label_new("Label String");
    return(widget);
}
```

Figure 21-1: A GtkAccelLabel widget
displaying its default string

GtkAdjustment

This object stores geometry information, such as upper and lower bounds, step
and page increments, and the size of a page. Other objects use a GtkAdjustment
object to store their internal dimension settings. It also is passed as an argument to
specify geometry.

A call to gtk_adjustment_changed() issues a "changed" signal; a call to
gtk_adjustment_value_changed() issues a "value changed" signal, if there
is a change in a value since the last signal was emitted.

Inheritance

```
GtkAdjustment->GtkData->GtkObject
```

Functions

```
void gtk_adjustment_changed(GtkAdjustment *adjustment)
void gtk_adjustment_clamp_page(GtkAdjustment *adjustment,
    gfloat lower, gfloat upper)
GtkType gtk_adjustment_get_type(void)
GtkObject *gtk_adjustment_new(gfloat value, gfloat lower,
    gfloat upper, gfloat step_increment, gfloat page_increment,
    gfloat page_size)
void gtk_adjustment_set_value(GtkAdjustment *adjustment,
    gfloat value)
void gtk_adjustment_value_changed(GtkAdjustment *adjustment)
```

There is an example of using a pair of GtkAdjustment objects to control vertical and horizontal scroll bars in "The Layout Container" section in Chapter 5.

GtkAlignment

This is a container widget that is capable of controlling the size of a single child widget. The scale values are from 0.0 to 1.0, indicating the maximum amount the child can expand to fill the space allocated to the GtkAlignment widget. The align values determine the *x* and *y* positions relative to the top left and bottom right corners of the GtkAlignment rectangle. The align values are from 0.0 to the top or left side, and 1.0 for the bottom or right side.

Inheritance

```
GtkAlignment->GtkBin->GtkContainer->GtkWidget->GtkObject
```

Functions

```
GtkType gtk_alignment_get_type(void)
GtkWidget *gtk_alignment_new(gfloat xalign, gfloat yalign,
    gfloat xscale, gfloat yscale)
void gtk_alignment_set(GtkAlignment *alignment, gfloat xalign,
    gfloat yalign, gfloat xscale, gfloat yscale)
```

The following code inserts a GtkButton widget into a GtkAlignment widget. The *x* alignment is set to 1.0, which keeps the button against the right edge. The *y* alignment is 0.5, keeping the widget vertically centered. The scale value is set to 0.15 in both directions, which limits the expansion of the button to no more than 15 percent of the area made available to it. Figure 21-2 shows the default size on the left where the GtkAlignment widget sized itself to the size that the button requested. The window on the right shows the result of expanding the window.

```
static GtkWidget *makeWidget()
{
    GtkWidget *alignment;
    GtkWidget *button;

    button = gtk_button_new_with_label("The Button Label");
    alignment = gtk_alignment_new(1.0,0.5,0.15,0.15);
    gtk_container_add(GTK_CONTAINER(alignment),button);
    return(alignment);
}
```

 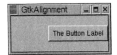

Figure 21-2: A GtkAlignment widget controls size and position of a child

GtkArrow

This is a simple arrowhead widget that points up, left, down, or right.

Inheritance

```
GtkArrow->GtkMisc->GtkWidget->GtkObject
```

Functions

```
GtkType gtk_arrow_get_type(void)
GtkWidget *gtk_arrow_new(GtkArrowType arrow_type,
    GtkShadowType shadow_type)
void gtk_arrow_set(GtkArrow *arrow, GtkArrowType arrow_type,
    GtkShadowType shadow_type)
```

Enums

```
typedef enum {
  GTK_ARROW_UP,
  GTK_ARROW_DOWN,
  GTK_ARROW_LEFT,
  GTK_ARROW_RIGHT
} GtkArrowType;

typedef enum {
  GTK_SHADOW_NONE,
  GTK_SHADOW_IN,
  GTK_SHADOW_OUT,
  GTK_SHADOW_ETCHED_IN,
  GTK_SHADOW_ETCHED_OUT
} GtkShadowType;
```

The following function creates the left-pointing arrow in Figure 21-3, drawn so that the shadowing makes it appear indented.

```
static GtkWidget *makeWidget()
{
    GtkWidget *arrow;

    arrow = gtk_arrow_new(GTK_ARROW_LEFT,GTK_SHADOW_IN);
    return(arrow);
}
```

Figure 21-3: A GtkArrow widget pointing left and shadowed in

GtkAspectFrame

This container widget wraps a single widget in a frame with a label, and imposes an aspect ratio on the child widget.

Inheritance

```
GtkAspectFrame->GtkFrame->GtkBin->GtkContainer->GtkWidget->
        GtkObject
```

Functions

```
GtkType gtk_aspect_frame_get_type(void)
GtkWidget *gtk_aspect_frame_new(const gchar *label,
    gfloat xalign, gfloat yalign, gfloat ratio,
    gint obey_child)
void gtk_aspect_frame_set(GtkAspectFrame *aspect_frame,
    gfloat xalign, gfloat yalign, gfloat ratio,
    gint obey_child)
```

The following example encloses a GtkLabel inside a GtkAspectFrame. The Boolean value obey_child is set to TRUE, so the value of ratio is ignored; instead, the ratio value is derived from the label's preferred size. Values of xalign and yalign set the preferred position as 60 percent of the distance from the top and the left. Figure 21-4 shows the widget as it first appears, and after it is resized. The window is stretched further horizontally than vertically. Essentially, the widget resized itself so that it is as large as possible, while maintaining the same aspect ratio (leaving 60 percent of the space on the left and 40 percent on the right).

```
static GtkWidget *makeWidget()
{
    GtkWidget *aspectframe;
    GtkWidget *label;

    label = gtk_label_new("The Label Text");
    aspectframe = gtk_aspect_frame_new("Flable",
            0.6,0.6,1.0,TRUE);
    gtk_container_add(GTK_CONTAINER(aspectframe),label);
    return(aspectframe);
}
```

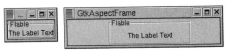

Figure 21-4: An aspect frame maintains the aspect ratio of child widgets

GtkBin

This is a base class for a container widget that has only one child. This class contains code common to all widgets that contain only a single child widget.

Inheritance

```
GtkBin->GtkContainer->GtkWidget->GtkObject
```

Function

```
GtkType gtk_bin_get_type(void)
```

GtkBox

This is the base class of GtkHBox and GtkVBox. It has the code necessary to maintain the contained list of widgets, but it does not position them.

Inheritance

```
GtkBox->GtkContainer->GtkWidget->GtkObject
```

Functions

```
GtkType gtk_box_get_type(void)
void gtk_box_pack_end(GtkBox *box, GtkWidget *child,
    gboolean expand, gboolean fill, guint padding)
void gtk_box_pack_end_defaults(GtkBox *box, GtkWidget *child)
void gtk_box_pack_start(GtkBox *box, GtkWidget *child,
    gboolean expand, gboolean fill, guint padding)
void gtk_box_pack_start_defaults(GtkBox *box, GtkWidget *child)
void gtk_box_query_child_packing(GtkBox *box, GtkWidget *child,
    gboolean *expand, gboolean *fill, guint *padding,
    GtkPackType *pack_type)
void gtk_box_reorder_child(GtkBox *box, GtkWidget *child,
    gint position)
void gtk_box_set_child_packing(GtkBox *box, GtkWidget *child,
    gboolean expand, gboolean fill, guint padding,
    GtkPackType pack_type)
void gtk_box_set_homogeneous(GtkBox *box, gboolean homogeneous)
void gtk_box_set_spacing(GtkBox *box, gint spacing)
```

Enum

```
typedef enum {
  GTK_PACK_START,
  GTK_PACK_END
} GtkPackType;
```

GtkButton

This is a window with a text or pixmap label inside a frame. It can respond to the mouse.

Inheritance

```
GtkButton->GtkBin->GtkContainer->GtkWidget->GtkObject
```

Functions

```
void gtk_button_clicked(GtkButton *button)
void gtk_button_enter(GtkButton *button)
GtkReliefStyle gtk_button_get_relief(GtkButton *button)
GtkType gtk_button_get_type(void)
void gtk_button_leave(GtkButton *button)
GtkWidget *gtk_button_new(void)
GtkWidget *gtk_button_new_with_label(const gchar *label)
void gtk_button_pressed(GtkButton *button)
void gtk_button_released(GtkButton *button)
void gtk_button_set_relief(GtkButton *button,
    GtkReliefStyle newrelief)
```

Enum

```
typedef enum {
  GTK_RELIEF_NORMAL,
  GTK_RELIEF_HALF,
  GTK_RELIEF_NONE,
} GtkReliefStyle;
```

Signals

```
"clicked"      void cb(GtkWidget *, gpointer)
"enter"        void cb(GtkWidget *, gpointer)
"leave"        void cb(GtkWidget *, gpointer)
"pressed"      void cb(GtkWidget *, gpointer)
"released"     void cb(GtkWidget *, gpointer)
```

The GtkButton object was used throughout the book, so there are examples of it in almost every chapter. In particular, see Chapters 3 and 4.

GtkButtonBox

This is the base class that holds the common functions for GtkHButtonBox and GtkVButtonBox. These are container widgets specifically designed to manage a collection of buttons. GtkButtonBox has a number of control functions that you can use to set the sizes and positions of the buttons.

Inheritance

```
GtkButtonBox->GtkBox->GtkContainer->GtkWidget->GtkObject
```

Functions

```
void gtk_button_box_child_requisition(GtkWidget *widget,
    int *nvis_children, int *width, int *height)
void gtk_button_box_get_child_ipadding(GtkButtonBox *widget,
    gint *ipad_x, gint *ipad_y)
void gtk_button_box_get_child_ipadding_default(gint *ipad_x,
    gint *ipad_y)
void gtk_button_box_get_child_size(GtkButtonBox *widget,
    gint *width, gint *height)
void gtk_button_box_get_child_size_default(gint *width,
    gint *height)
GtkButtonBoxStyle gtk_button_box_get_layout(
    GtkButtonBox *widget)
gint gtk_button_box_get_spacing(GtkButtonBox *widget)
GtkType gtk_button_box_get_type(void)
void gtk_button_box_set_child_ipadding(GtkButtonBox *widget,
    gint ipad_x, gint ipad_y)
void gtk_button_box_set_child_ipadding_default(gint ipad_x,
    gint ipad_y)
void gtk_button_box_set_child_size(GtkButtonBox *widget,
    gint width, gint height)
void gtk_button_box_set_child_size_default(gint width,
    gint height)
void gtk_button_box_set_layout(GtkButtonBox *widget,
    GtkButtonBoxStyle layout_style)
void gtk_button_box_set_spacing(GtkButtonBox *widget,
    gint spacing)
```

Enum

```
typedef enum {
  GTK_BUTTONBOX_DEFAULT_STYLE,
  GTK_BUTTONBOX_SPREAD,
  GTK_BUTTONBOX_EDGE,
  GTK_BUTTONBOX_START,
  GTK_BUTTONBOX_END
} GtkButtonBoxStyle;
```

GtkCalendar

The GtkCalendar widget displays one month. The user can select the month, year, and then select a specific day of the month.

Inheritance

```
GtkCalendar->GtkWidget->GtkObject
```

Functions

```
void gtk_calendar_clear_marks(GtkCalendar *calendar)
void gtk_calendar_display_options(GtkCalendar *calendar,
    GtkCalendarDisplayOptions flags)
```

```
void gtk_calendar_freeze(GtkCalendar *calendar)
void gtk_calendar_get_date(GtkCalendar *calendar, guint *year,
    guint *month, guint *day)
GtkType gtk_calendar_get_type(void)
gint gtk_calendar_mark_day(GtkCalendar *calendar, guint day)
GtkWidget *gtk_calendar_new(void)
void gtk_calendar_select_day(GtkCalendar *calendar, guint day)
gint gtk_calendar_select_month(GtkCalendar *calendar,
    guint month, guint year)
void gtk_calendar_thaw(GtkCalendar *calendar)
gint gtk_calendar_unmark_day(GtkCalendar *calendar, guint day)
```

Enum

```
typedef enum {
  GTK_CALENDAR_SHOW_HEADING,
  GTK_CALENDAR_SHOW_DAY_NAMES,
  GTK_CALENDAR_NO_MONTH_CHANGE,
  GTK_CALENDAR_SHOW_WEEK_NUMBERS,
  GTK_CALENDAR_WEEK_START_MONDAY
} GtkCalendarDisplayOptions;
```

Whenever a new calendar widget is created, it defaults to the current date and time and is displayed as shown in Figure 21-5.

```
static GtkWidget *makeWidget()
{
    GtkWidget *widget;

    widget = gtk_calendar_new();
    return(widget);
}
```

Figure 21-5: A displayed GtkCalendar widget

GtkCheckButton

A GtkCheckButton widget displays a small button with a label next to it. The button can be toggled on or off by the mouse, and will retain its state until it is toggled again.

Inheritance

```
GtkCheckButton->GtkToggleButton->GtkButton->GtkBin->
        GtkContainer->GtkWidget->GtkObject
```

Functions

```
GtkType gtk_check_button_get_type(void)
GtkWidget *gtk_check_button_new(void)
GtkWidget *gtk_check_button_new_with_label(
    const gchar *label)
```

The following example displays the window shown in Figure 21-6.

```
static GtkWidget *makeWidget()
{
    GtkWidget *widget;

    widget = gtk_check_button_new_with_label(
            "Check Button Label");
    return(widget);
}
```

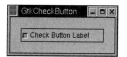

Figure 21-6: A GtkCheckButton widget with a label

GtkCheckMenuItem

This widget displays a toggle button and a label. Because it inherits from GtkMenuItem, it is intended for use as a toggle button on a menu.

Inheritance

```
GtkCheckMenuItem->GtkMenuItem->GtkItem->GtkBin->GtkContainer->
        GtkWidget->GtkObject
```

Functions

```
GtkType gtk_check_menu_item_get_type(void)
GtkWidget *gtk_check_menu_item_new(void)
GtkWidget *gtk_check_menu_item_new_with_label(
    const gchar *label)
void gtk_check_menu_item_set_active(
    GtkCheckMenuItem *check_menu_item, gboolean is_active)
void gtk_check_menu_item_set_show_toggle(
    GtkCheckMenuItem *menu_item, gboolean always)
void gtk_check_menu_item_toggled(
    GtkCheckMenuItem *check_menu_item)
```

Signal

```
"toggled"        void cb(GtkWidget *, gpointer)
```

The following example displays the window shown in Figure 21-7.

```
static GtkWidget *makeWidget()
{
    GtkWidget *widget;

    widget = gtk_check_menu_item_new_with_label(
        " Check Label");
    gtk_check_menu_item_set_show_toggle(
            GTK_CHECK_MENU_ITEM(widget),TRUE);
    return(widget);
}
```

Figure 21-7: A GtkCheckMenuItem with the toggle button displayed

GtkCList

The GtkCList widget contains one or more text lists and enables the user to select one or more rows. A large number of control functions make this a very flexible widget.

Inheritance

```
GtkCList->GtkContainer->GtkWidget->GtkObject
```

Functions

```
gint gtk_clist_append(GtkCList *clist, gchar *text [ ])
void gtk_clist_clear(GtkCList *clist)
void gtk_clist_column_title_active(GtkCList *clist,
    gint column)
void gtk_clist_column_title_passive(GtkCList *clist,
    gint column)
void gtk_clist_column_titles_active(GtkCList *clist)
void gtk_clist_column_titles_hide(GtkCList *clist)
void gtk_clist_column_titles_passive(GtkCList *clist)
void gtk_clist_column_titles_show(GtkCList *clist)
gint gtk_clist_columns_autosize(GtkCList *clist)
void gtk_clist_construct(GtkCList *clist, gint columns,
    gchar *titles [ ])
gint gtk_clist_find_row_from_data(GtkCList *clist,
    gpointer data)
void gtk_clist_freeze(GtkCList *clist)
GtkStyle *gtk_clist_get_cell_style(GtkCList *clist, gint row,
    gint column)
GtkCellType gtk_clist_get_cell_type(GtkCList *clist, gint row,
```

```
    gint column)
gchar *gtk_clist_get_column_title(GtkCList *clist, gint column)
GtkWidget *gtk_clist_get_column_widget(GtkCList *clist,
    gint column)
GtkAdjustment *gtk_clist_get_hadjustment(GtkCList *clist)
gint gtk_clist_get_pixmap(GtkCList *clist, gint row,
    gint column, GdkPixmap **pixmap, GdkBitmap **mask)
gint gtk_clist_get_pixtext(GtkCList *clist, gint row,
    gint column, gchar **text, guint8 *spacing,
    GdkPixmap **pixmap, GdkBitmap **mask)
gpointer gtk_clist_get_row_data(GtkCList *clist, gint row)
GtkStyle *gtk_clist_get_row_style(GtkCList *clist, gint row)
gboolean gtk_clist_get_selectable(GtkCList *clist, gint row)
gint gtk_clist_get_selection_info(GtkCList *clist, gint x,
    gint y, gint *row, gint *column)
gint gtk_clist_get_text(GtkCList *clist, gint row, gint column,
    gchar **text)
GtkType gtk_clist_get_type(void)
GtkAdjustment *gtk_clist_get_vadjustment(GtkCList *clist)
gint gtk_clist_insert(GtkCList *clist, gint row,
    gchar *text [ ])
void gtk_clist_moveto(GtkCList *clist, gint row, gint column,
    gfloat row_align, gfloat col_align)
GtkWidget *gtk_clist_new(gint columns)
GtkWidget *gtk_clist_new_with_titles(gint columns,
    gchar *titles [ ])
gint gtk_clist_optimal_column_width(GtkCList *clist,
    gint column)
gint gtk_clist_prepend(GtkCList *clist, gchar *text [ ])
void gtk_clist_remove(GtkCList *clist, gint row)
GtkVisibility gtk_clist_row_is_visible(GtkCList *clist,
    gint row)
void gtk_clist_row_move(GtkCList *clist, gint source_row,
    gint dest_row)
void gtk_clist_select_all(GtkCList *clist)
void gtk_clist_select_row(GtkCList *clist, gint row,
    gint column)
void gtk_clist_set_auto_sort(GtkCList *clist,
    gboolean auto_sort)
void gtk_clist_set_background(GtkCList *clist, gint row,
    GdkColor *color)
void gtk_clist_set_button_actions(GtkCList *clist,
    guint button, guint8 button_actions)
void gtk_clist_set_cell_style(GtkCList *clist, gint row,
    gint column, GtkStyle *style)
void gtk_clist_set_column_auto_resize(GtkCList *clist,
    gint column, gboolean auto_resize)
void gtk_clist_set_column_justification(GtkCList *clist,
    gint column, GtkJustification justification)
void gtk_clist_set_column_max_width(GtkCList *clist,
    gint column, gint max_width)
```

```
void gtk_clist_set_column_min_width(GtkCList *clist,
    gint column, gint min_width)
void gtk_clist_set_column_resizeable(GtkCList *clist,
    gint column, gint resizeable)
void gtk_clist_set_column_title(GtkCList *clist, gint column,
    const gchar *title)
void gtk_clist_set_column_visibility(GtkCList *clist,
    gint column, gboolean visible)
void gtk_clist_set_column_widget(GtkCList *clist, gint column,
    GtkWidget *widget)
void gtk_clist_set_column_width(GtkCList *clist, gint column,
    gint width)
void gtk_clist_set_compare_func(GtkCList *clist,
    GtkCListCompareFunc cmp_func)
void gtk_clist_set_foreground(GtkCList *clist, gint row,
    GdkColor *color)
void gtk_clist_set_hadjustment(GtkCList *clist,
    GtkAdjustment *adjustment)
void gtk_clist_set_pixmap(GtkCList *clist, gint row,
    gint column, GdkPixmap *pixmap, GdkBitmap *mask)
void gtk_clist_set_pixtext(GtkCList *clist, gint row,
    gint column, const gchar *text, guint8 spacing,
    GdkPixmap *pixmap, GdkBitmap *mask)
void gtk_clist_set_reorderable(GtkCList *clist,
    gboolean reorderable)
void gtk_clist_set_row_data(GtkCList *clist, gint row,
    gpointer data)
void gtk_clist_set_row_data_full(GtkCList *clist, gint row,
    gpointer data, GtkDestroyNotify destroy)
void gtk_clist_set_row_height(GtkCList *clist, guint height)
void gtk_clist_set_row_style(GtkCList *clist, gint row,
    GtkStyle *style)
void gtk_clist_set_selectable(GtkCList *clist, gint row,
    gboolean selectable)
void gtk_clist_set_selection_mode(GtkCList *clist,
    GtkSelectionMode mode)
void gtk_clist_set_shadow_type(GtkCList *clist,
    GtkShadowType type)
void gtk_clist_set_shift(GtkCList *clist, gint row,
    gint column, gint vertical, gint horizontal)
void gtk_clist_set_sort_column(GtkCList *clist, gint column)
void gtk_clist_set_sort_type(GtkCList *clist,
    GtkSortType sort_type)
void gtk_clist_set_text(GtkCList *clist, gint row, gint column,
    const gchar *text)
void gtk_clist_set_use_drag_icons(GtkCList *clist,
    gboolean use_icons)
void gtk_clist_set_vadjustment(GtkCList *clist,
    GtkAdjustment *adjustment)
void gtk_clist_sort(GtkCList *clist)
void gtk_clist_swap_rows(GtkCList *clist, gint row1, gint row2)
```

```
      void gtk_clist_thaw(GtkCList *clist)
      void gtk_clist_undo_selection(GtkCList *clist)
      void gtk_clist_unselect_all(GtkCList *clist)
      void gtk_clist_unselect_row(GtkCList *clist, gint row,
         gint column)
```

Enums

```
      typedef enum {
        GTK_SHADOW_NONE,
        GTK_SHADOW_IN,
        GTK_SHADOW_OUT,
        GTK_SHADOW_ETCHED_IN,
        GTK_SHADOW_ETCHED_OUT
      } GtkShadowType;

      typedef enum {
        GTK_SELECTION_SINGLE,
        GTK_SELECTION_BROWSE,
        GTK_SELECTION_MULTIPLE,
        GTK_SELECTION_EXTENDED
      } GtkSelectionMode;

      typedef enum {
        GTK_SORT_ASCENDING,
        GTK_SORT_DESCENDING
      } GtkSortType;
```

Signals

```
"abort_column_resize"      void cb(GtkWidget *, gpointer)
"click_column"             void cb(GtkWidget *, gint, gpointer)
"end_selection"            void cb(GtkWidget *, gpointer)
"extend_selection"         void cb(GtkWidget *, GtkScrollType, gfloat, gboolean,
gpointer)
"resize_column"            void cb(GtkWidget *, gint, gint, gpointer)
"row_move"                 void cb(GtkWidget *, gint, gint, gpointer)
"scroll_horizontal"        void cb(GtkWidget *, GtkScrollType, gfloat, gpointer)
"scroll_vertical"          void cb(GtkWidget *, GtkScrollType, gfloat, gpointer)
"select_all"               void cb(GtkWidget *, gpointer)
"select_row"               void cb(GtkWidget *, gint, gint, GdkEvent *, gpointer)
"set_scroll_adjustments"   void cb(GtkWidget *, GtkAdjustment *, GtkAdjustment *,
gpointer)
"start_selection"          void cb(GtkWidget *, gpointer)
"toggle_add_mode"          void cb(GtkWidget *, gpointer)
"toggle_focus_row"         void cb(GtkWidget *, gpointer)
"undo_selection"           void cb(GtkWidget *, gpointer)
"unselect_all"             void cb(GtkWidget *, gpointer)
"unselect_row"             void cb(GtkWidget *, gint, gint, GdkEvent *, gpointer)
```

This example creates a two-column `GtkCList` object and inserts three rows of data into each column. In Figure 21-8, it is shown with the second row selected. The optional column heading buttons also are included, and you can resize the columns by dragging the mouse pointer between the two buttons.

```
static GtkWidget *makeWidget()
{
    GtkWidget *widget;
    static gchar *titles[] = {
        "Column 1","Column 2"
    };
    static char *row1[] = {
        "Apple","Orange"
    };
    static char *row2[] = {
        "Car","Truck"
    };
    static char *row3[] = {
        "Airplane","Bird"
    };

    widget = gtk_clist_new_with_titles(2,titles);
    gtk_clist_append(GTK_CLIST(widget),row1);
    gtk_clist_append(GTK_CLIST(widget),row2);
    gtk_clist_append(GTK_CLIST(widget),row3);
    return(widget);
}
```

Figure 21-8: A two-column GtkCList with headings

GtkClock

This widget is an elapsed timer that either counts up or down. You also can set it to display the current time.

Inheritance
```
GtkClock->GtkLabel->GtkMisc->GtkWidget->GtkObject
```

Functions
```
guint gtk_clock_get_type(void)
GtkWidget *gtk_clock_new(GtkClockType type)
void gtk_clock_set_format(GtkClock *clock, gchar *fmt)
void gtk_clock_set_seconds(GtkClock *clock, time_t seconds)
```

```
void gtk_clock_set_update_interval(GtkClock *clock,
    gint seconds)
void gtk_clock_start(GtkClock *clock)
void gtk_clock_stop(GtkClock *clock)
```

Enum

```
typedef enum {
  GTK_CLOCK_INCREASING,
  GTK_CLOCK_DECREASING,
  GTK_CLOCK_REALTIME
} GtkClockType;
```

This example creates an elapsed timer that starts at zero and continuously counts upward. The finest granularity is one second, as you can see in Figure 21-9.

```
static GtkWidget *makeWidget()
{
    GtkWidget *widget;

    widget = gtk_clock_new(GTK_CLOCK_INCREASING);
    gtk_clock_start(GTK_CLOCK(widget));
    return(widget);
}
```

Figure 21-9: A GtkClock widget measuring elapsed time

GtkColorSelection

This widget displays color information in such a way that the user can specify, with the mouse, any available color.

Inheritance

```
GtkColorSelection->GtkVBox->GtkBox->GtkContainer->GtkWidget->
        GtkObject
```

Functions

```
void gtk_color_selection_get_color(
    GtkColorSelection *colorsel, gdouble *color)
guint gtk_color_selection_get_type(void)
GtkWidget *gtk_color_selection_new(void)
void gtk_color_selection_set_color(
    GtkColorSelection *colorsel, gdouble *color)
void gtk_color_selection_set_opacity(
```

```
        GtkColorSelection *colorsel, gint use_opacity)
    void gtk_color_selection_set_update_policy(
        GtkColorSelection *colorsel, GtkUpdateType policy)
```

Enum

```
    typedef enum {
      GTK_UPDATE_CONTINUOUS,
      GTK_UPDATE_DISCONTINUOUS,
      GTK_UPDATE_DELAYED
    } GtkUpdateType;
```

Signal

```
    "color_changed"        void cb(GtkWidget *, gpointer)
```

The following example displays the window shown in Figure 21-10.

```
    static GtkWidget *makeWidget()
    {
        GtkWidget *widget;

        widget = gtk_color_selection_new();
        return(widget);
    }
```

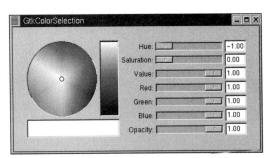

Figure 21-10: A GtkColorSelection widget with its default settings

GtkColorSelectionDialog

This is a GtkColorSelection widget that appears in its own dialog window.

Inheritance

```
    GtkColorSelectionDialog->GtkWindow->GtkBin->GtkContainer->
        GtkWidget->GtkObject
```

Functions

```
guint gtk_color_selection_dialog_get_type(void)
GtkWidget *gtk_color_selection_dialog_new(const gchar *title)
```

Creating the dialog box for GtkColorSelectionDialog generates the same display shown in Figure 21-10 for the GtkColorSelection widget.

```
static void makeWidget()
{
    GtkWidget *widget;

    widget = gtk_color_selection_dialog_new("Color Title");
    gtk_widget_show(widget);
}
```

GtkCombo

The GtkCombo box displays a single item and provides a pull-down list of items that can be selected. When it displays a single item, it is the one currently selected.

Inheritance

```
GtkCombo->GtkHBox->GtkBox->GtkContainer->GtkWidget->GtkObject
```

Functions

```
void gtk_combo_disable_activate(GtkCombo *combo)
guint gtk_combo_get_type(void)
GtkWidget *gtk_combo_new(void)
void gtk_combo_set_case_sensitive(GtkCombo *combo, gint val)
void gtk_combo_set_item_string(GtkCombo *combo, GtkItem *item,
    const gchar *item_value)
void gtk_combo_set_popdown_strings(GtkCombo *combo,
    GList *strings)
void gtk_combo_set_use_arrows(GtkCombo *combo, gint val)
void gtk_combo_set_use_arrows_always(GtkCombo *combo, gint val)
void gtk_combo_set_value_in_list(GtkCombo *combo, gint val,
    gint ok_if_empty)
```

The following example creates a GtkCombo widget with a total of five available selections. Figure 21-11 shows the widget with a pull-down list, and the third item in the list selected.

```
static GtkWidget *makeWidget()
{
    GtkWidget *widget;
    GList *glist;
```

```
        glist = NULL;
        glist = g_list_append(glist,"Selection 1");
        glist = g_list_append(glist,"Selection 2");
        glist = g_list_append(glist,"Selection 3");
        glist = g_list_append(glist,"Selection 4");
        glist = g_list_append(glist,"Selection 5");

        widget = gtk_combo_new();
        gtk_combo_set_popdown_strings(GTK_COMBO(widget),
                glist);
        return(widget);
    }
```

Figure 21-11: A GtkCombo with the third item selected

GtkContainer

The GtkContainer widget is a base class for container widgets. Widgets that inherit from GtkContainer have the ability to contain, position, size, and display one or more other widgets.

Inheritance

```
GtkContainer->GtkWidget->GtkObject
```

Functions

```
void gtk_container_add(GtkContainer *container,
    GtkWidget *widget)
void gtk_container_add_child_arg_type(const gchar *arg_name,
    GtkType arg_type, guint arg_flags, guint arg_id)
void gtk_container_add_with_args(GtkContainer *container,
    GtkWidget *widget, const gchar *first_arg_name, ...)
void gtk_container_addv(GtkContainer *container,
    GtkWidget *widget, guint n_args, GtkArg *args)
void gtk_container_arg_get(GtkContainer *container,
    GtkWidget *child, GtkArg *arg, GtkArgInfo *info)
void gtk_container_arg_set(GtkContainer *container,
    GtkWidget *child, GtkArg *arg, GtkArgInfo *info)
void gtk_container_check_resize(GtkContainer *container)
gchar *gtk_container_child_arg_get_info(GtkType object_type,
    const gchar *arg_name, GtkArgInfo **info_p)
gchar *gtk_container_child_args_collect(GtkType object_type,
```

```
        GSList **arg_list_p, GSList **info_list_p,
        const gchar *first_arg_name, va_list var_args)
gchar *gtk_container_child_composite_name(
        GtkContainer *container, GtkWidget *child)
void gtk_container_child_getv(GtkContainer *container,
        GtkWidget *child, guint n_args, GtkArg *args)
void gtk_container_child_set(GtkContainer *container,
        GtkWidget *child, const gchar *first_arg_name, ...)
void gtk_container_child_setv(GtkContainer *container,
        GtkWidget *child, guint n_args, GtkArg *args)
GtkType gtk_container_child_type(GtkContainer *container)
GList *gtk_container_children(GtkContainer *container)
void gtk_container_clear_resize_widgets(
        GtkContainer *container)
gint gtk_container_focus(GtkContainer *container,
        GtkDirectionType direction)
void gtk_container_forall(GtkContainer *container,
        GtkCallback callback, gpointer callback_data)
void gtk_container_foreach(GtkContainer *container,
        GtkCallback callback, gpointer callback_data)
void gtk_container_foreach_full(GtkContainer *container,
        GtkCallback callback, GtkCallbackMarshal marshal,
        gpointer callback_data, GtkDestroyNotify notify)
GList *gtk_container_get_toplevels(void)
GtkType gtk_container_get_type(void)
GtkArg *gtk_container_query_child_args(GtkType class_type,
        guint32 **arg_flags, guint *n_args)
void gtk_container_queue_resize(GtkContainer *container)
void gtk_container_real_set_focus_child(
        GtkContainer *container, GtkWidget *child)
void gtk_container_register_toplevel(GtkContainer *container)
void gtk_container_remove(GtkContainer *container,
        GtkWidget *widget)
void gtk_container_resize_children(GtkContainer *container)
void gtk_container_set_border_width(GtkContainer *container,
        guint border_width)
void gtk_container_set_focus_child(GtkContainer *container,
        GtkWidget *widget)
void gtk_container_set_focus_hadjustment(
        GtkContainer *container, GtkAdjustment *adjustment)
void gtk_container_set_focus_vadjustment(
        GtkContainer *container, GtkAdjustment *adjustment)
void gtk_container_set_resize_mode(GtkContainer *container,
        GtkResizeMode resize_mode)
void gtk_container_unregister_toplevel(
        GtkContainer *container)
```

Enums

```
typedef enum {
  GTK_DIR_TAB_FORWARD,
  GTK_DIR_TAB_BACKWARD,
```

```
    GTK_DIR_UP,
    GTK_DIR_DOWN,
    GTK_DIR_LEFT,
    GTK_DIR_RIGHT
} GtkDirectionType;

typedef enum {
    GTK_RESIZE_PARENT,
    GTK_RESIZE_QUEUE,
    GTK_RESIZE_IMMEDIATE
} GtkResizeMode;
```

Signals

```
"add"               void cb(GtkWidget *, GtkWidget *, gpointer)
"check_resize"      void cb(GtkWidget *, gpointer)
"focus"             gint cb(GtkWidget *, GtkDirectionType,
GtkDirectionType, gpointer)
"remove"            void cb(GtkWidget *, GtkWidget *, gpointer)
"set-focus-child"   void cb(GtkWidget *, GtkWidget *, gpointer)
```

GtkCTree

This widget displays a hierarchical tree (such as a directory tree) and enables the user to traverse the tree using the mouse.

Inheritance

```
GtkCTree->GtkCList->GtkContainer->GtkWidget->GtkObject
```

Functions

```
void gtk_ctree_collapse(GtkCTree *ctree, GtkCTreeNode *node)
void gtk_ctree_collapse_recursive(GtkCTree *ctree,
    GtkCTreeNode *node)
void gtk_ctree_collapse_to_depth(GtkCTree *ctree,
    GtkCTreeNode *node, gint depth)
void gtk_ctree_construct(GtkCTree *ctree, gint columns,
    gint tree_column, gchar *titles [ ])
void gtk_ctree_expand(GtkCTree *ctree, GtkCTreeNode *node)
void gtk_ctree_expand_recursive(GtkCTree *ctree,
    GtkCTreeNode *node)
void gtk_ctree_expand_to_depth(GtkCTree *ctree,
    GtkCTreeNode *node, gint depth)
GNode *gtk_ctree_export_to_gnode(GtkCTree *ctree,
    GNode *parent, GNode *sibling, GtkCTreeNode *node,
    GtkCTreeGNodeFunc func, gpointer data)
gboolean gtk_ctree_find(GtkCTree *ctree, GtkCTreeNode *node,
    GtkCTreeNode *child)
GList *gtk_ctree_find_all_by_row_data(GtkCTree *ctree,
    GtkCTreeNode *node, gpointer data)
GList *gtk_ctree_find_all_by_row_data_custom(GtkCTree *ctree,
    GtkCTreeNode *node, gpointer data, GCompareFunc func)
```

```
GtkCTreeNode *gtk_ctree_find_by_row_data(GtkCTree *ctree,
    GtkCTreeNode *node, gpointer data)
GtkCTreeNode *gtk_ctree_find_by_row_data_custom(
    GtkCTree *ctree, GtkCTreeNode *node, gpointer data,
    GCompareFunc func)
GtkCTreeNode *gtk_ctree_find_node_ptr(GtkCTree *ctree,
    GtkCTreeRow *ctree_row)
gint gtk_ctree_get_node_info(GtkCTree *ctree,
    GtkCTreeNode *node, gchar **text, guint8 *spacing,
    GdkPixmap **pixmap_closed, GdkBitmap **mask_closed,
    GdkPixmap **pixmap_opened, GdkBitmap **mask_opened,
    gboolean *is_leaf, gboolean *expanded)
GtkType gtk_ctree_get_type(void)
GtkCTreeNode *gtk_ctree_insert_gnode(GtkCTree *ctree,
    GtkCTreeNode *parent, GtkCTreeNode *sibling, GNode *gnode,
    GtkCTreeGNodeFunc func, gpointer data)
GtkCTreeNode *gtk_ctree_insert_node(GtkCTree *ctree,
    GtkCTreeNode *parent, GtkCTreeNode *sibling,
    gchar *text [ ], guint8 spacing, GdkPixmap *pixmap_closed,
    GdkBitmap *mask_closed, GdkPixmap *pixmap_opened,
    GdkBitmap *mask_opened, gboolean is_leaf,
    gboolean expanded)
gboolean gtk_ctree_is_ancestor(GtkCTree *ctree,
    GtkCTreeNode *node, GtkCTreeNode *child)
gboolean gtk_ctree_is_hot_spot(GtkCTree *ctree, gint x, gint y)
gboolean gtk_ctree_is_viewable(GtkCTree *ctree,
    GtkCTreeNode *node)
GtkCTreeNode *gtk_ctree_last(GtkCTree *ctree,
    GtkCTreeNode *node)
void gtk_ctree_move(GtkCTree *ctree, GtkCTreeNode *node,
    GtkCTreeNode *new_parent, GtkCTreeNode *new_sibling)
GtkWidget *gtk_ctree_new(gint columns, gint tree_column)
GtkWidget *gtk_ctree_new_with_titles(gint columns,
    gint tree_column, gchar *titles [ ])
GtkStyle *gtk_ctree_node_get_cell_style(GtkCTree *ctree,
    GtkCTreeNode *node, gint column)
GtkCellType gtk_ctree_node_get_cell_type(GtkCTree *ctree,
    GtkCTreeNode *node, gint column)
gint gtk_ctree_node_get_pixmap(GtkCTree *ctree,
    GtkCTreeNode *node, gint column, GdkPixmap **pixmap,
    GdkBitmap **mask)
gint gtk_ctree_node_get_pixtext(GtkCTree *ctree,
    GtkCTreeNode *node, gint column, gchar **text,
    guint8 *spacing, GdkPixmap **pixmap, GdkBitmap **mask)
gpointer gtk_ctree_node_get_row_data(GtkCTree *ctree,
    GtkCTreeNode *node)
GtkStyle *gtk_ctree_node_get_row_style(GtkCTree *ctree,
    GtkCTreeNode *node)
gboolean gtk_ctree_node_get_selectable(GtkCTree *ctree,
    GtkCTreeNode *node)
gint gtk_ctree_node_get_text(GtkCTree *ctree,
    GtkCTreeNode *node, gint column, gchar **text)
GtkVisibility gtk_ctree_node_is_visible(GtkCTree *ctree,
    GtkCTreeNode *node)
```

```
void gtk_ctree_node_moveto(GtkCTree *ctree, GtkCTreeNode *node,
    gint column, gfloat row_align, gfloat col_align)
GtkCTreeNode *gtk_ctree_node_nth(GtkCTree *ctree, guint row)
void gtk_ctree_node_set_background(GtkCTree *ctree,
    GtkCTreeNode *node, GdkColor *color)
void gtk_ctree_node_set_cell_style(GtkCTree *ctree,
    GtkCTreeNode *node, gint column, GtkStyle *style)
void gtk_ctree_node_set_foreground(GtkCTree *ctree,
    GtkCTreeNode *node, GdkColor *color)
void gtk_ctree_node_set_pixmap(GtkCTree *ctree,
    GtkCTreeNode *node, gint column, GdkPixmap *pixmap,
    GdkBitmap *mask)
void gtk_ctree_node_set_pixtext(GtkCTree *ctree,
    GtkCTreeNode *node, gint column, const gchar *text,
    guint8 spacing, GdkPixmap *pixmap, GdkBitmap *mask)
void gtk_ctree_node_set_row_data(GtkCTree *ctree,
    GtkCTreeNode *node, gpointer data)
void gtk_ctree_node_set_row_data_full(GtkCTree *ctree,
    GtkCTreeNode *node, gpointer data,
    GtkDestroyNotify destroy)
void gtk_ctree_node_set_row_style(GtkCTree *ctree,
    GtkCTreeNode *node, GtkStyle *style)
void gtk_ctree_node_set_selectable(GtkCTree *ctree,
    GtkCTreeNode *node, gboolean selectable)
void gtk_ctree_node_set_shift(GtkCTree *ctree,
    GtkCTreeNode *node, gint column, gint vertical,
    gint horizontal)
void gtk_ctree_node_set_text(GtkCTree *ctree,
    GtkCTreeNode *node, gint column, const gchar *text)
void gtk_ctree_post_recursive(GtkCTree *ctree,
    GtkCTreeNode *node, GtkCTreeFunc func, gpointer data)
void gtk_ctree_post_recursive_to_depth(GtkCTree *ctree,
    GtkCTreeNode *node, gint depth, GtkCTreeFunc func,
    gpointer data)
void gtk_ctree_pre_recursive(GtkCTree *ctree,
    GtkCTreeNode *node, GtkCTreeFunc func, gpointer data)
void gtk_ctree_pre_recursive_to_depth(GtkCTree *ctree,
    GtkCTreeNode *node, gint depth, GtkCTreeFunc func,
    gpointer data)
void gtk_ctree_real_select_recursive(GtkCTree *ctree,
    GtkCTreeNode *node, gint state)
void gtk_ctree_remove_node(GtkCTree *ctree, GtkCTreeNode *node)
void gtk_ctree_select(GtkCTree *ctree, GtkCTreeNode *node)
void gtk_ctree_select_recursive(GtkCTree *ctree,
    GtkCTreeNode *node)
void gtk_ctree_set_drag_compare_func(GtkCTree *ctree,
    GtkCTreeCompareDragFunc cmp_func)
void gtk_ctree_set_expander_style(GtkCTree *ctree,
    GtkCTreeExpanderStyle expander_style)
void gtk_ctree_set_indent(GtkCTree *ctree, gint indent)
void gtk_ctree_set_line_style(GtkCTree *ctree,
    GtkCTreeLineStyle line_style)
void gtk_ctree_set_node_info(GtkCTree *ctree,
    GtkCTreeNode *node, const gchar *text, guint8 spacing,
```

```
        GdkPixmap *pixmap_closed, GdkBitmap *mask_closed,
        GdkPixmap *pixmap_opened, GdkBitmap *mask_opened,
        gboolean is_leaf, gboolean expanded)
    void gtk_ctree_set_show_stub(GtkCTree *ctree,
        gboolean show_stub)
    void gtk_ctree_set_spacing(GtkCTree *ctree, gint spacing)
    void gtk_ctree_sort_node(GtkCTree *ctree, GtkCTreeNode *node)
    void gtk_ctree_sort_recursive(GtkCTree *ctree,
        GtkCTreeNode *node)
    void gtk_ctree_toggle_expansion(GtkCTree *ctree,
        GtkCTreeNode *node)
    void gtk_ctree_toggle_expansion_recursive(GtkCTree *ctree,
        GtkCTreeNode *node)
    void gtk_ctree_unselect(GtkCTree *ctree, GtkCTreeNode *node)
    void gtk_ctree_unselect_recursive(GtkCTree *ctree,
        GtkCTreeNode *node)
```

Enums

```
    typedef enum {
      GTK_CTREE_POS_BEFORE,
      GTK_CTREE_POS_AS_CHILD,
      GTK_CTREE_POS_AFTER
    } GtkCTreePos;

    typedef enum {
      GTK_CTREE_LINES_NONE,
      GTK_CTREE_LINES_SOLID,
      GTK_CTREE_LINES_DOTTED,
      GTK_CTREE_LINES_TABBED
    } GtkCTreeLineStyle;

    typedef enum {
      GTK_CTREE_EXPANDER_NONE,
      GTK_CTREE_EXPANDER_SQUARE,
      GTK_CTREE_EXPANDER_TRIANGLE,
      GTK_CTREE_EXPANDER_CIRCULAR
    } GtkCTreeExpanderStyle;

    typedef enum {
      GTK_CTREE_EXPANSION_EXPAND,
      GTK_CTREE_EXPANSION_EXPAND_RECURSIVE,
      GTK_CTREE_EXPANSION_COLLAPSE,
      GTK_CTREE_EXPANSION_COLLAPSE_RECURSIVE,
      GTK_CTREE_EXPANSION_TOGGLE,
      GTK_CTREE_EXPANSION_TOGGLE_RECURSIVE
    } GtkCTreeExpansionType;

    typedef enum {
      GTK_SELECTION_SINGLE,
      GTK_SELECTION_BROWSE,
      GTK_SELECTION_MULTIPLE,
      GTK_SELECTION_EXTENDED
    } GtkSelectionMode;
```

Signals

```
"change_focus_row_expansion"  void cb(GtkWidget *, GtkCTreeExpansionType,
gpointer)
"tree_collapse"               void cb(GtkWidget *, GtkCTreeNode *, gpointer)
"tree_expand"                 void cb(GtkWidget *, GtkCTreeNode *, gpointer)
"tree_move"                   void cb(GtkWidget *, GtkCTreeNode *, GtkCTreeNode
*, GtkCTreeNode *, gpointer)
"tree_select_row"             void cb(GtkWidget *, GtkCTreeNode *, gint,
gpointer)
"tree_unselect_row"           void cb(GtkWidget *, GtkCTreeNode, gint, gpointer)
```

Each node in a `GtkCTree` is a `GtkCTreeNode` struct. This struct contains pointers to sibling, parent, and child nodes. If the parent node is `NULL`, it is the root node. Whenever a new node is added to the tree, and it is not the root node, it is added to either a parent node or a sibling node. The following example produces the simple two-level tree shown in Figure 21-12.

```
static GtkWidget *makeWidget()
{
    GtkCTreeNode *node1_1;
    GtkCTreeNode *node1_3;
    GtkWidget *widget;
    static gchar *titles[] = {
        "First Column",
        "Second Column"
    };

    widget = gtk_ctree_new_with_titles(2,0,titles);
    node1_1 = makeNode(widget,NULL,NULL,1,1);
    makeNode(widget,NULL,node1_1,1,2);
    node1_3 = makeNode(widget,NULL,node1_1,1,3);
    makeNode(widget,NULL,node1_1,1,4);
    makeNode(widget,node1_1,NULL,2,1);
    makeNode(widget,node1_1,NULL,2,2);
    makeNode(widget,node1_3,NULL,2,1);
    makeNode(widget,node1_3,NULL,2,2);
    return(widget);
}
static GtkCTreeNode *makeNode(GtkWidget *widget,
        GtkCTreeNode *parent,GtkCTreeNode *sibling,
        gint level,gint count)
{
    GtkCTreeNode *node;
    gchar *text[2];
    gchar line1[20];
    gchar line2[20];
    text[0] = line1;
    text[1] = line2;

    sprintf(line1,"Level %d",level);
    sprintf(line2,"Number %d",count);
```

```
        node = gtk_ctree_insert_node(GTK_CTREE(widget),
                parent,
                sibling,
                text,
                0,
                NULL,NULL,NULL,NULL,
                FALSE,TRUE);
        return(node);
}
```

Figure 21-12: A two-level GtkCTree showing selection and expansion

GtkCurve

This widget displays a grid and traces a graph on it following a set of points. There are three kinds of traces available. You can add new points, and move existing points, interactively with the mouse.

Inheritance

```
GtkCurve->GtkDrawingArea->GtkWidget->GtkObject
```

Functions

```
GtkType gtk_curve_get_type(void)
void gtk_curve_get_vector(GtkCurve *c, int veclen,
    gfloat vector [ ])
GtkWidget *gtk_curve_new(void)
void gtk_curve_reset(GtkCurve *c)
void gtk_curve_set_curve_type(GtkCurve *c,
    GtkCurveType new_type)
void gtk_curve_set_gamma(GtkCurve *c, gfloat gamma)
void gtk_curve_set_range(GtkCurve *curve, gfloat min_x,
    gfloat max_x, gfloat min_y, gfloat max_y)
void gtk_curve_set_vector(GtkCurve *c, int veclen,
    gfloat vector [ ])
```

Enum

```
typedef enum {
  GTK_CURVE_TYPE_LINEAR,
  GTK_CURVE_TYPE_SPLINE,
  GTK_CURVE_TYPE_FREE
} GtkCurveType;
```

Signal
```
"curve_type_changed"      void cb(GtkWidget *, gpointer)
```

The following example creates a 100x100 display area. The mouse is used to add and position the points shown in Figure 21-13. The curve is a spline, so it creates smooth, curved lines passing through each point.

```
static GtkWidget *makeWidget()
{
    GtkWidget *widget;

    widget = gtk_curve_new();
    gtk_curve_set_range(GTK_CURVE(widget),
            0.0,100.0,0.0,100.0);
    gtk_curve_set_curve_type(GTK_CURVE(widget),
            GTK_CURVE_TYPE_SPLINE);
    return(widget);
}
```

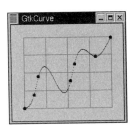

Figure 21-13: A GtkCurve widget displaying a spline curve

GtkData

Widgets inheriting from the base class GtkData have the ability to contain data that is shared among two or more widgets. Examples include GtkAdjustment, GtkTooltips, and GtkAdjustment.

Inheritance
```
GtkData->GtkObject
```

Function
```
GtkType gtk_data_get_type(void)
```

Signal
```
"disconnect"      void cb(GtkWidget *, gpointer)
```

GtkDial

The GtkDial widget displays a dial representing a value from 0 percent to 100 percent. If not in the view-only mode, you can use the mouse to adjust the dial.

Inheritance

```
GtkDial->GtkWidget->GtkObject
```

Functions

```
GtkAdjustment *gtk_dial_get_adjustment(GtkDial *dial)
gfloat gtk_dial_get_percentage(GtkDial *dial)
guint gtk_dial_get_type()
gfloat gtk_dial_get_value(GtkDial *dial)
GtkWidget *gtk_dial_new(GtkAdjustment *adjustment)
void gtk_dial_set_adjustment(GtkDial *dial,
    GtkAdjustment *adjustment)
gfloat gtk_dial_set_percentage(GtkDial *dial, gfloat percent)
void gtk_dial_set_update_policy(GtkDial *dial,
    GtkUpdateType policy)
gfloat gtk_dial_set_value(GtkDial *dial, gfloat value)
void gtk_dial_set_view_only(GtkDial *dial, gboolean view_only)
```

Enum

```
typedef enum {
  GTK_UPDATE_CONTINUOUS,
  GTK_UPDATE_DISCONTINUOUS,
  GTK_UPDATE_DELAYED
} GtkUpdateType;
```

The following example builds the GtkDial widget shown in Figure 21-14. The current setting of 44 is 22 percent of the distance from the 0 minimum and the 200 maximum.

```
static GtkWidget *makeWidget()
{
    GtkWidget *widget;
    GtkObject *adjustment;

    adjustment = gtk_adjustment_new(44.0,
            0.0,200.00,1.0,0.0,0.0);
    widget = gtk_dial_new(GTK_ADJUSTMENT(adjustment));
    return(widget);
}
```

Figure 21-14: A GtkDial widget at 22 percent

GtkDialog

A GtkDialog widget is a window with some preinstalled and configured containers that you can use to create your own popup dialog boxes.

Inheritance

```
GtkDialog->GtkWindow->GtkBin->GtkContainer->GtkWidget->
       GtkObject
```

Functions

```
GtkType gtk_dialog_get_type(void)
GtkWidget *gtk_dialog_new(void)
```

The following example, shown in Figure 21-15, places three buttons in each of the two available containers. The vertical box, named vbox, is configured at the top and is designed for use by toolbars and menus. Also, you can use the vertical box as a container for pixmap windows and text labels. The horizontal box, named action_area, spaces widgets out in the center and is designed for response buttons.

```
static void makeWidget()
{
    GtkWidget *dialog;
    GtkWidget *button;
    GtkWidget *vbox;
    GtkWidget *hbox;

    dialog = gtk_dialog_new();

    vbox = GTK_DIALOG(dialog)->vbox;
    button = gtk_button_new_with_label("VBOX First");
    gtk_box_pack_start(GTK_BOX(vbox),button,TRUE,TRUE,0);
    button = gtk_button_new_with_label("VBOX Second");
    gtk_box_pack_start(GTK_BOX(vbox),button,TRUE,TRUE,0);
    button = gtk_button_new_with_label("VBOX Third");
    gtk_box_pack_start(GTK_BOX(vbox),button,TRUE,TRUE,0);

    hbox = GTK_DIALOG(dialog)->action_area;
    button = gtk_button_new_with_label("HBOX First");
    gtk_box_pack_start(GTK_BOX(hbox),button,TRUE,TRUE,0);
    button = gtk_button_new_with_label("HBOX Second");
    gtk_box_pack_start(GTK_BOX(hbox),button,TRUE,TRUE,0);
    button = gtk_button_new_with_label("HBOX Third");
    gtk_box_pack_start(GTK_BOX(hbox),button,TRUE,TRUE,0);

    gtk_widget_show_all(dialog);
}
```

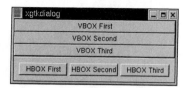

Figure 21-15: A GtkDialog widget displaying buttons vertically and horizontally

GtkDrawingArea

This is a very simple widget that provides access to a window used by primitive drawing and painting commands.

Inheritance

```
GtkDrawingArea->GtkWidget->GtkObject
```

Functions

```
guint gtk_drawing_area_get_type(void)
GtkWidget *gtk_drawing_area_new(void)
void gtk_drawing_area_size(GtkDrawingArea *darea, gint width,
    gint height)
```

Chapters 10 and 11 provide numerous examples of the GtkDrawingArea widget.

GtkEditable

The GtkEditable widget is used as a base class used in the creation of widgets that are capable of editing text. As such, it is used as the base class of GtkEntry, GtkSpinButton, and GtkText

Inheritance

```
GtkEditable->GtkWidget->GtkObject
```

Functions

```
void gtk_editable_changed(GtkEditable *editable)
void gtk_editable_claim_selection(GtkEditable *editable,
    gboolean claim, guint32 time)
void gtk_editable_copy_clipboard(GtkEditable *editable)
void gtk_editable_cut_clipboard(GtkEditable *editable)
void gtk_editable_delete_selection(GtkEditable *editable)
void gtk_editable_delete_text(GtkEditable *editable,
    gint start_pos, gint end_pos)
gchar *gtk_editable_get_chars(GtkEditable *editable,
    gint start, gint end)
gint gtk_editable_get_position(GtkEditable *editable)
```

```
GtkType gtk_editable_get_type(void)
void gtk_editable_insert_text(GtkEditable *editable,
    const gchar *new_text, gint new_text_length,
    gint *position)
void gtk_editable_paste_clipboard(GtkEditable *editable)
void gtk_editable_select_region(GtkEditable *editable,
    gint start, gint end)
void gtk_editable_set_editable(GtkEditable *editable,
    gboolean is_editable)
void gtk_editable_set_position(GtkEditable *editable,
    gint position)
```

Signals

```
"activate"          void cb(GtkWidget *, gpointer)
"changed"           void cb(GtkWidget *, gpointer)
"copy_clipboard"    void cb(GtkWidget *, gpointer)
"cut_clipboard"     void cb(GtkWidget *, gpointer)
"delete_text"       void cb(GtkWidget *, gint, gint, gpointer)
"insert_text"       void cb(GtkWidget *, gchar *, gint, gpointer,
gpointer)
"kill_char"         void cb(GtkWidget *, gint, gpointer)
"kill_line"         void cb(GtkWidget *, gint, gpointer)
"kill_word"         void cb(GtkWidget *, gint, gpointer)
"move_cursor"       void cb(GtkWidget *, gint, gint, gpointer)
"move_page"         void cb(GtkWidget *, gint, gint, gpointer)
"move_to_column"    void cb(GtkWidget *, gint, gint, gpointer)
"move_to_row"       void cb(GLkWidget *, gint, gpointer)
"move_word"         void cb(GtkWidget *, gint, gpointer)
"paste_clipboard"   void cb(GtkWidget *, gpointer)
"set-editable"      void cb(GtkWidget *, gbolean, gpointer)
```

GtkEntry

The GtkEntry widget provides a data-entry window for a single line of text.

Inheritance

```
GtkEntry->GtkEditable->GtkWidget->GtkObject
```

Functions

```
void gtk_entry_append_text(GtkEntry *entry, const gchar *text)
gchar *gtk_entry_get_text(GtkEntry *entry)
GtkType gtk_entry_get_type(void)
GtkWidget *gtk_entry_new(void)
GtkWidget *gtk_entry_new_with_max_length(guint16 max)
void gtk_entry_prepend_text(GtkEntry *entry, const gchar *text)
void gtk_entry_select_region(GtkEntry *entry, gint start,
    gint end)
void gtk_entry_set_editable(GtkEntry *entry, gboolean editable)
```

```
void gtk_entry_set_max_length(GtkEntry *entry, guint16 max)
void gtk_entry_set_position(GtkEntry *entry, gint position)
void gtk_entry_set_text(GtkEntry *entry, const gchar *text)
void gtk_entry_set_visibility(GtkEntry *entry,
    gboolean visible)
```

This example creates the text-entry window shown in Figure 21-16. It is 40 characters wide and initialized with text.

```
static GtkWidget *makeWidget()
{
    GtkWidget *widget;

    widget = gtk_entry_new_with_max_length(40);
    gtk_entry_set_text(GTK_ENTRY(widget),"Edit me!");
    return(widget);
}
```

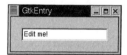

Figure 21-16: A data-entry box containing editable text

GtkEventBox

The GtkEventBox widget is a container with a see-through window that can receive events for the contained widget — normally one that cannot receive its own. Events are sent to windows, so a widget without windows cannot receive events.

Inheritance
```
GtkEventBox->GtkBin->GtkContainer->GtkWidget->GtkObject
```
Functions
```
GtkType gtk_event_box_get_type(void)
GtkWidget *gtk_event_box_new(void)
```

This example wraps a GtkEventBox around a GtkLabel to make the label sensitive to mouse movements. The callbacks are used to change the text of the label, as shown in Figure 21-17, to indicate whether or not the mouse pointer is inside the label.

```
static GtkWidget *makeWidget()
{
    GtkWidget *eventbox;
    GtkWidget *label;
```

```
        eventbox = gtk_event_box_new();
        label = gtk_label_new("Mouse Outside");
        gtk_container_add(GTK_CONTAINER(eventbox),label);
        gtk_signal_connect(GTK_OBJECT(eventbox),
                "enter_notify_event",
                GTK_SIGNAL_FUNC(mouseEnter),label);
        gtk_signal_connect(GTK_OBJECT(eventbox),
                "leave_notify_event",
                GTK_SIGNAL_FUNC(mouseLeave),label);

        return(eventbox);
    }
    static gboolean mouseEnter(GtkWidget *widget,
            GdkEvent *event,gpointer data)
    {
        gtk_label_set_text(GTK_LABEL(data),"Mouse Inside");
        return(TRUE);
    }
    static gboolean mouseLeave(GtkWidget *widget,
            GdkEvent *event,gpointer data)
    {
        gtk_label_set_text(GTK_LABEL(data),"Mouse Outside");
        return(TRUE);
    }
```

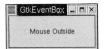

Figure 21-17: An event box supplying events to a label

GtkFileSelection

The GtkFileSelection widget lists all the files and directories in the current working directory and enables the user to select one of the file names. As shown in Figure 21-18, there are a number of navigation controls that enable the user to browse through the entire file system. There also are buttons that create directories, delete files, and rename files.

Inheritance

```
GtkFileSelection->GtkWindow->GtkBin->GtkContainer->GtkWidget->
        GtkObject
```

Functions

```
void gtk_file_selection_complete(GtkFileSelection *filesel,
    const gchar *pattern)
gchar *gtk_file_selection_get_filename(
```

```
        GtkFileSelection *filesel)
    GtkType gtk_file_selection_get_type(void)
    void gtk_file_selection_hide_fileop_buttons(
        GtkFileSelection *filesel)
    GtkWidget *gtk_file_selection_new(const gchar *title)
    void gtk_file_selection_set_filename(
        GtkFileSelection *filesel, const gchar *filename)
    void gtk_file_selection_show_fileop_buttons(
        GtkFileSelection *filesel)
    int translate_win32_path(GtkFileSelection *filesel)
```

The following example displays a `GtkFileSelection` widget with the file
`xgtkfileselection.c` as the preselected default, as shown in Figure 21-18. There
are three callbacks that need to be handled. The Cancel button closes the window
without making a selection, and the OK button returns the name of the selected file
and closes the window. Because this widget is in its own top-level window, you need
to call `gtk_main_quit()` to close it.

```
static void makeWidget()
{
    GtkWidget *fileselection;
    GtkWidget *okButton;
    GtkWidget *cancelButton;

    fileselection =
        gtk_file_selection_new("GtkFileSelection");

    okButton = GTK_FILE_SELECTION(fileselection)->ok_button;
    cancelButton =
            GTK_FILE_SELECTION(fileselection)->cancel_button;

    gtk_signal_connect (GTK_OBJECT(fileselection),"destroy",
            (GtkSignalFunc)gtk_widget_destroy,
            fileselection);
    gtk_signal_connect(GTK_OBJECT(okButton),"clicked",
            (GtkSignalFunc)eventOk,fileselection);
    gtk_signal_connect(GTK_OBJECT(cancelButton),"clicked",
            (GtkSignalFunc)eventCancel,fileselection);

    gtk_file_selection_set_filename(
            GTK_FILE_SELECTION(fileselection),
            "xgtkfileselection.c");
    gtk_widget_show(fileselection);
}
void eventOk(GtkWidget *widget,gpointer data)
{
    GtkFileSelection *fileselection;
    gchar *filename;

    fileselection = GTK_FILE_SELECTION(data);
```

```
            filename = gtk_file_selection_get_filename(fileselection);
            g_print("Selected File: %s\n",filename);
            gtk_main_quit();
    }
    void eventCancel(GtkWidget *widget,gpointer data)
    {
            gtk_main_quit();
    }
```

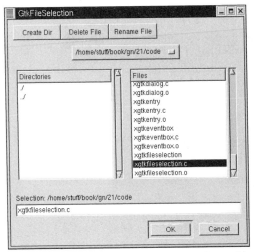

Figure 21-18: The GtkFileSelection widget with a file selected

GtkFixed

The GtkFixed container enables your program to place widgets at fixed locations, and to move widgets from one location to another.

Inheritance

```
GtkFixed->GtkContainer->GtkWidget->GtkObject
```

Functions

```
GtkType gtk_fixed_get_type(void)
void gtk_fixed_move(GtkFixed *fixed, GtkWidget *widget,
    gint16 x, gint16 y)
GtkWidget *gtk_fixed_new(void)
void gtk_fixed_put(GtkFixed *fixed, GtkWidget *widget,
    gint16 x, gint16 y)
```

Chapter 5 provides examples of GtkFixed.

GtkFontSelection

The GtkFontSelection widget can be used by your application to enable the user
to select a font.

Using this widget, it is up to your application to determine when a selection is made
and call the gtk_font_selection_get_font() function. The
GtkFontSelectionDialog widget uses this widget and adds selection buttons and
callbacks.

Inheritance
```
GtkFontSelection->GtkNotebook->GtkContainer->GtkWidget->
        GtkObject
```

Functions
```
GdkFont *gtk_font_selection_get_font(
    GtkFontSelection *fontsel)
gchar *gtk_font_selection_get_font_name(
    GtkFontSelection *fontsel)
gchar *gtk_font_selection_get_preview_text(
    GtkFontSelection *fontsel)
GtkType gtk_font_selection_get_type()
GtkWidget *gtk_font_selection_new()
void gtk_font_selection_set_filter(GtkFontSelection *fontsel,
    GtkFontFilterType filter_type, GtkFontType font_type,
    gchar **foundries, gchar **weights, gchar **slants,
    gchar **setwidths, gchar **spacings, gchar **charsets)
gboolean gtk_font_selection_set_font_name(
    GtkFontSelection *fontsel, const gchar *fontname)
void gtk_font_selection_set_preview_text(
    GtkFontSelection *fontsel, const gchar *text)
```

Enums
```
typedef enum {
  GTK_FONT_FILTER_BASE,
  GTK_FONT_FILTER_USER
} GtkFontFilterType;

typedef enum {
  GTK_FONT_BITMAP,
  GTK_FONT_SCALABLE,
  GTK_FONT_SCALABLE_BITMAP,
  GTK_FONT_ALL
} GtkFontFilterType;
```

The GtkFontSelection widget shown in Figure 21-19 following the example code is
the default configuration (there is no filtering) that shows a selected font, along
with its weight and size. The selected font is displayed in the window across the

bottom. The tab labeled *Font Information* displays a detailed list of the currently selected font and the long form of the font name, as described in Chapter 13. The tab labeled *Filter* exposes a window that you can use to set filtering controls used to restrict the displayed font names. The filtering operates on each of the parts of the long-font file names.

```
static GtkWidget *makeWidget()
{
    GtkWidget *widget;

    widget = gtk_font_selection_new();
    return(widget);
}
```

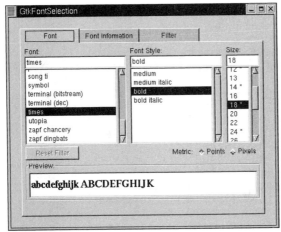

Figure 21-19: A GtkFontSelection widget showing a selected font

The call to font_selection_set_filter() can be used to specify the same sort of filtering that the user can impose under the *Filter* tab. Each filter is a pointer to an array of filter value strings. Passing a NULL pointer removes all filtering for that item.

GtkFontSelectionDialog

This widget uses a GtkFontSelection widget as its main window and adds buttons so the user can accept or cancel font selection.

Inheritance

```
GtkFontSelectionDialog->GtkWindow->GtkBin->GtkContainer->
      GtkWidget->GtkObject
```

Functions

```
GdkFont *gtk_font_selection_dialog_get_font(
    GtkFontSelectionDialog *fsd)
gchar *gtk_font_selection_dialog_get_font_name(
    GtkFontSelectionDialog *fsd)
gchar *gtk_font_selection_dialog_get_preview_text(
    GtkFontSelectionDialog *fsd)
guint gtk_font_selection_dialog_get_type(void)
GtkWidget *gtk_font_selection_dialog_new(const gchar *title)
void gtk_font_selection_dialog_set_filter(
    GtkFontSelectionDialog *fsd, GtkFontFilterType filter_type,
    GtkFontType font_type, gchar **foundries, gchar **weights,
    gchar **slants, gchar **setwidths, gchar **spacings,
    gchar **charsets)
gboolean gtk_font_selection_dialog_set_font_name(
    GtkFontSelectionDialog *fsd, const gchar *fontname)
void gtk_font_selection_dialog_set_preview_text(
    GtkFontSelectionDialog *fsd, const gchar *text)
```

Enums

```
typedef enum {
  GTK_FONT_FILTER_BASE,
  GTK_FONT_FILTER_USER
} GtkFontFilterType;

typedef enum {
  GTK_FONT_BITMAP,
  GTK_FONT_SCALABLE,
  GTK_FONT_SCALABLE_BITMAP,
  GTK_FONT_ALL
} GtkFontFilterType;
```

The following example displays the default configuration of the
GtkFontSelectionDialog window, as shown in Figure 21-20. To see an example of
responding to the dialog buttons, read the earlier section on GtkDialog. For more
information on font filtering and other controls, see GtkFontSelection. For
general information on fonts, refer to Chapter 13.

```
static void makeWidget()
{
    GtkWidget *widget;

    widget = gtk_font_selection_dialog_new(
            "GtkFontSelectionDialog");
    gtk_widget_show(widget);
}
```

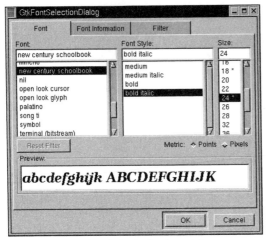

Figure 21-20: The default display of the GtkFontSelectionDialog window

GtkFrame

GtkFrame is a container that holds one widget and places a frame around it.

Inheritance
```
GtkFrame->GtkBin->GtkContainer->GtkWidget->GtkObject
```

Functions
```
GtkType gtk_frame_get_type(void)
GtkWidget *gtk_frame_new(const gchar *label)
void gtk_frame_set_label(GtkFrame *frame, const gchar *label)
void gtk_frame_set_label_align(GtkFrame *frame, gfloat xalign,
    gfloat yalign)
void gtk_frame_set_shadow_type(GtkFrame *frame,
    GtkShadowType type)
```

Enum
```
typedef enum {
  GTK_SHADOW_NONE,
  GTK_SHADOW_IN,
  GTK_SHADOW_OUT,
  GTK_SHADOW_ETCHED_IN,
  GTK_SHADOW_ETCHED_OUT
} GtkShadowType;
```

The following example uses a GtkFrame widget to enclose a label. The frame itself has a text label that can be suppressed by passing NULL to gtk_frame_new().

Chapter 5 includes examples showing the different shadow styles. The following example displays the window shown in Figure 21-21.

```
static GtkWidget *makeWidget()
{
    GtkWidget *label;
    GtkWidget *frame;

    label = gtk_label_new(
            "The string of characters in the label");
    frame = gtk_frame_new("Frame Text");
    gtk_container_add(GTK_CONTAINER(frame),label);
    return(frame);
}
```

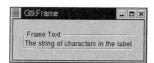

Figure 21-21: A GtkFrame with default shadowing and a label

GtkGammaCurve

The GtkGammaCurve widget displays an interactive window that enables the mouse to insert and move points. The points can be plotted as curves or linearly. Selecting the button with the gamma symbol enables you to alter the gamma value.

Inheritance

```
GtkGammaCurve->GtkVBox->GtkBox->GtkContainer->GtkWidget->
        GtkObject
```

Functions

```
guint gtk_gamma_curve_get_type(void)
GtkWidget *gtk_gamma_curve_new(void)
```

The following example displays the window shown in Figure 21-22.

```
static GtkWidget *makeWidget()
{
    GtkWidget *widget;

    widget = gtk_gamma_curve_new();
    return(widget);
}
```

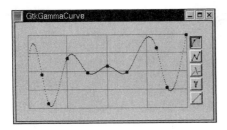

Figure 21-22: A GtkGammaCurve window with nine points and a gamma value of one

GtkHandleBox

A GtkHandleBox is a container that has a handle on one of its four sides; the mouse uses the handle to move the widget to another location. It can be moved completely outside the application window.

Inheritance

```
GtkHandleBox->GtkBin->GtkContainer->GtkWidget->GtkObject
```

Functions

```
guint gtk_handle_box_get_type(void)
GtkWidget *gtk_handle_box_new(void)
void gtk_handle_box_set_handle_position(
    GtkHandleBox *handle_box, GtkPositionType position)
void gtk_handle_box_set_shadow_type(GtkHandleBox *handle_box,
    GtkShadowType type)
void gtk_handle_box_set_snap_edge(GtkHandleBox *handle_box,
    GtkPositionType edge)
```

Enums

```
typedef enum {
  GTK_POS_LEFT,
  GTK_POS_RIGHT,
  GTK_POS_TOP,
  GTK_POS_BOTTOM
} GtkPositionType;

typedef enum {
  GTK_SHADOW_NONE,
  GTK_SHADOW_IN,
  GTK_SHADOW_OUT,
  GTK_SHADOW_ETCHED_IN,
  GTK_SHADOW_ETCHED_OUT
} GtkShadowType;
```

Signals

```
"child_attached"        void cb(GtkWidget *, GtkWidget *,
gpointer)
"child_detached"        void cb(GtkWidget *, GtkWidget *,
gpointer)
```

The follow example inserts a horizontal box, containing a row of three buttons, into a GtkHandleBox widget. The default position of the handle is on the left. Figure 21-23 shows the buttons and the handle as they appear when the application is started. Figure 21-24 shows the results of dragging the handle with the mouse. The handle box also can be dragged back to its original location. Notice that the sizes of the buttons are different—this is because, in this example, the parent windows control much of the button sizing and these controls are not active when the handle bar is in another location.

```
static GtkWidget *makeWidget()
{
    GtkWidget *handlebox;
    GtkWidget *box;
    GtkWidget *button;

    box = gtk_hbox_new(FALSE,0);
    button = gtk_button_new_with_label("First");
    gtk_box_pack_start(GTK_BOX(box),button,TRUE,TRUE,0);
    button = gtk_button_new_with_label("Second");
    gtk_box_pack_start(GTK_BOX(box),button,TRUE,TRUE,0);
    button = gtk_button_new_with_label("Third");
    gtk_box_pack_start(GTK_BOX(box),button,TRUE,TRUE,0);

    handlebox = gtk_handle_box_new();
    gtk_container_add(GTK_CONTAINER(handlebox),box);

    return(handlebox);
}
```

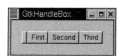

Figure 21-23: A GtkHandleBox with three buttons and a handle on the left

Figure 21-24: A GtkHandleBox dragged off its parent window

GtkHBox

GtkHBox is a container widget that organizes its contained widgets horizontally (side by side).

Inheritance
```
GtkHBox->GtkBox->GtkContainer->GtkWidget->GtkObject
```

Functions
```
GtkType gtk_hbox_get_type(void)
GtkWidget *gtk_hbox_new(gboolean homogeneous, gint spacing)
```

Chapter 4 includes a number of examples of `GtkHBox`.

GtkHButtonBox

`GtkHButtonBox` is a container designed to display a collection of buttons horizontally (side by side).

Inheritance
```
GtkHButtonBox->GtkButtonBox->GtkBox->GtkContainer->GtkWidget->
      GtkObject
```

Functions
```
GtkButtonBoxStyle gtk_hbutton_box_get_layout_default(void)
gint gtk_hbutton_box_get_spacing_default(void)
guint gtk_hbutton_box_get_type(void)
GtkWidget *gtk_hbutton_box_new(void)
void gtk_hbutton_box_set_layout_default(
    GtkButtonBoxStyle layout)
void gtk_hbutton_box_set_spacing_default(ginL spacing)
```

Enum
```
typedef enum {
  GTK_BUTTONBOX_DEFAULT_STYLE,
  GTK_BUTTONBOX_SPREAD,
  GTK_BUTTONBOX_EDGE,
  GTK_BUTTONBOX_START,
  GTK_BUTTONBOX_END
} GtkButtonBoxStyle;
```

See Chapter 5 for a number of examples of `GtkHButtonBox`.

GtkHPaned

`GtkHPaned` is a container with one left and one right pane. Each pane can contain a widget; you can use the mouse on the bar separating the panes to adjust the amount showing in each pane without changing the size of the overall window.

Inheritance
```
GtkHPaned->GtkPaned->GtkContainer->GtkWidget->GtkObject
```

Functions

```
guint gtk_hpaned_get_type(void)
GtkWidget *gtk_hpaned_new(void)
```

See Chapter 5 for an example of GtkHPaned.

GtkHRuler

GtkHRuler displays a horizontally-oriented scale that optionally can contain tic marks and a current-position pointer. You can set the pointer position from inside the program; it follows the mouse.

Inheritance

```
GtkHRuler->GtkRuler->GtkWidget->GtkObject
```

Functions

```
guint gtk_hruler_get_type(void)
GtkWidget *gtk_hruler_new(void)
```

The following example displays the window shown in Figure 21-25.

```
static GtkWidget *makeWidget()
{
    GtkWidget *widget;

    widget = gtk_hruler_new();
    gtk_ruler_set_range(GTK_RULER(widget),0.0,100.0,
            20.0,10.0);
    return(widget);
}
```

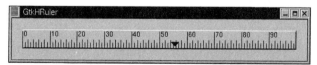

Figure 21-25: A horizontal ruler with tics and a position pointer

GtkHScale

This widget is a horizontal slot containing a slider that can be moved by the mouse.

Inheritance

```
GtkHScale->GtkScale->GtkRange->GtkWidget->GtkObject
```

Functions

```
GtkType gtk_hscale_get_type(void)
GtkWidget *gtk_hscale_new(GtkAdjustment *adjustment)
```

The following example creates a horizontal scale that ranges from 0 to 100 and has an initial value of 45, as shown in Figure 21-26.

```
static GtkWidget *makeWidget()
{
    GtkWidget *widget;
    GtkObject *adjustment;

    adjustment = gtk_adjustment_new(45.0,0.0,100.0,
        1.0,0.0,0.0);
    widget = gtk_hscale_new(GTK_ADJUSTMENT(adjustment));
    return(widget);
}
```

Figure 21-26: A horizontal scale with the slider set to 45

GtkHScrollbar

The GtkHScrollbar displays a horizontal scrollbar with a slider and a pair of arrow buttons. To create a scrollbar, you must specify the beginning and ending values, the size of the slider, an initial slider position, and how far the slider moves when the mouse clicks the slot.

Inheritance

```
GtkHScrollbar->GtkScrollbar->GtkRange->GtkWidget->GtkObject
```

Functions

```
GtkType gtk_hscrollbar_get_type(void)
GtkWidget *gtk_hscrollbar_new(GtkAdjustment *adjustment)
```

The following example creates a horizontal scrollbar that ranges from 0 to 100, as shown in Figure 21-27. The setting of the range specifies that there are 100 units from one end to the other (the difference between the beginning and ending values). Clicking an arrow at one end moves the slider one unit. Clicking the slot moves the slider 5 units. The slider is set to be 20 units wide.

```
static GtkWidget *makeWidget()
{
    GtkWidget *widget;
    GtkObject *adjustment;
```

```
        adjustment = gtk_adjustment_new(45.0,0.0,100.0,
            1.0,5.0,20.0);
        widget = gtk_hscrollbar_new(GTK_ADJUSTMENT(adjustment));
        return(widget);
    }
```

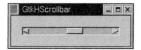

Figure 21-27: A horizontal scrollbar with the slider sized at 20 percent

GtkHSeparator

The GtkHSeparator widget draws a horizontal line that serves as a divider among a collection of vertically organized widgets. It is used commonly in menus.

Inheritance
```
    GtkHSeparator->GtkSeparator->GtkWidget->GtkObject
```
Functions
```
    GtkType gtk_hseparator_get_type(void)
    GtkWidget *gtk_hseparator_new(void)
```

The following example packs a horizontal separator into a box between two buttons, as shown in Figure 21-28. If the container does not resize the separator, its height must be set because the separator defaults to a height of zero and cannot be seen.

```
    static GtkWidget *makeWidget()
    {
        GtkWidget *box;
        GtkWidget *button;
        GtkWidget *separator;

        box = gtk_vbox_new(FALSE,0);

        button = gtk_button_new_with_label("Button 1");
        gtk_box_pack_start(GTK_BOX(box),button,FALSE,FALSE,0);

        separator = gtk_hseparator_new();
        gtk_box_pack_start(GTK_BOX(box),separator,FALSE,FALSE,0);
        gtk_widget_set_usize(separator,0,20);

        button = gtk_button_new_with_label("Button 2");
        gtk_box_pack_start(GTK_BOX(box),button,FALSE,FALSE,0);

        return(box);
    }
```

Figure 21-28: A horizontal separator between two buttons

GtkImage

The GtkImage widget contains and displays a GdkImage.

Inheritance

```
GtkImage->GtkMisc->GtkWidget->GtkObject
```

Functions

```
void gtk_image_get(GtkImage *image, GdkImage **val,
    GdkBitmap **mask)
GtkType gtk_image_get_type(void)
GtkWidget *gtk_image_new(GdkImage *val, GdkBitmap *mask)
void gtk_image_set(GtkImage *image, GdkImage *val,
    GdkBitmap *mask)
```

The following example creates a GdkImage object and creates a GtkImage widget to display it. Because the default GdkImage is all black; the *x* and *y* loop draws a white corner-to-corner X resulting in the display in Figure 21-29.

```
static GtkWidget *makeWidget()
{
    int x;
    int y;
    GtkWidget *widget;
    GdkVisual *visual;
    GdkImage *gdkimage;

    visual = gdk_visual_get_system();
    gdkimage = gdk_image_new(GDK_IMAGE_NORMAL,visual,100,100);

    for(x=0; x<100; x++) {
        y = x;
        gdk_image_put_pixel(gdkimage,x,y,0xFFFFFFFF);
        y = 100 - x;
        gdk_image_put_pixel(gdkimage,x,y,0xFFFFFFFF);
    }
    widget = gtk_image_new(gdkimage,NULL);
    return(widget);
}
```

Figure 21-29: A GdkImage displayed by a GtkWidget

GtkInputDialog

The GtkInputDialog window is designed specifically to be used in software that controls access to XInput devices (input devices other than the mouse and keyboard).

Inheritance

```
GtkInputDialog->GtkDialog->GtkWindow->GtkBin->GtkContainer->
        GtkWidget->GtkObject
```

Functions

```
GtkType gtk_input_dialog_get_type(void)
GtkWidget *gtk_input_dialog_new(void)
```

Signals

```
"disable_device"     void cb(GtkWidget *, gint, gpointer)
"enable_device"      void cb(GtkWidget *, gint, gpointer)
```

The following example displays the window shown in Figure 21-30.

```
static void makeWidget()
{
    GtkWidget *dialog;

    dialog = gtk_input_dialog_new();
    gtk_widget_show_all(dialog);
}
```

Figure 21-30: The default GtkInputDialog window

GtkInvisible

The GtkInvisible widget displays a blank window. It can act as a placeholder. For example, it can be sized with a call to gtk_widget_usize(), and used inside a container to help position other widgets.

Inheritance

```
GtkInvisible->GtkBin->GtkContainer->GtkWidget->GtkObject
```

Functions

```
GtkType gtk_invisible_get_type(void)
GtkWidget *gtk_invisible_new(void)
```

The following example inserts a pair of buttons into a horizontal box, as shown in Figure 21-31. The two buttons are separated by a GtkInvisible widget that is 30 pixels wide and 60 pixels high. Because the GtkInvisible widget is tallest, the box container uses it to determine the overall height. This causes the buttons to be stretched vertically to fill the box.

```
GtkWidget *makeWidget() {
    GtkWidget *box;
    GtkWidget *button;
    GtkWidget *invisible;

    box = gtk_hbox_new(FALSE,0);

    button = gtk_button_new_with_label("Left Button");
    gtk_box_pack_start(GTK_BOX(box),button,FALSE,FALSE,0);

    invisible = gtk_invisible_new();
    gtk_widget_set_usize(invisible,30,60);
    gtk_box_pack_start(GTK_BOX(box),invisible,FALSE,FALSE,0);

    button = gtk_button_new_with_label("Right Button");
    gtk_box_pack_end(GTK_BOX(box),button,FALSE,FALSE,0);

    return(box);
}
```

Figure 21-31: An invisible widget separating two buttons

GtkItem

This widget is designed to be a base class for widgets that can be selected and deselected. The widgets that inherit from GtkItem are GtkCheckMenuItem, GtkListItem, GtkMenuItem, GtkPixmapMenuItem, GtkRadioMenuItem, GtkTearoffMenuItem, and GtkTreeItem.

Inheritance

```
GtkItem->GtkBin->GtkContainer->GtkWidget->GtkObject
```

Functions

```
void gtk_item_deselect(GtkItem *item)
GtkType gtk_item_get_type(void)
void gtk_item_select(GtkItem *item)
void gtk_item_toggle(GtkItem *item)
```

Signals

```
"deselect"      void cb(GtkWidget *, gpointer)
"select"        void cb(GtkWidget *, gpointer)
"toggle"        void cb(GtkWidget *, gpointer)
```

GtkItemFactory

GtkItemFactory is a utility object designed to create menus. It reads the data found in an array of GtkItemFactoryEntry structs to determine the contents of the menu.

Inheritance

```
GtkItemFactory->GtkObject
```

Functions

```
void gtk_item_factories_path_delete(
    const gchar *ifactory_path, const gchar *path)
void gtk_item_factory_add_foreign(GtkWidget *accel_widget,
    const gchar *full_path, GtkAccelGroup *accel_group,
    guint keyval, GdkModifierType modifiers)
void gtk_item_factory_construct(GtkItemFactory *ifactory,
    GtkType container_type, const gchar *path,
    GtkAccelGroup *accel_group)
void gtk_item_factory_create_item(GtkItemFactory *ifactory,
    GtkItemFactoryEntry *entry, gpointer callback_data,
    guint callback_type)
void gtk_item_factory_create_items(GtkItemFactory *ifactory,
    guint n_entries, GtkItemFactoryEntry *entries,
    gpointer callback_data)
void gtk_item_factory_create_items_ac(
    GtkItemFactory *ifactory, guint n_entries,
    GtkItemFactoryEntry *entries, gpointer callback_data,
    guint callback_type)
void gtk_item_factory_create_menu_entries(guint n_entries,
    GtkMenuEntry *entries)
void gtk_item_factory_delete_entries(
    GtkItemFactory *ifactory, guint n_entries,
    GtkItemFactoryEntry *entries)
```

```
void gtk_item_factory_delete_entry(GtkItemFactory *ifactory,
    GtkItemFactoryEntry *entry)
void gtk_item_factory_delete_item(GtkItemFactory *ifactory,
    const gchar *path)
void gtk_item_factory_dump_items(GtkPatternSpec *path_pspec,
    gboolean modified_only, GtkPrintFunc print_func,
    gpointer func_data)
void gtk_item_factory_dump_rc(const gchar *file_name,
    GtkPatternSpec *path_pspec, gboolean modified_only)
GtkItemFactory *gtk_item_factory_from_path(const gchar *path)
GtkItemFactory *gtk_item_factory_from_widget(
    GtkWidget *widget)
GtkWidget *gtk_item_factory_get_item(
    GtkItemFactory *ifactory, const gchar *path)
GtkWidget *gtk_item_factory_get_item_by_action(
    GtkItemFactory *ifactory, guint action)
GtkType gtk_item_factory_get_type(void)
GtkWidget *gtk_item_factory_get_widget(
    GtkItemFactory *ifactory, const gchar *path)
GtkWidget *gtk_item_factory_get_widget_by_action(
    GtkItemFactory *ifactory, guint action)
GtkItemFactory *gtk_item_factory_new(GtkType container_type,
    const gchar *path, GtkAccelGroup *accel_group)
void gtk_item_factory_parse_rc(const gchar *file_name)
void gtk_item_factory_parse_rc_scanner(GScanner *scanner)
void gtk_item_factory_parse_rc_string(const gchar *rc_string)
gchar *gtk_item_factory_path_from_widget(GtkWidget *widget)
void gtk_item_factory_popup(GtkItemFactory *ifactory, guint x,
    guint y, guint mouse_button, guint32 time)
gpointer gtk_item_factory_popup_data(
    GtkItemFactory *ifactory)
gpointer gtk_item_factory_popup_data_from_widget(
    GtkWidget *widget)
void gtk_item_factory_popup_with_data(
    GtkItemFactory *ifactory, gpointer popup_data,
    GtkDestroyNotify destroy, guint x, guint y,
    guint mouse_button, guint32 time)
void gtk_item_factory_print_func(gpointer FILE_pointer,
    gchar *string)
void gtk_item_factory_set_translate_func(
    GtkItemFactory *ifactory, GtkTranslateFunc func,
    gpointer data, GtkDestroyNotify notify)
```

The GtkItemFactory is being retained as part of GTK only for backward
compatibility. A better way of creating menus has been devised. Chapter 8 contains
examples of creating both menus and toolbars.

GtkLabel

The GtkLabel widget displays a string of text.

Inheritance

```
GtkLabel->GtkMisc->GtkWidget->GtkObject
```

Functions

```
void gtk_label_get(GtkLabel *label, char **str)
GtkType gtk_label_get_type(void)
GtkWidget *gtk_label_new(const char *str)
guint gtk_label_parse_uline(GtkLabel *label,
    const gchar *string)
void gtk_label_set_justify(GtkLabel *label,
    GtkJustification jtype)
void gtk_label_set_line_wrap(GtkLabel *label, gboolean wrap)
void gtk_label_set_pattern(GtkLabel *label,
    const gchar *pattern)
void gtk_label_set_text(GtkLabel *label, const char *str)
```

Enum

```
typedef enum {
  GTK_JUSTIFY_LEFT,
  GTK_JUSTIFY_RIGHT,
  GTK_JUSTIFY_CENTER,
  GTK_JUSTIFY_FILL
} GtkJustification;
The following example displays the window displayed in Figure
21-32.static GtkWidget *makeWidget()
{
    GtkWidget *widget;

    widget = gtk_label_new("Label String");
    return(widget);
}
```

Figure 21-32: A GtkLabel widget
displaying text

GtkLayout

You can use this container widget to position widgets on a virtual window that is
much larger than the currently visible area. You also can use horizontal and vertical
scrollbars to make any portion of the window visible.

Inheritance

```
GtkLayout->GtkContainer->GtkWidget->GtkObject
```

Functions

```
void gtk_layout_freeze(GtkLayout *layout)
GtkAdjustment *gtk_layout_get_hadjustment(GtkLayout *layout)
GtkType gtk_layout_get_type(void)
GtkAdjustment *gtk_layout_get_vadjustment(GtkLayout *layout)
void gtk_layout_move(GtkLayout *layout,
    GtkWidget *child_widget, gint x, gint y)
GtkWidget *gtk_layout_new(GtkAdjustment *hadjustment,
    GtkAdjustment *vadjustment)
void gtk_layout_put(GtkLayout *layout, GtkWidget *child_widget,
    gint x, gint y)
void gtk_layout_set_hadjustment(GtkLayout *layout,
    GtkAdjustment *adjustment)
void gtk_layout_set_size(GtkLayout *layout, guint width,
    guint height)
void gtk_layout_set_vadjustment(GtkLayout *layout,
    GtkAdjustment *adjustment)
void gtk_layout_thaw(GtkLayout *layout)
```

Signal

```
"set_scroll_adjustments"     void cb(GtkWidget *, GtkAdjustment
*, GtkAdjustment *, gpointer)
```

Chapter 5 provides an example of the GtkLayout container.

GtkList

The GtkList container manages a list of text items and enables the selection of one or more items.

Inheritance

```
GtkList->GtkContainer->GtkWidget->GtkObject
```

Functions

```
void gtk_list_append_items(GtkList *list, GList *items)
gint gtk_list_child_position(GtkList *list, GtkWidget *child)
void gtk_list_clear_items(GtkList *list, gint start, gint end)
void gtk_list_end_drag_selection(GtkList *list)
void gtk_list_end_selection(GtkList *list)
void gtk_list_extend_selection(GtkList *list,
    GtkScrollType scroll_type, gfloat position,
    gboolean auto_start_selection)
GtkType gtk_list_get_type(void)
void gtk_list_insert_items(GtkList *list, GList *items,
```

```
      gint position)
GtkWidget *gtk_list_new(void)
void gtk_list_prepend_items(GtkList *list, GList *items)
void gtk_list_remove_items(GtkList *list, GList *items)
void gtk_list_remove_items_no_unref(GtkList *list,
    GList *items)
void gtk_list_scroll_horizontal(GtkList *list,
    GtkScrollType scroll_type, gfloat position)
void gtk_list_scroll_vertical(GtkList *list,
    GtkScrollType scroll_type, gfloat position)
void gtk_list_select_all(GtkList *list)
void gtk_list_select_child(GtkList *list, GtkWidget *child)
void gtk_list_select_item(GtkList *list, gint item)
void gtk_list_set_selection_mode(GtkList *list,
    GtkSelectionMode mode)
void gtk_list_start_selection(GtkList *list)
void gtk_list_toggle_add_mode(GtkList *list)
void gtk_list_toggle_focus_row(GtkList *list)
void gtk_list_toggle_row(GtkList *list, GtkWidget *item)
void gtk_list_undo_selection(GtkList *list)
void gtk_list_unselect_all(GtkList *list)
void gtk_list_unselect_child(GtkList *list, GtkWidget *child)
void gtk_list_unselect_item(GtkList *list, gint item)
```

Enums

```
typedef enum {
  GTK_SCROLL_NONE,
  GTK_SCROLL_STEP_BACKWARD,
  GTK_SCROLL_STEP_FORWARD,
  GTK_SCROLL_PAGE_BACKWARD,
  GTK_SCROLL_PAGE_FORWARD,
  GTK_SCROLL_JUMP
} GtkScrollType;

typedef enum {
  GTK_SELECTION_SINGLE,
  GTK_SELECTION_BROWSE,
  GTK_SELECTION_MULTIPLE,
  GTK_SELECTION_EXTENDED
} GtkSelectionMode;
```

Signals

```
"select_child"        void cb(GtkWidget *, GtkWidget *, gpointer)
"selection_changed"   void cb(GtkWidget *, gpointer)
"unselect_child"      void cb(GtkWidget *, GtkWidget *, gpointer)
```

The following example creates a list of GtkListItem widgets and inserts them into
a GtkList. The GtkListItem widget has the ability to display itself as selected or
unselected, and the GtkList responds to the mouse to toggle the selection on and
off, as shown in Figure 21-33.

```
static GtkWidget *makeWidget()
{
    GtkWidget *list;
    GList *glist;

    glist=NULL;
    glist = g_list_append(glist,
            gtk_list_item_new_with_label("Maximum"));
    glist = g_list_append(glist,
            gtk_list_item_new_with_label("Minimum"));
    glist = g_list_append(glist,
            gtk_list_item_new_with_label("Average"));
    glist = g_list_append(glist,
            gtk_list_item_new_with_label("Projection"));

    list = gtk_list_new();
    gtk_list_append_items(GTK_LIST(list),glist);
    return(list);
}
```

Figure 21-33: A GtkList with one item selected

GtkListItem

A `GtkListItem` can be included in a `GtkList` that allows you to select items. It normally contains text but, as it inherits from `GtkBin`, it is capable of containing any widget.

Inheritance

```
GtkListItem->GtkItem->GtkBin->GtkContainer->GtkWidget->
      GtkObject
```

Functions

```
void gtk_list_item_deselect(GtkListItem *list_item)
GtkType gtk_list_item_get_type(void)
GtkWidget *gtk_list_item_new(void)
GtkWidget *gtk_list_item_new_with_label(const gchar *label)
void gtk_list_item_select(GtkListItem *list_item)
```

Signals

```
"end_selection"        void cb(GtkWidget *, gpointer)
```

```
"extend_selection"   void cb(GtkWidget *, gint, gfloat,
gboolean, gpointer)
"scroll_horizontal"  void cb(GtkWidget *, gint, gfloat,
gpointer)
"scroll_vertical"    void cb(GtkWidget *, gint, gfloat,
gpointer)
"select_all"         void cb(GtkWidget *, gpointer)
"start_selection"    void cb(GtkWidget *, gpointer)
"toggle_add_mode"    void cb(GtkWidget *, gpointer)
"toggle_focus_row"   void cb(GtkWidget *, gpointer)
"undo_selection"     void cb(GtkWidget *, gpointer)
"unselect_all"       void cb(GtkWidget *, gpointer)
```

For an example, see the GtkList description earlier in this chapter.

GtkMenu

This is a container designed to operate as a pull-down menu.

Inheritance

```
GtkMenu->GtkMenuShell->GtkContainer->GtkWidget->GtkObject
```

Functions

```
void gtk_menu_append(GtkMenu *menu, GtkWidget *child)
void gtk_menu_attach_to_widget(GtkMenu *menu,
    GtkWidget *attach_widget, GtkMenuDetachFunc detacher)
void gtk_menu_detach(GtkMenu *menu)
GtkAccelGroup *gtk_menu_ensure_uline_accel_group(
    GtkMenu *menu)
GtkAccelGroup *gtk_menu_get_accel_group(GtkMenu *menu)
GtkWidget *gtk_menu_get_active(GtkMenu *menu)
GtkWidget *gtk_menu_get_attach_widget(GtkMenu *menu)
GtkType gtk_menu_get_type(void)
GtkAccelGroup *gtk_menu_get_uline_accel_group(GtkMenu *menu)
void gtk_menu_insert(GtkMenu *menu, GtkWidget *child,
    gint position)
GtkWidget *gtk_menu_new(void)
void gtk_menu_popdown(GtkMenu *menu)
void gtk_menu_popup(GtkMenu *menu,
    GtkWidget *parent_menu_shell, GtkWidget *parent_menu_item,
    GtkMenuPositionFunc func, gpointer data, guint button,
    guint32 activate_time)
void gtk_menu_prepend(GtkMenu *menu, GtkWidget *child)
void gtk_menu_reorder_child(GtkMenu *menu, GtkWidget *child,
    gint position)
void gtk_menu_reposition(GtkMenu *menu)
void gtk_menu_set_accel_group(GtkMenu *menu,
```

```
        GtkAccelGroup *accel_group)
    void gtk_menu_set_active(GtkMenu *menu, guint index)
    void gtk_menu_set_tearoff_state(GtkMenu *menu,
        gboolean torn_off)
    void gtk_menu_set_title(GtkMenu *menu, const gchar *title)
```

The following example creates a menu bar containing a single menu, which, in turn, contains a submenu (as shown in Figure 21-34). The creation of a menu is a matter of creating each of the individual parts and attaching them together.

The call to gtk_menu_new() produces a GtkMenu that is capable of holding a list of menu items. Each item to be added to a menu is created by a call to gtk_menu_item_new_with_label(). Once the menus are created, the submenu is attached to a parent menu with a call to gtk_menu_append(). Each menu is attached to the main menu bar with a call to gtk_menu_bar_append().

```
static GtkWidget *makeWidget()
{
    GtkWidget *fileMenu;
    GtkWidget *fileNewMenu;
    GtkWidget *fileItem;
    GtkWidget *fileNewItem;
    GtkWidget *menuBar;

    /* Create the 'new' menu */
    fileNewMenu = gtk_menu_new();
    fileNewItem = gtk_menu_item_new_with_label("Template");
    gtk_menu_append(GTK_MENU(fileNewMenu),fileNewItem);
    fileNewItem = gtk_menu_item_new_with_label("Empty");
    gtk_menu_append(GTK_MENU(fileNewMenu),fileNewItem);

    /* Create the 'file' menu */
    fileMenu = gtk_menu_new();
    fileItem = gtk_menu_item_new_with_label("Open");
    gtk_menu_append(GTK_MENU(fileMenu),fileItem);
    fileItem = gtk_menu_item_new_with_label("Close");
    gtk_menu_append(GTK_MENU(fileMenu),fileItem);
    fileItem = gtk_menu_item_new_with_label("Save");
    gtk_menu_append(GTK_MENU(fileMenu),fileItem);

    /* Attach 'new' menu to 'file' menu */
    fileItem = gtk_menu_item_new_with_label("New");
    gtk_menu_append(GTK_MENU(fileMenu),fileItem);
    gtk_menu_item_set_submenu(GTK_MENU_ITEM(fileItem),
            fileNewMenu);

    /* Add the label on top of the 'file' menu */
    fileItem = gtk_menu_item_new_with_label("File");
    gtk_menu_item_set_submenu(GTK_MENU_ITEM(fileItem),
            fileMenu);
```

```
        /* Append the 'file' menu to the menu bar */
        menuBar = gtk_menu_bar_new();
        gtk_menu_bar_append(GTK_MENU_BAR(menuBar),fileItem);

        return(menuBar);
}
```

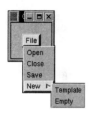

Figure 21-34: A menu with a submenu

GtkMenuBar

A GtkMenuBar is a container widget designed to manage a collection of pull-down
menus. It displays a label for each menu it contains.

Inheritance
    GtkMenuBar->GtkMenuShell->GtkContainer->GtkWidget->GtkObject
Functions
```
    void gtk_menu_bar_append(GtkMenuBar *menu_bar,
        GtkWidget *child)
    GtkType gtk_menu_bar_get_type(void)
    void gtk_menu_bar_insert(GtkMenuBar *menu_bar,
        GtkWidget *child, gint position)
    GtkWidget *gtk_menu_bar_new(void)
    void gtk_menu_bar_prepend(GtkMenuBar *menu_bar,
        GtkWidget *child)
    void gtk_menu_bar_set_shadow_type(GtkMenuBar *menu_bar,
        GtkShadowType type)
```
Enum
```
    typedef enum {
      GTK_SHADOW_NONE,
      GTK_SHADOW_IN,
      GTK_SHADOW_OUT,
      GTK_SHADOW_ETCHED_IN,
      GTK_SHADOW_ETCHED_OUT
    } GtkShadowType;
```

See the description of GtkMenu for an example of GtkMenuBar.

GtkMenuItem

A GtkMenuItem is a widget that can be inserted into a menu. It is capable of displaying text and acting as the head of submenu.

Inheritance

```
GtkMenuItem->GtkItem->GtkBin->GtkContainer->GtkWidget->
     GtkObject
```

Functions

```
void gtk_menu_item_activate(GtkMenuItem *menu_item)
void gtk_menu_item_configure(GtkMenuItem *menu_item,
    gint show_toggle_indicator, gint show_submenu_indicator)
void gtk_menu_item_deselect(GtkMenuItem *menu_item)
GtkType gtk_menu_item_get_type(void)
GtkWidget *gtk_menu_item_new(void)
GtkWidget *gtk_menu_item_new_with_label(const gchar *label)
void gtk_menu_item_remove_submenu(GtkMenuItem *menu_item)
void gtk_menu_item_right_justify(GtkMenuItem *menuitem)
void gtk_menu_item_select(GtkMenuItem *menu_item)
void gtk_menu_item_set_placement(GtkMenuItem *menu_item,
    GtkSubmenuPlacement placement)
void gtk_menu_item_set_submenu(GtkMenuItem *menu_item,
    GtkWidget *submenu)
```

Enums

```
typedef enum {
  GTK_DIRECTION_LEFT,
  GTK_DIRECTION_RIGHT
} GtkSubmenuDirection;
```

Signal

```
"activate"      void cb(GtkWidget *, gpointer)
```

For an example of GtkMenuItem, see the description of GtkMenu.

GtkMenuShell

This is the base class for GtkMenu and GtkMenuBar.

Inheritance

```
GtkMenuShell->GtkContainer->GtkWidget >GtkObject
```

Functions

```
void gtk_menu_shell_activate_item(GtkMenuShell *menu_shell,
    GtkWidget *menu_item, gboolean force_deactivate)
```

```
    void gtk_menu_shell_append(GtkMenuShell *menu_shell,
        GtkWidget *child)
    void gtk_menu_shell_deactivate(GtkMenuShell *menu_shell)
    void gtk_menu_shell_deselect(GtkMenuShell *menu_shell)
    GtkType gtk_menu_shell_get_type(void)
    void gtk_menu_shell_insert(GtkMenuShell *menu_shell,
        GtkWidget *child, gint position)
    void gtk_menu_shell_prepend(GtkMenuShell *menu_shell,
        GtkWidget *child)
    void gtk_menu_shell_select_item(GtkMenuShell *menu_shell,
        GtkWidget *menu_item)
```

Signals

```
    "activate_current"    void cb(GtkWidget *, gboolean, gpointer)
    "cancel"              void cb(GtkWidget *, gpointer)
    "deactivate"         void cb(GtkWidget *, gpointer)
    "move_current"       void cb(GtkWidget *, GtkMenuDirectionType,
    gpointer)
    "selection-done"     void cb(GtkWidget *, gpointer)
```

GtkMisc

This is a base class providing alignment and spacing to a number of displayable widgets.

Inheritance

```
    GtkMisc->GtkWidget->GtkObject
```

Functions

```
    GtkType gtk_misc_get_type(void)
    void gtk_misc_set_alignment(GtkMisc *misc, gfloat xalign,
        gfloat yalign)
    void gtk_misc_set_padding(GtkMisc *misc, gint xpad, gint ypad)
```

GtkNotebook

A GtkNotebook object is a container widget that displays its contained widgets one at a time. There is a row of tabs at the top of the display that provides mouse access to each of the individual widgets.

Inheritance

```
    GtkNotebook->GtkContainer->GtkWidget->GtkObject
```

Functions

```
void gtk_notebook_append_page(GtkNotebook *notebook,
    GtkWidget *child, GtkWidget *tab_label)
void gtk_notebook_append_page_menu(GtkNotebook *notebook,
    GtkWidget *child, GtkWidget *tab_label,
    GtkWidget *menu_label)
gint gtk_notebook_get_current_page(GtkNotebook *notebook)
GtkWidget *gtk_notebook_get_menu_label(GtkNotebook *notebook,
    GtkWidget *child)
GtkWidget *gtk_notebook_get_nth_page(GtkNotebook *notebook,
    gint page_num)
GtkWidget *gtk_notebook_get_tab_label(GtkNotebook *notebook,
    GtkWidget *child)
GtkType gtk_notebook_get_type(void)
void gtk_notebook_insert_page(GtkNotebook *notebook,
    GtkWidget *child, GtkWidget *tab_label, gint position)
void gtk_notebook_insert_page_menu(GtkNotebook *notebook,
    GtkWidget *child, GtkWidget *tab_label,
    GtkWidget *menu_label, gint position)
GtkWidget *gtk_notebook_new(void)
void gtk_notebook_next_page(GtkNotebook *notebook)
gint gtk_notebook_page_num(GtkNotebook *notebook,
    GtkWidget *child)
void gtk_notebook_popup_disable(GtkNotebook *notebook)
void gtk_notebook_popup_enable(GtkNotebook *notebook)
void gtk_notebook_prepend_page(GtkNotebook *notebook,
    GtkWidget *child, GtkWidget *tab_label)
void gtk_notebook_prepend_page_menu(GtkNotebook *notebook,
    GtkWidget *child, GtkWidget *tab_label,
    GtkWidget *menu_label)
void gtk_notebook_prev_page(GtkNotebook *notebook)
void gtk_notebook_query_tab_label_packing(
    GtkNotebook *notebook, GtkWidget *child, gboolean *expand,
    gboolean *fill, GtkPackType *pack_type)
void gtk_notebook_remove_page(GtkNotebook *notebook,
    gint page_num)
void gtk_notebook_reorder_child(GtkNotebook *notebook,
    GtkWidget *child, gint position)
void gtk_notebook_set_homogeneous_tabs(GtkNotebook *notebook,
    gboolean homogeneous)
void gtk_notebook_set_menu_label(GtkNotebook *notebook,
    GtkWidget *child, GtkWidget *menu_label)
void gtk_notebook_set_menu_label_text(GtkNotebook *notebook,
    GtkWidget *child, const gchar *menu_text)
void gtk_notebook_set_page(GtkNotebook *notebook,
    gint page_num)
void gtk_notebook_set_scrollable(GtkNotebook *notebook,
    gint scrollable)
void gtk_notebook_set_show_border(GtkNotebook *notebook,
    gint show_border)
```

```
void gtk_notebook_set_show_tabs(GtkNotebook *notebook,
    gboolean show_tabs)
void gtk_notebook_set_tab_border(GtkNotebook *notebook,
    guint tab_border)
void gtk_notebook_set_tab_hborder(GtkNotebook *notebook,
    guint tab_hborder)
void gtk_notebook_set_tab_label(GtkNotebook *notebook,
    GtkWidget *child, GtkWidget *tab_label)
void gtk_notebook_set_tab_label_packing(
    GtkNotebook *notebook, GtkWidget *child, gboolean expand,
    gboolean fill, GtkPackType pack_type)
void gtk_notebook_set_tab_label_text(GtkNotebook *notebook,
    GtkWidget *child, const gchar *tab_text)
void gtk_notebook_set_tab_pos(GtkNotebook *notebook,
    GtkPositionType pos)
void gtk_notebook_set_tab_vborder(GtkNotebook *notebook,
    guint tab_vborder)
```

Enums

```
typedef enum {
  GTK_POS_LEFT,
  GTK_POS_RIGHT,
  GTK_POS_TOP,
  GTK_POS_BOTTOM
} GtkPositionType;

typedef enum {
  GTK_PACK_START,
  GTK_PACK_END
} GtkPackType;
```

Signal

```
"switch_page"      void cb(GtkWidget *, gpointer, guint,
gpointer)
```

Refer to Chapter 5 for an example of GtkNotebook.

GtkObject

This is the base class of all objects in GTK+.

Inheritance

```
GtkObject
```

Functions

```
gchar *Gtk_object_args_collect(GtkType object_type,
    GSList **arg_list_p, GSList **info_list_p,
    const gchar *first_arg_name, va_list var_args)
```

```
void gtk_object_add_arg_type(const char *arg_name,
    GtkType arg_type, guint arg_flags, guint arg_id)
void gtk_object_arg_get(GtkObject *object, GtkArg *arg,
    GtkArgInfo *info)
gchar *gtk_object_arg_get_info(GtkType object_type,
    const gchar *arg_name, GtkArgInfo **info_p)
void gtk_object_arg_set(GtkObject *object, GtkArg *arg,
    GtkArgInfo *info)
void gtk_object_class_add_signals(GtkObjectClass *class,
    guint *signals, guint nsignals)
guint gtk_object_class_user_signal_new(GtkObjectClass *class,
    const gchar *name, GtkSignalRunType signal_flags,
    GtkSignalMarshaller marshaller, GtkType return_val,
    guint nparams, ...)
guint gtk_object_class_user_signal_newv(
    GtkObjectClass *class, const gchar *name,
    GtkSignalRunType signal_flags,
    GtkSignalMarshaller marshaller, GtkType return_val,
    guint nparams, GtkType *params)
void gtk_object_constructed(GtkObject *object)
void gtk_object_default_construct(GtkObject *object)
void gtk_object_destroy(GtkObject *object)
gpointer gtk_object_get_data(GtkObject *object,
    const gchar *key)
gpointer gtk_object_get_data_by_id(GtkObject *object,
    GQuark data_id)
GtkType gtk_object_get_type(void)
gpointer gtk_object_get_user_data(GtkObject *object)
void gtk_object_getv(GtkObject *object, guint n_args,
    GtkArg *args)
void gtk_object_init_type(void)
GtkObject *gtk_object_new(GtkType object_type,
    const gchar *first_arg_name, ...)
GtkObject *gtk_object_newv(GtkType object_type, guint n_args,
    GtkArg *args)
void gtk_object_post_arg_parsing_init(void)
GtkArg *gtk_object_query_args(GtkType class_type,
    guint32 **arg_flags, guint *n_args)
void gtk_object_ref(GtkObject *object)
void gtk_object_remove_data(GtkObject *object,
    const gchar *key)
void gtk_object_remove_data_by_id(GtkObject *object,
    GQuark data_id)
void gtk_object_remove_no_notify(GtkObject *object,
    const gchar *key)
void gtk_object_remove_no_notify_by_id(GtkObject *object,
    GQuark key_id)
void gtk_object_set(GtkObject *object,
    const gchar *first_arg_name, ...)
void gtk_object_set_data(GtkObject *object, const gchar *key,
    gpointer data)
```

```
void gtk_object_set_data_by_id(GtkObject *object,
    GQuark data_id, gpointer data)
void gtk_object_set_data_by_id_full(GtkObject *object,
    GQuark data_id, gpointer data, GtkDestroyNotify destroy)
void gtk_object_set_data_full(GtkObject *object,
    const gchar *key, gpointer data, GtkDestroyNotify destroy)
void gtk_object_set_user_data(GtkObject *object, gpointer data)
void gtk_object_setv(GtkObject *object, guint n_args,
    GtkArg *args)
void gtk_object_sink(GtkObject *object)
void gtk_object_unref(GtkObject *object)
void gtk_object_weakref(GtkObject *object,
    GtkDestroyNotify notify, gpointer data)
void gtk_object_weakunref(GtkObject *object,
    GtkDestroyNotify notify, gpointer data)
void gtk_trace_referencing(GtkObject *object,
    const gchar *func, guint dummy, guint line,
    gboolean do_ref)
```

Enums

```
typedef enum {
  GTK_RUN_FIRST,
  GTK_RUN_LAST,
  GTK_RUN_BOTH,
  GTK_RUN_NO_RECURSE,
  GTK_RUN_ACTION,
  GTK_RUN_NO_HOOKS
} GtkSignalRunType;
```

Signal

```
"switch_page"        void cb(GtkWidget *, gpointer, guint,
gpointer)
```

GtkOptionMenu

This container is capable of controlling a single-level menu that you can use for
multiple choice selection. The widget normally is collapsed with only the current
selection displayed.

Inheritance

```
GtkOptionMenu->GtkButton->GtkBin->GtkContainer->GtkWidget->
        GtkObject
```

Functions

```
GtkWidget *gtk_option_menu_get_menu(
    GtkOptionMenu *option_menu)
GtkType gtk_option_menu_get_type(void)
GtkWidget *gtk_option_menu_new(void)
```

```
void gtk_option_menu_remove_menu(GtkOptionMenu *option_menu)
void gtk_option_menu_set_history(GtkOptionMenu *option_menu,
    guint index)
void gtk_option_menu_set_menu(GtkOptionMenu *option_menu,
    GtkWidget *menu)
```

This example creates a three-button menu and installs it into a `GtkOptionMenu` widget to be displayed and controlled. Figure 21-35 shows the appearance of the widget in both collapsed and expanded states.

```
static GtkWidget *makeWidget()
{
    GtkWidget *optionmenu;
    GtkWidget *menu;
    GtkWidget *item;

    menu = gtk_menu_new();
    item = gtk_menu_item_new_with_label("Open");
    gtk_menu_append(GTK_MENU(menu),item);
    item = gtk_menu_item_new_with_label("Close");
    gtk_menu_append(GTK_MENU(menu),item);
    item = gtk_menu_item_new_with_label("Save");
    gtk_menu_append(GTK_MENU(menu),item);

    optionmenu = gtk_option_menu_new();
    gtk_option_menu_set_menu(GTK_OPTION_MENU(optionmenu),menu);

    return(optionmenu);
}
```

Figure 21-35: The two states of the GtkOptionMenu widget

GtkPacker

The `GtkPacker` is a container widget providing functions that give your program detailed control over the rules which position and space widgets. The spacing and sizing rules are all relative values, so the layout will automatically adjust to the height and width of the container.

Inheritance

```
GtkPacker->GtkContainer->GtkWidget->GtkObject
```

Functions

```
void gtk_packer_add(GtkPacker *packer, GtkWidget *child,
    GtkSideType side, GtkAnchorType anchor,
    GtkPackerOptions options, guint border_width, guint pad_x,
    guint pad_y, guint i_pad_x, guint i_pad_y)
void gtk_packer_add_defaults(GtkPacker *packer,
    GtkWidget *child, GtkSideType side, GtkAnchorType anchor,
    GtkPackerOptions options)
GtkType gtk_packer_get_type(void)
GtkWidget *gtk_packer_new(void)
void gtk_packer_reorder_child(GtkPacker *packer,
    GtkWidget *child, gint position)
void gtk_packer_set_child_packing(GtkPacker *packer,
    GtkWidget *child, GtkSideType side, GtkAnchorType anchor,
    GtkPackerOptions options, guint border_width, guint pad_x,
    guint pad_y, guint i_pad_x, guint i_pad_y)
void gtk_packer_set_default_border_width(GtkPacker *packer,
    guint border)
void gtk_packer_set_default_ipad(GtkPacker *packer,
    guint i_pad_x, guint i_pad_y)
void gtk_packer_set_default_pad(GtkPacker *packer, guint pad_x,
    guint pad_y)
void gtk_packer_set_spacing(GtkPacker *packer, guint spacing)
```

Enums

```
typedef enum {
    GTK_PACK_EXPAND,
    GTK_FILL_X,
    GTK_FILL_Y
} GtkPackerOptions;

typedef enum {
    GTK_SIDE_TOP,
    GTK_SIDE_BOTTOM,
    GTK_SIDE_LEFT,
    GTK_SIDE_RIGHT
} GtkSideType;

typedef enum {
  GTK_ANCHOR_CENTER,
  GTK_ANCHOR_NORTH,
  GTK_ANCHOR_NORTH_WEST,
  GTK_ANCHOR_NORTH_EAST,
  GTK_ANCHOR_SOUTH,
  GTK_ANCHOR_SOUTH_WEST,
  GTK_ANCHOR_SOUTH_EAST,
  GTK_ANCHOR_WEST,
  GTK_ANCHOR_EAST,
  GTK_ANCHOR_N,
  GTK_ANCHOR_NW,
```

```
    GTK_ANCHOR_NE,
    GTK_ANCHOR_S,
    GTK_ANCHOR_SW,
    GTK_ANCHOR_SE,
    GTK_ANCHOR_W,
    GTK_ANCHOR_E
} GtkAnchorType;
```

The following example creates the window displayed in Figure 21-36. Two buttons are added to the container, but the rules are different for each one.

```
static GtkWidget *makeWidget()
{
    GtkWidget *packer;
    GtkWidget *button;

    packer = gtk_packer_new();

    button = gtk_button_new_with_label("First Button");
    gtk_packer_add_defaults(GTK_PACKER(packer),button,
            GTK_SIDE_LEFT,GTK_ANCHOR_SOUTH,GTK_FILL_Y);

    button = gtk_button_new_with_label("Second Button");
    gtk_packer_add_defaults(GTK_PACKER(packer),button,
            GTK_SIDE_LEFT,GTK_ANCHOR_CENTER,GTK_PACK_EXPAND);

    gtk_widget_set_usize(GTK_WIDGET(packer),200,200);

    return(packer);
}
```

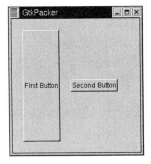

Figure 21-36: A GtkPacker widget containing two buttons using different rules

GtkPaned

This is the base class for GtkHPaned and GtkVPaned.

Inheritance

```
GtkPaned->GtkContainer->GtkWidget->GtkObject
```

Functions

```
void gtk_paned_add1(GtkPaned *paned, GtkWidget *widget)
void gtk_paned_add2(GtkPaned *paned, GtkWidget *widget)
void gtk_paned_compute_position(GtkPaned *paned,
    gint allocation, gint child1_req, gint child2_req)
GtkType gtk_paned_get_type(void)
void gtk_paned_pack1(GtkPaned *paned, GtkWidget *widget,
    gboolean resize, gboolean shrink)
void gtk_paned_pack2(GtkPaned *paned, GtkWidget *widget,
    gboolean resize, gboolean shrink)
void gtk_paned_set_gutter_size(GtkPaned *paned, guint16 size)
void gtk_paned_set_handle_size(GtkPaned *paned, guint16 size)
void gtk_paned_set_position(GtkPaned *paned, gint position)
```

GtkPixmap

The GtkPixmap widget contains a RAM-based window. You can render graphics on it just as if it were a window, but it does not display anything.

Inheritance

```
GtkPixmap->GtkMisc->GtkWidget->GtkObject
```

Functions

```
void gtk_pixmap_get(GtkPixmap *pixmap, GdkPixmap **val,
    GdkBitmap **mask)
GtkType gtk_pixmap_get_type(void)
GtkWidget *gtk_pixmap_new(GdkPixmap *val, GdkBitmap *mask)
void gtk_pixmap_set(GtkPixmap *pixmap, GdkPixmap *val,
    GdkBitmap *mask)
void gtk_pixmap_set_build_insensitive(GtkPixmap *pixmap,
    guint build)
```

Refer to Chapter 7 for GtkPixmap examples.

GtkPixmapMenuItem

A GtkPixmapMenuItem widget is used to adjust the position of the menu buttons to make room for the appearance of a pixmap or a toggle button to the left of the text. A GtkPixmapMenuItem automatically is created as needed for GNOME menus.

Inheritance

```
GtkPixmapMenuItem->GtkMenuItem->GtkItem->GtkBin->GtkContainer->
        GtkWidget->GtkObject
```

Functions

```
GtkType gtk_pixmap_menu_item_get_type(void)
GtkWidget *gtk_pixmap_menu_item_new(void)
void gtk_pixmap_menu_item_set_pixmap(
    GtkPixmapMenuItem *menu_item, GtkWidget *pixmap)
```

The GtkPixmapMenuItem is used internally by the menu generation software, with examples in Chapter 8.

GtkPlug

A GtkPlug widget is a top-level window that can be made available to a separate process from the one that created it. The separate process uses a GtkSocket to access the widget just as if it were local.

Inheritance

```
GtkPlug->GtkWindow->GtkBin->GtkContainer->GtkWidget->
        GtkObject
```

Functions

```
void gtk_plug_construct(GtkPlug *plug, guint32 socket_id)
guint gtk_plug_get_type()
GtkWidget *gtk_plug_new(guint32 socket_id)
```

GtkPreview

The GtkPreview widget provides a graphic window and some functions that manage it. Applications use it to preview graphic operations and display available colors.

Inheritance

```
GtkPreview->GtkWidget->GtkObject
```

Functions

```
void gtk_preview_draw_row(GtkPreview *preview, guchar *data,
    gint x, gint y, gint w)
GdkColormap *gtk_preview_get_cmap(void)
GtkPreviewInfo *gtk_preview_get_info(void)
guint gtk_preview_get_type(void)
GdkVisual *gtk_preview_get_visual(void)
GtkWidget *gtk_preview_new(GtkPreviewType type)
void gtk_preview_put(GtkPreview *preview, GdkWindow *window,
    GdkGC *gc, gint srcx, gint srcy, gint destx, gint desty,
    gint width, gint height)
void gtk_preview_reset(void)
void gtk_preview_set_color_cube(guint nred_shades,
    guint ngreen_shades, guint nblue_shades,
    guint ngray_shades)
void gtk_preview_set_dither(GtkPreview *preview,
    GdkRgbDither dither)
void gtk_preview_set_expand(GtkPreview *preview, gint expand)
void gtk_preview_set_gamma(double _gamma)
void gtk_preview_set_install_cmap(gint _install_cmap)
void gtk_preview_set_reserved(gint nreserved)
void gtk_preview_size(GtkPreview *preview, gint width,
    gint height)
void gtk_preview_uninit(void)
```

Enums

```
typedef enum {
  GTK_PREVIEW_COLOR,
  GTK_PREVIEW_GRAYSCALE
} GtkPreviewType;

typedef enum {
  GDK_RGB_DITHER_NONE,
  GDK_RGB_DITHER_NORMAL,
  GDK_RGB_DITHER_MAX
} GdkRgbDither;
```

This example creates a `GtkPreview` object and then sets up a callback function to draw a rectangle into its window, as shown in Figure 21-37. It is necessary for the drawing to occur in a callback function after the window is displayed because the actual window must exist.

```
static GtkWidget *makeWidget()
{
    GtkWidget *preview;

    preview = gtk_preview_new(GTK_PREVIEW_COLOR);
    gtk_preview_size(GTK_PREVIEW(preview),200,100);
    gtk_signal_connect(GTK_OBJECT(preview),"event",
            GTK_SIGNAL_FUNC(eventDraw),NULL);
```

```
        return(preview);
}
static gboolean eventDraw(GtkWidget *widget,
        GdkEvent *event,gpointer data) {
    GdkGC *gc;
    GdkColor foreground;
    GdkColormap *colormap;

    colormap = gdk_colormap_get_system();
    gc = gdk_gc_new(widget->window);
    gdk_color_parse("blue",&foreground);
    gdk_color_alloc(colormap,&foreground);
    gdk_gc_set_foreground(gc,&foreground);

    gdk_draw_rectangle(widget->window,gc,
            TRUE,20,10,160,80);
    return(TRUE);
}
```

Figure 21-37: A GtkPreview window displaying a rectangle

GtkProgress

The GtkProgress widget is the base class of GtkProgressBar.

Inheritance

```
GtkProgress->GtkWidget->GtkObject
```

Functions

```
void gtk_progress_configure(GtkProgress *progress,
    gfloat value, gfloat min, gfloat max)
gfloat gtk_progress_get_current_percentage(
    GtkProgress *progress)
gchar *gtk_progress_get_current_text(GtkProgress *progress)
gfloat gtk_progress_get_percentage_from_value(
    GtkProgress *progress, gfloat value)
gchar *gtk_progress_get_text_from_value(
    GtkProgress *progress, gfloat value)
GtkType gtk_progress_get_type(void)
gfloat gtk_progress_get_value(GtkProgress *progress)
```

```
void gtk_progress_set_activity_mode(GtkProgress *progress,
    guint activity_mode)
void gtk_progress_set_adjustment(GtkProgress *progress,
    GtkAdjustment *adjustment)
void gtk_progress_set_format_string(GtkProgress *progress,
    gchar *format)
void gtk_progress_set_percentage(GtkProgress *progress,
    gfloat percentage)
void gtk_progress_set_show_text(GtkProgress *progress,
    gint show_text)
void gtk_progress_set_text_alignment(GtkProgress *progress,
    gfloat x_align, gfloat y_align)
void gtk_progress_set_value(GtkProgress *progress,
    gfloat value)
```

GtkProgressBar

The GtkProgressBar widget displays a moving indicator that represents a percentage of completion of some tasks.

Inheritance

```
GtkProgressBar->GtkProgress->GtkWidget->GtkObject
```

Functions

```
GtkType gtk_progress_bar_get_type(void)
GtkWidget *gtk_progress_bar_new(void)
GtkWidget *gtk_progress_bar_new_with_adjustment(
    GtkAdjustment *adjustment)
void gtk_progress_bar_set_activity_blocks(
    GtkProgressBar *pbar, guint blocks)
void gtk_progress_bar_set_activity_step(GtkProgressBar *pbar,
    guint step)
void gtk_progress_bar_set_bar_style(GtkProgressBar *pbar,
    GtkProgressBarStyle bar_style)
void gtk_progress_bar_set_discrete_blocks(
    GtkProgressBar *pbar, guint blocks)
void gtk_progress_bar_set_orientation(GtkProgressBar *pbar,
    GtkProgressBarOrientation orientation)
void gtk_progress_bar_update(GtkProgressBar *pbar,
    gfloat percentage)
```

Enums

```
typedef enum {
  GTK_PROGRESS_CONTINUOUS,
  GTK_PROGRESS_DISCRETE
} GtkProgressBarStyle;

typedef enum {
```

```
    GTK_PROGRESS_LEFT_TO_RIGHT,
    GTK_PROGRESS_RIGHT_TO_LEFT,
    GTK_PROGRESS_BOTTOM_TO_TOP,
    GTK_PROGRESS_TOP_TO_BOTTOM
} GtkProgressBarOrientation;
```

As shown in Figure 21-38, this example creates a horizontal progress bar that moves from 0 on the left to 100 on the right. The GtkAdjustment widget is used to initialize the limits and the current progress setting. Your application needs to call the gtk_progress_bar_update() function to cause the bar to move.

```
static GtkWidget *makeWidget()
{
    GtkWidget *bar;
    GtkObject *adjustment;

    adjustment = gtk_adjustment_new(70.25,0.0,100.0,
            0.25,0.0,0.0);
    bar = gtk_progress_bar_new_with_adjustment(
            GTK_ADJUSTMENT(adjustment));
    gtk_progress_bar_set_bar_style(GTK_PROGRESS_BAR(bar),
            GTK_PROGRESS_CONTINUOUS);
    gtk_progress_bar_set_orientation(GTK_PROGRESS_BAR(bar),
            GTK_PROGRESS_LEFT_TO_RIGHT);

    return(bar);
}
```

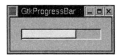

Figure 21-38: A progress bar showing 70 percent completion

GtkRadioButton

GtkRadioButton widgets are toggle buttons intended for use in a group in which only one item of the group can be selected at a time.

Inheritance
```
GtkRadioButton->GtkCheckButton->GtkToggleButton->GtkButton->
        GtkBin->GtkContainer->GtkWidget->GtkObject
```

Functions
```
GtkType gtk_radio_button_get_type(void)
GSList *gtk_radio_button_group(GtkRadioButton *radio_button)
GtkWidget *gtk_radio_button_new(GSList *group)
```

```
GtkWidget *gtk_radio_button_new_from_widget(
    GtkRadioButton *group)
GtkWidget *gtk_radio_button_new_with_label(GSList *group,
    const gchar *label)
GtkWidget *gtk_radio_button_new_with_label_from_widget(
    GtkRadioButton *group, const gchar *label)
void gtk_radio_button_set_group(GtkRadioButton *radio_button,
    GSList *group)
```

This example creates the collection of radio buttons shown in Figure 21-39. The first button is created by calling gtk_radio_button_new_with_label(), passing NULL as the group pointer. To create the next button, it is necessary to retrieve the GSList pointer to the group and use it instead of NULL on the call to gtk_radio_button_new_with_label(). In building the third button, it is necessary to retrieve the group pointer again because the previous pointer may no longer be valid.

The normal default is for the first button in the group to be active, but the call to gtk_toggle_button_active() specifies that the third button is to be active.

```
static GtkWidget *makeWidget()
{
    GtkWidget *box;
    GSList *group;
    GtkWidget *radiobutton;

    box = gtk_vbox_new(FALSE,0);

    radiobutton = gtk_radio_button_new_with_label(NULL,
            "Apples");
    gtk_box_pack_start(GTK_BOX(box),radiobutton,
            FALSE,TRUE,0);

    group = gtk_radio_button_group(
            GTK_RADIO_BUTTON(radiobutton));
    radiobutton = gtk_radio_button_new_with_label(group,
            "Bananas");
    gtk_box_pack_start(GTK_BOX(box),radiobutton,
            FALSE,TRUE,0);

    group = gtk_radio_button_group(
            GTK_RADIO_BUTTON(radiobutton));
    radiobutton = gtk_radio_button_new_with_label(group,
            "Oranges");
    gtk_toggle_button_set_active(
            GTK_TOGGLE_BUTTON(radiobutton),TRUE);
    gtk_box_pack_start(GTK_BOX(box),radiobutton,
            FALSE,TRUE,0);

    return(box);
}
```

Figure 21-39: Three radio buttons in a vertical box

GtkRadioMenuItem

You can add a group of two or more of these buttons to a menu. Selecting any one of the buttons in a group causes the other buttons to be unselected.

Inheritance

```
GtkRadioMenuItem->GtkCheckMenuItem->GtkMenuItem->GtkItem->
    GtkBin->GtkContainer->GtkWidget->GtkObject
```

Functions

```
GtkType gtk_radio_menu_item_get_type(void)
GSList *gtk_radio_menu_item_group(
    GtkRadioMenuItem *radio_menu_item)
GtkWidget *gtk_radio_menu_item_new(GSList *group)
GtkWidget *gtk_radio_menu_item_new_with_label(GSList *group,
    const gchar *label)
void gtk_radio_menu_item_set_group(
    GtkRadioMenuItem *radio_menu_item, GSList *group)
```

This example creates a menu that contains three radio buttons (as shown in Figure 21-40). The first button is created with the group pointer set to NULL. Then the GSlist pointer is returned and used in the call to create the next button. If the group is used more than once, it is necessary to retrieve GSlist each time.

```
static GtkWidget *makeWidget()
{
    GtkWidget *menu;
    GtkWidget *item;
    GtkWidget *menubar;
    GSList *group;

    /* Create the menu */
    menu = gtk_menu_new();
    item = gtk_radio_menu_item_new_with_label(NULL,
            "First Radio");
    gtk_menu_append(GTK_MENU(menu),item);
    group = gtk_radio_menu_item_group(
            GTK_RADIO_MENU_ITEM(item));
    item = gtk_radio_menu_item_new_with_label(group,
            "Second Radio");
```

```
gtk_menu_append(GTK_MENU(menu),item);
group = gtk_radio_menu_item_group(
        GTK_RADIO_MENU_ITEM(item));
item = gtk_radio_menu_item_new_with_label(group,
        "Third Radio");
gtk_menu_append(GTK_MENU(menu),item);

/* Add the label on top of the menu */
item = gtk_menu_item_new_with_label("RadioMenu");
gtk_menu_item_set_submenu(GTK_MENU_ITEM(item),
        menu);

/* Append the menu to the menu bar */
menubar = gtk_menu_bar_new();
gtk_menu_bar_append(GTK_MENU_BAR(menubar),item);

return(menubar);
}
```

Figure 21-40: A set of three radio buttons on a menu

GtkRange

This is the base class for the group of widgets that involve graphic display and manipulation of a value bounded within a specific minimum and maximum value. These widgets are GtkHScale, GtkHScrollbar, GtkVScale, and GtkVScrollbar.

Inheritance
```
GtkRange->GtkWidget->GtkObject
```

Functions
```
void gtk_range_clear_background(GtkRange *range)
void gtk_range_default_hmotion(GtkRange *range, gint xdelta,
    gint ydelta)
void gtk_range_default_hslider_update(GtkRange *range)
gint gtk_range_default_htrough_click(GtkRange *range, gint x,
    gint y, gfloat *jump_perc)
void gtk_range_default_vmotion(GtkRange *range, gint xdelta,
    gint ydelta)
void gtk_range_default_vslider_update(GtkRange *range)
gint gtk_range_default_vtrough_click(GtkRange *range, gint x,
    gint y, gfloat *jump_perc)
```

```
void gtk_range_draw_background(GtkRange *range)
void gtk_range_draw_slider(GtkRange *range)
void gtk_range_draw_step_back(GtkRange *range)
void gtk_range_draw_step_forw(GtkRange *range)
void gtk_range_draw_trough(GtkRange *range)
GtkAdjustment *gtk_range_get_adjustment(GtkRange *range)
GtkType gtk_range_get_type(void)
void gtk_range_set_adjustment(GtkRange *range,
    GtkAdjustment *adjustment)
void gtk_range_set_update_policy(GtkRange *range,
    GtkUpdateType policy)
void gtk_range_slider_update(GtkRange *range)
gint gtk_range_trough_click(GtkRange *range, gint x, gint y,
    gfloat *jump_perc)
```

GtkRuler

This widget is the base class for `GtkHRuler` and `GtkVRuler`. It contains the configuration and calculation software, but has no ability to display the results.

Inheritance

```
GtkRuler->GtkWidget->GtkObject
```

Functions

```
void gtk_ruler_draw_pos(GtkRuler *ruler)
void gtk_ruler_draw_ticks(GtkRuler *ruler)
guint gtk_ruler_get_type(void)
void gtk_ruler_set_metric(GtkRuler *ruler,
    GtkMetricType metric)
void gtk_ruler_set_range(GtkRuler *ruler, gfloat lower,
    gfloat upper, gfloat position, gfloat max_size)
```

Enum

```
typedef enum {
  GTK_PIXELS,
  GTK_INCHES,
  GTK_CENTIMETERS
} GtkMetricType;
```

GtkScale

This is the base class for `GtkHScale` and `GtkVScale`.

Inheritance

```
GtkScale->GtkRange->GtkWidget->GtkObject
```

Functions

```
void gtk_scale_draw_value(GtkScale *scale)
GtkType gtk_scale_get_type(void)
gint gtk_scale_get_value_width(GtkScale *scale)
void gtk_scale_set_digits(GtkScale *scale, gint digits)
void gtk_scale_set_draw_value(GtkScale *scale,
    gboolean draw_value)
void gtk_scale_set_value_pos(GtkScale *scale,
    GtkPositionType pos)
```

Enum

```
typedef enum
{
  GTK_POS_LEFT,
  GTK_POS_RIGHT,
  GTK_POS_TOP,
  GTK_POS_BOTTOM
} GtkPositionType;
```

GtkScrollbar

The GtkScrollbar **class is the base class for** GtkHScrollbar **and** GtkVScrollbar.

Inheritance

```
GtkScrollbar->GtkRange->GtkWidget->GtkObject
```

Function

```
GtkType gtk_scrollbar_get_type(void)
```

GtkScrolledWindow

A GtkScrolledWindow is a container that does not resize to fit in the space allotted to it. Instead, it adds scrollbars (as necessary) so you can view any part of the window.

Inheritance

```
GtkScrolledWindow->GtkBin->GtkContainer->GtkWidget->GtkObject
```

Functions

```
void gtk_scrolled_window_add_with_viewport(
    GtkScrolledWindow *scrolled_window, GtkWidget *child)
GtkAdjustment *gtk_scrolled_window_get_hadjustment(
    GtkScrolledWindow *scrolled_window)
GtkType gtk_scrolled_window_get_type(void)
```

```
GtkAdjustment *gtk_scrolled_window_get_vadjustment(
    GtkScrolledWindow *scrolled_window)
GtkWidget *gtk_scrolled_window_new(
    GtkAdjustment *hadjustment, GtkAdjustment *vadjustment)
void gtk_scrolled_window_set_hadjustment(
    GtkScrolledWindow *scrolled_window,
    GtkAdjustment *hadjustment)
void gtk_scrolled_window_set_placement(
    GtkScrolledWindow *scrolled_window,
    GtkCornerType window_placement)
void gtk_scrolled_window_set_policy(
    GtkScrolledWindow *scrolled_window,
    GtkPolicyType hscrollbar_policy,
    GtkPolicyType vscrollbar_policy)
void gtk_scrolled_window_set_vadjustment(
    GtkScrolledWindow *scrolled_window,
    GtkAdjustment *vadjustment)
```

Enums

```
typedef enum {
  GTK_POLICY_ALWAYS,
  GTK_POLICY_AUTOMATIC,
  GTK_POLICY_NEVER
} GtkPolicyType;

typedef enum {
  GTK_CORNER_TOP_LEFT,
  GTK_CORNER_BOTTOM_LEFT,
  GTK_CORNER_TOP_RIGHT,
  GTK_CORNER_BOTTOM_RIGHT
} GtkCornerType;
```

For examples of GtkScrolledWindow, see Chapter 5.

GtkSeparator

The GtkSeparator class is the base class for GtkHSeparator and GTKVSeparator.

Inheritance

```
GtkSeparator->GtkWidget->GtkObject
```

Function

```
GtkType gtk_separator_get_type(void)
```

GtkSocket

A GtkSocket widget can access widget windows from a remote process and display them as if they were local. The remote process creates a GtkPlug widget as the window to be made available to the GtkSocket of this process.

Inheritance

```
GtkSocket->GtkContainer->GtkWidget->GtkObject
```

Functions

```
guint gtk_socket_get_type()
GtkWidget *gtk_socket_new()
void gtk_socket_steal(GtkSocket *socket, guint32 id)
```

GtkSpinButton

A GtkSpinButton widget displays a single numeric value that you can change by using the two arrow buttons to its right, or by editing the number directly.

Inheritance

```
GtkSpinButton->GtkEntry->GtkEditable->GtkWidget->GtkObject
```

Functions

```
void gtk_spin_button_configure(GtkSpinButton *spin_button,
    GtkAdjustment *adjustment, gfloat climb_rate, guint digits)
GtkAdjustment *gtk_spin_button_get_adjustment(
    GtkSpinButton *spin_button)
GtkType gtk_spin_button_get_type(void)
gfloat gtk_spin_button_get_value_as_float(
    GtkSpinButton *spin_button)
gint gtk_spin_button_get_value_as_int(
    GtkSpinButton *spin_button)
GtkWidget *gtk_spin_button_new(GtkAdjustment *adjustment,
    gfloat climb_rate, guint digits)
void gtk_spin_button_set_adjustment(
    GtkSpinButton *spin_button, GtkAdjustment *adjustment)
void gtk_spin_button_set_digits(GtkSpinButton *spin_button,
    guint digits)
void gtk_spin_button_set_numeric(GtkSpinButton *spin_button,
    gboolean numeric)
void gtk_spin_button_set_shadow_type(
    GtkSpinButton *spin_button, GtkShadowType shadow_type)
void gtk_spin_button_set_snap_to_ticks(
    GtkSpinButton *spin_button, gboolean snap_to_ticks)
```

```
void gtk_spin_button_set_update_policy(
    GtkSpinButton *spin_button,
    GtkSpinButtonUpdatePolicy policy)
void gtk_spin_button_set_value(GtkSpinButton *spin_button,
    gfloat value)
void gtk_spin_button_set_wrap(GtkSpinButton *spin_button,
    gboolean wrap)
void gtk_spin_button_spin(GtkSpinButton *spin_button,
    GtkSpinType direction, gfloat increment)
void gtk_spin_button_update(GtkSpinButton *spin_button)
```

Signals

```
"input"     void cb(GtkWidget *, gpointer, gpointer)
"output"    gboolean cb(GtkWidget *, gpointer)
```

The following example creates a spin button with its initial value set to 80, as shown in Figure 21-41. According to the GtkAdjustment, the values can range from 100 to -100 in increments of 1. On the call to gtk_spin_button_new(), the increment/decrement buttons are set to change the value by 3, and there is 1 digit to the right of the decimal point.

```
static GtkWidget *makeWidget()
{
    GtkWidget *spin;
    GtkObject *adjustment;

    adjustment = gtk_adjustment_new(80.0,
            -100.0,100.0,1.0,0.0,0.0);
    spin =
gtk_spin_button_new(GTK_ADJUSTMENT(adjustment),3.0,1);
    return(spin);
}
```

Figure 21-41: A spin button showing its value and its adjustment arrows

GtkStatusbar

The GtkStatusbar widget has a window that can display textual status information. Internally, it maintains a separate list of status messages for any number of context ID numbers; each of these lists is managed separately. Also, each text message is assigned an ID that can be used to remove it.

Inheritance

```
GtkStatusbar->GtkHBox->GtkBox->GtkContainer->GtkWidget->
        GtkObject
```

Functions

```
guint gtk_statusbar_get_context_id(GtkStatusbar *statusbar,
    const gchar *context_description)
guint gtk_statusbar_get_type(void)
GtkWidget *gtk_statusbar_new(void)
void gtk_statusbar_pop(GtkStatusbar *statusbar,
    guint context_id)
guint gtk_statusbar_push(GtkStatusbar *statusbar,
    guint context_id, const gchar *text)
void gtk_statusbar_remove(GtkStatusbar *statusbar,
    guint context_id, guint message_id)
```

Signals

```
"text_popped"       void cb(GtkWidget *, guint, gchar *,
gpointer)
"text_pushed"       void cb(GtkWidget *, guint, gchar *,
gpointer)
```

Refer to Chapter 8 for examples of GtkStatusBar.

GtkTable

The GtkTable widget is a container that creates a grid of flexible or static rectangles that you can use to position and size widgets.

Inheritance

```
GtkTable->GtkContainer->GtkWidget->GtkObject
```

Functions

```
void gtk_table_attach(GtkTable *table, GtkWidget *child,
    guint left_attach, guint right_attach, guint top_attach,
    guint bottom_attach, GtkAttachOptions xoptions,
    GtkAttachOptions yoptions, guint xpadding, guint ypadding)
void gtk_table_attach_defaults(GtkTable *table,
    GtkWidget *widget, guint left_attach, guint right_attach,
    guint top_attach, guint bottom_attach)
GtkType gtk_table_get_type(void)
GtkWidget *gtk_table_new(guint rows, guint columns,
    gboolean homogeneous)
void gtk_table_resize(GtkTable *table, guint n_rows,
    guint n_cols)
void gtk_table_set_col_spacing(GtkTable *table, guint column,
    guint spacing)
void gtk_table_set_col_spacings(GtkTable *table, guint spacing)
void gtk_table_set_homogeneous(GtkTable *table,
    gboolean homogeneous)
void gtk_table_set_row_spacing(GtkTable *table, guint row,
    guint spacing)
void gtk_table_set_row_spacings(GtkTable *table, guint spacing)
```

Enum
```
typedef enum {
  GTK_EXPAND,
  GTK_SHRINK,
  GTK_FILL
} GtkAttachOptions;
```

Chapter 4 provides examples using `GtkTable`.

GtkTearOffMenuItem

GNOME uses this widget to add a handle on the left end of a menu bar. This enables you to move the menu to another location and have it remain accessible even when its window is not visible.

Inheritance
```
GtkTearoffMenuItem->GtkMenuItem->GtkItem->GtkBin->
      GtkContainer->GtkWidget->GtkObject
```

Functions
```
GtkType gtk_tearoff_menu_item_get_type(void)
GtkWidget *gtk_tearoff_menu_item_new(void)
```

The following example creates a menu bar and adds a menu to it. The first member of the menu is a `GtkTearoffMenuItem`, which appears as a dashed line on the menu. This example places the `GtkTearoffMenuItem` at the top of the menu, but it can be placed anywhere on the menu and it will still work as a tear-off handle for the entire menu.

```
static GtkWidget *makeWidget()
{
    GtkWidget *menu;
    GtkWidget *item;
    GtkWidget *menuBar;

    /* Create the 'transform' menu */
    menu = gtk_menu_new();
    item = gtk_tearoff_menu_item_new();
    gtk_menu_append(GTK_MENU(menu),item);
    item = gtk_menu_item_new_with_label("Rotate");
    gtk_menu_append(GTK_MENU(menu),item);
    item = gtk_menu_item_new_with_label("Resize");
    gtk_menu_append(GTK_MENU(menu),item);
    item = gtk_menu_item_new_with_label("Select Color");
    gtk_menu_append(GTK_MENU(menu),item);
```

```
        /* Add the label on top of the 'transform' menu */
        item = gtk_menu_item_new_with_label("Transform");
        gtk_menu_item_set_submenu(GTK_MENU_ITEM(item),
                menu);

        /* Append the 'transform' menu to the menu bar */
        menuBar = gtk_menu_bar_new();
        gtk_menu_bar_append(GTK_MENU_BAR(menuBar),item);

        return(menuBar);
    }
```

Figure 21-42 shows the tear-off menu in its two states. On the left is the menu as it appears while attached to its menu bar. On the right is the appearance of the menu, in its own top-level window, after the mouse is used to tear it off. A menu is torn off by using the mouse to select the dashed line of the menu while it is still attached.

Figure 21-42: A menu before and after being torn off

GtkTed

GtkTed is a container widget that is expected to be deleted from a future version of GTK+.

Inheritance
```
GtkTed->GtkTable->GtkContainer->GtkWidget->GtkObject
```
Functions
```
void gtk_ted_add(GtkTed *ted, GtkWidget *widget,
    char *original_name)
guint gtk_ted_get_type()
GtkWidget *gtk_ted_new(char *name)
GtkWidget *gtk_ted_new_layout(char *name, char *layout)
void gtk_ted_prepare(GtkTed *ted)
void gtk_ted_set_app_name(char *str)
```

GtkText

The GtkText widget can be used to simply display text, or it can be used to enable the user to edit text. The editing capabilities are quite simple. It wraps lines longer than it can display.

Inheritance

```
GtkText->GtkEditable->GtkWidget->GtkObject
```

Functions

```
gint gtk_text_backward_delete(GtkText *text, guint nchars)
gint gtk_text_forward_delete(GtkText *text, guint nchars)
void gtk_text_freeze(GtkText *text)
guint gtk_text_get_length(GtkText *text)
guint gtk_text_get_point(GtkText *text)
GtkType gtk_text_get_type(void)
void gtk_text_insert(GtkText *text, GdkFont *font,
    GdkColor *fore, GdkColor *back, const char *chars,
    gint nchars)
GtkWidget *gtk_text_new(GtkAdjustment *hadj,
    GtkAdjustment *vadj)
void gtk_text_set_adjustments(GtkText *text,
    GtkAdjustment *hadj, GtkAdjustment *vadj)
void gtk_text_set_editable(GtkText *text, gboolean is_editable)
void gtk_text_set_line_wrap(GtkText *text, gint line_wrap)
void gtk_text_set_point(GtkText *text, guint index)
void gtk_text_set_word_wrap(GtkText *text, gint word_wrap)
void gtk_text_thaw(GtkText *text)
```

Signal

```
"set_scroll_adjustments"    void cb(GtkWidget *, GtkTypeAdjustment *,
GtkTypeAdjustment *, gpointer)
```

You can find examples of GtkText in Chapters 5 and 16.

GtkTipsQuery

The GtkTipsQuery widget is a label with added ability to switch into *query* mode. In this mode, the cursor changes to a question mark and, as the mouse passes over widgets, the tooltips are displayed immediately. If the user selects a widget, the GtkTipsQuery object issues a "widget_selected" signal giving your program the opportunity to display some specific information.

Inheritance

```
GtkTipsQuery->GtkLabel->GtkMisc->GtkWidget->GtkObject
```

Functions

```
guint gtk_tips_query_get_type(void)
GtkWidget *gtk_tips_query_new(void)
void gtk_tips_query_set_caller(GtkTipsQuery *tips_query,
    GtkWidget *caller)
void gtk_tips_query_set_labels(GtkTipsQuery *tips_query,
    const gchar *label_inactive, const gchar *label_no_tip)
```

```
void gtk_tips_query_start_query(GtkTipsQuery *tips_query)
void gtk_tips_query_stop_query(GtkTipsQuery *tips_query)
```

Signals

```
"start_query"     void cb(GtkWidget *, gpointer)
"stop_query"      void cb(GtkWidget *, gpointer)
"widget_entered"  void cb(GtkWidget *, GtkWidget *, gchar *,
gchar *, gpointer)
"widget_selected" gboolean cb(GtkWidget *, GdkWdiget *, gchar
*, gchar *, GdkEvent *, gpointer)
```

GtkToggleButton

A GtkToggleButton is a button that changes, and retains, its on or off state each time it is selected with the mouse.

Inheritance

```
GtkToggleButton->GtkButton->GtkBin->GtkContainer->GtkWidget->
       GtkObject
```

Functions

```
gboolean gtk_toggle_button_get_active(
    GtkToggleButton *toggle_button)
GtkType gtk_toggle_button_get_type(void)
GtkWidget *gtk_toggle_button_new(void)
GtkWidget *gtk_toggle_button_new_with_label(
    const gchar *label)
void gtk_toggle_button_set_active(
    GtkToggleButton *toggle_button, gboolean is_active)
void gtk_toggle_button_set_mode(
    GtkToggleButton *toggle_button, gboolean draw_indicator)
void gtk_toggle_button_toggled(
    GtkToggleButton *toggle_button)
```

Signal

```
"toggled"      void cb(GtkWidget *, gpointer)
```

Refer to Chapter 8 for examples of GtkToggleButtons.

GtkToolbar

The GtkToolbar is used to construct a toolbar. It is the container that controls the position of a set of icons that are mouse sensitive.

Inheritance

```
GtkToolbar->GtkContainer->GtkWidget->GtkObject
```

Functions

```
GtkWidget *gtk_toolbar_append_element(GtkToolbar *toolbar,
    GtkToolbarChildType type, GtkWidget *widget,
    const char *text, const char *tooltip_text,
    const char *tooltip_private_text, GtkWidget *icon,
    GtkSignalFunc callback, gpointer user_data)
GtkWidget *gtk_toolbar_append_item(GtkToolbar *toolbar,
    const char *text, const char *tooltip_text,
    const char *tooltip_private_text, GtkWidget *icon,
    GtkSignalFunc callback, gpointer user_data)
void gtk_toolbar_append_space(GtkToolbar *toolbar)
void gtk_toolbar_append_widget(GtkToolbar *toolbar,
    GtkWidget *widget, const gchar *tooltip_text,
    const gchar *tooltip_private_text)
GtkReliefStyle gtk_toolbar_get_button_relief(
    GtkToolbar *toolbar)
guint gtk_toolbar_get_type(void)
GtkWidget *gtk_toolbar_insert_element(GtkToolbar *toolbar,
    GtkToolbarChildType type, GtkWidget *widget,
    const char *text, const char *tooltip_text,
    const char *tooltip_private_text, GtkWidget *icon,
    GtkSignalFunc callback, gpointer user_data, gint position)
GtkWidget *gtk_toolbar_insert_item(GtkToolbar *toolbar,
    const char *text, const char *tooltip_text,
    const char *tooltip_private_text, GtkWidget *icon,
    GtkSignalFunc callback, gpointer user_data, gint position)
void gtk_toolbar_insert_space(GtkToolbar *toolbar,
    gint position)
void gtk_toolbar_insert_widget(GtkToolbar *toolbar,
    GtkWidget *widget, const char *tooltip_text,
    const char *tooltip_private_text, gint position)
GtkWidget *gtk_toolbar_new(GtkOrientation orientation,
    GtkToolbarStyle style)
GtkWidget *gtk_toolbar_prepend_element(GtkToolbar *toolbar,
    GtkToolbarChildType type, GtkWidget *widget,
    const char *text, const char *tooltip_text,
    const char *tooltip_private_text, GtkWidget *icon,
    GtkSignalFunc callback, gpointer user_data)
GtkWidget *gtk_toolbar_prepend_item(GtkToolbar *toolbar,
    const char *text, const char *tooltip_text,
    const char *tooltip_private_text, GtkWidget *icon,
    GtkSignalFunc callback, gpointer user_data)
void gtk_toolbar_prepend_space(GtkToolbar *toolbar)
void gtk_toolbar_prepend_widget(GtkToolbar *toolbar,
    GtkWidget *widget, const gchar *tooltip_text,
    const gchar *tooltip_private_text)
void gtk_toolbar_set_button_relief(GtkToolbar *toolbar,
    GtkReliefStyle relief)
void gtk_toolbar_set_orientation(GtkToolbar *toolbar,
    GtkOrientation orientation)
```

```
void gtk_toolbar_set_space_size(GtkToolbar *toolbar,
    gint space_size)
void gtk_toolbar_set_space_style(GtkToolbar *toolbar,
    GtkToolbarSpaceStyle space_style)
void gtk_toolbar_set_style(GtkToolbar *toolbar,
    GtkToolbarStyle style)
void gtk_toolbar_set_tooltips(GtkToolbar *toolbar, gint enable)
```

Enums

```
typedef enum {
  GTK_TOOLBAR_ICONS,
  GTK_TOOLBAR_TEXT,
  GTK_TOOLBAR_BOTH
} GtkToolbarStyle;

typedef enum {
  GTK_TOOLBAR_CHILD_SPACE,
  GTK_TOOLBAR_CHILD_BUTTON,
  GTK_TOOLBAR_CHILD_TOGGLEBUTTON,
  GTK_TOOLBAR_CHILD_RADIOBUTTON,
  GTK_TOOLBAR_CHILD_WIDGET
} GtkToolbarChildType;

typedef enum {
  GTK_TOOLBAR_SPACE_EMPTY,
  GTK_TOOLBAR_SPACE_LINE
} GtkToolbarSpaceStyle;

typedef enum {
  GTK_ORIENTATION_HORIZONTAL,
  GTK_ORIENTATION_VERTICAL
} GtkOrientation;
```

Signals

```
"orientation_changed"      void cb(GtkWidget *, gint, gpointer)
"style_changed"            void cb(GtkWidget *, gint, gpointer)
```

You can find examples of creating GNOME toolbars in Chapter 8.

GtkTooltips

You can add a GtkTooltips object to any widget. When the mouse lingers over the widget for a few seconds, a box appears that contains a brief description of the actions of the widget.

Inheritance

```
GtkTooltips->GtkData->GtkObject
```

Functions
```
GtkTooltipsData *gtk_tooltips_data_get(GtkWidget *widget)
void gtk_tooltips_disable(GtkTooltips *tooltips)
void gtk_tooltips_enable(GtkTooltips *tooltips)
void gtk_tooltips_force_window(GtkTooltips *tooltips)
GtkType gtk_tooltips_get_type(void)
GtkTooltips *gtk_tooltips_new(void)
void gtk_tooltips_set_colors(GtkTooltips *tooltips,
    GdkColor *background, GdkColor *foreground)
void gtk_tooltips_set_delay(GtkTooltips *tooltips, guint delay)
void gtk_tooltips_set_tip(GtkTooltips *tooltips,
    GtkWidget *widget, const gchar *tip_text,
    const gchar *tip_private)
```

This example creates a button widget and attaches a tooltip to it. Whenever the mouse pointer remains inside the rectangle of the button for a few seconds, the window looks like the one in Figure 21-43.

```
static GtkWidget *makeWidget()
{
    GtkTooltips *tooltips;
    GtkWidget *button;

    button = gtk_button_new_with_label("Button");
    tooltips = gtk_tooltips_new();
    gtk_tooltips_set_tip(tooltips,button,
            "Button Tool Tip Text",NULL);

    return(button);
}
```

Figure 21-43: A button with a tooltip

GtkTree

The GtkTree widget is a container of GtkTreeItem widgets and other GtkTree widgets to create and display a tree of names that you can traverse with the mouse.

Inheritance
```
GtkTree->GtkContainer->GtkWidget->GtkObject
```

Functions

```
void gtk_tree_append(GtkTree *tree, GtkWidget *tree_item)
gint gtk_tree_child_position(GtkTree *tree, GtkWidget *child)
void gtk_tree_clear_items(GtkTree *tree, gint start, gint end)
GtkType gtk_tree_get_type(void)
void gtk_tree_insert(GtkTree *tree, GtkWidget *tree_item,
    gint position)
GtkWidget *gtk_tree_new(void)
void gtk_tree_prepend(GtkTree *tree, GtkWidget *tree_item)
void gtk_tree_remove_item(GtkTree *container,
    GtkWidget *widget)
void gtk_tree_remove_items(GtkTree *tree, GList *items)
void gtk_tree_select_child(GtkTree *tree, GtkWidget *tree_item)
void gtk_tree_select_item(GtkTree *tree, gint item)
void gtk_tree_set_selection_mode(GtkTree *tree,
    GtkSelectionMode mode)
void gtk_tree_set_view_lines(GtkTree *tree, guint flag)
void gtk_tree_set_view_mode(GtkTree *tree,
    GtkTreeViewMode mode)
void gtk_tree_unselect_child(GtkTree *tree,
    GtkWidget *tree_item)
void gtk_tree_unselect_item(GtkTree *tree, gint item)
```

Enum

```
typedef enum {
  GTK_TREE_VIEW_LINE,
  GTK_TREE_VIEW_ITEM
} GtkTreeViewMode;
```

Signals

```
"select_child"        void cb(GtkWidget *, GtkWidget *, gpointer)
"selection_changed"   void cb(GtkWidget *, gpointer)
"unselect_child"      void cb(GtkWidget *, GtkWidget *, gpointer)
```

A GtkTree widget contains a list of one or more GtkTreeItem widgets. A
GtkTreeItem widget can contain a label; it also can contain another GtkTree
widget, which becomes a subtree. This example tree has two items at the top level,
both of which have subtrees underneath them (as shown in Figure 21-44). Note that
whenever each tree or subtree is completed (that is, all of its items are inserted),
you need to call gtk_widget_show_all() to make the items displayable.

```
static GtkWidget *makeWidget()
{
    GtkWidget *tree;
    GtkWidget *subtree;
    GtkWidget *treeitem;

    tree = gtk_tree_new();
```

```
treeitem = gtk_tree_item_new_with_label("One");
gtk_tree_append(GTK_TREE(tree),treeitem);
subtree = gtk_tree_new();
gtk_tree_item_set_subtree(GTK_TREE_ITEM(treeitem),subtree);
treeitem = gtk_tree_item_new_with_label("First One");
gtk_tree_append(GTK_TREE(subtree),treeitem);
treeitem = gtk_tree_item_new_with_label("Second One");
gtk_tree_append(GTK_TREE(subtree),treeitem);
treeitem = gtk_tree_item_new_with_label("Third One");
gtk_tree_append(GTK_TREE(subtree),treeitem);
gtk_widget_show_all(subtree);

treeitem = gtk_tree_item_new_with_label("Two");
gtk_tree_append(GTK_TREE(tree),treeitem);
subtree = gtk_tree_new();
gtk_tree_item_set_subtree(GTK_TREE_ITEM(treeitem),subtree);
treeitem = gtk_tree_item_new_with_label("First Two");
gtk_tree_append(GTK_TREE(subtree),treeitem);
treeitem = gtk_tree_item_new_with_label("Second Two");
gtk_tree_append(GTK_TREE(subtree),treeitem);
gtk_widget_show_all(subtree);

gtk_widget_show_all(tree);

return(tree);
}
```

Figure 21-44: A GtkTree with two subtrees and five leaf nodes

GtkTreeItem

This widget, capable of being contained in a GtkTree, is a container that can hold a single child widget.

Inheritance
```
GtkTreeItem->GtkItem->GtkBin->GtkContainer->GtkWidget->
     GtkObject
```

Functions

```
void gtk_tree_item_collapse(GtkTreeItem *tree_item)
void gtk_tree_item_deselect(GtkTreeItem *tree_item)
void gtk_tree_item_expand(GtkTreeItem *tree_item)
GtkType gtk_tree_item_get_type(void)
GtkWidget *gtk_tree_item_new(void)
GtkWidget *gtk_tree_item_new_with_label(gchar *label)
void gtk_tree_item_remove_subtree(GtkTreeItem *item)
void gtk_tree_item_select(GtkTreeItem *tree_item)
void gtk_tree_item_set_subtree(GtkTreeItem *tree_item,
    GtkWidget *subtree)
```

Signals

```
"collapse"      void cb(GtkWidget *, gpointer)
"expand"        void cb(GtkWidget *, gpointer)
```

For an example of `GtkTreeItem`, see the description of `GtkTree`.

GtkVBox

`GtkVBox` is a container widget that organizes its contained widgets vertically (one on top of the other).

Inheritance

```
GtkVBox->GtkBox->GtkContainer->GtkWidget->GtkObject
```

Functions

```
GtkType gtk_vbox_get_type(void)
GtkWidget *gtk_vbox_new(gboolean homogeneous, gint spacing)
```

Refer to Chapter 4 for a number of examples of `GtkVBox`.

GtkVButtonBox

`GtkVButtonBox` is a container designed to display a collection of buttons vertically (one on top of the other).

Inheritance

```
GtkVButtonBox->GtkButtonBox->GtkBox->GtkContainer->GtkWidget->
    GtkObject
```

Functions

```
GtkButtonBoxStyle gtk_vbutton_box_get_layout_default(void)
gint gtk_vbutton_box_get_spacing_default(void)
guint gtk_vbutton_box_get_type(void)
GtkWidget *gtk_vbutton_box_new(void)
void gtk_vbutton_box_set_layout_default(
    GtkButtonBoxStyle layout)
void gtk_vbutton_box_set_spacing_default(gint spacing)
```

Enum

```
typedef enum {
  GTK_BUTTONBOX_DEFAULT_STYLE,
  GTK_BUTTONBOX_SPREAD,
  GTK_BUTTONBOX_EDGE,
  GTK_BUTTONBOX_START,
  GTK_BUTTONBOX_END
} GtkButtonBoxStyle;
```

You can find a number of examples of `GtkVButtonBox` in Chapter 5.

GtkViewport

A `GtkViewport` is a container that does not resize to fit in the space allotted to it. Instead, it adds scrollbars as necessary so you can view any part of the window.

Inheritance

```
GtkViewport->GtkBin->GtkContainer->GtkWidget->GtkObject
```

Functions

```
GtkAdjustment *gtk_viewport_get_hadjustment(
    GtkViewport *viewport)
GtkType gtk_viewport_get_type(void)
GtkAdjustment *gtk_viewport_get_vadjustment(
    GtkViewport *viewport)
GtkWidget *gtk_viewport_new(GtkAdjustment *hadjustment,
    GtkAdjustment *vadjustment)
void gtk_viewport_set_hadjustment(GtkViewport *viewport,
    GtkAdjustment *adjustment)
void gtk_viewport_set_shadow_type(GtkViewport *viewport,
    GtkShadowType type)
void gtk_viewport_set_vadjustment(GtkViewport *viewport,
    GtkAdjustment *adjustment)
```

Enum

```
typedef enum {
  GTK_SHADOW_NONE,
  GTK_SHADOW_IN,
```

```
        GTK_SHADOW_OUT,
        GTK_SHADOW_ETCHED_IN,
        GTK_SHADOW_ETCHED_OUT
   } GtkShadowType;
```

Signal

```
   "set_scroll_adjustments"     void cb(GtkWidget *, GtkAdjustment
   *, GtkAdjustment *, gpointer)
```

The GtkViewport widget normally is not used directly; it is used inside GtkScrolledWindow. Chapter 5 has examples of GtkViewport.

GtkVPaned

GtkVPaned is a container with two panes—one above the other. Each pane can contain a widget, and you can use the mouse on the bar separating the panes to adjust the amount showing in each pane without changing the size of the overall window.

Inheritance

```
   GtkVPaned->GtkPaned->GtkContainer->GtkWidget->GtkObject
```

Functions

```
   guint gtk_vpaned_get_type(void)
   GtkWidget *gtk_vpaned_new(void)
```

Refer to Chapter 5 for an example of GtkVPaned.

GtkVRuler

GtkVRuler displays a vertically-oriented scale that optionally can contain tic marks and a current-position pointer. You can set the pointer position from inside the program; it follows the mouse.

Inheritance

```
   GtkVRuler->GtkRuler->GtkWidget->GtkObject
```

Functions

```
   guint gtk_vruler_get_type(void)
   GtkWidget *gtk_vruler_new(void)
```

The following example displays the window shown in Figure 21-45.

```
static GtkWidget *makeWidget()
{
    GtkWidget *widget;

    widget = gtk_vruler_new();
    gtk_ruler_set_range(GTK_RULER(widget),0.0,100.0,
            20.0,10.0);
    return(widget);
}
```

Figure 21-45: A vertical ruler with tic marks and a position pointer

GtkVScale

The GtkVScale widget is a vertical slot containing a slider that can be moved by the mouse.

Inheritance
```
GtkVScale->GtkScale->GtkRange->GtkWidget->GtkObject
```
Functions
```
GtkType gtk_vscale_get_type(void)
GtkWidget *gtk_vscale_new(GtkAdjustment *adjustment)
```

The following example creates a vertical scale that ranges from 0 to 100, and has an initial value of 45, as shown in Figure 21-46.

```
static GtkWidget *makeWidget()
{
    GtkWidget *widget;
    GtkObject *adjustment;
```

```
    adjustment = gtk_adjustment_new(45.0,0.0,100.0,
        1.0,0.0,0.0);
    widget = gtk_vscale_new(GTK_ADJUSTMENT(adjustment));
    return(widget);
}
```

Figure 21-46: A vertical scale with the slider set to 45

GtkVScrollbar

The GtkVScrollbar displays a vertical scrollbar with a slider and a pair of arrow buttons. To create a scrollbar, you must specify the beginning and ending values, the size of the slider, an initial slider position, and how far the slider should move when the mouse clicks the slot.

Inheritance
```
GtkVScrollbar->GtkScrollbar->GtkRange->GtkWidget->GtkObject
```
Functions
```
GtkType gtk_vscrollbar_get_type(void)
GtkWidget *gtk_vscrollbar_new(GtkAdjustment *adjustment)
```

The following example creates a vertical scrollbar that ranges from 0 to 100, as shown in Figure 21-47. The setting of the range specifies that there are 100 units from one end to the other (the difference between the beginning and ending values). Clicking an arrow at one end moves the slider one unit. Clicking the slot moves the slider 5 units. The slider is set to a width of 20 units.

```
static GtkWidget *makeWidget()
{
    GtkWidget *widget;
    GtkObject *adjustment;

    adjustment = gtk_adjustment_new(45.0,0.0,100.0,
        1.0,5.0,20.0);
    widget = gtk_vscrollbar_new(GTK_ADJUSTMENT(adjustment));
    return(widget);
}
```

Figure 21-47: A vertical scrollbar with the slider sized at 20 percent

GtkVSeparator

The GtkVSeparator widget draws a vertical line that you can use as a divider among a collection of horizontally organized widgets.

Inheritance

```
GtkVSeparator->GtkSeparator->GtkWidget->GtkObject
```

Functions

```
GtkType gtk_vseparator_get_type(void)
GtkWidget *gtk_vseparator_new(void)
```

The following example packs a vertical separator into a box between two buttons, as shown in Figure 21-48. If the container does not resize the separator, you must set its width because it defaults to a zero and cannot be seen.

```
static GtkWidget *makeWidget()
{
    GtkWidget *box;
    GtkWidget *button;
    GtkWidget *separator;

    box = gtk_hbox_new(FALSE,0);

    button = gtk_button_new_with_label("Button One");
    gtk_box_pack_start(GTK_BOX(box),button,FALSE,FALSE,0);

    separator = gtk_vseparator_new();
    gtk_box_pack_start(GTK_BOX(box),separator,FALSE,FALSE,0);
    gtk_widget_set_usize(separator,20,0);

    button = gtk_button_new_with_label("Button Two");
    gtk_box_pack_start(GTK_BOX(box),button,FALSE,FALSE,0);

    return(box);
}
```

Figure 21-48: A vertical separator between two buttons

GtkWidget

GtkWidget is the base class of all widgets.

Inheritance

    GtkWidget->GtkObject

Functions

    guint gtk_widget_accelerator_signal(GtkWidget *widget,
        GtkAccelGroup *accel_group, guint accel_key,
        guint accel_mods)
    gboolean gtk_widget_accelerators_locked(GtkWidget *widget)
    gboolean gtk_widget_activate(GtkWidget *widget)
    void gtk_widget_add_accelerator(GtkWidget *widget,
        const gchar *accel_signal, GtkAccelGroup *accel_group,
        guint accel_key, guint accel_mods,
        GtkAccelFlags accel_flags)
    void gtk_widget_add_events(GtkWidget *widget, gint events)
    void gtk_widget_class_path(GtkWidget *widget,
        guint *path_length_p, gchar **path_p,
        gchar **path_reversed_p)
    void gtk_widget_destroy(GtkWidget *widget)
    void gtk_widget_destroyed(GtkWidget *widget,
        GtkWidget **widget_pointer)
    void gtk_widget_draw(GtkWidget *widget, GdkRectangle *area)
    void gtk_widget_draw_default(GtkWidget *widget)
    void gtk_widget_draw_focus(GtkWidget *widget)
    void gtk_widget_ensure_style(GtkWidget *widget)
    gint gtk_widget_event(GtkWidget *widget, GdkEvent *event)
    void gtk_widget_get(GtkWidget *widget, GtkArg *arg)
    GtkWidget *gtk_widget_get_ancestor(GtkWidget *widget,
        GtkType widget_type)
    void gtk_widget_get_child_requisition(GtkWidget *widget,
        GtkRequisition *requisition)
    GdkColormap *gtk_widget_get_colormap(GtkWidget *widget)
    gchar *gtk_widget_get_composite_name(GtkWidget *widget)
    GdkColormap *gtk_widget_get_default_colormap(void)
    GtkStyle *gtk_widget_get_default_style(void)
    GdkVisual *gtk_widget_get_default_visual(void)
    gint gtk_widget_get_events(GtkWidget *widget)
    GdkExtensionMode gtk_widget_get_extension_events(
        GtkWidget *widget)
    gchar *gtk_widget_get_name(GtkWidget *widget)

```
GdkWindow *gtk_widget_get_parent_window(GtkWidget *widget)
void gtk_widget_get_pointer(GtkWidget *widget, gint *x,
    gint *y)
GtkStyle *gtk_widget_get_style(GtkWidget *widget)
GtkWidget *gtk_widget_get_toplevel(GtkWidget *widget)
GtkType gtk_widget_get_type(void)
GdkVisual *gtk_widget_get_visual(GtkWidget *widget)
void gtk_widget_getv(GtkWidget *widget, guint nargs,
    GtkArg *args)
void gtk_widget_grab_default(GtkWidget *widget)
void gtk_widget_grab_focus(GtkWidget *widget)
void gtk_widget_hide(GtkWidget *widget)
void gtk_widget_hide_all(GtkWidget *widget)
gint gtk_widget_hide_on_delete(GtkWidget *widget)
gint gtk_widget_intersect(GtkWidget *widget,
    GdkRectangle *area, GdkRectangle *intersection)
gint gtk_widget_is_ancestor(GtkWidget *widget,
    GtkWidget *ancestor)
void gtk_widget_lock_accelerators(GtkWidget *widget)
void gtk_widget_map(GtkWidget *widget)
void gtk_widget_modify_style(GtkWidget *widget,
    GtkRcStyle *style)
GtkWidget *gtk_widget_new(GtkType widget_type,
    const gchar *first_arg_name, ...)
GtkWidget *gtk_widget_newv(GtkType type, guint nargs,
    GtkArg *args)
void gtk_widget_path(GtkWidget *widget, guint *path_length_p,
    gchar **path_p, gchar **path_reversed_p)
void gtk_widget_pop_colormap(void)
void gtk_widget_pop_composite_child(void)
void gtk_widget_pop_style(void)
void gtk_widget_pop_visual(void)
void gtk_widget_popup(GtkWidget *widget, gint x, gint y)
void gtk_widget_push_colormap(GdkColormap *cmap)
void gtk_widget_push_composite_child(void)
void gtk_widget_push_style(GtkStyle *style)
void gtk_widget_push_visual(GdkVisual *visual)
void gtk_widget_queue_clear(GtkWidget *widget)
void gtk_widget_queue_clear_area(GtkWidget *widget, gint x,
    gint y, gint width, gint height)
void gtk_widget_queue_draw(GtkWidget *widget)
void gtk_widget_queue_draw_area(GtkWidget *widget, gint x,
    gint y, gint width, gint height)
void gtk_widget_queue_resize(GtkWidget *widget)
void gtk_widget_realize(GtkWidget *widget)
void gtk_widget_ref(GtkWidget *widget)
void gtk_widget_remove_accelerator(GtkWidget *widget,
    GtkAccelGroup *accel_group, guint accel_key,
    guint accel_mods)
void gtk_widget_remove_accelerators(GtkWidget *widget,
    const gchar *accel_signal, gboolean visible_only)
void gtk_widget_reparent(GtkWidget *widget,
    GtkWidget *new_parent)
```

```
void gtk_widget_reset_rc_styles(GtkWidget *widget)
void gtk_widget_reset_shapes(GtkWidget *widget)
void gtk_widget_restore_default_style(GtkWidget *widget)
void gtk_widget_set(GtkWidget *widget,
    const gchar *first_arg_name, ...)
void gtk_widget_set_app_paintable(GtkWidget *widget,
    gboolean app_paintable)
void gtk_widget_set_colormap(GtkWidget *widget,
    GdkColormap *colormap)
void gtk_widget_set_composite_name(GtkWidget *widget,
    gchar *name)
void gtk_widget_set_default_colormap(GdkColormap *colormap)
void gtk_widget_set_default_style(GtkStyle *style)
void gtk_widget_set_default_visual(GdkVisual *visual)
void gtk_widget_set_events(GtkWidget *widget, gint events)
void gtk_widget_set_extension_events(GtkWidget *widget,
    GdkExtensionMode mode)
void gtk_widget_set_name(GtkWidget *widget, const gchar *name)
void gtk_widget_set_parent(GtkWidget *widget,
    GtkWidget *parent)
void gtk_widget_set_parent_window(GtkWidget *widget,
    GdkWindow *parent_window)
void gtk_widget_set_rc_style(GtkWidget *widget)
gboolean gtk_widget_set_scroll_adjustments(GtkWidget *widget,
    GtkAdjustment *hadjustment, GtkAdjustment *vadjustment)
void gtk_widget_set_sensitive(GtkWidget *widget,
    gint sensitive)
void gtk_widget_set_state(GtkWidget *widget,
    GtkStateType state)
void gtk_widget_set_style(GtkWidget *widget, GtkStyle *style)
void gtk_widget_set_uposition(GtkWidget *widget, gint x,
    gint y)
void gtk_widget_set_usize(GtkWidget *widget, gint width,
    gint height)
void gtk_widget_set_visual(GtkWidget *widget,
    GdkVisual *visual)
void gtk_widget_setv(GtkWidget *widget, guint nargs,
    GtkArg *args)
void gtk_widget_shape_combine_mask(GtkWidget *widget,
    GdkBitmap *shape_mask, gint offset_x, gint offset_y)
void gtk_widget_show(GtkWidget *widget)
void gtk_widget_show_all(GtkWidget *widget)
void gtk_widget_show_now(GtkWidget *widget)
void gtk_widget_size_allocate(GtkWidget *widget,
    GtkAllocation *allocation)
void gtk_widget_size_request(GtkWidget *widget,
    GtkRequisition *requisition)
void gtk_widget_unlock_accelerators(GtkWidget *widget)
void gtk_widget_unmap(GtkWidget *widget)
void gtk_widget_unparent(GtkWidget *widget)
void gtk_widget_unrealize(GtkWidget *widget)
void gtk_widget_unref(GtkWidget *widget)
```

Enums

```
typedef enum {
  GTK_ACCEL_VISIBLE,
  GTK_ACCEL_SIGNAL_VISIBLE,
  GTK_ACCEL_LOCKED,
  GTK_ACCEL_MASK
} GtkAccelFlags;

typedef enum {
  GTK_STATE_NORMAL,
  GTK_STATE_ACTIVE,
  GTK_STATE_PRELIGHT,
  GTK_STATE_SELECTED,
  GTK_STATE_INSENSITIVE
} GtkStateType;
```

Signals

```
"button_press_event"       gboolean cb(GtkWidget *, GdkEvent *, gpointer)
"button_release_event"     gboolean cb(GtkWidget *, GdkEvent *, gpointer)
"client_event"             gboolean cb(GtkWidget *, GdkEvent *, gpointer)
"configure_event"          gboolean cb(GtkWidget *, GdkEvent *, gpointer)
"debug_msg"                void cb(GtkWidget *, gchar *, gpointer)
"delete_event"             gboolean cb(GtkWidget *, GdkEvent *, gpointer)
"destroy_event"            gboolean cb(GtkWidget *, GdkEvent *, gpointer)
"drag_begin"               void cb(GtkWidget *, GdkDragContext *, gpointer)
"drag_data_delete"         void cb(GtkWidget *, GdkDragContext *, gpointer)
"drag_data_get"            void cb(GtkWidget *, GdkDragContext *,
GtkSelectionData *, guint, guint, gpointer)
"drag_data_received"       void cb(GtkWidget *, GdkDragContext *, gint, gint,
GtkSelectionData *, guint, guint, gpointer)
"drag_drop"                gboolean cb(GtkWidget *, GdkDragContext *, gint, gint,
guint, gpointer)
"drag_end"                 void cb(GtkWidget *, GdkDragContext *, gpointer)
"drag_leave"               void cb(GtkWidget *, GdkDragContext *, gpointer)
"drag_motion"              gboolean cb(GtkWidget *, GdkDragContext *, gint, gint,
guint, gpointer)
"draw"                     void cb(GtkWidget *, gpointer, gpointer)
"draw_default"             void cb(GtkWidget *, gpointer)
"draw_focus"               void cb(GtkWidget *, gpointer)
"enter_notify_event"       gboolean cb(GtkWidget *, GdkEvent *, gpointer)
"event"                    gboolean cb(GtkWidget *, GdkEvent *, gpointer)
"expose_event"             gboolean cb(GtkWidget *, GdkEvent *, gpointer)
"focus_in_event"           gboolean cb(GtkWidget *, GdkEvent *, gpointer)
"focus_out_event"          gboolean cb(GtkWidget *, GdkEvent *, gpointer)
"grab_focus"               void cb(GtkWidget *, gpointer)
"hide"                     void cb(GtkWidget *, gpointer)
"key_press_event"          gboolean cb(GtkWidget *, GdkEvent *, gpointer)
"key_release_event"        gboolean cb(GtkWidget *, GdkEvent *, gpointer)
"leave_notify_event"       gboolean cb(GtkWidget *, GdkEvent *, gpointer)
"map"                      void cb(GtkWidget *, gpointer)
"map_event"                gboolean cb(GtkWidget *, GdkEvent *, gpointer)
"motion_notify_event"      gboolean cb(GtkWidget *, GdkEvent *, gpointer)
"no_expose_event"          gboolean cb(GtkWidget *, GdkEvent *, gpointer)
```

```
"parent_set"              void cb(GtkWidget *, GtkObject *, gpointer)
"property_notify_event"   gboolean cb(GtkWidget *, GdkEvent *, gpointer)
"proximity_in_event"      gboolean cb(GtkWidget *, GdkWidget *, gpointer)
"proximity_out_event"     gboolean cb(GtkWidget *, GdkEvent *, gpointer)
"realize"                 void cb(GtkWidget *, gpointer)
"selection_clear_event"   gboolean cb(GtkWidget *, GdkEvent *, gpointer)
"selection_get"           void cb(GtkWidget *, GtkSelectionData *, guint, guint,
gpointer)
"selection_notify_event"  gboolean cb(GtkWidget *, GdkEvent *, gpointer)
"selection_received"      void cb(GtkWidget *, GtkSelectionData *, gpointer)
"selection_request_event" gboolean cb(GtkWidget *, GdkEvent *, gpointer)
"show"         void cb(GtkWidget *, gpointer)
"size_allocate"           void cb(GtkWidget *, gpointer, gpointer)
"size_request"            void cb(GtkWidget *, gpointer, gpointer)
"state_changed"           void cb(GtkWidget *, GtkStateType, gpointer)
"style_set"               void cb(GtkWidget *, GtkStyle *, gpointer)
"unmap"                   void cb(GtkWidget *, gpointer)
"unmap_event"             gboolean cb(GtkWidget *, GtkEvent *, gpointer)
"unrealize"               void cb(GtkWidget *, gpointer)
"visibility_notify_event" gboolean cb(GtkWidget *, GdkEvent *, gpointer)
```

GtkWindow

A GtkWindow is a window that can be displayed on the screen. It also is a container that can hold a single child widget. It is common to have the window in GtkWindow supply the margin around the window of the contained widget.

Inheritance

```
GtkWindow->GtkBin->GtkContainer->GtkWidget->GtkObject
```

Functions

```
gint gtk_window_activate_default(GtkWindow *window)
gint gtk_window_activate_focus(GtkWindow *window)
void gtk_window_add_accel_group(GtkWindow *window,
    GtkAccelGroup *accel_group)
void gtk_window_add_embedded_xid(GtkWindow *window, guint xid)
GtkType gtk_window_get_type(void)
GtkWidget *gtk_window_new(GtkWindowType type)
void gtk_window_remove_accel_group(GtkWindow *window,
    GtkAccelGroup *accel_group)
void gtk_window_remove_embedded_xid(GtkWindow *window,
    guint xid)
void gtk_window_set_default(GtkWindow *window,
    GtkWidget *default_widget)
void gtk_window_set_default_size(GtkWindow *window, gint width,
    gint height)
void gtk_window_set_focus(GtkWindow *window, GtkWidget *focus)
void gtk_window_set_geometry_hints(GtkWindow *window,
    GtkWidget *geometry_widget, GdkGeometry *geometry,
    GdkWindowHints geom_mask)
```

```
void gtk_window_set_modal(GtkWindow *window, gboolean modal)
void gtk_window_set_policy(GtkWindow *window,
    gint allow_shrink, gint allow_grow, gint auto_shrink)
void gtk_window_set_position(GtkWindow *window,
    GtkWindowPosition position)
void gtk_window_set_title(GtkWindow *window,
    const gchar *title)
void gtk_window_set_transient_for(GtkWindow *window,
    GtkWindow *parent)
void gtk_window_set_wmclass(GtkWindow *window,
    const gchar *wmclass_name, const gchar *wmclass_class)
```

Enum

```
typedef enum {
  GTK_WINDOW_TOPLEVEL,
  GTK_WINDOW_DIALOG,
  GTK_WINDOW_POPUP
} GtkWindowType;
```

Signal

```
"set_focus"        void cb(GtkWidget *, GtkWidget *, gpointer)
```

Because every GUI application must have one, examples of creating top-level windows can be found throughout the book. In particular, you can see a popup dialog window being created in Chapter 3.

Summary

This chapter provided an alphabetical listing of every GTK+ widget, and a number of the other GTK+ objects that are used to construct an application. Each class was listed along with:

✦ The list of signals, enumerated types, and functions defined for an object

✦ The inheritance of each object so you can track down all of the signals and functions defined for any specific widget

✦ Examples of displayable widgets and container widgets, and references to other chapters in the book where examples are located

The next chapter is an alphabetic listing of the GNOME objects and widgets. Every GNOME widget is based on a GTK+. This means that it will be necessary to trace the inheritance of a GNOME widget in the next chapter back to its GTK+ ancestor in this chapter.

✦   ✦   ✦

The Widgets of GNOME

◆ ◆ ◆ ◆

In This Chapter

Listing and
explaining the
widgets, and some
other objects, of
GNOME

Determining all of the
signals and functions
defined for each
object

Determining all of the
inherited functions
available in an object
by examining its
inheritance

Determining the enum
constants defined for
passing configuration
settings to the
functions

Starting you off by
including a simple
example of each
widget

◆ ◆ ◆ ◆

This chapter provides an alphabetical listing of the GNOME
widgets (and some other objects). Each widget is listed
with its inheritance, all of the functions that are available to
your application, and a simple example.

The example code included with each widget is, in most cases,
a function that creates a displayable widget and returns its
address. The beginning of Chapter 21 describes the mainline
of the program that displays the widgets.

GnomeAbout

The GnomeAbout widget dialog window is designed to pop up
from the About button on an application menu. Its purpose is
to standardize the form and content.

Inheritance

```
GnomeAbout->GnomeDialog->GtkWindow->GtkBin-
>GtkContainer->
        GtkWidget->GtkObject
```

Functions

```
void gnome_about_construct(GnomeAbout *about,
    const gchar *title, const gchar *version,
    const gchar *copyright, const gchar
**authors,
    const gchar *comments, const gchar *logo)
guint gnome_about_get_type()
GtkWidget *gnome_about_new(const gchar *title,
    const gchar *version, const gchar
*copyright,
    const gchar **authors, const gchar
*comments,
    const gchar *logo)
```

Chapter 2 shows an example of a Menu button starting an
About box.

GnomeAnimator

The GnomeAnimator widget displays a list of images one at a time in such a way that, if the images are drawn correctly, an animated sequence is displayed. The sequence can be continuous and loop from the last back to the first image, stop after the last image is displayed, or display images one at a time.

> **Note** Currently, the GnomeAnimation widget is incomplete so you may find some differences in the information here and a newer version.

Inheritance

```
GnomeAnimator->GtkWidget->GtkObject
```

Functions

```
gboolean gnome_animator_advance(GnomeAnimator *animator,
    gint num)
gboolean gnome_animator_append_frame_from_file(
    GnomeAnimator *animator, const gchar *name, gint x_offset,
    gint y_offset, guint32 interval)
gboolean gnome_animator_append_frame_from_file_at_size(
    GnomeAnimator *animator, const gchar *name, gint x_offset,
    gint y_offset, guint32 interval, guint width, guint height)
gboolean gnome_animator_append_frame_from_gnome_pixmap(
    GnomeAnimator *animator, GnomePixmap *pixmap,
    gint x_offset, gint y_offset, guint32 interval)
gboolean gnome_animator_append_frame_from_imlib(
    GnomeAnimator *animator, GdkImlibImage *image,
    gint x_offset, gint y_offset, guint32 interval)
gboolean gnome_animator_append_frame_from_imlib_at_size(
    GnomeAnimator *animator, GdkImlibImage *image,
    gint x_offset, gint y_offset, guint32 interval,
    guint width, guint height)
gboolean gnome_animator_append_frames_from_file(
    GnomeAnimator *animator, const gchar *name, gint x_offset,
    gint y_offset, guint32 interval, gint x_unit)
gboolean gnome_animator_append_frames_from_file_at_size(
    GnomeAnimator *animator, const gchar *name, gint x_offset,
    gint y_offset, guint32 interval, gint x_unit, guint width,
    guint height)
gboolean gnome_animator_append_frames_from_imlib(
    GnomeAnimator *animator, GdkImlibImage *image,
    gint x_offset, gint y_offset, guint32 interval,
    gint x_unit)
gboolean gnome_animator_append_frames_from_imlib_at_size(
    GnomeAnimator *animator, GdkImlibImage *image,
    gint x_offset, gint y_offset, guint32 interval,
    gint x_unit, guint width, guint height)
guint gnome_animator_get_current_frame_number(
```

```
        GnomeAnimator *animator)
GnomeAnimatorLoopType gnome_animator_get_loop_type(
        GnomeAnimator *animator)
gint gnome_animator_get_playback_direction(
        GnomeAnimator *animator)
double gnome_animator_get_playback_speed(
        GnomeAnimator *animator)
GnomeAnimatorStatus gnome_animator_get_status(
        GnomeAnimator *animator)
guint gnome_animator_get_type(void)
void gnome_animator_goto_frame(GnomeAnimator *animator,
        guint frame_number)
GtkWidget *gnome_animator_new_with_size(guint width,
        guint height)
void gnome_animator_set_loop_type(GnomeAnimator *animator,
        GnomeAnimatorLoopType loop_type)
void gnome_animator_set_playback_direction(
        GnomeAnimator *animator, gint playback_direction)
void gnome_animator_set_playback_speed(
        GnomeAnimator *animator, double speed)
void gnome_animator_start(GnomeAnimator *animator)
void gnome_animator_stop(GnomeAnimator *animator)
```

Enums

```
typedef enum {
  GNOME_ANIMATOR_LOOP_NONE,
  GNOME_ANIMATOR_LOOP_RESTART,
  GNOME_ANIMATOR_LOOP_PING_PONG
GnomeAnimatorLoopType;

GnomeAnimatorStatus {
  GNOME_ANIMATOR_STATUS_STOPPED,
  GNOME_ANIMATOR_STATUS_RUNNING
} GnomeAnimationStatus;
```

The following example animates the modulation-like graph shown in Figure 22-1.
The frames of the sequence are stored as XPM data in the file named
"animator.xpm", and the address of each frame is stored in an array named anim.
This is done at the top of the program and looks like this:

```
#include "animator.xpm"

static char **anim[] = {
    anim1,anim2,anim3,anim4,anim5
};
```

There is a loop that creates a GnomePixmap for each frame, and appends each
pixmap as a frame in the sequence. The animator is set to show the frames in order
and then loop back to the beginning to start over. You also can set the animator to

sequence through the frames only once, or it you can set it to show only the first frame and wait for the application to switch frames.

```
static GtkWidget *makeWidget()
{
    int i;
    GtkWidget *animator;
    GtkWidget *pixmap;

    animator = gnome_animator_new_with_size(100,100);

    for(i=0; i<5; i++) {
        pixmap = gnome_pixmap_new_from_xpm_d(anim[i]);
        gnome_animator_append_frame_from_gnome_pixmap(
                GNOME_ANIMATOR(animator),GNOME_PIXMAP(pixmap),
                0,0,50);
    }
    gnome_animator_set_loop_type(GNOME_ANIMATOR(animator),
            GNOME_ANIMATOR_LOOP_RESTART);
    gnome_animator_start(GNOME_ANIMATOR(animator));

    return(animator);
}
```

Figure 22-1: One frame of a GNOME animation

GnomeApp

The GnomeApp widget is the main window of a GNOME application. It is a container widget that can hold a single child widget. It also includes facilities for attaching menus, toolbars, a status bar, and widgets that can be docked.

Inheritance

```
GnomeApp->GtkWindow->GtkBin->GtkContainer->GtkWidget->
        GtkObject
```

Functions

```
void gnome_app_add_dock_item(GnomeApp *app,
    GnomeDockItem *item, GnomeDockPlacement placement,
    gint band_num, gint band_position, gint offset)
void gnome_app_add_docked(GnomeApp *app, GtkWidget *widget,
    const gchar *name, GnomeDockItemBehavior behavior,
    GnomeDockPlacement placement, gint band_num,
    gint band_position, gint offset)
void gnome_app_add_toolbar(GnomeApp *app, GtkToolbar *toolbar,
    const gchar *name, GnomeDockItemBehavior behavior,
```

```
    GnomeDockPlacement placement, gint band_num,
    gint band_position, gint offset)
void gnome_app_construct(GnomeApp *app, gchar *appname,
    char *title)
void gnome_app_enable_layout_config(GnomeApp *app,
    gboolean enable)
GnomeDock *gnome_app_get_dock(GnomeApp *app)
GnomeDockItem *gnome_app_get_dock_item_by_name(GnomeApp *app,
    const gchar *name)
GtkType gnome_app_get_type(void)
GtkWidget *gnome_app_new(gchar *appname, char *title)
void gnome_app_set_contents(GnomeApp *app, GtkWidget *contents)
void gnome_app_set_menus(GnomeApp *app, GtkMenuBar *menubar)
void gnome_app_set_statusbar(GnomeApp *app,
    GtkWidget *statusbar)
void gnome_app_set_statusbar_custom(GnomeApp *app,
    GtkWidget *container, GtkWidget *statusbar)
void gnome_app_set_toolbar(GnomeApp *app, GtkToolbar *toolbar)
```

Enums

```
typedef enum {
  GNOME_DOCK_ITEM_BEH_NORMAL = 0,
  GNOME_DOCK_ITEM_BEH_EXCLUSIVE = 1 << 0,
  GNOME_DOCK_ITEM_BEH_NEVER_FLOATING = 1 << 1,
  GNOME_DOCK_ITEM_BEH_NEVER_VERTICAL = 1 << 2,
  GNOME_DOCK_ITEM_BEH_NEVER_HORIZONTAL = 1 << 3,
  GNOME_DOCK_ITEM_BEH_LOCKED = 1 << 4
} GnomeDockItemBehavior;

typedef enum {
  GNOME_DOCK_TOP,
  GNOME_DOCK_RIGHT,
  GNOME_DOCK_BOTTOM,
  GNOME_DOCK_LEFT,
  GNOME_DOCK_FLOATING
} GnomeDockPlacement;
```

Chapter 2 provides some introductory examples of the GnomeApp widget.

GnomeAppBar

The GnomeAppBar widget is a progress bar with a textual annotation.

Inheritance

```
GnomeAppBar->GtkHBox->GtkBox->GtkContainer->GtkWidget->
    GtkObject
```

Functions

```
void gnome_appbar_clear_prompt(GnomeAppBar *appbar)
void gnome_appbar_clear_stack(GnomeAppBar *appbar)
```

```
void gnome_appbar_construct(GnomeAppBar *ab,
    gboolean has_progress, gboolean has_status,
    GnomePreferencesType interactivity)
GtkProgress *gnome_appbar_get_progress(GnomeAppBar *ab)
gchar *gnome_appbar_get_response(GnomeAppBar *appbar)
guint gnome_appbar_get_type()
GtkWidget *gnome_appbar_new(gboolean has_progress,
    gboolean has_status, GnomePreferencesType interactivity)
void gnome_appbar_pop(GnomeAppBar *appbar)
void gnome_appbar_push(GnomeAppBar *appbar,
    const gchar *status)
void gnome_appbar_refresh(GnomeAppBar *appbar)
void gnome_appbar_set_default(GnomeAppBar *appbar,
    const gchar *default_status)
void gnome_appbar_set_progress(GnomeAppBar *ab,
    gfloat percentage)
void gnome_appbar_set_prompt(GnomeAppBar *appbar,
    const gchar *prompt, gboolean modal)
void gnome_appbar_set_status(GnomeAppBar *appbar,
    const gchar *status)
```

Enum

```
typedef enum {
  GNOME_PREFERENCES_NEVER,
  GNOME_PREFERENCES_USER,
  GNOME_PREFERENCES_ALWAYS
} GnomePreferencesType;
```

A `GnomeAppBar` displays two pieces of data. As shown in Figure 22-2, there is a descriptive string on the left and a progress bar on the right. Calling the function `gnome_set_progress()` sets the progress value and calling `gnome_appbar_set_prompt()` sets the string.

```
static GtkWidget *makeWidget()
{
    GtkWidget *appbar;

    appbar = gnome_appbar_new(TRUE,TRUE,
            GNOME_PREFERENCES_ALWAYS);
    gnome_appbar_set_progress(GNOME_APPBAR(appbar),0.63);
    gnome_appbar_set_prompt(GNOME_APPBAR(appbar),
            "Showing 63 Percent",TRUE);

    return(appbar);
}
```

Figure 22-2: A GnomeAppBar displays text and a progress bar

GnomeCalculator

The `GomeCalculator` widget is a popup window that contains a completely functional scientific calculator.

Inheritance

```
GnomeCalculator->GtkVBox->GtkBox->GtkContainer->GtkWidget->
        GtkObject
```

Functions

```
void gnome_calculator_clear(GnomeCalculator *gc,
    const gboolean reset)
guint gnome_calculator_get_type(void)
GtkWidget *gnome_calculator_new(void)
void gnome_calculator_set(GnomeCalculator *gc, gdouble result)
```

The programmatic interface to `GnomeCalculator` is very simple because it handles all of the user input and output. Figure 22-3 shows the calculator face.

```
static GtkWidget *makeWidget()
{
    GtkWidget *calculator;

    calculator = gnome_calculator_new();

    return(calculator);
}
```

Figure 22-3: The layout of the GnomeCalculator widget

GnomeCanvas

You can use the `GnomeCanvas` widget to draw figures, display graphics, position widgets, and more.

Inheritance

`GnomeCanvas->GtkLayout->GtkContainer->GtkWidget->GtkObject`

Functions

```
void gnome_canvas_c2w(GnomeCanvas *canvas, int cx, int cy,
    double *wx, double *wy)
int gnome_canvas_get_color(GnomeCanvas *canvas, char *spec,
    GdkColor *color)
GnomeCanvasItem *gnome_canvas_get_item_at(
    GnomeCanvas *canvas, double x, double y)
void gnome_canvas_get_scroll_offsets(GnomeCanvas *canvas,
    int *cx, int *cy)
void gnome_canvas_get_scroll_region(GnomeCanvas *canvas,
    double *x1, double *y1, double *x2, double *y2)
GtkType gnome_canvas_get_type(void)
GtkWidget *gnome_canvas_new(void)
GtkWidget *gnome_canvas_new_aa(void)
void gnome_canvas_request_redraw(GnomeCanvas *canvas, int x1,
    int y1, int x2, int y2)
void gnome_canvas_request_redraw_uta(GnomeCanvas *canvas,
    ArtUta *uta)
GnomeCanvasGroup *gnome_canvas_root(GnomeCanvas *canvas)
void gnome_canvas_scroll_to(GnomeCanvas *canvas, int cx,
    int cy)
void gnome_canvas_set_pixels_per_unit(GnomeCanvas *canvas,
    double n)
void gnome_canvas_set_scroll_region(GnomeCanvas *canvas,
    double x1, double y1, double x2, double y2)
void gnome_canvas_set_stipple_origin(GnomeCanvas *canvas,
    GdkGC *gc)
void gnome_canvas_update_now(GnomeCanvas *canvas)
void gnome_canvas_w2c(GnomeCanvas *canvas, double wx,
    double wy, int *cx, int *cy)
void gnome_canvas_w2c_affine(GnomeCanvas *canvas,
    double affine [ 6 ])
void gnome_canvas_w2c_d(GnomeCanvas *canvas, double wx,
    double wy, double *cx, double *cy)
void gnome_canvas_window_to_world(GnomeCanvas *canvas,
    double winx, double winy, double *worldx, double *worldy)
void gnome_canvas_world_to_window(GnomeCanvas *canvas,
    double worldx, double worldy, double *winx, double *winy)
```

Chapter 9 focuses on using the `GnomeCanvas` widget.

GnomeCanvasEllipse

The `GnomeCanvasEllipse` **is a** `GnomeCanvasItem` that draws itself as an ellipse on a `GnomeCanvas`.

Inheritance
    GnomeCanvasEllipse->GnomeCanvasRE->GnomeCanvasItem->GtkObject

Function
    GtkType gnome_canvas_ellipse_get_type(void)

Chapter 9 provides examples of the `GnomeCanvasEllipse` widget.

GnomeCanvasGroup

Objects of this class are created and managed inside a `GnomeCanvas` widget. Its purpose is to contain and control a collection of `CanvasItem` objects displayed by the `GnomeCanvas`. The only way to add a `GnomeCanvasItem` to a `GnomeCanvas` is to add it to a `GnomeCanvasGroup` object. And, because the `GnomeCanvasGroup` also is a `GnomeCanvasItem`, it can contain other `GnomeCanvasGroups`. There is always one `GnomeCanvasGroup` (the *root* group) in a `GnomeCanvas`.

Inheritance
    GnomeCanvasGroup->GnomeCanvasItem->GtkObject

Functions
    void gnome_canvas_group_child_bounds(GnomeCanvasGroup *group,
        GnomeCanvasItem *item)
    GtkType gnome_canvas_group_get_type(void)

Chapter 9 includes examples of the `GnomeCanvasGroup`.

GnomeCanvasImage

A `GnomeCanvasImage` displays an image on a `GnomeCanvas`.

Inheritance
    GnomeCanvasImage->GnomeCanvasItem->GtkObject

Function
    GtkType gnome_canvas_image_get_type(void)

You can see examples of using `GnomeCanvasImage` in Chapter 9.

GnomeCanvasItem

The `GnomeCanvasItem` **is the base class of all items that a** `GnomeCanvas` **displays.**

Inheritance

```
GnomeCanvasItem->GtkObject
```

Functions

```
void gnome_canvas_item_affine_absolute(GnomeCanvasItem *item,
    const double affine [ 6 ])
void gnome_canvas_item_affine_relative(GnomeCanvasItem *item,
    const double affine [ 6 ])
void gnome_canvas_item_construct(GnomeCanvasItem *item,
    GnomeCanvasGroup *parent, const gchar *first_arg_name,
    va_list args)
void gnome_canvas_item_constructv(GnomeCanvasItem *item,
    GnomeCanvasGroup *parent, guint nargs, GtkArg *args)
void gnome_canvas_item_get_bounds(GnomeCanvasItem *item,
    double *x1, double *y1, double *x2, double *y2)
GtkType gnome_canvas_item_get_type(void)
int gnome_canvas_item_grab(GnomeCanvasItem *item,
    guint event_mask, GdkCursor *cursor, guint32 etime)
void gnome_canvas_item_grab_focus(GnomeCanvasItem *item)
void gnome_canvas_item_hide(GnomeCanvasItem *item)
void gnome_canvas_item_i2c_affine(GnomeCanvasItem *item,
    double affine [ 6 ])
void gnome_canvas_item_i2w(GnomeCanvasItem *item, double *x,
    double *y)
void gnome_canvas_item_i2w_affine(GnomeCanvasItem *item,
    double affine [ 6 ])
void gnome_canvas_item_lower(GnomeCanvasItem *item,
    int positions)
void gnome_canvas_item_lower_to_bottom(GnomeCanvasItem *item)
void gnome_canvas_item_move(GnomeCanvasItem *item, double dx,
    double dy)
GnomeCanvasItem *gnome_canvas_item_new(
    GnomeCanvasGroup *parent, GtkType type,
    const gchar *first_arg_name, ...)
GnomeCanvasItem *gnome_canvas_item_newv(
    GnomeCanvasGroup *parent, GtkType type, guint nargs,
    GtkArg *args)
void gnome_canvas_item_raise(GnomeCanvasItem *item,
    int positions)
void gnome_canvas_item_raise_to_top(GnomeCanvasItem *item)
void gnome_canvas_item_reparent(GnomeCanvasItem *item,
    GnomeCanvasGroup *new_group)
void gnome_canvas_item_request_redraw_svp(
    GnomeCanvasItem *item, const ArtSVP *svp)
void gnome_canvas_item_request_update(GnomeCanvasItem *item)
void gnome_canvas_item_reset_bounds(GnomeCanvasItem *item)
```

```
void gnome_canvas_item_set(GnomeCanvasItem *item,
    const gchar *first_arg_name, ...)
void gnome_canvas_item_set_valist(GnomeCanvasItem *item,
    const gchar *first_arg_name, va_list args)
void gnome_canvas_item_setv(GnomeCanvasItem *item, guint nargs,
    GtkArg *args)
void gnome_canvas_item_show(GnomeCanvasItem *item)
void gnome_canvas_item_ungrab(GnomeCanvasItem *item,
    guint32 etime)
void gnome_canvas_item_update_svp(GnomeCanvasItem *item,
    ArtSVP **p_svp, ArtSVP *new_svp)
void gnome_canvas_item_update_svp_clip(GnomeCanvasItem *item,
    ArtSVP **p_svp, ArtSVP *new_svp, ArtSVP *clip_svp)
void gnome_canvas_item_w2i(GnomeCanvasItem *item, double *x,
    double *y)
```

See Chapter 9 for examples of creating different kinds of GnomeCanvasItems.

GnomeCanvasLine

The GnomeCanvasLine is a GnomeCanvasItem that draws a line on a GnomeCanvas. The line can contain multiple segments.

Inheritance
```
GnomeCanvasLine->GnomeCanvasItem->GtkObject
```
Function
```
GtkType gnome_canvas_line_get_type(void)
```

You can find examples of GnomeCanvasLine in Chapter 9.

GnomeCanvasPolygon

A GnomeCanvasPolygon is a GnomeCanvasItem that draws a filled polygon on a GnomeCanvas.

Inheritance
```
GnomeCanvasPolygon->GnomeCanvasItem->GtkObject
```
Functions
```
GtkType gnome_canvas_polygon_get_type(void)
double gnome_canvas_polygon_to_point(double *poly,
    int num_points, double x, double y)
```

Refer to Chapter 9 for examples of GnomeCanvasPolygon.

GnomeCanvasRE

This is a base class that acts as a parent for both GnomeCanvasRectangle and GnomeCanvasEllipse. This base class includes information pertaining to colors and sizes, but the two descendents contain the drawing details.

Inheritance
```
GnomeCanvasRE->GnomeCanvasItem->GtkObject
```
Functions
```
GtkType gnome_canvas_re_get_type(void)
```

Chapter 9 provides examples of GnomeCanvasEllipse and GnomeCanvasRect.

GnomeCanvasRect

The GnomeCanvasRect is a GnomeCanvasItem that draws itself as a rectangle on a GnomeCanvas.

Inheritance
```
GnomeCanvasRect->GnomeCanvasRE->GnomeCanvasItem->GtkObject
```
Function
```
GtkType gnome_canvas_rect_get_type(void)
```

You can see examples of GnomeCanvasRect in Chapter 9.

GnomeCanvasText

A GnomeCanvasText is a GnomeCanvasItem that displays a line of text on a GnomeCanvas.

Inheritance
```
GnomeCanvasText->GnomeCanvasItem->GtkObject
```
Function
```
GtkType gnome_canvas_text_get_type(void)
```

Chapter 9 has examples of GnomeCanvasText.

GnomeCanvasWidget

The `GnomeCanvasWidget` is not a widget — it is a `GnomeCanvasItem` that is capable of containing a widget. You can use a `GnomeCanvasWidget` to display any widget in a `GnomeCanvas` as if the widget were a `GnomeCanvasItem`.

Inheritance

```
GnomeCanvasWidget->GnomeCanvasItem->GtkObject
```

Function

```
GtkType gnome_canvas_widget_get_type(void)
```

You can find an example of using the `GnomeCanvasWidget` in Chapter 9.

GnomeClient

The `GnomeClient` object makes it possible for your application to save session information when the user logs out. If, when logging out, the user chooses to save the current settings, a `"save_yourself"` signal is sent to each application. Then an application can save information in such a way that it is supplied on the command line whenever the program automatically restarts by a user login.

Inheritance

```
GnomeClient->GtkObject
```

Functions

```
void gnome_client_add_static_arg(GnomeClient *client, ...)
void gnome_client_connect(GnomeClient *client)
void gnome_client_disable_master_connection(void)
void gnome_client_disconnect(GnomeClient *client)
void gnome_client_flush(GnomeClient *client)
gchar *gnome_client_get_config_prefix(GnomeClient *client)
GnomeClientFlags gnome_client_get_flags(GnomeClient *client)
gchar *gnome_client_get_global_config_prefix(
    GnomeClient *client)
gchar *gnome_client_get_id(GnomeClient *client)
gchar *gnome_client_get_previous_id(GnomeClient *client)
GtkType gnome_client_get_type(void)
void gnome_client_init(void)
GnomeClient *gnome_client_new(void)
GnomeClient *gnome_client_new_without_connection(void)
void gnome_client_request_interaction(GnomeClient *client,
    GnomeDialogType dialog_type,
    GnomeInteractFunction function, gpointer data)
void gnome_client_request_interaction_interp(
```

```
        GnomeClient *client, GnomeDialogType dialog_type,
        GtkCallbackMarshal function, gpointer data,
        GtkDestroyNotify destroy)
void gnome_client_request_phase_2(GnomeClient *client)
void gnome_client_request_save(GnomeClient *client,
        GnomeSaveStyle save_style, gboolean shutdown,
        GnomeInteractStyle interact_style, gboolean fast,
        gboolean global)
void gnome_client_save_any_dialog(GnomeClient *client,
        GnomeDialog *dialog)
void gnome_client_save_error_dialog(GnomeClient *client,
        GnomeDialog *dialog)
void gnome_client_set_clone_command(GnomeClient *client,
        gint argc, gchar *argv[])
void gnome_client_set_current_directory(GnomeClient *client,
        const gchar *dir)
void gnome_client_set_discard_command(GnomeClient *client,
        gint argc, gchar *argv[])
void gnome_client_set_environment(GnomeClient *client,
        const gchar *name, const gchar *value)
void gnome_client_set_global_config_prefix(
        GnomeClient *client, gchar *prefix)
void gnome_client_set_id(GnomeClient *client, const gchar *id)
void gnome_client_set_priority(GnomeClient *client,
        guint priority)
void gnome_client_set_process_id(GnomeClient *client,
        pid_t pid)
void gnome_client_set_program(GnomeClient *client,
        const gchar *program)
void gnome_client_set_resign_command(GnomeClient *client,
        gint argc, gchar *argv[])
void gnome_client_set_restart_command(GnomeClient *client,
        gint argc, gchar *argv[])
void gnome_client_set_restart_style(GnomeClient *client,
        GnomeRestartStyle style)
void gnome_client_set_shutdown_command(GnomeClient *client,
        gint argc, gchar *argv[])
void gnome_client_set_user_id(GnomeClient *client,
        const gchar *id)
GnomeClient *gnome_cloned_client(void)
void gnome_interaction_key_return(gint tag,
        gboolean cancel_shutdown)
GnomeClient *gnome_master_client(void)
```

Enums

```
typedef enum {
  GNOME_INTERACT_NONE,
  GNOME_INTERACT_ERRORS,
  GNOME_INTERACT_ANY
} GnomeInteractStyle;
```

```
typedef enum {
  GNOME_DIALOG_ERROR,
  GNOME_DIALOG_NORMAL
} GnomeDialogType;

typedef enum {
  GNOME_SAVE_GLOBAL,
  GNOME_SAVE_LOCAL,
  GNOME_SAVE_BOTH
} GnomeSaveStyle;

typedef enum {
  GNOME_RESTART_IF_RUNNING,
  GNOME_RESTART_ANYWAY,
  GNOME_RESTART_IMMEDIATELY,
  GNOME_RESTART_NEVER
} GnomeRestartStyle;

typedef enum {
  GNOME_CLIENT_IDLE,
  GNOME_CLIENT_SAVING_PHASE_1,
  GNOME_CLIENT_WAITING_FOR_PHASE_2,
  GNOME_CLIENT_SAVING_PHASE_2,
  GNOME_CLIENT_FROZEN,
  GNOME_CLIENT_DISCONNECTED,
  GNOME_CLIENT_REGISTERING
} GnomeClientState;

typedef enum {
  GNOME_CLIENT_IS_CONNECTED,
  GNOME_CLIENT_RESTARTED,
  GNOME_CLIENT_RESTORED
} GnomeClientFlags;
```

The following examples responds to the "save_yourself" signal in GtkObject
when the user logs out, and calls the function eventSaveYourself(). This
function creates an array of command-line arguments that are used to restart the
program at the point where it left off.

```
/** gnomeclient.c **/
#include <gnome.h>

gint eventDelete(GtkWidget *widget,
      GdkEvent *event,gpointer data);
gint eventDestroy(GtkWidget *widget,
      GdkEvent *event,gpointer data);
gint eventSaveYourself(GnomeClient *client,gint phase,
      GnomeSaveStyle sStyle,gint isShutdown,
      GnomeInteractStyle iStyle,gint isFast,gpointer data);
```

```
int main(int argc,char *argv[])
{
    int i;
    GtkWidget *app;
    GnomeClient *client;
    GtkWidget *label;
    GtkWidget *box;
    gchar string[80];

    gnome_init("gnomeclient","1.0",argc,argv);
    app = gnome_app_new("gnomeclient","GnomeClient");
    gtk_container_set_border_width(GTK_CONTAINER(app),20);
    gtk_signal_connect(GTK_OBJECT(app),"delete_event",
            GTK_SIGNAL_FUNC(eventDelete),NULL);
    gtk_signal_connect(GTK_OBJECT(app),"destroy",
            GTK_SIGNAL_FUNC(eventDestroy),NULL);

    client = gnome_master_client();
    gtk_signal_connect(GTK_OBJECT(client),"save_yourself",
            GTK_SIGNAL_FUNC(eventSaveYourself),argv[0]);

    box = gtk_vbox_new(FALSE,0);
    for(i=0; i<argc; i++) {
        sprintf(string,"argv[%d]=%s",i,argv[i]);
        label = gtk_label_new(string);
        gtk_box_pack_start(GTK_BOX(box),label,FALSE,FALSE,0);
    }

    gnome_app_set_contents(GNOME_APP(app),box);
    gtk_widget_show_all(app);
    gtk_main();
    exit(0);
}
gint eventDelete(GtkWidget *widget,
        GdkEvent *event,gpointer data) {
    return(FALSE);
}
gint eventDestroy(GtkWidget *widget,
        GdkEvent *event,gpointer data) {
    gtk_main_quit();
    return(0);
}
gint eventSaveYourself(GnomeClient *client,gint phase,
        GnomeSaveStyle sStyle,gint isShutdown,
        GnomeInteractStyle iStyle,gint isFast,gpointer data)
{
    guint argc;
    gchar *argv[2];

    argc = 2;
    argv[0] = (gchar *)data;
```

```
        argv[1] = "MyRestartValue";

        gnome_client_set_clone_command(client,argc,argv);
        gnome_client_set_restart_command(client,argc,argv);

        return(TRUE);
    }
```

This example uses a vertical box to hold a column of labels with each label showing one of the arguments on the command line. When the program is first run, its window looks like the one in Figure 22-4. If the user shuts down the program (with the Close option from a menu, or the button in the upper-right corner), no configuration information is saved. If, on the other hand, the user logs off and chooses to save the configuration, then the "save_yourself" signal is sent to the program. The next time the user logs in, the program starts automatically and is passed the saved information. The information on the command line causes the window to look like the one in Figure 22-5.

Figure 22-4: The command line with no client arguments

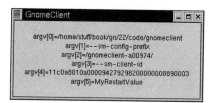

Figure 22-5: The command line with previously saved arguments

GnomeColorPicker

The GnomeColorPicker button pops up a GtkColorSelectionDialog and allows a color to be selected. The button changes color to match the currently selected color.

Inheritance

```
GnomeColorPicker->GtkButton->GtkBin->GtkContainer->GtkWidget->
    GtkObject
```

Functions

```
void gnome_color_picker_get_d(GnomeColorPicker *cp, gdouble *r,
    gdouble *g, gdouble *b, gdouble *a)
```

```
void gnome_color_picker_get_i16(GnomeColorPicker *cp,
    gushort *r, gushort *g, gushort *b, gushort *a)
void gnome_color_picker_get_i8(GnomeColorPicker *cp, guint8 *r,
    guint8 *g, guint8 *b, guint8 *a)
GtkType gnome_color_picker_get_type(void)
GtkWidget *gnome_color_picker_new(void)
void gnome_color_picker_set_d(GnomeColorPicker *cp, gdouble r,
    gdouble g, gdouble b, gdouble a)
void gnome_color_picker_set_dither(GnomeColorPicker *cp,
    gboolean dither)
void gnome_color_picker_set_i16(GnomeColorPicker *cp,
    gushort r, gushort g, gushort b, gushort a)
void gnome_color_picker_set_i8(GnomeColorPicker *cp, guint8 r,
    guint8 g, guint8 b, guint8 a)
void gnome_color_picker_set_title(GnomeColorPicker *cp,
    const gchar *title)
void gnome_color_picker_set_use_alpha(GnomeColorPicker *cp,
    gboolean use_alpha)
```

The default initial color for a GnomeColorPicker is black. There are functions that you can use to set and retrieve the current color. The following example creates a GnomeColorPicker that displays itself as a button. When selected, it pops up the color selection dialog box, as shown in Figure 22-6.

```
static GtkWidget *makeWidget()
{
    GtkWidget *colorpicker;

    colorpicker = gnome_color_picker_new();

    return(colorpicker);
}
```

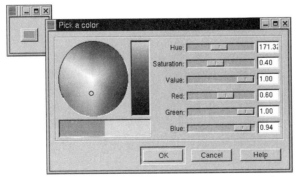

Figure 22-6: A color selection dialog box controlled by a GnomeColorPicker

GnomeDEntryEdit

A GnomeDEntryEdit object can be inserted as two pages in a GtkNotebook. These two pages enable the user to edit the application and directory information that appears in the system menu. This includes the program name, the command to start the program, and the location of the help documentation.

Inheritance

```
GnomeDEntryEdit->GtkObject
```

Functions

```
void gnome_dentry_edit_clear(GnomeDEntryEdit *dee)
gchar *gnome_dentry_edit_get_icon(GnomeDEntryEdit *dee)
gchar *gnome_dentry_edit_get_name(GnomeDEntryEdit *dee)
guint gnome_dentry_edit_get_type(void)
void gnome_dentry_edit_load_file(GnomeDEntryEdit *dee,
    const gchar *path)
GtkObject *gnome_dentry_edit_new(void)
GtkObject *gnome_dentry_edit_new_notebook(
    GtkNotebook *notebook)
void gnome_dentry_edit_set_dentry(GnomeDEntryEdit *dee,
    GnomeDesktopEntry *dentry)
GtkWidget *gnome_dentry_get_comment_entry(
    GnomeDEntryEdit *dee)
GnomeDesktopEntry *gnome_dentry_get_dentry(
    GnomeDEntryEdit *dee)
GtkWidget *gnome_dentry_get_doc_entry(GnomeDEntryEdit *dee)
GtkWidget *gnome_dentry_get_exec_entry(GnomeDEntryEdit *dee)
GtkWidget *gnome_dentry_get_icon_entry(GnomeDEntryEdit *dee)
GtkWidget *gnome_dentry_get_name_entry(GnomeDEntryEdit *dee)
GtkWidget *gnome_dentry_get_tryexec_entry(
    GnomeDEntryEdit *dee)
```

While the GnomeDEntryEdit object is not a widget, it does contain some widgets. These widgets are organized so they form the two pages that are inserted into the GtkNotebook. The GtkNotebook widget is used to display the two pages that are added by the GnomeDEntryEdit object. The following example creates an empty GnomeDEntryEdit object and inserts it into a notebook, as shown in Figure 22-7.

```
static GtkWidget *makeWidget()
{
    GtkObject *dentryedit;
    GtkWidget *notebook;

    notebook = gtk_notebook_new();
    dentryedit = gnome_dentry_edit_new_notebook(
            GTK_NOTEBOOK(notebook));

    return(notebook);
}
```

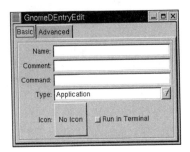

Figure 22-7: The two-page GnomeDEntryEdit object inside a GtkNotebook

GnomeDialog

You can use a GnomeDialog widget to construct a customized dialog box. The dialog box is created in its own top-level window. It uses a vertical box as a container and is capable of inserting a horizontal row of standard buttons in the bottom of the box. Your application can pack other widgets into the top of the box.

A GnomeMessageBox is a wrapper around GnomeDialog that simplifies the interface. Also, Chapter 3 provides examples and information on a set of predefined dialog boxes.

Inheritance

```
GnomeDialog->GtkWindow->GtkBin->GtkContainer->GtkWidget->
     GtkObject
```

Functions

```
void gnome_dialog_append_button(GnomeDialog *dialog,
    const gchar *button_name)
void gnome_dialog_append_button_with_pixmap(
    GnomeDialog *dialog, const gchar *button_name,
    const gchar *pixmap_name)
void gnome_dialog_append_buttons(GnomeDialog *dialog,
    const gchar *first, ...)
void gnome_dialog_append_buttons_with_pixmaps(
    GnomeDialog *dialog, const gchar **names,
    const gchar **pixmaps)
void gnome_dialog_append_buttonsv(GnomeDialog *dialog,
    const gchar **buttons)
void gnome_dialog_button_connect(GnomeDialog *dialog,
    gint button, GtkSignalFunc callback, gpointer data)
void gnome_dialog_button_connect_object(GnomeDialog *dialog,
    gint button, GtkSignalFunc callback, GtkObject *obj)
void gnome_dialog_close(GnomeDialog *dialog)
void gnome_dialog_close_hides(GnomeDialog *dialog,
    gboolean just_hide)
```

```
void gnome_dialog_close_real(GnomeDialog *dialog)
void gnome_dialog_construct(GnomeDialog *dialog,
    const gchar *title, va_list ap)
void gnome_dialog_constructv(GnomeDialog *dialog,
    const gchar *title, const gchar **buttons)
void gnome_dialog_editable_enters(GnomeDialog *dialog,
    GtkEditable *editable)
guint gnome_dialog_get_type()
GtkWidget *gnome_dialog_new(const gchar *title, ...)
GtkWidget *gnome_dialog_newv(const gchar *title,
    const gchar **buttons)
gint gnome_dialog_run(GnomeDialog *dialog)
gint gnome_dialog_run_and_close(GnomeDialog *dialog)
void gnome_dialog_set_accelerator(GnomeDialog *dialog,
    gint button, const guchar accelerator_key,
    guint8 accelerator_mods)
void gnome_dialog_set_close(GnomeDialog *dialog,
    gboolean click_closes)
void gnome_dialog_set_default(GnomeDialog *dialog, gint button)
void gnome_dialog_set_parent(GnomeDialog *dialog,
    GtkWindow *parent)
void gnome_dialog_set_sensitive(GnomeDialog *dialog,
    gint button, gboolean setting)
```

This example displays a GtkLabel widget at the top and uses two of the standard buttons at the bottom, as shown in Figure 22-8.

Figure 22-8: A dialog box with a label and two stock buttons

The buttons are added to the dialog box from left to right in the order you name them on the gnome_dialog_new() function. To get a response from the buttons, a "clicked" callback is connected to the entire dialog box. Inside the callback function, the selected button is specified by its number — the first button is zero, the second is one, and so on. Also, a call to gtk_widget_destroy() is made in the callback function to delete the dialog box.

```
/** gnomedialog.c **/
#include <gnome.h>

static void dialogCallback(GtkWidget *widget,
        gint button,gpointer data);

int main(int argc,char *argv[])
{
```

```
    GtkWidget *dialog;
    GtkWidget *box;
    GtkWidget *label;

    gnome_init("gnomedialog","1.0",argc,argv);

    dialog = gnome_dialog_new("GnomeDialog",
            GNOME_STOCK_BUTTON_OK,
            GNOME_STOCK_BUTTON_CANCEL,
            NULL);
    label = gtk_label_new("Text of the dialog box");
    box = GNOME_DIALOG(dialog)->vbox;
    gnome_dialog_set_default(GNOME_DIALOG(dialog),0);
    gtk_box_pack_start(GTK_BOX(box),label,TRUE,TRUE,0);

    gtk_signal_connect(GTK_OBJECT(dialog),"clicked",
            dialogCallback,NULL);

    gtk_widget_show_all(dialog);
    gtk_main();
    exit(0);
}
static void dialogCallback(GtkWidget *widget,
        gint button,gpointer data)
{
    switch(button) {
    case 0:
        g_print("The OK Button\n");
        break;
    case 1:
        g_print("The CANCEL Button\n");
        break;
    }
    gtk_widget_destroy(widget);
}
```

The following is the list of stock buttons that you can include in a dialog box.

```
GNOME_STOCK_BUTTON_OK
GNOME_STOCK_BUTTON_CANCEL
GNOME_STOCK_BUTTON_YES
GNOME_STOCK_BUTTON_NO
GNOME_STOCK_BUTTON_CLOSE
GNOME_STOCK_BUTTON_APPLY
GNOME_STOCK_BUTTON_HELP
GNOME_STOCK_BUTTON_NEXT
GNOME_STOCK_BUTTON_PREV
GNOME_STOCK_BUTTON_UP
GNOME_STOCK_BUTTON_DOWN
GNOME_STOCK_BUTTON_FONT
```

GnomeDock

You can add the `GnomeDock` widget to a window to manage the docking and undocking of widgets. It actually manages a set of `GnomeDockBands`, and each `GnomeDockBand` can contain one or more `GnomeDockItems`.

Inheritance

```
GnomeDock->GtkContainer->GtkWidget->GtkObject
```

Functions

```
void gnome_dock_add_floating_item(GnomeDock *dock,
    GnomeDockItem *item, gint x, gint y,
    GtkOrientation orientation)
gboolean gnome_dock_add_from_layout(GnomeDock *dock,
    GnomeDockLayout *layout)
void gnome_dock_add_item(GnomeDock *dock, GnomeDockItem *item,
    GnomeDockPlacement placement, guint band_num,
    gint position, guint offset, gboolean in_new_band)
void gnome_dock_allow_floating_items(GnomeDock *dock,
    gboolean enable)
GtkWidget *gnome_dock_get_client_area(GnomeDock *dock)
GnomeDockItem *gnome_dock_get_item_by_name(GnomeDock *dock,
    const gchar *name, GnomeDockPlacement *placement_return,
    guint *num_band_return, guint *band_position_return,
    guint *offset_return)
GnomeDockLayout *gnome_dock_get_layout(GnomeDock *dock)
GtkType gnome_dock_get_type(void)
GtkWidget *gnome_dock_new(void)
void gnome_dock_set_client_area(GnomeDock *dock,
    GtkWidget *widget)
```

Enum

```
typedef enum {
  GNOME_DOCK_TOP,
  GNOME_DOCK_RIGHT,
  GNOME_DOCK_BOTTOM,
  GNOME_DOCK_LEFT,
  GNOME_DOCK_FLOATING
} GnomeDockPlacement;
```

Signal

```
"layout_changed"       void cb(GtkWidget *, gpointer)
```

The following example creates a `GnomeDock` widget and adds it to the main window of the application. The function `makeWidget()` creates the widget and installs three toolbars into it. When the window first appears, it has one toolbar at the top, one on the right, and one free-floating, as shown in Figure 22-9.

```
/** gnomedock.c **/
#include <gnome.h>
```

```
gint eventDelete(GtkWidget *widget,
        GdkEvent *event,gpointer data);
gint eventDestroy(GtkWidget *widget,
        GdkEvent *event,gpointer data);
static GtkWidget *makeWidget();
static GtkWidget *makeToolbar();
static void uib_signal(GnomeUIInfo *uiinfo,gchar *signal_name,
        GnomeUIBuilderData *uibdata);

static GnomeUIInfo toolbarDef[] = {
    { GNOME_APP_UI_ITEM,"New",
      "Create a new file",NULL,NULL,NULL,
      GNOME_APP_PIXMAP_STOCK,GNOME_STOCK_PIXMAP_NEW,
      0,0,NULL },
    { GNOME_APP_UI_ITEM,"Open",
      "Open an existing file",NULL,NULL,NULL,
      GNOME_APP_PIXMAP_STOCK,GNOME_STOCK_PIXMAP_OPEN,
      0,0,NULL },
    { GNOME_APP_UI_ITEM,"Save",
      "Save the current file",NULL,NULL,NULL,
      GNOME_APP_PIXMAP_STOCK,GNOME_STOCK_PIXMAP_SAVE,
      0,0,NULL },
    { GNOME_APP_UI_ITEM,"Save as",
      "Save to a new file",NULL,NULL,NULL,
      GNOME_APP_PIXMAP_STOCK,GNOME_STOCK_PIXMAP_SAVE_AS,
      0,0,NULL },
    GNOMEUIINFO_END
};


int main(int argc,char *argv[])
{
    GtkWidget *app;
    GtkWidget *widget;

    gnome_init("gnomedock","1.0",argc,argv);
    app = gnome_app_new("gnomedock","GnomeDock");
    gtk_widget_set_usize(GTK_WIDGET(app),350,350);
    gtk_signal_connect(GTK_OBJECT(app),"delete_event",
            GTK_SIGNAL_FUNC(eventDelete),NULL);
    gtk_signal_connect(GTK_OBJECT(app),"destroy",
            GTK_SIGNAL_FUNC(eventDestroy),NULL);

    widget = makeWidget();

    gnome_app_set_contents(GNOME_APP(app),widget);
    gtk_widget_show_all(app);
    gtk_main();
    exit(0);
}
gint eventDelete(GtkWidget *widget,
```

```
            GdkEvent *event,gpointer data) {
        return(FALSE);
    }
    gint eventDestroy(GtkWidget *widget,
            GdkEvent *event,gpointer data) {
        gtk_main_quit();
        return(0);
    }
    static GtkWidget *makeWidget()
    {
        GtkWidget *dock;
        GnomeDockLayout *layout;
        GtkWidget *item;
        GtkWidget *toolbar;

        dock = gnome_dock_new();
        layout = gnome_dock_layout_new();

        toolbar = makeToolbar();
        item = gnome_dock_item_new("Item1",
                GNOME_DOCK_ITEM_BEH_EXCLUSIVE);
        gtk_container_add(GTK_CONTAINER(item),toolbar);
        gnome_dock_layout_add_item(layout,GNOME_DOCK_ITEM(item),
                GNOME_DOCK_TOP,0,0,0);

        toolbar = makeToolbar();
        item = gnome_dock_item_new("Item2",
                GNOME_DOCK_ITEM_BEH_NORMAL);
        gtk_container_add(GTK_CONTAINER(item),toolbar);
        gnome_dock_layout_add_item(layout,GNOME_DOCK_ITEM(item),
                GNOME_DOCK_RIGHT,0,0,0);

        toolbar = makeToolbar();
        item = gnome_dock_item_new("Item3",
                GNOME_DOCK_ITEM_BEH_NORMAL);
        gtk_container_add(GTK_CONTAINER(item),toolbar);
        gnome_dock_layout_add_item(layout,GNOME_DOCK_ITEM(item),
                GNOME_DOCK_FLOATING,0,0,0);

        gtk_widget_show(toolbar);
        gtk_widget_show(item);

        gnome_dock_layout_add_to_dock(GNOME_DOCK_LAYOUT(layout),
                GNOME_DOCK(dock));

        return(dock);
    }
    static GtkWidget *makeToolbar()
    {
        GtkWidget *toolbar;
        GnomeUIBuilderData uibdata;
```

```
toolbar = gtk_toolbar_new(GTK_ORIENTATION_HORIZONTAL,
        GTK_TOOLBAR_ICONS);
gtk_container_set_border_width(GTK_CONTAINER(toolbar),1);

uibdata.connect_func = uib_signal;
uibdata.data = NULL;
uibdata.is_interp = FALSE;
uibdata.relay_func = NULL;
uibdata.destroy_func = NULL;
gnome_app_fill_toolbar_custom(GTK_TOOLBAR(toolbar),
        toolbarDef,&uibdata,NULL);

return(toolbar);
}
static void uib_signal(GnomeUIInfo *uiinfo,gchar *signal_name,
        GnomeUIBuilderData *uibdata)
{
}
```

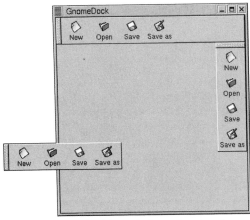

Figure 22-9: A docking window showing three toolbars

As each toolbar is created, it is inserted into GnomeDockItem with a call to gtk_container_add(). Then, in turn, the GnomeDockItem is added to the GnomeDockLayout. Finally, the GnomeDockLayout is added to the GnomeDock with the call to gnome_dock_layout_add_to_dock().

The GnomeApp window provides a simpler way to create toolbars. You can see some examples of this in Chapter 8.

GnomeDockBand

A GnomeDockBand is a container widget that is specifically used to contain a group of widgets for a GnomeDock widget.

Inheritance

```
GnomeDockBand->GtkContainer->GtkWidget->GtkObject
```

Functions

```
gboolean gnome_dock_band_append(GnomeDockBand *band,
    GtkWidget *child, guint offset)
void gnome_dock_band_drag_begin(GnomeDockBand *band,
    GnomeDockItem *item)
void gnome_dock_band_drag_end(GnomeDockBand *band,
    GnomeDockItem *item)
gboolean gnome_dock_band_drag_to(GnomeDockBand *band,
    GnomeDockItem *item, gint x, gint y)
guint gnome_dock_band_get_child_offset(GnomeDockBand *band,
    GtkWidget *child)
GnomeDockItem *gnome_dock_band_get_item_by_name(
    GnomeDockBand *band, const char *name,
    guint *position_return, guint *offset_return)
guint gnome_dock_band_get_num_children(GnomeDockBand *band)
GtkOrientation gnome_dock_band_get_orientation(
    GnomeDockBand *band)
GtkType gnome_dock_band_get_type(void)
gboolean gnome_dock_band_insert(GnomeDockBand *band,
    GtkWidget *child, guint offset, gint position)
void gnome_dock_band_layout_add(GnomeDockBand *band,
    GnomeDockLayout *layout, GnomeDockPlacement placement,
    guint band_num)
void gnome_dock_band_move_child(GnomeDockBand *band,
    GList *old_child, guint new_num)
GtkWidget *gnome_dock_band_new(void)
gboolean gnome_dock_band_prepend(GnomeDockBand *band,
    GtkWidget *child, guint offset)
void gnome_dock_band_set_child_offset(GnomeDockBand *band,
    GtkWidget *child, guint offset)
void gnome_dock_band_set_orientation(GnomeDockBand *band,
    GtkOrientation orientation)
```

Enums

```
typedef enum {
  GTK_ORIENTATION_HORIZONTAL,
  GTK_ORIENTATION_VERTICAL,
} GtkOrientation;

typedef enum {
  GNOME_DOCK_TOP,
```

```
    GNOME_DOCK_RIGHT,
    GNOME_DOCK_BOTTOM,
    GNOME_DOCK_LEFT,
    GNOME_DOCK_FLOATING
} GnomeDockPlacement;
```

For an example of docking, see the GnomeDock widget earlier in this chapter.

GnomeDockItem

The GnomeDockItem is a container with the ability of containing one widget. The GnomeDockItem is contained in a GnomeDockBand widget, which is contained in a GnomeDock widget.

Inheritance

```
GnomeDockItem->GtkBin->GtkContainer->GtkWidget->GtkObject
```

Functions

```
void gnome_dock_item_attach(GnomeDockItem *item,
    GtkWidget *parent, gint x, gint y)
gboolean gnome_dock_item_detach(GnomeDockItem *item, gint x,
    gint y)
void gnome_dock_item_drag_floating(GnomeDockItem *item, gint x,
    gint y)
GnomeDockItemBehavior gnome_dock_item_get_behavior(
    GnomeDockItem *dock_item)
GtkWidget *gnome_dock_item_get_child(GnomeDockItem *item)
void gnome_dock_item_get_floating_position(
    GnomeDockItem *item, gint *x, gint *y)
gchar *gnome_dock_item_get_name(GnomeDockItem *item)
GtkOrientation gnome_dock_item_get_orientation(
    GnomeDockItem *dock_item)
GtkShadowType gnome_dock_item_get_shadow_type(
    GnomeDockItem *dock_item)
guint gnome_dock_item_get_type(void)
void gnome_dock_item_grab_pointer(GnomeDockItem *item)
void gnome_dock_item_handle_size_request(GnomeDockItem *item,
    GtkRequisition *requisition)
GtkWidget *gnome_dock_item_new(const gchar *name,
    GnomeDockItemBehavior behavior)
gboolean gnome_dock_item_set_orientation(
    GnomeDockItem *dock_item, GtkOrientation orientation)
void gnome_dock_item_set_shadow_type(
    GnomeDockItem *dock_item, GtkShadowType type)
```

Enum

```
typedef enum {
    GNOME_DOCK_ITEM_BEH_NORMAL,
    GNOME_DOCK_ITEM_BEH_EXCLUSIVE,
    GNOME_DOCK_ITEM_BEH_NEVER_FLOATING,
```

```
        GNOME_DOCK_ITEM_BEH_NEVER_VERTICAL,
        GNOME_DOCK_ITEM_BEH_NEVER_HORIZONTAL,
        GNOME_DOCK_ITEM_BEH_LOCKED
    } GnomeDockItemBehavior;
```

Signals

```
"dock_detach"       void cb(GtkWidget *, gpointer)
"dock_drag_begin"   void cb(GtkWidget *, gpointer)
"dock_drag_end"     void cb(GtkWidget *, gpointer)
"dock_drag_motion"  void cb(GtkWidget *, gint, gint, gpointer)
```

For an example of docking, see the GnomeDock widget earlier in this chapter.

GnomeDockLayout

The GnomeDockLayout object is a container that holds widgets in place in a
GnomeDock widget.

Inheritance

```
GnomeDockLayout->GtkObject
```

Functions

```
gboolean gnome_dock_layout_add_floating_item(
    GnomeDockLayout *layout, GnomeDockItem *item, gint x,
    gint y, GtkOrientation orientation)
gboolean gnome_dock_layout_add_item(GnomeDockLayout *layout,
    GnomeDockItem *item, GnomeDockPlacement placement,
    gint band_num, gint band_position, gint offset)
gboolean gnome_dock_layout_add_to_dock(
    GnomeDockLayout *layout, GnomeDock *dock)
gchar *gnome_dock_layout_create_string(
    GnomeDockLayout *layout)
GnomeDockLayoutItem *gnome_dock_layout_get_item(
    GnomeDockLayout *layout, GnomeDockItem *item)
GnomeDockLayoutItem *gnome_dock_layout_get_item_by_name(
    GnomeDockLayout *layout, const gchar *name)
guint gnome_dock_layout_get_type(void)
GnomeDockLayout *gnome_dock_layout_new(void)
gboolean gnome_dock_layout_parse_string(
    GnomeDockLayout *layout, const gchar *string)
gboolean gnome_dock_layout_remove_item(
    GnomeDockLayout *layout, GnomeDockItem *item)
gboolean gnome_dock_layout_remove_item_by_name(
    GnomeDockLayout *layout, const gchar *name)
```

Enum

```
typedef enum {
  GNOME_DOCK_TOP,
  GNOME_DOCK_RIGHT,
  GNOME_DOCK_BOTTOM,
```

```
        GNOME_DOCK_LEFT,
        GNOME_DOCK_FLOATING
} GnomeDockPlacement;
```

For an example of docking, see the GnomeDock widget earlier in this chapter.

GnomeEntry

The GnomeEntry widget accepts user input; once accepted, the entry is included in the history of items previously entered (or added internally by the application). You can save this history information so it can be restored the next time the widget appears.

Inheritance

```
GnomeEntry->GtkCombo->GtkHBox->GtkBox->GtkContainer->
        GtkWidget->GtkObject
```

Functions

```
void gnome_entry_append_history(GnomeEntry *gentry,
    gboolean save, const gchar *text)
guint gnome_entry_get_type(void)
GtkWidget *gnome_entry_gtk_entry(GnomeEntry *gentry)
void gnome_entry_load_history(GnomeEntry *gentry)
GtkWidget *gnome_entry_new(const gchar *history_id)
void gnome_entry_prepend_history(GnomeEntry *gentry,
    gboolean save, const gchar *text)
void gnome_entry_save_history(GnomeEntry *gentry)
void gnome_entry_set_history_id(GnomeEntry *gentry,
    const gchar *history_id)
void gnome_entry_set_max_saved(GnomeEntry *gentry,
    guint max_saved)
```

The following example displays a GnomeEntry window with three items added to the history list, as shown in Figure 22-10. The saved history is tagged with an ID string that you can use to recover previously saved history information.

```
static GtkWidget *makeWidget()
{
    GtkWidget *entry;

    entry = gnome_entry_new("idstring");
    gnome_entry_append_history(GNOME_ENTRY(entry),
            TRUE,"First Append");
    gnome_entry_append_history(GNOME_ENTRY(entry),
            TRUE,"Second Append");
    gnome_entry_append_history(GNOME_ENTRY(entry),
```

```
            TRUE,"Third Append");
      gnome_entry_save_history(GNOME_ENTRY(entry));

      return(entry);
}
```

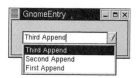

Figure 22-10: A GnomeEntry widget with three history entries

GnomeFileEntry

The GnomeFileEntry widget enables the user to select the name of a file. A user can enter the file name from the keyboard, select it from the pull-down list of previously selected file names, or find it by browsing the file system.

Inheritance

```
GnomeFileEntry->GtkHBox->GtkBox->GtkContainer->GtkWidget->
      GtkObject
```

Functions

```
char *gnome_file_entry_get_full_path(GnomeFileEntry *fentry,
    int file_must_exist)
guint gnome_file_entry_get_type(void)
GtkWidget *gnome_file_entry_gnome_entry(
    GnomeFileEntry *fentry)
GtkWidget *gnome_file_entry_gtk_entry(GnomeFileEntry *fentry)
GtkWidget *gnome_file_entry_new(char *history_id,
    char *browse_dialog_title)
void gnome_file_entry_set_default_path(
    GnomeFileEntry *fentry, char *path)
void gnome_file_entry_set_directory(GnomeFileEntry *fentry,
    int directory_entry)
void gnome_file_entry_set_modal(GnomeFileEntry *fentry,
    int is_modal)
void gnome_file_entry_set_title(GnomeFileEntry *fentry,
    char *browse_dialog_title)
```

The following code creates the GnomeFileEntry window shown in Figure 22-11. The widget has a drop-down list of previously selected files. The entry window and the pull-down list are GnomeEntry widgets, so the names of the files are retained from one invocation of the program to the next. The Browse button pops up a

`GtkFileSelection` widget (described in Chapter 21) that enables the user to select a file.

```
static GtkWidget *makeWidget()
{
    GtkWidget *fileentry;

    fileentry = gnome_file_entry_new("fseekid","File Seeking");

    return(fileentry);
}
```

The string `"fseekid"` is the ID used to save the list of previously selected file names. The second string is for the title bar of the `GtkFileSelection` window.

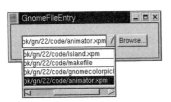

Figure 22-11: A GnomeFileEntry widget with four remembered file names

GnomeFontPicker

The `GnomeFontPicker` widget is a button that, when selected, presents a window that enables the user to select from among the many available fonts.

Inheritance
```
GnomeFontPicker->GtkButton->GtkBin->GtkContainer->GtkWidget->
        GtkObject
```

Functions
```
GtkWidget *gnome_font_picker_create_inside(
    GnomeFontPicker *gfp)
void gnome_font_picker_dialog_destroy(GtkWidget *widget,
    gpointer data)
void gnome_font_picker_fi_set_show_size(GnomeFontPicker *gfp,
    gboolean show_size)
void gnome_font_picker_fi_set_use_font_in_label(
    GnomeFontPicker *gfp, gboolean use_font_in_label,
    gint size)
void gnome_font_picker_font_extract_attr(gchar *font_name,
    gchar *attr, gint i)
void gnome_font_picker_font_set_attr(gchar **font_name,
    const gchar *attr, gint i)
GdkFont *gnome_font_picker_get_font(GnomeFontPicker *gfp)
```

```
gchar *gnome_font_picker_get_font_name(GnomeFontPicker *gfp)
GnomeFontPickerMode gnome_font_picker_get_mode(
    GnomeFontPicker *gfp)
gchar *gnome_font_picker_get_preview_text(
    GnomeFontPicker *gfp)
GtkType gnome_font_picker_get_type(void)
void gnome_font_picker_label_use_font_in_label(
    GnomeFontPicker *gfp)
GtkWidget *gnome_font_picker_new(void)
gboolean gnome_font_picker_set_font_name(
    GnomeFontPicker *gfp, const gchar *fontname)
void gnome_font_picker_set_mode(GnomeFontPicker *gfp,
    GnomeFontPickerMode mode)
void gnome_font_picker_set_preview_text(GnomeFontPicker *gfp,
    const gchar *text)
void gnome_font_picker_set_title(GnomeFontPicker *gfp,
    const gchar *title)
void gnome_font_picker_update_font_info(GnomeFontPicker *gfp)
void gnome_font_picker_uw_set_widget(GnomeFontPicker *gfp,
    GtkWidget *widget)
```

Enum

```
typedef enum {
    GNOME_FONT_PICKER_MODE_PIXMAP,
    GNOME_FONT_PICKER_MODE_FONT_INFO,
    GNOME_FONT_PICKER_MODE_USER_WIDGET,
    GNOME_FONT_PICKER_MODE_UNKNOWN
} GnomeFontPickerMode;
```

Chapter 13 provides examples of `GnomeFontPicker`.

GnomeFontSelector

The `GnomeFontSelector` widget is a dialog box that manages all the details of popping up, accepting input, and returning the name of the selected font.

Inheritance

```
GnomeFontSelector->GtkDialog->GtkWindow->GtkBin->GtkContainer->
    GtkWidget->GtkObject
```

Functions

```
gchar *gnome_font_select(void)
gchar *gnome_font_select_with_default(
    const gchar *default_font)
gchar *gnome_font_selector_get_selected(
    GnomeFontSelector *text_tool)
guint gnome_font_selector_get_type(void)
GtkWidget *gnome_font_selector_new(void)
```

This example demonstrates how your application can make a single function call that returns the selected font. You can call either gnome_font_select() or gnome_font_select_with_default() from anywhere in your program, and the dialog shown in Figure 22-12 appears. The function call contains its own event loop, so it does not return until the user selects a font or closes the dialog box.

```
/** gnomefontpicker.c **/
#include <gnome.h>

int main(int argc,char *argv[])
{
    gchar *font;

    gnome_init("gnomefontpicker","1.0",argc,argv);

    font = gnome_font_select();
    if(font == NULL)
        g_print("No font selected\n");
    else
        g_print("Selected: %s\n",font);

    exit(0);
}
```

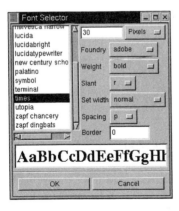

Figure 22-12: A GnomeFontSelector dialog box

GnomeGuru

This is an unfinished widget. When finished, it will be a tool for constructing a wizard (a list of steps that changes according to which branch you take).

Inheritance
```
GnomeGuru->GtkVBox->GtkBox->GtkContainer->GtkWidget->
        GtkObject
```

Functions

```
void gnome_guru_append_page(GnomeGuru *guru, const gchar *name,
    GtkWidget *widget)
void gnome_guru_back_set_sensitive(GnomeGuru *guru,
    gboolean sensitivity)
void gnome_guru_construct(GnomeGuru *guru, const gchar *name,
    GtkWidget *graphic, GnomeDialog *dialog)
GtkWidget *gnome_guru_current_page(GnomeGuru *guru)
guint gnome_guru_get_type()
GtkWidget *gnome_guru_new(const gchar *name,
    GtkWidget *graphic, GnomeDialog *dialog)
void gnome_guru_next_set_sensitive(GnomeGuru *guru,
    gboolean sensitivity)
```

GnomeHRef

The GnomeHRef widget displays a frameless button that, when selected, issues a command for the web browser to connect to a Web site. The actual command to the browser is defined globally as the default member of URL Handler list in the GNOME Control Center.

Inheritance

```
GnomeHRef->GtkButton->GtkBin->GtkContainer->GtkWidget->
    GtkObject
```

Functions

```
gchar *gnome_href_get_label(GnomeHRef *self)
guint gnome_href_get_type(void)
gchar *gnome_href_get_url(GnomeHRef *self)
GtkWidget *gnome_href_new(const gchar *url, const gchar *label)
void gnome_href_set_label(GnomeHRef *self, const gchar *label)
void gnome_href_set_url(GnomeHRef *self, const gchar *url)
```

This example creates a widget with the label Gnome's start page and attaches a URL to it. The widget appears as normal text, as shown in Figure 22-13, which is blue and underlined. This way, you can include it in the body of text among other widgets and it should be recognized as a link. Also, a frame appears around it when the mouse passes over it.

```
static GtkWidget *makeWidget()
{
    GtkWidget *href;

    href = gnome_href_new("http://www.gnome.org/start",
        "Gnome's start page");

    return(href);
}
```

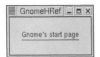

Figure 22-13: A GnomeHRef widget is a link to a Web site

GnomeIconEntry

A GnomeIconEntry is a button that pops up a window displaying a collection of icons. The user can select one of the icons found in /usr/share/pixmaps or browse the file system to find icons in other directories. The pull-down list of directory names maintains a history of previously opened directories.

Inheritance

```
GnomeIconEntry->GtkVBox->GtkBox->GtkContainer->GtkWidget->
     GtkObject
```

Functions

```
char *gnome_icon_entry_get_filename(GnomeIconEntry *ientry)
guint gnome_icon_entry_get_type(void)
GtkWidget *gnome_icon_entry_gnome_entry(
     GnomeIconEntry *ientry)
GtkWidget *gnome_icon_entry_gnome_file_entry(
     GnomeIconEntry *ientry)
GtkWidget *gnome_icon_entry_gtk_entry(GnomeIconEntry *ientry)
GtkWidget *gnome_icon_entry_new(char *history_id,
     char *browse_dialog_title)
void gnome_icon_entry_set_icon(GnomeIconEntry *ientry,
     const char *filename)
void gnome_icon_entry_set_pixmap_subdir(
     GnomeIconEntry *ientry, const char *subdir)
```

The following example creates a button that, when clicked, displays the dialog box shown in Figure 22-14. If the user selects an icon, the button changes to display the icon — as shown in Figure 22-15.

```
static GtkWidget *makeWidget()
{
    GtkWidget *iconentry;
    GtkWidget *entry;

    iconentry = gnome_icon_entry_new("historyID",
            "Select an Icon");
    entry = gnome_icon_entry_gtk_entry(
            GNOME_ICON_ENTRY(iconentry));
    gtk_signal_connect(GTK_OBJECT(entry),"changed",
            GTK_SIGNAL_FUNC(eventIconChanged),iconentry);
```

```
        return(iconentry);
}
void eventIconChanged(GtkWidget *widget,
        GnomeIconEntry *iconentry)
{
    GtkWidget *dialog;

    dialog = GNOME_ICON_ENTRY(iconentry)->pick_dialog;
    if(dialog != NULL) {
        gtk_signal_handlers_destroy(GTK_OBJECT(dialog));
        gtk_signal_connect(GTK_OBJECT(dialog),"clicked",
                eventIconSelected,iconentry);
    }
}
void eventIconSelected(GtkWidget *widget,gint button,
        GnomeIconEntry *iconentry)
{
    gchar *iconfile;

    switch(button) {
    case 0:
        iconfile = gnome_icon_entry_get_filename(iconentry);
        g_print("Icon file name: %s\n",iconfile);
        break;
    case 1:
        g_print("No icon selection was made\n");
    }
}
```

Figure 22-14: The Icon Selection dialog box of the GnomeIconEntry widget

Figure 22-15: The Activation button of the GnomeIconEntry widget

There really are two widgets involved here. The first one is the button that pops up the selection dialog box. The other is the selection dialog box that is constructed as a `GnomeDialog` widget. Whenever the button is selected, the dialog window appears for the user to select an icon. The following example connects a `"changed"` signal to the `GnomeEntry` widget inside the `GnomeIconEntry` widget; this executes the callback `eventIconChanged()` every time the user selects an icon with the mouse or types an icon name.

You can retrieve the name of the icon inside the callback `eventIconChanged()`, but it really doesn't matter until the OK button is selected. To wait until a button is clicked, it is necessary to add the `"clicked"` callback to the `GnomeDialog` widget. This signal is set to execute the `eventIconSelected()` callback whenever the user selects either the OK or Cancel button. If the user selects the OK button, the name of the selected icon can be retrieved. All signals are removed from the button before the new one is attached because the `eventIconChanged()` callback can be called a number of times before the `"clicked"` signal arrives.

Note   This double callback sequence is necessary only because the callback function `eventIconChanged()` is called every time the user clicks an icon in the browse window. While the new icon file name is available at that point, you need the other callback to determine whether the user has clicked the OK or Cancel button.

GnomeIconSelection

This widget loads and displays a set of icons and enables the user to select one. The application must specify the directory, or directories, containing the icons to be displayed. This widget is used as the selection window in the `GnomeIconEntry` widget.

Inheritance

```
GnomeIconSelection->GtkVBox->GtkBox->GtkContainer >GtkWidget->
    GtkObject
```

Functions

```
void gnome_icon_selection_add_defaults(
    GnomeIconSelection *gis)
void gnome_icon_selection_add_directory(
    GnomeIconSelection *gis, const gchar *dir)
```

```
void gnome_icon_selection_clear(GnomeIconSelection *gis,
    gboolean not_shown)
const gchar *gnome_icon_selection_get_icon(
    GnomeIconSelection *gis, gboolean full_path)
guint gnome_icon_selection_get_type()
GtkWidget *gnome_icon_selection_new(void)
void gnome_icon_selection_select_icon(
    GnomeIconSelection *gis, const gchar *filename)
void gnome_icon_selection_show_icons(GnomeIconSelection *gis)
void gnome_icon_selection_stop_loading(
    GnomeIconSelection *gis)
```

The following example loads the default set of icons into a GnomeIconSelection widget and displays it, as shown in Figure 22-16.

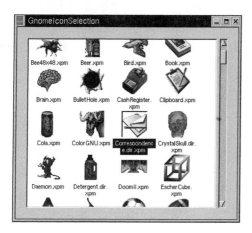

Figure 22-16: A GnomeIcon Selection widget displaying the default set of icons

This example doesn't include the buttons or other mechanisms necessary to determine when the user selects a widget. You can do this by adding a button with a callback function that makes a call to gnome_icon_selection_get_icon() to retrieve the file name of the icon.

GnomeLess

The GnomeLess widget displays the contents of a text file.

Inheritance

```
GnomeLess->GtkVBox->GtkBox->GtkContainer->GtkWidget->
    GtkObject
```

Functions

```
void gnome_less_clear(GnomeLess *gl)
void gnome_less_fixed_font(GnomeLess *gl)
guint gnome_less_get_type()
GtkWidget *gnome_less_new(void)
void gnome_less_reshow(GnomeLess *gl)
void gnome_less_set_fixed_font(GnomeLess *gl, gboolean fixed)
void gnome_less_set_font(GnomeLess *gl, GdkFont *font)
gboolean gnome_less_show_command(GnomeLess *gl,
    const gchar *command_line)
gboolean gnome_less_show_fd(GnomeLess *gl, int file_descriptor)
gboolean gnome_less_show_file(GnomeLess *gl, const gchar *path)
gboolean gnome_less_show_filestream(GnomeLess *gl, FILE *f)
void gnome_less_show_string(GnomeLess *gl, const gchar *s)
gboolean gnome_less_write_fd(GnomeLess *gl, int fd)
gboolean gnome_less_write_file(GnomeLess *gl,
    const gchar *path)
```

The following example program uses a GnomeLess widget to display its own source code, as shown in Figure 22-17.

```
static GtkWidget *makeWidget()
{
    GtkWidget *less;

    less = gnome_less_new();
    gnome_less_show_file(GNOME_LESS(less),"gnomeless.c");

    return(less);
}
```

Figure 22-17: A GnomeLess widget displays the contents of a text file

GnomeMDI

The GnomeMDI object keeps track of multiple widgets comprising the various windows of a *Multiple Document Interface (MDI)*.

Inheritance

```
GnomeMDI->GtkObject
```

Functions

```
gint gnome_mdi_add_child(GnomeMDI *mdi, GnomeMDIChild *child)
gint gnome_mdi_add_toplevel_view(GnomeMDI *mdi,
    GnomeMDIChild *child)
gint gnome_mdi_add_view(GnomeMDI *mdi, GnomeMDIChild *child)
GnomeMDIChild *gnome_mdi_find_child(GnomeMDI *mdi, gchar *name)
GnomeMDIChild *gnome_mdi_get_active_child(GnomeMDI *mdi)
GtkWidget *gnome_mdi_get_active_view(GnomeMDI *mdi)
GnomeApp *gnome_mdi_get_active_window(GnomeMDI *mdi)
GnomeApp *gnome_mdi_get_app_from_view(GtkWidget *view)
GnomeMDIChild *gnome_mdi_get_child_from_view(GtkWidget *view)
GnomeUIInfo *gnome_mdi_get_child_menu_info(GnomeApp *app)
GnomeUIInfo *gnome_mdi_get_menubar_info(GnomeApp *app)
GnomeUIInfo *gnome_mdi_get_toolbar_info(GnomeApp *app)
guint gnome_mdi_get_type()
GtkWidget *gnome_mdi_get_view_from_window(GnomeMDI *mdi,
    GnomeApp *app)
GtkObject *gnome_mdi_new(gchar *appname, gchar *title)
void gnome_mdi_open_toplevel(GnomeMDI *mdi)
void gnome_mdi_register(GnomeMDI *mdi, GtkObject *object)
gint gnome_mdi_remove_all(GnomeMDI *mdi, gint force)
gint gnome_mdi_remove_child(GnomeMDI *mdi,
    GnomeMDIChild *child, gint force)
gint gnome_mdi_remove_view(GnomeMDI *mdi, GtkWidget *view,
    gint force)
void gnome_mdi_set_active_view(GnomeMDI *mdi, GtkWidget *view)
void gnome_mdi_set_child_list_path(GnomeMDI *mdi,
    const gchar *path)
void gnome_mdi_set_child_menu_path(GnomeMDI *mdi,
    const gchar *path)
void gnome_mdi_set_menubar_template(GnomeMDI *mdi,
    GnomeUIInfo *menu_tmpl)
void gnome_mdi_set_mode(GnomeMDI *mdi, GnomeMDIMode mode)
void gnome_mdi_set_toolbar_template(GnomeMDI *mdi,
    GnomeUIInfo *tbar_tmpl)
void gnome_mdi_unregister(GnomeMDI *mdi, GtkObject *object)
void gnome_mdi_update_child(GnomeMDI *mdi,
    GnomeMDIChild *child)
```

Chapter 17 provides examples of GnomeMDI.

GnomeMDIChild

The GnomeMDIChild object is a base class used to create widgets that GnomeMDI can manage as MDI windows. Unless you have some special need, you can use a GnomeMDIGenericChild, which is based on GnomeMDIChild.

Inheritance

```
GnomeMDIChild->GtkObject
```

Functions
```
GtkWidget *gnome_mdi_child_add_view(GnomeMDIChild *mdi_child)
guint gnome_mdi_child_get_type()
void gnome_mdi_child_remove_view(GnomeMDIChild *mdi_child,
    GtkWidget *view)
void gnome_mdi_child_set_menu_template(
    GnomeMDIChild *mdi_child, GnomeUIInfo *menu_tmpl)
void gnome_mdi_child_set_name(GnomeMDIChild *mdi_child,
    gchar *name)
```

GnomeMDIGenericChild

The GnomeMDIGenericChild widget is a generalized form of a child window that can be used in an MDI.

Inheritance
```
GnomeMDIGenericChild->GnomeMDIChild->GtkObject
```

Functions
```
guint gnome_mdi_generic_child_get_type()
GnomeMDIGenericChild *gnome_mdi_generic_child_new(
    gchar *name)
void gnome_mdi_generic_child_set_config_func(
    GnomeMDIGenericChild *child, GnomeMDIChildConfigFunc func,
    gpointer data)
void gnome_mdi_generic_child_set_config_func_full(
    GnomeMDIGenericChild *child, GnomeMDIChildConfigFunc func,
    GtkCallbackMarshal marshal, gpointer data,
    GtkDestroyNotify notify)
void gnome_mdi_generic_child_set_label_func(
    GnomeMDIGenericChild *child, GnomeMDIChildLabelFunc func,
    gpointer data)
void gnome_mdi_generic_child_set_label_func_full(
    GnomeMDIGenericChild *child, GnomeMDIChildLabelFunc func,
    GtkCallbackMarshal marshal, gpointer data,
    GtkDestroyNotify notify)
void gnome_mdi_generic_child_set_menu_creator(
    GnomeMDIGenericChild *child, GnomeMDIChildMenuCreator func,
    gpointer data)
void gnome_mdi_generic_child_set_menu_creator_full(
    GnomeMDIGenericChild *child, GnomeMDIChildMenuCreator func,
    GtkCallbackMarshal marshal, gpointer data,
    GtkDestroyNotify notify)
void gnome_mdi_generic_child_set_view_creator(
    GnomeMDIGenericChild *child, GnomeMDIChildViewCreator func,
    gpointer data)
void gnome_mdi_generic_child_set_view_creator_full(
```

```
GnomeMDIGenericChild *child, GnomeMDIChildViewCreator func,
GtkCallbackMarshal marshal, gpointer data,
GtkDestroyNotify notify)
```

See Chapter 17 for examples of `GnomeMDIGenericChild`.

GnomeMessageBox

A `GnomeMessageBox` is a dialog box you can use to display a simple message and get a response. The dialog box is created as its own top-level window. It displays a standard icon, a text message, and a row of buttons.

Inheritance
```
GnomeMessageBox->GnomeDialog->GtkWindow->GtkBin->GtkContainer->
        GtkWidget->GtkObject
```

Functions
```
guint gnome_message_box_get_type()
GtkWidget *gnome_message_box_new(const gchar *message,
    const gchar *message_box_type, ...)
GtkWidget *gnome_message_box_newv(const gchar *message,
    const gchar *message_box_type, const gchar **buttons)
void gnome_message_box_set_default(
    GnomeMessageBox *message_box, gint button)
void gnome_message_box_set_modal(
    GnomeMessageBox *message_box)
```

A `GnomeMessageBox` is a wrapper around `GnomeDialog` for the purpose of simplifying the interface. It automatically includes the text message and an appropriate icon. Also, after responding to the mouse and the callback, it shuts itself down. Chapter 3 has examples and information on a set of predefined dialog boxes.

The following example asks a question and provides three buttons for the user to choose (as shown in Figure 22-18).

```
/** gnomemessagebox.c **/
#include <gnome.h>

static void messageboxCallback(GtkWidget *widget,
        gint button,gpointer data);

int main(int argc,char *argv[])
{
    GtkWidget *messagebox;

    gnome_init("gnomemessagebox","1.0",argc,argv);
```

```
    messagebox = gnome_message_box_new(
        "Is this the question being displayed?",
        GNOME_MESSAGE_BOX_QUESTION,
        GNOME_STOCK_BUTTON_YES,
        GNOME_STOCK_BUTTON_NO,
        GNOME_STOCK_BUTTON_CLOSE,
        NULL);
    gtk_signal_connect(GTK_OBJECT(messagebox),"clicked",
        messageboxCallback,NULL);
    gtk_widget_show_all(messagebox);

    gtk_main();
    exit(0);
}
static void messageboxCallback(GtkWidget *widget,
        gint button,gpointer data)
{
    switch(button) {
    case 0:
        g_print("The YES Button\n");
        break;
    case 1:
        g_print("The NO Button\n");
        break;
    case 2:
        g_print("The CLOSE Button\n");
        break;
    }
}
```

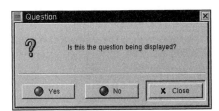

Figure 22-18: A GnomeMessageBox

The following is the list of the different types of message boxes:

```
GNOME_MESSAGE_BOX_INFO
GNOME_MESSAGE_BOX_WARNING
GNOME_MESSAGE_BOX_ERROR
GNOME_MESSAGE_BOX_QUESTION
GNOME_MESSAGE_BOX_GENERIC
```

The following is the list of stock buttons that you can include as part of the dialog box:

```
GNOME_STOCK_BUTTON_OK
GNOME_STOCK_BUTTON_CANCEL
GNOME_STOCK_BUTTON_YES
GNOME_STOCK_BUTTON_NO
GNOME_STOCK_BUTTON_CLOSE
GNOME_STOCK_BUTTON_APPLY
GNOME_STOCK_BUTTON_HELP
GNOME_STOCK_BUTTON_NEXT
GNOME_STOCK_BUTTON_PREV
GNOME_STOCK_BUTTON_UP
GNOME_STOCK_BUTTON_DOWN
GNOME_STOCK_BUTTON_FONT
```

GnomeNumberEntry

The GnomeNumberEntry widget enables the user to enter numeric values.

Inheritance

```
GnomeNumberEntry->GtkHBox->GtkBox->GtkContainer->GtkWidget->
        GtkObject
```

Functions

```
gdouble gnome_number_entry_get_number(
    GnomeNumberEntry *nentry)
guint gnome_number_entry_get_type(void)
GtkWidget *gnome_number_entry_gnome_entry(
    GnomeNumberEntry *nentry)
GtkWidget *gnome_number_entry_gtk_entry(
    GnomeNumberEntry *nentry)
GtkWidget *gnome_number_entry_new(char *history_id,
    char *calc_dialog_title)
void gnome_number_entry_set_title(GnomeNumberEntry *nentry,
    char *calc_dialog_title)
```

The following function creates a GnomeNumberEntry widget, shown in Figure 22-19, that uses the "histid" string to fill its pull-down list with recently chosen numbers. The string "Minimum Distance" is used on the title bar of the calculator; if popped up, it stores its results as the text in the GnomeNumberEntry window. The calculator is a GnomeCalculator, as described in this chapter.

```
static GtkWidget *makeWidget()
{
    GtkWidget *numberentry;
```

```
numberentry = gnome_number_entry_new("histid",
        "Minimum Distance");

return(numberentry);
}
```

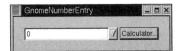

Figure 22-19: A GnomeNumberEntry widget showing a data window and a Calculator button

GnomePaperSelector

The `GnomePaperSelector` widget prompts the user for the type and size of paper for a printer.

Inheritance

```
GnomePaperSelector->GtkVBox->GtkBox->GtkContainer->GtkWidget->
        GtkObject
```

Functions

```
gfloat gnome_paper_selector_get_bottom_margin(
    GnomePaperSelector *gspaper)
gfloat gnome_paper_selector_get_height(
    GnomePaperSelector *gspaper)
gfloat gnome_paper_selector_get_left_margin(
    GnomePaperSelector *gspaper)
gchar *gnome_paper_selector_get_name(
    GnomePaperSelector *gspaper)
gfloat gnome_paper_selector_get_right_margin(
    GnomePaperSelector *gspaper)
gfloat gnome_paper_selector_get_top_margin(
    GnomePaperSelector *gspaper)
guint gnome_paper_selector_get_type(void)
gfloat gnome_paper_selector_get_width(
    GnomePaperSelector *gspaper)
GtkWidget *gnome_paper_selector_new(void)
void gnome_paper_selector_set_height(
    GnomePaperSelector *gspaper, gfloat height)
void gnome_paper_selector_set_name(
    GnomePaperSelector *gspaper, gchar *name)
void gnome_paper_selector_set_width(
    GnomePaperSelector *gspaper, gfloat width)
```

The following code creates the `GnomePaperSelector` widget shown in Figure 22-20. The button at the bottom changes the values in the widget to those of the system default paper size. The search for the default occurs in this order: the environment variable `PAPERCONF`, the contents of the file named by the environment variable `PAPERSIZE`, the file `/etc/conf`, and, finally, the default built into the widget.

```
static GtkWidget *makeWidget()
{
    GtkWidget *paperselector;

    paperselector = gnome_paper_selector_new();

    return(paperselector);
}
```

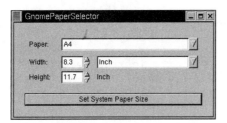

Figure 22-20: A GnomePaperSelector widget showing the default paper setting

GnomePixmap

This is a pixmap in the form of a window. Because it is a widget, you can include it directly in a container, and you can use the primitive drawing and painting functions to modify its appearance.

Inheritance
```
GnomePixmap->GtkWidget->GtkObject
```

Functions
```
guint gnome_pixmap_get_type(void)
void gnome_pixmap_load_file(GnomePixmap *gpixmap,
    const char *filename)
void gnome_pixmap_load_file_at_size(GnomePixmap *gpixmap,
    const char *filename, int width, int height)
void gnome_pixmap_load_imlib(GnomePixmap *gpixmap,
    GdkImlibImage *im)
void gnome_pixmap_load_imlib_at_size(GnomePixmap *gpixmap,
    GdkImlibImage *im, int width, int height)
void gnome_pixmap_load_rgb_d(GnomePixmap *gpixmap,
    unsigned char *data, unsigned char *alpha, int rgb_width,
    int rgb_height)
void gnome_pixmap_load_rgb_d_at_size(GnomePixmap *gpixmap,
    unsigned char *data, unsigned char *alpha, int rgb_width,
    int rgb_height, int width, int height)
void gnome_pixmap_load_rgb_d_shaped(GnomePixmap *gpixmap,
    unsigned char *data, unsigned char *alpha, int rgb_width,
    int rgb_height, GdkImlibColor *shape_color)
void gnome_pixmap_load_rgb_d_shaped_at_size(
    GnomePixmap *gpixmap, unsigned char *data,
    unsigned char *alpha, int rgb_width, int rgb_height,
```

```
                int width, int height, GdkImlibColor *shape_color)
     void gnome_pixmap_load_xpm_d(GnomePixmap *gpixmap,
        char **xpm_data)
     void gnome_pixmap_load_xpm_d_at_size(GnomePixmap *gpixmap,
        char **xpm_data, int width, int height)
     GtkWidget *gnome_pixmap_new_from_file(const char *filename)
     GtkWidget *gnome_pixmap_new_from_file_at_size(
        const char *filename, int width, int height)
     GtkWidget *gnome_pixmap_new_from_gnome_pixmap(
        GnomePixmap *gpixmap_old)
     GtkWidget *gnome_pixmap_new_from_imlib(GdkImlibImage *im)
     GtkWidget *gnome_pixmap_new_from_imlib_at_size(
        GdkImlibImage *im, int width, int height)
     GtkWidget *gnome_pixmap_new_from_rgb_d(unsigned char *data,
        unsigned char *alpha, int rgb_width, int rgb_height)
     GtkWidget *gnome_pixmap_new_from_rgb_d_at_size(
        unsigned char *data, unsigned char *alpha, int rgb_width,
        int rgb_height, int width, int height)
     GtkWidget *gnome_pixmap_new_from_rgb_d_shaped(
        unsigned char *data, unsigned char *alpha, int rgb_width,
        int rgb_height, GdkImlibColor *shape_color)
     GtkWidget *gnome_pixmap_new_from_rgb_d_shaped_at_size(
        unsigned char *data, unsigned char *alpha, int rgb_width,
        int rgb_height, int width, int height,
        GdkImlibColor *shape_color)
     GtkWidget *gnome_pixmap_new_from_xpm_d(char **xpm_data)
     GtkWidget *gnome_pixmap_new_from_xpm_d_at_size(
        char **xpm_data, int width, int height)
```

The following example creates a GnomePixmap widget from an XPM file. Chapter 7 describes the format of the XPM file. In this example, the XPM data has a width of 64 pixels and a height of 38, but the loaded version is expanded to twice that size when loaded at 128 by 72. The resulting widget display is shown in Figure 22-21.

```
     static GtkWidget *makeWidget()
     {
         GtkWidget *widget;

         widget = gnome_pixmap_new_from_file_at_size("island.xpm",
             128,72);

         return(widget);
     }
```

Figure 22-21: A GnomePixmap widget

GnomePixmapEntry

The GnomePixmapEntry is a window that enables the user to enter the file name of a pixmap, choose the name from a history list of those previously chosen, or browse through pixmap files to select one.

Inheritance

```
GnomePixmapEntry->GtkVBox->GtkBox->GtkContainer->GtkWidget->
      GtkObject
```

Functions

```
char *gnome_pixmap_entry_get_filename(
    GnomePixmapEntry *pentry)
guint gnome_pixmap_entry_get_type(void)
GtkWidget *gnome_pixmap_entry_gnome_entry(
    GnomePixmapEntry *pentry)
GtkWidget *gnome_pixmap_entry_gnome_file_entry(
    GnomePixmapEntry *pentry)
GtkWidget *gnome_pixmap_entry_gtk_entry(
    GnomePixmapEntry *pentry)
GtkWidget *gnome_pixmap_entry_new(char *history_id,
    char *browse_dialog_title, int do_preview)
void gnome_pixmap_entry_set_pixmap_subdir(
    GnomePixmapEntry *pentry, const char *subdir)
void gnome_pixmap_entry_set_preview(GnomePixmapEntry *pentry,
    int do_preview)
void gnome_pixmap_entry_set_preview_size(
    GnomePixmapEntry *pentry, int preview_w, int preview_h)
```

The following example produces the windows shown in Figure 22-22. The currently selected pixmap is displayed in the widget's window. Selecting the Browse button pops up the selection window. Because the call to gnome_pixmap_entry_new() specified TRUE as its last argument, the preview window appears on the right side of the browser window.

```
static GtkWidget *makeWidget()
{
    GtkWidget *pixmapentry;
    GtkWidget *entry;

    pixmapentry = gnome_pixmap_entry_new("historyID",
            "Select a Pixmap",TRUE);
    entry = gnome_pixmap_entry_gtk_entry(
            GNOME_PIXMAP_ENTRY(pixmapentry));
    gtk_signal_connect(GTK_OBJECT(entry),"changed",
            GTK_SIGNAL_FUNC(eventPixmapChanged),pixmapentry);

    return(pixmapentry);
}
```

```
void eventPixmapChanged(GtkWidget *widget,
        GnomePixmapEntry *pixmapentry)
{
    char *filename;

    filename = gnome_pixmap_entry_get_filename(pixmapentry);
    g_print("Selection: %s\n",filename);
}
```

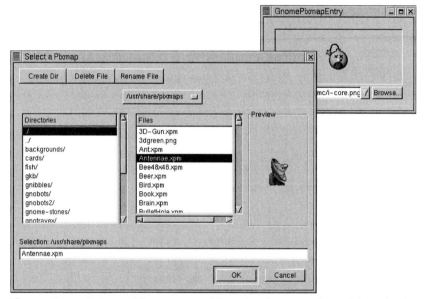

Figure 22-22: A GnomePixmapEntry widget showing a preview of the selection

An internal GtkEntry widget is used to accept the name of the pixmap file. The "changed" signal is connected to it so there is a callback no matter how the change is made (data entry, history selection, or with the browser).GnomeProcBar

The GnomeProcBar widget graphically presents a percentage of completion of one or more processes.

Inheritance
```
GnomeProcBar->GtkHBox->GtkBox->GtkContainer->GtkWidget->
        GtkObject
```
Functions
```
GtkWidget *gnome_proc_bar_new(GtkWidget *label,
    gint n, GdkColor *colors, gint (*cb)())
```

```
guint gnome_proc_bar_get_type(void)
void gnome_proc_bar_set_orient(GnomeProcBar *pb,
    gboolean vertical)
void gnome_proc_bar_set_values(GnomeProcBar *pb,
    unsigned val[])
void gnome_proc_bar_start(GnomeProcBar *pb, gint gtime,
    gpointer data)
void gnome_proc_bar_stop(GnomeProcBar *pb)
void gnome_proc_bar_update(GnomeProcBar *pb, GdkColor *colors)
```

Normally, a `GnomeProcBar` is used as a progress bar to display a moving bar of color, which displays the percentage of completion. The `GnomeProcBar` can do this, but it also can display the progress rate of several tasks at once. The following example shows the appearance of multiple color bars all expanding from left to right, as shown in Figure 22-23. To determine the bar positions, all of the values are summed and each is assigned space according to its percentage of the total.

```
static GdkColor barColors[5] = {
    {0, 0x4fff, 0x0fff, 0xffff},
    {0, 0xffff, 0xffff, 0x4fff},
    {0, 0xdfff, 0xdfff, 0xdfff},
    {0, 0xafff, 0xafff, 0xafff},
    {0, 0, 0, 0},
};

static GtkWidget *procbar;

static GtkWidget *makeWidget()
{
    GtkWidget *label;

    label = gtk_label_new("Label Text");
    procbar = gnome_proc_bar_new(
            label,4,barColors,updateValue);
    gtk_widget_set_usize(procbar,400,15);
    gnome_proc_bar_start(GNOME_PROC_BAR(procbar),1000,NULL);

    return(procbar);
}
static gint updateValue()
{
    static gint values[4] = { 0, 0, 0, 0};

    values[0]++;
    values[1] += 2;
    values[2] += 3;
    values[3] = 200 - values[0] - values[1] - values[2];
    if(values[3] < 0) {
        values[0] = 0;
        values[1] = 0;
```

```
            values[2] = 0;
            values[3] = 200;
    }
    gnome_proc_bar_set_values(GNOME_PROC_BAR(procbar),values);

    return(TRUE);
}
```

Figure 22-23: A GnomeProcBar showing multiple progress bars

There is a unique color assigned to each value; both the colors and the values are defined as arrays. The array of GdkColor objects passed to gnome_proc_bar_ new() do not have to be allocated in the color map because the GnomeProcBar widget does it.

This widget generates its own callbacks according to a timer. In this example, 1000 milliseconds is specified on the call to gnome_proc_bar_new(). This means the function updateValue() is called once each second. Because there are no arguments to updateValue(), and its job is to update the display, the GnomeProcBar itself must be declared as a global value. This example simply cycles through some values and then returns to the beginning.

GnomePropertyBox

A GnomePropertyBox is a popup dialog box that can contain multiple pages of widgets for setting property values. The pages are placed one on top of another (using a GtkNotebook) and can be selected with tabs at the top. The buttons at the bottom enable the user to update the property values and/or close the window.

Inheritance

```
GnomePropertyBox->GnomeDialog->GtkWindow->GtkBin->
        GtkContainer->GtkWidget->GtkObject
```

Functions

```
gint gnome_property_box_append_page(
    GnomePropertyBox *property_box, GtkWidget *child,
    GtkWidget *tab_label)
void gnome_property_box_changed(
    GnomePropertyBox *property_box)
guint gnome_property_box_get_type(void)
```

```
GtkWidget *gnome_property_box_new(void)
void gnome_property_box_set_modified(
    GnomePropertyBox *property_box, gboolean state)
void gnome_property_box_set_state(
    GnomePropertyBox *property_box, gboolean state)
```

The following example program creates a GnomePropertyBox with two pages of radio buttons. These pages can contain any widget that is capable of retaining an input value, such as a text widget or a toggle button. When the dialog box first appears, the buttons labeled OK and Apply are disabled. If any change is made (in this case, toggling a radio button) then the OK and Apply buttons become enabled. The window produced by this example is shown in Figure 22-24. Clicking the Apply button causes the values from all of the pages to update the properties. Clicking the Close button immediately closes the dialog box, whether or not changes are made. Clicking OK is the same as clicking Apply the Close.

```
/** gnomepropertybox.c **/
#include <gnome.h>

static void propertyboxCallback(GtkWidget *widget,
        gint page,gpointer data);
static GtkWidget *makeRadioButtonBox();
void radioCallback(GtkWidget *widget,
        GnomePropertyBox *propertybox);

int main(int argc,char *argv[])
{
    GtkWidget *propertybox;
    GtkWidget *pageWidget;
    GtkWidget *label;

    gnome_init("gnomepropertybox","1.0",argc,argv);

    propertybox = gnome_property_box_new();
    gtk_window_set_title(GTK_WINDOW(propertybox),
            "GnomePropertyBox");

    pageWidget = makeRadioButtonBox("Apples",
            "Oranges","Peaches",propertybox);
    label = gtk_label_new("Radio Buttons");
    gnome_property_box_append_page(
            GNOME_PROPERTY_BOX(propertybox),
            pageWidget,label);

    pageWidget = makeRadioButtonBox("Light Blue",
            "Dark Blue","Black",propertybox);
    label = gtk_label_new("More Radio Buttons");
    gnome_property_box_append_page(
            GNOME_PROPERTY_BOX(propertybox),
            pageWidget,label);
```

```
        gtk_signal_connect(GTK_OBJECT(propertybox),"apply",
                propertyboxCallback,NULL);
        gtk_widget_show_all(propertybox);
        gtk_main();
        exit(0);
}
static void propertyboxCallback(GtkWidget *widget,
        gint page,gpointer data)
{
    switch(page) {
    case 0:
        g_print("Page 0 has changed\n");
        break;
    case 1:
        g_print("Page 1 has changed\n");
        break;
    default:
        g_print("Apply all pages\n");
        break;
    }
}
static GtkWidget *makeRadioButtonBox(
        gchar *label1,gchar *label2,gchar *label3,
        GtkWidget *propertybox)
{
    GtkWidget *box;
    GSList *group;
    GtkWidget *radiobutton;

    box = gtk_vbox_new(FALSE,0);

    radiobutton = gtk_radio_button_new_with_label(NULL,
            label1);
    gtk_box_pack_start(GTK_BOX(box),radiobutton,
            FALSE,TRUE,0);
    gtk_signal_connect(GTK_OBJECT(radiobutton),"toggled",
            radioCallback,propertybox);

    group = gtk_radio_button_group(
            GTK_RADIO_BUTTON(radiobutton));
    radiobutton = gtk_radio_button_new_with_label(group,
            label2);
    gtk_signal_connect(GTK_OBJECT(radiobutton),"toggled",
            radioCallback,propertybox);
    gtk_box_pack_start(GTK_BOX(box),radiobutton,
            FALSE,TRUE,0);

    group = gtk_radio_button_group(
            GTK_RADIO_BUTTON(radiobutton));
    radiobutton = gtk_radio_button_new_with_label(group,
            label3);
```

```
    gtk_signal_connect(GTK_OBJECT(radiobutton),"toggled",
            radioCallback,propertybox);
    gtk_box_pack_start(GTK_BOX(box),radiobutton,
            FALSE,TRUE,0);

    return(box);
}
void radioCallback(GtkWidget *widget,
        GnomePropertyBox *propertybox)
{
    gnome_property_box_changed(propertybox);
}
```

Figure 22-24: A GnomePropertyBox with two pages of radio buttons

The property box is created by the call to gnome_property_box_new(). The call to property_box_append_page() adds a new page along with the label that appears as its tab. The "apply" callback signal is connected to the GnomePropertyBox, and the function propertyboxCallback() is called whenever one or more values are changed and they need to be stored as the new property values.

The propertyboxCallback() is called whenever the OK or Apply button is clicked. In fact, it gets called more than once. It is called once with the number of each page that changes, and then it is called again with a page number of -1. For example, if there are changes on pages 0 and 3, but pages 1, 2, and 4 stay the same, the callback is called with the page number 0, then again with the number 3, and finally with -1. In most cases, all you need to concern yourself with is the -1 call. However, there may be circumstances that require special processing for some pages, and it would be inefficient to do it every time the callback executes.

The buttons OK and Apply remain inactive until something changes on one of the pages. It is up to your application to let the GnomePropertyBox know when a change occurs. In this example, all of the radio buttons cause the callback function radioCallback() to execute, which, in turn, calls gnome_property_box_changed() to register the fact that something has changed. And, because the GnomePropertyBox knows which is the current page, it records that information so it can be passed to the "apply" signal callback.

GnomeScores

The GnomeScores widget displays a list of names and scores for the players of a game.

Inheritance

```
GnomeScores->GnomeDialog->GtkWindow->GtkBin->GtkContainer->
    GtkWidget->GtkObject
```

Functions

```
void gnome_scores_display(gchar *title, gchar *app_name,
    gchar *level, int pos)
guint gnome_scores_get_type()
GtkWidget *gnome_scores_new(guint n_scores, gchar **names,
    gfloat *scores, time_t *times, guint clear)
void gnome_scores_set_color(GnomeScores *gs, guint n,
    GdkColor *col)
void gnome_scores_set_colors(GnomeScores *gs, GdkColor *col)
void gnome_scores_set_current_player(GnomeScores *gs, gint i)
void gnome_scores_set_def_color(GnomeScores *gs, GdkColor *col)
void gnome_scores_set_logo_label(GnomeScores *gs, gchar *txt,
    gchar *font, GdkColor *col)
void gnome_scores_set_logo_label_title(GnomeScores *gs,
    gchar *txt)
void gnome_scores_set_logo_pixmap(GnomeScores *gs,
    gchar *pix_name)
void gnome_scores_set_logo_widget(GnomeScores *gs,
    GtkWidget *w)
```

The following example creates a GnomeScores popup dialog box that displays three names, dates, and scores (as shown in Figure 22-25).

```
/** gnomescores.c **/
#include <gnome.h>

static gchar *names[3] = { "Peter","Laura","Norton" };
static gfloat values[3] = { 93781.0,99751.0,4429.0 };
static time_t times[3];


int main(int argc,char *argv[])
{
    GtkWidget *scores;

    gnome_init("gnomescores","1.0",argc,argv);

    times[0] = time(NULL);
    times[1] = times[0] - 100000;
    times[2] = times[1] - 100000;
```

```
    scores = gnome_scores_new(3,names,values,times,FALSE);
    gtk_widget_show_all(scores);

    gtk_main();
    exit(0);
}
```

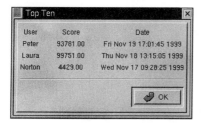

Figure 22-25: A GnomeScores dialog box showing the top three entries

GnomeSpell

This is an incomplete widget. When completed, it will use the Linux ispell program to scan text for words not found in the dictionary, and then display the words — possibly along with some suggested alternatives — so the user can correct the spelling.

Inheritance
```
GnomeSpell->GtkVBox->GtkBox->GtkContainer->GtkWidget->
     GtkObject
```

Functions
```
void gdk_child_register(pid_t pid, GChildFunc func,
    gpointer user_data)
void gnome_spell_accept(GnomeSpell *spell, gchar *word)
gint gnome_spell_check(GnomeSpell *spell, gchar *str)
guint gnome_spell_get_type()
void gnome_spell_insert(GnomeSpell *spell, gchar *word,
    gint lowercase)
void gnome_spell_kill(GnomeSpell *spell)
GtkWidget *gnome_spell_new()
int gnome_spell_next(GnomeSpell *spell)
```

GnomeStock

The GnomeStock widget is used to create buttons, pixmaps, and other objects, and to register them with the set of predefined stock objects. An application also can use it to add new pixmaps for its own purposes.

Inheritance

```
GnomeStock->GnomePixmap->GtkWidget->GtkObject
```

Functions

```
void gnome_button_can_default(GtkButton *button,
    gboolean can_default)
GtkWidget *gnome_pixmap_button(GtkWidget *pixmap,
    const char *text)
GtkWidget *gnome_stock_button(const char *type)
guint gnome_stock_get_type(void)
gboolean gnome_stock_menu_accel(const char *type, guchar *key,
    guint8 *mod)
void gnome_stock_menu_accel_dlg(char *section)
void gnome_stock_menu_accel_parse(const char *section)
GtkWidget *gnome_stock_menu_item(const char *type,
    const char *text)
GtkWidget *gnome_stock_new(void)
GtkWidget *gnome_stock_new_with_icon(const char *icon)
GtkWidget *gnome_stock_or_ordinary_button(const char *type)
gint gnome_stock_pixmap_change(const char *icon,
    const char *subtype, GnomeStockPixmapEntry *entry)
GnomeStockPixmapEntry *gnome_stock_pixmap_checkfor(
    const char *icon, const char *subtype)
void gnome_stock_pixmap_gdk(const char *icon,
    const char *subtype, GdkPixmap **pixmap, GdkPixmap **mask)
gint gnome_stock_pixmap_register(const char *icon,
    const char *subtype, GnomeStockPixmapEntry *entry)
gboolean gnome_stock_set_icon(GnomeStock *stock,
    const char *icon)
GtkWidget *gnome_stock_transparent_window(const char *icon,
    const char *subtype)
```

The following example creates buttons and other widgets using the facilities of the GnomeStock widget. Then it packs them into a vertical box, as displayed in Figure 22-26.

```
static GtkWidget *makeWidget()
{
    GtkWidget *box;
    GtkWidget *widget;

    box = gtk_vbox_new(FALSE,0);

    widget = gnome_stock_button(GNOME_STOCK_PIXMAP_REVERT);
    gtk_box_pack_start(GTK_BOX(box),widget,FALSE,FALSE,0);

    widget = gnome_stock_menu_item(GNOME_STOCK_PIXMAP_REVERT,
            "Menu Revert");
    gtk_box_pack_start(GTK_BOX(box),widget,FALSE,FALSE,0);
```

```
    widget = gnome_stock_or_ordinary_button("Scores");
    gtk_box_pack_start(GTK_BOX(box),widget,FALSE,FALSE,0);

    widget = gnome_stock_or_ordinary_button("High Scores");
    gtk_box_pack_start(GTK_BOX(box),widget,FALSE,FALSE,0);

    widget = gnome_stock_new_with_icon(
            GNOME_STOCK_PIXMAP_OPEN);
    gtk_box_pack_start(GTK_BOX(box),widget,FALSE,FALSE,0);

    return(box);
}
```

Figure 22-26: A collection of widgets produced by a GnomeStock widget

The function calls involved do not require that you create your own version of the GnomeStock widget because one is created internally. In fact, about the only reason you would create a GnomeStock widget in your application is if you wanted to make additions to the list of available stock widgets.

The first widget created is a button that contains both text and a pixmap. GnomeStock performs the job of creating two pixmaps: one for the normal appearance of the button and the other for its appearance when the mouse selects it. This involves using a different color background and changing the colors of the frame to make the button appear to be either raised or indented.

The stock pixmap names are strings. For example, the name GNOME_STOCK_ PIXMAP_REVERT is defined as "Revert". The call to gnome_stock_or_ordinary_ button() with "Scores" is the same as if the argument were GNOME_STOCK_ PIXMAP_SCORES. This produces a button with both the named pixmap and the string. However, the call to the same function with the argument "High Scores" does not match a stock pixmap, so only the text appears.

The last entry in the box is a GnomeStock widget itself. It can be displayed this way because it is a widget, and its only displayable content is the pixmap.

GnomeStockPixmapWidget

The `GnomeStockPixmapWidget` is a utility widget used for operations with the `GnomeStock` widget.

Inheritance
```
GnomeStockPixmapWidget->GtkVBox->GtkBox->GtkContainer->
      GtkWidget->GtkObject
```

Functions
```
GtkWidget *gnome_stock_pixmap_widget(GtkWidget *window,
    const char *icon)
GtkWidget *gnome_stock_pixmap_widget_at_size(
    GtkWidget *window, const char *icon, guint width,
    guint height)
guint gnome_stock_pixmap_widget_get_type(void)
GtkWidget *gnome_stock_pixmap_widget_new(GtkWidget *window,
    const char *icon)
void gnome_stock_pixmap_widget_set_icon(GnomeStock *widget,
    const char *icon)
```

A `GnomeStockPixmapWidget` can be used by your application to display any one of the stock pixmaps. The folowing example displays the window in Figure 22-27 containing the stock pixmap named `GNOME_STOCK_PIXMAP_REVERT`.

```
static GtkWidget *makeWidget()
{
    GtkWidget *widget;

    widget = gnome_stock_pixmap_widget_new(NULL,
            GNOME_STOCK_PIXMAP_REVERT);

    return(widget);
}
```

Figure 22-27: The display of a GNOME stock pixmap

Summary

This chapter provided an alphabetical listing of every Gnome widget, and a number of the other Gnome objects that can be used to construct an application. Each class was listed along with:

✦ The signals, enumerated types, and functions defined for an object

✦ The inheritance of each object so you can track down all of the signals and functions defined for any specific widget

✦ Examples of the displayable widgets and container widgets and references to other chapters in the book where examples are located

Even a GNOME application has to use some of the facilities of the operating system. The next chapter takes a look at some of the more commonly needed facilities that are built into Linux.

✦   ✦   ✦

Some Linux Mechanics

✦   ✦   ✦   ✦

In This Chapter

Deciphering
Linux status and
error codes

Spawning new
processes from
within a process

Executing a
command line
from within
a process

Communicating
by using pipes

Accessing the current
system date and time

Handling files

✦   ✦   ✦   ✦

Most of the work in writing an application has to do with managing the windows, and managing the data the windows display and accept. This chapter is not about windows and GUI interfaces — rather it describes some of the function calls that provide access to the operating system, and to some special capabilities. There is very little here about the standard C library (although, because C was born to a UNIX environment, some of what is standard C derives from UNIX system calls).

The functions presented in this chapter represent a small percentage of the functions available. I chose some that have shown to be the most useful to programmers over the years, including myself. The explanations are a bit brief, but the purpose of this chapter is to let you know that they exist and give you an idea of how they work. For more information on each one, use the man pages.

Linux Error Codes

Whenever a system call encounters an error, the error number is stored in a global variable named errno. Every system call can modify this value; if you want the number, you need to read it immediately following the error. There are three things you can do. The simplest thing to do is log or display the number, but some functions translate it into a descriptive string for you.

```
/* error.c */
#include <sys/types.h>
#include <sys/stat.h>
#include <stdio.h>
#include <fcntl.h>
#include <errno.h>

int main(int argc,char *argv[])
```

```
{
    int fd;
    char *filename = "/invalid/path/name";

    fd = creat(filename,S_IRWXU | S_IRWXG);
    if(fd < 0) {
        fprintf(stderr,"Error code: %d\n",errno);
        perror("Unable to create file");
        fprintf(stderr,"Unable to create %s: %s\n",
            filename,strerror(errno));
    }
}
```

The call to creat() attempts to create a new file (user and group are granted all permissions), but the attempt fails because the path is not valid. The error code is displayed on standard error in three different ways. The output looks like this:

```
Error code: 2
Unable to create file: No such file or directory
Unable to create /invalid/path/name: No such file or directory
```

The function perror() combines the string you supply with the current value of errno to create a description of the error. Then it writes the string to stderr. The function strerror() simply translates the error code into a string. The function perror() has the advantage of simplicity, and the function strerror() has the advantage of providing maximum flexibility.

Spawning Processes

The Linux way of having one process spawn another is a two-step procedure called *fork and exec*.

The first step is for your program to fork to create a duplicate of itself. A call to the function fork() creates two completely separate copies of the same program running, each with its own unique process ID number. Because executable code can be shared among programs, forking results in only one copy if it is stored in memory. The things that are peculiar to each process — such as data, the current program location, certain CPU register values, and the stack — are duplicated. Forking a process is such a fundamental part of the Linux operating system that, even though it can be a complicated procedure, it is very fast. Once a process is forked, the original is called the *parent* process and the new one is called the *child* process.

The second step is for the child process to replace itself with a new process. That is, a new program is loaded from disk and starts to run as the child process. You can accomplish this by calling one of the exec() family functions. All of the exec() functions do the same thing — the only difference is the organization of the arguments that are passed to the new program via its command line.

The following program forks, then the child resulting from the fork execs a new program:

```
 1 /* forkexec.c */
 2 #include <unistd.h>
 3
 4 int main(int argc,char *argv[])
 5 {
 6     int pid;
 7     int childpid;
 8     int status;
 9
10     if((pid = fork()) == 0) {
11         printf("Child: pid=%d parentpid=%d\n",
12             getpid(),getppid());
13         execlp("showargs","first","second","third",NULL);
14         printf("Child: This should never print\n");
15     }
16     printf("Parent: pid=%d childpid=%d\n",
17             getpid(),pid);
18     childpid = wait(&status);
19     printf("Parent: child %d died\n",childpid);
20     exit(0);
21 }
```

The fork takes place with the call to fork() on line 10. During execution of the function, the running program is split into two so there actually are two returns from the function: one for the parent and one for the child. The returned process ID number is used to determine which is the child and which is the parent; the parent process is returned the process ID of the child and the child is returned a zero process ID. This means that the statements on lines 11 through 14 are executed only by the child process. And, because the call to execlp() on line 13 never returns, only the parent process executes lines 16 through 20.

On line 11, the child process displays its process ID and the process ID of its parent. Neither of these are returned from the fork() call, so it is necessary to call getpid() and getppid() to retrieve them.

On line 12, a call is made to execlp() to start a new process that takes the place of this one (the child process) and assumes the same process ID number. This program immediately stops running and the new program starts. If the execlp() function returns, it has failed. The first argument to execlp() is the name of the program to run. The other arguments are things you should include on the command line of the child program. There are several versions of the exec() function — with different ways to pass the arguments — and you can get details on them by typing man exec.

On line 16, the parent process displays its own process ID and the process ID of the new child process. A call is made to getpid() for the parent to get its own ID number, but the ID of the child process is the one returned from the call to fork().

Line 18 is a call to a function named wait(). This function blocks and does not return until a child process dies. If you have no child processes, it returns immediately. If you have more than one child process, you have to call wait() for each one of them. There are a number of approaches you can take to wait for child processes to die, but you do need to acknowledge them with some form of the wait() function call. This is because every process continues to exist until it reports its status to its parent process. If you are in a situation in which you are spawning a lot of child processes, you need to set up some procedure by which you check for child processes that die. There are four functions designed to wait in different ways and return different values — you can see them by entering man wait and man wait3. The status value returned by these functions contains the return code from the program, along with some flags that explain how the child died.

The following program is spawned by the fork and exec:

```
/* showargs */
int main(int argc,char *argv[])
{
    int i;

    for(i=0; i<argc; i++)
        printf("    %d %s\n",i,argv[i]);
    return(66);
}
```

All this program does is display each of the arguments found on the command line. The output can look like this:

```
Parent: pid=23018 childpid=23019
Child: pid=23019 parentpid=23018
    0 first
    1 second
    2 third
Parent: child 23019 died
```

Immediately following the fork, the parent process displays its process ID, and the ID of the child, and calls wait() to detect child termination. Simultaneously, the child process is displaying its information and forking to another process that also displays some strings. The order of the statements shown may vary because the two processes are asynchronous — for example, if the child is faster than the parent, both of the parent's display lines may appear at the bottom.

Note   The first argument passed to showargs is not, as you might expect, the name of the program. It is the first argument string you passed to the execlp() function. To correct this, you can pass the name of the program or you can use one of the other exec() functions.

Executing a Command Line

Using the function `system()`, you can enter the same kind of commands from inside a program that you can enter from the command line. The following example demonstrates the sort of things that you can do:

```
/* system.c */
#include <unistd.h>

int main(int argc,char *argv[])
{
    int pid1;
    int pid2;

    pid1 = system("grep print *.c\n");
    pid2 = system("grep include *.c >inclist &\n");
    wait(pid2);
    exit(0);
}
```

A `system()` function call executes a fork and exec to get a command shell that runs the command. The first one instructs `grep` to run in the foreground and display its results to the standard output, as it normally does. The second `system()` call both redirects the output and, by including an ampersand, runs the command as a child process. The call to `system()` waits until the command completes, unless it is run as a child process.

A return value of -1 indicates there is an error with the command passed to it. A return value of 127 indicates that the command line shell could not be started. If there are no errors, and the command is not being run in the background, the value resulting from the execution of the command is returned. If, however, the program is run in the background (as in the second `system()` call in the example), the process ID of the child is returned and you need to call `wait()` just as with fork and exec.

Note   There is something a bit odd about the return value from `system()`. It has an error return code of 127. A valid return value from a command also can be 127. If this poses a problem, use fork and exec.

Pipes

A *pipe* is a one-way connection between a pair of processes. The function `popen()` spawns a child process and creates a pipe connected to it. Depending on the direction of the pipe, the child process either can read from it by reading its own standard input or write to it by writing to its own standard output. For example, the ls command writes to its standard output. Therefore, a pipe can be created enabling you to capture the output of ls inside your program:

```
/* pipein.c */
#include <stdio.h>

int main(int argc,char *argv[])
{
    FILE *pd;
    char instring[100];

    if((pd = popen("ls\n","r")) == NULL) {
        perror("Cannot open pipe");
        exit(1);
    }
    while(fgets(instring,sizeof(instring),pd) != NULL) {
        printf("                    %s",instring);
    }
    pclose(pd);
    exit(0);
}
```

The call to popen() requires a command-line string and the specification of whether the pipe is for reading or writing. The only options are "r" and "w" because pipes are only one way.

The return value from popen() is a FILE structure representing a stream; it can be used just as if it had been opened by fopen(). Any function that you can use to read a file, you can use to read from a pipe. The only difference is, to close it, you must use pclose() instead of fclose().

The previous example reads and displays the file names found by ls. Notice that there is no newline character required on the printf() statement This is because fgets() operates on a pipe exactly the way it does on a file, and includes the newline with the incoming line.

The following example shows a pipe being opened in the opposite direction. The cat command, when started with no arguments, reads from the standard input and writes to standard output. This program opens a pipe that sends characters to cat just as if you typed them in from the terminal:

```
/* pipeout.c */
#include <stdio.h>

int main(int argc,char *argv[])
{
    FILE *pd;
    char instring[100];

    if((pd = popen("cat\n","w")) == NULL) {
        perror("Cannot open pipe");
```

```
        exit(1);
    }
    fputs("The first string to cat\n",pd);
    fflush(pd);
    sleep(5);
    fputs("The second string to cat\n",pd);
    fflush(pd);
    pclose(pd);
    exit(0);
}
```

Because the pipe is opened in `"w"` mode, this program is able to write to it. The call to `fputs()` sends strings to the `cat` command, which writes them to standard output so they appear on the display. The reason for the `fflush()` function call is because pipes are buffered fully, and actual output data is sent only when either the buffer fills up or the pipe is closed. This buffering of pipe data has no size limitation because it stores data on disk, so writing to a pipe never blocks. This means you can queue up all the commands and data you like and the child process will read them at its own pace.

Time

Linux stores the time as a count of the number of seconds since midnight January 1, 1970. The following example retrieves and displays the current time:

```
/* showtime.c */
#include <time.h>
#include <limits.h>

int main(int argc,char *argv[])
{
    time_t binarytime;
    struct tm *nowtm;

    binarytime = time(NULL);
    printf("now=%d\n",binarytime);
    printf("ctime=%s",ctime(&binarytime));

    nowtm = localtime(&binarytime);
    printf("asctime=%s",asctime(nowtm));

    printf("\n");
    printf("  HHMMSS %d:%02d:%02d\n",
            nowtm->tm_hour,nowtm->tm_min,nowtm->tm_sec);
    printf("  MMDDYY %d/%d/%d\n",
            nowtm->tm_mon + 1,nowtm->tm_mday,
            nowtm->tm_year + 1900);
    printf("  Weekday=%d\n",
            nowtm->tm_wday);
    printf("  Yearday=%d\n",
```

```
                nowtm->tm_yday);
        printf("  Daylight time=%d\n",
                nowtm->tm_isdst);
        printf("  Offset from GMT=%d\n",
                nowtm->tm_gmtoff / 3600);
        printf("  Time zone=%s\n",
                nowtm->tm_zone);
        printf("\n");
        binarytime = INT_MIN;
        printf("minimum=%s",ctime(&binarytime));
        binarytime = INT_MAX;
        printf("maximum=%s",ctime(&binarytime));
}
```

The call to the function time() returns the 32-bit integer representing the current time. This is a convenient form because it is easy to adjust by addition and subtraction, and it only requires four bytes for storage. The call to ctime() converts the time into a string that is always 25 characters long—the 24 visible characters with a newline character at the end.

Another storage format for time data is the tm struct. In this example, the call to localtime() converts the binary time into a tm struct. The struct has one field for each piece of information:

```
struct tm
{
    int tm_sec;    /* Seconds [0-60] (1 leap second) */
    int tm_min;    /* Minutes [0-59] */
    int tm_hour    /* Hours [0-23] */
    int tm_mday;   /* Day [1-31] */
    int tm_mon;    /* Month [0-11] */
    int tm_year;   /* Year - 1900. */
    int tm_wday;   /* Day of week [0-6] */
    int tm_yday;   /* Days in year.[0-365]    */
    int tm_isdst;  /* Daylight time [-1/0/1]*/
    long int tm_gmtoff; /* Seconds east of UTC. */
    const char *tm_zone; /* Timezone abbreviation. */
};
```

The months of the year are numbered 0 through 11, with January being the 0 month. The year is stored by subtracting 1900 from the actual year value (this is left over from an earlier version of tm in which each field was a single byte). The days of the week are numbered beginning with Sunday as 0, Monday as 1, and so on. The daylight time indicator is set to 1 if daylight time is in effect, 0 if it is not, and -1 if it cannot be determined. The offset from *UTC (Universal Time Coordinate)*, or *Greenwich Mean Time*, is in seconds because there are places that adjust local times by amounts smaller than an hour. The time zone is specified as an ASCII string.

The following is example output from this program:

```
now=942345478
ctime=Thu Nov 11 09:37:58 1999
asctime=Thu Nov 11 09:37:58 1999

    HHMMSS 9:37:58
    MMDDYY 11/11/1999
    Weekday=4
    Yearday=314
    Daylight time=0
    Offset from GMT=-9
    Time zone=AKST

minimum=Fri Dec 13 10:45:52 1901
maximum=Mon Jan 18 18:14:07 2038
```

The last two lines display the extreme dates that the 32-bit number can represent. As you can see, there is a year 2038 problem.

There is a function call that not only returns the number of seconds since January 1, 1970, but also returns a count of the number of microseconds that have passed in the current second. This is very useful for putting time stamps on things because it is almost impossible for the same time value to be returned twice—the length of time required by the function call is enough to cause the value to change. The values are returned as two members of a struct, as shown by the following example:

```
/* microtime.c */
#include <sys/time.h>
#include <unistd.h>

int main(int argc,char *argv[])
{
    struct timeval tv;

    gettimeofday(&tv,NULL);
    printf("     Seconds: %d\n",tv.tv_sec);
    printf("Microseconds: %d\n",tv.tv_usec);
}
```

The gettimeofday() function inserts the current time into the timeval struct. The second argument to gettimeofday() is always NULL (an artifact of the original version). Calling gettimeofday() returns the same count of seconds as you get by calling time(), but there is also the count of a number of microseconds. The output looks like this:

```
    Seconds: 942369385
Microseconds: 127905
```

The microsecond value shows that time has progressed about 12.7 percent of the distance to the next second.

Unless you use a special, real-time version of Linux, the count of microseconds is only good for comparison. By using a `timeval` struct to attach a time stamp to things, a quick comparison always indicates which came first (or, at least, which was time stamped first). There is a macro that you can use to compare two structs:

```
if(timercmp(tv1,tv2,<)) {
    printf("tv1 is less than tv2\n");
else
    printf("tv1 is not less than tv2\n");

if(timercmp(tv1,tv2,>)) {
    printf("tv1 is greater than tv2\n");
else
    printf("tv1 is not greater than tv2\n");
```

The third argument may look a bit odd, but it is a macro; the comparison operator simply is substituted into the expanded expression.

File Information

Not only is it possible to get a listing of the file and directory names, it also is possible to get quite a bit of information about them. The following program lists the names of all the files and subdirectories in a directory, and displays a bit of information on each one.

```
 1 /* showdir.c */
 2 #include <sys/types.h>
 3 #include <sys/stat.h>
 4 #include <errno.h>
 5 #include <unistd.h>
 6 #include <dirent.h>
 7 #include <stdio.h>
 8
 9 int main(int argc,char *argv[])
10 {
11     DIR *dir;
12     struct dirent *dent;
13     struct stat st;
14     char *directory_name = ".";
15     char file_name[120];
16
17     if(argc > 1)
18         directory_name = argv[1];
19
20     if((dir = opendir(directory_name)) ==  NULL) {
21         perror("Cannot open directory");
22         exit(1);
```

```
23      }
24      while(dent = readdir(dir)) {
25          printf("%s\n",dent->d_name);
26          sprintf(file_name,"%s/%s",
27                  directory_name,dent->d_name);
28          if(stat(file_name,&st) < 0) {
29              perror("Cannot get file status");
30              errno = 0;
31              continue;
32          }
33          printf("    A");
34          if(S_ISLNK(st.st_mode))
35              printf(" symbolic link");
36          if(S_ISREG(st.st_mode))
37              printf(" regular file");
38          if(S_ISDIR(st.st_mode))
39              printf(" directory");
40          if(S_ISCHR(st.st_mode))
41              printf(" character device");
42          if(S_ISBLK(st.st_mode))
43              printf(" block device");
44          if(S_ISFIFO(st.st_mode))
45              printf(" fifo");
46          if(S_ISSOCK(st.st_mode))
47              printf(" socket");
48          printf("\n");
49          printf("    Owner group: %d   user: %d\n",
50                  st.st_gid,st.st_uid);
51          printf("    File size in bytes: %d\n",st.st_size);
52          printf("    Accessed: %s",ctime(&st.st_atime));
53          printf("    Modified: %s",ctime(&st.st_mtime));
54          errno = 0;
55      }
56      if(errno != 0)
57          perror("Cannot read directory entry");
58      closedir(dir);
59      exit(0);
60  }
```

In earlier days, a *directory* was a regular disk file that contained a list of file names and disk locations. You could open and read a directory file just like any other file. In the quest for efficiency, and because of all the different file systems, developers created special functions to open, read, and close a directory.

The directory is opened on line 20 by the call to opendir(). A DIR data type is returned to the handle for operations on the directory. The top of the loop on line 24 calls readdir() to read each member of the directory (the first two members are always "." and ".."). After all the file information is read and displayed, the call to closedir() on line 58 closes the directory.

Inside the loop on line 28, the stat() function is called to retrieve information about the file. The returned information is stored in the stat struct on line 13. Lines 33 through 53 format and display the data.

```
showdir
    A regular file
    Owner group: 39    user: 500
    File size in bytes: 8793
    Accessed: Fri Nov 12 11:54:45 1999
    Modified: Fri Nov 12 11:52:26 1999
```

The name of the file is followed by some descriptive information. This is by no means all the information available in the stat struct. To find additional information that is available, and other ways to call this function, enter:

```
man 2 stat
```

Lines 30 and 54 set errno to zero. This is because readdir() does not change the value of errno unless there is an actual error condition, so an old error code could have been left in it. Also, because readdir() returns NULL for both an error and end-of-file condition, ensuring that errno is set to zero is the only correct way to detect the end of file.

System Information

The following program retrieves and displays information about the system. If your program needs to know things about its environment, there almost certainly is a function you can call to get the information.

```
/* systeminfo.c */
#include <stdio.h>
#include <stdlib.h>
#include <unistd.h>
#include <sys/utsname.h>
#include <sys/time.h>
#include <sys/resource.h>
#include <linux/kernel.h>

int main(int argc,char *argv[])
{
    struct utsname uts;
    char cwd[120];
    char *env;
    struct rlimit rlim;
    struct sysinfo s_info;

    if(uname(&uts) >= 0){
        printf("                        System name: %s\n",
                uts.sysname);
        printf("                            Release: %s\n",
                uts.release);
        printf("                            Version: %s\n",
                uts.version);
        printf("                           Hardware: %s\n",
```

```
                    uts.machine);
        printf("                          Node name: %s\n",
                    uts.nodename);
#ifdef USE_GNU
        printf("                        Domain name: %s\n",
                uts.domainname);
#else
        printf("                        Domain name: %s\n",
                uts.__domainname);
#endif
    }

    if(getcwd(cwd,sizeof(cwd)))
        printf("              Current directory: %s\n",
            cwd);

    if((env = getenv("SHELL")) != NULL)
        printf("    Environment variable SHELL: %s\n",
            env);
    printf("                           User ID: %d\n",
            getuid());
    printf("                          Group ID: %d\n",
            getgid());
    printf("                        Process ID: %d\n",
            getpid());
    printf("                 Parent process ID: %d\n",
            getppid());
    printf("                             Login: %s\n",
            getlogin());
    printf("                        User shell: %s\n",
            getusershell());
    printf(" Maximum arg length for exec(): %ld\n",
            sysconf(_SC_ARG_MAX));
    printf("     Maximum processes per user: %ld\n",
            sysconf(_SC_CHILD_MAX));
    printf("           Clock ticks per second: %ld\n",
            sysconf(_SC_CLK_TCK));
    printf("    Maximum streams per process: %ld\n",
            sysconf(_SC_STREAM_MAX));
    printf("Maximum open files per process: %ld\n",
            sysconf(_SC_OPEN_MAX));
    printf("Maximum chars in timezone name: %ld\n",
            sysconf(_SC_TZNAME_MAX));
    printf("   Maximum command line length: %ld\n",
            sysconf(_SC_LINE_MAX));
    printf("   POSIX job control supported: %s\n",
            sysconf(_SC_CHILD_MAX) ? "true" : "false");
    printf("   POSIX.1 compliance (YYYYMM): %ld\n",
            sysconf(_SC_VERSION));
    printf("   POSIX.2 compliance (YYYYMM): %ld\n",
            sysconf(_SC_2_VERSION));
    printf("    POSIX.2 locale by localedef: %s\n",
            sysconf(_SC_2_LOCALEDEF) ? "true" : "false");
    printf("  POSIX.2 software development: %s\n",
```

```
                        sysconf(_SC_2_SW_DEV) ? "true" : "false");

        sysinfo(&s_info);
        printf("              Uptime in seconds: %d\n",
            s_info.uptime);
        printf("        Load for past 1 minute: %d\n",
            s_info.loads[0]);
        printf("       Load for past 5 minutes: %d\n",
            s_info.loads[1]);
        printf("      Load for past 15 minutes: %d\n",
            s_info.loads[2]);
        printf("            Total amount of RAM: %d\n",
            s_info.totalram);
        printf("              Amount of free RAM: %d\n",
            s_info.freeram);
        printf("            Amount of shared RAM: %d\n",
            s_info.sharedram);
        printf("       Amount of RAM in buffers: %d\n",
            s_info.bufferram);
        printf("               Total swap space: %d\n",
            s_info.totalswap);
        printf("                Free swap space: %d\n",
            s_info.freeswap);
        printf("      Total number of processes: %d\n",
            s_info.procs);

        exit(0);
    }
```

This program is self-explanatory—system calls are made that return values, and the values are displayed. The following is an example of the output produced by this program:

```
                  System name: Linux
                      Release: 2.0.36
                      Version: #1 Tue Oct 13 22:17:11 EDT 1998
                     Hardware: i586
                    Node name: arlin.athome.com
                  Domain name:
            Current directory: /home/stuff/book/gn/23/code
  Environment variable SHELL: /bin/bash
                      User ID: 0
                     Group ID: 0
                   Process ID: 18859
            Parent process ID: 17091
                        Login: root
                   User shell: /bin/bash
  Maximum arg length for exec(): 131072
        Maximum processes per user: 999
           Clock ticks per second: 100
        Maximum streams per process: 256
     Maximum open files per process: 256
   Maximum chars in timezone name: 4
```

```
        Maximum command line length: 2048
        POSIX job control supported: true
        POSIX.1 compliance (YYYYMM): 199309
        POSIX.2 compliance (YYYYMM): 199912
         POSIX.2 locale by localdef: true
      POSIX.2 software development: true
                Uptime in seconds: 618899
             Load for past 1 minute: 178656
            Load for past 5 minutes: 146560
           Load for past 15 minutes: 139680
              Total amount of RAM: 64655360
               Amount of free RAM: 1880064
             Amount of shared RAM: 23175168
          Amount of RAM in buffers: 23179264
                  Total swap space: 98664448
                   Free swap space: 59662336
       Total number of processes: 77
```

This program does not include nearly all the possibilities. You may find what you are looking for in this example, but if not, use the man utility to get more information about a function that resembles what you need. For example, the man page for getenv(), a function to retrieve the value of an environment variable, also leads you to setenv(), which can define an environment variable, and to unsetenv(), which can remove an environment variable. Also, there are system calls that I do not include in this example. To get a list of them, enter:

```
man 2 syscalls
```

Summary

This book concerns itself almost entirely with the user interface. This chapter described some techniques your program can use to interface with the operating system:

✦ All system calls (and some utility function calls) use the global value errno to store an error code number. An errno value of zero indicates no error. There are special functions designed to format the error codes into human-readable form.

✦ Any process can use fork and exec to start another process. In fact, every process on Linux has started using this technique. The system process init starts running at boot time; it assumes the task of starting the other processes. The process ID number of init is always 1.

✦ Any command that you can type in from the terminal can be issued from inside a program.

✦ A parent and child process can communicate with each other through a pipe that redirects standard input and standard output.

✦ It is possible to retrieve and display time values with more accuracy than most hardware is capable of producing.

✦ Additionally, it is possible to open a directory and read all of the information about it. This includes all of its files and subdirectories.

✦ A large family of system calls can give you information on the current user, the computer status, the CPU usage history, and much more.

The following chapter compares a small application written for GNOME with the same application written for Windows. It is intended to serve as a sort of Rosetta stone for a Windows programmer to get started with GNOME.

✦   ✦   ✦

Comparative Anatomy: Win32 and GNOME

◆   ◆   ◆   ◆

In This Chapter

Writing a simple
GNOME program
that draws squares
on a window

Writing a simple
Win32 program that
draws squares on a
window

Comparing the two
programs point by
point

◆   ◆   ◆   ◆

If you are familiar with programming using the Win32 API, this chapter can help you understand the structure of a GNOME/GTK+ application. At the lowest levels, the two programming models are very similar. They both operate using a main loop that waits for events to arrive; when an event does arrive, a function is called to notify the application.

To make the comparison as simple as possible, this chapter implements the same short program for both Win32 and GNOME/GTK+.

Note The comparison in this chapter has nothing to do with which windowing system is better. And there is no attempt to use any kind of standard optimal programming techniques. These two programs are contrived to be as much alike as possible so a person that understands one of them easily can see the structure of the other.

A Win32 Program

The following example is a Windows program that fills a window with concentric boxes. Whenever the window resizes, the boxes also resize to fit it. The display looks like the one shown in Figure 24-1.

```
1 /* boxbox.c  (win32) */
2 #include <windows.h>
3
4 #define STEP 3
5
6 static char name[] = "BoxBox";
7 static int xBox1;
8 static int yBox1;
```

```
 9 static int xBox2;
10 static int yBox2;
11
12 LRESULT CALLBACK callback(HWND,UINT,WPARAM,LPARAM);
13
14 int WINAPI WinMain(HINSTANCE instance,
15         HINSTANCE prev,PSTR commandLine,int showCommand)
16 {
17     HWND window;
18     MSG message;
19     WNDCLASSEX winclass;
20
21     winclass.cbSize = sizeof (winclass);
22     winclass.style = CS_HREDRAW | CS_VREDRAW;
23     winclass.lpfnWndProc = callback;
24     winclass.cbClsExtra = 0;
25     winclass.cbWndExtra = 0;
26     winclass.hInstance = instance;
27     winclass.hIcon = LoadIcon(NULL,IDI_APPLICATION);
28     winclass.hCursor = LoadCursor(NULL,IDC_ARROW);
29     winclass.lpszMenuName = NULL;
30     winclass.lpszClassName = name;
31     winclass.hIconSm = LoadIcon(NULL,IDI_APPLICATION);
32     winclass.hbrBackground =
33             (HBRUSH)GetStockObject(WHITE_BRUSH);
34
35     RegisterClassEx(&winclass);
36     window = CreateWindow (name,"Boxes in Boxes",
37             WS_OVERLAPPEDWINDOW,
38             CW_USEDEFAULT,CW_USEDEFAULT,
39             CW_USEDEFAULT,CW_USEDEFAULT,
40             NULL,NULL,instance,NULL);
41     ShowWindow(window,showCommand);
42     UpdateWindow (window);
43
44     while(GetMessage(&message,NULL,0,0)) {
45         TranslateMessage(&message);
46         DispatchMessage(&message);
47     }
48     return(message.wParam);
49 }
50
51 LRESULT CALLBACK callback(HWND window,UINT messageType,
52         WPARAM wParam,LPARAM lParam)
53 {
54     int x1;
55     int y1;
56     int x2;
57     int y2;
58     HDC hdc;
59     PAINTSTRUCT ps;
60
```

```
61      switch (messageType) {
62      case WM_SIZE:
63          xBox1 = 10;
64          yBox1 = 10;
65          xBox2 = LOWORD(lParam) - 10;
66          yBox2 = HIWORD(lParam) - 10;
67          return(0);
68      case WM_PAINT:
69          hdc = BeginPaint(window,&ps);
70          SetViewportOrgEx(hdc,0,0,NULL);
71          x1 = xBox1;
72          x2 = xBox2;
73          y1 = yBox1;
74          y2 = yBox2;
75          while((x1 < x2) && (y1 < y2)) {
76              MoveToEx(hdc,x1,y1,NULL);
77              LineTo(hdc,x2,y1);
78              LineTo(hdc,x2,y2);
79              LineTo(hdc,x1,y2);
80              LineTo(hdc,x1,y1);
81              x1 += STEP;
82              y1 += STEP;
83              x2 -= STEP;
84              y2 -= STEP;
85          }
86          EndPaint(window,&ps);
87          return(0);
88      case WM_DESTROY:
89          PostQuitMessage(0);
90          return(0);
91      }
92      return(DefWindowProc(window,messageType,
93              wParam,lParam));
94  }
```

The program has only two functions. The function WinMain(), beginning on line 14, is the original one called by the operating system to start the program. The function callback(), on line 51, is called by the operating system whenever an event arrives.

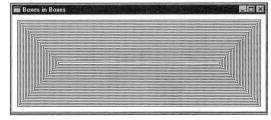

Figure 24-1: A Win32 main window

A GNOME Program

The following example is a GNOME/GTK+ program that fills a window with concentric boxes. If the size of the window changes, the size of the boxes also changes. The window looks like the one shown in Figure 24-2.

```
 1 /** boxbox.c (Gnome) **/
 2 #include <gnome.h>
 3
 4 gint eventDelete(GtkWidget *widget,
 5         GdkEvent *event,gpointer data);
 6 gint eventDestroy(GtkWidget *widget,
 7         GdkEvent *event,gpointer data);
 8 gboolean eventExpose(GtkWidget *widget,
 9         GdkEvent *event,gpointer data);
10 gint eventConfigure(GtkWidget *widget,
11         GdkEventConfigure *event,gpointer data);
12
13 #define STEP 3
14
15 static char name[] = "BoxBox";
16 static int xBox1;
17 static int yBox1;
18 static int xBox2;
19 static int yBox2;
20
21 int main(int argc,char *argv[])
22 {
23     GtkWidget *app;
24     GtkWidget *area;
25
26     gnome_init(name,"1.0",argc,argv);
27     app = gnome_app_new(name,"Boxes in Boxes");
28     gtk_signal_connect(GTK_OBJECT(app),"delete_event",
29         GTK_SIGNAL_FUNC(eventDelete),NULL);
30     gtk_signal_connect(GTK_OBJECT(app),"destroy",
31         GTK_SIGNAL_FUNC(eventDestroy),NULL);
32
33     area = gtk_drawing_area_new();
34     gnome_app_set_contents(GNOME_APP(app),area);
35
36     gtk_signal_connect(GTK_OBJECT(area),"expose_event",
37         GTK_SIGNAL_FUNC(eventExpose),NULL);
38     gtk_signal_connect(GTK_OBJECT(area),"configure_event",
39         GTK_SIGNAL_FUNC(eventConfigure),NULL);
40
41     gtk_widget_show_all(app);
42     gtk_main();
43     exit(0);
44 }
45 gboolean eventExpose(GtkWidget *widget,
```

```
46              GdkEvent *event,gpointer data) {
47      int x1;
48      int y1;
49      int x2;
50      int y2;
51
52      x1 = xBox1;
53      y1 = yBox1;
54      x2 = xBox2;
55      y2 = yBox2;
56      while((x1 < x2) && (y1 < y2)) {
57          gdk_draw_line(widget->window,
58                  widget->style->black_gc,
59                  x1,y1,x2,y1);
60          gdk_draw_line(widget->window,
61                  widget->style->black_gc,
62                  x2,y1,x2,y2);
63          gdk_draw_line(widget->window,
64                  widget->style->black_gc,
65                  x2,y2,x1,y2);
66          gdk_draw_line(widget->window,
67                  widget->style->black_gc,
68                  x1,y2,x1,y1);
69          x1 += STEP;
70          y1 += STEP;
71          x2 -= STEP;
72          y2 -= STEP;
73      }
74      return(TRUE);
75 }
76 gint eventConfigure(GtkWidget *widget,
77          GdkEventConfigure *event,gpointer data)
78 {
79      xBox1 = 10;
80      yBox1 = 10;
81      xBox2 = event->width - 10;
82      yBox2 = event->height - 10;
83      return(TRUE);
84 }
85 gint eventDelete(GtkWidget *widget,
86          GdkEvent *event,gpointer data) {
87      return(FALSE);
88 }
89 gint eventDestroy(GtkWidget *widget,
90          GdkEvent *event,gpointer data) {
91      gtk_main_quit();
92      return(0);
93 }
```

This program has a `main()` function that is used to initialize GNOME, create the window to be displayed, specify the callbacks, and go into an execution loop. There are four other functions, each of which executes on the arrival of a specific event.

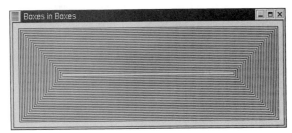

Figure 24-2: A GNOME main window

A Point-by-Point Comparison

This description shows the similarities and differences between the GNOME and Win32 programs by detailing some specifics. As you can see, the difference lies in the details — not in the underlying technology.

Initialization

Line 26 of the GNOME program is a call to gnome_init() to initialize the GUI interface and other parts of the underlying graphics software. There is no counterpart to this function in the Win32 program because the Win32 API is part of the operating system and already is initialized. However, GNOME is not a part of the operating system, so it is necessary to initialize windowing software.

The Main Window

Line 27 of the GNOME program is a call to gnome_app_new() to create a new, top-level application window. This function call assigns the program its name, and supplies a title that appears at the top of the window. The parallel action in the Win32 version is the call to CreateWindow() on line 36. Lines 21 through 35 of the Win32 version define the main window, and the call to RegisterClassEx() on line 35 registers it with the operating system. As you can see, a lot more setup is required to create a Win32 top-level window than a GNOME top-level window. This is because all of the settings must be specified up front for Win32; GNOME, however, uses a standard set of defaults for everything and has functions available so your program can change things after the window is built.

Responding to Events

Both the GNOME and Win32 programs are event-driven. In other words, once both programs are initialized and their windows are displayed, GNOME and Win32 wait until an event (mouse, keyboard, or whatever) occurs. When an event does occur, a function is called to pass the information from the system to the application. Lines 36 and 39 of the GNOME program call `gtk_signal_connect()` to tell the system which functions to call for which events. This event-by-event specification step is unnecessary for the Win32 program because a catchall callback function is assigned to the top-level window on line 23.

Both of the programs need to respond to two events: when the size of the window changes and when all or part of the window has been exposed and should be drawn.

On line 38, the GNOME program assigns the `"configure_event"` signal to the callback function `eventConfigure()`. This function uses the size of the window to calculate the coordinate position of the outermost box. The same thing is achieved in the function `callback()` of the Win32 program with the `case` statement on line 62.

On line 36, the GNOME program assigns the `"expose_event"` signal to the callback function `eventExpose()`. This function draws a set of nested boxes using the size and location values that are retrieved from the latest configure event. The Win32 program does the same thing with the `case` statement on line 68.

> **Note** These two methods of handling events are more alike than they are different. A GNOME application specifies the same callback function for all of its events and then sorts them out with `case` statements. In the Win32 program, the callback function can be used as a dispatcher that contains only function calls for each event — thus requiring a separate function for each event.

The Main Loop

The GNOME program calls `gtk_main()` on line 42. This function does not return until it is time for the program to exit. It has the job of waiting for events and then causing the appropriate function to be called. The function `gtk_signal_connect()` relates a window, a callback function, and a specific event. This means the `gtk_main()` loop also has the responsibility of deciding which window is the source of the event.

The main loop of the Win32 program is on lines 44 through 47. The function `GetMessage()` waits until it receives an event, and then it returns. The call to `TranslateMessage()` translates keyboard codes into characters and `DispatchMessage()` forwards the event to the correct window.

Program Shutdown

When shutting down the Win32 program, the callback function is called with a `WM_DESTROY` message. A call to `PostQuitMessage()` is made on line 89; this call places a `quit` message in the input queue and, when it is read, the program terminates. This gives you the opportunity to clean things up before shutting down, or (by failure to post the `quit` message) refusing to quit.

The GNOME application, on lines 28 through 31, specifies two functions as callbacks for shutting down the program. The "delete_event" signal causes the function eventDelete() to be called immediately before the program shuts down. If you return FALSE from this function, indicating the shutdown may proceed, a "destroy" event is issued, causing a callback to eventDestroy(). This, in turn, calls gtk_main_quit() to shut down the program. If this program returns TRUE from eventDelete(), the shutdown does not happen.

Note   These GNOME callbacks are important. Without them, an application cannot be stopped by the button on the right of the title bar, or by the menu on the left.

Global Data

Both of these examples use globally declared data to retain information from one callback to the next. Also, they both provide alternatives to this, but in different ways.

In a Win32 program, you simply declare the data as static inside the callback function. This way, every callback has access to the data. Even if you choose to call other functions to do the actual work, the data is available to be passed as arguments.

GNOME takes a different approach. Notice that there is a third argument — always NULL in this example — on the calls to gtk_signal_connect(). You can use this third argument to pass a pointer to the callback. In other words, every time the callback function is executed, the last argument passed to it is the pointer you specify in your call to gtk_signal_connect(). A common way of handling this is to create a struct that contains all the global data and pass around its address to the places you need it.

Summary

The underlying architecture of a Win32 application and a GNOME application are the same. They both are based on events. In this chapter, a comparison of the two showed:

✦ Both Win32 and GNOME use the concept of an infinite loop waiting for the arrival of events.

✦ They seem to require about the same amount of code, but one may require more detail in a particular area.

✦ Win32 and GNOME share the concept of a top-level window as the main display, and both top-level windows are capable of receiving events.

✦ They each supply a method for guaranteeing that an application closes down cleanly.

This chapter is the conclusion of the third, and final, part of the book. The following appendixes serve two purposes. Appendixes A and B explain where and how to load and install the software. Appendixes C through G are some cross-reference listings that can be quite handy when programming GNOME.

✦   ✦   ✦

What's on the CD-ROM

This appendix describes the contents of the CD-ROM accompanying this book. This is a complete set of the libraries and utilities you will need to create GNOME applications. Also, all the examples from the book are included.

Note　This is all open software so it is being continuously updated. There are later versions of the software than those on the CD-ROM. However, if you are relatively new to GNOME and GTK+, it will be simpler and safer to use the software on the CD-ROM. As software moves from one version to another, incompatibilities pop up here and there, but the CD-ROM versions all work together.

If you prefer to get the latest versions of everything, the URLs are listed in Appendix B. Also, if you use the software supplied on the CD-ROM, Appendix B supplies the information you will want if you decide to upgrade your installation to a later version.

CD Contents

The files on the CD-ROM are divided into the three directories listed in Table A-1.

Table A-1
Contents of the CD-ROM

Directory	Contains
examples	The source code of the examples in the book. Each chapter has its own subdirectory.
gnome/base	The source code of the base GNOME/GTK+ development libraries.
gnome/core	The source code of the core GNOME/GTK+ development libraries.
tools	This contains the compiler, autoconf, and automake.

Examples

The examples from the book—located in the examples directory on the CD-ROM— are organized according to the chapter in which they appear in the book. There are no executables included because different Linux platforms require different formats for binary executables. Each directory can be copied to a hard drive and compiled. Also, if you want to compile them all, simply copy the entire tree to your hard drive and use the makefile in the root directory.

Note

There is a Web site for the book, and the example code is available there also. If you find something wrong, or something that should be changed, in one of the examples, please check this Web site for updates:

```
http://www.belugalake.com/book/gnomebible
```

GNOME

The files in the gnome and tools directories are of the type often referred to as *tarballs*. These are tar files that have been compressed with the gzip utility. They all contain the source and makefiles that can be used to compile and install the files on your system. You can install the GNOME files anywhere you would like. My personal preference is to create a directory in /usr/local like this:

```
mkdir /usr/local/gnome
```

Next, make the new directory your current directory:

```
cd /usr/local/gnome
```

Then, assuming your CD-ROM drive is `/mnt/cdrom`, each of the files can be installed in its own subdirectory. For example, to install the GTK+ library, enter this command:

```
tar -xvzf /mnt/cdrom/gnome/base/gtk+-1.2.6.tar.gz
```

The `tar` command will (x) extract the files and store them in a local directory named `gtk+-1.2.6`. The (v) verbose option specifies that every file and directory name should be displayed. The file will first be (z) `gunzipped` and then untarred. The (f) input file is the one named on the command line.

There are three steps to compiling and installing each of the packages. The first step is to establish the configuration for your system. This is mostly automatic because there is a shell script that detects the necessary information and creates the makefiles. Once the makefiles are created, you will still need to compile and install the software. This is done with these three commands:

```
configure
make
make install
```

The first command creates the makefiles, the second compiles the source into object code, and the third stores binary files in the appropriate locations.

Note You will be better off if you get to know the process. There are README and INSTALL files in each of the source directories, and you should read them. This is especially true if you have some sort of special Linux installation. After you have read through two or three of these, the process should become clear.

Tools

The tools supplied on the CD-ROM are also tarballs including the source code. They install in much the same way as the GNOME software, but you will probably want to pay more attention to the README and INSTALL files. In particular, gcc has a number of options that allow you to configure it for your preferences.

✦　　✦　　✦

Setting Up for Software Development

There are a number of software components you need to install before you can write a GNOME/GTK+ application. If you have a relatively recent Linux CD, you certainly have a lot of what you need—and you may have it all. The following checklist helps you to make sure you have it all.

> **Note** Like everything else in the world of open source, things are subject to change. The names and URLs listed here may change. Also, a newer version of something may operate differently and have slightly different requirements than those outlined here.

Linux

If you do not have Linux, you probably will purchase a CD. A commercial CD has the advantages of containing most of the items you need, being easier to install than a downloaded version, and providing telephone support to get you started.

If, however, you want to get a copy over the Internet, then you should be careful which version you choose. Mainly, you don't want to get an experimental version. A Linux version number indicates whether it is a stable or developmental version. Unless you are working on the Linux kernel itself, use a stable version. If the second digit following the version number is even (2.0, 2.2, and so on), it is a stable version. There may be a third number in the version number (like 2.2.8) that indicates bug fixes. To get the latest version of the kernel, get the highest even-numbered version.

The following are some of the more popular Linux distributions:

Caldera	`http://www.caldera.com`
Corel	`http://linux.corel.com`
Debian	`http://www.debian.org/`
LinuxPro	`http://www.wgs.com`
Red Hat	`http://www.redhat.com`
Slackware	`http://www.slackware.com`
StormLinux	`http://stormlinux.com`
SuSE	`http://www.suse.com`
TurboLinux	`http://www.turbolinux.com`

While any one of these can run GNOME successfully and can be used as a GNOME development platform, Red Hat Linux seems the most committed to a GNOME environment.

gcc (egcs)

This is the C compiler that you need to compile your programs. In April of 1999, because of future plans, the Free Software Foundation appointed the *egcs Steering Committee* to maintain gcc. At that time, the name was changed from gcc to egcs. But the executable of the program is still named gcc because it has to work with all the existing make files.

There certainly will be a version of the gcc compiler included in your Linux distribution. But new features are added from time to time, so you need to make sure you have a version that is as current as your GNOME software. You can get the latest version from any number of locations on the Internet. The home page is:

`http://www.gnu.ai.mit.edu/software/gcc/gcc.html`

XFree86

This is the low-level windowing software used by GTK+ and GDK. All Linux distributions include this software, and install it during normal installation. This is very stable software, but there are occasional releases (as of this writing, the latest version is X11R6.4). If you find that you need to get a new version (or need to find out more information about it), the XFree86 home page is:

`http://www.xfree86.org`

autoconf and automake

If you compile the GNOME distribution source code, you need these utility programs. These utilities are used to automatically create the make files and then compile the programs. If you have some difficulty with the compilation process, you should make certain you have the latest versions. If they are not available in your Linux distribution, you can download them from:

```
ftp://ftp.gnu.org/pub/gnu/automake/
ftp://ftp.gnu.org/pub/gnu/autoconf/
```

You can use these utility programs to compile your own programs. In fact, if you intend to write a large application, it is a good idea. Chapter 20 describes the process.

GNOME, glib, GDK, and GTK+

You want the source code. As you write your application, a moment will come when you must take a peek to see what is going on. If you don't want to go to the trouble of compiling and installing GNOME, you also can download a binary version. You should find everything you need at the GNOME Web site:

```
http://www.gnome.org
```

You can find information, and the latest version, of the other components separately at their own Web sites:

```
http://www.glib.org
http://www.gdk.org
http://www.gtk.org
```

There are a lot of options. Some of the software is specific to one Linux distribution, while all of it is specific to a single CPU. If you can't find a match for your system, download the source code and compile your own. Exactly which parts you download and install should depend on what you intend to do:

✦ If you simply want to install and use the GNOME interface without doing any programming, you just need to load the base system and install it.

✦ If you want to write GTK+ applications without using GNOME, you only need to load the GTK+ libraries.

✦ If you want to write GNOME applications, you need to download GTK+, as well as the GNOME base and development systems. GTK+ is not a separate download — it is included as part of the GNOME development download.

✦ If you want to try to use the cutting edge version of GNOME and GTK+, you need to get a current copy of the developer's source from the CVS (Concurrent Version System) archive and compile it for your system.

✦ If you want to participate in the GNOME project and modify the GNOME system itself, you need to get the developer's source from the CVS archive and take actions to keep it updated.

If you use Red Hat Linux, you may have some (or all) of these pieces already installed from the CD. Fortunately, the installation procedure automatically takes care of this situation. If you use the rpm system, the part that is installed already does not get installed again. On the other hand, if you have an older version installed, the installation procedure updates your installation to a new version.

Start by taking a look at the Web site:

```
http://www.gnome.org/start
```

Among other things, this Web page has the latest information on how to install GNOME and what files you need to download.

Installing GTK+ from Source

If you want to write programs that use GTK+ without the addition of GNOME, you only need to load the GTK+ portion of the software. You can get a copy of GTK+ at their FTP site:

```
ftp.gtk.org/pub/gtk
```

You can download the libraries in a binary form, or you can load it as source. If you elect to load source, you need to compile the libraries. This is a simple procedure.

```
configure
make
```

Getting GTK+ and GNOME Source Files

You can get the source files from a number of locations. The primary location is:

```
ftp://ftp.gnome.org/pub/GNOME
```

In this directory, a file named MIRRORS lists all of the locations that also have the GNOME files.

This is an optional step. You can get the latest source files for GTK+ and GNOME, and update your source files as often as you wish. These are the source files that are updated constantly by the GNOME developers. You only need this if you are considering contributing to the GNOME project.

Note The latest source may not compile successfully. This is because it remains a work-in-progress and, with multiple programmers modifying multiple files, any given snapshot may be incomplete or incompatible with itself. If you want to build GNOME and GTK+ libraries from scratch, you may need to update the source a few times before you get a viable version.

If you download the libraries in their binary form, having the source is not a requirement for applications development. However, it can be very useful to have the source on hand so you can refer to it for answers to those sticky questions. The truth of open source is that the software is updated much faster and more often than the documentation. Not only is the code itself informative, but there are comments in the code and in some text files that can prove very useful.

The source is stored in CVS archives. CVS was designed for software development and is used to track source-code changes. It enables each programmer to check out a source file, make changes, and check it back in to CVS. If two programmers change the same source file, CVS merges the changes. If the changes overlap, a manual merge may be necessary. If you do not work inside the GNOME code, you only need to get the current copy of the source.

To get your copy of the source, follow these steps:

1. There is CVS software on your system. Use it to get a copy of the source by writing a script with these instructions:

```
export CVSROOT=':pserver:anonymous@anoncvs.gnome.org:/cvs/gnome'
cvs login
cvs -z3 checkout glib gtk+ imlib ORBit gnome-libs gnome-core
```

2. Change to a directory that is to be the root directory of all the ones holding the source files.

3. Establish a connection to the Internet.

4. Execute the script.

5. The first line of the script defines the environment variable CVSROOT with the location of the CVS source files. The cvs program expects this variable to be set.

6. The cvs login prompts you for a password. There is no password, so just press Enter.

7. The files are downloaded. Several directories — one for each library — are created inside the current directory and the source for all of them is retrieved.

Updating the Source

After you download the source files, you can keep up with the latest version by creating a script to update your source files. The script is very much like the one that performs the initial download:

```
export
CVSROOT=':pserver:anonymous@anoncvs.gnome.org:/cvs/gnome'
cvs login
cvs -z3 update -Pd glib gtk+ imlib ORBit gnome-libs gnome-core
```

The cvs command is update instead of checkout. The -P option causes cvs to remove any directories that are left empty after the update is complete. It takes a bit of time because it has to check the version of every file, but it is a lot quicker than downloading the whole thing.

Keeping up with Changes

You can subscribe to a mailing list that notifies you of updates by sending a message with the word subscribe as the entire body of the text. Send the message to:

```
cvs-commits-list-request@gnome.org
```

Once you subscribe, you will receive an e-mail every time one or more modules is updated.

Viewing the Source Online

If, instead of downloading the source files, you prefer to execute an online search of the CVS archives, go to this Web site:

```
http://cvs.gnome.org
```

At this site, you can search the archives using a variety of search parameters.

✦   ✦   ✦

Inheritance

Every widget inherits the functions and capabilities of the base class `GtkWidget`. In turn, `GtkWidget` inherits the functions and capabilities of `GtkObject`. Anything that inherits from `GtkObject` is an object. Anything that inherits from `GtkWidget` is both an object and a widget.

Each defined object also has a class defined for it, and there is a parallel inheritance tree for the classes. They have the same name and inheritance path as the widgets, except the names all end with '`Class`'. For example, the following widget hierarchy:

```
GnomePixmap->GtkWidget->GtkObject
```

has a class hierarchy that looks like this:

```
GnomePixmapClass->GtkWidgetClass-
    >GtkObjectClass
```

There is a macro that you can use to cast an object to any type in its inheritance chain. For example, the `GnomeAbout` widget inherits from `GnomeDialog`, so you can treat the pointer to a `GnomeAbout` widget like a `GnomeDialog` pointer with the macro `GNOME_DIALOG(widget)`. It also can be used as a `GtkWindow` widget by using the macro `GTK_WINDOW(widget)`. There is a macro for every widget type, all the way up to `GTK_OBJECT(widget)`. Using these macros provides access to the functions of any widget included in the family tree.

The following lists all the GNOME and GTK+ widgets, with their parentage traced back to `GtkObject`.

```
GnomeAbout->GnomeDialog->GtkWindow->GtkBin-
    >GtkContainer->
        GtkWidget->GtkObject
GnomeAnimator->GtkWidget->GtkObject
GnomeApp->GtkWindow->GtkBin->GtkContainer-
    >GtkWidget->
        GtkObject
```

```
GnomeAppBar->GtkHBox->GtkBox->GtkContainer->GtkWidget->
        GtkObject
GnomeCalculator->GtkVBox->GtkBox->GtkContainer->GtkWidget->
        GtkObject
GnomeCanvas->GtkLayout->GtkContainer->GtkWidget->GtkObject
GnomeCanvasEllipse->GnomeCanvasRE->GnomeCanvasItem->GtkObject
GnomeCanvasGroup->GnomeCanvasItem->GtkObject
GnomeCanvasImage->GnomeCanvasItem->GtkObject
GnomeCanvasItem->GtkObject
GnomeCanvasLine->GnomeCanvasItem->GtkObject
GnomeCanvasPolygon->GnomeCanvasItem->GtkObject
GnomeCanvasRE->GnomeCanvasItem->GtkObject
GnomeCanvasRect->GnomeCanvasRE->GnomeCanvasItem->GtkObject
GnomeCanvasText->GnomeCanvasItem->GtkObject
GnomeCanvasWidget->GnomeCanvasItem->GtkObject
GnomeClient->GtkObject
GnomeColorPicker->GtkButton->GtkBin->GtkContainer->GtkWidget->
        GtkObject
GnomeDEntryEdit->GtkObject
GnomeDialog->GtkWindow->GtkBin->GtkContainer->GtkWidget->
        GtkObject
GnomeDock->GtkContainer->GtkWidget->GtkObject
GnomeDockBand->GtkContainer->GtkWidget->GtkObject
GnomeDockItem->GtkBin->GtkContainer->GtkWidget->GtkObject
GnomeDockLayout->GtkObject
GnomeEntry->GtkCombo->GtkHBox->GtkBox->GtkContainer->
        GtkWidget->GtkObject
GnomeFileEntry->GtkHBox->GtkBox->GtkContainer->GtkWidget->
        GtkObject
GnomeFontPicker->GtkButton->GtkBin->GtkContainer->GtkWidget->
        GtkObject
GnomeFontSelector->GtkDialog->GtkWindow->GtkBin->GtkContainer->
        GtkWidget->GtkObject
GnomeGuru->GtkVBox->GtkBox->GtkContainer->GtkWidget->
        GtkObject
GnomeHRef->GtkButton->GtkBin->GtkContainer->GtkWidget->
        GtkObject
GnomeIconEntry->GtkVBox->GtkBox->GtkContainer->GtkWidget->
        GtkObject
GnomeIconSelection->GtkVBox->GtkBox->GtkContainer->GtkWidget->
        GtkObject
GnomeLess->GtkVBox->GtkBox->GtkContainer->GtkWidget->
        GtkObject
GnomeMDI->GtkObject
GnomeMDIChild->GtkObject
GnomeMDIGenericChild->GnomeMDIChild->GtkObject
GnomeMessageBox->GnomeDialog->GtkWindow->GtkBin->GtkContainer->
        GtkWidget->GtkObject
GnomeNumberEntry->GtkHBox->GtkBox->GtkContainer->GtkWidget->
        GtkObject
GnomePaperSelector->GtkVBox->GtkBox->GtkContainer->GtkWidget->
        GtkObject
```

```
GnomePixmap->GtkWidget->GtkObject
GnomePixmapEntry->GtkVBox->GtkBox->GtkContainer->GtkWidget->
        GtkObject
GnomeProcBar->GtkHBox->GtkBox->GtkContainer->GtkWidget->
        GtkObject
GnomePropertyBox->GnomeDialog->GtkWindow->GtkBin->
        GtkContainer->GtkWidget->GtkObject
GnomeScores->GnomeDialog->GtkWindow->GtkBin->GtkContainer->
        GtkWidget->GtkObject
GnomeSpell->GtkVBox->GtkBox->GtkContainer->GtkWidget->
        GtkObject
GnomeStock->GnomePixmap->GtkWidget->GtkObject
GnomeStockPixmapWidget->GtkVBox->GtkBox->GtkContainer->
        GtkWidget->GtkObject
GtkAccelLabel->GtkLabel->GtkMisc->GtkWidget->GtkObject
GtkAdjustment->GtkData->GtkObject
GtkAlignment->GtkBin->GtkContainer->GtkWidget->GtkObject
GtkArrow->GtkMisc->GtkWidget->GtkObject
GtkAspectFrame->GtkFrame->GtkBin->GtkContainer->GtkWidget->
        GtkObject
GtkBin->GtkContainer->GtkWidget->GtkObject
GtkBox->GtkContainer->GtkWidget->GtkObject
GtkButton->GtkBin->GtkContainer->GtkWidget->GtkObject
GtkButtonBox->GtkBox->GtkContainer->GtkWidget->GtkObject
GtkCList->GtkContainer->GtkWidget->GtkObject
GtkCTree->GtkCList->GtkContainer->GtkWidget->GtkObject
GtkCalendar->GtkWidget->GtkObject
GtkCheckButton->GtkToggleButton->GtkButton->GtkBin->
        GtkContainer->GtkWidget->GtkObject
GtkCheckMenuItem->GtkMenuItem->GtkItem->GtkBin->GtkContainer->
        GtkWidget->GtkObject
GtkClock->GtkLabel->GtkMisc->GtkWidget->GtkObject
GtkColorSelection->GtkVBox->GtkBox->GtkContainer->GtkWidget->
        GtkObject
GtkColorSelectionDialog->GtkWindow->GtkBin->GtkContainer->
        GtkWidget->GtkObject
GtkCombo->GtkHBox->GtkBox->GtkContainer->GtkWidget->GtkObject
GtkContainer->GtkWidget->GtkObject
GtkCurve->GtkDrawingArea->GtkWidget->GtkObject
GtkData->GtkObject
GtkDial->GtkWidget->GtkObject
GtkDialog->GtkWindow->GtkBin->GtkContainer->GtkWidget->
        GtkObject
GtkDrawingArea->GtkWidget->GtkObject
GtkEditable->GtkWidget->GtkObject
GtkEntry->GtkEditable->GtkWidget->GtkObject
GtkEventBox->GtkBin->GtkContainer->GtkWidget->GtkObject
GtkFileSelection->GtkWindow->GtkBin->GtkContainer->GtkWidget->
        GtkObject
GtkFixed->GtkContainer->GtkWidget->GtkObject
GtkFontSelection->GtkNotebook->GtkContainer->GtkWidget->
        GtkObject
```

```
GtkFontSelectionDialog->GtkWindow->GtkBin->GtkContainer->
        GtkWidget->GtkObject
GtkFrame->GtkBin->GtkContainer->GtkWidget->GtkObject
GtkGammaCurve->GtkVBox->GtkBox->GtkContainer->GtkWidget->
        GtkObject
GtkHBox->GtkBox->GtkContainer->GtkWidget->GtkObject
GtkHButtonBox->GtkButtonBox->GtkBox->GtkContainer->GtkWidget->
        GtkObject
GtkHPaned->GtkPaned->GtkContainer->GtkWidget->GtkObject
GtkHRuler->GtkRuler->GtkWidget->GtkObject
GtkHScale->GtkScale->GtkRange->GtkWidget->GtkObject
GtkHScrollbar->GtkScrollbar->GtkRange->GtkWidget->GtkObject
GtkHSeparator->GtkSeparator->GtkWidget->GtkObject
GtkHandleBox->GtkBin->GtkContainer->GtkWidget->GtkObject
GtkImage->GtkMisc->GtkWidget->GtkObject
GtkInputDialog->GtkDialog->GtkWindow->GtkBin->GtkContainer->
        GtkWidget->GtkObject
GtkInvisible->GtkBin->GtkContainer->GtkWidget->GtkObject
GtkItem->GtkBin->GtkContainer->GtkWidget->GtkObject
GtkItemFactory->GtkObject
GtkLabel->GtkMisc->GtkWidget->GtkObject
GtkLayout->GtkContainer->GtkWidget->GtkObject
GtkList->GtkContainer->GtkWidget->GtkObject
GtkListItem->GtkItem->GtkBin->GtkContainer->GtkWidget->
        GtkObject
GtkMenu->GtkMenuShell->GtkContainer->GtkWidget->GtkObject
GtkMenuBar->GtkMenuShell->GtkContainer->GtkWidget->GtkObject
GtkMenuItem->GtkItem->GtkBin->GtkContainer->GtkWidget->
        GtkObject
GtkMenuShell->GtkContainer->GtkWidget->GtkObject
GtkMisc->GtkWidget->GtkObject
GtkNotebook->GtkContainer->GtkWidget->GtkObject
GtkObject
GtkOptionMenu->GtkButton->GtkBin->GtkContainer->GtkWidget->
        GtkObject
GtkPacker->GtkContainer->GtkWidget->GtkObject
GtkPaned->GtkContainer->GtkWidget->GtkObject
GtkPixmap->GtkMisc->GtkWidget->GtkObject
GtkPixmapMenuItem->GtkMenuItem->GtkItem->GtkBin->GtkContainer->
        GtkWidget->GtkObject
GtkPlug->GtkWindow->GtkBin->GtkContainer->GtkWidget->
        GtkObject
GtkPreview->GtkWidget->GtkObject
GtkProgress->GtkWidget->GtkObject
GtkProgressBar->GtkProgress->GtkWidget->GtkObject
GtkRadioButton->GtkCheckButton->GtkToggleButton->GtkButton->
        GtkBin->GtkContainer->GtkWidget->GtkObject
GtkRadioMenuItem->GtkCheckMenuItem->GtkMenuItem->GtkItem->
        GtkBin->GtkContainer->GtkWidget->GtkObject
GtkRange->GtkWidget->GtkObject
GtkRuler->GtkWidget->GtkObject
```

```
GtkScale->GtkRange->GtkWidget->GtkObject
GtkScrollbar->GtkRange->GtkWidget->GtkObject
GtkScrolledWindow->GtkBin->GtkContainer->GtkWidget->GtkObject
GtkSeparator->GtkWidget->GtkObject
GtkSocket->GtkContainer->GtkWidget->GtkObject
GtkSpinButton->GtkEntry->GtkEditable->GtkWidget->GtkObject
GtkStatusbar->GtkHBox->GtkBox->GtkContainer->GtkWidget->
        GtkObject
GtkTable->GtkContainer->GtkWidget->GtkObject
GtkTearoffMenuItem->GtkMenuItem->GtkItem->GtkBin->
        GtkContainer->GtkWidget->GtkObject
GtkTed->GtkTable->GtkContainer->GtkWidget->GtkObject
GtkText->GtkEditable->GtkWidget->GtkObject
GtkTipsQuery->GtkLabel->GtkMisc->GtkWidget->GtkObject
GtkToggleButton->GtkButton->GtkBin->GtkContainer->GtkWidget->
        GtkObject
GtkToolbar->GtkContainer->GtkWidget->GtkObject
GtkTooltips->GtkData->GtkObject
GtkTree->GtkContainer->GtkWidget->GtkObject
GtkTreeItem->GtkItem->GtkBin->GtkContainer->GtkWidget->
        GtkObject
GtkVBox->GtkBox->GtkContainer->GtkWidget->GtkObject
GtkVButtonBox->GtkButtonBox->GtkBox->GtkContainer->GtkWidget->
        GtkObject
GtkVPaned->GtkPaned->GtkContainer->GtkWidget->GtkObject
GtkVRuler->GtkRuler->GtkWidget->GtkObject
GtkVScale->GtkScale->GtkRange->GtkWidget->GtkObject
GtkVScrollbar->GtkScrollbar->GtkRange->GtkWidget->GtkObject
GtkVSeparator->GtkSeparator->GtkWidget->GtkObject
GtkViewport->GtkBin->GtkContainer->GtkWidget->GtkObject
GtkWidget->GtkObject
GtkWindow->GtkBin->GtkContainer->GtkWidget->GtkObject
GtkXmHTML->GtkContainer->GtkWidget->GtkObject
GtkXmHTMLParser->GtkObject
```

✦   ✦   ✦

Arg Setting and Getting

An *arg* is a value inside an object, and it can be addressed by its name. Each widget that has one or more arg values has a function to read the value, write the value, or both. For example, a GtkWidget object has the following function that you can use to set an arg value:

```
gtk_widget_set_arg(GtkObject *object,GtkArg
*arg,guint id);
```

Also, a GtkWidget object provides the following function that enables you to read the values:

```
gtk_widget_get_arg(GtkObject *object,GtkArg
*arg,guint id);
```

Table D-1 lists the arg names, types, and the operations that are valid for each.

Table D-1
The Arguments

Arg Name	Data Type	Operation
GnomeCanvasGroup::x	gdouble	read/write
GnomeCanvasGroup::y	gdouble	read/write
GnomeCanvasImage::anchor	GtkAnchorType	read/write
GnomeCanvasImage::height	gdouble	read/write
GnomeCanvasImage::image	GdkImlibImage	read/write
GnomeCanvasImage::width	gdouble	read/write
GnomeCanvasImage::x	gdouble	read/write
GnomeCanvasImage::y	gdouble	read/write
GnomeCanvasLine::arrow_shape_a	gdouble	read/write
GnomeCanvasLine::arrow_shape_b	gdouble	read/write
GnomeCanvasLine::arrow_shape_c	gdouble	read/write
GnomeCanvasLine::cap_style	GdkCapStyle	read/write
GnomeCanvasLine::fill_color	gchar*	write-only
GnomeCanvasLine::fill_color_gdk	GdkColor	read/write
GnomeCanvasLine::fill_color_rgba	guint	read/write
GnomeCanvasLine::fill_stipple	GdkWindow	read/write
GnomeCanvasLine::first_arrowhead	gboolean	read/write
GnomeCanvasLine::join_style	GdkJoinStyle	read/write
GnomeCanvasLine::last_arrowhead	gboolean	read/write
GnomeCanvasLine::line_style	GdkLineStyle	read/write
GnomeCanvasLine::points	GnomeCanvas Points	read/write
GnomeCanvasLine::smooth	gboolean	read/write
GnomeCanvasLine::spline_steps	guint	read/write
GnomeCanvasLine::width_pixels	guint	write-only
GnomeCanvasLine::width_units	gdouble	write-only
GnomeCanvasPolygon::fill_color	gchar*	write-only
GnomeCanvasPolygon::fill_color_gdk	GdkColor	read/write

Arg Name	Data Type	Operation
GnomeCanvasPolygon::fill_ color_rgba	guint	read/write
GnomeCanvasPolygon::fill_stipple	GdkWindow	read/write
GnomeCanvasPolygon::outline_color	gchar*	write-only
GnomeCanvasPolygon::outline_ color_gdk	GdkColor	read/write
GnomeCanvasPolygon::outline_ color_rgba	guint	read/write
GnomeCanvasPolygon::outline_ stipple	GdkWindow	read/write
GnomeCanvasPolygon::points	GnomeCanvas Points	read/write
GnomeCanvasPolygon::width_pixels	guint	write-only
GnomeCanvasPolygon::width_units	gdouble	write-only
GnomeCanvasRE::fill_color	gchar*	write-only
GnomeCanvasRE::fill_color_gdk	GdkColor	read/write
GnomeCanvasRE::fill_color_rgba	guint	read/write
GnomeCanvasRE::fill_stipple	GdkWindow	read/write
GnomeCanvasRE::outline_color	gchar*	write-only
GnomeCanvasRE::outline_color_gdk	GdkColor	read/write
GnomeCanvasRE::outline_color_rgba	guint	read/write
GnomeCanvasRE::outline_stipple	GdkWindow	read/write
GnomeCanvasRE::width_pixels	guint	write-only
GnomeCanvasRE::width_units	gdouble	write-only
GnomeCanvasRE::x1	gdouble	read/write
GnomeCanvasRE::x2	gdouble	read/write
GnomeCanvasRE::y1	gdouble	read/write
GnomeCanvasRE::y2	gdouble	read/write
GnomeCanvasText::anchor	GtkAnchorType	read/write
GnomeCanvasText::clip	gboolean	read/write
GnomeCanvasText::clip_height	gdouble	read/write
GnomeCanvasText::clip_width	gdouble	read/write

Continued

Table D-1 (continued)		
Arg Name	**Data Type**	**Operation**
GnomeCanvasText::fill_color	gchar*	write-only
GnomeCanvasText::fill_color_gdk	GdkColor	read/write
GnomeCanvasText::fill_color_rgba	guint	read/write
GnomeCanvasText::fill_stipple	GdkWindow	read/write
GnomeCanvasText::font	gchar*	write-only
GnomeCanvasText::font_gdk	GdkFont	read/write
GnomeCanvasText::fontset	gchar*	write-only
GnomeCanvasText::justification	Gtk Justification	read/write
GnomeCanvasText::text	gchar*	read/write
GnomeCanvasText::text_height	gdouble	read-only
GnomeCanvasText::text_width	gdouble	read-only
GnomeCanvasText::x	gdouble	read/write
GnomeCanvasText::x_offset	gdouble	read/write
GnomeCanvasText::y	gdouble	read/write
GnomeCanvasText::y_offset	gdouble	read/write
GnomeCanvasWidget::anchor	GtkAnchorType	read/write
GnomeCanvasWidget::height	gdouble	read/write
GnomeCanvasWidget::size_pixels	gboolean	read/write
GnomeCanvasWidget::widget	GtkObject	read/write
GnomeCanvasWidget::width	gdouble	read/write
GnomeCanvasWidget::x	gdouble	read/write
GnomeCanvasWidget::y	gdouble	read/write
GnomeDockItem::orientation	GtkOrientation	read/write
GnomeDockItem::shadow	GtkShadowType	read/write
GnomeIconList::hadjustment	GtkAdjustment	read/write
GnomeIconList::vadjustment	GtkAdjustment	read/write
GtkAccelLabel::accel_widget	GtkWidget	read/write
GtkAlignment::xalign	gfloat	read/write
GtkAlignment::xscale	gfloat	read/write

Arg Name	Data Type	Operation
GtkAlignment::yalign	gfloat	read/write
GtkAlignment::yscale	gfloat	read/write
GtkArrow::arrow_type	GtkArrowType	read/write
GtkArrow::shadow_type	GtkShadowType	read/write
GtkBox::expand	gboolean	read/write
GtkBox::fill	gboolean	read/write
GtkBox::homogeneous	gboolean	read/write
GtkBox::pack_type	GtkPackType	read/write
GtkBox::padding	gulong	read/write
GtkBox::position	glong	read/write
GtkBox::spacing	gint	read/write
GtkButton::label	gchar*	read/write
GtkButton::relief	GtkRelief Style	read/write
GtkCList::n_columns	guint	read/write
GtkCList::reorderable	gboolean	read/write
GtkCList::row_height	guint	read/write
GtkCList::selection_mode	GtkSelection Mode	read/write
GtkCList::shadow_type	GtkShadowType	read/write
GtkCList::titles_active	gboolean	read/write
GtkCList::use_drag_icons	gboolean	read/write
GtkCTree::expander_style	GtkCtree Expander-Style	read/write
GtkCTree::indent	guint	read/write
GtkCTree::line_style	GtkCtreeLine Style	read/write
GtkCTree::n_columns	guint	read/write
GtkCTree::show_stub	gboolean	read/write
GtkCTree::spacing	guint	read/write
GtkCTree::tree_column	guint	read/write

Continued

Table D-1 *(continued)*

Arg Name	Data Type	Operation
GtkContainer::border_width	gulong	read/write
GtkContainer::child	GtkWidget	write-only
GtkContainer::resize_mode	GtkResizeMode	read/write
GtkEditable::editable	gboolean	read/write
GtkEditable::text_position	gint	read/write
GtkEntry::max_length	guint	read/write
GtkEntry::visibility	gboolean	read/write
GtkFrame::label	gchar*	read/write
GtkFrame::label_xalign	gfloat	read/write
GtkFrame::label_yalign	gfloat	read/write
GtkFrame::shadow	GtkShadowType	read/write
GtkHScale::adjustment	GtkAdjustment	read/write
GtkHScrollbar::adjustment	GtkAdjustment	read/write
GtkHandleBox::shadow	GtkShadowType	read/write
GtkLabel::justify	GtkJustification	read/write
GtkLabel::label	gchar*	read/write
GtkLabel::pattern	gchar*	read/write
GtkMenuBar::shadow	GtkShadowType	read/write
GtkMisc::xalign	gfloat	read/write
GtkMisc::xpad	gint	read/write
GtkMisc::yalign	gfloat	read/write
GtkMisc::ypad	gint	read/write
GtkNotebook::enable_popup	gboolean	read/write
GtkNotebook::menu_label	gchar*	read/write
GtkNotebook::page	gint	read/write
GtkNotebook::position	gint	read/write
GtkNotebook::scrollable	gboolean	read/write
GtkNotebook::show_border	gboolean	read/write
GtkNotebook::show_tabs	gboolean	read/write

Arg Name	Data Type	Operation
GtkNotebook::tab_border	guint	write-only
GtkNotebook::tab_fill	gboolean	read/write
GtkNotebook::tab_hborder	guint	read/write
GtkNotebook::tab_label	gchar*	read/write
GtkNotebook::tab_pack	gboolean	read/write
GtkNotebook::tab_pos	GtkPosition Type	read/write
GtkNotebook::tab_vborder	guint	read/write
GtkObject::object_signal	GtkSignal	write-only
GtkObject::object_signal_after	GtkSignal	write-only
GtkObject::signal	GtkSignal	write-only
GtkObject::signal_after	GtkSignal	write-only
GtkObject::user_data	gpointer	read/write
GtkPacker::anchor	GtkAnchorType	read/write
GtkPacker::border_width	guint	read/write
GtkPacker::default_border_width	guint	read/write
GtkPacker::default_ipad_x	guint	read/write
GtkPacker::default_ipad_y	guint	read/write
GtkPacker::default_pad_x	guint	read/write
GtkPacker::default_pad_y	guint	read/write
GtkPacker::expand	gboolean	read/write
GtkPacker::fill_x	gboolean	read/write
GtkPacker::fill_y	gboolean	read/write
GtkPacker::ipad_x	guint	read/write
GtkPacker::ipad_y	guint	read/write
GtkPacker::pad_x	guint	read/write
GtkPacker::pad_y	guint	read/write
GtkPacker::position	glong	read/write
GtkPacker::side	GtkSideType	read/write
GtkPacker::spacing	guint	read/write

Continued

Table D-1 *(continued)*

Arg Name	Data Type	Operation
GtkPacker::use_default	gboolean	read/write
GtkProgress::activity_mode	gboolean	read/write
GtkProgress::show_text	gboolean	read/write
GtkProgress::text_xalign	gfloat	read/write
GtkProgress::text_yalign	gfloat	read/write
GtkProgressBar::activity_blocks	guint	read/write
GtkProgressBar::activity_step	guint	read/write
GtkProgressBar::adjustment	GtkAdjustment	read/write
GtkProgressBar::bar_style	GtkProgress Bar-Style	read/write
GtkProgressBar::discrete_blocks	guint	read/write
GtkProgressBar::orientation	GtkProgress Bar- Orientation	read/write
GtkRadioButton::group	GtkRadioButton	write-only
GtkRange::update_policy	GtkUpdateType	read/write
GtkScale::digits	gint	read/write
GtkScale::draw_value	gboolean	read/write
GtkScale::value_pos	GtkPosition Type	read/write
GtkScrolledWindow::hadjustment	GtkAdjustment	read/write
GtkScrolledWindow::hscrollbar_ policy	GtkPolicyType	read/write
GtkScrolledWindow::vadjustment	GtkAdjustment	read/write
GtkScrolledWindow::vscrollbar_ policy	GtkPolicyType	read/write
GtkScrolledWindow::window_ placement	GtkCornerType	read/write
GtkSpinButton::adjustment	GtkAdjustment	read/write
GtkSpinButton::climb_rate	gfloat	read/write
GtkSpinButton::digits	guint	read/write
GtkSpinButton::numeric	gboolean	read/write

Arg Name	Data Type	Operation
GtkSpinButton::shadow_type	GtkShadowType	read/write
GtkSpinButton::snap_to_ticks	gboolean	read/write
GtkSpinButton::update_policy	GtkSpinButton Update-Policy	read/write
GtkSpinButton::value	gfloat	read/write
GtkSpinButton::wrap	gboolean	read/write
GtkTable::bottom_attach	guint	read/write
GtkTable::column_spacing	guint	read/write
GtkTable::homogeneous	gboolean	read/write
GtkTable::left_attach	guint	read/write
GtkTable::n_columns	guint	read/write
GtkTable::n_rows	guint	read/write
GtkTable::right_attach	guint	read/write
GtkTable::row_spacing	guint	read/write
GtkTable::top_attach	guint	read/write
GtkTable::x_options	GtkAttach Options	read/write
GtkTable::x_padding	guint	read/write
GtkTable::y_options	GtkAttach Options	read/write
GtkTable::y_padding	guint	read/write
GtkText::hadjustment	GtkAdjustment	read/write
GtkText::line_wrap	gboolean	read/write
GtkText::vadjustment	GtkAdjustment	read/write
GtkText::word_wrap	gboolean	read/write
GtkTipsQuery::caller	GtkWidget	read/write
GtkTipsQuery::emit_always	gboolean	read/write
GtkTipsQuery::label_inactive	gchar*	read/write
GtkTipsQuery::label_no_tip	gchar*	read/write
GtkToggleButton::active	gboolean	read/write
GtkToggleButton::draw_indicator	gboolean	read/write
GtkVScale::adjustment	GtkAdjustment	read/write

Continued

Table D-1 *(continued)*

Arg Name	Data Type	Operation
GtkVScrollbar::adjustment	GtkAdjustment	read/write
GtkViewport::hadjustment	GtkAdjustment	read/write
GtkViewport::shadow_type	GtkShadowType	read/write
GtkViewport::vadjustment	GtkAdjustment	read/write
GtkWidget::app_paintable	gboolean	read/write
GtkWidget::can_default	gboolean	read/write
GtkWidget::can_focus	gboolean	read/write
GtkWidget::composite_child	gboolean	read/write
GtkWidget::events	GdkEventMask	read/write
GtkWidget::extension_events	GdkEventMask	read/write
GtkWidget::has_default	gboolean	read/write
GtkWidget::has_focus	gboolean	read/write
GtkWidget::height	gint	read/write
GtkWidget::name	gchar*	read/write
GtkWidget::parent	GtkContainer	read/write
GtkWidget::receives_default	gboolean	read/write
GtkWidget::sensitive	gboolean	read/write
GtkWidget::style	GtkStyle	read/write
GtkWidget::visible	gboolean	read/write
GtkWidget::width	gint	read/write
GtkWidget::x	gint	read/write
GtkWidget::y	gint	read/write
GtkWindow::allow_grow	gboolean	read/write
GtkWindow::allow_shrink	gboolean	read/write
GtkWindow::auto_shrink	gboolean	read/write
GtkWindow::modal	gboolean	read/write
GtkWindow::title	gchar*	read/write
GtkWindow::type	GtkWindow	read/write
GtkWindow::window_position	GtkWindow Position	read/write

✦   ✦   ✦

Enumerated Types

Many of the function calls require that one or more int values be passed to it as a flag or mode indicator. Each constant is declared as an enum, which gives the constant a data type and assigns a name to each of its possible values. Table E-1 contains all of the value names for each of the enumerated types.

Table E-1
Enumerated Type and Value Names

Type Name	Value Names
GdkAxisUse	GDK_AXIS_IGNORE, GDK_AXIS_X, GDK_AXIS_Y, GDK_AXIS_PRESSURE, GDK_AXIS_XTILT, GDK_AXIS_YTILT, GDK_AXIS_LAST
GdkByteOrder	GDK_LSB_FIRST, GDK_MSB_FIRST
GdkCapStyle	GDK_CAP_NOT_LAST, GDK_CAP_BUTT, GDK_CAP_ROUND, GDK_CAP_PROJECTING
GdkColorContextMode	GDK_CC_MODE_UNDEFINED, GDK_CC_MODE_BW, GDK_CC_MODE_STD_CMAP, GDK_CC_MODE_TRUE, GDK_CC_MODE_MY_GRAY, GDK_CC_MODE_PALETTE
GdkColorInfoFlags	GDK_COLOR_WRITEABLE
GdkCrossingMode	GDK_CROSSING_NORMAL, GDK_CROSSING_GRAB, GDK_CROSSING_UNGRAB
GdkCursorType	GDK_LAST_CURSOR, GDK_CURSOR_IS_PIXMAP
GdkDebugFlag	GDK_DEBUG_MISC, GDK_DEBUG_EVENTS, GDK_DEBUG_DND, GDK_DEBUG_COLOR_CONTEXT, GDK_DEBUG_XIM
GdkDragAction	GDK_ACTION_DEFAULT, GDK_ACTION_COPY, GDK_ACTION_MOVE, GDK_ACTION_LINK, GDK_ACTION_PRIVATE, GDK_ACTION_ASK
GdkDragProtocol	GDK_DRAG_PROTO_MOTIF, GDK_DRAG_PROTO_XDND, GDK_DRAG_PROTO_ROOTWIN, GDK_DRAG_PROTO_NONE, GDK_DRAG_PROTO_WIN32_DROPFILES, GDK_DRAG_PROTO_OLE2
GdkEventMask	GDK_EXPOSURE_MASK, GDK_POINTER_MOTION_MASK, GDK_POINTER_MOTION_HINT_MASK, GDK_BUTTON_MOTION_MASK, GDK_BUTTON1_MOTION_MASK, GDK_BUTTON2_MOTION_MASK, GDK_BUTTON3_MOTION_MASK, GDK_BUTTON_PRESS_MASK, GDK_BUTTON_RELEASE_MASK, GDK_KEY_PRESS_MASK, GDK_KEY_RELEASE_MASK,

Type Name	Value Names
	GDK_ENTER_NOTIFY_MASK, GDK_LEAVE_NOTIFY_MASK, GDK_FOCUS_CHANGE_MASK, GDK_STRUCTURE_MASK, GDK_PROPERTY_CHANGE_MASK, GDK_VISIBILITY_NOTIFY_MASK, GDK_PROXIMITY_IN_MASK, GDK_PROXIMITY_OUT_MASK, GDK_SUBSTRUCTURE_MASK, GDK_ALL_EVENTS_MASK
GdkEventType	GDK_NOTHING, GDK_DELETE, GDK_DESTROY, GDK_EXPOSE, GDK_MOTION_NOTIFY, GDK_BUTTON_PRESS, GDK_2BUTTON_PRESS, GDK_3BUTTON_PRESS, GDK_BUTTON_RELEASE, GDK_KEY_PRESS, GDK_KEY_RELEASE, GDK_ENTER_NOTIFY, GDK_LEAVE_NOTIFY, GDK_FOCUS_CHANGE, GDK_CONFIGURE, GDK_MAP, GDK_UNMAP, GDK_PROPERTY_NOTIFY, GDK_SELECTION_CLEAR, GDK_SELECTION_REQUEST, GDK_SELECTION_NOTIFY, GDK_PROXIMITY_IN, GDK_PROXIMITY_OUT, GDK_DRAG_ENTER, GDK_DRAG_LEAVE, GDK_DRAG_MOTION, GDK_DRAG_STATUS, GDK_DROP_START, GDK_DROP_FINISHED, GDK_CLIENT_EVENT, GDK_VISIBILITY_NOTIFY, GDK_NO_EXPOSE
GdkExtensionMode	GDK_EXTENSION_EVENTS_NONE, GDK_EXTENSION_EVENTS_ALL, GDK_EXTENSION_EVENTS_CURSOR
GdkFill	GDK_SOLID, GDK_TILED, GDK_STIPPLED, GDK_OPAQUE_STIPPLED
GdkFillRule	GDK_EVEN_ODD_RULE, GDK_WINDING_RULE
GdkFilterReturn	GDK_FILTER_CONTINUE, GDK_FILTER_TRANSLATE, GDK_FILTER_REMOVE
GdkFontType	GDK_FONT_FONT, GDK_FONT_FONTSET

Continued

Table E-1 *(continued)*

Type Name	*Value Names*
GdkFunction	GDK_COPY, GDK_INVERT, GDK_XOR, GDK_CLEAR, GDK_AND, GDK_AND_REVERSE, GDK_AND_INVERT, GDK_NOOP, GDK_OR, GDK_EQUIV, GDK_OR_REVERSE, GDK_COPY_INVERT, GDK_OR_INVERT, GDK_NAND, GDK_SET
GdkGCValuesMask	GDK_GC_FOREGROUND, GDK_GC_BACKGROUND, GDK_GC_FONT, GDK_GC_FUNCTION, GDK_GC_FILL, GDK_GC_TILE, GDK_GC_STIPPLE, GDK_GC_CLIP_MASK, GDK_GC_SUBWINDOW, GDK_GC_TS_X_ORIGIN, GDK_GC_TS_Y_ORIGIN, GDK_GC_CLIP_X_ORIGIN, GDK_GC_CLIP_Y_ORIGIN, GDK_GC_EXPOSURES, GDK_GC_LINE_WIDTH, GDK_GC_LINE_STYLE, GDK_GC_CAP_STYLE, GDK_GC_JOIN_STYLE
GdkICAttributesType	GDK_IC_STYLE, GDK_IC_CLIENT_WINDOW, GDK_IC_FOCUS_WINDOW, GDK_IC_FILTER_EVENTS, GDK_IC_SPOT_LOCATION, GDK_IC_LINE_SPACING, GDK_IC_CURSOR, GDK_IC_PREEDIT_FONTSET, GDK_IC_PREEDIT_AREA, GDK_IC_PREEDIT_AREA_NEEDED, GDK_IC_PREEDIT_FOREGROUND, GDK_IC_PREEDIT_BACKGROUND, GDK_IC_PREEDIT_PIXMAP, GDK_IC_PREEDIT_COLORMAP, GDK_IC_STATUS_FONTSET, GDK_IC_STATUS_AREA, GDK_IC_STATUS_AREA_NEEDED, GDK_IC_STATUS_FOREGROUND, GDK_IC_STATUS_BACKGROUND, GDK_IC_STATUS_PIXMAP, GDK_IC_STATUS_COLORMAP, GDK_IC_ALL_REQ, GDK_IC_PREEDIT_AREA_REQ, GDK_IC_PREEDIT_POSITION_REQ, GDK_IC_STATUS_AREA_REQ

Type Name	Value Names
GdkIMStyle	GDK_IM_PREEDIT_AREA, GDK_IM_PREEDIT_CALLBACKS, GDK_IM_PREEDIT_POSITION, GDK_IM_PREEDIT_NOTHING, GDK_IM_PREEDIT_NONE, GDK_IM_PREEDIT_MASK, GDK_IM_STATUS_AREA, GDK_IM_STATUS_CALLBACKS, GDK_IM_STATUS_NOTHING, GDK_IM_STATUS_NONE, GDK_IM_STATUS_MASK
GdkImageType	GDK_IMAGE_NORMAL, GDK_IMAGE_SHARED, GDK_IMAGE_FASTEST, GDK_IMAGE_SHARED_PIXMAP
GdkInputCondition	GDK_INPUT_READ, GDK_INPUT_WRITE, GDK_INPUT_EXCEPTION
GdkInputMode	GDK_MODE_DISABLED, GDK_MODE_SCREEN, GDK_MODE_WINDOW
GdkInputSource	GDK_SOURCE_MOUSE, GDK_SOURCE_PEN, GDK_SOURCE_ERASER, GDK_SOURCE_CURSOR
GdkJoinStyle	GDK_JOIN_MITER, GDK_JOIN_ROUND, GDK_JOIN_BEVEL
GdkLineStyle	GDK_LINE_SOLID, GDK_LINE_ON_OFF_DASH, GDK_LINE_DOUBLE_DASH
GdkModifierType	GDK_SHIFT_MASK, GDK_LOCK_MASK, GDK_CONTROL_MASK, GDK_MOD1_MASK, GDK_MOD2_MASK, GDK_MOD3_MASK, GDK_MOD4_MASK, GDK_MOD5_MASK, GDK_BUTTON1_MASK, GDK_BUTTON2_MASK, GDK_BUTTON3_MASK, GDK_BUTTON4_MASK, GDK_BUTTON5_MASK, GDK_RELEASE_MASK, GDK_MODIFIER_MASK
GdkNotifyType	GDK_NOTIFY_ANCESTOR, GDK_NOTIFY_VIRTUAL, GDK_NOTIFY_INFERIOR, GDK_NOTIFY_NONLINEAR, GDK_NOTIFY_NONLINEAR_VIRTUAL, GDK_NOTIFY_UNKNOWN

Continued

Table E-1 (continued)

Type Name	Value Names
GdkOverlapType	GDK_OVERLAP_RECTANGLE_IN, GDK_OVERLAP_RECTANGLE_OUT, GDK_OVERLAP_RECTANGLE_PART
GdkPropMode	GDK_PROP_MODE_REPLACE, GDK_PROP_MODE_PREPEND, GDK_PROP_MODE_APPEND
GdkPropertyState	GDK_PROPERTY_NEW_VALUE, GDK_PROPERTY_DELETE
GdkRgbDither	GDK_RGB_DITHER_NONE, GDK_RGB_DITHER_NORMAL, GDK_RGB_DITHER_MAX
GdkSelection	GDK_SELECTION_PRIMARY, GDK_SELECTION_SECONDARY
GdkSelectionType	GDK_SELECTION_TYPE_ATOM, GDK_SELECTION_TYPE_BITMAP, GDK_SELECTION_TYPE_COLORMAP, GDK_SELECTION_TYPE_DRAWABLE, GDK_SELECTION_TYPE_INTEGER, GDK_SELECTION_TYPE_PIXMAP, GDK_SELECTION_TYPE_WINDOW, GDK_SELECTION_TYPE_STRING
GdkStatus	GDK_OK, GDK_ERROR, GDK_ERROR_PARAM, GDK_ERROR_FILE, GDK_ERROR_MEM
GdkSubwindowMode	GDK_CLIP_BY_CHILDREN, GDK_INCLUDE_INFERIORS
GdkTarget	GDK_TARGET_BITMAP, GDK_TARGET_COLORMAP, GDK_TARGET_DRAWABLE, GDK_TARGET_PIXMAP, GDK_TARGET_STRING
GdkVisibilityState	GDK_VISIBILITY_UNOBSCURED, GDK_VISIBILITY_PARTIAL, GDK_VISIBILITY_FULLY_OBSCURED
GdkVisualType	GDK_VISUAL_STATIC_GRAY, GDK_VISUAL_GRAYSCALE, GDK_VISUAL_STATIC_COLOR, GDK_VISUAL_PSEUDO_COLOR, GDK_VISUAL_TRUE_COLOR, GDK_VISUAL_DIRECT_COLOR

Type Name	Value Names
GdkWMDecoration	GDK_DECOR_ALL, GDK_DECOR_BORDER, GDK_DECOR_RESIZEH, GDK_DECOR_TITLE, GDK_DECOR_MENU, GDK_DECOR_MINIMIZE, GDK_DECOR_MAXIMIZE
GdkWMFunction	GDK_FUNC_ALL, GDK_FUNC_RESIZE, GDK_FUNC_MOVE, GDK_FUNC_MINIMIZE, GDK_FUNC_MAXIMIZE, GDK_FUNC_CLOSE
GdkWindowAttributesType	GDK_WA_TITLE, GDK_WA_X, GDK_WA_Y, GDK_WA_CURSOR, GDK_WA_COLORMAP, GDK_WA_VISUAL, GDK_WA_WMCLASS, GDK_WA_NOREDIR
GdkWindowClass	GDK_INPUT_OUTPUT, GDK_INPUT_ONLY
GdkWindowHints	GDK_HINT_POS, GDK_HINT_MIN_SIZE, GDK_HINT_MAX_SIZE, GDK_HINT_BASE_SIZE, GDK_HINT_ASPECT, GDK_HINT_RESIZE_INC
GdkWindowType	GDK_WINDOW_ROOT, GDK_WINDOW_TOPLEVEL, GDK_WINDOW_CHILD, GDK_WINDOW_DIALOG, GDK_WINDOW_TEMP, GDK_WINDOW_PIXMAP, GDK_WINDOW_FOREIGN
GnomeAnimatorLoopType	GNOME_ANIMATOR_LOOP_NONE, GNOME_ANIMATOR_LOOP_RESTART, GNOME_ANIMATOR_LOOP_PING_PONG
GnomeAnimatorStatus	GNOME_ANIMATOR_STATUS_STOPPED, GNOME_ANIMATOR_STATUS_RUNNING
GnomeCalculatorMode	GNOME_CALCULATOR_DEG, GNOME_CALCULATOR_RAD, GNOME_CALCULATOR_GRAD
GnomeClientFlags	GNOME_CLIENT_IS_CONNECTED, GNOME_CLIENT_RESTARTED, GNOME_CLIENT_RESTORED
GnomeClientState	GNOME_CLIENT_IDLE, GNOME_CLIENT_SAVING_PHASE_1, GNOME_CLIENT_WAITING_FOR_PHASE_2, GNOME_CLIENT_SAVING_PHASE_2, GNOME_CLIENT_FROZEN, GNOME_CLIENT_DISCONNECTED, GNOME_CLIENT_REGISTERING

Continued

Table E-1 (continued)

Type Name	Value Names
GnomeDateEditFlags	GNOME_DATE_EDIT_SHOW_TIME, GNOME_DATE_EDIT_24_HR, GNOME_DATE_EDIT_WEEK_STARTS_ON_MONDAY
GnomeDialogType	GNOME_DIALOG_ERROR, GNOME_DIALOG_NORMAL
GnomeDockItemBehavior	GNOME_DOCK_ITEM_BEH_NORMAL, GNOME_DOCK_ITEM_BEH_EXCLUSIVE, GNOME_DOCK_ITEM_BEH_NEVER_FLOATING, GNOME_DOCK_ITEM_BEH_NEVER_VERTICAL, GNOME_DOCK_ITEM_BEH_NEVER_HORIZONTAL, GNOME_DOCK_ITEM_BEH_LOCKED
GnomeDockPlacement	GNOME_DOCK_TOP, GNOME_DOCK_RIGHT, GNOME_DOCK_BOTTOM, GNOME_DOCK_LEFT, GNOME_DOCK_FLOATING
GnomeFontPickerMode	GNOME_FONT_PICKER_MODE_PIXMAP, GNOME_FONT_PICKER_MODE_FONT_INFO, GNOME_FONT_PICKER_MODE_USER_WIDGET, GNOME_FONT_PICKER_MODE_UNKNOWN
GnomeIconListMode	GNOME_ICON_LIST_ICONS, GNOME_ICON_LIST_TEXT_BELOW, GNOME_ICON_LIST_TEXT_RIGHT
GnomeInteractStyle	GNOME_INTERACT_NONE, GNOME_INTERACT_ERRORS, GNOME_INTERACT_ANY
GnomeMDIMode	GNOME_MDI_NOTEBOOK, GNOME_MDI_TOPLEVEL, GNOME_MDI_MODAL, GNOME_MDI_DEFAULT_MODE
GnomeMagicType	T_END, T_BYTE, T_SHORT, T_LONG, T_STR, T_DATE, T_BESHORT, T_BELONG, T_BEDATE, T_LESHORT, T_LELONG, T_LEDATE
GnomeMetadataError_t	GNOME_METADATA_OK, GNOME_METADATA_IO_ERROR, GNOME_METADATA_NOT_FOUND
GnomePreferencesType	GNOME_PREFERENCES_NEVER, GNOME_PREFERENCES_USER, GNOME_PREFERENCES_ALWAYS

Type Name	Value Names
GnomePropertyAction	GNOME_PROPERTY_ACTION_APPLY, GNOME_PROPERTY_ACTION_UPDATE, GNOME_PROPERTY_ACTION_LOAD, GNOME_PROPERTY_ACTION_SAVE, GNOME_PROPERTY_ACTION_LOAD_TEMP, GNOME_PROPERTY_ACTION_SAVE_TEMP, GNOME_PROPERTY_ACTION_DISCARD_TEMP, GNOME_PROPERTY_ACTION_CHANGED
GnomeRestartStyle	GNOME_RESTART_IF_RUNNING, GNOME_RESTART_ANYWAY, GNOME_RESTART_IMMEDIATELY, GNOME_RESTART_NEVER
GnomeSaveStyle	GNOME_SAVE_GLOBAL, GNOME_SAVE_LOCAL, GNOME_SAVE_BOTH
GnomeStockPixmapType	GNOME_STOCK_PIXMAP_TYPE_NONE, GNOME_STOCK_PIXMAP_TYPE_DATA, GNOME_STOCK_PIXMAP_TYPE_FILE, GNOME_STOCK_PIXMAP_TYPE_PATH, GNOME_STOCK_PIXMAP_TYPE_WIDGET, GNOME_STOCK_PIXMAP_TYPE_IMLIB, GNOME_STOCK_PIXMAP_TYPE_IMLIB_SCALED, GNOME_STOCK_PIXMAP_TYPE_GPIXMAP
GnomeUIInfo-ConfigurableTypes	GNOME_APP_CONFIGURABLE_ITEM_NEW, GNOME_APP_CONFIGURABLE_ITEM_OPEN, GNOME_APP_CONFIGURABLE_ITEM_SAVE, GNOME_APP_CONFIGURABLE_ITEM_SAVE_AS, GNOME_APP_CONFIGURABLE_ITEM_REVERT, GNOME_APP_CONFIGURABLE_ITEM_PRINT, GNOME_APP_CONFIGURABLE_ITEM_PRINT_SETUP, GNOME_APP_CONFIGURABLE_ITEM_CLOSE, GNOME_APP_CONFIGURABLE_ITEM_EXIT, GNOME_APP_CONFIGURABLE_ITEM_CUT, GNOME_APP_CONFIGURABLE_ITEM_COPY, GNOME_APP_CONFIGURABLE_ITEM_PASTE, GNOME_APP_CONFIGURABLE_ITEM_CLEAR, GNOME_APP_CONFIGURABLE_ITEM_UNDO, GNOME_APP_CONFIGURABLE_ITEM_REDO, GNOME_APP_CONFIGURABLE_ITEM_FIND, GNOME_APP_CONFIGURABLE_ITEM_FIND_AGAIN, GNOME_APP_CONFIGURABLE_ITEM_REPLACE, GNOME_APP_CONFIGURABLE_ITEM_PROPERTIES, GNOME_APP_CONFIGURABLE_ITEM_PREFERENCES,

Continued

Table E-1 *(continued)*

Type Name	Value Names
	GNOME_APP_CONFIGURABLE_ITEM_ABOUT, GNOME_APP_CONFIGURABLE_ITEM_SELECT_ALL, GNOME_APP_CONFIGURABLE_ITEM_NEW_WINDOW, GNOME_APP_CONFIGURABLE_ITEM_CLOSE_WINDOW, GNOME_APP_CONFIGURABLE_ITEM_NEW_GAME, GNOME_APP_CONFIGURABLE_ITEM_PAUSE_GAME, GNOME_APP_CONFIGURABLE_ITEM_RESTART_GAME, GNOME_APP_CONFIGURABLE_ITEM_UNDO_MOVE, GNOME_APP_CONFIGURABLE_ITEM_REDO_MOVE, GNOME_APP_CONFIGURABLE_ITEM_HINT, GNOME_APP_CONFIGURABLE_ITEM_SCORES, GNOME_APP_CONFIGURABLE_ITEM_END_GAME
GnomeUIInfoType	GNOME_APP_UI_ENDOFINFO, GNOME_APP_UI_ITEM, GNOME_APP_UI_TOGGLEITEM, GNOME_APP_UI_RADIOITEMS, GNOME_APP_UI_SUBTREE, GNOME_APP_UI_SEPARATOR, GNOME_APP_UI_HELP, GNOME_APP_UI_BUILDER_DATA, GNOME_APP_UI_ITEM_CONFIGURABLE, GNOME_APP_UI_SUBTREE_STOCK
GnomeUIPixmapType	GNOME_APP_PIXMAP_NONE, GNOME_APP_PIXMAP_STOCK, GNOME_APP_PIXMAP_DATA, GNOME_APP_PIXMAP_FILENAME

Type Name	Value Names
GnomeWinAppState	WIN_APP_STATE_NONE, WIN_APP_STATE_ACTIVE1, WIN_APP_STATE_ACTIVE2, WIN_APP_STATE_ERROR1, WIN_APP_STATE_ERROR2, WIN_APP_STATE_FATAL_ERROR1, WIN_APP_STATE_FATAL_ERROR2, WIN_APP_STATE_IDLE1, WIN_APP_STATE_IDLE2, WIN_APP_STATE_WAITING1, WIN_APP_STATE_WAITING2, WIN_APP_STATE_WORKING1, WIN_APP_STATE_WORKING2, WIN_APP_STATE_NEED_USER_INPUT1, WIN_APP_STATE_NEED_USER_INPUT2, WIN_APP_STATE_STRUGGLING1, WIN_APP_STATE_STRUGGLING2, WIN_APP_STATE_DISK_TRAFFIC1, WIN_APP_STATE_DISK_TRAFFIC2, WIN_APP_STATE_NETWORK_TRAFFIC1, WIN_APP_STATE_NETWORK_TRAFFIC2, WIN_APP_STATE_OVERLOADED1, WIN_APP_STATE_OVERLOADED2, WIN_APP_STATE_PERCENT000_1, WIN_APP_STATE_PERCENT000_2, WIN_APP_STATE_PERCENT010_1, WIN_APP_STATE_PERCENT010_2, WIN_APP_STATE_PERCENT020_1, WIN_APP_STATE_PERCENT020_2, WIN_APP_STATE_PERCENT030_1, WIN_APP_STATE_PERCENT030_2, WIN_APP_STATE_PERCENT040_1, WIN_APP_STATE_PERCENT040_2, WIN_APP_STATE_PERCENT050_1, WIN_APP_STATE_PERCENT050_2, WIN_APP_STATE_PERCENT060_1, WIN_APP_STATE_PERCENT060_2, WIN_APP_STATE_PERCENT070_1, WIN_APP_STATE_PERCENT070_2, WIN_APP_STATE_PERCENT080_1, WIN_APP_STATE_PERCENT080_2, WIN_APP_STATE_PERCENT090_1, WIN_APP_STATE_PERCENT090_2, WIN_APP_STATE_PERCENT100_1, WIN_APP_STATE_PERCENT100_2

Continued

Table E-1 *(continued)*

Type Name	Value Names
GnomeWinHints	WIN_HINTS_SKIP_FOCUS, WIN_HINTS_SKIP_WINLIST, WIN_HINTS_SKIP_TASKBAR, WIN_HINTS_GROUP_TRANSIENT, WIN_HINTS_FOCUS_ON_CLICK, WIN_HINTS_DO_NOT_COVER
GnomeWinLayer	WIN_LAYER_DESKTOP, WIN_LAYER_BELOW, WIN_LAYER_NORMAL, WIN_LAYER_ONTOP, WIN_LAYER_DOCK, WIN_LAYER_ABOVE_DOCK
GnomeWinState	WIN_STATE_STICKY, WIN_STATE_MINIMIZED, WIN_STATE_MAXIMIZED_VERT, WIN_STATE_MAXIMIZED_HORIZ, WIN_STATE_HIDDEN, WIN_STATE_SHADED, WIN_STATE_HID_WORKSPACE, WIN_STATE_HID_TRANSIENT, WIN_STATE_FIXED_POSITION, WIN_STATE_ARRANGE_IGNORE
GtkAccelFlags	GTK_ACCEL_VISIBLE, GTK_ACCEL_SIGNAL_VISIBLE, GTK_ACCEL_LOCKED, GTK_ACCEL_MASK
GtkAnchorType	GTK_ANCHOR_CENTER, GTK_ANCHOR_NORTH, GTK_ANCHOR_NORTH_WEST, GTK_ANCHOR_NORTH_EAST, GTK_ANCHOR_SOUTH, GTK_ANCHOR_SOUTH_WEST, GTK_ANCHOR_SOUTH_EAST, GTK_ANCHOR_WEST, GTK_ANCHOR_EAST, GTK_ANCHOR_N, GTK_ANCHOR_NW, GTK_ANCHOR_NE, GTK_ANCHOR_S, GTK_ANCHOR_SW, GTK_ANCHOR_SE, GTK_ANCHOR_W, GTK_ANCHOR_E
GtkArgFlags	GTK_ARG_READABLE, GTK_ARG_WRITABLE, GTK_ARG_CONSTRUCT, GTK_ARG_CONSTRUCT_ONLY, GTK_ARG_CHILD_ARG, GTK_ARG_MASK, GTK_ARG_READWRITE
GtkArrowType	GTK_ARROW_UP, GTK_ARROW_DOWN, GTK_ARROW_LEFT, GTK_ARROW_RIGHT
GtkAttachOptions	GTK_EXPAND, GTK_SHRINK, GTK_FILL

Type Name	Value Names
GtkButtonAction	GTK_BUTTON_IGNORED, GTK_BUTTON_SELECTS, GTK_BUTTON_DRAGS, GTK_BUTTON_EXPANDS
GtkButtonBoxStyle	GTK_BUTTONBOX_DEFAULT_STYLE, GTK_BUTTONBOX_SPREAD, GTK_BUTTONBOX_EDGE, GTK_BUTTONBOX_START, GTK_BUTTONBOX_END
GtkCListDragPos	GTK_CLIST_DRAG_NONE, GTK_CLIST_DRAG_BEFORE, GTK_CLIST_DRAG_INTO, GTK_CLIST_DRAG_AFTER
GtkCTreeExpanderStyle	GTK_CTREE_EXPANDER_NONE, GTK_CTREE_EXPANDER_SQUARE, GTK_CTREE_EXPANDER_TRIANGLE, GTK_CTREE_EXPANDER_CIRCULAR
GtkCTreeExpansionType	GTK_CTREE_EXPANSION_EXPAND, GTK_CTREE_EXPANSION_EXPAND_RECURSIVE, GTK_CTREE_EXPANSION_COLLAPSE, GTK_CTREE_EXPANSION_COLLAPSE_RECURSIVE, GTK_CTREE_EXPANSION_TOGGLE, GTK_CTREE_EXPANSION_TOGGLE_RECURSIVE
GtkCTreeLineStyle	GTK_CTREE_LINES_NONE, GTK_CTREE_LINES_SOLID, GTK_CTREE_LINES_DOTTED, GTK_CTREE_LINES_TABBED
GtkCTreePos	GTK_CTREE_POS_BEFORE, GTK_CTREE_POS_AS_CHILD, GTK_CTREE_POS_AFTER
GtkCalendarDisplay Options	GTK_CALENDAR_SHOW_HEADING, GTK_CALENDAR_SHOW_DAY_NAMES, GTK_CALENDAR_NO_MONTH_CHANGE, GTK_CALENDAR_SHOW_WEEK_NUMBERS, GTK_CALENDAR_WEEK_START_MONDAY
GtkCellType	GTK_CELL_EMPTY, GTK_CELL_TEXT, GTK_CELL_PIXMAP, GTK_CELL_PIXTEXT, GTK_CELL_WIDGET
GtkClockType	GTK_CLOCK_INCREASING, GTK_CLOCK_DECREASING, GTK_CLOCK_REALTIME
GtkCornerType	GTK_CORNER_TOP_LEFT, GTK_CORNER_BOTTOM_LEFT, GTK_CORNER_TOP_RIGHT, GTK_CORNER_BOTTOM_RIGHT

Continued

Table E-1 *(continued)*

Type Name	Value Names
GtkCurveType	GTK_CURVE_TYPE_LINEAR, GTK_CURVE_TYPE_SPLINE, GTK_CURVE_TYPE_FREE
GtkDebugFlag	GTK_DEBUG_OBJECTS, GTK_DEBUG_MISC, GTK_DEBUG_SIGNALS, GTK_DEBUG_DND, GTK_DEBUG_PLUGSOCKET
GtkDestDefaults	GTK_DEST_DEFAULT_MOTION, GTK_DEST_DEFAULT_HIGHLIGHT, GTK_DEST_DEFAULT_DROP, GTK_DEST_DEFAULT_ALL
GtkDirectionType	GTK_DIR_TAB_FORWARD, GTK_DIR_TAB_BACKWARD, GTK_DIR_UP, GTK_DIR_DOWN, GTK_DIR_LEFT, GTK_DIR_RIGHT
GtkFontFilterType	GTK_FONT_FILTER_BASE, GTK_FONT_FILTER_USER
GtkFontMetricType	GTK_FONT_METRIC_PIXELS, GTK_FONT_METRIC_POINTS
GtkFontType	GTK_FONT_BITMAP, GTK_FONT_SCALABLE, GTK_FONT_SCALABLE_BITMAP, GTK_FONT_ALL
GtkFundamentalType	GTK_TYPE_INVALID, GTK_TYPE_NONE, GTK_TYPE_CHAR, GTK_TYPE_UCHAR, GTK_TYPE_BOOL, GTK_TYPE_INT, GTK_TYPE_UINT, GTK_TYPE_LONG, GTK_TYPE_ULONG, GTK_TYPE_FLOAT, GTK_TYPE_DOUBLE, GTK_TYPE_STRING, GTK_TYPE_ENUM, GTK_TYPE_FLAGS, GTK_TYPE_BOXED, GTK_TYPE_POINTER, GTK_TYPE_SIGNAL, GTK_TYPE_ARGS, GTK_TYPE_CALLBACK, GTK_TYPE_C_CALLBACK, GTK_TYPE_FOREIGN, GTK_TYPE_OBJECT
GtkJustification	GTK_JUSTIFY_LEFT, GTK_JUSTIFY_RIGHT, GTK_JUSTIFY_CENTER, GTK_JUSTIFY_FILL
GtkMatchType	GTK_MATCH_ALL, GTK_MATCH_ALL_TAIL, GTK_MATCH_HEAD, GTK_MATCH_TAIL, GTK_MATCH_EXACT, GTK_MATCH_LAST
GtkMenuDirectionType	GTK_MENU_DIR_PARENT, GTK_MENU_DIR_CHILD, GTK_MENU_DIR_NEXT, GTK_MENU_DIR_PREV

Type Name	Value Names
GtkMenuFactoryType	GTK_MENU_FACTORY_MENU, GTK_MENU_FACTORY_MENU_BAR, GTK_MENU_FACTORY_OPTION_MENU
GtkMetricType	GTK_PIXELS, GTK_INCHES, GTK_CENTIMETERS
GtkObjectFlags	GTK_DESTROYED, GTK_FLOATING, GTK_CONNECTED, GTK_CONSTRUCTED
GtkOrientation	GTK_ORIENTATION_HORIZONTAL, GTK_ORIENTATION_VERTICAL
GtkPackType	GTK_PACK_START, GTK_PACK_END
GtkPackerOptions	GTK_PACK_EXPAND, GTK_FILL_X, GTK_FILL_Y
GtkPathPriorityType	GTK_PATH_PRIO_LOWEST, GTK_PATH_PRIO_GTK, GTK_PATH_PRIO_APPLICATION, GTK_PATH_PRIO_RC, GTK_PATH_PRIO_HIGHEST, GTK_PATH_PRIO_MASK
GtkPathType	GTK_PATH_WIDGET, GTK_PATH_WIDGET_CLASS, GTK_PATH_CLASS
GtkPolicyType	GTK_POLICY_ALWAYS, GTK_POLICY_AUTOMATIC, GTK_POLICY_NEVER
GtkPositionType	GTK_POS_LEFT, GTK_POS_RIGHT, GTK_POS_TOP, GTK_POS_BOTTOM
GtkPreviewType	GTK_PREVIEW_COLOR, GTK_PREVIEW_GRAYSCALE
GtkPrivateFlags	PRIVATE_GTK_USER_STYLE, PRIVATE_GTK_REDRAW_PENDING, PRIVATE_GTK_RESIZE_PENDING, PRIVATE_GTK_RESIZE_NEEDED, PRIVATE_GTK_LEAVE_PENDING, PRIVATE_GTK_HAS_SHAPE_MASK, PRIVATE_GTK_IN_REPARENT, PRIVATE_GTK_IS_OFFSCREEN
GtkProgressBar Orientation	GTK_PROGRESS_LEFT_TO_RIGHT, GTK_PROGRESS_RIGHT_TO_LEFT, GTK_PROGRESS_BOTTOM_TO_TOP, GTK_PROGRESS_TOP_TO_BOTTOM
GtkProgressBarStyle	GTK_PROGRESS_CONTINUOUS, GTK_PROGRESS_DISCRETE

Continued

Table E-1 (continued)

Type Name	Value Names
GtkRcFlags	GTK_RC_FG, GTK_RC_BG, GTK_RC_TEXT, GTK_RC_BASE
GtkRcTokenType	GTK_RC_TOKEN_INVALID, GTK_RC_TOKEN_INCLUDE, GTK_RC_TOKEN_NORMAL, GTK_RC_TOKEN_ACTIVE, GTK_RC_TOKEN_PRELIGHT, GTK_RC_TOKEN_SELECTED, GTK_RC_TOKEN_INSENSITIVE, GTK_RC_TOKEN_FG, GTK_RC_TOKEN_BG, GTK_RC_TOKEN_BASE, GTK_RC_TOKEN_TEXT, GTK_RC_TOKEN_FONT, GTK_RC_TOKEN_FONTSET, GTK_RC_TOKEN_BG_PIXMAP, GTK_RC_TOKEN_PIXMAP_PATH, GTK_RC_TOKEN_STYLE, GTK_RC_TOKEN_BINDING, GTK_RC_TOKEN_BIND, GTK_RC_TOKEN_WIDGET, GTK_RC_TOKEN_WIDGET_CLASS, GTK_RC_TOKEN_CLASS, GTK_RC_TOKEN_LOWEST, GTK_RC_TOKEN_GTK, GTK_RC_TOKEN_APPLICATION, GTK_RC_TOKEN_RC, GTK_RC_TOKEN_HIGHEST, GTK_RC_TOKEN_ENGINE, GTK_RC_TOKEN_MODULE_PATH, GTK_RC_TOKEN_LAST
GtkReliefStyle	GTK_RELIEF_NORMAL, GTK_RELIEF_HALF, GTK_RELIEF_NONE
GtkResizeMode	GTK_RESIZE_PARENT, GTK_RESIZE_QUEUE, GTK_RESIZE_IMMEDIATE
GtkScrollType	GTK_SCROLL_NONE, GTK_SCROLL_STEP_BACKWARD, GTK_SCROLL_STEP_FORWARD, GTK_SCROLL_PAGE_BACKWARD, GTK_SCROLL_PAGE_FORWARD, GTK_SCROLL_JUMP
GtkSelectionMode	GTK_SELECTION_SINGLE, GTK_SELECTION_BROWSE, GTK_SELECTION_MULTIPLE, GTK_SELECTION_EXTENDED
GtkShadowType	GTK_SHADOW_NONE, GTK_SHADOW_IN, GTK_SHADOW_OUT, GTK_SHADOW_ETCHED_IN, GTK_SHADOW_ETCHED_OUT

Type Name	Value Names
GtkSideType	GTK_SIDE_TOP, GTK_SIDE_BOTTOM, GTK_SIDE_LEFT, GTK_SIDE_RIGHT
GtkSignalRunType	GTK_RUN_FIRST, GTK_RUN_LAST, GTK_RUN_BOTH, GTK_RUN_NO_RECURSE, GTK_RUN_ACTION, GTK_RUN_NO_HOOKS
GtkSortType	GTK_SORT_ASCENDING, GTK_SORT_DESCENDING
GtkSpinButtonUpdate Policy	GTK_UPDATE_ALWAYS, GTK_UPDATE_IF_VALID
GtkSpinType	GTK_SPIN_STEP_FORWARD, GTK_SPIN_STEP_BACKWARD, GTK_SPIN_PAGE_FORWARD, GTK_SPIN_PAGE_BACKWARD, GTK_SPIN_HOME, GTK_SPIN_END, GTK_SPIN_USER_DEFINED
GtkStateType	GTK_STATE_NORMAL, GTK_STATE_ACTIVE, GTK_STATE_PRELIGHT, GTK_STATE_SELECTED, GTK_STATE_INSENSITIVE
GtkSubmenuDirection	GTK_DIRECTION_LEFT, GTK_DIRECTION_RIGHT
GtkSubmenuPlacement	GTK_TOP_BOTTOM, GTK_LEFT_RIGHT
GtkTargetFlags	GTK_TARGET_SAME_APP, GTK_TARGET_SAME_WIDGET
GtkToolbarChildType	GTK_TOOLBAR_CHILD_SPACE, GTK_TOOLBAR_CHILD_BUTTON, GTK_TOOLBAR_CHILD_TOGGLEBUTTON, GTK_TOOLBAR_CHILD_RADIOBUTTON, GTK_TOOLBAR_CHILD_WIDGET
GtkToolbarSpaceStyle	GTK_TOOLBAR_SPACE_EMPTY, GTK_TOOLBAR_SPACE_LINE
GtkToolbarStyle	GTK_TOOLBAR_ICONS, GTK_TOOLBAR_TEXT, GTK_TOOLBAR_BOTH
GtkTreeViewMode	GTK_TREE_VIEW_LINE, GTK_TREE_VIEW_ITEM
GtkTroughType	GTK_TROUGH_NONE, GTK_TROUGH_START, GTK_TROUGH_END, GTK_TROUGH_JUMP
GtkUpdateType	GTK_UPDATE_CONTINUOUS, GTK_UPDATE_DISCONTINUOUS, GTK_UPDATE_DELAYED

Continued

Table E-1 *(continued)*

Type Name	*Value Names*
GtkVisibility	GTK_VISIBILITY_NONE, GTK_VISIBILITY_PARTIAL, GTK_VISIBILITY_FULL
GtkWidgetFlags	GTK_TOPLEVEL, GTK_NO_WINDOW, GTK_REALIZED, GTK_MAPPED, GTK_VISIBLE, GTK_SENSITIVE, GTK_PARENT_SENSITIVE, GTK_CAN_FOCUS, GTK_HAS_FOCUS, GTK_CAN_DEFAULT, GTK_HAS_DEFAULT, GTK_HAS_GRAB, GTK_RC_STYLE, GTK_COMPOSITE_CHILD, GTK_NO_REPARENT, GTK_APP_PAINTABLE, GTK_RECEIVES_DEFAULT
GtkWindowPosition	GTK_WIN_POS_NONE, GTK_WIN_POS_CENTER, GTK_WIN_POS_MOUSE
GtkWindowType	GTK_WINDOW_TOPLEVEL, GTK_WINDOW_DIALOG, GTK_WINDOW_POPUP

◆   ◆   ◆

Signals

Every event received from a hardware device, as the result of some action by the user, is capable of signaling the application program by making a call to a callback function. Table F-1 lists the classes that have signals, the names of the signals, and the prototypes for their corresponding callback functions.

All callback functions have at least two arguments, but they may have more. The first argument is always a pointer to the widget that issues the signal. The last argument is always the pointer that the application program passes to the function to register the callback with the widget. Some callback functions have other arguments; these arguments are included between the widget pointer and the data pointer.

Table F-1
Signals and Their Callback Prototypes

Signal Name	Name	Callback Prototype
"abort_column_resize"	GtkCList	void cb(GtkWidget *, gpointer)
"activate"	GtkEditable	void cb(GtkWidget *, gpointer)
"activate"	GtkMenuItem	void cb(GtkWidget *, gpointer)
"activate_current"	GtkMenuShell	void cb(GtkWidget *, gboolean, gpointer)
"add"	GtkContainer	void cb(GtkWidget *, GtkWidget *, gpointer)
"button_press_event"	GtkWidget	gboolean cb(GtkWidget *, GdkEvent *, gpointer)
"button_release_event"	GtkWidget	gboolean cb(GtkWidget *, GdkEvent *, gpointer)
"cancel"	GtkMenuShell	void cb(GtkWidget *, gpointer)
"change_focus_row_expansion"	GtkCTree	void cb(GtkWidget *, GtkCTreeExpansionType, gpointer)
"changed"	GtkAdjustment	void cb(GtkWidget *, gpointer)
"changed"	GtkEditable	void cb(GtkWidget *, gpointer)
"check_resize"	GtkContainer	void cb(GtkWidget *, gpointer)
"child_detached"	GtkHandleBox	void cb(GtkWidget *, GtkWidget *, gpointer)
"click_column"	GtkCList	void cb(GtkWidget *, gint, gpointer)
"clicked"	GtkButton	void cb(GtkWidget *, gpointer)

Signal Name	Name	Callback Prototype
"client_event"	GtkWidget	gboolean cb(GtkWidget *, GdkEvent *, gpointer)
"collapse"	GtkTreeItem	void cb(GtkWidget *, gpointer)
"color_changed"	GtkColorSelection	void cb(GtkWidget *, gpointer)
"configure_event"	GtkWidget	gboolean cb(GtkWidget *, GdkEvent *, gpointer)
"copy_clipboard"	GtkEditable	void cb(GtkWidget *, gpointer)
"curve_type_changed"	GtkCurve	void cb(GtkWidget *, gpointer)
"cut_clipboard"	GtkEditable	void cb(GtkWidget *, gpointer)
"deactivate"	GtkMenuShell	void cb(GtkWidget *, gpointer)
"debug_msg"	GtkWidget	void cb(GtkWidget *, gchar *, gpointer)
"delete_event"	GtkWidget	gboolean cb(GtkWidget *, GdkEvent *, gpointer)
"delete_text"	GtkEditable	void cb(GtkWidget *, gint, gint, gpointer)
"deselect"	GtkItem	void cb(GtkWidget *, gpointer)
"destroy"	GtkObject	void cb(GtkWidget *, gpointer)
"destroy_event"	GtkWidget	gboolean cb(GtkWidget *, GdkEvent *, gpointer)
"disable_device"	GtkInputDialog	void cb(GtkWidget *, gint, gpointer)

Continued

Table F-1 *(continued)*

Signal Name	Name	Callback Prototype
"disconnect"	GtkData	void cb(GtkWidget *, gpointer)
"dock_detach"	GnomeDockItem	void cb(GtkWidget *, gpointer)
"dock_drag_begin"	GnomeDockItem	void cb(GtkWidget *, gpointer)
"dock_drag_end"	GnomeDockItem	void cb(GtkWidget *, gpointer)
"dock_drag_motion"	GnomeDockItem	void cb(GtkWidget *, gint, gint, gpointer)
"drag_begin"	GtkWidget	void cb(GtkWidget *, GdkDragContext *, gpointer)
"drag_data_delete"	GtkWidget	void cb(GtkWidget *, GdkDragContext *, gpointer)
"drag_data_get"	GtkWidget	void cb(GtkWidget *, GdkDragContext *, GtkSelectionData *, guint, guint, gpointer)
"drag_data_received"	GtkWidget	void cb(GtkWidget *, GdkDragContext *, gint, gint, GtkSelectionData *, guint, guint, gpointer)
"drag_drop"	GtkWidget	gboolean cb(GtkWidget *, GdkDragContext *, gint, gint, guint, gpointer)
"drag_end"	GtkWidget	void cb(GtkWidget *, GdkDragContext *, gpointer)

Signal Name	Name	Callback Prototype
"drag_leave"	GtkWidget	void cb(GtkWidget *, GdkDragContext *, gpointer)
"drag_motion"	GtkWidget	gboolean cb(GtkWidget *, GdkDragContext *, gint, gint, guint, gpointer)
"draw"	GtkWidget	void cb(GtkWidget *, gpointer, gpointer)
"draw_default"	GtkWidget	void cb(GtkWidget *, gpointer)
"draw_focus"	GtkWidget	void cb(GtkWidget *, gpointer)
"editing_started"	GnomeIconTextItem	void cb(GtkWidget *, gpointer)
"editing_stopped"	GnomeIconTextItem	void cb(GtkWidget *, gpointer)
"enable_device"	GtkInputDialog	void cb(GtkWidget *, gint, gpointer)
"end_selection"	GtkCList	void cb(GtkWidget *, gpointer)
"end_selection"	GtkListItem	void cb(GtkWidget *, gpointer)
"enter"	GtkButton	void cb(GtkWidget *, gpointer)
"enter_notify_event"	GtkWidget	gboolean cb(GtkWidget *, GdkEvent *, gpointer)
"event"	GtkWidget	gboolean cb(GtkWidget *, GdkEvent *, gpointer)

Continued

Table F-1 *(continued)*

Signal Name	Name	Callback Prototype
"expand"	GtkTreeItem	void cb(GtkWidget *, gpointer)
"expose_event"	GtkWidget	gboolean cb(GtkWidget *, GdkEvent *, gpointer)
"extend_selection"	GtkCList	void cb(GtkWidget *, GtkScrollType, gfloat, gboolean, gpointer)
"extend_selection"	GtkListItem	void cb(GtkWidget *, gint, gfloat, gboolean, gpointer)
"focus"	GtkContainer	gint cb(GtkWidget *, GtkDirectionType, GtkDirectionType, gpointer)
"focus_in_event"	GtkWidget	gboolean cb(GtkWidget *, GdkEvent *, gpointer)
"focus_out_event"	GtkWidget	gboolean cb(GtkWidget *, GdkEvent *, gpointer)
"grab_focus"	GtkWidget	void cb(GtkWidget *, gpointer)
"height_changed"	GnomeIconTextItem	void cb(GtkWidget *, gpointer)
"hide"	GtkWidget	void cb(GtkWidget *, gpointer)
"input"	GtkSpinButton	void cb(GtkWidget *, gpointer, gpointer)
"insert_text"	GtkEditable	void cb(GtkWidget *, gchar *, gint, gpointer, gpointer)
"key_press_event"	GtkWidget	gboolean cb(GtkWidget *, GdkEvent *, gpointer)

Signal Name	Name	Callback Prototype
"key_release_event"	GtkWidget	gboolean cb(GtkWidget *, GdkEvent *, gpointer)
"kill_char"	GtkEditable	void cb(GtkWidget *, gint, gpointer)
"kill_line"	GtkEditable	void cb(GtkWidget *, gint, gpointer)
"kill_word"	GtkEditable	void cb(GtkWidget *, gint, gpointer)
"layout_changed"	GnomeDock	void cb(GtkWidget *, gpointer)
"leave"	GtkButton	void cb(GtkWidget *, gpointer)
"leave_notify_event"	GtkWidget	gboolean cb(GtkWidget *, GdkEvent *, gpointer)
"map"	GtkWidget	void cb(GtkWidget *, gpointer)
"map_event"	GtkWidget	gboolean cb(GtkWidget *, GdkEvent *, gpointer)
"motion_notify_event"	GtkWidget	gboolean cb(GtkWidget *, GdkEvent *, gpointer)
"move_current"	GtkMenuShell	void cb(GtkWidget *, GtkMenuDirectionType, gpointer)
"move_cursor"	GtkEditable	void cb(GtkWidget *, gint, gint, gpointer)
"move_page"	GtkEditable	void cb(GtkWidget *, gint, gint, gpointer)

Continued

Table F-1 (continued)

Signal Name	Name	Callback Prototype
"move_to_column"	GtkEditable	void cb(GtkWidget *, gint, gint, gpointer)
"move_to_row"	GtkEditable	void cb(GtkWidget *, gint, gpointer)
"move_word"	GtkEditable	void cb(GtkWidget *, gint, gpointer)
"no_expose_event"	GtkWidget	gboolean cb(GtkWidget *, GdkEvent *, gpointer)
"orientation_changed"	GtkToolbar	void cb(GtkWidget *, gint, gpointer)
"output"	GtkSpinButton	gboolean cb(GtkWidget *, gpointer)
"parent_set"	GtkWidget	void cb(GtkWidget *, GtkObject *, gpointer)
"paste_clipboard"	GtkEditable	void cb(GtkWidget *, gpointer)
"pressed"	GtkButton	void cb(GtkWidget *, gpointer)
"property_notify_event"	GtkWidget	gboolean cb(GtkWidget *, GdkEvent *, gpointer)
"proximity_in_event"	GtkWidget	gboolean cb(GtkWidget *, GdkWidget *, gpointer)
"proximity_out_event"	GtkWidget	gboolean cb(GtkWidget *, GdkEvent *, gpointer)
"realize"	GtkWidget	void cb(GtkWidget *, gpointer)

Signal Name	Name	Callback Prototype
"released"	GtkButton	void cb(GtkWidget *, gpointer)
"remove"	GtkContainer	void cb(GtkWidget *, GtkWidget *, gpointer)
"resize_column"	GtkCList	void cb(GtkWidget *, gint, gint, gpointer)
"row_move"	GtkCList	void cb(GtkWidget *, gint, gint, gpointer)
"scroll_horizontal"	GtkCList	void cb(GtkWidget *, GtkScrollType, gfloat, gpointer)
"scroll_horizontal"	GtkListItem	void cb(GtkWidget *, gint, gfloat, gpointer)
"scroll_vertical"	GtkCList	void cb(GtkWidget *, GtkScrollType, gfloat, gpointer)
"scroll_vertical"	GtkListItem	void cb(GtkWidget *, gint, gfloat, gpointer)
"select"	GtkItem	void cb(GtkWidget *, gpointer)
"select_all"	GtkCList	void cb(GtkWidget *, gpointer)
"select_all"	GtkListItem	void cb(GtkWidget *, gpointer)
"select_child"	GtkList	void cb(GtkWidget *, GtkWidget *, gpointer)
"select_child"	GtkTree	void cb(GtkWidget *, GtkWidget *, gpointer)

Continued

Table F-1 *(continued)*

Signal Name	Name	Callback Prototype
"select_icon"	GnomeIconList	void cb(GtkWidget *, gint, GdkEvent *, gpointer)
"select_row"	GtkCList	void cb(GtkWidget *, gint, gint, GdkEvent *, gpointer)
"selection_changed"	GtkList	void cb(GtkWidget *, gpointer)
"selection_changed"	GtkTree	void cb(GtkWidget *, gpointer)
"selection_clear_event"	GtkWidget	gboolean cb(GtkWidget *, GdkEvent *, gpointer)
"selection_get"	GtkWidget	void cb(GtkWidget *, GtkSelectionData *, guint, guint, gpointer)
"selection_notify_event"	GtkWidget	gboolean cb(GtkWidget *, GdkEvent *, gpointer)
"selection_received"	GtkWidget	void cb(GtkWidget *, GtkSelectionData *, gpointer)
"selection_request_event"	GtkWidget	gboolean cb(GtkWidget *, GdkEvent *, gpointer)
"selection_started"	GnomeIconTextItem	void cb(GtkWidget *, gpointer)
"selection_stopped"	GnomeIconTextItem	void cb(GtkWidget *, gpointer)
"selection-done"	GtkMenuShell	void cb(GtkWidget *, gpointer)
"set_focus"	GtkWindow	void cb(GtkWidget *, GtkWidget *, gpointer)

Signal Name	Name	Callback Prototype
"set_scroll_adjustments"	GtkCList	void cb(GtkWidget *, GtkAdjustment *, GtkAdjustment *, gpointer)
"set_scroll_adjustments"	GtkLayout	void cb(GtkWidget *, GtkAdjustment *, GtkAdjustment *, gpointer)
"set_scroll_adjustments"	GtkText	void cb(GtkWidget *, GtkTypeAdjustment *, GtkTypeAdjustment *, gpointer)
"set_scroll_adjustments"	GtkViewport	void cb(GtkWidget *, GtkAdjustment *, GtkAdjustment *, gpointer)
"set-editable"	GtkEditable	void cb(GtkWidget *, gboolean, gpointer)
"set-focus-child"	GtkContainer	void cb(GtkWidget *, GtkWidget *, gpointer)
"show"	GtkWidget	void cb(GtkWidget *, gpointer)
"size_allocate"	GtkWidget	void cb(GtkWidget *, gpointer, gpointer)
"size_request"	GtkWidget	void cb(GtkWidget *, gpointer, gpointer)
"start_query"	GtkTipsQuery	void cb(GtkWidget *, gpointer)
"start_selection"	GtkCList	void cb(GtkWidget *, gpointer)
"start_selection"	GtkListItem	void cb(GtkWidget *, gpointer)
"state_changed"	GtkWidget	void cb(GtkWidget *, GtkStateType, gpointer)

Continued

Table F-1 (continued)

Signal Name	Name	Callback Prototype
"stop_query"	GtkTipsQuery	void cb(GtkWidget *, gpointer)
"style_changed"	GtkToolbar	void cb(GtkWidget *, gint, gpointer)
"style_set"	GtkWidget	void cb(GtkWidget *, GtkStyle *, gpointer)
"switch_page"	GtkNotebook	void cb(GtkWidget *, gpointer, guint, gpointer)
"text_changed"	GnomeIconTextItem	gboolean cb(GtkWidget *, gpointer)
"text_popped"	GtkStatusbar	void cb(GtkWidget *, guint, gchar *, gpointer)
"text_pushed"	GtkStatusbar	void cb(GtkWidget *, guint, gchar *, gpointer)
"toggle"	GtkItem	void cb(GtkWidget *, gpointer)
"toggle_add_mode"	GtkCList	void cb(GtkWidget *, gpointer)
"toggle_add_mode"	GtkListItem	void cb(GtkWidget *, gpointer)
"toggle_focus_row"	GtkCList	void cb(GtkWidget *, gpointer)
"toggle_focus_row"	GtkListItem	void cb(GtkWidget *, gpointer)
"toggled"	GtkCheckMenuItem	void cb(GtkWidget *, gpointer)
"toggled"	GtkToggleButton	void cb(GtkWidget *, gpointer)
"tree_collapse"	GtkCTree	void cb(GtkWidget *, GtkCTreeNode *, gpointer)

Signal Name	Name	Callback Prototype
"tree_expand"	GtkCTree	void cb(GtkWidget *, GtkCTreeNode *, gpointer)
"tree_move"	GtkCTree	void cb(GtkWidget *, GtkCTreeNode *, GtkCTreeNode *, GtkCTreeNode *, gpointer)
"tree_select_row"	GtkCTree	void cb(GtkWidget *, GtkCTreeNode *, gint, gpointer)
"tree_unselect_row"	GtkCTree	void cb(GtkWidget *, GtkCTreeNode, gint, gpointer)
"undo_selection"	GtkCList	void cb(GtkWidget *, gpointer)
"undo_selection"	GtkListItem	void cb(GtkWidget *, gpointer)
"unmap"	GtkWidget	void cb(GtkWidget *, gpointer)
"unmap_event"	GtkWidget	gboolean cb(GtkWidget *, GtkEvent*, gpointer)
"unrealize"	GtkWidget	void cb(GtkWidget *, gpointer)
"unselect_all"	GtkCList	void cb(GtkWidget *, gpointer)
"unselect_all"	GtkListItem	void cb(GtkWidget *, gpointer)
"unselect_child"	GtkList	void cb(GtkWidget *, GtkWidget *, gpointer)
"unselect_child"	GtkTree	void cb(GtkWidget *, GtkWidget *, gpointer)

Continued

Table F-1 *(continued)*

Signal Name	Name	Callback Prototype
"unselect_icon"	GnomeIconList	void cb(GtkWidget *, gint, GdkEvent *, gpointer)
"unselect_row"	GlkCList	void cb(GtkWidget *, gint, gint, GdkEvent *, gpointer)
"value_changed"	GtkAdjustment	void cb(GtkWidget *, gpointer)
"visibility_notify_event"	GtkWidget	gboolean cb(GtkWidget *, GdkEvent *, gpointer)
"widget_entered"	GtkTipsQuery	void cb(GtkWidget *, GtkWidget *, gchar *, gchar *, gpointer)
"widget_selected"	GtkTipsQuery	gboolean cb(GtkWidget *, GdkWdiget *, gchar *, gchar *, GdkEvent *, gpointer)
"width_changed"	GnomeIconTextItem	void cb(GtkWidget *, gpointer)

✦   ✦   ✦

Functions by Return Type

This appendix lists each data type, along with the functions that return it (or a pointer to it). The fundamental types (`int`, `gint`, `gboolean`, `guint32`, and so on) are not included.

GdkAtom
```
gdk_atom_intern(const gchar *atom_name,
    gint only_if_exists)
```

```
gdk_drag_get_selection(GdkDragContext *context)
```

GdkBitmap *
```
gdk_bitmap_ref(GdkBitmap *bitmap)
```

GdkColor *
```
gdk_color_copy(GdkColor *color)
```

GdkColorContext *
```
gdk_color_context_new(GdkVisual *visual,
    GdkColormap *colormap)
```

```
gdk_color_context_new_mono(GdkVisual *visual,

    GdkColormap *colormap)
```

GdkColormap *
```
gdk_colormap_get_system(void)
```

```
gdk_colormap_lookup(Colormap xcolormap)
```

```
gdk_colormap_new(GdkVisual *visual,
    gint private_cmap)
```

```
gdk_colormap_ref(GdkColormap *cmap)

gdk_rgb_get_cmap(void)

gdk_window_get_colormap(GdkWindow *window)

gdkx_colormap_get(Colormap xcolormap)

gtk_preview_get_cmap(void)

gtk_widget_get_colormap(GtkWidget *widget)

gtk_widget_get_default_colormap(void)
```

GdkCursor *
```
gdk_cursor_new(GdkCursorType cursor_type)

gdk_cursor_new_from_pixmap(GdkPixmap *source, GdkPixmap *mask,

    GdkColor *fg, GdkColor *bg, gint x, gint y)
```

GdkDragContext *
```
gdk_drag_begin(GdkWindow *window, GList *targets)

gdk_drag_context_new(void)

gtk_drag_begin(GtkWidget *widget, GtkTargetList *target_list,

    GdkDragAction actions, gint button, GdkEvent *event)
```

GdkEvent *
```
gdk_event_copy(GdkEvent *event)

gdk_event_get(void)

gdk_event_get_graphics_expose(GdkWindow *window)

gdk_event_peek(void)

gtk_get_current_event(void)
```

GdkEventMask
```
gdk_ic_get_events(GdkIC *ic)

gdk_window_get_events(GdkWindow *window)
```

GdkExtensionMode

gtk_widget_get_extension_events(GtkWidget *widget)

GdkFilterReturn

gdk_wm_protocols_filter(GdkXEvent *xev, GdkEvent *event,

    gpointer data)

motif_dnd_filter(GdkXEvent *xev, GdkEvent *event,

    gpointer data)

motif_drag_status(GdkEvent *event, guint16 flags,

    guint32 timestamp)

motif_drag_window_filter(GdkXEvent *xevent, GdkEvent *event,

    gpointer data)

motif_drop_start(GdkEvent *event, guint16 flags,

    guint32 timestamp, guint32 source_window, guint32 atom,

    gint16 x_root, gint16 y_root)

motif_motion(GdkEvent *event, guint16 flags, guint32 timestamp,

    gint16 x_root, gint16 y_root)

motif_operation_changed(GdkEvent *event, guint16 flags,

    guint32 timestamp)

motif_top_level_leave(GdkEvent *event, guint16 flags,

    guint32 timestamp)

GdkFont *

gdk_font_load(const gchar *font_name)

gdk_font_ref(GdkFont *font)

gdk_fontset_load(gchar *fontset_name)

```
gnome_font_picker_get_font(GnomeFontPicker *gfp)

gtk_font_selection_dialog_get_font

    (GtkFontSelectionDialog *fsd)

gtk_font_selection_get_font(GtkFontSelection *fontsel)
```

GdkGC *
```
gdk_gc_new(GdkWindow *window)

gdk_gc_new_with_values(GdkWindow *window, GdkGCValues *values,

    GdkGCValuesMask values_mask)

gdk_gc_ref(GdkGC *gc)

gtk_gc_get(gint depth, GdkColormap *colormap,

    GdkGCValues *values, GdkGCValuesMask values_mask)
```

GdkIC *
```
gdk_ic_new(GdkICAttr *attr, GdkICAttributesType mask)
```

GdkICAttr *
```
gdk_ic_attr_new(void)
```

GdkICAttributesType
```
gdk_ic_get_attr(GdkIC *ic, GdkICAttr *attr,

    GdkICAttributesType mask)

gdk_ic_set_attr(GdkIC *ic, GdkICAttr *attr,

    GdkICAttributesType mask)
```

GdkImage *
```
gdk_image_get(GdkWindow *window, gint x, gint y, gint width,

    gint height)

gdk_image_new(GdkImageType type, GdkVisual *visual, gint width,
```

```
    gint height)
```

gdk_image_new_bitmap(GdkVisual *visual, gpointer data, gint w,

    gint h)

GdkIMlibImage *
gnome_canvas_load_alpha(char *file)

GdkIMStyle
gdk_ic_get_style(GdkIC *ic)

gdk_im_decide_style(GdkIMStyle supported_style)

gdk_im_set_best_style(GdkIMStyle style)

GdkOverlapType
gdk_region_rect_in(GdkRegion *region, GdkRectangle *rect)

GdkPixmap *
gdk_bitmap_create_from_data(GdkWindow *window,

    const gchar *data, gint width, gint height)

gdk_pixmap_colormap_create_from_xpm(GdkWindow *window,

    GdkColormap *colormap, GdkBitmap **mask,

    GdkColor *transparent_color, const gchar *filename)

gdk_pixmap_colormap_create_from_xpm_d(GdkWindow *window,

    GdkColormap *colormap, GdkBitmap **mask,

    GdkColor *transparent_color, gchar **data)

gdk_pixmap_create_from_data(GdkWindow *window,

    const gchar *data, gint width, gint height, gint depth,

    GdkColor *fg, GdkColor *bg)

gdk_pixmap_create_from_xpm(GdkWindow *window, GdkBitmap **mask,

```
        GdkColor *transparent_color, const gchar *filename)
gdk_pixmap_create_from_xpm_d(GdkWindow *window,
    GdkBitmap **mask, GdkColor *transparent_color,
    gchar **data)
gdk_pixmap_foreign_new(guint32 anid)
gdk_pixmap_new(GdkWindow *window, gint width, gint height,
    gint depth)
gdk_pixmap_ref(GdkPixmap *pixmap)
gtk_rc_load_image(GdkColormap *colormap,
    GdkColor *transparent_color, const gchar *filename)
```

GdkRegion *
```
gdk_region_new(void)
gdk_region_polygon(GdkPoint *points, gint npoints,
    GdkFillRule fill_rule)
gdk_region_union_with_rect(GdkRegion *region,
    GdkRectangle *rect)
gdk_regions_intersect(GdkRegion *source1, GdkRegion *source2)
gdk_regions_subtract(GdkRegion *source1, GdkRegion *source2)
gdk_regions_union(GdkRegion *source1, GdkRegion *source2)
gdk_regions_xor(GdkRegion *source1, GdkRegion *source2)
```

GdkRgbCmap *
```
gdk_rgb_cmap_new(guint32 *colors, gint n_colors)
```

GdkTimeCoord *
```
gdk_input_motion_events(GdkWindow *window, guint32 deviceid,
    guint32 start, guint32 stop, gint *nevents_return)
```

GdkVisual *

```
gdk_colormap_get_visual(GdkColormap *colormap)

gdk_rgb_get_visual(void)

gdk_visual_get_best(void)

gdk_visual_get_best_with_both(gint depth,
    GdkVisualType visual_type)

gdk_visual_get_best_with_depth(gint depth)

gdk_visual_get_best_with_type(GdkVisualType visual_type)

gdk_visual_get_system(void)

gdk_visual_lookup(Visual *xvisual)

gdk_visual_ref(GdkVisual *visual)

gdk_window_get_visual(GdkWindow *window)

gdkx_visual_get(VisualID xvisualid)

gtk_preview_get_visual(void)

gtk_widget_get_default_visual(void)

gtk_widget_get_visual(GtkWidget *widget)
```

GdkVisualType

```
gdk_visual_get_best_type(void)
```

GdkWindow *

```
gdk_selection_owner_get(GdkAtom selection)

gdk_window_at_pointer(gint *win_x, gint *win_y)

gdk_window_foreign_new(guint32 anid)

gdk_window_get_parent(GdkWindow *window)

gdk_window_get_pointer(GdkWindow *window, gint *x, gint *y,
    GdkModifierType *mask)
```

```
gdk_window_get_toplevel(GdkWindow *window)

gdk_window_new(GdkWindow *parent, GdkWindowAttr *attributes,
    gint attributes_mask)

gdk_window_ref(GdkWindow *window)

gtk_widget_get_parent_window(GtkWidget *widget)
```

GdkWindowType
```
gdk_window_get_type(GdkWindow *window)
```

GList *
```
gdk_input_list_devices(void)

gdk_list_visuals(void)

gdk_window_get_children(GdkWindow *window)

gdk_window_get_toplevels(void)

gnome_history_get_recently_used(void)

gnome_i18n_get_language_list(const gchar *category_name)

gnome_mime_get_keys(const char *mime_type)

gnome_paper_name_list(void)

gnome_unit_name_list(void)

gnome_uri_list_extract_filenames(const gchar *uri_list)

gnome_uri_list_extract_uris(const gchar *uri_list)

gnome_win_hints_get_client_window_ids(void)

gnome_win_hints_get_workspace_names(void)

gtk_container_children(GtkContainer *container)

gtk_container_get_toplevels(void)
```

```
gtk_ctree_find_all_by_row_data(GtkCTree *ctree,

    GtkCTreeNode *node, gpointer data)

gtk_ctree_find_all_by_row_data_custom(GtkCTree *ctree,

    GtkCTreeNode *node, gpointer data, GCompareFunc func)

gtk_type_children_types(GtkType type)
```

GNode *
```
gtk_ctree_export_to_gnode(GtkCTree *ctree, GNode *parent,

    GNode *sibling, GtkCTreeNode *node, GtkCTreeGNodeFunc func,

    gpointer data)
```

GnomeAnimatorLoopType
```
gnome_animator_get_loop_type(GnomeAnimator *animator)
```

GnomeAnimatorStatus
```
gnome_animator_get_status(GnomeAnimator *animator)
```

GnomeApp *
```
gnome_mdi_get_active_window(GnomeMDI *mdi)

gnome_mdi_get_app_from_view(GtkWidget *view)
```

GnomeAppProgressKey
```
gnome_app_progress_manual(GnomeApp *app,

    const gchar *description,

    GnomeAppProgressCancelFunc cancel_cb, gpointer data)

gnome_app_progress_timeout(GnomeApp *app,

    const gchar *description, guint32 interval,

    GnomeAppProgressFunc percentage_cb,

    GnomeAppProgressCancelFunc cancel_cb, gpointer data)
```

GnomeCanvasGroup *
```
gnome_canvas_root(GnomeCanvas *canvas)
```

GnomeCanvasItem *
```
gnome_canvas_get_item_at(GnomeCanvas *canvas, double x,

    double y)

gnome_canvas_item_new(GnomeCanvasGroup *parent, GtkType type,

    const gchar *first_arg_name, . . .)

gnome_canvas_item_newv(GnomeCanvasGroup *parent, GtkType type,

    guint nargs, GtkArg *args)
```

GnomeCanvasPoints *
```
gnome_canvas_points_new(int num_points)

gnome_canvas_points_ref(GnomeCanvasPoints *points)
```

GnomeClient *
```
gnome_client_new(void)

gnome_client_new_without_connection(void)

gnome_cloned_client(void)

gnome_master_client(void)
```

GnomeClientFlags
```
gnome_client_get_flags(GnomeClient *client)
```

GnomeDesktopEntry *
```
gnome_dentry_get_dentry(GnomeDEntryEdit *dee)

gnome_desktop_entry_copy(GnomeDesktopEntry *source)

gnome_desktop_entry_load(const char *file)

gnome_desktop_entry_load_flags(const char *file,

    int clean_from_memory_after_load)
```

```
gnome_desktop_entry_load_flags_conditional(const char *file,

    int clean_from_memory_after_load, int unconditional)

gnome_desktop_entry_load_unconditional(const char *file)
```

GnomeDock *

```
gnome_app_get_dock(GnomeApp *app)
```

GnomeDockItem *

```
gnome_app_get_dock_item_by_name(GnomeApp *app,

    const gchar *name)

gnome_dock_band_get_item_by_name(GnomeDockBand *band,

    const char *name, guint *position_return,

    guint *offset_return)

gnome_dock_get_item_by_name(GnomeDock *dock, const gchar *name,

    GnomeDockPlacement *placement_return,

    guint *num_band_return, guint *band_position_return,

    guint *offset_return)
```

GnomeDockItemBehavior

```
gnome_dock_item_get_behavior(GnomeDockItem *dock_item)
```

GnomeDockLayout *

```
gnome_dock_get_layout(GnomeDock *dock)

gnome_dock_layout_new(void)
```

GnomeDockLayoutItem *

```
gnome_dock_layout_get_item(GnomeDockLayout *layout,

    GnomeDockItem *item)

gnome_dock_layout_get_item_by_name(GnomeDockLayout *layout,

    const gchar *name)
```

GnomeFontPickerMode
gnome_font_picker_get_mode(GnomeFontPicker *gfp)

GnomeIconTextInfo *
gnome_icon_layout_text(GdkFont *font, char *text,

    char *separators, int max_width, int confine)

GnomeMagicEntry *
gnome_magic_parse(const gchar *filename, gint *nents)

GnomeMDIChild *
gnome_mdi_find_child(GnomeMDI *mdi, gchar *name)

gnome_mdi_get_active_child(GnomeMDI *mdi)

gnome_mdi_get_child_from_view(GtkWidget *view)

GnomeMDIGenericChild *
gnome_mdi_generic_child_new(gchar *name)

GnomeMDIMode
gnome_preferences_get_mdi_mode()

GnomePaper *
gnome_paper_with_name(const gchar *papername)

gnome_paper_with_size(const double pswidth,

    const double psheight)

GnomePlugin *
gnome_plugin_use(const char *plugin_id)

GnomePropertyObject *
gnome_property_object_new

    (GnomePropertyDescriptor *descriptor,

    gpointer property_data_ptr)

GnomeRegexCache *

```
gnome_regex_cache_new(void)
```

GnomeStockPixmapEntry *

```
gnome_stock_pixmap_checkfor(const char *icon,

    const char *subtype)
```

GnomeUIInfo *

```
gnome_mdi_get_child_menu_info(GnomeApp *app)

gnome_mdi_get_menubar_info(GnomeApp *app)

gnome_mdi_get_toolbar_info(GnomeApp *app)
```

GnomeUnit *

```
gnome_unit_with_name(const gchar *unitname)
```

GnomeWinAppState

```
gnome_win_hints_get_app_state(GtkWidget *window)
```

GnomeWinHints

```
gnome_win_hints_get_hints(GtkWidget *window)
```

GnomeWinLayer

```
gnome_win_hints_get_layer(GtkWidget *window)
```

GnomeWinState

```
gnome_win_hints_get_state(GtkWidget *window)
```

GSList *

```
gtk_accel_group_entries_from_object(GtkObject *object)

gtk_accel_groups_from_object(GtkObject *object)

gtk_radio_button_group(GtkRadioButton *radio_button)

gtk_radio_menu_item_group(GtkRadioMenuItem *radio_menu_item)
```

GtkAccelEntry *

```
gtk_accel_group_get_entry(GtkAccelGroup *accel_group,

    guint accel_key, GdkModifierType accel_mods)
```

GtkAccelGroup *

```
gnome_popup_menu_get_accel_group(GtkMenu *menu)

gtk_accel_group_get_default(void)

gtk_accel_group_new(void)

gtk_accel_group_ref(GtkAccelGroup *accel_group)

gtk_menu_ensure_uline_accel_group(GtkMenu *menu)

gtk_menu_get_accel_group(GtkMenu *menu)

gtk_menu_get_uline_accel_group(GtkMenu *menu)
```

GtkAdjustment *

```
gtk_clist_get_hadjustment(GtkCList *clist)

gtk_clist_get_vadjustment(GtkCList *clist)

gtk_dial_get_adjustment(GtkDial *dial)

gtk_layout_get_hadjustment(GtkLayout *layout)

gtk_layout_get_vadjustment(GtkLayout *layout)

gtk_range_get_adjustment(GtkRange *range)

gtk_scrolled_window_get_hadjustment

    (GtkScrolledWindow *scrolled_window)

gtk_scrolled_window_get_vadjustment

    (GtkScrolledWindow *scrolled_window)

gtk_spin_button_get_adjustment(GtkSpinButton *spin_button)

gtk_viewport_get_hadjustment(GtkViewport *viewport)

gtk_viewport_get_vadjustment(GtkViewport *viewport)
```

GtkArg *
gtk_arg_copy(GtkArg *src_arg, GtkArg *dest_arg)

gtk_arg_new(GtkType arg_type)

gtk_args_query(GtkType class_type,

    GHashTable *arg_info_hash_table, guint32 **arg_flags,

    guint *n_args_p)

gtk_container_query_child_args(GtkType class_type,

    guint32 **arg_flags, guint *n_args)

gtk_object_query_args(GtkType class_type, guint32 **arg_flags,

    guint *n_args)

GtkArgInfo *
gtk_arg_type_new_static(GtkType base_class_type,

    const gchar *arg_name, guint class_n_args_offset,

    GHashTable *arg_info_hash_table, GtkType arg_type,

    guint arg_flags, guint arg_id)

GtkBindingSet *
gtk_binding_set_by_class(gpointer object_class)

gtk_binding_set_find(const gchar *set_name)

gtk_binding_set_new(const gchar *set_name)

GtkButtonBoxStyle
gnome_preferences_get_button_layout(void)

gtk_button_box_get_layout(GtkButtonBox *widget)

gtk_hbutton_box_get_layout_default(void)

gtk_vbutton_box_get_layout_default(void)

GtkCellType

gtk_clist_get_cell_type(GtkCList *clist, gint row, gint column)

gtk_ctree_node_get_cell_type(GtkCTree *ctree,

    GtkCTreeNode *node, gint column)

GtkCTreeNode *

gtk_ctree_find_by_row_data(GtkCTree *ctree, GtkCTreeNode *node,

    gpointer data)

gtk_ctree_find_by_row_data_custom(GtkCTree *ctree,

    GtkCTreeNode *node, gpointer data, GCompareFunc func)

gtk_ctree_find_node_ptr(GtkCTree *ctree,

    GtkCTreeRow *ctree_row)

gtk_ctree_insert_gnode(GtkCTree *ctree, GtkCTreeNode *parent,

    GtkCTreeNode *sibling, GNode *gnode,

    GtkCTreeGNodeFunc func, gpointer data)

gtk_ctree_insert_node(GtkCTree *ctree, GtkCTreeNode *parent,

    GtkCTreeNode *sibling, gchar *text[], guint8 spacing,

    GdkPixmap *pixmap_closed, GdkBitmap *mask_closed,

    GdkPixmap *pixmap_opened, GdkBitmap *mask_opened,

    gboolean is_leaf, gboolean expanded)

gtk_ctree_last(GtkCTree *ctree, GtkCTreeNode *node)

gtk_ctree_node_nth(GtkCTree *ctree, guint row)

GtkEnumValue *

gtk_type_enum_find_value(GtkType enum_type,

    const gchar *value_name)

gtk_type_enum_get_values(GtkType enum_type)

GtkFlagValue *
```
gtk_type_flags_find_value(GtkType flag_type,

    const gchar *value_name)

gtk_type_flags_get_values(GtkType flags_type)
```

GtkItemFactory *
```
gtk_item_factory_from_path(const gchar *path)

gtk_item_factory_from_widget(GtkWidget *widget)

gtk_item_factory_new(GtkType container_type, const gchar *path,

    GtkAccelGroup *accel_group)
```

GtkMenuFactory *
```
gtk_menu_factory_new(GtkMenuFactoryType type)
```

GtkMenuPath *
```
gtk_menu_factory_find(GtkMenuFactory *factory,

    const char *path)
```

GtkObject *
```
gnome_dentry_edit_new(void)

gnome_dentry_edit_new_notebook(GtkNotebook *notebook)

gnome_mdi_new(gchar *appname, gchar *title)

gtk_adjustment_new(gfloat value, gfloat lower, gfloat upper,

    gfloat step_increment, gfloat page_increment,

    gfloat page_size)

gtk_object_new(GtkType object_type,

    const gchar *first_arg_name, . . .)

gtk_object_newv(GtkType object_type, guint n_args,

    GtkArg *args)

gtk_xmhtml_parser_new()
```

GtkOrientation
```
gnome_dock_band_get_orientation(GnomeDockBand *band)

gnome_dock_item_get_orientation(GnomeDockItem *dock_item)
```

GtkPositionType
```
gnome_preferences_get_mdi_tab_pos()
```

GtkPreviewInfo *
```
gtk_preview_get_info(void)
```

GtkProgress *
```
gnome_appbar_get_progress(GnomeAppBar *ab)
```

GtkRcStyle *
```
gtk_rc_style_new(void)
```

GtkReliefStyle
```
gtk_button_get_relief(GtkButton *button)

gtk_toolbar_get_button_relief(GtkToolbar *toolbar)
```

GtkSelectionData *
```
gtk_selection_data_copy(GtkSelectionData *data)
```

GtkShadowType
```
gnome_dock_item_get_shadow_type(GnomeDockItem *dock_item)
```

GtkSignalQuery *
```
gtk_signal_query(guint signal_id)
```

GtkStyle *
```
gtk_clist_get_cell_style(GtkCList *clist, gint row,
    gint column)

gtk_clist_get_row_style(GtkCList *clist, gint row)

gtk_ctree_node_get_cell_style(GtkCTree *ctree,
    GtkCTreeNode *node, gint column)

gtk_ctree_node_get_row_style(GtkCTree *ctree,
```

```
    GtkCTreeNode *node)
```

```
gtk_rc_get_style(GtkWidget *widget)
```

```
gtk_style_attach(GtkStyle *style, GdkWindow *window)
```

```
gtk_style_copy(GtkStyle *style)
```

```
gtk_style_new(void)
```

```
gtk_style_ref(GtkStyle *style)
```

```
gtk_widget_get_default_style(void)
```

```
gtk_widget_get_style(GtkWidget *widget)
```

GtkTargetList *
```
gtk_target_list_new(const GtkTargetEntry *targets,

    guint ntargets)
```

GtkThemeEngine *
```
gtk_theme_engine_get(gchar *name)
```

GtkTooltips *
```
gtk_tooltips_new(void)
```

GtkTooltipsData *
```
gtk_tooltips_data_get(GtkWidget *widget)
```

GtkType
```
gnome_app_get_type(void)
```

```
gnome_canvas_ellipse_get_type(void)
```

```
gnome_canvas_get_type(void)
```

```
gnome_canvas_group_get_type(void)
```

```
gnome_canvas_image_get_type(void)
```

```
gnome_canvas_item_get_type(void)
```

```
gnome_canvas_line_get_type(void)
```

```
gnome_canvas_polygon_get_type(void)
```

```
gnome_canvas_re_get_type(void)

gnome_canvas_rect_get_type(void)

gnome_canvas_text_get_type(void)

gnome_canvas_widget_get_type(void)

gnome_client_get_type(void)

gnome_color_picker_get_type(void)

gnome_dock_band_get_type(void)

gnome_dock_get_type(void)

gnome_font_picker_get_type(void)

gnome_icon_text_item_get_type(void)

gtk_accel_label_get_type(void)

gtk_adjustment_get_type(void)

gtk_alignment_get_type(void)

gtk_arrow_get_type(void)

gtk_aspect_frame_get_type(void)

gtk_bin_get_type(void)

gtk_box_get_type(void)

gtk_button_box_get_type(void)

gtk_button_get_type(void)

gtk_calendar_get_type(void)

gtk_check_button_get_type(void)

gtk_check_menu_item_get_type(void)

gtk_clist_get_type(void)

gtk_container_child_type(GtkContainer *container)

gtk_container_get_type(void)
```

```
gtk_ctree_get_type(void)

gtk_curve_get_type(void)

gtk_data_get_type(void)

gtk_dialog_get_type(void)

gtk_editable_get_type(void)

gtk_entry_get_type(void)

gtk_event_box_get_type(void)

gtk_file_selection_get_type(void)

gtk_fixed_get_type(void)

gtk_font_selection_get_type()

gtk_frame_get_type(void)

gtk_hbox_get_type(void)

gtk_hscale_get_type(void)

gtk_hscrollbar_get_type(void)

gtk_hseparator_get_type(void)

gtk_identifier_get_type(void)

gtk_image_get_type(void)

gtk_input_dialog_get_type(void)

gtk_invisible_get_type(void)

gtk_item_factory_get_type(void)

gtk_item_get_type(void)

gtk_label_get_type(void)

gtk_layout_get_type(void)

gtk_list_get_type(void)

gtk_list_item_get_type(void)
```

```
gtk_menu_bar_get_type(void)

gtk_menu_get_type(void)

gtk_menu_item_get_type(void)

gtk_menu_shell_get_type(void)

gtk_misc_get_type(void)

gtk_notebook_get_type(void)

gtk_object_get_type(void)

gtk_option_menu_get_type(void)

gtk_packer_get_type(void)

gtk_paned_get_type(void)

gtk_pixmap_get_type(void)

gtk_pixmap_menu_item_get_type(void)

gtk_progress_bar_get_type(void)

gtk_progress_get_type(void)

gtk_radio_button_get_type(void)

gtk_radio_menu_item_get_type(void)

gtk_range_get_type(void)

gtk_scale_get_type(void)

gtk_scrollbar_get_type(void)

gtk_scrolled_window_get_type(void)

gtk_separator_get_type(void)

gtk_spin_button_get_type(void)

gtk_table_get_type(void)
```

```
gtk_tearoff_menu_item_get_type(void)

gtk_text_get_type(void)

gtk_toggle_button_get_type(void)

gtk_tooltips_get_type(void)

gtk_tree_get_type(void)

gtk_tree_item_get_type(void)

gtk_type_from_name(const gchar *name)

gtk_type_get_varargs_type(GtkType foreign_type)

gtk_type_parent(GtkType type)

gtk_type_register_enum(const gchar *type_name,
    GtkEnumValue *values)

gtk_type_register_flags(const gchar *type_name,
    GtkFlagValue *values)

gtk_type_unique(GtkType parent_type,
    const GtkTypeInfo *type_info)

gtk_vbox_get_type(void)

gtk_viewport_get_type(void)

gtk_vscale_get_type(void)

gtk_vscrollbar_get_type(void)

gtk_vseparator_get_type(void)

gtk_widget_get_type(void)

gtk_window_get_type(void)
```

GtkTypeClass *
```
gtk_type_check_class_cast(GtkTypeClass *klass,

    GtkType cast_type)
```

GtkTypeObject *
```
gtk_type_check_object_cast(GtkTypeObject *type_object,

    GtkType cast_type)
```

GtkTypeQuery *
```
gtk_type_query(GtkType type)
```

GtkVisibility
```
gnome_icon_list_icon_is_visible(GnomeIconList *gil, int pos)

gtk_clist_row_is_visible(GtkCList *clist, gint row)

gtk_ctree_node_is_visible(GtkCTree *ctree, GtkCTreeNode *node)
```

GtkWidget *
```
gnome_about_new(const gchar *title, const gchar *version,

    const gchar *copyright, const gchar **authors,

    const gchar *comments, const gchar *logo)

gnome_animator_new_with_size(guint width, guint height)

gnome_app_error(GnomeApp *app, const gchar *error)

gnome_app_find_menu_pos(GtkWidget *parent, gchar *path,

    gint *pos)

gnome_app_message(GnomeApp *app, const gchar *message)

gnome_app_new(gchar *appname, char *title)

gnome_app_ok_cancel(GnomeApp *app, const gchar *message,

    GnomeReplyCallback callback, gpointer data)

gnome_app_ok_cancel_modal(GnomeApp *app, const gchar *message,

    GnomeReplyCallback callback, gpointer data)
```

gnome_app_question(GnomeApp *app, const gchar *question,

    GnomeReplyCallback callback, gpointer data)

gnome_app_question_modal(GnomeApp *app, const gchar *question,

    GnomeReplyCallback callback, gpointer data)

gnome_app_request_password(GnomeApp *app, const gchar *prompt,

    GnomeStringCallback callback, gpointer data)

gnome_app_request_string(GnomeApp *app, const gchar *prompt,

    GnomeStringCallback callback, gpointer data)

gnome_app_warning(GnomeApp *app, const gchar *warning)

gnome_appbar_new(gboolean has_progress, gboolean has_status,

    GnomePreferencesType interactivity)

gnome_calculator_new(void)

gnome_canvas_new(void)

gnome_canvas_new_aa(void)

gnome_color_picker_new(void)

gnome_date_edit_new(time_t the_time, int show_time,

    int use_24_format)

gnome_date_edit_new_flags(time_t the_time,

    GnomeDateEditFlags flags)

gnome_dentry_get_comment_entry(GnomeDEntryEdit *dee)

gnome_dentry_get_doc_entry(GnomeDEntryEdit *dee)

gnome_dentry_get_exec_entry(GnomeDEntryEdit *dee)

gnome_dentry_get_icon_entry(GnomeDEntryEdit *dee)

gnome_dentry_get_name_entry(GnomeDEntryEdit *dee)

gnome_dentry_get_tryexec_entry(GnomeDEntryEdit *dee)

```
gnome_dialog_new(const gchar *title, . . .)

gnome_dialog_newv(const gchar *title, const gchar **buttons)

gnome_dock_band_new(void)

gnome_dock_get_client_area(GnomeDock *dock)

gnome_dock_item_get_child(GnomeDockItem *item)

gnome_dock_item_new(const gchar *name,
    GnomeDockItemBehavior behavior)

gnome_dock_new(void)

gnome_entry_gtk_entry(GnomeEntry *gentry)

gnome_entry_new(const gchar *history_id)

gnome_error_dialog(const gchar *error)

gnome_error_dialog_parented(const gchar *error,
    GtkWindow *parent)

gnome_file_entry_gnome_entry(GnomeFileEntry *fentry)

gnome_file_entry_gtk_entry(GnomeFileEntry *fentry)

gnome_file_entry_new(char *history_id,
    char *browse_dialog_title)

gnome_font_picker_create_inside(GnomeFontPicker *gfp)

gnome_font_picker_new(void)

gnome_font_selector_new(void)

gnome_guru_current_page(GnomeGuru *guru)

gnome_guru_new(const gchar *name, GtkWidget *graphic,
    GnomeDialog *dialog)

gnome_href_new(const gchar *url, const gchar *label)

gnome_icon_entry_gnome_entry(GnomeIconEntry *ientry)
```

gnome_icon_entry_gnome_file_entry(GnomeIconEntry *ientry)

gnome_icon_entry_gtk_entry(GnomeIconEntry *ientry)

gnome_icon_entry_new(char *history_id,

    char *browse_dialog_title)

gnome_icon_list_new(guint icon_width, GtkAdjustment *adj,

    int flags)

gnome_icon_list_new_flags(guint icon_width, GtkAdjustment *adj,

    int flags)

gnome_icon_selection_new(void)

gnome_less_new(void)

gnome_mdi_child_add_view(GnomeMDIChild *mdi_child)

gnome_mdi_get_active_view(GnomeMDI *mdi)

gnome_mdi_get_view_from_window(GnomeMDI *mdi, GnomeApp *app)

gnome_message_box_new(const gchar *message,

    const gchar *message_box_type, . . .)

gnome_message_box_newv(const gchar *message,

    const gchar *message_box_type, const gchar **buttons)

gnome_number_entry_gnome_entry(GnomeNumberEntry *nentry)

gnome_number_entry_gtk_entry(GnomeNumberEntry *nentry)

gnome_number_entry_new(char *history_id,

    char *calc_dialog_title)

gnome_ok_cancel_dialog(const gchar *message,

    GnomeReplyCallback callback, gpointer data)

gnome_ok_cancel_dialog_modal(const gchar *message,

    GnomeReplyCallback callback, gpointer data)

```
gnome_ok_cancel_dialog_modal_parented(const gchar *message,

    GnomeReplyCallback callback, gpointer data,

    GtkWindow *parent)

gnome_ok_cancel_dialog_parented(const gchar *message,

    GnomeReplyCallback callback, gpointer data,

    GtkWindow *parent)

gnome_ok_dialog(const gchar *message)

gnome_ok_dialog_parented(const gchar *message,

    GtkWindow *parent)

gnome_paper_selector_new(void)

gnome_pixmap_button(GtkWidget *pixmap, const char *text)

gnome_pixmap_entry_gnome_entry(GnomePixmapEntry *pentry)

gnome_pixmap_entry_gnome_file_entry(GnomePixmapEntry *pentry)

gnome_pixmap_entry_gtk_entry(GnomePixmapEntry *pentry)

gnome_pixmap_entry_new(char *history_id,

    char *browse_dialog_title, int do_preview)

gnome_pixmap_new_from_file(const char *filename)

gnome_pixmap_new_from_file_at_size(const char *filename,

    int width, int height)

gnome_pixmap_new_from_gnome_pixmap(GnomePixmap *gpixmap_old)

gnome_pixmap_new_from_imlib(GdkImlibImage *im)

gnome_pixmap_new_from_imlib_at_size(GdkImlibImage *im,

    int width, int height)

gnome_pixmap_new_from_rgb_d(unsigned char *data,

    unsigned char *alpha, int rgb_width, int rgb_height)
```

```
gnome_pixmap_new_from_rgb_d_at_size(unsigned char *data,
    unsigned char *alpha, int rgb_width, int rgb_height,
    int width, int height)
gnome_pixmap_new_from_rgb_d_shaped(unsigned char *data,
    unsigned char *alpha, int rgb_width, int rgb_height,
    GdkImlibColor *shape_color)
gnome_pixmap_new_from_rgb_d_shaped_at_size
    (unsigned char *data, unsigned char *alpha, int rgb_width,
    int rgb_height, int width, int height,
    GdkImlibColor *shape_color)
gnome_pixmap_new_from_xpm_d(char **xpm_data)
gnome_pixmap_new_from_xpm_d_at_size(char **xpm_data, int width,
    int height)
gnome_popup_menu_new(GnomeUIInfo *uiinfo)
gnome_popup_menu_new_with_accelgroup(GnomeUIInfo *uiinfo,
    GtkAccelGroup *accelgroup)
gnome_property_box_new(void)
gnome_property_entry_colors(GnomePropertyObject *object,
    const gchar *label, gint num_colors, gint columns,
    gint *table_pos, GdkColor *colors, const gchar *texts[])
gnome_property_entry_font(GnomePropertyObject *object,
    const gchar *label, gchar **font_name_ptr,
    GdkFont **font_ptr)
gnome_question_dialog(const gchar *question,
    GnomeReplyCallback callback, gpointer data)
```

```
gnome_question_dialog_modal(const gchar *question,
    GnomeReplyCallback callback, gpointer data)
gnome_question_dialog_modal_parented(const gchar *question,
    GnomeReplyCallback callback, gpointer data,
    GtkWindow *parent)
gnome_question_dialog_parented(const gchar *question,
    GnomeReplyCallback callback, gpointer data,
    GtkWindow *parent)
gnome_request_dialog(gboolean password, const gchar *prompt,
    const gchar *default_text, const guint16 max_length,
    GnomeStringCallback callback, gpointer data,
    GtkWindow *parent)
gnome_request_password_dialog(const gchar *prompt,
    GnomeStringCallback callback, gpointer data)
gnome_request_password_dialog_parented(const gchar *prompt,
    GnomeStringCallback callback, gpointer data,
    GtkWindow *parent)
gnome_request_string_dialog(const gchar *prompt,
    GnomeStringCallback callback, gpointer data)
gnome_request_string_dialog_parented(const gchar *prompt,
    GnomeStringCallback callback, gpointer data,
    GtkWindow *parent)
gnome_scores_new(guint n_scores, gchar **names, gfloat *scores,
    time_t *times, guint clear)
gnome_spell_new()
```

```
gnome_stock_button(const char *type)

gnome_stock_menu_item(const char *type, const char *text)

gnome_stock_new(void)

gnome_stock_new_with_icon(const char *icon)

gnome_stock_or_ordinary_button(const char *type)

gnome_stock_pixmap_widget(GtkWidget *window, const char *icon)

gnome_stock_pixmap_widget_at_size(GtkWidget *window,
    const char *icon, guint width, guint height)

gnome_stock_pixmap_widget_new(GtkWidget *window,
    const char *icon)

gnome_stock_transparent_window(const char *icon,
    const char *subtype)

gnome_warning_dialog(const gchar *warning)

gnome_warning_dialog_parented(const gchar *warning,
    GtkWindow *parent)

gtk_accel_label_new(const gchar *string)

gtk_alignment_new(gfloat xalign, gfloat yalign, gfloat xscale,
    gfloat yscale)

gtk_arrow_new(GtkArrowType arrow_type,
    GtkShadowType shadow_type)

gtk_aspect_frame_new(const gchar *label, gfloat xalign,
    gfloat yalign, gfloat ratio, gint obey_child)

gtk_button_new(void)

gtk_button_new_with_label(const gchar *label)

gtk_calendar_new(void)
```

```
gtk_check_button_new(void)

gtk_check_button_new_with_label(const gchar *label)

gtk_check_menu_item_new(void)

gtk_check_menu_item_new_with_label(const gchar *label)

gtk_clist_get_column_widget(GtkCList *clist, gint column)

gtk_clist_new(gint columns)

gtk_clist_new_with_titles(gint columns, gchar *titles[])

gtk_clock_new(GtkClockType type)

gtk_color_selection_dialog_new(const gchar *title)

gtk_color_selection_new(void)

gtk_combo_new(void)

gtk_ctree_new(gint columns, gint tree_column)

gtk_ctree_new_with_titles(gint columns, gint tree_column,
    gchar *titles[])

gtk_curve_new(void)

gtk_dial_new(GtkAdjustment *adjustment)

gtk_dialog_new(void)

gtk_drag_get_source_widget(GdkDragContext *context)

gtk_drawing_area_new(void)

gtk_entry_new(void)

gtk_entry_new_with_max_length(guint16 max)

gtk_event_box_new(void)

gtk_file_selection_new(const gchar *title)

gtk_fixed_new(void)

gtk_font_selection_dialog_new(const gchar *title)
```

```
gtk_font_selection_new()

gtk_frame_new(const gchar *label)

gtk_gamma_curve_new(void)

gtk_get_event_widget(GdkEvent *event)

gtk_grab_get_current(void)

gtk_handle_box_new(void)

gtk_hbox_new(gboolean homogeneous, gint spacing)

gtk_hbutton_box_new(void)

gtk_hpaned_new(void)

gtk_hruler_new(void)

gtk_hscale_new(GtkAdjustment *adjustment)

gtk_hscrollbar_new(GtkAdjustment *adjustment)

gtk_hseparator_new(void)

gtk_image_new(GdkImage *val, GdkBitmap *mask)

gtk_input_dialog_new(void)

gtk_invisible_new(void)

gtk_item_factory_get_item(GtkItemFactory *ifactory,
    const gchar *path)

gtk_item_factory_get_item_by_action(GtkItemFactory *ifactory,
    guint action)

gtk_item_factory_get_widget(GtkItemFactory *ifactory,
    const gchar *path)

gtk_item_factory_get_widget_by_action
    (GtkItemFactory *ifactory, guint action)

gtk_label_new(const char *str)
```

```
gtk_layout_new(GtkAdjustment *hadjustment,

    GtkAdjustment *vadjustment)

gtk_list_item_new(void)

gtk_list_item_new_with_label(const gchar *label)

gtk_list_new(void)

gtk_menu_bar_new(void)

gtk_menu_get_active(GtkMenu *menu)

gtk_menu_get_attach_widget(GtkMenu *menu)

gtk_menu_item_new(void)

gtk_menu_item_new_with_label(const gchar *label)

gtk_menu_new(void)

gtk_notebook_get_menu_label(GtkNotebook *notebook,

    GtkWidget *child)

gtk_notebook_get_nth_page(GtkNotebook *notebook, gint page_num)

gtk_notebook_get_tab_label(GtkNotebook *notebook,

    GtkWidget *child)

gtk_notebook_new(void)

gtk_option_menu_get_menu(GtkOptionMenu *option_menu)

gtk_option_menu_new(void)

gtk_packer_new(void)

gtk_pixmap_menu_item_new(void)

gtk_pixmap_new(GdkPixmap *val, GdkBitmap *mask)

gtk_plug_new(guint32 socket_id)

gtk_preview_new(GtkPreviewType type)

gtk_progress_bar_new(void)
```

```
gtk_progress_bar_new_with_adjustment

    (GtkAdjustment *adjustment)

gtk_radio_button_new(GSList *group)

gtk_radio_button_new_from_widget(GtkRadioButton *group)

gtk_radio_button_new_with_label(GSList *group,

    const gchar *label)

gtk_radio_button_new_with_label_from_widget

    (GtkRadioButton *group, const gchar *label)

gtk_radio_menu_item_new(GSList *group)

gtk_radio_menu_item_new_with_label(GSList *group,

    const gchar *label)

gtk_scrolled_window_new(GtkAdjustment *hadjustment,

    GtkAdjustment *vadjustment)

gtk_socket_new()

gtk_spin_button_new(GtkAdjustment *adjustment,

    gfloat climb_rate, guint digits)

gtk_statusbar_new(void)

gtk_table_new(guint rows, guint columns, gboolean homogeneous)

gtk_tearoff_menu_item_new(void)

gtk_ted_new(char *name)

gtk_ted_new_layout(char *name, char *layout)

gtk_text_new(GtkAdjustment *hadj, GtkAdjustment *vadj)

gtk_tips_query_new(void)

gtk_toggle_button_new(void)

gtk_toggle_button_new_with_label(const gchar *label)
```

```
gtk_toolbar_append_element(GtkToolbar *toolbar,

    GtkToolbarChildType type, GtkWidget *widget,

    const char *text, const char *tooltip_text,

    const char *tooltip_private_text, GtkWidget *icon,

    GtkSignalFunc callback, gpointer user_data)

gtk_toolbar_append_item(GtkToolbar *toolbar, const char *text,

    const char *tooltip_text, const char *tooltip_private_text,

    GtkWidget *icon, GtkSignalFunc callback,

    gpointer user_data)

gtk_toolbar_insert_element(GtkToolbar *toolbar,

    GtkToolbarChildType type, GtkWidget *widget,

    const char *text, const char *tooltip_text,

    const char *tooltip_private_text, GtkWidget *icon,

    GtkSignalFunc callback, gpointer user_data, gint position)

gtk_toolbar_insert_item(GtkToolbar *toolbar, const char *text,

    const char *tooltip_text, const char *tooltip_private_text,

    GtkWidget *icon, GtkSignalFunc callback,

    gpointer user_data, gint position)

gtk_toolbar_new(GtkOrientation orientation,

    GtkToolbarStyle style)

gtk_toolbar_prepend_element(GtkToolbar *toolbar,

    GtkToolbarChildType type, GtkWidget *widget,

    const char *text, const char *tooltip_text,

    const char *tooltip_private_text, GtkWidget *icon,
```

```
        GtkSignalFunc callback, gpointer user_data)
    gtk_toolbar_prepend_item(GtkToolbar *toolbar, const char *text,
        const char *tooltip_text, const char *tooltip_private_text,
        GtkWidget *icon, GtkSignalFunc callback,
        gpointer user_data)
    gtk_tree_item_new(void)
    gtk_tree_item_new_with_label(gchar *label)
    gtk_tree_new(void)
    gtk_vbox_new(gboolean homogeneous, gint spacing)
    gtk_vbutton_box_new(void)
    gtk_viewport_new(GtkAdjustment *hadjustment,
        GtkAdjustment *vadjustment)
    gtk_vpaned_new(void)
    gtk_vruler_new(void)
    gtk_vscale_new(GtkAdjustment *adjustment)
    gtk_vscrollbar_new(GtkAdjustment *adjustment)
    gtk_vseparator_new(void)
    gtk_widget_get_ancestor(GtkWidget *widget, GtkType widget_type)
    gtk_widget_get_toplevel(GtkWidget *widget)
    gtk_widget_new(GtkType widget_type,
        const gchar *first_arg_name, . . .)
    gtk_widget_newv(GtkType type, guint nargs, GtkArg *args)
    gtk_window_new(GtkWindowType type)
    gtk_xmhtml_new(void)
```

GtkWindowPosition

`gnome_preferences_get_dialog_position()`

GtkWindowType

`gnome_preferences_get_dialog_type()`

poptContext

`gnomelib_parse_args(int argc, char *argv[], int popt_flags)`

regex_t *

`gnome_regex_cache_compile(GnomeRegexCache *rxc,`

`    const char *pattern, int flags)`

time_t

`gnome_date_edit_get_date(GnomeDateEdit *gde)`

Window

`gdk_window_xid_at(Window base, gint bx, gint by, gint x,`

`    gint y, GList *excludes, gboolean excl_child)`

`gdk_window_xid_at_coords(gint x, gint y, GList *excludes,`

`    gboolean excl_child)`

`motif_find_drag_window(gboolean create)`

XmHTMLForm *

`_XmHTMLFormAddInput(XmHTMLWidget html, String attributes)`

`_XmHTMLFormAddSelect(XmHTMLWidget html, String attributes)`

`_XmHTMLFormAddTextArea(XmHTMLWidget html, String attributes,`

`    String text)`

✦   ✦   ✦

Glossary

app Short for *application*

applet An application program like any other GNOME application, except its main window is small and is displayed on the panel instead of a free-floating, top-level window

application A user-level program that runs within a specific environment (in this case, the GNOME desktop environment), but is not an integral part of that environment

arg There are values that can be set inside widgets by calling a function and passing the name and value of the argument. Their value also can be retrieved by name.

base class Used only as an ancestor of another class. For example, the `GtkWidget` class inherits characteristics from its base class `GtkObject`.

bitmap A pixmap with one bit per pixel

callback You can give an object the address of a function to call to report on an action. Most commonly, a program passes the address of one of its own functions to a GNOME or GTK+ library utility so the program will be called back with the results.

child The windows for an application are in a hierarchical tree. Any window that has one or more subwindows is called a *parent* window; the subwindows are called *child* windows.

class Every object is the member of a class. The class contains information that is common to all objects derived from it. For example, every `GtkButton` widget is a member of the `GtkButtonClass` class. The class contains the functions that are called to react to mouse activity because that is common to all buttons. A `GtkCheckButton` widget has its indicator size and spacing in the class, so changing it once changes it for all instances of `GtkCheckButton`.

color map A mapping between actual RGB values and the colors stored in display memory. The stored colors can take many forms (depending on the hardware), so a color is an index into the color map array.

container A widget that has the job of positioning, sizing, and displaying one or more other widgets is a *container* widget.

convenience function A function that calls another function. Usually, the convenience function requires a subset of the arguments required by the more complicated function, and inserts standard default values when calling it. This happens most often in graphics programming because there are so many options to consider.

CVS Concurrent Version System. An archive of source code that enables multiple programmers to work on the same project simultaneously. If possible, CVS automatically merges the changes made by one programmer with all the changes made by others.

dialog box A window that displays text and/or graphics data and enables user input from the mouse, the keyboard, or both. It looks and acts like a main window because the window manager includes a title bar and window controls.

DND Drag-and-drop

dpi Dots per inch. A measurement of resolution of a monitor — the more dots (pixels) per inch, the higher the resolution. Some have a different number of dots vertically and horizontally.

drawable An object that has the ability to accept paint and draw commands to create a rectangle of displayable pixel values is said to be a *drawable*. A GtkWidget is a drawable with a window; a GtkPixmap is a drawable that keeps its pixels in memory.

ELF The *Extensible Executable and Linking Format* (also known as *Extensible ELF*) is the binary format of the object files produced by the compiler. Files of this type are linked together to create a binary executable. This format can be stored in static libraries and shared libraries.

focus The input from the keyboard is routed to a single window. This window is said to have the keyboard focus. The mouse normally chooses the window; usually, you can identify the window because its title bar is a different color than that of all the other windows.

gc See graphics context

GDK A library of functions that are wrappers around the Xlib functions; also makes use of glib functions

GIMP GNU Image Manipulation Project. The GIMP is a graphical editor written using GTK+. Its Web site is www.gimp.org.

glib A collection of functions and definitions used in the development of GDK and GTK+ applications. The library originally was created to implement GIMP.

GNOME The GNU Network Object Model Environment. A GUI interface built on top of GTK+

GNU A recursive acronym that means GNU's Not UNIX. It is the organization at the center of the open-source software movement. Among its many achievements is the GPL software license.

GPL GNU Public License

graphics context Defines the color, fill method, fill pattern, clipping region, and other details of a graphics operation. Its defined type is `GdkGC`.

GTK+ The GIMP Toolkit. A GPL GUI library for the X Window System that provides the look and feel of Motif. It is comprised of objects written in C. The plus was appended when GTK was modified to use the signal callback mechanism and to enable one widget to inherit the characteristics of another.

GTK– A library of C++ language wrappers for the GTK+ classes

hint The window manager has the responsibility of positioning and sizing all windows. Any request from an application to the window manager for a certain size and position is considered a *hint* because it may not be honored due to conflicts with windows unknown to the application.

homogeneous A group of widgets is homogeneous if the container displays each one as the same width, the same height, or both.

i18n This is an abbreviation of *internationalization*. It was derived from "i(eighteen letters)n".

idle function A function that executes during the idle times that the application otherwise would wait for input from the event queue

inherit When a new class is constructed based on another class, the new class has access to the resources of the existing widget — it is said to *inherit* from the existing widget.

instance An actual object. For example, a window may contain several `GtkButton` objects. Each of these is an *instance* of the `GtkButton` class.

internationalization The act of creating software that responds to its *locale*. This can be as simple as changing date formats and the currency symbol, or as complicated as translating all the buttons, menus, help, and other text displayed by the application. Internationalization also is called *i18n*.

locale The time and date format, currency symbol, numeric format, and character set, for a specific region. An international program may be able to switch to one of several locales.

marshal A process that dynamically organizes a collection of arguments and makes a function call. A GNOME signal makes its callbacks by *marshaling* the data to be passed to the callback function, and then using that data to call the function.

MDI Multiple Document Interface. A single window contains a number of subwindows, and you can switch among them. In other words, any one of the subwindows can be displayed.

MIME Multipurpose Internet Mail Extension. A method by which data can be encoded into a form that is transmitted easily over the Internet, or some other connection, and decoded into its original form by the receiver. Designed for handling attachments on e-mail, it is used for other things, such as drag-and-drop.

Multiple Document Interface See MDI

modal While it is displayed, a modal window prevents mouse or keyboard access to any other window displayed by the same application.

object A data structure and the collection of functions that operate on it. This is the code organization used by GNOME and GTK+ — but not by GDK and X.

parent The windows for an application are in a hierarchical tree. Any window that has one or more subwindows is called a *parent* window, and the subwindows are called *child* windows.

parented A child window also is called a parented window. That is, it has a parent.

pixmap A rectangular array of pixel values that accepts drawing commands. To draw a pixmap to a window, you simply copy its pixels to the display. Also, a program can draw onto a pixmap in RAM the same way it can draw to a window on the display — just treat it like a window in RAM.

popt A GNOME library package for reading arguments from the command line

popup The same as a dialog box, except the window manager does not include the frame with the title and controls.

root window The parent window of all the windows on the display. It fills the entire display area and provides a place to display icons and background to fill places not used by other windows.

rpm Red Hat Package Manager. Creates and manipulates packages for distributing software packages. You can use it to build new software packages; install software from an existing package; update to a newer, installed version; query the status of the installed package; and uninstall a package.

spline An algorithm that uses piecewise refinement to construct a polynomial that will smoothly connect a set of points. It is often used to visually interpolate between data points in a graph.

visual A visual is the format of displayable screen data. There usually is a single default visual (stored as GdkVisual struct) that displays all windows. However, some screens allow multiple visuals to be active simultaneously—different windows displayed using different color and pixel-painting methods.

widget A single unit of a code-data combination in GTK+ and GNOME that facilitates windowing. Normally, a widget is displayable, but some widgets do not display a window. A widget can be very simple, such as a label that displays a text string; or it can be complex, such as a color selector that displays color graphics, buttons, and sliders. Widgets commonly contain other widgets, such as a button widget that contains a label widget to display its text.

X or X11 Also called the X Window System. It is a set of library routines that you can use to implement a graphical user interface. The Linux version of X is XFree86, which is used on both BSD and Linux. You can get more information from this Web site: XFree86.org.

XInput An extension of X that allows input devices other than the mouse and keyboard

XPM A graphics file format in the form of C source code. You can compile it directly into a program, or use an XPM file as an independent graphics file.

Index

Continued

T

tab character and make utility, 23
tables
    adding space between widgets, 96–97
    combining with boxes, 104–108
    homogeneous, 100
    homogeneous cells, 94
    packing, 91–104
    positioning buttons, 91–94
    positioning widgets, 92, 615–616
    sizing widgets, 94
    stretching widgets across cells, 94
    three buttons, 94–97
tag file, 16–17
talking to widgets, 419–422
tbdisable.c program, 230–231
tbhide.c program, 234–236
tbradio.c program, 239–241
tbtoggle.c program, 245–247
tbxpm.h header file, 241, 247
tear-off menus, 198, 616–617
tenSecondCallback() callback function, 168
text
    anchor point, 275
    canvas, 273–276, 648
    cutting and pasting, 460–462
    displaying, 617–618
    drag-and-drop, 449–452
    drawing, 319–322
    editing, 617–618
    managing list, 586–588
    string, 585
    widgets for editing, 563–564
text files, 526–527, 675–676
text label inside frame, 540
text lists, 544–548
text statements, 529
text.c program, 319–321
textdomain() function, 516
thrice.c program, 94–96
tile pixmap, 345
time, 548–549, 705–708
time() function, 706
timers, 166–168
timeval struct, 707
timing.c program, 166–168
tm struct, 706
TODO file, 527
toggle buttons
    menus, 242–245
    toolbars, 245–247

toggleOne() callback function, 244, 247
toolbar.c program, 217–218
toolbarcustom.c program, 225–226
toolbarmdi.c program, 475–477
toolbars, 197, 662
    constructing, 619–621
    creation of, 217–219
    docking, 218–219
    enabling/disabling items, 230–232
    hiding and showing items, 234–236
    macros, 206
    MDI (Multiple Document Interface), 474–478
    moving on-screen, 218
    non-standard icons, 225–227
    radio buttons, 239–242
    stock icons, 220–224
    toggle buttons, 245–247
    tooltip, or hint, 218
    without identifying text, 219
top level windows, 24
topic.dat file, 214
toplevel widget, 178
top-level windows, 31
    available to separate process, 602
    displaying, 25
toplevelCallback() callback function, 478
tracing graph on grids, 559–560
translate.c program, 514–515
translated string data type, 511
translated_string functions, 513
TranslateMessage() function, 721
tree structure, 622–625
TRUE macro, 14, 15
true or false condition, 14
typedef
    defining names of structs, 485
    struct, 290–291
typednd.c program, 453–457

U

#undef statements, 527–527
underscore(_) macro, 516
ungrabMouse() callback function, 382, 385
unsetenv() function, 713
updateCallback() function, 442
updateValue() function, 688
user category, 510
user-created
    cursors, 188–191
    popup dialog boxes, 562
users, 667–668

IDG Books Worldwide, Inc.
End-User License Agreement

READ THIS. You should carefully read these terms and conditions before opening the software packet(s) included with this book ("Book"). This is a license agreement ("Agreement") between you and IDG Books Worldwide, Inc. ("IDGB"). By opening the accompanying software packet(s), you acknowledge that you have read and accept the following terms and conditions. If you do not agree and do not want to be bound by such terms and conditions, promptly return the Book and the unopened software packet(s) to the place you obtained them for a full refund.

1. **License Grant**. IDGB grants to you (either an individual or entity) a nonexclusive license to use one copy of the enclosed software program(s) (collectively, the "Software") solely for your own personal or business purposes on a single computer (whether a standard computer or a workstation component of a multiuser network). The Software is in use on a computer when it is loaded into temporary memory (RAM) or installed into permanent memory (hard disk, CD-ROM, or other storage device). IDGB reserves all rights not expressly granted herein.

2. **Ownership**. IDGB is the owner of all right, title, and interest, including copyright, in and to the compilation of the Software recorded on the disk(s) or CD-ROM ("Software Media"). Copyright to the individual programs recorded on the Software Media is owned by the author or other authorized copyright owner of each program. Ownership of the Software and all proprietary rights relating thereto remain with IDGB and its licensers.

3. **Restrictions On Use and Transfer**.

   (a) You may only (i) make one copy of the Software for backup or archival purposes, or (ii) transfer the Software to a single hard disk, provided that you keep the original for backup or archival purposes. You may not (i) rent or lease the Software, (ii) copy or reproduce the Software through a LAN or other network system or through any computer subscriber system or bulletin-board system, or (iii) modify, adapt, or create derivative works based on the Software.

   (b) You may not reverse engineer, decompile, or disassemble the Software. You may transfer the Software and user documentation on a permanent basis, provided that the transferee agrees to accept the terms and conditions of this Agreement and you retain no copies. If the Software is an update or has been updated, any transfer must include the most recent update and all prior versions.

(b) In no event shall IDGB or the author be liable for any damages whatsoever (including without limitation damages for loss of business profits, business interruption, loss of business information, or any other pecuniary loss) arising from the use of or inability to use the Book or the Software, even if IDGB has been advised of the possibility of such damages.

(c) Because some jurisdictions do not allow the exclusion or limitation of liability for consequential or incidental damages, the above limitation or exclusion may not apply to you.

7. **U.S. Government Restricted Rights.** Use, duplication, or disclosure of the Software by the U.S. Government is subject to restrictions stated in paragraph (c)(1)(ii) of the Rights in Technical Data and Computer Software clause of DFARS 252.227-7013, and in subparagraphs (a) through (d) of the Commercial Computer — Restricted Rights clause at FAR 52.227-19, and in similar clauses in the NASA FAR supplement, when applicable.

8. **General.** This Agreement constitutes the entire understanding of the parties and revokes and supersedes all prior agreements, oral or written, between them and may not be modified or amended except in a writing signed by both parties hereto that specifically refers to this Agreement. This Agreement shall take precedence over any other documents that may be in conflict herewith. If any one or more provisions contained in this Agreement are held by any court or tribunal to be invalid, illegal, or otherwise unenforceable, each and every other provision shall remain in full force and effect.

GNU General Public License

Version 2, June 1991

Copyright (c) 1989, 1991 Free Software Foundation, Inc.

675 Mass Ave., Cambridge, MA 02139, USA

Preamble

The licenses for most software are designed to take away your freedom to share and change it. By contrast, the GNU General Public License is intended to guarantee your freedom to share and change free software — to make sure the software is free for all its users. This General Public License applies to most of the Free Software Foundation's software and to any other program whose authors commit to using it. (Some other Free Software Foundation software is covered by the GNU Library General Public License instead.) You can apply it to your programs, too.

When we speak of *free software*, we are referring to freedom, not price. Our General Public Licenses are designed to make sure that you have the freedom to distribute copies of free software (and charge for this service if you wish), that you receive source code or can get it if you want it, that you can change the software or use pieces of it in new free programs, and that you know you can do these things.

To protect your rights, we need to make restrictions that forbid anyone to deny you these rights or to ask you to surrender the rights. These restrictions translate to certain responsibilities for you if you distribute copies of the software, or if you modify it.

For example, if you distribute copies of such a program, whether gratis or for a fee, you must give the recipients all the rights that you have. You must make sure that they, too, receive or can get the source code. And you must show them these terms so they know their rights.

We protect your rights with two steps: (1) copyright the software, and (2) offer you this license, which gives you legal permission to copy, distribute, and/or modify the software.

Also, for each author's protection and ours, we want to make certain that everyone understands that there is no warranty for this free software. If the software is modified by someone else and passed on, we want its recipients to know that what they have is not the original, so that any problems introduced by others will not reflect on the original authors' reputations.

Finally, any free program is threatened constantly by software patents. We wish to avoid the danger that redistributors of a free program will individually obtain patent licenses, in effect making the program proprietary. To prevent this, we have made it clear that any patent must be licensed for everyone's free use or not licensed at all.

The precise terms and conditions for copying, distribution and modification follow.

Terms and Conditions for Copying, Distribution, and Modification

0. This License applies to any program or other work that contains a notice placed by the copyright holder saying it may be distributed under the terms of this General Public License. The "Program," below, refers to any such program or work, and a "work based on the Program" means either the Program or any derivative work under copyright law: that is to say, a work containing the Program or a portion of it, either verbatim or with modifications and/or translated into another language. (Hereinafter, translation is included without limitation in the term "modification.") Each licensee is addressed as "you."

Activities other than copying, distribution, and modification are not covered by this License; they are outside its scope. The act of running the Program is not restricted, and the output from the Program is covered only if its contents constitute a work based on the Program (independent of having been made by running the Program). Whether that is true depends on what the Program does.

1. You may copy and distribute verbatim copies of the Program's source code as you receive it, in any medium, provided that you conspicuously and appropriately publish on each copy an appropriate copyright notice and disclaimer of warranty; keep intact all the notices that refer to this License and to the absence of any warranty; and give any other recipients of the Program a copy of this License along with the Program.

You may charge a fee for the physical act of transferring a copy, and you may at your option offer warranty protection in exchange for a fee.

2. You may modify your copy or copies of the Program or any portion of it, thus forming a work based on the Program, and copy and distribute such modifications or work under the terms of Section 1 above, provided that you also meet all of these conditions:

    (a) You must cause the modified files to carry prominent notices stating that you changed the files and the date of any change.

    (b) You must cause any work that you distribute or publish, that in whole or in part contains or is derived from the Program or any part thereof, to be licensed as a whole at no charge to all third parties under the terms of this License.

(c) If the modified program normally reads commands interactively when run, you must cause it, when started running for such interactive use in the most ordinary way, to print or display an announcement including an appropriate copyright notice and a notice that there is no warranty (or else, saying that you provide a warranty) and that users may redistribute the program under these conditions, and telling the user how to view a copy of this License. (Exception: If the Program itself is interactive but does not normally print such an announcement, your work based on the Program is not required to print an announcement.)

These requirements apply to the modified work as a whole. If identifiable sections of that work are not derived from the Program, and can be reasonably considered independent and separate works in themselves, then this License, and its terms, do not apply to those sections when you distribute them as separate works. But when you distribute the same sections as part of a whole that is a work based on the Program, the distribution of the whole must be on the terms of this License, whose permissions for other licensees extend to the entire whole, and thus to each and every part regardless of who wrote it.

Thus, it is not the intent of this section to claim rights or contest your rights to work written entirely by you; rather, the intent is to exercise the right to control the distribution of derivative or collective works based on the Program.

In addition, mere aggregation of another work not based on the Program with the Program (or with a work based on the Program) on a volume of a storage or distribution medium does not bring the other work under the scope of this License.

3. You may copy and distribute the Program (or a work based on it, under Section 2) in object code or executable form under the terms of Sections 1 and 2 above provided that you also do one of the following:

(a) Accompany it with the complete corresponding machine-readable source code, which must be distributed under the terms of Sections 1 and 2 above on a medium customarily used for software interchange; or,

(b) Accompany it with a written offer, valid for at least three years, to give any third party, for a charge no more than your cost of physically performing source distribution, a complete, machine-readable copy of the corresponding source code, to be distributed under the terms of Sections 1 and 2 above on a medium customarily used for software interchange; or,

(c) Accompany it with the information you received as to the offer to distribute corresponding source code. (This alternative is allowed only for noncommercial distribution and only if you received the program in object code or executable form with such an offer, in accord with Subsection (b) above.)

The source code for a work means the preferred form of the work for making modifications to it. For an executable work, complete source code means all the source code for all modules it contains, plus any associated interface definition files, plus the scripts used to control compilation and installation of the executable. However, as a special exception, the source code distributed need not include anything that is normally distributed (in either source or binary form) with the major components (compiler, kernel, and so forth) of the operating system on which the executable runs, unless that component itself accompanies the executable.

If distribution of executable or object code is made by offering access to copy from a designated place, then offering equivalent access to copy the source code from the same place counts as distribution of the source code, even though third parties are not compelled to copy the source along with the object code.

4. You may not copy, modify, sublicense, or distribute the Program except as expressly provided under this License. Any attempt otherwise to copy, modify, sublicense, or distribute the Program is void, and will automatically terminate your rights under this License.

However, parties who have received copies, or rights, from you under this License will not have their licenses terminated so long as such parties remain in full compliance.

5. You are not required to accept this License, since you have not signed it. However, nothing else grants you permission to modify or distribute the Program or its derivative works. These actions are prohibited by law if you do not accept this License. Therefore, by modifying or distributing the Program (or any work based on the Program), you indicate your acceptance of this License to do so, and all its terms and conditions for copying, distributing or modifying the Program or works based on it.

6. Each time you redistribute the Program (or any work based on the Program), the recipient automatically receives a license from the original licensor to copy, distribute, or modify the Program subject to these terms and conditions. You may not impose any further restrictions on the recipients' exercise of the rights granted herein. You are not responsible for enforcing compliance by third parties to this License.

7. If, as a consequence of a court judgment or allegation of patent infringement or for any other reason (not limited to patent issues), conditions are imposed on you (whether by court order, agreement or otherwise) that contradict the conditions of this License, they do not excuse you from the conditions of this License. If you cannot distribute so as to satisfy simultaneously your obligations under this License and any other pertinent obligations, then as a

consequence you may not distribute the Program at all. For example, if a patent license would not permit royalty-free redistribution of the Program by all those who receive copies directly or indirectly through you, then the only way you could satisfy both it and this License would be to refrain entirely from distribution of the Program.

If any portion of this section is held invalid or unenforceable under any particular circumstance, the balance of the section is intended to apply and the section as a whole is intended to apply in other circumstances.

It is not the purpose of this section to induce you to infringe any patents or other property right claims or to contest validity of any such claims; this section has the sole purpose of protecting the integrity of the free software distribution system, which is implemented by public license practices. Many people have made generous contributions to the wide range of software distributed through that system in reliance on consistent application of that system; it is up to the author/donor to decide if he or she is willing to distribute software through any other system and a licensee cannot impose that choice.

This section is intended to make thoroughly clear what is believed to be a consequence of the rest of this License.

8. If the distribution and/or use of the Program is restricted in certain countries either by patents or by copyrighted interfaces, the original copyright holder who places the Program under this License may add an explicit geographical distribution limitation excluding those countries, so that distribution is permitted only in or among countries not thus excluded. In such case, this License incorporates the limitation as if written in the body of this License.

9. The Free Software Foundation may publish revised and/or new versions of the General Public License from time to time. Such new versions will be similar in spirit to the present version, but may differ in detail to address new problems or concerns.

Each version is given a distinguishing version number. If the Program specifies a version number of this License which applies to it and "any later version," you have the option of following the terms and conditions either of that version or of any later version published by the Free Software Foundation. If the Program does not specify a version number of this License, you may choose any version ever published by the Free Software Foundation.

10. If you wish to incorporate parts of the Program into other free programs whose distribution conditions are different, write to the author to ask for permission. For software which is copyrighted by the Free Software Foundation, write to the Free Software Foundation; we sometimes make exceptions for this. Our decision will be guided by the two goals of preserving the free status of all derivatives of our free software and of promoting the sharing and reuse of software generally.

No Warranty

11. BECAUSE THE PROGRAM IS LICENSED FREE OF CHARGE, THERE IS NO WARRANTY FOR THE PROGRAM, TO THE EXTENT PERMITTED BY APPLICABLE LAW. EXCEPT WHEN OTHERWISE STATED IN WRITING, THE COPYRIGHT HOLDERS AND/OR OTHER PARTIES PROVIDE THE PROGRAM "AS IS" WITHOUT WARRANTY OF ANY KIND, EITHER EXPRESSED OR IMPLIED, INCLUDING, BUT NOT LIMITED TO, THE IMPLIED WARRANTIES OF MERCHANTABILITY AND FITNESS FOR A PARTICULAR PURPOSE. THE ENTIRE RISK AS TO THE QUALITY AND PERFORMANCE OF THE PROGRAM IS WITH YOU. SHOULD THE PROGRAM PROVE DEFECTIVE, YOU ASSUME THE COST OF ALL NECESSARY SERVICING, REPAIR, OR CORRECTION.

12. IN NO EVENT UNLESS REQUIRED BY APPLICABLE LAW OR AGREED TO IN WRITING WILL ANY COPYRIGHT HOLDER, OR ANY OTHER PARTY WHO MAY MODIFY AND/OR REDISTRIBUTE THE PROGRAM AS PERMITTED ABOVE, BE LIABLE TO YOU FOR DAMAGES, INCLUDING ANY GENERAL, SPECIAL, INCIDENTAL, OR CONSEQUENTIAL DAMAGES ARISING OUT OF THE USE OR INABILITY TO USE THE PROGRAM (INCLUDING BUT NOT LIMITED TO LOSS OF DATA OR DATA BEING RENDERED INACCURATE OR LOSSES SUSTAINED BY YOU OR THIRD PARTIES OR A FAILURE OF THE PROGRAM TO OPERATE WITH ANY OTHER PROGRAMS), EVEN IF SUCH HOLDER OR OTHER PARTY HAS BEEN ADVISED OF THE POSSIBILITY OF SUCH DAMAGES.

End of Terms and Conditions

How to Apply These Terms to Your New Programs

If you develop a new program, and you want it to be of the greatest possible use to the public, the best way to achieve this is to make it free software that everyone can redistribute and change under these terms.

To do so, attach the following notices to the program. It is safest to attach them to the start of each source file to most effectively convey the exclusion of warranty; and each file should have at least the "copyright" line and a pointer to where the full notice is found:

<One line to give the program's name and a brief idea of what it does.>

Copyright (c) 19yy (name of author)

This program is free software; you can redistribute it and/or modify it under the terms of the GNU General Public License as published by the Free Software Foundation; either Version 2 of the License or (at your option) any later version.

This program is distributed in the hope that it will be useful, but WITHOUT ANY WARRANTY; without even the implied warranty of MERCHANTABILITY or FITNESS FOR A PARTICULAR PURPOSE. See the GNU General Public License for more details.

You should have received a copy of the GNU General Public License along with this program; if not, write to the Free Software Foundation, Inc., 675 Mass Ave., Cambridge, MA 02139, USA.

Also add information on how to contact you by electronic and paper mail.

If the program is interactive, make it output a short notice like this when it starts in an interactive mode:

```
Gnomovision version 69, Copyright (c) 19yy name of author
Gnomovision comes with ABSOLUTELY NO WARRANTY; for details type
'show w'
This is free software, and you are welcome to redistribute it
under certain conditions; type 'show c' for details.
```

The hypothetical commands show w and show c should show the appropriate parts of the General Public License. Of course, the commands you use may be called something other than show w and show c; they could even be mouse-clicks or menu items — whatever suits your program.

You should also get your employer (if you work as a programmer) or your school, if any, to sign a "copyright disclaimer" for the program, if necessary. Here is a sample; alter the names:

Yoyodyne, Inc., hereby disclaims all copyright interest in the program "Gnomovision" (which makes passes at compilers) written by James Hacker.

(signature of Ty Coon), 1 April 1989

Ty Coon, President of Vice

This General Public License does not permit incorporating your program into proprietary programs. If your program is a subroutine library, you may consider it more useful to permit linking proprietary applications with the library. If this is what you want to do, use the GNU Library General Public License instead of this License.

my2cents.idgbooks.com

Register This Book — And Win!

Visit **http://my2cents.idgbooks.com** to register this book and we'll automatically enter you in our fantastic monthly prize giveaway. It's also your opportunity to give us feedback: let us know what you thought of this book and how you would like to see other topics covered.

Discover IDG Books Online!

The IDG Books Online Web site is your online resource for tackling technology — at home and at the office. Frequently updated, the IDG Books Online Web site features exclusive software, insider information, online books, and live events!

10 Productive & Career-Enhancing Things You Can Do at www.idgbooks.com

- Nab source code for your own programming projects.

- Download software.

- Read Web exclusives: special articles and book excerpts by IDG Books Worldwide authors.

- Take advantage of resources to help you advance your career as a Novell or Microsoft professional.

- Buy IDG Books Worldwide titles or find a convenient bookstore that carries them.

- Register your book and win a prize.

- Chat live online with authors.

- Sign up for regular e-mail updates about our latest books.

- Suggest a book you'd like to read or write.

- Give us your 2¢ about our books and about our Web site.

You say you're not on the Web yet? It's easy to get started with IDG Books' *Discover the Internet,* available at local retailers everywhere.

CD-ROM Installation Instructions

Insert the CD-ROM into your CD-ROM drive. If it does not automatically mount, you can mount it manually with the following two commands:

```
cd /mnt
mount cdrom
```

However it is mounted, the contents of the CD-ROM will appear as the directory /mnt/cdrom. You can have Linux automatically mount the CD-ROM by adding the following line to the file /etc/fstab:

```
/dev/cdrom /mnt/cdrom iso9660 noauto,owner,ro 0 0
```

There is a README file on the CD-ROM that explains the contents.

The example source code from the book is stored in the directory named examples. You can view or copy the source directly from the CD-ROM. Each individual directory can be copied and compiled using the makefile that is in the directory. Also, you can duplicate the entire example source tree by using the tar utility to extract the tree from the file examples.tgz.

The source code of GNOME and GTK+ is contained in a number of tarred and zipped files. The directories /mnt/cdrom/gnome/base and /mnt/cdrom/gnome/core contain the source code of the development libraries for both GNOME and GTK+. To use these, select a working directory in your hard drive and use tar to unpack the source. There are installation instructions with each file.

The source code of the software development utilities are in the tar files found in /mnt/cdrom/tools.

Appendix A contains information on unpacking and installing the CD-ROM files.

To remove the CD-ROM, it must be unmounted. This can be done by entering one of the following commands:

```
umount /mnt/cdrom
```

or

```
eject
```